McKIE'S GAZETTEER

Also by David McKie

Jabez: The Rise and Fall of a Victorian Rogue
Great British Bus Journeys: Travels Through Unfamous Places

McKIE'S GAZETTEER

A LOCAL HISTORY OF BRITAIN

DAVID McKIE

Atlantic Books
London

First published in hardback in Great Britain in 2008 by Atlantic Books, an imprint of Grove Atlantic Ltd.

1 3 5 7 9 8 6 4 2

A CIP catalogue record for this book is available from the British Library.

ISBN: 978 1 84354 654 2

Printed in Malta

Designed by www.fivetwentyfive.com

Index compiled by Meg Davies (Fellow of the Society of Indexers)

Atlantic Books
An imprint of Grove Atlantic Ltd
Ormond House 26–27 Boswell Street London WC1N 3JZ

www.atlantic-books.co.uk

CONTENTS

ix Contents by Region
xiii List of Illustrations
xv Preface

3 Aan
5 Abbeycwmhir
8 Aberdeen
14 Abney Park
17 Ashford
22 Ashwell
25 Aston

31 Balham
32 Barbaraville
36 Bedford
41 Bishop's Castle
48 Blennerhasset
52 Boothville
53 Bossenden
60 Boston
64 Broadstairs
67 Burrow

73 Caernarfon
77 Cape Wrath
80 Castle Dangerous
83 Castle Gloom
86 Castle Spiritual
88 Chelsea
94 City of Three Waters
98 Clevedon
102 Clydebank
106 Compton Verney

113 Debatable Land
116 Defiance Platform
119 Devil's Quoits
122 Devizes
127 Dolbadarn Castle
132 Durham

139 Eardisland
144 Edwinstowe
149 Enville
152 Etruria

159 Foulness
164 Frinton and Walton
169 Frodsham

175 Gatton
177 Gipton
183 Goyt
186 Grimsthorpe

191 Halifax
196 Hay-on-Wye
199 Helmsdale
202 High Cross
204 Houghton Hall
209 Humber
211 Huntingdon
215 Hurstpierpoint

223 Ilkeston
230 Inverewe
232 Ipswich
235 Irk

CONTENTS

239 Isle of Whithorn
245 Islip
250 Iwerne Courtney, or Shroton

255 Jackfield
259 Jacob's Island
262 Jaywick

271 Keighley
276 Kettering
279 Kinlochleven
284 Knockin
285 Knoweside

289 Lambeth
295 Leverburgh
302 Llanthony
308 Llanwrda
311 Llanyblodwel
316 Lochgelly
320 Lowther
327 Lydiard Park
330 Lyme Regis

337 Machynlleth
340 Market Harborough
341 Marston, South
347 Marwick Head
348 Marylebone
352 Mawgan-in-Pydar
354 Middlesbrough
359 Middlesex
362 Milngavie
366 Montgomery
369 Mortlake
375 Morwenstow

383 Neath
387 Neptune's Staircase
390 New Brighton
394 Newtown
395 Norwich
399 Nowheresville

403 Orford
406 Orkney

415 Peacehaven
421 Peterborough
425 Pontlottyn
427 Port Appin
430 Portsdown
436 Port Sunlight
440 Poverty Bottom

445 Quarr Abbey
449 Quebec
452 Queen's Park

459 Ramsbottom
463 Richmond
466 Rivington
470 Rothbury
475 Rothley

485 St Elvis
488 St Marychurch
494 Sandtoft
498 Senghenydd
502 Shipden
506 Sidmouth
509 Snig's End
515 Steeple Ashton

CONTENTS

518 Streatlam
523 Stromness
524 Stroud
527 Sunderland Point
529 Sutton-under-Whitestonecliffe
533 Swansea

537 Talbot Village
541 Tattenhoe
545 Temperance Town
548 Tenterden
553 Tewkesbury
557 Tockholes
558 Tonbridge
562 Tottington
566 Tremadog

575 Ullapool
579 Unthank
581 Upper Upham

587 Ventnor
593 Verney Junction

599 Whiteway
606 Whitwell
611 Widmerpool
615 Wigan
620 Wolverhampton
621 Wythenshawe

627 XI Towns

631 Yarm
634 Yarrow

641 Zouch
642 Zoze Point

645 A Bartholomew Glossary
647 Bibliography
653 Index

CONTENTS BY REGION

Scotland

3 Aan
8 Aberdeen
32 Barbaraville
77 Cape Wrath
80 Castle Dangerous
83 Castle Gloom
86 Castle Spiritual
102 Clydebank
113 Debatable Land
199 Helmsdale
230 Inverewe
239 Isle of Whithorn
279 Kinlochleven
285 Knoweside
295 Leverburgh
316 Lochgelly
347 Marwick Head
362 Milngavie
387 Neptune's Staircase
399 Nowheresville
406 Orkney
427 Port Appin
523 Stromness
575 Ullapool
634 Yarrow

North West

48 Blennerhasset
113 Debatable Land
169 Frodsham
183 Goyt
235 Irk
320 Lowther
390 New Brighton
436 Port Sunlight
459 Ramsbottom
466 Rivington
527 Sunderland Point
557 Tockholes
579 Unthank
615 Wigan
621 Wythenshawe

Yorkshire and North East

132 Durham
177 Gipton
191 Halifax
209 Humber
271 Keighley
354 Middlesbrough
449 Quebec
463 Richmond
470 Rothbury
518 Streatlam
529 Sutton-under-Whitestonecliffe

Wales

5 Abbeycwmhir
73 Caernarfon
127 Dolbadarn Castle
196 Hay-on-Wye

302 Llanthony
308 Llanwrda
311 Llanyblodwel
337 Machynlleth
366 Montgomery
383 Neath
394 Newtown
425 Pontlottyn
485 St Elvis
498 Senghenydd
533 Swansea
545 Temperance Town
566 Tremadog

West Midlands

25 Aston
41 Bishop's Castle
106 Compton Verney
139 Eardisland
149 Enville
152 Etruria
255 Jackfield
284 Knockin
620 Wolverhampton
627 XI Towns

East Midlands

52 Boothville
60 Boston
94 City of Three Waters
144 Edwinstowe
183 Goyt
186 Grimsthorpe
202 High Cross
223 Ilkeston
276 Kettering
340 Market Harborough
475 Rothley
494 Sandtoft
606 Whitwell
611 Widmerpool
641 Zouch

East of England

22 Ashwell
36 Bedford
159 Foulness
164 Frinton and Walton
204 Houghton Hall
211 Huntingdon
232 Ipswich
262 Jaywick
395 Norwich
403 Orford
421 Peterborough
502 Shipden
562 Tottington

Devon and Cornwall

116 Defiance Platform
352 Mawgan-in-Pydar
375 Morwenstow
488 St Marychurch
506 Sidmouth
642 Zoze Point

Wessex

67 Burrow
98 Clevedon
122 Devizes
250 Iwerne Courtney, or Shroton
327 Lydiard Park
330 Lyme Regis
341 Marston, South
509 Snig's End
515 Steeple Ashton
524 Stroud
537 Talbot Village
553 Tewkesbury
581 Upper Upham
599 Whiteway

Thames and Solent

14 Abney Park
31 Balham
88 Chelsea
119 Devil's Quoits
175 Gatton
245 Islip
259 Jacob's Island
289 Lambeth
348 Marylebone
359 Middlesex
369 Mortlake
430 Portsdown
445 Quarr Abbey
452 Queen's Park
541 Tattenhoe
587 Ventnor
593 Verney Junction

South East

17 Ashford
53 Bossenden
64 Broadstairs
215 Hurstpierpoint
415 Peacehaven
440 Poverty Bottom
548 Tenterden
558 Tonbridge

LIST OF ILLUSTRATIONS

5 Abbeycwmhir Church
15 Statue of Dr Watts
19 *The Garden that I Love* by Alfred Austin
26 Mountford Rubber Co. Ltd sign
34 Barbaraville caravan
42 Train on the Bishop's Castle railway
54 Sir William Courtenay
62 Boston windmill
68 Burrow Mump
79 Cape Wrath lighthouse
84 Castle Gloom
96 Hare and Hounds pub
99 Clevedon bandstand
104 Singer clock
117 Royal Albert Bridge
123 Devizes market cross
128 Dolbadarn Castle
139 Eardisley Church font
150 Cricket bat and ball
153 Etruria Wedgwood urn
162 Barbed wire
166 Frinton gates
170 Frodsham Main Street Community Church
178 Gipton estate flats
187 Grimsthorpe Castle decoration
192 Saltaire United Reformed Church
197 Hay-on-Wye Booksellers
199 Triumphal arch
210 Andrew Marvell in the Humber estuary
216 Hurstpierpoint sign
223 Ilkeston cinema
234 Ipswich Town Football Club scarf
242 Isle of Whithorn from the harbour
251 Iwerne Courtnay, Iwerne Courtney and Shroton signpost
257 The Boat Inn sign
265 Abandoned slot machine
272 *Keighley News and Bingley Chronicle*
280 Loch Leven
284 The Knockin Shop
291 Horatio Herbert Kitchener
303 Llanthony Priory
314 St Michael's Church window
326 Lowther Castle
330 Icthyosaurus fossil skeleton
338 Machynlleth town centre
343 Alfred Williams's meadow of flowers
357 The Riverside Stadium
363 The Bennie railplane
370 Sir Richard Burton's tomb
388 Neptune's Staircase
393 New Brighton clown
396 William Crotch
404 Ministry of Defence pagoda
407 London Brighton and South Coast Railway coat of arms
422 Peterborough Guildhall
428 Castle Stalker
435 Panama hat
437 Port Sunlight houses

447 Quarr Abbey
453 Droop Street house
460 Ramsbottom paper mill
468 Rivington Pike Pigeon Tower
471 Cragside
486 Elvis
495 Sandtoft trolleybus
503 Hotel de Paris
507 Sidmouth crab
516 St Mary's Church interior carving
525 Stroud clock with four faces
530 Claymore sword
543 Interested sheep at the church of St Giles
549 Tenterden station signal box
559 Solitary walker
566 Tremadog town centre
576 Bag of potatoes
582 Ruined cottage
588 Ventnor cottage
595 Letter addressed to Miss Nightingale
600 Burning title deeds
609 Monument to Robert Kelwey
615 Wigan pier
621 Statue of Oliver Cromwell
628 Talbot Inn sign
632 Yarm viaduct
643 National Trust Zone Point sign

PREFACE

THIS IS A BOOK of discoveries: some now quite ancient, from childhood, when taking refuge in distant and barely imagined territory from the V2s falling on London I first saw Wigan, and (though only by night) Halifax. Many more derive from almost fifty years in newspapers: some of what appears here is based on columns I wrote for the *Guardian*, though in every case I went back to these places – even to Sidmouth, which never changes – and discovered more than before. During 2006 and 2007 I visited every place in this Gazetteer apart from a very few – Boothville, Swansea, Tockholes, Wolverhampton, and naturally Nowheresville, which are here just the briefest of interludes.

Treasured spots such as Abbeycwmhir, in what used to be Radnorshire, and Bishop's Castle in Shropshire are discoveries from holidays in the 1950s and 1960s. Also chronicled here are places which I came across by accident while looking for something or somebody else. I found Blennerhasset in Cumbria, for instance, the scene of the brief doomed hyper-idealist experiment in rural cooperation devised by William Lawson, while researching his more famous brother, the pacifist and temperance campaigner Sir Wilfrid. Senghenydd was a name I saw on a road sign on my way up the Rhymney Valley en route to Pontlottyn, which awakened a distant memory of some dark epic event. I found the story of the supposed discovery of the corpse of Lord Kitchener by a man who called himself Frank Power while researching two of his sisters for a previous book.

Some places I chose in homage to lifelong heroes. Rothley is here because that great polymath and irresistible master of our language, Thomas Macaulay, was born there; Bedford, because it's the birthplace of the brilliant, tragic topographer Ian Nairn (who, as we'll see, deplored it). Nairn was one of those irreplaceable writers who travelled the land with his eyes wide open. John Betjeman and Nikolaus Pevsner keep cropping up in these pages for the same reason. Gillian Darley's *Villages of Vision*, happily now reprinted at last by Five Leaves Press, put me on to a string of places I later went to explore. The Kettering writer and publisher J. L. Carr keeps finding his way into these pages too, as, quite unexpectedly, do Sir Walter Scott and the super-rich soap magnate who rose from a humble start in Bolton to leave the world as Lord Leverhulme.

Chance discoveries in second-hand bookshops introduced me to the so-called Sir William Courtenay who died at Bossenden Wood, to Canon Townsend of Durham who hoped to convert the pope, to the journals of Captain Gronow who came from Neath though he didn't often go back there and, in the scholarly pages of E. Royston Pike, to that one-time centre of squalor and pestilence, now mostly a yuppie kingdom, Jacob's Island, south east of Tower Bridge.

But the source to which I have turned most – which indeed has shaped this whole book – is one that the *Guardian*'s kindly librarians offered me one day when they found they had no further use for it: the ninth edition of John Bartholomew's *Gazetteer of the British Isles*, published in 1943. The book's stated purpose is bleakly practical, even prosaic: it sets out to list every place in these islands that is worthy of consideration, according to an order of service set out in the opening pages: name, county, status, docks, industries, university, special features, airport. Bartholomew, an Edinburgh man, produced his first edition in 1883, and this ninth is clearly the work of hundreds of different hands over more than half a century. Yet one is always aware of a personality behind it, which, though he died twenty-six years before this edition was published, must be Bartholomew's own, reflecting his own passions, priorities and quirky obsessions.

'I would spend long hours poring over the atlas,' says Hector Berlioz (whom we shall meet at Marylebone), looking back on his childhood in his entrancing *Memoirs*, 'examining the intricate system of islands, straits and promontories in the South Seas and the Indian archipelago, pondering on the origins of these remote regions, their climate and vegetation, the people who lived there, and filled with the desire to visit them.' Bartholomew, when I discovered him, had much that effect on me. Here are almost 800 pages, listing 90,000 places in England, Scotland, Wales and across the island of Ireland, from the Aan, or Water of Aven (*streamlet, E. Grampians*) to Zoze Point (*at the SW. extremity of Gerrans Bay, Cornwall, 3m. SE. of Falmouth*). In homage to Bartholomew, his starting point, the Aan, is my starting point; his last entry, Zoze Point, is my last entry too. The introductions for each of the places in this collection are taken from Bartholomew, though not always in full – I have spared readers some of his now poignant celebrations of railway stations where the lines were ripped up long ago, and post and telegraph offices which have closed or are doomed to close. His standard abbreviations – *ry. sta, G.W.R.* and *L.M.S., mkt.-town, spt.* and so on – are explained in a glossary at the end of the book. There are also in this book, which there aren't in Bartholomew, a series of signposts, put there for those who may wish to plot their way around the country geographically rather than alphabetically; who, for instance, having dallied in Stroud, may yearn to move on to nearby Tewkesbury rather than, as alphabetical order ordains, to distant Sunderland Point in Lancashire and Sutton-under-Whitestonecliffe, Yorkshire.

Maps can show you the shape of these places, create within the mind's eye the islands and straits and promontories as the gazetteer cannot; but the gazetteer will begin to uncover their secrets. '*Clevedon, urb. dist., seaside town and par., with ry. stas., G.W.R. and Weston, Clevedon and Portishead R., NW. Somerset, 15½m. WSW. of Bristol by rail; 3,292 ac., pop. 8,000...*' See? It is taking shape already. '*On the pier-head is a fixed light, seen 7m; there is a rocket apparatus...*' Bartholomew is obsessed with these lights. *Cleethorpes, Lincs, mun. bor., and par., with ry. terminus, L.N.E.*, '*shows 2 fixed red lights on the sewer outfall*'. '*Cape Wrath* [which we shall come to] *is crowned by a lighthouse with white and red alternating flashing light 400 ft. above high water and seen 27m.*' Also, for some reason I cannot discern, he seems fascinated by paper mills, most of them closed long ago. I had not guessed there would have been so many.

And among the assembled statistics there is poetry too. How can life be complete until one has deviated to investigate, say, Swacking Cuckoo, Slapfaggot Green or Twitty Fee; or, if you're across the sea in County Wexford, where this book does not venture, Forlorn Point? Then there is Temperance Town in Glamorgan: does this reflect a community dedicated to teetotalism, or is it, as with so many place names, a mere corruption of some older, forgotten, name? We shall see.

That the book is so out of date (Milton Keynes is a *par. and vil., Bucks, on the r. Ouzel, pop. 192*; we'll see later on what it has done to Tattenhoe) simply enhances its charm and feeds one's eagerness to go out and discover how places have changed in the sixty-five years since Bartholomew's ninth edition was completed. There are mysteries, too, which it isn't Bartholomew's task to investigate but which cry out for elucidation. Why are three hamlets in the old county of Cumberland – there are others in Northumberland and in Yorkshire – called Unthank? Why is Iwerne Courtnay (as he spells it) in Dorset, known also as Shroton? And whatever became of the settlements which had disappeared from Bartholomew's pages when the 1943 edition was updated twenty-five years later? Did they, like Snap in Wiltshire (*locality, Wilts, in Ramsbury rural dist.*: it comes in my book under Upper Upham), simply cease to exist? The pages which follow will try to unravel some of these mysteries. Others, I fear, will remain where he left them: lost in the mists of perplexity – for ever, perhaps.

My other debts are to people who offered hospitality, guidance, and often both. Patricia Long, who first alerted me to the importance of Samuel Laing, conducted me on such an instructive and enjoyable tour of Orkney, under which heading you will find him, that I began to believe she must even have fixed the fine weather. Martin Wainwright in Leeds put me on to the case of the Milngavie railplane; Alistair and Bud Macbeth in Helensburgh pointed me to, and equipped me with information on, Port Appin and the West Highland railway, and introduced me to Stewart Noble, who not only remembered the railplane but incited me to investigate Kinlochleven. Paul Alldred advised me on Leverburgh. Robert Waller, who knows more about more places in England than anyone I have ever met, came up with countless recommendations. I owe Quarr to my *Guardian* colleague, Jonathan Glancey. Julia Langdon took me to see the extraordinary tomb of the Burtons at Mortlake. Jill Crewe, on learning I had never seen Jaywick, Essex, advised me to go there immediately: you will scarcely believe what you see, she said; she was right. Alison and Julian Drury and Tom Humble acquainted me with the story of Tattenhoe, Dan and Fay Howison with the history of Exton, Rutland, and Whitwell's twinning with Paris; and Stephen Boyle and Maggie Gjessing helped me to understand the past and present of the Gipton and Seacroft estates in East Leeds. Janice Bailey of the Whitwick Historical Group and Janet Smith of the Ramsbottom Heritage Society dug out answers to questions, and David Harvey discovered the reason, which neither the National Trust nor the Ordnance Survey was able to tell me, why Zoze Point is nowadays Zone Point. Victor and Rosie Keegan in Herefordshire,

Matthew Parris and Julian Glover in Derbyshire, Kathy and Adrian Ham in Gloucestershire, Tim and Pat Cook in Cumbria were kind, considerate and informative hosts during my journeys. My wife Beryl came with me to the north of Scotland, and to some other destinations closer to hand, tolerated my constant changes of plan, and rescued my earliest text from innumerable errors. Toby Mundy at Atlantic Books was as ever hugely encouraging, as were his editorial director, Louisa Joyner (whose enthusiasm for the project reached the point of coming with me to the Wirral, her childhood territory) and her colleagues Fran Owen and Sarah Norman; also, as ever my agent at Curtis Brown, Jonathan Pegg.

Alexander Cruden, sole author of that extraordinary work, *A Complete Concordance to the Old and New Testaments*, whom we shall meet in Aberdeen, disavowed the word 'complete', declaring that it was appropriate only in a comparative sense, since 'poor sinful man can do nothing absolutely perfectly and completely'. That is certainly true of this book. There will be those who know these 150 places much better than I ever could on the basis of mere fleeting visits, and will ruefully note its omissions and errors. So it ought to be said that there would have been many more errors here but for the sharp and practised eye and tireless research of Jane Robertson, copy editor for this as for my two previous books.

Thinking back now the book is done, I have come to recognize how much I owe, in this and other respects, to three teachers at Christ's Hospital who made my schooldays into a true education. David Roberts (1900–1956), an ebullient extrovert Welshman, and Michael Cherniavsky (1920–1992), modest, shy and diffident but no less inspiring, took me into territories well beyond the history syllabus: I can still remember the thrill of hearing Michael declaim the passage of Carlyle lavishly lauding the Normans and condemning the Saxons that appear in the entry for Islip. (Not that he endorsed it; but he revelled in its sonorities.) David Jesson-Dibley (1924–2006), who died while I was at work on this book, introduced me in English classes to many of the writers and books I still most revere. 'The Planster's Vision' (see Jackfield) was one among many of his discoveries which had David hurtling into the classroom, bursting to share them with his class. In each case, their passion resembled Hector's in Alan Bennett's *The History*

Boys: 'Pass it on, boys. That's the game I want you to learn. Pass it on.' As a small acknowledgement of what I, and so many like me, gained from them, this book is dedicated to their memories; but also to that of my mother, who on a Rogers of Roundhay coach trip from Leeds to the Lake District in around 1949, told me it was high time I put down my book and started looking out of the window.

A B C D

E F G H

I J K L

M N O P

Q R S T

U V W X Y Z

AAN

AAN, or Aven, streamlet, E. Grampians, forms part of boundary between Aberdeenshire and Kincardineshire; runs into the Feugh.

I STARTED MY JOURNEYS where John Bartholomew started his book: at the river Aan, which rises on the northern slopes of the Grampian hills, south-west of the town of Banchory, beginning the journey that will merge it before very long, near the Feughside Inn, with the Water of Feugh; which in turn, having passed beneath the pretty bridge at Banchory, close to which there's a spot where people come to watch salmon leaping, it will join with the Dee on its way to Aberdeen and the sea. The clouds hung over the hills as I came to plot the course of the Aan, a not uncommon event, one assumes, since one of these hills is called by a Gaelic name that means 'Clouds Knob'. It was March, and well out of season. 'It's not like this in summer,' said a local man surveying all this serenity. 'Then, it's all motor bikes.' So many come to walk the greatest of local hills, Clachnaben, which is said to give views of the east of Scotland from Peterhead down to the Lammermuirs, that the surface is being eroded.

The river while I was there looked peaceful enough, but the Dee, with the Aan as contributing accomplice, has staged some spectacular scenes in its time, and people still talk of the Muckle Spate in the year 1829, when the water at Banchory rose to 27 feet above its normal level. It spread devastation all down the Dee, destroying most of the bridges away from Aberdeen, including one which Thomas Telford had erected at Ballater twenty years earlier.

I call it the Aan, because my mentor Bartholomew does, but the latest maps name it the Water of Aven, no doubt because someone thought that sounded more douce and alluring. I think they should have stuck to the ancient form Aan, not least because that puts it ahead of most contenders in the race to be first in gazetteers. As it is, some authorities put Ab Kettleby, Leicestershire, first, treating it as a place called 'Ab' to which Kettleby is a mere appendage. I went there to check out its charms against those I found near Banchory, and I think that on aesthetic grounds as well as historic practice, Aberdeenshire wins.

Ab Kettleby is a village which, apart from a pub called the Sugar Loaf which is just on it, is just off the main road from Nottingham to that famous progenitor of pork pies, Melton Mowbray. I was there on a gentle evening in spring. Daffodils flourished in gardens, birds sang, an early mower whirred into action, dutiful labradors were out for their evening walks. The ironstone church of St James, its solid tower topped by a spire, down the hill, past the pond and the old bakehouse (there are houses throughout the village which look as though they used to be shops, but such days are over) was not just shut, but heavily padlocked, having been declared a dangerous structure. The Anglicans were taking refuge, it seemed, in the Wesleyan Chapel (1843), the home of Ab Kettleby's Methodists.

Ab Kettleby's name reflects its ownership in the twelfth century by a person called Abbe, which is not a good qualification for coming first, since there are also scattered round England a collection of very small places whose names start with 'Aaron': Aaron Crags in Cumbria, Aaron Hill in Calderdale, Aaron's Hills in Surrey and Somerset, and Aaron Slack and Aaron's Town, again in Cumbria. The Ordnance Survey, the sacred text for such matters nowadays, puts the Aabe in Shetland ahead of them all: Bartholomew seems not to have heard of it. The British, as you can see, don't do too well in these matters. They have much to learn from the people of Norway, where there's a town with a name that is quite unchallengeable: Å.

ABBEYCWMHIR

ABBEYCWMHIR, par. and vil., NW. Radnorshire, 6m. NE. of Rhyader… has remains of Cistercian abbey founded in 1143… Abbey Hall is a seat.

A PLEASANTLY DEVIOUS ROAD, where a straight stretch of even a hundred yards is a matter for some amazement, off the A483 from Llandrindod Wells, county town of Powys, to one of the eighty-two places called Newtown known to Bartholomew, takes you slowly and reflectively westward into the almost ethereal calm of the village of Abbeycwmhir. A church, a pub, a stately hall, the ruins beside a stream of the twelfth-century Cistercian house which ushered it into existence, a huddle of houses, a Post Office, and even a petrol pump (though when I was there it didn't look to have discharged much petrol in the twenty-first century) are all set in a ring of hills, equipped with tempting paths inviting you to their summits. Though it's not by any means architecturally identical, the simple church with its belfry always makes me think of Samuel Palmer's picture Coming from Evening Church. Were the doors to open suddenly and the congregation to come blinking into the sunshine, I'd expect them to look like those in Palmer's picture: solemn, stately, with a holiness about them that suggests a procession of saints.

There was no one in the church when I went there, but the door, above which there's a simple carving of Christ ascending to heaven, was welcomingly unlocked – a notice asks you to close it behind you 'owing to birds' nests in the church'. In the Visitors' Book, people have written 'peaceful' and 'beautiful', which it is, but Visitors' Books in churches nearly always say that. The house is tucked away in the trees. David Verey's *Shell Guide to Mid Wales* says the house and the church are linked, built in the 1860s by the same architects in a style which Geoffrey Grigson called 'coniferous architecture of the purest Victorian conifer age'.

The abbey, like so many, especially here in the Marches, had a troubled history; Abbeycwmhir is not the stranger to turbulence that everything about it now tends to suggest. The monks were settled here by the sons of Madog, prince of what we now call Radnorshire, but Hugh Mortimer, and Roger, Earl of Hereford, drove them back to Trefgarne in Pembrokeshire. The most powerful figure in the south of Wales at the end of the twelfth century, Lord Rhys, brought them back again. When on his death the Mortimers returned, they came bearing charters and offering their protection; but the monks, beset with understandable doubts about their intentions, decamped dolefully to Dolgellau.

The abbey was a mighty construction, its nave comparable in size with that of Durham Cathedral and possibly exceeded only by Winchester. Llywelyn I, called the Great, asserting the independence of Wales in the 1220s, planned to turn the abbey into a cathedral. Any chance that Abbeycwmhir might have become a cathedral city was eradicated by the English king, Henry III, after it was brought to his notice that one of the monks of Abbeycwmhir had led his men into an ambush. The fines he imposed for this outrage precluded any further aggrandizement of the abbey.

Thereafter these lands fell into the grasp of the Mortimers, until they were taken back once more by Owain Glyndwr, whose supporters, seeing the abbey as an emblem of Norman dominance, ideologically looted some of its stone to build themselves houses. Henry VIII's dissolution of the monasteries and the ravages of the Civil War between them disposed of most of what remained. There is nothing left now but some fragments of a distinguished wall and a plaque which suggests that Llywelyn ap Gruffydd, the last native prince of Wales before the English appropriated the title, may lie buried here among the chomping sheep who are gathered on this warm afternoon under a shady tree.

All is stillness and silence, except for the little pub called the Happy Union which, for a pub, is quite still and silent too this afternoon. It's exactly the kind of unassuming hostelry one might hope to chance on, especially if attempting the Glyndwr's Way National Trail (Llwybr Cenedlaethol Fford Glyndwr), a walk of 135 miles which passes through the village on its circuitous route from Machynlleth to Knighton and Llanidloes, then up to Lake Vyrnwy and through to Welshpool. The walls are hung with pictures of great days in the village's history: the village *en fête* in 1893 under a banner which simply says 'Happiness'; and the same occasion re-created in 1993. John Charles of Leeds United and Wales, the hero of my childhood days on the Elland Road terraces and perhaps the most accomplished footballer that Wales has ever produced, is commemorated here too. There was huge enthusiasm for Leeds United here at one time, the landlord told me; unsurprisingly, it has faded since.

As I left the Happy Union, a man at the door asked what had brought me here. I said I had come to revisit a favourite place which I hoped to put into a book. 'It's such a lovely place,' he begged, 'please don't tell the world about it.' So I said that I wouldn't. Nor have I told the world: only that tiny segment of it that happens to read this book.

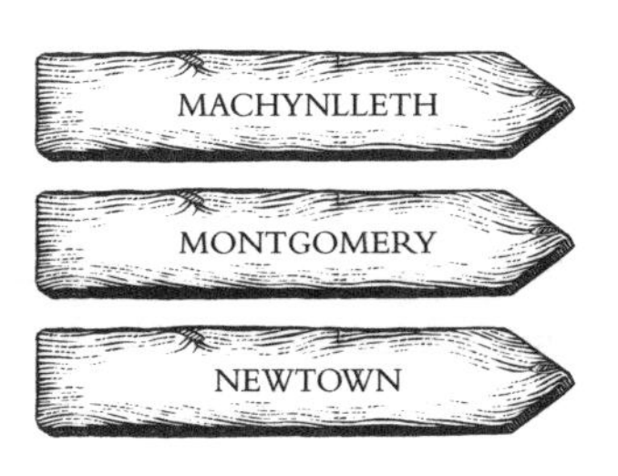

ABERDEEN

ABERDEEN, co. town of Aberdeenshire, city, parl. and roy. bur., and principal spt. in the N. of Scotland, between the mouths of the Dee and the Don… the fourth largest town in Scotland… The seat of a University formed by the union of the University and King's College of Old A. and the Marischal College of New A. … On N. pier is a fixed light visible 8m., and on S. breakwater, red, white and green lights, 88, 84 and 80 ft. above high water.

IN AN INCONSPICUOUS CORNER of Aberdeen, off Broad Street, close to the imposing presence of Marischal College, there's a drab little spot called Cruden's Court, where those with sharp eyes might possibly spot an acknowledgement – the only one I could find in the place – that out of this city, and out of this college, there emerged the sole creator of one of the world's most remarkable reference books: Cruden's *Complete Concordance to the Old and New Testaments.*

Until the computer age, which has made such endeavours look commonplace, this was an aid like no other, and is a work of quite awesome scholarship. Cruden's fellow eccentric, J. L. Carr, novelist, historian, aphorist and publisher of very small books, whom we'll encounter at Kettering, pays this characteristic terse tribute on the back of his *Welbourn's Dictionary of Prelates, Parsons, Vergers, Wardens, Sidesmen & Preachers, Sunday-School Teachers, Hermits, Ecclesiastical Flower-arrangers, Fifth Monarchy Men and False Prophets*:

> Alexander Cruden, MA, a Calvinist dissenter, d. 1770, between spells chained to an asylum bedstead, compiled references, chapter and verse, to every noun, verb, adjective and adverb in the Holy Bible. This great work, Cruden's Concordance to the Scriptures, inherited from his father, stands by this publisher's bedside, a constant inspiration to the compilation of similarly valuable Works of Reference.

Exactly. And, odd though he was, I'd have thought his native city might have considered him worth a statue; especially when, as we shall see, he left all his money to it. Why he hasn't got one is a matter of doubt. It could be because at an early opportunity he left the city and spent most of his time in distant, alien London – despite the dissipation which this God-fearing son of God-fearing parents in God-fearing Aberdeen saw all around him in the capital all the time. It might also be because his life was so full of turbulence, punctuated by episodes which suggested, at the least, a degree of mental imbalance, and landed him at times in asylums.

Alexander Cruden was born in 1699, the second of eleven children, to a respected bailie of Aberdeen, William Cruden, and his wife Isabel. The oldest son, a boy of precocious intellect, became Professor of Greek at Marischal College at the age of twenty. Bright as he was, Alexander was never likely to emulate that. And his training for the ministry was disrupted, and then abandoned, when he fell in love with the daughter of an Aberdeen minister. Her rejection of him led to a mental breakdown, and the fact of that breakdown would tilt the scales against him in moments of crisis later in life.

Cruden left Aberdeen by boat for London where his search for work took him into the service of the Earl of Derby, who wished to be read to in French. Unfortunately, though he had a good understanding of French, Cruden had no idea how to pronounce it, which led the earl to dismiss him. His attempts to get his job back, despite the overwhelming evidence of his unsuitability, can only be construed as obsessional. He found a job as a proof-reader, and after a while opened a bookshop under the Royal Exchange. On the death of the official bookseller to Queen Caroline in 1735, Cruden was given the post, which brought him a dependable income. But that was merely a sideline. By now he was well embarked on his extraordinary project: a kind of super-index to the Bible.

Such an enterprise had rarely been attempted before, and when it was, it was carried out by a team which numbered fifty scholars at least: some accounts say 500. Yet Cruden worked absolutely alone, compiling some 2 million entries, beginning with 'Aaron' and ending with 'Zurishaddai (see Shelumiel)', and the 'Zuzims' of Genesis 14:5, making his book, it was estimated, three times as long as the Authorized Version of King James's Bible. Nor did he content himself with simply listing each word and citing where one could find it. Sometimes he launched into reverential soliloquies on concepts he considered of special importance to every believer; for example, 'Heart – the word heart is used in Scripture as the seat of one's life or strength; hence it means mind, soul, spirit, or one's entire emotional nature and understanding. It is also used as the centre or inner part of a thing'. No other book known to man at that time matched the *Concordance*. Nevertheless Cruden himself was far from satisfied. It was talked of as being 'complete'; but that, he protested, was true 'only in a comparative sense' since 'poor sinful man can do nothing absolutely perfectly and completely'.

Unhappily, poor sinful men failed to accord him the recognition he deserved. Anglicans distrusted the book as the work of a dissenter. Queen Caroline, to whom he dedicated it, died just a few days after he had presented it to her, thus depriving him of his expected reward. Soon after, according to standard versions of his biography, he lapsed once more into insanity. The occasion this time was his pursuit of a widow called Mrs Pain. She and her husband, who had a business in Piccadilly, had taken Cruden on as a kind of spiritual counsellor. When in 1737 Mrs Pain was widowed, Cruden began to pursue her with pledges of love. She took offence and called in a friend (who, it seems, was intent on wedding the widow too) to assist her. Cruden was apprehended and taken to a private asylum at Bethnal Green.

It was here, as J. L. Carr describes, that he was chained for spells to a bedstead. Somehow he managed to get hold of a knife, sawed through the leg of the bed, and escaped. When recaptured, he demanded to be taken before the Lord Mayor of London to assert his right to freedom. The Lord Mayor, having examined him, declared that Cruden was sane. Had he left it at that his miseries might have been over. Instead, he pursued his captors at law through the courts, where he wrecked his case by the way he pleaded it, misconstruing the law and alienating the court. And here the episode with the girl he had wooed in Aberdeen came back to blight him: a letter written by Cruden's father, referring to his serious state of disturbance nearly twenty years before, was procured and produced in court.

After years of earning his living as a proof corrector, Cruden now decided that he ought to extend his talent for the elimination of error on to a wider stage. Having observed and been shocked by what he saw around him in London, he thought that God had called him to act as a censor of morals. 'Alexander the Corrector', he styled himself, in a declaration of intent written in the third person. He stated his wish to be appointed 'Corrector of the People'; he knew from his studies that just such a post had existed in ancient Rome. Ambition now fed on ambition. Surely, he told himself, his chance of success in the role would be greatly enhanced were he given a knighthood. 'Sir Alexander the Corrector' had a ring about it that mere 'Alexander the Corrector' did not. He took to attending the court of King George with a £100 note in his pocket, hoping it might prove persuasive. Again, to be MP for the City of London would be a dramatic boost for his aspirations; so he proceeded to seek nomination. His cause was not helped by a third contentious incident, which began when the corrector intervened in a brawl to rebuke one of the participants for using bad language. The altercation which followed led again to his arrest – at the instigation, he believed, of his sister and brother-in-law – and a further spell in a private asylum ensued, this time in Chelsea, constrained by a straitjacket.

There followed an obsessive pursuit of a woman called Elizabeth Abney (see Abney Park). True, he had never met her, but he explained to her in a letter that he was fifty-six, it was time that he settled down, and she was the woman for him. Though rich, she was still unmarried at fifty-one, and Cruden seemed fully satisfied that the match would be good for her too. He seems also to have been convinced that God was in favour of this arrangement. Miss Abney, however, was not, and understandably felt that (to use a term not yet then in circulation) Cruden was stalking her. When he got no response to his pleadings he issued what he called a 'declaration of war', renewing his campaign. Still the lady was not won over. In other senses, however, events had turned in his favour. The *Concordance* was now recognized as the superb, if eccentric, feat that it was. George III, to whom he sent a revised edition, made him a gift of £100. With £500 from a bookseller and sales of his new edition making him £300 more, he was now a man of means. The King entertained him at court, taking avidly to him while shunning the novelist and creator of Tristram Shandy, Laurence Sterne, who was standing close by. Both Oxford and Cambridge honoured him.

He was now a man of some substance; but still not, perhaps, an entirely sane one. In 2004, Julia Keay published a book of revisionist biography called: *Alexander the Corrector: the tormented genius who unwrote the Bible*. In contradiction of most previous accounts, she argued that Cruden was never the mentally unstable figure which his misadventures suggested. She contended that previous analyses had been seriously flawed, that his episodes of curious behaviour were largely explicable in terms of his grievous life experiences. The girl he had adored in his Aberdeen youth had rejected him not because of his oddity but because she was involved in an incestuous relationship with her brother – by whom she was pregnant. This was a man whom Cruden knew well, by whom he had been bullied at school, and who nevertheless had gone on to become an honoured figure in Aberdeen. Alexander's subsequent incarceration when he pursued the widow Pain had been engineered by his rival for her affections; as the Lord Mayor had said at the time, there was no good reason to think he was mad. And the third occasion, the one which followed the street brawl? That, said Julia Keay, had been confected by his irresponsible, malevolent sister and her husband.

The case she makes is plausible, but not to my mind persuasive. The really significant evidence is the *Concordance*. He may not have been mad: but like the account of his pursuit of Mrs Pain and Miss Abney, his masterpiece shrieks out the word 'obsessive'. Only a seriously obsessional person could have conceived it and brought it as near to perfection as sinful man could achieve. In his classic book *A Social History of Madness* Roy Porter says Cruden's remonstrances against those he believed had misused him 'command an important place in the history of mad people's writings'. Yet on his assessment the issue of madness isn't really the point. These outpourings deserve our respect and attention, Porter says, because 'they stand at the headwaters of a long and honourable tradition of protest against arbitrary confinement and the evils of asylum'. He catches Cruden's tortured way of looking at life with these words from among his writings: 'Joseph the son of Jacob was called a Dreamer, hated by his brethren, let down into the pit, sold to the Midianites, and by them sold to Potiphar an officer of Pharaoh, and was afterwards falsely accused by Potiphar's wife and cast into prison. And Alexander the son of William was falsely accused of insanity by some unthinking persons, who little expected that he who behaved with the mildness and meekness of a Moses could upon proper occasion act with the undaunted courage and resolution of an Alexander...'

In 1769, Cruden returned at last to the city of Aberdeen, where his first great woe had overtaken him almost fifty years before, and stayed for a year. As the author of the celebrated *Concordance*, the old man (he was seventy now) was given a kindly and courteous reception, but detected – his old corrector instincts still at work – that the place was growing ungodly. Yet he then went back to London. On 1 November the following year, he failed to appear for breakfast. A woman servant who went to look for him found him dead, on his knees. He had hoped to be buried in the graveyard of the Kirk of St Nicholas in his native town, but that was refused: a space was found for him in a dissenters' churchyard in Southwark.

Aberdeen may have named an inconspicuous street after its awkward, uneasy son (there's a street called Correction Wynd too but that seems unconnected with Cruden) but unless you know where to look, you are never likely to find it as the street name is nowhere displayed. Few, unless forewarned, will spot the plaque the city erected to him, on a walkway through to a car park. In far from compelling lettering on a dim grey background, not much above knee level, it says: 'Alexander Cruden 1699–1770. Master of Arts Marischal College, Compiler of the Concordance to the Bible, was born in a house in Cruden's Court near this spot'.

Yet maybe this obscurity would have suited him. If he came to Aberdeen nowdays, no longer the strict and dutiful place of its reputation, no longer immune to permissiveness seeping up from the south, it might very well put him in mind of St Matthew 10:14 'When ye depart out of that house or city, shake off the dust of your feet'. Not least when he came to the deconsecrated church that's now known as the Soul Casino.

ABNEY PARK

ABNEY PARK, dist. and cem'y., N. London,
in Stoke Newington met. bor.

ON THE DULL AND shabby A10, not the loveliest road out of London, close to the point where Stoke Newington High Street gives up and becomes Stamford Hill, imposing gates announce Abney Park cemetery. This is one of the group of London cemeteries which used to be known as 'the magnificent seven', long before that term reached the cinema, but many years of neglect, from which it is still being rescued by the Abney Park Cemetery Trust and the London Borough of Hackney, betrayed the high ambitions of those who created it. This was the second home – their first was eleven miles further out of London, at Theobalds Park in Hertfordshire – of Sir Thomas Abney, alderman of the City of London, and Mary, his wife, who inherited what became Abney Park and its newly constructed manor house from her brother. She was thirty-six years younger than Sir Thomas, and on his death resolved to make a new life for herself. She left Theobalds and moved into Abney Park, taking with her her daughter Elizabeth and the celebrated hymnodist Isaac Watts, an ailing and vulnerable figure whom the Abneys had rescued and invited in as a permanent house-guest. Here they created a place that, uniquely in Britain, was both a cemetery and a garden full of fine trees: a cemetery, too, open to dissenters of every persuasion.

Few people whose graves you will find here are famous, unlike those of Highgate, where Karl Marx is buried, or Kensal Green. You cannot roam it, as you can the Père Lachaise in Paris, in the full and certain assurance that you'll come upon somebody famous which ever path you may take: Chopin or Cherubini, Corot or Callas, Beaumarchais or Oscar Wilde, Pissarro and Piaf, the gloriously talented jazz pianist Michel Petrucciani or Jim Morrison of The Doors. By far the most honoured figure at Abney Park now, with his statue commanding the heart of it (though in fact he is buried elsewhere, in Bunhill Fields), is Dr Watts, who wrote hymns as revered as 'When I survey the wondrous Cross' and 'Our God, our help in ages past', sung nowadays as 'Oh God…' after John Wesley changed it. Watts was also the author of many improving works for children: the verses 'How doth the little busy bee/ Improve the shining hour/ And gather honey all the day/ From every opening flower!' and 'Tis the voice of the sluggard, I heard him complain: "You have waked me too soon! I must slumber again!"' dutifully committed to memory by generations of children, and joyously mocked in *Alice in Wonderland* by Lewis Carroll.

Watts stands now in majesty in the centre of the park, his left hand clutching a book; his right hand is lost. His back is turned to the chapel, which means that he's spared the distressing site of its present condition – its interior gone, its windows empty, with plants growing out of what's left of its roof. You come to him down muddy pathways, lined with trees and enveloping foliage. Here and there an obstreperous tree has roughly uprooted a tombstone. Walk on, and here is a clutch of Salvationists: General William Booth, who founded the Army, his wife and the son who succeeded him, Bramwell, flanked by their senior acolytes, a host of Commissioners and Mrs Commissioners: 'promoted to glory' their memorials say, though with William and Catherine Booth it is 'went to heaven' as simply and surely as 'went to lunch'.

Elsewhere there are City of London dignitaries, and the Chartist leader James Bronterre O'Brien, described at Abney Park as the 'intellectual leader' of Chartism, as if to set him apart from the hot-headed firebrand Feargus O'Connor, whom we will meet at Snig's End; and Emily Gosse, wife of the naturalist Philip Gosse and mother of Edmund, who wrote the chilling account of his childhood, *Father and Son*, to which we shall come at St Marychurch. But this is more a place for the graves of the unfamous, along paths frequented by strollers, joggers, friends locked in serious conversation, mothers with children freshly collected from school – though also, it has to be said, the odd slightly sinister, prowling invader. The place has a melancholy charm: everywhere there are chronicles of lives full of sorrow. Here is the family grave of Frederick and

Emily Mean, of Clapton just up the road: 'In loving memory of our dear children, Frederick William, 13 months (1879); Emily Maud, 1 year 8 months (1884); Hubert Arthur, 1 year 10 months'. Their mother, the older Emily, died in 1903, in her fifty-first year; three years later her grandson Cyril lived for only five weeks. A further son, Ted, having survived childhood, fell in France in July 1916: he was twenty-six. Frederick himself, husband and father, lived on until he was ninety: he died in March 1942, nearly forty years after his wife. At the foot of their catalogue is the inscription: 'Love lives on'.

Some of the inscriptions along these paths are almost joyful. The 'sure and certain hope of resurrection' of the funeral service flourishes among the foliage. 'On that happy Easter morning' says one inscription, 'All the graves their dead restore/ Father, sister, child and mother/ Meet once more'. There's also a great sense here of London as a cosmopolitan city. The names are an eloquent mix of old London and refugee London – nowhere more so than on the memorial to over ninety people, some never identified, who died when one of Hitler's bombs fell on flats in Coronation Avenue, London N16, on Sunday, 13 October 1940. Names like Cooperstein, Danziger, Krakosky, Muscovitch, Serkovitch (many of them would have been Jewish refugees from Nazi Germany) are interspersed with the Ballards and Beams and Bulls and Chalkleys and Ponds and Smiths – and someone who was known both as Black and as Swart.

As Dr Watts perceptively noted, time like an ever-rolling stream bears all its sons away; its daughters, too, for Elizabeth Abney, who inherited the estate from her mother, and who, despite the relentless attentions of Alexander Cruden of Aberdeen, never married, directed that on her death everything she owned should be sold and the proceeds given to Nonconformist charities. Thus she proved her fidelity to the principle urged on her in childhood by Dr Watts ('Your most Affectionate Monitor', as he signed himself, 'and obliged Servant in the daily Views of a future World'): 'Remember what God Himself will expect at your hands, from whose Grace you have received plentiful Distributions in the Beginning of your Days.'

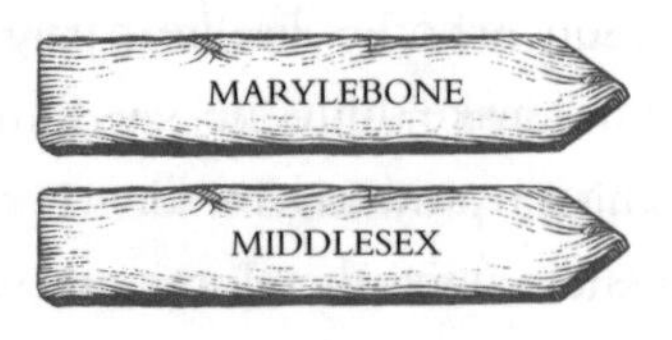

ASHFORD

ASHFORD, urb. dist., par. and mkt. town, with ry. sta., S.R., E. Kent, on r. Stour… The locomotive and carriage works of the S.R. Co. are principally in this par.

JOHN MASEFIELD, POET LAUREATE in my youth, lived at tidy Tetbury, Gloucestershire. That is just the sort of rarefied rural place you'd expect a poet of those days to choose. The town most associated with his predecessor but one, however, was less predictable: the railway town of Ashford, Kent. But that in some ways seems appropriate. It's a familiar assumption that of all the nineteen incumbents from the time the office was established for John Dryden in 1668, Alfred Austin, solemnly responding to the promptings of his muse in his house and garden at Swinford Old Manor, some three miles out of the centre of Ashford, is the unchallenged worst.

This honour should not be given away too lightly, and there's certainly competition – from Laurence Eusden, for instance, born in 1688, offered the post at thirty, dead at forty-two in May 1730. Eusden, a serious scholar, ordained late in life, became the unhappily drink-sodden rector of Coningsby, Lincolnshire, of whom Thomas Gray (one of many good poets who was offered the post but rejected it) wrote: 'Eusden was a person of great hopes in his youth, though at last he turned out a drunken parson.' Or from Colley Cibber, a dramatist of some note, but a very indifferent poet; or perhaps, above all, from Henry Pye, another military man and one-time Tory MP, who owed his job less to his talent than to the services he had rendered to the Prime Minister, Pitt the Younger. And it has to be said that some of the lines for which Alfred Austin was most mocked and despised were never written (or as he would have said, penn'd) by him.

E. F. Benson, whose tales are partly so entertaining because when in doubt he would sometimes make things up, says in his wonderful memoir, *As We Were* (1930), that the lines which were said to have been written by Austin on the illness of the Prince of Wales – 'Across the wires the gloomy message came: / "He is no better; he is much the same"' – may not have been written by him. They certainly weren't. They were foisted on the poor man by an Oxford parodist. Yet Benson – and others have followed him – unconditionally accused Austin of having written in his poem on the Jameson Raid: 'They went across the veldt/ As hard as they could pelt'; whereas had he bothered to check he would have found that the genuine version says: 'So we forded and galloped forward,/ As fast as our beasts could pelt,/ First eastward, then trending northwards,/ Right over the rolling veldt' – which at least has a pounding rhythm and swagger about it.

Still, some of the verse he wrote, and boasted of having written, was scarcely better. 'A disdain of habitual frivolity, ostentatious opulence, material worldliness and vulgar ambition', he said of his poems, 'is, I truly assert, their prevailing mark, together with the love of a rural and simple life, tempered only by some acquaintance with – permit me again the phrase – things in general and public affairs.' Others have been less kind. Quite apart from the bulbousness of his verse, and his weakness for words like 'blent', 'girt' and 'enjoined', he clearly had a cloth ear. How otherwise could he have written: 'When with staid mothers' milk and sunshine warmed/ The pasture's frisky innocents bucked up'; or 'Love, though an egotist, can deify/ A vulgar fault, and drape the gross with grace' (true though that is); or the characteristic claim: 'Nor would I shape for fame my lay.'

It didn't help that he was in most eyes a preposterous figure. That he stood only five feet tall was hardly his fault (and Alexander Pope was shorter, at four feet six inches) but somehow it magnified his pomposity. He derided his predecessor, Tennyson. He had, he liked to confide, pointed out Tennyson's faults to the poet, and Tennyson had acknowledged that his strictures were merited. And, like many vain people, he liked to boast of his modesty: having inscribed his autograph in somebody's book he added beneath it: 'humility is the window of the heart'. He did, however, accept (when the critics fell on it and savaged it) that what he'd considered one of his greatest works, *The Human Tragedy*, had been produced too fast (or as he preferred to put it, 'written with reckless rapidity'). The failure of this epic even led to a bout of writer's block; or in Austin-speak, 'a prolonged pause in poetic procedures'.

So why did he get the job? Tennyson had died, and who could ever be fit to follow Tennyson? For more than three years the post remained vacant. Gladstone procrastinated;

Lord Rosebery too failed to act; for a while the new Conservative leader, the Marquees of Salisbury, brooded too. Queen Victoria was thought to favour Swinburne, though she wouldn't have done had she known of the scurrilous verse he had written about her and circulated to friends, alleging forms of sexual malpractice of which she was not merely guiltless but probably quite unaware. Then Salisbury sent for Austin, whom he knew well. Andrew Roberts, in his life of Salisbury, says that, when taken to task for this curious choice, he replied: 'No one else applied for the laurel crown' – and Austin, he added, seemed so very keen to have it. In fact, this was Austin's reward for making himself useful. For years he had been writing leaders for a Tory daily paper, *The Standard*. What he wrote was invariably tailored to Salisbury's taste; indeed, Roberts says that Austin used to allow the politician to redraft what he had written, a practice of which his editor appeared to approve.

From his youth, Alfred had been an unwavering Tory. In 1865 he stood for the party at Taunton, where he finished fourth in a field of four. Fifteen years later, as a favour to Disraeli, he put up for Dewsbury in his native county of Yorkshire but was soundly beaten again. For several years he also edited the staunchly Conservative *National Review*. It was almost, therefore, as if Tony Blair had awarded the office of Laureate to Peter Mandelson. Here, Salisbury could say to himself, is a man I can trust. So it was at the least a fine irony that the very first poem he wrote as Laureate – hailing the brave defiance of Dr Leander Starr Jameson's unauthorized attack on the Boers – caused an outcry, and greatly displeased the Queen, to whom Salisbury had to apologize.

Austin had, as he might have put it, a second string to his bow. He was, in his own estimation, a poet of talent and consequence; he was also a gifted gardener. That is why he had settled at Swinford. The gardens there were what attracted him first: it was only when he'd already decided he wanted the place that he took any real account of the manor house that went with them. In a bestselling book called *The Garden that I Love* (1894), he described, in the kind of language that England had come to expect of him, his journey to Ashford (in Austinese terminology, 'thither I betook myself').

Reaching the station, 'I found myself unable to obtain a conveyance of any sort, by reason of some high ecclesiastical function that had set the little town agog.' Fortunately, a 'genial though suspiciously rubicund' porter accosted him and accompanied him on the three-mile journey to Swinford. Down the old elm avenue the pair of them marched, until soon 'the umbrageous branches came to an end', and they found themselves in a park 'indifferently cared for', but full of fine trees. 'If there be a wood reeve of this well-timbered domain, he must be, I thought to myself, a good old Tory, indeed, who does not allow trunk to be axed or bough to be lopped.' At this point, his companion pointed out to him 'a goodly Jacobean mansion of red brick', which he swiftly recognized as 'the haven of my hopes'. They were joined at this point by two others: a bent, bareheaded man with a scythe – 'Father Time'– and his wife, 'who with the exception of her raiment, seemed the very double of himself, in hue, age, manner and toothless speech'. There was not (apart perhaps from the ancient couple) an eyesore anywhere: ' "Suum quisque domum spatio circumdat" (Each person surrounds his house with a space), I reiterated to myself, with a contentment rivalling that of the wood pigeons.'

He commemorated his garden in a series of mildly fictionalized books, in which he appears as 'The Poet'; his companion, Veronica, is based on Hester, his wife. The Austins, strutting around London and Kent, seemed an ill-assorted couple: he tiny and birdlike, she in time growing vast and majestic. The public loved these books and bought them in their thousands, and indeed one of the kindlier accounts of Austin's life suggests that he deserves to be celebrated more for his aubrietas and hydrangeas than for his umbrageous verse. So I went to Ashford in the hope of inspecting his horticultural legacy. But Swinford Old Manor is now a special needs school for boys, and when I was there the builders were at work on a substantial extension. It was Easter school holiday time, and the staff and the boys were away. A children's holiday project had taken over the place, one of whose leaders assured me there was now very little to see. Even Poet's Walk, Austin's particular pride, no longer survived, he said. So Austin has, I'm afraid, to stand or fall by the poetry.

Ashford does not seem to have honoured him. There is no street named after him, which makes him second best to a foreigner, another unlikely Ashfordian, the French philosopher and theologian, Simone Weil. She lived in Ashford during the Second World War, though making frequent forays to London, the railway service being then as now one boon of living in Ashford. It was in this uncelebrated town that she died in 1943, and in the saddest of circumstances. She had vowed to eat no more than she would have been able to do as a prisoner of the Nazis; as a result, she ate little or nothing and, in effect, she wasted away. At the time it was described as a death brought on by her principles, although nowadays the invocation of prison conditions would be portrayed in the tabloids as a cover for anorexia. Ashford, at any rate, has named part of its ring road after her. For many Ashfordians now the name 'Simone Weil' now means something you drive down, often with the accelerator pressed as close to the floor as you dare.

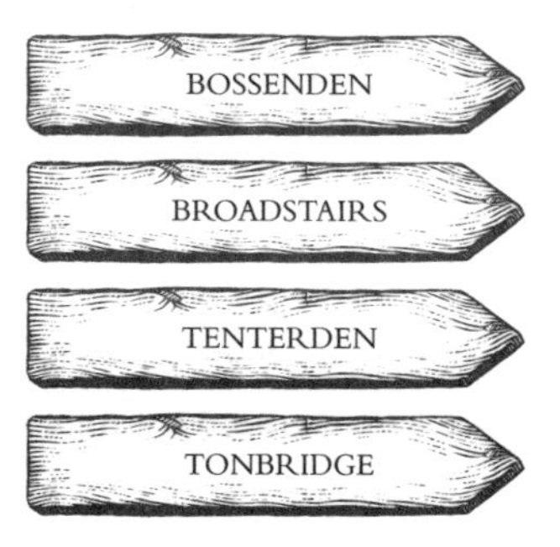

ASHWELL

ASHWELL, par., vil. and ry. sta. (A. and Morden)
L. N. E., Herts, 4½m. NE. of Baldock…

AS YOU DRIVE THOUGH the prairie landscapes of the A505 east of Baldock, you start to see signs to the north offering Ashwell. Unless you're impossibly pressed for time, accept this invitation. It will introduce you to a very endearing small town. True, these days Ashwell calls itself a village, as Bartholomew does, but they're wrong: it's a town. It's too full of the sense of centuries of accumulated experience of being a town to surrender that status. Indeed, Ashwell was once – though admittedly as far back as the reign of William Rufus – the fourth town of Hertfordshire, a county to which it only just belongs. Go a mile to the east and you're in Cambridgeshire; perhaps two miles west, you're in Bedfordshire. Go north and you could be in either.

St Mary's church, just back from the main street, gives you a solid sense of the place as it used to be. It's a big bold church, built like so much of Ashwell out of chalk, a substance that does not wear well and keeps local builders busy. It's fine fourteenth-century tower looms presidentially over the village. It was always substantial, but they added more when they heard of Henry V's success at Agincourt. There's a spire on the top of the tower which looks like an afterthought, and not necessarily a sensible one. What lures some people to Ashwell church is the writing on the wall. Someone whose name will never be known but clearly had talent etched on the walls a picture of St Paul's in London – not Wren's cathedral, but the one, bigger than Wren's, which stood there until the Great Fire of London did what even Hitler's bombers failed to do to its successor – reduced it to rubble. Alongside it are messages scrawled on the chalk: one from the plague year, reflecting the misery of those who survived; another recording the great storms of January 1361 which blew off the spire of Norwich Cathedral. A plaque on the wall emphasizes that sense of continuity that is always with you here, listing rectors of Ashwell from 1218 (Alan) through Odode Wathyngton (1308), William Clarivant (1509), John Libanus (1668), Samuel J. Panjotti-Webb (1892: he was there for thirty-three years) to 1998, when Jacqueline Birdseye took over; though the Reverend Birdseye has now been succeeded by a priest in charge.

When you leave the church for the streets, whichever route you take should delight you. Best of all is the long and rambling main street, the geographical equivalent of some wholly unstructured but enjoyable conversation, a happy jumble of houses, hardly any two the same, some colour-washed, some dour, and yet all in sympathy. Sometimes fortunate towns attain, without the aid of planners or architects, what even the best of planners and architects often can't. There is harmony in this disharmony; like one of those people whose faces break all the rules yet are undeniably lovely, the sequence looks beautiful. I'm not alone in this judgement. R. M. Healey, who wrote the *Shell Guide to Hertfordshire*, published in 1982, was clearly swept away by the place, as were his editors who, shunning their usual rules of balance, filled page after page, not to mention the dustjacket cover, with pictures of this small town: the church, the Georgian houses great and small, the assortment of happy domestic building, a butcher's shop seen through a lych gate… 'Yet the beauty,' Healey says, 'is robust. This is no Lavenham or Lacock.'

The little museum – the village museum, as they mistakenly call it – helps establish the sense of the place, reviewing its characteristic buildings and their construction, its traditional occupations, its breweries and its pubs, among which at various times it has boasted the Jester, the Fox, the Cricketers, the Wagon and Horses, the Australian Cow, the Six Bells, the White Horse, the Greyhound, the Swan, the Bull's Head, the Stag's Head, the Bushel and Strike, the Engine, the Chaffcutter, the Rose and Crown, the Bear, the Three Brewers, and the Chalkman's Knoll. Today there are three: the Rose and Crown, the Three Tuns and the Bushel and Strike (the strike being the board you used for sweeping off surplus wheat). The museum, in a building formely known as the Town House, was given to Ashwell by one of its sons who made good, or at least became Mayor of Brighton. 'A scene almost worthy of a fairy story was enacted in the old-world town of Ashwell on Saturday,' a local paper reported, 'when, after going out into the world to make his fortune as a boy of fifteen half a century ago, Sir William Benjamin Gentle returned to the place of his boyhood and opened the half-timbered Tudor building which he has restored and presented to the town as a museum.' Note that it says the town, not the village – twice.

Yet the High Street itself is a museum: a historical record as well as a working street. Walk only a little way west and you're in the country. Walk east and you come to the spot where it all began: the spring from which it derives its name where the river Rhee starts, which in time will become the Cam and glorify the city of Cambridge. It's a dell-like spot below the main road with a backdrop of good-looking houses beyond. Goodness knows how Gentle could drag himself off to Brighton. *The Shell Guide* went overboard; so do I. Unreservedly, this place, this *town*, is a joy.

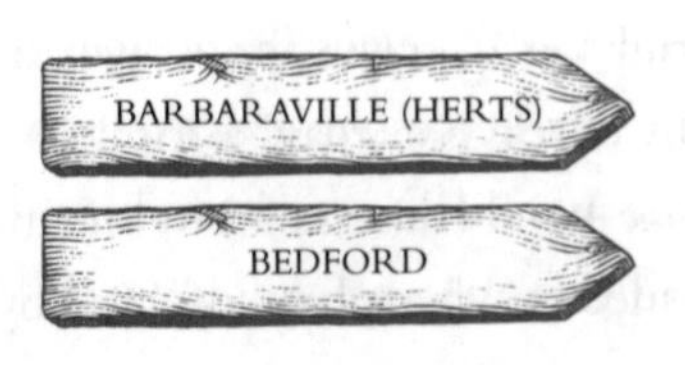

ASTON

ASTON, ward and ry. sta., L.M.S., Warwickshire, in bor. of Birmingham. At Aston Hall Charles I was entertained prior to the battle of Edge Hill.

IN THE SHADOW OF the Aston Expressway which carries the raging A38 out of the centre of obsessively motorized Birmingham, there's a little thicket of streets, once the homes of the poor, now dominated by light industry: the Mountford Rubber Company, M. P. Manipulated Tubes, Radshape Sheet Ltd, Engineering Consistency Services Ltd, City Electrical Factors Ltd. And among them, Aston Manor School, a technology college – all reassuring evidence in these post-industrial times that this city still makes and mends things. Here in January 1883, at the point where Bracebridge Street crosses Miller Street, the police apprehended a man whom they named as John Hartwell, although he preferred to be known as, variously, Methratton, the Great Seer of England, Anna Ross, the seeress of New York, the Philosophical Astrologer, Grand Master of Mysteries, or Enchanter, Sorcerer and Dealer in Magic and Spells. The police, who had been keeping watch to see if his post was being delivered, intercepted four letters and then took charge of a further two to three hundred which had been left at 139 Miller Street, the home of Betty Foxley, next door to the house where he lodged.

The *Birmingham Daily Post* reported the outcome. John Hartwell, twenty-nine, writer, alias Methratton, the Great Seer of England, described on the court sheet as 'of imperfect education', was brought up for sentence, having been committed by the stipendiary to the sessions as a rogue and vagabond. 'The prisoner, who wore a faded blue ribbon, presented a somewhat dejected appearance. Evidence was given that Elizabeth Miller, of Leicester, a well-dressed young woman, having answered an advertisement in a Leicester newspaper, sent "Methratton" 2s 6d in stamps. In return, he stated that she would be very wealthy (laughter) but that she was not to marry yet (laughter), and that when she did marry, it would be to someone of great wealth.'

MOUNTFORD RUBBER CO. LTD.

This was one of a series of court appearances which uncovered the methods employed by the prophet. 'I have given my best attention to the particulars of your destiny,' he had written to one subscriber, 'and find that by mysterious omens the sign Libra (the balance) bears rule over your fate, which tells of the hazards of chance – a rise beyond your expectations, a pompous name, and the gifts of wealth.' Another customer was treated to a stream of watery advice: 'Your fate is at present unsettled. Choose mostly the westward rivers, and the sea, and places where navigable rivers and large bodies of water are.'

The accused was said to have come from Daventry, Northants, and to claim descent from Lord Lovell. He believed he was divinely inspired, and asserted that in 1876 he had foretold a terrible storm three months before it occurred. He further claimed that what he was doing was perfectly legal, so long as his forecasts were made within his own house and he made no charge above his costs. He knew this was so because he had seen it stated in the *Daily Telegraph*. The seer warned the court that were he to be convicted, the country and its rulers would be ruined.

The law remained unimpressed. At the Magistrates' Court, the scene of his first appearance in the series (though he'd been jailed in the previous year on a charge of practising mystic arts, so he wasn't new to the process) the bench had expressed amazement at the credulity of the women who had dealt with the seer. Mr Herbert (magistrates' clerk) said he had not thought so many fools were to be found in the country. In the end, at Warwick Assizes, Hartwell was jailed for six months. His offence as listed upon the charge sheet was defrauding a large number of people by professing to reveal the future.

No doubt he should have foreseen this. And maybe he reflected as he was taken down on his misfortune in getting nailed for false prophecy when men of greater eminence, in politics and elsewhere, some earning far more than he was, were constantly uttering false prophecies. The issue which Hartwell's case raises today is this: is the offence of defrauding people by professing to reveal the future still on the statute book? If it is, there are several prosperous persons who might well be called to account at the Assizes with a very good chance of spending a spell in prison. Why, open-minded people may wonder, is Lord Rees-Mogg, whose prophecies on political and economic events are such a matter for wonder that *Private Eye* long ago nicknamed him 'Mystic Mogg', still at liberty? My favourite case of his legendary predictive skills is the piece he wrote in *The Times* shortly before the ousting of Iain Duncan Smith from the Conservative leadership, headed: 'We don't need a hero: bring on the Quiet Man'. ('The quiet man' was how the doomed Duncan Smith had recently designated himself.) 'I must hold myself back from exaggerating for effect,' he wrote, 'but I look forward to the lashings of humble pie that are about to be served up to the more supercilious commentators and above all, to the BBC, always ready to write a premature obituary for a Conservative leader.' Before long, the humble pie, you might say, was on the other foot. Then there's the *Daily Telegraph* columnist, a gung-ho supporter of the war against Saddam Hussein and a big fan of Donald Rumsfeld, who in the spring of 2003 prophesied: 'There will be terrible acts of suicide-bomber depravity in the months ahead, but no widespread resentment at or resistance of the western military presence.' Within a year, this seer foretold, Basra would have a lower crime rate than most London boroughs. And Iraq as a whole would be, at a bare minimum, the least badly governed state in the Arab world and at best pleasant, civilized and thriving. In the *Spectator* nine months later he treated readers to this New Year prediction: 'Another six weeks of insurgency sounds about right, after which it will peter out.' Is it only the fact that Mark Steyn lives in Canada that has saved him from being hauled up before the magistrates? And why are the courts not jammed with cases against astrologers and those who commission them?

Exploiting the fears of the credulous has for centuries been regarded as serious wickedness in civilized societies. The penalties sometimes exacted for such offences makes Hartwell's six months' hard labour seem merciful. The Scythians, says Montaigne, had a way with makers of false predictions: they bound them hand and foot, laid them in an ox-drawn cart filled with brushwood, and burned them. Here in Britain, as recently as the reign of King John, Peter Pontefract, a hermit, having foretold the death of the king within a twelvemonth, was hanged as a false prophet on day 366.

In India in 2005, thousands flocked to a village to see if an astrologer who had forecast his own death would die as he had predicted. The deadline he'd set passed without any fatality; but the seer was spared any punishment, on the grounds that his death must have been prevented by the prayers of the crowd that his forecast might be falsified. The stars, it seemed, had failed to foresee this. 'In the past,' said the *Guardian* sombrely, 'crowds have beaten up astrologers whose predictions of demise proved false.' And perhaps, on occasion, it might have added, had killed them. Even though such punitive measures must now be considered excessive, why is it that those who constantly proffer these wonky prophecies are still avidly published and read? The wonder of the Birmingham magistrate's clerk at the gullibility of so many is scarcely less appropriate now. All sensible people should repeat to themselves every morning over their newspapers the wise teaching of George Eliot: 'Among all the forms of mistake, prophecy is the most gratuitous.'

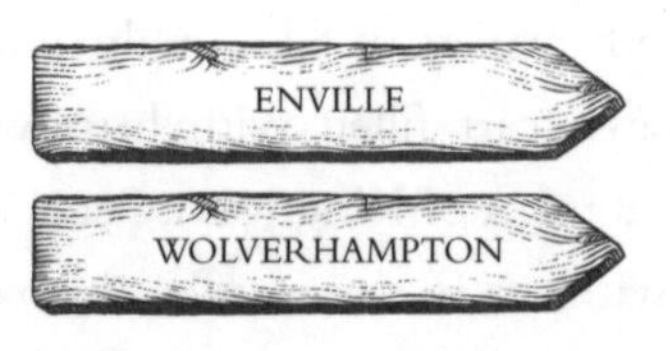

A B C D
E F G H
I J K L
M N O P
Q R S T
U V W X Y Z

BALHAM

BALHAM, 2 eccl. dists. and ry. stas.… co. of London…

ON THE VERY CUSP of Balham, just where it transmogrifies into superior Clapham, there used to be a caff called the Balham Hill Restaurant, under whose name board there appeared the claim: 'Where the Elite Meet to Eat.' You couldn't avoid the sight of it as you came out of Clapham South underground station, and I always intended to cross the road and put the claim to the test. Might I, I wondered, catch sight of Professor A. J. Ayer, scribbling away over his baked beans on toast on a book that would one day be talked about as avidly as his *Language, Truth and Logic*? Or perhaps Michael Tippett, humming away to himself and noting down what he was humming, his tea and Chelsea bun left untouched in this spasm of creative excitement? Or would the proprietor, rubbing his hands on his greasy apron, tell me whom I'd just missed. 'See that pool of tea on the table?… Bertrand Russell. He always leaves the place in a bit of a mess. Then that Jean-Paul Sartre was in here with Simone de Someone-or-Other…'

Then one day I came out of Clapham South station and saw that the restaurant had gone, its name board replaced by a big red sign which said only: 'Hoover'. My chance had been lost and would never return; and the poor old elite would have to find some other place to philosophize over their egg, bacon and chips. Still, with all that intelligence, they shouldn't find it too difficult. What a shame that they hadn't posted up notices to tell us poor gawpers where the elite would be meeting to eat from now on.

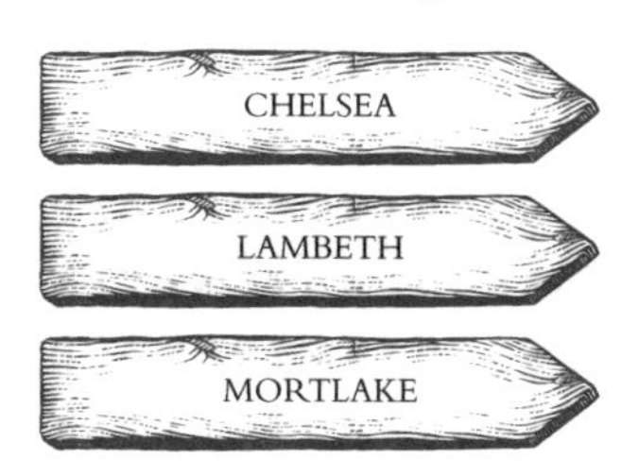

BARBARAVILLE

BARBARAVILLE, vil., Ross and Cromarty, 3½m.
NE. of Invergordon; pop. 186.

A LOT MORE THAN 186 people live in Barbaraville today, as you'll find if you leave the A9 as it runs north-east out of Inverness on its way to the northernmost tracts of these islands. On the way you pass Invergordon, where in September 1931, when Ramsay MacDonald's government was trying to fight its way out of a financial crisis by slashing pay in the public sector, men of the Atlantic Fleet resorted to mutiny – a mutiny which succeeded, for the Admiralty rescinded the cuts. The oldest part of what is now Barbaraville was there long before that name was invented, and was known as Portleich. Then a developer expanded the place, and renamed it after his wife. That was a popular practice in this region of Scotland. There's a place called Jemimaville on the other side of the Cromarty Firth, and an Arabella, with no 'ville' attached, some five miles beyond Barbaraville. (In Wester Ross, Bartholomew says, there's a village that used to be known both as Janetown and Jeantown, but it's now resolved that discrepancy by calling itself Lochcarron.) There are other such acts of devotion scattered about the place: even dignified upmarket Helensburgh on the west coast is a name-it-after-the-missus town.

But the core of Barbaraville today has nothing to do with Barbara or her loving husband. Much of the heart of the place consists of a modern development, partly of retirement homes and partly of a care home. This arrangement ensures that those who have moved in good health to retirement housing, but who, having grown old and frail, can no longer cope on their own, can move a little distance away and not lose contact with the friends they have made over the years. This is such a sensible arrangement that it's sad it doesn't happen more often, or indeed, become a general rule. 'Let us emulate Barbaraville, 3½ miles north-east of Invergordon,' planners should invariably say to themselves.

In the centre of this double development, where the two communities meet, is a small but excellent shop that also serves as an information and gossip centre. I asked in the shop if anyone knew who Barbara was. The woman at the counter thought Barbara and Jemima might have been sisters, but reference books fail to confirm that. We know who Jemima was: she was the wife of George Munro of Poyntzfield. But of Barbaraville, David Ross in his *Scottish Place-names* (2001) says only that it was one of the new villages created in the late eighteeth and early nineteenth centuries by lairds who named them after their wives and thought -'ville' was better than -'ton' because it sounded more sophisticated.

That this Barbaraville (there's another we'll come to later) has been heard of much outside the town itself is attributable to a singer-songwriter called Martin Stephenson who, looking down on Barbaraville and seeing, as he later recalled, 'a bus stop, a row of houses, and then suddenly a llama in a field', was inspired to fashion a tribute to it with the help of his accomplice Joe Guillan. He gave it the title: 'Barbaraville: heed this advice for all that it's worth, steer clear of the village on Cromarty Firth named Barbaraville'. I dare not reproduce the lyrics, since that sort of thing gets one's publisher into trouble with the Performing Rights Society, but I think I can paraphrase Stephenson's argument thus: if you visit this village, its restless presence will instil in you (I'm not quite sure how that process works, but let us press on) as you see a weird shine from the roadside and perceive a peering llama. Eerie sounds can be expected at dead of night, hitchhikers will tap at the window, people are liable to disappear without trace, sinister signs of radiation may manifest themselves, naked serpents may on past evidence attempt to solicit your cash, and the villagers are likely to strike you as closely resembling the cast of a movie made by the American director Ed Wood. Oh, and another sound you'll hear is that of Captain Boocock (who sounds like something out of *Under Milk Wood*) banging away at his drum. My own time exploring Barbaraville failed to confirm even one of these allegations.

There's a second Barbaraville, though, which Bartholomew's ninth edition does not know about, since it didn't exist until twenty years after publication. It's a caravan site just off the Hatfield–Hertford road which owes its existence to the pink-clad, mightily coiffured romantic novelist Barbara Cartland, the list of whose publications by the time she died in 2000 was taking up over 300 lines in *Who's Who*. She was thought to have published 723 books in all, though some were on other themes, such as cookery and the restorative virtues of vitamins. Despite her reputation for frothy fantasy, her interests were never confined to heaving bosoms among the bougainvilleas. Dame Barbara – as she became in 1981 – had been a Chief Lady Welfare Officer for Bedfordshire during the Second World War, and after the war was over she maintained both a philanthropic and a practical interest in people who needed help. In the early 1960s when problems arose in finding sites for Gypsy communities she not only campaigned both nationally and in Hertfordshire, where she was a Conservative councillor, to get permanent sites for travellers in order to give them and their children access to schools and local health services, but provided land of her own to house the caravans of nine Romany families. They asked if they might call the place she had made for them Barbaraville, and Barbara assented.

It's not an easy place to find, nor an especially desirable one. It's sandwiched between the ostentatious salubrity and abundant rabbits of the Mill Green Golf Club and a site which shyly announces itself as Thames Water but which the map calls a sewage works. The mobile homes of the Gypsies, which look pretty immobile to me, are arranged in a yard on a sideway which runs from the Thames Water site. Relations between the water company and the Gypsies of Barbaraville Camp deteriorated when in 2006 the company revealed its plans to put a composting plant next to its sewage works, alarming the Gypsy community which feared an invasion of heavy lorries and the inescapable smells of compost. The keeper of the Cartland flame, Dame Barbara's son Ian McCorquodale, was aghast on his own behalf and that of his mother, while the local Tory MP, Grant Shapps, said Thames Water would never have dared to propose such a scheme had the neighbours lived in suburban houses. The protests were successful; to the delight of Barbaraville, the plans were abandoned early in 2008.

The name Barbara, by the way, means a foreign woman, which doesn't apply to most Barbaras in my experience and was not, I imagine, at all appropriate to either of those who inspired the naming of the two Barbaravilles. It also has just a hint of 'barbarian', which is no doubt why one of the graffiti in Ashwell church, disconsolately etched, one supposes, by a man disappointed in love, declares: 'Barbara barbara est', which is taken to mean he thinks she's treated him barbarously.

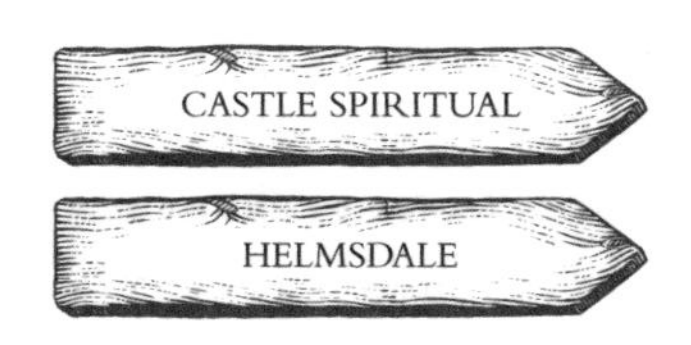

BEDFORD

BEDFORD, co. town of Bedfordshire, par. and mun. bor. with ry. stas. on both sides of r. Ouse… the town contains many relics of John Bunyan (1628-1688).

IN A PLEASANT SUBURBAN avenue just outside the centre of Bedford, the sort of location which newspapers like to call 'leafy', you will come across 4 Milton Road, where on 24 August 1930 there was born the master topographer, scourge of planners and architects, popularizer though not inventor of the concept called Subtopia, qualified pilot (and so devoted a lover of aircraft that he wanted his ashes scattered under the flight path out of Heathrow), depressive and, fatally in the end, spectacular drunk, Ian Nairn. He first made his name with a series of articles, later a book, called *Outrage*, which helped to wake the world up to some of the horrors which architects and planners imposed on us as Britain began its recovery after the Second World War. It's tempting, as you leave the quiet, substantial late Victorian and early Edwardian houses of Milton Road and the streets around it (Chaucer and Shakespeare and Spenser are there as well as Milton, and rather more rarely, Sidney) and walk past a good many pubs that Nairn might have stopped at, and some sinister Gothic almshouses which might have been modelled on some dark tale out of Grimm, to think that the boiling rage and resentment that infected *Outrage* might partly have come from having had to grow up in Bedford. 'The most characterless county town in England,' he called it; and he would have known them all.

A county town demands a sense of occasion. Bedford has only its river. The river, as you walk on its spacious boulevard from the bridge past the Swan Hotel (1794) and the rowing club on the southern side, with delicate willows and good green spaces to sit and reflect and possibly picnic on, is a delight. It might have migrated from Cambridge, a sense that becomes even stronger when you come to Newnham Road, close to another of Bedford's allurements, the Cecil Higgins Art Gallery, which, when I was there on a glorious spring afternoon in 2007, had an exhibition on called *Blake to*

Sutherland: the Romantic Tradition. (That's another thing about Bedford: it lacks romance.) It's best if you are exploring the town to start in the north. If you start in the south, the river sets up expectations which are going to be disappointed. Start in the north and the river seems like a kind of redemption.

What it lacks, above all, is a square, something to give the place a focus and a sense of what the town is about. There's a square of sorts between the old school (now a shopping centre) and the splendid 1836 classical Harpur Suite, built as the town's Assembly Rooms, later a gentlemen's club, and later still Bedford Public Library, whose modern replacement stands next door; but it's simply too cramped to do the job that needs to be done. St Paul's Square, just around the corner towards the bridge, has a lot of the necessary attributes: the church of St Paul itself, in the centre, the old municipal buildings mostly superseded today by newer ones tucked in behind them, the market stalls, the Corn Exchange, where Glenn Miller so often came over from Cambridge to play; and a statue I thought would be Bunyan, but in fact is the penal reformer John Howard, who settled in the area and became high sheriff of Bedfordshire. Bunyan does have his statue, but it's a little out of the centre of town, as if the civic authorities feared he might rear up at the heart of the place and denounce it. As he would, I dare say, if he came back today and found, on the way to the station, a pub called the Pilgrim's Progress.

The church needs more room to breathe, and the people of Bedford need more space to sit in peace and contemplate their inheritance. What it's got is merciless traffic, and the clutter that breeds, and the orgies of signage which used to drive Nairn to distraction. If you want to know why he railed so much at street furniture you will find your answer in Bedford. This potential town square is a territory that belongs to the car and the van and the heavy lorry rather than to the people, and the bullying signage is inescapable, simply because there's no way of dispersing the traffic. There is nowhere else for it to go.

At school and university Ian Nairn was a mathematician. He was called up for National Service and found more satisfaction in that experience than most of his fellow pressed men. He learned to fly, which he continued to do after being demobbed, both for enjoyment and because it was a fresh way of looking at towns. (Sometimes, unsure where he was, he would dip down over the railway station in the hope of discerning its name.) But by now he felt driven to write about architecture, and began to pester the editors of the *Architectural Review* to give him his chance. As a colleague wrote later: 'The editors had little choice in the matter. Calling at Queen Anne's Gate almost daily, still wearing a dyed RAF overcoat, and constantly submitting articles, he demanded a job and in the face of such conviction an intrigued H de C Hastings (the magazine's editor) gave him a job.'

Nairn wrote the words for *Outrage*, which were illustrated by the talented Gordon Cullen (it was probably Cullen who coined the word 'Subtopia'). The key definition, though, was provided by Nairn. England, he said, was being reduced to a universal Subtopia, a mean and indeterminate state which was neither country nor town. You would know it, he advised, by its abandoned aerodromes, fake rusticity, wire fences, traffic roundabouts, gratuitous notice boards, car parks, and 'things in fields'. To these he then added posters, disused petrol pumps, conifers, cement works, sanitation plants, generator stations, the wreckage of war and the works of the War Department. At one point he journeyed from Southampton to Carlisle, charting all that demeaned the townscape (townscape: an invaluable term, invented by the *Review* in the late 1940s) and landscape, and deviating off the main road into the Lake District to discover whether the blight had affected that too. Finding that it had, he then raged at what he called 'a ferocious display of municipal gardening beside lake Windermere' in poor benighted Bowness. Recovering, he pushed on northwards. 'You might as well', he said as he looked out from Stirling, 'be looking south from Mill Hill' (the northern suburb of London, which I shall not defend even though I was born there). He was stricken by the thought that soon the last refuge, the Highlands, would succumb to the process too. Don't, he begged, destroy the 'genius loci' (a favourite Nairnian term.) What he feared above all was the process he could see all over Britain in which almost every place was becoming more and more like everywhere else.

There's a problem with *Outrage*, though. It's not so much that the language is often over the top (though it is), for this is the fruit of a young man's justified anguish. It's more that remembering Nairn for *Outrage* associates him with the negatives, whereas the whole point about this great twentieth-century hero is his bounding enthusiasm, his immense and unfailing capacity for delight. Nairn wrote columns for a time for both the *Sunday Times* and the *Observer*. I read one of these, I think in the *Times*, on a somnolent Sunday morning: it was Nairn's recommendation for twenty-five places or so that you could easily visit from London. So infectious was his joy in these places that I bundled the family into the car and set off for Brockham Green, near Dorking in Surrey – not as well known in those days as the Sunday crowds in the two pubs on the green suggest it is now, but worth every mile of my journey – along with another of Nairn's private passions, Gatton, which is how Gatton comes to be in this book. That restless, all-encompassing eye and the glorious exuberance of his language make him a matchless companion. Open at random his book *Nairn's London*, which he followed up with *Nairn's Paris*, and could have continued with, home and abroad, almost ad infinitum, had illness and drink not done for him. The judgements leap off the page and lodge deep in your brain.

Here are a few: Finsbury Savings Bank, Sekforde Street: 'an extraordinary *overwrought* building [my italics, not his]... the style is more or less Barry's, but with every detail screwed into place comprehensively.' St Nicholas, Deptford Green: 'a *chubby* brick church of 1697'. 12 Langford Place, St John's Wood: 'Sheer horror: a Francis Bacon shriek in these affluent, uncomplicated surroundings... The design radiates malevolence as unforgettably as Iago.' (No wonder readers with eyes to see and hearts to respond loved Ian Nairn; no wonder architects consulted their lawyers.) Scotland Yard: 'Norman Shaw's beefy heartlessness'. Soon he feels better again. The tower of St Anne's, Soho, is 'louche', not, I think, a term of disparagement: this is Nairn, this is Soho. He has a good hot taste for the louche, and even more for the vulgar. 'The jolliest public building in London,' he says of Deptford Town Hall, 'dashed off by an Edwardian genius, Charles Rickards, who could overturn classical rules and – like Wilde – make a masterpiece out of the paradoxes... Edwardian England meant many things to many people. One of them, undoubtedly, was gaiety; and here it is.'

Even within the cloistered pages of Pevsner's *Buildings of England* (Nairn wrote Surrey, and collaborated on Sussex) the language rampages, the choices are bold and exuberant. At Christ's Hospital, Horsham, where I went to school, it's the railway station, rather than the school buildings, that he thinks one should go to see. Petworth's a joy, as it should be, but so in its way is Bognor, which many despise. The collaboration, probably engineered by his second wife, who spent many years working on Pevsner's series, did not last. He felt too confined and he would far rather spend his time on cattle markets and tram depots than in diligent detailed contemplation of clerestories and triforia. He made television and radio series too, all infected with passion – I remember him almost in tears at the coming destruction of a fine old arcade in Northampton – and free from the posturing gimmick-crazed personalization of successors like Jonathan Meades.

By now it was the doctrine among producers that you got what you could out of Nairn before lunchtime struck and the alcohol took effect. Newspapers too were cooling on him. He could be, as even his friends and admirers accepted, touchy and stubborn and difficult. Depression and drink fed off each other. At the end of his life he spent his days – his talent locked up or boozed out – in the pubs of Chelsea. He died on 14 August 1983 at a mere fifty-three. In the new *Oxford Dictionary of National Biography*, Gavin Stamp says of him: 'During his short, furious, productive career, Ian Nairn had a more beneficial effect on the face of Britain than any other architectural writer of his generation.' I was one of his beneficiaries. The boy from the poets' quarter in Bedford grew up to open my eyes and enrich my life.

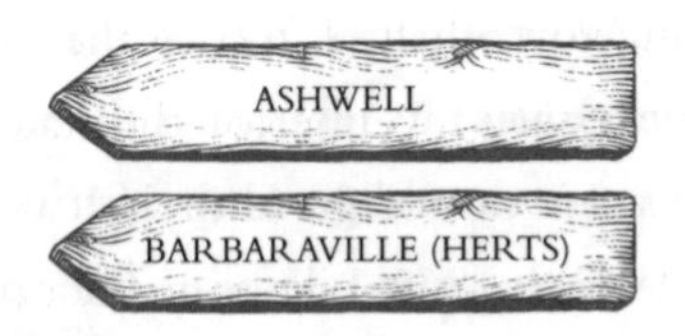

BISHOP'S CASTLE

BISHOP'S CASTLE, mun. bor., par. and mkt.-town, SW. Salop, 18m. SW. from Shrewsbury and 7½m. NW. of Craven Arms sta. …

INTO THIS BORDER TOWN, until Nemesis overtook it long before Dr Beeching, there used to run perhaps the most endearingly incompetent railway ever to operate on this island. This was a line of which an inspector once said: 'It is a matter of surprise that the trains ever reach their journey's end.' Or, as one high authority, the *Oxford Companion to British Railway History*, was later to put it, the Bishop's Castle line was 'a byword for decrepitude'.

It began with a grand design. Bishop's Castle, long the smallest municipal borough in England, feared it might become smaller still unless it was served by a railway. The Central Wales line had shunned it, preferring to go through Knighton. What was needed for economic lift-off in this part of the world was a new line from Craven Arms – open since 1852 on the route from Manchester to South Wales – through Montgomery, just over the border in Wales, and then in a glorious sweep round to Minsterley, Shropshire, to join the line west out of Shrewsbury. Bishop's Castle itself would be a kind of addendum to that, served by a spur, down which the trains would need to reverse. It was in Montgomery rather than Bishop's Castle that the first public meetings took place, and subsequently it was even suggested, to the chagrin of Bishop's Castle, that the line through to Montgomery should be completed first, with their town being tacked on later. Bishop's Castle, though, had other ideas.

Then as now, this was a highly individual, even eccentric small town; at its heart is a high street that runs down from its engaging town hall (1762) to the church. It still has a cattle market, in its time a source of necessary revenue for the station, traces of which are still perceptible at the end of a side street east of the church. It was out of this station that the first train ran on Tuesday, 25 October 1865. Like so many on this railway,

that departure was well behind schedule, and the first contractor – somewhat hastily hired and discovered to be working at the same time for some of this railway's rivals – went bankrupt. And some of the day's events confirmed the view of local sceptics that the new Bishop's Castle railway (BCR) had little chance of success. 'The promoters of the line', the *Shrewsbury Chronicle* had noted at the outset, 'are very sensitive when one says anything to them upon the subject of money, and well they may, for their prospects in this respect are very gloomy indeed.' It did not seem a good omen that having none of their own they'd had to borrow an engine to haul their first train; nor that, after this inaugural journey, no further trains were able to run for some time, because the line had yet to be cleared for use by a government inspector. When he did arrive, this high official found so much wrong with the enterprise, and particularly with its level crossings, that he declared the line to be a danger to the travelling public.

Its predicament grew still worse the following year. The financial crisis that ruined so many after the crash of the Overend and Gurney bank wiped out any remaining chance of completing the Montgomery–Minsterley sections. Potential backers withdrew, and the dreadful word 'bankruptcy' began to be used for the first time, though certainly not for the last. Sure enough, by the end of the year the BCR was unable to meet its debts and a force of bailiffs moved in, with one posted at each of the terminal stations and a third deputed to ride on its trains. From then on, for the whole of its life, the BCR was run by receivers. It had to sell off much of its rolling stock, including two of its engines, for a fraction of what it had paid for them. Even that was not enough to meet the demands of its creditors, though their clamour abated when one who'd obtained a judgment against the company was told that his agents had failed to find any goods or chattels worth seizing.

There were signs of the railway's indigence everywhere. Only Plowden, which served one of the principal local families, had anything much to offer by way of a station. That at Bishop's Castle itself was vestigial: since the funds did not even run to providing a clock, the staff had to listen out for the church clock striking to know when to wave their green flags. Even then, departure times were erratic. If some bigwig was on the way, the train was held until he arrived. It was also well known that one of the railway's supervisors liked to stop off for a couple of glasses of stout before he turned up at the station: you could always delay the train on behalf of some friend who had not yet arrived by treating him to a third.

As a market town with a smattering of local industry, Bishop's Castle could provide the line with both passengers and remunerative freight. That could hardly be said of the intervening stations on the line through to Craven Arms, which were no more than hamlets, and in some cases not even that. One of them, Stretford Bridge Halt, could be reached only by making your way across a meadow in the middle of which stood a sign saying trespassers would be prosecuted. The debts were persistent and crushing. One of the line's main creditors was a doctor called Beddoes, who, since he also had a seat on the board, made no attempt to recover his money. When he died, his family proved to be less indulgent. They demanded the £1,300 (about £83,000 today) they claimed they were owed. The court ordered the debt be paid within twenty-eight days, but the BCR simply could not raise a vast sum like that. So the bailiffs removed a couple of rails and built a barrier blocking the line near the village of Horderley. The BCR was reduced to running its trains as far as the barrier, disembarking the goods and the passengers, and completing the journey by road. Trade in the borough suffered, and businesses feared for their future. What happened next was described in a railway magazine by another Beddoes, superintendent of a railway in Ireland:

> As things were growing desperate, a certain coal merchant... called a secret council of war in the back parlour of the well known hostelry at Craven Arms... The 'council' decided to make a bold bid, and after the shunting engine at the 'Arms' had been very busy, every truck labelled for the Castle was ready for a journey. In the meantime a couple of men had crossed the line near Horderley, where the faithful 'bums' were keeping watch over the vacant spaces in the 'iron road' and took pity on them in their cold and lonely job. The visitors

> suggested a drink at the 'village pub' and thither the bailiffs went. A gallon or two of mulled beer, tempered with a drop of gin, was served out in front of the blazing fire…
>
> In the meantime a gang of men, by the aid of dark lanterns, had placed the rails back in position, and soon after, an engine with all the empties crept quietly down from Bishop's Castle into Craven Arms, picked up a trainload of goods and coal, and steamed off hard as she could 'pelt' for the beleaguered town. The bailiffs, however, had by this time recovered a little, in fact, sufficiently to hear the snort of the engine, and reeling out of 'The Lion', shouted and waved their lanterns and tried in vain to stop the train as she sped by…

This triumph lifted and sustained the spirits of Bishop's Castle. A new company was floated in 1884 which came up with grandiose plans not only for the fabled Montgomery–Minsterley section but for a line which would link it with Wolverhampton and Bridgnorth. That, though, needed parliamentary approval, and the House of Lords, which seemed to have a shrewder sense of the problems of running these minor railways than the optimists of Bishop's Castle, blocked the legislation. The plans were abandoned.

So the line pottered on in unaltered form. When the trains ran, this was one of the prettiest lines in Britain, following the course of the river Onny which it here and there crossed and recrossed. The *Daily Mail* sent a reporter to observe what he seemed to consider poetry in motion. Under the headline: 'Puffing Through Fairyland: Delights of a Rustic Railway' he wrote:

> A few minutes out of Craven Arms, our chuffing tank engine turns gleefully from the smooth, artificial setting of the Great Western Railway and London, Midland and Scottish main line, and plunges along grass-covered miles into undergrowth and woodland – Nature at her choicest.
>
> For many minutes foliage of every shade of green caresses the window of the carriage and emphasises the folly of leaning out of

> carriage windows; then an avenue gives way to meadow, backed by green and purple-garbed hills...
>
> A strutting cock pheasant pauses in his stride to regard us haughtily; drowsy cattle eyes us phlegmatically. Almost, it seems, we are in an unbounded zoological garden – with ourselves the exhibits, not the sightseers...

There was plenty of time to savour such journeys. Top speed on these trains was 20 mph, with a limit of 7 mph at some places. Sometimes there were long contemplative pauses. One problem was taking on water. When necessary, drivers stopped to collect it from the river, with the fish still swimming about in it. At times, passengers, it was said, would get out and pick mushrooms. Other journeys were more eventful. As early as 1866 the service had to be suspended when heavy flooding washed away an embankment at Plowden and the track was left hanging in mid-air. Five years later a driver took the bend at Stretford Bridge, where the BCR line joined the Craven Arms mainline, so fast that he could not stop and a crash ensued, in which fortunately no one was killed. It should be said in defence of this 'byword for decrepitude' that the BCR never killed anyone, which was more than could be said for some other Victorian railways. The worst that seems to have happened was the incident when the stationmaster at Plowden fell on the line and a train passed over his foot, costing him his big toe.

Passengers might not have been so fortunate had it not been for the inspectors who came to check on the line and found it not just deficient but dangerous. 'I feel it my duty', wrote one inspector in 1878, 'to report, in consequence of the defective state of the Bishop's Castle line as regards the sleepers, keys and fish bolts, the lack of proper attention to the packing of rails and the condition of the timbers on the tops of many of the bridges, I consider that the public are exposed to constant danger in travelling on the line...' That led to the suspension of passenger travel until October the following year, the fourth such suspension in the BCR's history, and when running resumed, it was subject to further reductions in permitted speeds, about which users complained. In 1895 another inspector discovered that because the signals at level crossings weren't working properly, the company had set them permanently at danger and told drivers to pass them anyway. As for the track, 'the sleepers are so decayed and the rails so much worse that it is a matter of surprise that the trains ever reach their journey's end, and I have never seen in England or elsewhere a railway in such bad condition'.

From time to time, officials came from Wrexham, where the receivers were based, to check on the line's performance. The local staff knew how to deal with that. The driver would give a pre-arranged signal as the train approached its terminus, so that by the time the eminent visitors reached the station, the staff were in a frenzy of activity. These supervisors seem to have missed a good deal. A man called Pearce Higgins who poked about in the early 1930s, established that in almost seventy years the BCR had not sold even one first-class return between Bishop's Castle and Plowden. Yet even he missed another significant clue to the railway's decrepitude. Like every other railway, this one had been required by legislation brought in by Gladstone when he was still a Conservative and in charge of the Board of Trade to run one train a day in each direction on which the fares must not exceed a penny a mile.

This rule had faded out in the 1880s, yet the BCR went on selling these 'parliamentary' tickets to the end of its life. Moving from booking offices out on to the track, Higgins discovered a signal at Horderley which was not being used because a wire had broken and no one had come to repair it. A second signal was out of use because (he was told) they'd been having such frosty weather. When another curious visitor asked the station mistress at Eaton why no timetables or posters were displayed on the walls, she said the goat must have eaten them.

There were very few years in this railway's life when there wasn't some talk of closure, alarming the local people who protested that such little trade and development there had been in Bishop's Castle over the years could not have occurred but for the railway. At one point, the trains were supplemented, even supplanted, by buses, until critics persuaded the company that they were in effect competing against themselves. The Great Western Railway (GWR), wheedled to take it over, responded with granite indifference. They were professionals, and they knew that the line was unsavable.

By the start of the 1930s, a sense of doom had settled over the sleepy stations, the substandard sleepers and fallible fishplates. The company's financial plight was terminal and its dereliction incurable. Bridges appeared unsafe; sleepers, cut from alder trees alongside the track and never treated, were sprouting leaves, even branches. 'So overgrown was the track during the last years', wrote Edward Griffith in a wonderfully evocative history of the railway, 'that it was always said that one could tell which way the last train had passed by looking at the grass growing between the rails, and the ground was so uneven that a passenger looking out of the window of the first coach would see the one behind rising and falling like a ship in a slight swell.'

What was said to be the last train steamed out on 20 April 1935, though in the way of the BCR, the last train was not the last: several were seen on the tracks thereafter as the melancholy process of clearing up and demolishing got under way. As late as December, attempts were made to try to raise enough money to reopen the line and take it – that old romantic delusion – through to Montgomery. It wasn't until February 1937 that the final last journey was made through to Craven Arms. Three months later, the junction that linked the BCR with the mainline through Craven Arms was removed. And that was the end of that.

But perhaps not quite. The memory of this wretched and wonderful railway is kept alive in a small museum (not often open) in Bishop's Castle; by a poignant CD entitled, like the *Daily Mail*'s piece, *Puffing Through Fairyland*; and by two excellent histories, one by Edward Griffith (first published privately in 1948 and revised and reissued in 1969), and the other by John Scott Morgan (this too revised and reissued in 2003) – as well as by Bishop's Castle itself, balanced on the other side of the border by possibly even more enchanting Montgomery. Both places, now shorn of what Bartholomew calls their '*ry. stas.*', can now – for those not equipped with motor cars – be reached only by bus.

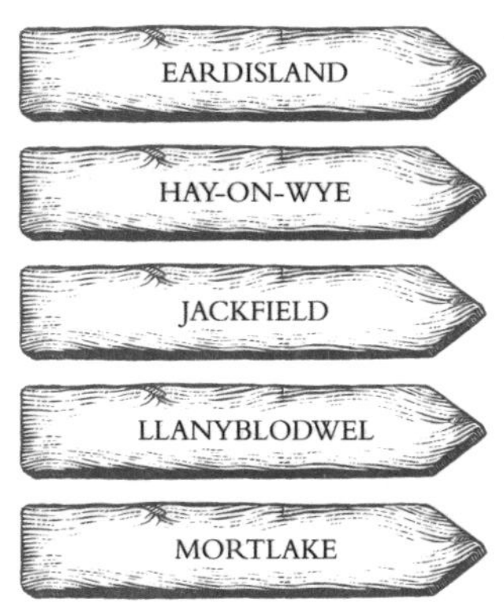

BLENNERHASSET

BLENNERHASSET AND KIRKLAND, par. W. Cumberland, 2m. E of Aspatria and ¼m. S of Baggrow sta. … P.O. at B.

A MILE OR SO down a quiet byway off the hectic A595 from Carlisle to Cockermouth there's a place that might, had things worked out differently, have become famous and feted: the village of Blennerhasset, where an unquenchable optimist set out to create an irresistible example both of pioneering farming methods and of what could be achieved by cooperation between master and men. It's a backwater now. There's a pleasant village green, and a school, and a bridge across the river Ellen; and there's what remains of the Post Office: to judge by the windows there haven't been any parcels accepted or stamps pushed under the grille for a good while now. But a plaque above the door establishes its former importance. 'This business', it says, 'was founded in 1867 by William Lawson of Brayton, gentleman, philanthropist, fourth son of Sir Wilfrid Wybergh Lawson of Brayton, baronet.' Below it is his coat of arms.

This Sir Wilfrid was the father of an even more eminent temperance man. The first Sir Wilfrid gave up drink after his butler returned from a temperance meeting and reported what he'd been told with such evangelical fervour that Sir Wilfrid collected every bottle of spirits he found in the house and poured their contents into a pond. (This became a historic moment for the temperance movement: Rosalind Frances, Countess of Carlisle, arriving to take up residence at Castle Howard in Yorkshire, outdid even Sir Wilfrid by pouring its whole array of fine wines into the lake.) The second Sir Wilfrid became the most famous and influential temperance campaigner in the land, presenting Bills every year in the House of Commons to permit the suppression of drink shops where a local majority willed it. His brother, William, fourth son of the household, was no less an idealist, but his passion took different forms. What he cared about most was farming, and for this reason his father, intending to leave the estate to the second Sir Wilfrid, set William up as a farmer at

Blennerhasset. In 1861, when he was twenty-five, William had visited a farm in Essex run by an Alderman Mechi and in tribute to Mechi's innovatory methods there he named his new base in the village of Blennerhasset Mechi Farm, later adding a second farm at Prior Hall.

He began as he meant to go on, by calling a village meeting to announce that from now on the agriculture of Blennerhasset would be run on a wholly different basis. He had in mind not only the daring modern equipment he planned to buy, including the first steam plough ever to ply its trade in the county, or the artificial manure works, the laboratory or the homes he intended to build for his workforce – but also the fact that, whereas until now they had worked for a master, in future he and they would be working together. *With* me, not *for* me, he said. And where profits accrued, they would have their share of them. As the leading champion of cooperative endeavour, George Jacob Holyoake, would later record, that made him the only gentleman in England at that time ever to have committed his fortune to such an enterprise.

To the agricultural poor of Blennerhasset, it must have sounded like revolution. They heard him courteously, but somewhat unbelievingly. As a recent local historian, Geoffrey Bremner, describes it, they admired the intentions of this son of the lord of the manor, but doubted his ability to deliver. They were certainly unprepared for the tides of democracy that now swept through Blennerhasset. Lawson established a village parliament, at which farmworkers (initially paid to attend) made ambitious demands which he then sought to satisfy, whatever the cost. So a free school was provided, and a night school, a free reading room and a library. When William left the village for a few months, the question of who should deputize was settled by ballot. The schoolmistress owed her job to public election. Her pupils were even invited to vote on which subjects they fancied. Sometimes votes went harshly against Lawson. The Congregationalist minister objected to the presence in the library of *The Age of Reason*, on the grounds that its author, Tom Paine, was an unrepentant atheist. Lawson stood up for Paine, but the minister's will prevailed, and the book was solemnly burned on the village green. There was trouble over Lawson's grocery shop (whose opening required him to register himself as a grocer: William Lawson, licensed dealer in tea and tobacco). Sabbatarians said it should not be open on Sundays. Lawson disagreed, but he lost the vote.

The early years were full of the buzz of progress. Lawson imported the farming methods he'd learned from Alderman Mechi in Tiptree (especially the use of liquid manure) and from the cooperative farm at Assington in Suffolk, established by a man called Gurdon. He was also in touch with the pioneering experiment in cooperative retailing in Rochdale. Additional shops were opened at Carlisle, Newcastle and Ireby. Festivals, fetes and other fine social occasions were staged in the village – though not all were entirely successful: at Christmas 1866 the food that Lawson had chosen was not to the taste of the villagers, and was even, it was later reported, left uneaten when fed to the pigs.

Trips were arranged to places which the people of Blennerhasset could never have hoped to see. There was even an excursion to the Great Exhibition in Paris in 1867. Lawson set aside £60 for this purpose, but where women were given £4.10s spending money, men were offered only £3, on the typically Lawsonian calculation that the women were much less likely to spend their money on drink. There was culture too: lecturers addressed the farmworkers of Blennerhasset on such subjects as Practical Education and Training, Phrenology and The Highest Good of the Nation. As Lawson would later record in his usual wry, self-deprecatory way, 'during the very earliest days of my farming one afternoon I called together a lot of the labourers and read the whole of Shakespere's [sic] Macbeth to them at a sitting. They all went to sleep except one.'

Inevitably things began to go wrong. Sometimes this was for reasons which might have blighted any agricultural enterprise: bad weather, disease (1869 saw a wretched outbreak of rinderpest), potato blight and a disastrous fire. But some of Blennerhasset's adversity was, as Lawson came to admit, his fault. The history of the experiment is described in a book called *Ten Years of Gentleman Farming at Blennerhasset*, part of it written by Lawson himself and part by his friend Charles Hunter. As Holyoake says in the Preface, William Lawson never holds back from telling a story against himself. His enthusiasm, his naivety, and his very goodness of heart weighed against him. As Geoffrey Bremner records, by 1871 such heavy losses were accumulating that the adventure was doomed. The following year he departed, handing over the shop which now bears his name to the People's Shop Co. Ltd. (The shops at Newcastle, Carlisle and Ireby had folded long before.) Lawson didn't even stay to complete the book, which was published in 1874: by then he was busy in Massachusetts. 'With hindsight,' says Bremner, 'the project looks like an uneasy combination of socialism and Victorian paternalism, democratic co-operation and benevolent management from above. Today, with the exception of the new buildings on the farm and in the village, it is as though it had never been.' Later, miners working in the pits of Aspatria, Mealsgate and Fletchertown came to live here, swelling the population of Blennerhasset at the end of the nineteenth century, but it dwindles again after the pits had gone.

In the end, the scepticism of the country people whom Lawson hoped would become his eager and thriving partners proved to be justified. And it may have been more than scepticism: Bremner writes of a 'mute resistance'. The genuine, exuberant, ideological thirst for, and trust in, cooperation in Blennerhasset seems, sadly, to have been confined to one man. Perhaps it was always destined to work out that way. The whole enterprise began with a moment so deeply ominous that a less optimistic adventurer would have probably turned then and there and fled. After his initial meeting with the village, Lawson had called together eleven of his farmworkers to see what they made of it. He recounts the result with his usual endearing candour:

> Agricultural labourers are not exactly like the inhabitants of Manchester: they are not, perhaps, so independent; and they may be thought generally to speak very much as their employers wish them to speak. However, these labourers showed independence very soon; for when the poll was taken they did not vote at all as they were expected. Our voting urns were two bottles. One was ticketed with the word 'Co-operation' and the other bore the inscription, 'Every man for himself'.
>
> In stating the issue, I did not wish to make the best of my case; I wanted their unbiased opinion. What, then, was the result with these eleven people? Actually, ten of them voted for 'Every man for himself', and only one put into the "co-operation" bottle.

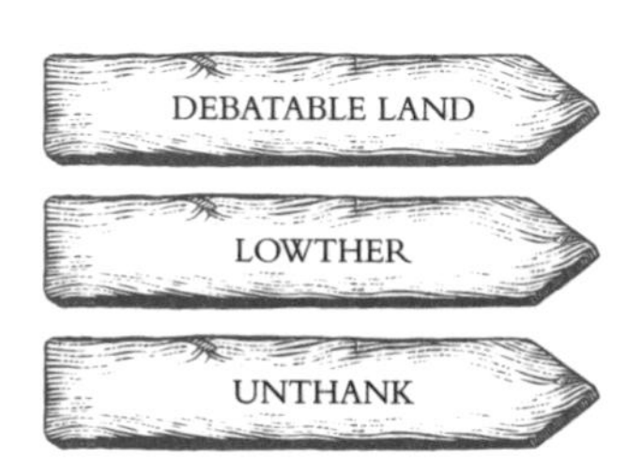

BOOTHVILLE

BOOTHVILLE, Northampton.

BOOTHVILLE, ON THE NORTHERN side of Northampton, is not listed in my *Bartholomew's Gazetteer.* This is probably because back in 1943 there was no such place as Boothville. Its name in those days, which persisted on Ordnance Survey maps though to the 1960s, was one which someone in authority in Northampton presumably found distasteful. So Buttocks Booth, as it had always been (still is, for some who live there), was banished, and Boothville brought in instead. Nearby is an area called Lumbertubs, but happily no one – so far – has monkeyed about with that.

BOSSENDEN

BOSSENDEN, pl., N. Kent, 1m. NE. of Dunkirk.
BOSSENDEN WOOD was the scene of a riot in 1838.

BARTHOLOMEW LISTS BOSSENDEN AS the scene of a riot, but in fact it was more than that. It has sometimes been portrayed as the site of a battle, in which eleven people died. It's even been nominated, replacing Sedgemoor, as the last battle fought on English soil. But that is to overstate the extent of the force commanded there by Sir William Courtenay against the armed authority. The *Annual Register*, chronicling the year 1838, wrote of 'a disturbance of an extraordinary and very serious character which… excited, both in that neighbourhood and throughout the kingdom, the greatest astonishment and sorrow'. That, from my reading of the event, gets it just about right.

In the year 1832 there appeared in the city of Canterbury a man who claimed to be Count Moses Rostopchein Rothschild, though some were aware that not long before he had called himself Squire Thompson: a swashbuckling figure, over six feet tall, always melodramatically dressed, with long hair and a formidable beard, and to judge from his lavish donations to worthy causes, a man of means. The Count swiftly became the object of attention and some admiration, though some less impressionable people doubted whether he was quite what he claimed to be. And their doubts were swiftly justified, for Rothschild soon confessed that he wasn't Rothschild at all. He was Sir William Percy Honeywood Courtenay, Knight of Malta, rightful heir to the Earldom of Devon and to the Kentish estates of Sir Edward Hales, King of the Gypsies and King of Jerusalem. Squire Thompson and Count Rothschild, he courteously explained, were simply two of his inseparable friends. (The man recognized by the rest of the world as the 9th Earl of Devon was at this time far away from the family mansion, Powderham, having fled the country in the hope of escaping the consequences of what were described as 'unspeakable offences'.)

The present time, Sir William informed the people of Canterbury, was one of unparalleled opportunity. The Great Reform Act had now been passed, which gave them the chance to elect to Parliament an independent free-thinking patriot to represent them at Westminster: viz. and to wit, himself. The Conservatives, anxious to baulk the Liberals, encouraged his candidacy; a nakedly cynical move, in that Sir William stood on a platform of universal suffrage, annual parliaments, the abolition of primogeniture, and a shift in the burden of tax from the poor to the rich, all of which seem to belong more to Chartism than to Conservatism. On the other hand, he also promised a return to the good old days of roast beef and mutton and plenty of prime, nut-brown ale.

The Canterbury mob, particularly active in this time of agricultural distress, enlisted behind him and set the tone for a hectic and bruising campaign. In the event, the Liberal candidates in a two-seat constituency got home with around 800 votes each, but Courtenay's haul of 375 votes reflected electors' responses to a degree of charisma rare in the city's usual candidates. Elections in those days were staggered, some constituencies voting while others were still in mid-campaign, and Courtenay, buoyed by his success in the city, now decided to stand in the county too. But his magic failed to enthral the great rural tracts of East Kent and his votes totalled only four.

A vivid and entertaining book called *English Messiahs*, by Ronald Matthews, in which I first discovered Sir William, says the Courtenay who appeared in the county constituency was utterly changed from the one who had caught the eye of the town: 'The Courtenay who the townspeople had known was a robust and gaily-dressed man, in the prime of his youth. The figure who appeared to claim the county electors' suffrage bore the appearance of an infirm veteran. Clothed in an old-fashioned costume of the strictest black, he hobbled on a stick; he seemed to nod his head with age while assumed wrinkles furrowed his brow.' This was because he had belatedly realized that the true

Earl of Devon must be very much older than he was. Matthews may have been led astray by an over-embroidered account of Courtenay published about that time by someone calling himself 'Canterburiensis'. This book was later discovered in a second-hand bookshop in Ramsgate by a writer called P. G. Rogers, who in 1961 published the definitive account of this astonishing and sorrowful tale: *Battle in Bossenden Wood: the strange story of Sir William Courtenay*.

The debacle in East Kent did little to dampen Sir William's ardour. He began to publish an inflammatory radical news-sheet, *The Lion*, a mixture, says Rogers, of wild fantasy and good common sense. But he overreached himself when he turned up in court offering to defend a gang of smugglers, rather than leave their fate to their lawyers. He entered the courtroom dressed in his usual buccaneering finery and waving a scimitar. Although claiming the office of defence counsel, in which role he departed from recognized legal procedures by challenging prosecution witnesses to a duel, he also demanded the right to appear as a witness. Since he hadn't been anywhere near the scenes he purported to describe, his evidence was easily shown to be pure invention. This led to a charge of perjury; in addition to which he now also faced accusations of swindling from a waiter at a pub in the city.

These threats to their hero's liberty agitated the mob, whose leaders pledged that if he were jailed they would rescue him. Hundreds gathered outside the courthouse when the knight came to trial, and were stirred to a paroxysm of excitement and rage when Sir William emerged to address them. The prosecution detected in these events a mood of senseless 'infatuation' – a word that would frequently recur as events developed. The jury at his perjury trial found him guilty – in the light of the evidence it had no real alternative – but added a recommendation for mercy. The accused now embarked on a long and emotional speech. 'Kent! Your God will see me done justice!' he cried. He was sentenced to three months in jail and to transportation. 'I forgive them,' he said, 'they know not what they do.'

The coverage of this case at last unravelled the mystery of who Rothschild/Thompson/Courtenay was. His real name was John Nichols Tom. The son of a publican at St Columb Major in Cornwall, he had begun his working life as a dealer in wines and spirits in Truro, where he married a woman called Catherine Fulpitt, of whom it was said by observers that her dowry was more attractive than she was. A fire destroyed his business, and his mother, to whom he was close, was committed to an asylum. By 1829, the year in which he was thirty, Tom became increasingly melancholic and odd, and in time he too was committed. Then he seemed to get better: well enough, he assured his wife, to undertake a business journey to Liverpool. Off he went; but he never returned.

The commotion over the Canterbury court case had poor Catherine hurrying up from Cornwall in the hope of retrieving her husband. Sir William denied any knowledge either of her or of the old Truro friend who came with her. At this point the decision was taken to commit him to an asylum. Among those who thought this both unjust and unwise was Charles Dickens, who warned that confining him was likely to make him worse, and convince him even more that he was God's chosen prophet.

He remained locked up for four years. In the General Election campaign of 1837 his treatment in distant London and Kent became enough of an issue in Truro to disquiet the Liberal Party. When the contest was over, the Home Secretary, Lord John Russell, ordered that Tom be released to the care of people who said they were ready to take him. But he still refused to acknowledge either his wife or his father, so instead he was taken in by a Mr Francis of Boughton near Canterbury, a resolute Courtenay supporter who was moved and impressed by Tom's expositions of scripture and seems to have rather hoped that the knight might marry his daughter.

By now, though, Sir William's preoccupation was less with the winning of votes than with the saving of souls. He no longer preached salvation through politics: the only true hope lay in religion, and specifically in religion as propounded by him. The adulation that had once been lavished on Sir William the candidate was now given in equal measure to Sir William the Kent Messiah, whose claim that he might be the reincarnation of Christ had all the more force for his devotees because he so resembled pictures of Christ. For the most part, it was observed, his infatuated adherents were poor, simple, uneducated folk, living in poverty and with little hope of escaping it. Among his disciples, however, were some professional people and tradesmen who, like his protector Mr Francis of Boughton, were established and prosperous. Among this latter class were a family called Culver, who gave him their hospitality at Bossenden Farm.

The final stage of the drama began at Dunkirk, the village closest to the farm and to Bossenden Woods, on 27 May 1839, when at an open-air meeting Courtenay was heard to mix religious teachings with violent denunciations of the oppression to which the rich subjected the poor. Two days later the knight took his place at the head of a march, armed with two pistols, a sword and a bugle, with a loaf of bread stuck on a pole to be carried ceremonially in front of him. Three of his followers were so alarmed at this point by the prospect of violence that they decamped. Next morning, at 3 a.m., he led his forces on a further march which he told them would bring new adherents; they returned disconsolate from their tramp through the villages having not even replaced the three they had lost.

By now, local landowners, alarmed by the marching and the violence it seemed to portend, had persuaded the police and the magistrates that Courtenay must be halted before the mischief went further. This commission was entrusted to a plumber, John Mears, who held the office of High Constable of Boughton. He set off for Bossenden with a warrant for Courtenay's arrest, accompanied by his brother Nicholas, and his assistant, Daniel Edwards. They were met by Courtenay, armed with his pistols and sword, and his unarmed followers. When they challenged him, Courtenay fired on them. John Mears and Edwards fled, but Nicholas Mears was shot, attacked with the sword and then shot again. 'Though I have killed the body,' Courtenay assured his adherents, 'I have saved the soul.' Then he threw the dead man's body into the ditch and warned his followers that any who tried to desert could expect the same treatment as Nicholas Mears.

Next day he took his troops to the home of a supporter for a communal breakfast, then ordered them to march back to Bossenden Wood. They must expect to come under further attack, he told them, but they need have no fear, for he was divine and therefore immortal. He could not be harmed or killed. Let a thousand soldiers attack him: he would strike them all dead. Some of his woebegone troops hailed this further proof of his divinity, though others sombrely pondered their choice: stay and fight, against armed and superior numbers; or desert, and Sir William himself would deal with them.

Soldiers had been summoned from Canterbury, but a local magistrate, Norton Knatchbull, was no longer willing to wait for them. He set off to confront Sir William, who challenged him to a duel. Then the local Anglican minister, the Reverend Mr

Handley, arrived with his brother, a major, whom Courtenay threatened to kill. 'You are a madman,' the major retorted. Courtenay shot at him, but missed. He then led his devotees back into Bossenden Wood. Knatchbull pursued them, and he and Courtenay fired at each other.

In the meantime, a Major Armstrong had arrived at Dunkirk with three junior officers and somewhere near 100 men. Crowds gathered outside the Red Lion pub as the army planned their attack and the Riot Act was read against the noise of a violent thunderstorm. The major sent Lieutenant Bennett to lead his forces into the wood. The young officer ordered Courtenay to surrender. Courtenay drew his gun, fired at Bennett at point-blank range, and killed him. As the knight's supporters, armed only with sticks and cudgels, made ready to charge the soldiers, Major Armstrong gave the order to fire.

The battle of Bossenden Wood – the well-armed and well-trained soldiery pitted again a rabble held together only by its blind trust in its leader – lasted perhaps three or four minutes. By then, eight of Courtenay's forces were dead and two more were fatally wounded. One was Courtenay himself. He was not, after all, his adherents discovered too late, divine and therefore immortal. 'I have Jesus in my heart,' he said as he fell. The bodies were taken to the Red Lion pub, where so many gawpers gathered that the landlord had to barricade it against intrusion. An auction began for segments of Courtenay's body. Even then, some of his faithful refused to believe that their leader was dead. The coffin was opened to prove it, yet some of the followers were still not convinced. He might be dead, they concluded, but that did not mean he was mortal. It would surely not be long before Sir William rose again.

That was the end of John Nichols Tom, alias Squire Thompson, Count Moses Rothschild, Knight of Malta, the true Earl of Devon and all the rest of it. But it wasn't quite the end of the story. The survivors among his adherents were tried and convicted of the wilful murders of Nicholas Mears and Lieutenant Bennett, though the jury recommended mercy on the grounds of infatuation (that word yet again), so none was sentenced to death. Some were jailed; a few were transported. But, just as the *Annual Register* says, there was astonishment and sorrow over the deaths in Bossenden Wood, not just in Kent but all over the kingdom. MPs declared in the Commons that the way the authorities had acted had made bloodshed unavoidable. The Church too was blamed.

Had the Courtenayites been given adequate religious instruction and leadership, it was complained, these poor gullible people would never have succumbed to their charismatic champion. In particular, Mr Handley, who buried the victims of Bossenden Wood with something close to disdain, was not thought to have come well out of this episode.

The Red Lion at Dunkirk is still there, on a road a little recessed from the busy A2. The name Bossenden Wood no longer appears at this point on the Ordnance Survey map, though it's still to be found just east of Bossenden Farm. If you walk back from the pub towards Faversham, east of the United Agricultural Products (UAP) depot, though not as far as the road running north – which, surprisingly in the circumstances, is called Courtenay Lane – you will come to a path which will take you into the heart of the woods where these wretched events occurred. There is nothing to mark the spot where Sir William and his disciples fell. But it's useful, perhaps, as you walk through these woods, to remember – in an age that's so often impressed, even overwhelmed, by charisma – that charisma alone ought not to become a basis for trust; that it's frequently part of the stock-in-trade of false prophets; and that, now as then, the diagnosis that ought to be made in the case of such intense and fevered public response, in politics or anywhere else, is simply infatuation.

BOSTON

BOSTON par., mun. bor. and spt.-town with ry. sta.,
L. N. E, Holland, Lincolnshire, on r. Witham… has 3 fixed lights.
Boston is the headquarters of a deep-sea fishery.

AT FIRST IT'S NO more than a vague apparition – so vague you cannot be sure that you've really seen it – across the limitless fen. Then it begins to take shape – a mysterious shape suggesting some kind of primitive monolith designed for simple people to marvel at. And then, bit by bit, it reveals itself in all its heroic magnificence: a fourteenth-century tower, built for the glory of God, to be sure, but also, one can't help thinking, for the glory of Boston. Officially, the tower of the church of St Botolph; informally and generally Boston Stump. This is one of the great sights of England.

I saw it first while driving east out of Sleaford, and marvelled. What I didn't record, and cannot remember, is precisely where this marvelling started, where the glimmering outline first became perceptible. So I went back to check. It was misty as I drove out of Leicestershire into Lincolnshire, mistier still in Sleaford, and by the time I reached Heckington, which I thought was the point where the magic was going to begin, mist was almost fog. It was not until I reached Boston itself, at some point near the curious old Swan Hotel (now, sadly, a hotel no more) near the station, that the Stump at last deigned to appear, shimmering in a brave shaft of sunlight. There is something to be said for reaching Boston in mist and letting the tower take you by surprise. There it is, without warning, high and magnificent, 272 feet of it thrusting towards the heavens, a thrilling *coup de théâtre*. Is it better to choose a clear day or a misty one? Best to try both.

The mist had something particular to contribute. It underlined a necessary truth about Boston: its sense of being cut off from the world. That's what makes it, even for those who enjoy it, an uneasy, edgy kind of a place. There's something withdrawn and suspicious in Boston. It was one of the places where violence broke out in the streets when England lost the World Cup to Portugal in 2006: there's a sizeable Portuguese presence in Boston, and it wasn't an easy time. The armies of migrant workers employed on the fenland farms in summer create a sense of invasion. For many years it was represented in Parliament by a man called Richard Body, the most Euro-sceptic of MPs. The Eurosceptical UKIP party took almost 10 per cent of the vote here in 2005, a figure which might have been higher had the BNP not netted a further thousand votes.

For all that, it's a fine town to wander through, especially when the market's in session on Wednesdays and Saturdays. Then it's just what market days ought to be – the customers who've come in by car, train and bus from all the surrounding villages bump into old friends and block the gangways with fruity Lincolnshire gossip in the shadow of the church of St Botolph. The church is on the edge of the marketplace. Behind it, in fine juxtaposition, is the river, though the scene would be better still if the buildings didn't crowd so close to the Witham that no space is left for a riverside walk. Before it, in prime place in the square, is a statue of Herbert Ingram, founder of the *Illustrated London News*, and Boston's Liberal Member of Parliament until he drowned in a boating accident on Lake Erie in 1860, now turning a little green, as statues do.

Once this marketplace was full of local businesses trading under distinctive local names: seedsmen, sellers of tractors and the like. Now the names on the fascias are much the ones you find everywhere: Barclays, H. Samuel, Dollond & Aitchison, Marks & Spencer, Jeans Station, Poundstretcher, Millets, Timpson, Specsavers, the Carphone Warehouse. The twentieth century has done a lot to erode the sense of the town as it used to be. To the south and east of the centre, a screeching ring road called John Adams Way (named after the eighteenth-century US president, not as one might otherwise have supposed, after the composer of *A Short Ride in a Fast Machine*) has slashed through the town, cutting the far end of South Street off from the rest and condemning its mingled shops to decline and closure. (Yet the streets in the centre are still congested and fume-ridden; without John Adams's wretched Way they'd presumably be even worse.)

Even so there's a lot to savour as you walk around Boston. There are fine evocative buildings in South Street: the fifteenth-century (much amended) Shodfriars Hall, which once housed the theatre; the handsome riverbank grain store, now noisily but harmoniously in business as a centre for musical education; and perhaps the most elegant building in the town, Fydell House, now Pilgrim College. The Guildhall, now a museum, which was closed for refurbishment when I visited Boston in 2002 and still closed for refurbishment when I went back in the spring of 2007, was due to reopen soon in a celebration of Boston's history. Meanwhile it's been proved by dendrochronology, a notice said, to have been built in the 1390s, far earlier than experts assumed. Narrow endearing alleys lead to secret squares, now badly in need of improvement and, a little distance away, in Red Lion Street, there is a pleasingly spunky Centenary Methodist church, where they seem to have said to themselves: OK, maybe we can't match the Stump, but we'll certainly have a go.

Beyond, at the north end of Bargate, is a broad urban space which was once the cattle market: mostly a sea of parked cars nowadays, redeemed and humanized on market days by an overspill of stalls from the square. And then – another fine townscape surprise – the Horncastle Road, with its prosperous houses and its waterway in the middle, in the manner of Bruges, with above it a great unexpected windmill: the only one left of fifteen which once flourished in Boston, and now a working mill again, with an excellent vegetarian tea room.

You can walk the town for an hour or more and, John Adams apart, enjoy almost every moment. That still doesn't quite atone for having been robbed by the mist of the distant view. You can get a sense of it, though, from a novel by Robert Shaw, the actor. His book, *The Flag*, was intended as the first part of a trilogy, but the two remaining parts were never completed. No doubt Shaw was too much in demand as an actor. He died in 1978, at fifty-one. *The Flag* is based on the life of Conrad Noel, the 'Red Vicar' of Thaxted, installed by a Socialist patron, Daisy, Countess of Warwick. Noel had made it clear that if appointed he would never compromise his Socialist faith, however much it might scandalize the local Conservative faithful, and on May Day he lived up to his promise by running up the red flag on the church tower.

Shaw's version of Noel is a working-class priest who has come from Houghton

(Shaw was born at Westhoughton, near Wigan) with his alienated and unstable wife and three children. The flag is brought from Lancashire by a miner called Rockingham, who is joined on his journey by a nervous, stuttering, pregnant girl called Jean. In Shaw's book the church for which they are heading is out on the Suffolk coast at a place he calls Eastwold, though it's clearly Southwold: there's a character in the book modelled on the young George Orwell, who grew up in that seaside town. The route from the north takes them through Boston.

> 'Is that what they call a mm… mirage, Mr Rockingham?'
>
> He looked up, lifted in eyes and heart. After mile upon mile of this plain on which nothing had been raised over their heads for more than thirty feet the massive silhouette rising up in the sky might indeed have been a mirage, it stood above like some prehistoric rock worn away from the land by the wind and the sea.
>
> 'Would that be the ocean beyond?'
>
> 'I can't tell.' She shaded her eyes with her hand. 'I've never seen the ocean… that place is Boston and that church tower dropping from heaven is what they call Boston "stump".'
>
> 'It's as… astonishing Mister Rockingham.'
>
> 'It is,' said Rockingham with pleasure. 'It is.'

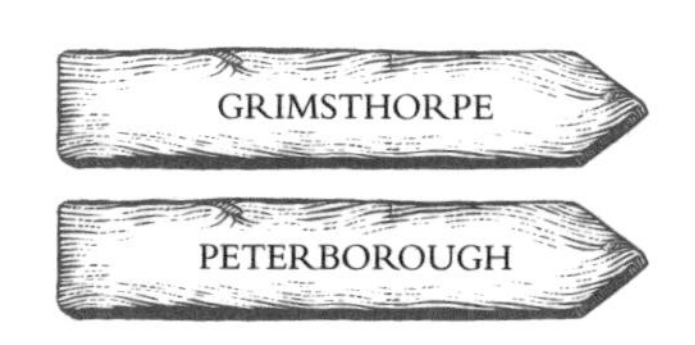

BROADSTAIRS

BROADSTAIRS AND ST PETER'S urb. dist. and par. and ry. sta., S. R., E. Kent… it is a much-frequented bathing-place.

ON THE WAY FROM the station, there's the Dickens in India Indian restaurant. Next comes the Dickens Pantry, purveyors of home-made cakes. Then the Charles Dickens pub, fine wines and ales, hot and cold food, in John Street. In this north-eastern corner of Kent, Charles Dickens is everywhere. Trotwood Place has a cottage which was said to be the model for Betsey's house in *David Copperfield*; Betsey herself is said to have been modelled on Mary Pearson Strong, who once lived here. There's an Old Curiosity Shop, of course, but at least it's not Ye Olde Curiosity Shoppe, as they so often are. And Bumble's Antiques, named after the beadle in *Oliver Twist*. And Nickleby's Takeaway (named after nasty old Uncle Ralph perhaps, in the light of his talent for taking away what does not belong to him). Fort Road has a Dickens Cottage, and Union Square a Barnaby's Lodge, and Harbour Street, just beyond, a pub called the Barnaby Rudge. One begins to look for Dickens connections even where there aren't any. Which book of his does the Tartar Frigate refer to? Or Owler's Nook? Or the Phileas Fogg restaurant? – wrong writer there, I think. I also looked long and hard at a spot called the Ritzy Retro. Probably not.

Broadstairs has a fair claim to Dickens. He wasn't born here (that honour belongs ineluctably to the city of Portsmouth); and even in Kent, the city of Rochester and Dickens's house at Gads Hill must have a superior claim. But he certainly holidayed here, and wrote here, and incorporated various aspects of the town into more books than just *David Copperfield*. Fort House, splendidly turreted on its height, is claimed to be the model for Bleak House, though Fort House looks rather grander than Ada Summerson's first impressions when invited into Bleak House, which in the book is not by the sea.

They haven't put up a statue to Dickens, but that is no doubt because Dickens ordained that no statue of him should be created, a rule broken, so far as I know, only by some over-enthusiastic Americans. Attempts to offer it to England were fought off by Dickens's descendants, so it now stands in Clark Park, west Philadelphia. Yet the town's devotion to Dickens seems not just respectful, but fulsome. Though I could not find it this time, there used to be a plaque attached to a wall by a local councillor, which said: 'This house has no connection with Dickens'.

There's much else to be said for Broadstairs besides the great man. I wandered through it on a Sunday afternoon in high summer: the harbour and beach looked irresistible, though sea-bathing was not much in evidence. People have taken to doing their bathing elsewhere since Bartholomew's description was written. Groups of diligent tourists responded with 'oohs' and even the occasional 'wow' as gobbets of Broadstairs history were fed to them.

It seems harsh to condemn this Dickens fixation in a town which lives by its tourism, but I just longed for some variation. Why wasn't I lured to see the site of the Thirty-Nine Steps in Buchan's novel? In Hitchcock's film – the thirty-nine steps, as the memory man repeats in his robotic monotone a moment before he gets shot – is 'an organization of spies, collecting information on behalf of the Foreign Office of…'; but in the Buchan original it's a staircase leading down to the sea that he's thought to have modelled on one at Broadstairs.

But the people I miss most of all here are Mr and Mrs Pooter, and possibly their son Lupin too, though in some of his moods I'm not sure I would savour his company. If and when they can bear to break free of The Laurels, Brickfield Terrace, Broadstairs is the place on which the keeper of *The Diary of a Nobody* and his family like to bestow their custom. 'I don't think we can do better than "good Old Broadstairs"' Pooter animadverts on 31 July, though distressingly Dear Carrie 'not only raised an objection to Broadstairs, for the first time, but begged me not to use the expression, "Good Old", but to leave it to Mr Stillbrook'.

She soon relents, and writes to Mrs Beck of Harbour View Terrace – who, however, having offered them rooms, then withdraws the offer as she needs to house someone else. Still, they have their week there in August: the weather is fitful, and Lupin, having said he would go to bed and read, turns out to have sloped off to the Assembly

Rooms, where Polly Presswell, England's 'Particular Spark', is appearing. They spend quite a lot of the time visiting Margate, where their great friends Cummings and Gowing behave somewhat childishly, and the Pooters miss the train back to Broadstairs and are forced to take a cab, which costs them a painful 7s 6d. Sadly the book ends early the following summer, but I bet they went to Broadstairs again. Yet where in this town is Pooter's Pet Shop, Carrie's Caff, or Lupin's Laundrette?

Sauntering back to the station, though, I came upon Daisy's Café Bar. Might that be named after Lupin's disturbing girlfriend, the reprehensible Daisy Mutlar, who troubles the senior Pooters so before she abandons Lupin for the better-off Murray Posh? The place was shut, so I couldn't ask. But I hope so.

BURROW

BURROW, ham., S. Somersetshire,
4½m. SSW. of Langport…

TRAVELLERS ON THE A361 out of Taunton (one of those roads which runs between two completely arbitrary destinations, in this case Barnstaple, Devon, and Beckhampton, Wilts, a place where racehorses are put through their paces), will find that there suddenly rears up before them a strange apparition: a hill with a tower on top, which the timid might fear has been put there to bar their way. Unwary drivers might assume that this is Glastonbury, for which the A361 is aiming and which also has a tor and a tower, but those who have been to Glastonbury will know better; it's a further five miles down the road. No, this is Burrow Mump, on the edge of the village of Burrow or Burrow Bridge; and it's a mump, they insist, not a tump, or even a hump or bump.

A notice board put up by the National Trust boringly claims that both words in 'Burrow Mump' simply mean hill: but although there's a place near Kirkby Lonsdale called Burrow with Burrow, I cannot believe that this place is no more than Hill Hill. According to *A Dictionary of Archaic and Provincial Words*, by James Orchard Halliwell, published in 1847, the word 'mump' had different meanings in different places. In the north, 'to mump' meant to beat or bruise; in the west, to cheat or intrude. More specifically, Gloucestershire people used mump to indicate a large piece of wood, while in Somerset it simply meant a protuberance, just as it does in the illness called mumps. Mumpinday, when the poor used to go around begging for money or corn, is 21 December, while 'mumpoker' is an expression used on the Isle of Wight to frighten naughty children, as in: 'I will send the mumpoker after you.' But let us, since we're in Somerset, settle for Burrow Protuberance.

It's probably a natural, rather than a man-made, protuberance, though it did form part of a line of defence around Alfred's stronghold, the Isle of Athelney. A chapel

which belonged to the Abbey of Athelney stood on this hill in the late twelfth century. It was rebuilt a century later and several times thereafter. It's thought that Royalists hid here after the battle of Langport in 1645, but the Parliamentarians caught up with them and made a horrible mess of their sanctuary. A further attempt to establish a working church on the hill was made in 1793, but failed for lack of money. Instead, a modest church was built at the foot of the Mump. When I was there, a group of exuberant schoolchildren was descending from a bus marked 'Cheam School'. This is the prep school, once in Cheam in Surrey but now moved to somewhere near Newbury, which Prince Charles attended, and his father before him, but this was holiday time, and these might may have been merely visitors. When they saw the hill they were required to climb, some of the girls let out little shrieks of 'Omigod', the most common word in the teenage female vocabulary nowadays after 'like', as in: 'I was like, Omigod.' But they bounded up it anyway.

A slow and slippery progress up the slope will reward you with an enormous view, in which, this being Somerset, you can pick out several church towers. If you want to go back and look at the village, be careful: there's no pavement, and the road is a series of bends around which urgent cars, propelled by men with fiercely resolute faces, come hurtling. At the bridge, you cross the river: the Parrett, though there are three rivers here, converging. A pleasant road running north by the river takes you to Westonzoyland, close to the site of the battle of Sedgemoor, where the Duke of Monmouth was routed. The church has a truly magnificent tower, one of those you see from the mump, but was locked when I tried to get in. The pub, which is close by the church, is, in contrast, open all day. The big lurid pub sign features both the Duke of Monmouth, who does not look like a man you'd enjoy doing business with, and his triumphant opponent at Sedgemoor, Louis de Duras, 2nd Earl of Feversham, who looks very nasty indeed. The artist could of course have added Judge Jeffreys, who sent so many men to their deaths after Sedgemoor, but that at least we are spared.

A B C D

E F G H

I J K L

M N O P

Q R S T

U V W XYZ

CAERNARFON

CARNARVON, co. town of Carnarvonshire, parl. (contributory to Carnarvon District of Boroughs) and mun. bor. and spt., with ry. sta., at mouth of r. Seiont…
The old castle, built by Edward I, is still almost entire.
On the Pile pier-head is a green fixed light…

QUITE APART FROM THE green fixed light, there is much to enjoy in Caernarfon (now the accepted spelling): its majestic castle – though if I were Welsh I might withhold a slice of my pleasure in it, because it is all about the English subduing the Welsh; the sturdy walls that accompany you everywhere; its jolly square, complete with funfair when I visited, over which the castle and church benignly preside; the statue to David Lloyd George, who represented this constituency from 1890 to 1945, looking out over the water; a magistrates' court which was once County Hall, very imposing and swaggery, as such buildings ought to be, with a figure on top whom I took for Britannia, but she's blindfold, and so she is Justice; and a spot where you pass through the wall and there is the sparkling sea and the harbour laid out before you in as dazzling a piece of townscape as I saw in all these journeys. There's also a tower, 28½ feet high, on the site where the Exchequer and Chancery of the Principality stood from 1284: another reminder, this, that for centuries the Princes of Wales have been those that the English ordained for them. A plaque in the centre of town records 'the generous deed of a loyal subject', Sir Charles Assheton-Smith Bt, who gave three houses to be demolished in order that his countrymen could witness the investiture of the Prince of Wales in July 1911; he also gave the land whereon they stood to the Crown. What the people who lived in the houses he gave thought of this generosity is of course not recorded.

What I couldn't find in Caernarfon, though, despite a prolonged inspection, was the offices of the Caernarfon and District branch of the United Nations Peacekeeping Force. I wouldn't have expected to find such an institution were it not that I had read about it in the *Guardian* newspaper. It might seem inexplicable to anyone who has never worked on a newspaper in the age of hot metal printing that such an unlikely organization should have been invoked, but to those who worked on the *Guardian* then, as I did, it was almost to be expected. In those days the words that went into the paper were spewed out line by line on linotype machines, and then fed into the page by men (women were never employed, by order of the print unions) called stonehands. Quite often an error would be found in a line: the process then was to tweezer out the offending line and substitute a corrected one. In practice, given the speed at which these lines were hammered out, the replacement line often contained its own error, sometimes odder than the one that was being extirpated. Even worse, a replacement line would sometimes be dropped into an inappropriate space; and in the case of the Caernarfon branch, this had happened twice. The story as written said that the Haldane Society of Socialist Lawyers had issued a statement defending the *Guardian* against some complaint made against it. 'It is not the *Guardian* that is to blame,' the paper had hoped to quote them as saying, 'it is…' – at which point the name of the culprits ought to have followed. But at this stage someone dropped in an inapplicable line about the Caernarfon and District branch of some organization or other, and then a second inappropriate line destined for a story about the UN.

These were difficult times for the friends of accuracy. Even if such a solecism was spotted, it wasn't always corrected. The supervisor known as the Head Printer, who ran the composing room, would stand behind the editor of the night, warning of what would happen if the paper was delayed by making further attempts to get things right. 'You realize you have just lost the whole of South Wales,' I was thunderously rebuked on one such occasion. Maybe someone noted on the night that we had inadvertently created a statesman called President Eisenhowever, but decided not to intervene for fears that the paper might never reach Rugby. Sometimes we felt that when we did succeed in eradicating errors, we denied many readers much pleasure. I felt a terrible killjoy in insisting that Mrs Whirley Williams ought to become Mrs Shirley Williams. And it probably cost us the whole of Scotland.

This was only one of the risks one took in those days in putting together a newspaper. One night I found a line in a proof which referred to the inventor of the Laffer curve as a 'two-headed American economist'. 'Tow-headed, I think,' I told the

Head Printer, but when the first edition came up poor Laffer still had both heads. 'I thought we were getting somebody to chip it,' I said to the Printer (chipping being a crude resort to eradicating a dud word by hitting it with a chisel). Mournfully he contemplated the evidence. 'I did,' he said, 'but he seems to have missed.'

But the errors for which the *Guardian* became famous were by no means all the fault of the print floor. Even journalists, in my experience, were not, you may be amazed to hear, entirely infallible. More perilous still was the system of copy-taking, where writers not in the office used to read what they had written to ranks of copy typists, a breed best known for their plangent cries after the first hundred words of: 'Is there much more of this?' Not all of them knew their way around the subjects involved. That was why the arts page, over the years, treated readers to reviews of such little known works as 'Lazy Luminations' by Benjamin Britten, 'Doris Gudonov', and Gilbert and Sullivan's 'Princess Aida'. The Selsey Marina once went through all editions as 'the self-same arena', and on a night when a weary copytaker switched from taking a piece for sport to taking a piece for the arts pages, the paper even gave birth to an Alfred Lawn Tennison.

Later the compositors and copytakers of the *Guardian* were swept away by a new technology which ensured that copy appeared in the paper as typed by journalists, who could no longer take refuge from their mistakes by blaming those who had gone. The daily feature called 'Corrections and Clarifications', introduced in 1997, regularly demonstrates that even today, no one is perfect. 'Australian cricketer Don Bradman', a column in late 2006 had to admit, 'was carried, not curried, off the field during the Ashes series in August 1938.' And in early 2008, the paper had to own up to having described the liaison between President Sarkozy of France and Carla Bruni as 'a very pubic romance'.

The march of new technology added new complications, undreamed of until then. There's a function on computers called 'Find and Replace' where, for instance, if you spell Beethoven as 'Batehoven' throughout your piece, a single instruction will correct every misspelling. One night, a sub-editor who was putting the results of elections for the European Parliament into the paper pointed out that we were using the formula 'percentage poll' to show the (meagre) proportion of electors who had bothered to vote, where the *Guardian* style book said we should use 'percentage turnout'. So a global change was ordered, switching every 'poll' to 'turnout'. That was why, where every other newspaper the next morning recorded the election of a candidate called Anita Pollak, the *Guardian* awarded the seat to Anita Turnoutak.

On the other hand, should you come across a branch of the UN Peacekeeping Force in delightful Caernarfon, I take it all back.

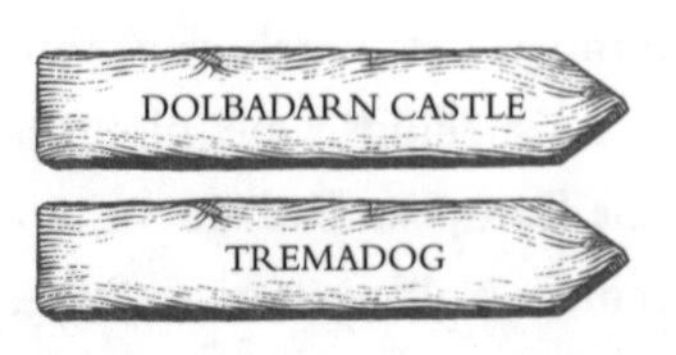

CAPE WRATH

CAPE WRATH, bold headland, on N. coast of Sutherlandshire, forming the NW. point of mainland of Scotland. Is crowned by a lighthouse with white and red alternating flashing light 400 ft. above high water and seen 27m.

A COUPLE OF MILES along the dramatic road that runs south-west out of Durness in the north of Scotland, there's a road sign that says: Cape Wrath, 12 miles. That makes it sound simple. Turn down this road, past the Cape Wrath Hotel on your right, continue for another 12 miles and there you are. But it isn't like that at all. You drive down the road only as far as the car park, then wander along the lane until you come to a kind of rudimentary slipway. From there, if conditions are right, you'll be able to cross the Kyle of Durness in Mr J. Morrison's boat and then ride away to the lighthouse in Mrs I. P. Mackay's minibus.

But that might not happen. It may be a day or two, sometimes more, before you arrive at the Cape Wrath lighthouse. Sometimes the weather can make the boat crossing too hazardous, and even if you got across there wouldn't be a minibus, and even if there was a minibus, the wind and rain on the edge of the cape above the high cliffs would batter you half to death. And then there's a notice board at the roadside which warns you that the place for which you are heading is also the Cape Wrath Bombardment Range. If you're lucky, it says that the road across the range is not subject to delay; but if you're unlucky, you may find that 'is not' has been changed to 'is'. Sometimes, when NATO air forces are in action, there is a delay. But sometimes, when the Navy is firing its heavy stuff at Garve Island, off the north of the headland, the whole area will be shut. Indeed, any civilians on it will have had to clear out.

Forewarned, I allowed two days for this expedition. On the first, the weather was wrathful: furious wind and torrential rain. No chance today of crossing the kyle in Mr J. Morrison's boat. There will be enough people drowned in this book, I told myself, without its author joining them. On the second morning, you couldn't at first be sure. The day was clear, but threatening. 'We can get you across,' said a man at the top of the slipway, who would later be revealed as the driver of Mrs I. P. Mackay's minibus, 'but can we get you back? That's the question.' If the boat was unable to bring us back, we would face a 4-mile walk on the other side of the water, and a difficult walk at that.

But maybe he was merely ratcheting up the sense of the journey's drama. Soon we could see a boat heading towards us which was clearly Mr J. Morrison's. This seemed hopeful – though rather less hopeful when we perceived that Mr Morrison (as we took him to be) was baling with muscular vigour as he approached, and was still baling vigorously when he reached the foot of the slipway. At which point he said he was sorry but he thought he had better go back and fetch another boat, and away he went over the tranquil kyle. Happily, the new boat didn't need so much baling, and a dozen intrepid travellers, some dressed for difficult weather, some not, settled into it, and off we went over the water, where Mrs Mackay's minibus was awaiting us.

The driver, whose name was Davy, issued us all with tickets imbued with a spirit of adventure: 'your ticket to the most remote part of Britain' they said. And away we went on a forty-minute journey which took us 11 miles to the lighthouse, every yard of the road, built in 1828 to service the lighthouse, pitted and potholed. Calm water today, maybe; but choppy land. But Mrs I. P. Mackay's driver smoothed our passage with a cheerful, informative commentary, pausing only to get out and open a gate and shut it behind him to keep the local sheep in their place. There were once, he said, not so very long since, families living on this austere and treeless territory with mountains towering above it. Until 1947, there was even a school. Now only five bothies remained in occupation, three reserved to the Ministry of Defence, the two others let out to visitors (except on days when the Navy was doing its worst to Garve Island).

At last, both shaken and stirred, we arrived at the lighthouse – the work of the first of the Stevensons, who built so many in Scotland – with a real sense of achievement, as if it was we who had got us here, rather than Mr Morrison's boat and Mrs Mackay's bumpety minibus. You can stand on a foghorn platform, with a sheer drop below you, 250 feet down to the water, and gaze out across the measureless sea. To the west there is no land until Canada. To the north, there is nothing for the space of more than 2,000 miles, between here and the pole.

Sir Walter Scott, who, wherever you go in Scotland, seems to have been there before you, came to the Cape in his role as a lighthouse commissioner. He saw the place from the sea; an even more awesome Old Testament kind of sight than the ones you get from the lighthouse. 'This dread cape,' he wrote, 'so fatal to mariners, is a high promontory whose steep sides go sheer down to the breakers which lash its feet. There is no land, except for a small creek about 1½ miles to the eastward. There the foam of the sea plays at "long bowl" with a huge collection of large stones, some of them a ton in weight, but which these fearful billows chuck up and down as a child tosses a ball.' No wonder, you think, contemplating this remote and primeval spot, they called it 'Cape Wrath', as if they could not pass this way without an instinctive calling to mind of the majestic anger of the Old Testament God. Yet wrath in that sense has nothing to do with it. The name is a corruption of a Norse word meaning 'a turning point': it was where mariners travelling west turned south, where mariners travelling north turned east, around the headland.

One cannot regret that these journeys can't always be made, and that some who aspire to go there may be disappointed. The Cape Wrath Hotel (closed and barred off when I visited) in its heyday had been attacked for having one year brought to this spot 240 persons whose vehicles had cut up the road. Perhaps seventeen times that number now come to the Cape in a season, not, fortunately, in their own vehicles, but on journeys made possible by Mr J. Morrison first and Mrs Mackay thereafter. If journeys to the most remote part of Britain endlessly multiply, that sense of utter remoteness, already eroded when you arrive in the comfort – well, relative comfort – of a minibus, will be gone for good. Let it remain as it is: some days, however bleak it may be in the wind by the lighthouse out on the headland, still accessible, even welcoming, thanks to Mr Morrison and Mrs Mackay; on others, undisturbed, unobserved, lost in its timeless solitude.

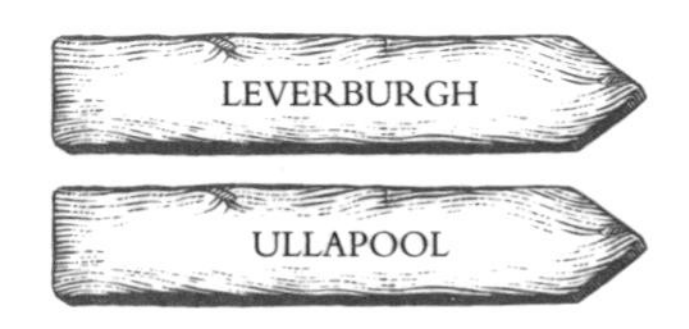

CASTLE DANGEROUS

CASTLE DANGEROUS, see Douglas Castle.

DOUGLAS CASTLE is a seat of the Earl of Home.

BARTHOLOMEW HAS A FINE collection of castles. With his usual liberality, he includes some names by which they are locally known as well as their official ones. Some are true fortified castles; some, like Castle Cluggy in Perthshire, are listed as fortalices, or in the case of Castle Drumin, Banffshire, baronial fortalices; some are no more than earthworks. A few of the most intriguing are located in Ireland, and so beyond the reach of this book: Castle Freke in Co. Cork; Castle Gore, Co. Mayo (though the Gore may reflect a family connection rather than buckets of blood spilled on the site); Castlelost, Co. Westmeath; Castle Matrix and Castle Troy, Limerick. I picked out three to sample in Scotland, not because they are famous but simply because of their names: Dangerous in Lanarkshire, Gloom in Clackmannanshire, and Spiritual at the northern end of Loch Ness.

Castle Dangerous waits at the end of a walk of less than a mile from the village of Douglas, south Lanarkshire, past a memorial to the Polish soldiers who took refuge here in the summer of 1940, some of whom stayed and settled. The castle, I have to say, doesn't look the least bit dangerous now, mainly because so little of it is left. One side of the building is gone entirely. What remains is roofless; grass grows on the window ledges. The remnants have been patched in places, and the doorways filled in. The first reference to a castle at Douglas – as so often in medieval Scottish history, to a murder – occurs in 1288. Wallace and Bruce fought the English here. The English repeatedly evicted the Scots, but Bruce's loyal accomplice James Douglas kept taking it back. It was in that time that the name 'Castle Dangerous' became attached to it.

Nothing is left of that castle: what you see on the site is the remnant of a building no earlier than the seventeenth century. That building in turn was destroyed by fire in

1755. The castle Bartholomew mentions as one of the homes of the Homes is a much later matter, built in 1757 on a separate site by Robert Adam. Much as, in the 1850s, the leading citizens of Leeds had the halls of other ambitious towns and cities measured up to make sure that their new town hall would outdo them, so Adam was under instructions to see the dimensions of this monument to the pride and power of the Homes exceeded in every respect those of the castle at Inveraray, which belonged to the Campbells. In the event, only one wing was finished, and that has now gone – knocked down in 1938, partly because of the damage done to the structure by mining. There is little left now but the meadows, the sheep, the birds on a little loch, and the Cameron memorial – which recalls that it was here in 1689 that James, Earl of Angus, raised a regiment to defend the Covenanters. 'Here on the 14th March 1968,' says an angry plaque, 'within a mile of the spot where the 20th Cameronian Regiment was raised by the Earl of Angus on 14th May 1689, the 1st Battalion Cameronians (Scottish Rifle) held a conventicle and lowered the regimental flag to mark its abandonment on order of the government.' A government in England, they did not need to add.

At the end of his life, in 1831, Sir Walter Scott set a novel here, one he had long hoped to write. He had by then suffered at least three strokes, possibly four, and insisted, despite the advice of friends and family, on not only trying to write this new book but on visiting Douglas to set an authentic scene. His son-in-law, J. G. Lockhart, includes in his vast biography of Sir Walter a grim account of this expedition. 'The state of his health at the time', Scott wrote of himself in a preface to his novel, 'was so feeble that he found himself incapable of pursuing his researches, as in better days he would have delighted to do, and was obliged to be contented with such a cursory view of scenes, in themselves most interesting, as could be snatched in a single morning, when any bodily exertion was painful.' It is not, by common consent, a good book. An opening sentence of more than 100 words sets the tone for it. E. Cobham Brewer, compiler of the immortal *Dictionary of Phrase and Fable*, whom we shall meet at Edwinstowe and an admirer of Scott, says in his *Reader's Handbook of Allusions, References, Plots and Stories*: 'Those who read it must remember they are the last notes of a dying swan, and forbear to scan its merits too strictly.'

The sense that you get at the castle, that though momentous and often terrible events once occurred here, many years have since passed in which nothing happened at all, is stronger still in the village. Groome says of it: 'Formerly a place of much political importance, a burgh of barony with high magisterial powers, and a seat of considerable trade and marketing, it has fallen into great decadence, and now presents an antique and irregular appearance. Its streets are narrow, some of the houses look as if they still belonged to the Middle Ages...' And so they still do today, with little beside the façade of the Co-op to hint at the twentieth century. There's a memorial here on the site of the house where he lived to a man called James Gavin, a Covenanter. The vengeful scourge of all Covenanters, John Graham of Claverhouse, came to the house, demanded to borrow Gavin's shears, and used them to cut off his ears. 'To commemorate and perpetuate this brutal outrage,' said an inscription on the front of the house, 'Gavin carved the stone with his own hand to put above the door of the house erected by him years after his return from banishment in the Island of Barbadoes.'

With the fate of poor Gavin, and others like him, fresh in my mind in this dour and solemn place, I turned back to the busy Ayr road on the edge of Douglas to catch my bus back to Lanark. Where the billboards jerked me roughly back into a world to which even time-locked Douglas is apparently no longer immune. '*Daily Record* exclusive,' they said. 'My fling with Brad Pitt, by Scots gangster's girlfriend.'

CASTLE GLOOM

CASTLE GLOOM, see Castle Campbell.
CASTLE CAMPBELL, old fortress of the Argyll family,
1m. N. Dollar, Clackmannanshire.

IT IS CASTLE CAMPBELL today, but for years it was Castle Gloom. The Campbells changed the name when they acquired it in the fifteenth century, though they had to get an Act of the Scottish Parliament to do so. It stands on a prominent hill, which seems, says Groome's *Ordnance Gazetteer of Scotland*, 'to have been partly formed by the hand of Nature, and partly finished by Art', overlooking the small town of Dollar, famous for its Academy. On one side of the castle, deep in a dark ravine, is a stream called the Burn of Sorrow, on the other, a stream called the Burn of Care; they join together to make the broader stream that runs down the glen and into the village. Much the best way to approach the castle is through a pleasant glen that runs north out of Dollar. It's easier to go by road, but you shouldn't. The road wheels round and ends above the castle and from there you come gently down to it, which isn't a gloomy experience at all. Go through the glen and it suddenly rears up above you, grave and daunting, creating that sense of menace which belongs in such a place.

The Campbells, Earls of Argyll, a clan grown rich on the forfeitures of its rivals, acquired the castle in the fifteenth century when the previous owners fell foul of the king, and held it until the seventeenth, when they miscalculated. Archibald, eighth Earl of Argyll, who had placed the crown on the head of King Charles at Scone, defected to Cromwell, inviting a bitter revenge at the hands of the royalist Marquess of Montrose, who set Castle Campbell on fire. What survived was the tower, with its fine barrel-vaulted hall, installed around 1600, with a spiral staircase to take you up to the top. There's a good model reconstruction in the cellar of the castle as it must have looked in its greatest days. Watch out too for the green man masks at the top of the house (they probably held lamps clenched in their teeth), and the slightly incongruous Italian-influenced loggia, not a common sight in wet and windy Scotland.

From the top of the tower you may look out over the village, across the Clackmannan plain, once a famous coal-mining territory, to the river Forth beyond, where, had I come on a less gloomy day, I might, a notice at the viewpoint informed me, have been able to pick out Longannet and Kincardine power stations and the Grangemouth refinery. Below the tower, perched on the edge of what seems like a precipice, is a curious doorway known as John Knox's pulpit, where the sixteenth-century Protestant firebrand is said to have preached in the open air, no doubt making this sombre place feel more sombre still. He undoubtedly preached here, but according to modern opinion not perhaps in this spot. Below is a kind of chasm leading back to the village, which, until the path through the glen was created in 1863, was the principal access. Needless to say, Scott came here; it was through this chasm that he had to make his laborious, painful way at this point to visit the castle.

And if modern teachings on the location of Knox dispose of one legend, here's something to dispose of another. It's the story of Cape so-called Wrath all over again. Castle Gloom has nothing to do with gloom. The name of the castle before the Campbells arrived, as its custodian explained to me (it's also confessed in the guidebook) was Gloume, probably derived from the Gaelic word 'glom' which indicates not gloom, but a chasm. But what, I indignantly asked, about the two burns, Care and Sorrow? He sighed. These were not their real names at all, but ones invented by the Victorians, with their weakness for melodrama.

So gloom, and care and sorrow – all are illusion. And indeed, had I picked a brilliant spring morning to come here, rather than a grave day in winter, it might all have been sweetness and light. And yet I was lucky to get in at all. Had I arrived the following day, a Thursday, I'd have found the great forbidding wooden door of the castle barred against me. Castle Gloom does not open on Thursdays or Fridays in winter. To have walked up the glen would still have been a pleasure, but to find oneself then restricted to the merest peep at the keep through the gun holes would have been to taste the rage and frustration which the Campbells visited over the years on their toiling would-be assailants. Be warned!

CASTLE SPIRITUAL

CASTLE SPIRITUAL, ancient fort, in co. and 6m. SW. of Inverness, on peninsula between Lochs Ness and Dochfour.

THE WORD 'SPIRITUAL' IS partly defined as being incorporeal, having no material form, so perhaps it's an entirely appropriate name for Bartholomew's ancient fort, which is neither visible or even, with any certainty, findable. 'The original building', says Groome's *Ordnance Gazetteer of Scotland*, 'is thought to have been a crannage or lake dwelling; either that building or one succeeding it is by some believed to have been a stronghold of the early Pictish kings, the place where St Columba visited King Bruisde nan Melchan (AD 565); and a later building, vestiges of which remain, appears to have been a small baronial keep of the feudal times, and to have completely commanded the adjoining ford across the river Ness.' *Some* believed that, note, which clearly implies that others did not. That was written in the 1880s. I could find no vestiges now. Later accounts say the original building was destroyed at the end of the fifteenth century, and the rest of it was eradicated by the navvies who worked for Thomas Telford when he linked up the lochs to create the Caledonian Canal.

If you drive down the road out of Inverness on the northern side of the loch, you will come to a place called Lochend, a largely twentieth-century settlement with a handful of earlier houses interspersed. There's a track on the Inverness side of the village which leads to the promontory, which takes you out to the narrowest point of the canal. There used to be a ferry here – it is easy to see where it might have docked on either side of the water. The nearest thing to a castle is a building which must have been in its day a well-loved family house – but it was all boarded up in the early summer of 2007 and apparently waiting for the demolition men to put it out of its misery.

Why this spot should ever have been known as Castle Spiritual is unclear. Groome knew it as such, and an Ordnance Survey map of 1905 gives it that name, but later accounts say the name was Castle Bona (the ferry was known as the Bona Ferry) or Caisteal Spioradain. Bona, in this case, is unlikely to have been derived from the word much used in Polari, a form of gay slang, which means, basically, good. The still fondly remembered radio comedy series *Round the Horne* used to feature a gay couple who worked for a shadowy outfit called Bona Enterprises.

Caisteal Spioradain, though, sounds a rather more serious matter; spiritual even. It means 'Castle of the Ghosts', and refers to bloody events in this now peaceful place in the mid fifteenth century. A book called *Discovering Inverness-shire* says the Macleans, later of Dochgarroch, under the chief of the clan, Hector, were at odds with the Camerons, who called Hector 'the robber baron of the north'. Details of their encounters vary, says the author (herself a Maclean), according to which clan history you read. The Maclean version says that their lot had been down to Glen Urquhart to avenge atrocities carried out by the Camerons. At the end of the day, there were dead Camerons hanging all over the battlements, while the Camerons had killed two of Hector's sons in front of their father. 'From that day,' writes Loraine Maclean of Dochgarroch, 'Bona Castle was Caisteal Spioradain, the Castle of the Ghosts, because of its haunting by the dead men.'

No such sense of ghostly presences was apparent when I was there: the sun kindly appeared after a morning of rain, and holiday boats passed peacefully down the waterway towards the succession of lochs at Neptune's Staircase and on to the western sea. Though finding a vestige or two might have been even better, it all made for an agreeable expedition. Quite bona, in fact.

CHELSEA

CHELSEA, parl. and met. bor. … chiefly famous for its hospital for invalid soldiers, built by Sir Christopher Wren. Cheyne Walk is associated with the name of Thomas Carlyle, the 'Philosopher of Chelsea', who resided there for many years, as did Turner, the famous painter.

ON THE EVENING OF Tuesday, 16 December 1930, two men left a pub called the Duke of Wellington in the heart of Belgravia and set off for Tite Street, close to Wren's hospital and no great distance from Cheyne Walk. Though not as eminent as Turner or Carlyle, they too belonged to the world of the arts – they were composers. The older man, the senior by seventeen years, was called Bernard van Dieren. The younger, a striking, dapper figure with his smooth black hair and pointed beard, had a double identity. Born Philip Heseltine, he had reinvented himself as Peter Warlock, a name which hinted, correctly, at an interest in the black arts. They were heading for Warlock's rented flat. The younger composer, always prone to depression, seemed that night, as van Dieren would later testify, to be in a state of more than habitual dejection. 'I felt terribly unhappy about him,' he said; but was saddened, as he remembered, rather than alarmed. The woman with whom Warlock lived, known to neighbours as Mrs Warlock but in fact his mistress Barbara Peache, had gone out for the evening, so when van Dieren said goodnight in the early hours of the morning, Warlock was alone.

Next morning, when Barbara returned to the flat – she had been to a dance, she explained to the police, and had stayed so late that it seemed best to spend the night in a hotel – she found the landlady, who lived upstairs, in a state of some agitation. She'd become aware of the smell of gas, and having failed to find a source of a leak, had summoned the gas company. When Barbara tried the door of her flat, she found that it would not open. When the door was finally opened, the place was full of gas and Peter Warlock – composer of the Capriol Suite and many songs, some gently sensitive, others roistering, that are still in the repertoire – was lying dead on a couch. He was thirty-six.

The inquest into his death was held three days before Christmas. The jury had to decide whether the death was an accident or whether in his depression he had chosen to end his life. Looking at the evidence now, an accident seemed out of the question. The door of the flat was locked. Warlock's cat had been put outside – the landlady found it distressed and mewing pitiably in the yard. A gas fitter told the coroner he had searched for a possible leak, but had found nothing. The landlady, Mrs Mary Venn, recalled that at around 6.40 that morning she had heard the sound of doors and windows in Warlock's flat being shut. When she got up some ninety minutes later, she smelled gas, and sent for the gasmen, who could not get into the flat and called in the police. Barbara Peache said Warlock had been very depressed and had more than once threatened to kill himself. The last of these threats had been made on the previous Sunday night. He had argued that he and Barbara ought to separate; when everyone was out of the way, he would be able to kill himself. In spite of all this, the jury failed to reach a conclusion. Possibly, it was speculated, they did not wish to upset the composer's mother, who had refused to accept that her son could have killed himself, by reaching what was otherwise the obvious verdict.

There was, however, another possibility, one specifically raised over fifty years later in a book by Warlock/Heseltine's son Nigel, the product of the composer's marriage to a woman called Minnie Lucy Channing, always known as Puma. At the close of this book, Heseltine suggested that his father could have been murdered – and by Bernard van Dieren. Heseltine had never been close to his father – he had never even met him until he was eight – and most of Warlock's friends dismissed his case with contempt. But there were some odd circumstances, not all of which came out at the inquest.

Van Dieren was man of multiple talents. His contemporary Constant Lambert named him alongside Sibelius and Busoni as the best and brightest hopes for the future of music. When he died, Lambert wrote that the world had recently lost two of its greatest composers: Van Dieren and Alban Berg. The critic Cecil Gray, in a piece for the *Radio Times*, called him 'the modern Leonardo'. Perhaps, Gray suggested, his importance as a composer was undervalued simply because his gifts were so rich and so varied. Van Dieren had a matchless grasp of instrumental technique. As a violinist, he was gifted enough to handle the trickiest Paganini. He was a talented writer, not just about music but about all kinds of art (he had written a study of Epstein). Having trained as a scientist he could well have made his name in medicine, mathematics or chemistry. He was also exceptionally good with his hands; he could have earned a living as a carpenter or a bookbinder.

As a chemist, working in London hospitals, he would have understood and had access to poisons. Partly because of his persistent ill-health, he was chronically short of money, and, so some of Warlock's other friends alleged, used to sponge off the younger man – despite the fact that Warlock's financial circumstances were frequently precarious too, and he regularly pestered his mother for money.

When the will was read it was found that Warlock had left everything to van Dieren – a bequest which the beneficiary claimed he had been wholly unaware of until informed by a solicitor shortly before the inquest. But Warlock was also close to a woman called Winifred Baker, a former nurse. Most of his friends could not understand this relationship. They thought her a joke. Yet he seemed to have some deep emotional need for her company. And a policeman called to the flat when the body was discovered found a sheet of paper on which Warlock had written the draft of a second will, in which nothing was left to van Dieren, and everything to Winifred Baker.

Warlock had spent what proved to be his final evening with Bernard van Dieren. Van Dieren, indisputably, was the last man to see him alive. Had the drafting of this new will been the result of their conversation? Or had van Dieren discovered it, already drafted, during the evening? These questions were never asked at the time by anyone in authority, but they did suggest that the issue of murder rather than suicide at least deserved some investigation.

Whatever the truth of the matter, which will never be known for certain, Warlock's death enlisted him in the sad galaxy of musicians who have died in strange or unexplained circumstances. As a composer you are putting your work on public trial and frequently having the world disparage or simply ignore it, so that the kind of depression – less endogenous apparently than reactive – which dogged Peter Warlock has perhaps accounted for other lives too.

Jeremiah Clarke, now recognized as the composer of the 'Trumpet Voluntary' that was once ascribed to Purcell, shot himself on 1 December 1707, apparently in a state of derangement, thought to have been brought on by a disappointment in love. Francesco Bianchi, an Italian composer who settled in London and had a string of successes, killed himself in Hammersmith in 1810. Tchaikovsky, according to most accounts, took his own life, though others have argued, quite credibly, that he was murdered.

The death of Mozart has frequently been attributed to the envy of the far less successful Salieri. Alessandro Stradella, who had talent enough to earn him six pages in the *New Grove Dictionary of Music and Musicians*, was attacked and left for dead in 1677, and then stabbed to death five years later, apparently through the agency of a rival for the affections of an actress whose preference was for Stradella. According to one account, two hired assassins had been sent at one point to Stradella's house with orders to kill him, but were so moved by the beauty of the music that he was making that they sneaked away with the deed undone.

Jean-Marie Leclair, one of a famous family of musicians, considered (says *Grove*) the founder of the French violin school, was murdered in 1764 as he entered his home. The police listed three suspects: his gardener, who had found the body; a nephew with whom he had fallen out; and the wife from whom he had recently parted. 'The murder', says *Grove*, 'is often said to be shrouded in mystery, but the evidence (in the French Archives Nationales) is so clearly against the nephew, who was a violinist and the author of *L'arbre généalogique de l'harmonie* (1767), that the only remaining mystery is that he was never brought to trial.' There were murderers among distinguished musicians too: Carlo Gesualdo, Prince of Venoza and Count of Conza, slew his faithless wife and her lover whom he found 'in flagrante delicto di fragrante peccato'. Other famous musicians died in accidents, some of them bizarre. Jean-Baptiste Lully used to conduct by banging a staff on the floor. One day in 1687 he jabbed it right through his foot, contracted gangrene and died. Samuel Arnold, a prolific eighteenth-century English composer of operas (more than seventy, including one called *Baron Kinkvervankotsdorsprakingatchdern*; all but one of them are now lost) died in 1802 after falling from a set of library steps. Charles-Valentin Alkan is frequently said to have died, like Leonard Bast in *Howards End*, when in 1888 a case of books fell on him as he reached out for the Talmud, although this is not well documented and other versions suggest the assassin may have been an umbrella rack. César Franck is said to have died two years later after being struck by a horse bus, though Grove gives his immediate cause of death as pleurisy. Alban Berg (d. 1935) was stung by a wasp and developed a fatal blood poisoning. The death of Maurice Ravel (1937) followed a blow to the head sustained while he was travelling in a taxi. Anton von Webern was shot in 1945 by an American soldier who thought he was a dealer on the black market – an allegation which might have been better directed against the composer's son-in-law, with whom he was staying. Maurice Duruflé (d. 1986), whose *Requiem* deserves to be rated with Fauré's, never fully recovered, and certainly never composed again, after a motoring accident.

Several composers drowned (Thomas Linley who might have been one of that rare breed, a great English composer, died at twenty-two in a boating accident: more of him when we get to Grimsthorpe). Enrique Granados drowned in March 1916 when a boat that was taking him across the English Channel was struck by a torpedo. He was picked up by a life raft, but seeing his wife struggling, went to her rescue and drowned alongside her. E. J. Moeran, a close friend of Warlock, was found dead in the river Kenmare in Ireland, but that was the result of a heart attack. Another poignant case was the death, at just thirty-seven, of Samuel Coleridge-Taylor, composer of *Hiawatha*, a huge favourite with choral societies down the years, on West Croydon railway station, though that too was from natural causes. He had a son called Hiawatha, who lived to be eighty.

More like Warlock's case perhaps is that of a composer from Manchester called Eric Fogg, entirely forgotten today, whose story, like that of William Crotch whom we shall meet in Norwich, is a reminder that early success and acclaim can carry its penalties. Fogg's father was the Halle Orchestra's organist; his mother was a singing teacher. At fifteen, he was organist of St John's, Deansgate. At seventeen he had one of his works played at a promenade concert (it was well enough received to be repeated there four years later) and conducted a concert of his own music at the Queen's Hall in London. His bassoon concerto, written for the instrument's most celebrated practitioner, Archie Camden, and still occasionally played nowadays, was performed at the Proms in 1931.

But that may have been the year when disappointment and disillusion began to set in. An ambitious choral work called *The Seasons*, a setting of poems by Blake, was picked out for performance at the Leeds triennial festival, but was severely overshadowed on the night by the premiere of a work by another talented young Lancastrian, William Walton. It was *Belshazzar's Feast*, not *The Seasons* that the audience came out talking about and which commandeered the attention of critics. The BBC, for which Fogg was working at this time as an accompanist – a promotion of sorts from his previous role playing solo piano under the pseudonym Keyboard Kitty – put him in charge of its newly created Empire Orchestra. But that went out only on short wave transmissions, so few in the UK heard it, and in any case they soon shut it down.

In subsequent years the sense must have invaded him that all the predictions that had thrilled him twenty years before were not to be fulfilled. On 19 December 1939, the day before that fixed for his second wedding, he fell to his death under a tube train at Waterloo. This death, like Warlock's nine years earlier, occurred in the days before Christmas, traditionally a bleak time for people afflicted by depression, and the inquest, like Warlock's, returned an open verdict. It might have been an accident; it might, as seems more probable, have been suicide.

The link between creativity and a tendency to melancholy was recognized early on by Aristotle. Artists of every kind are more likely than most to suffer as a result of rejection, as Warlock had done, and Fogg, and Felix Powell, whom we will meet at Peacehaven, whose death was plainly suicide. Maybe statisticians could show that other callings – horticulturalists, forgers, salesmen of second-hand cars, Members of Parliament, professional footballers – have been just as much the victims of odd unrepresentative deaths. But, aside from veterinary surgeons and cricketers, two groups that seem particularly prone to suicide, I have never seen much evidence that this was so.

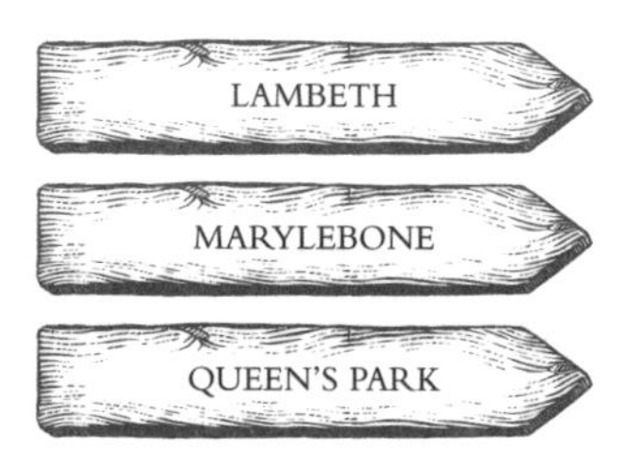

CITY OF THREE WATERS

CITY OF THREE WATERS,
locality, Leicestershire, in Coalville urb. dist.

ON PAGE 150 OF the 1943 *Bartholomew's Gazetteer of the British Isles* we find a strange anomaly: a city that's a mere locality – and one that, though called a city, does not appear on most conventional maps. Even Ordnance Survey map 129, Nottingham and Loughborough, does not to include it. In subsequent amendments to this edition, Bartholomew revealed a little bit more: the city, he informed us, was 1½ miles north-west of Whitwick. Turn to Whitwick, and you find it described as a small town, population 4,500, then with a railway station, between Ashby-de-la-Zouch and Loughborough. It's an old mining community. Coalville may be more important these days, but it took the Whitwick Colliery, established down the road in 1824, to engender Coalville, which the *Shell Guide to Leicestershire* describes as 'an unlovely name for an unlovely place'. Whitwick by then had been in existence for at least six centuries. And, by the way, the locals pronounce it "Whittick".

This is, or rather was until recently, an unrelentingly industrial slice of Leicestershire. It looks on the map like a kind of ganglion, extending from its centre – the marketplace – in all directions, and fusing almost imperceptibly here into Thringstone, there into New Swannington. Like many such mining villages it reflects what tended to be the twin preoccupations of those who worked in the pits: drink and religious devotions. Some colliers, perhaps, combined both. But strict Nonconformists were usually temperance men, if not total abstainers. They took one road, some of their comrades the other. So here, from my probing in Whitwick, is how to get a sense of what it must have been like, and how in time to discover its secret city – or cities.

Start at the car park by the Hermitage Leisure centre and walk downhill on Silver Street. Close by the King's Arms pub, not the last pub you'll see in Whitwick.

Just beyond, its name – well, some of it, anyway – picked out on the front in gold lettering, is the

WHITWI K
CON TITUTIONAL
CL B

– presumably not alcohol-free. At the foot of this street, on the marketplace, is the Three Crowns; 'good stabling', it promises over the arch. Turning left could bring you to the Three Horseshoes and the Forest Rock and the Foresters Arms in Leicester Road or the Lady Jane in Hall Lane. I eschewed the lot, turning right into the main street where you come in quick succession to a White Horse and then to a Black one on Church Lane. Here we enter the devotional quarter: the parish church of St John the Baptist on the northern side of the road, the Baptists just beyond on the southern, and back on the northern side a Wesleyan Methodist Chapel which bears the inscription: 'Ebenezer hitherto hath the Lord helped us'. What did they mean, 'hitherto'? Had He stopped?

The Whitwick North Street Working Men's Club, once the Whitwick Liberal Club, its frontage boasting of Coors and Carling, is here too, but that has also shut. Maybe it is going the way of previous lost pubs in Whitwick, which, according to one local website, include the Abbey Inn, Cademan Street; Blacksmith's Arms, Hall Lane; Cricketers, Leicester Road; Crown and Cushion, South Street; Duke of Newcastle, North Street; Duke of York, Leicester Road; Hastings Arms, Market Place; Hermitage Hotel, Hermitage Road; Marquis of Granby, Cademan Street; New Inn, Brooks Lane; Queen's Head, Thornborough Road; Royal George, North Street; Waggon and Horses, Church Lane; Beaumont Arms, Market Place; Boot Inn, Silver Street; Castle Inn, Castle Street; Crown and Cushion (the second one bearing this name), Silver Street; Hermitage Inn, Hermitage Road; Railway Hotel, South Street; Talbot Inn, Talbot Lane; and White Hart, South Street. Or maybe someone will step in and save it?

A stage further on and we come to a crossroads, close to which is the Oak. To the south is Brooks Lane, leading to Thornborough Road, down which you can find the Jolly Colliers; and down the hill to the north, Dumps Road, and beyond Dumps Road, the City of Three Waters for which I was searching. The fact that it doesn't appear on most maps suggests it is now little more than a street name, though a hundred years ago it might have felt like a separate community. There's a bridge across a small stream, presumably one of the Waters, though I could not find any others, and then houses on either side of the road, and, this being Whitwick, a pub – the Hare and Hounds. Just beyond, the street name changes to Gracedieu Road, named after a ruined priory. Alternatively you can follow the Loughborough road just a little further and find there a pub with the mysterious name, the Man Within Compass.

By now I had really taken to Whitwick, and the city is a prettier spot than most, though honesty compels one to say that it's hardly a city: even little St David's in Pembrokeshire is a Cardiff by comparison. Yet, apparently, it isn't the only city in Whitwick. There is also, it says on my AA map of Loughborough, Coalville, Melton Mowbray, Shepshed, Syston and various other places, a street just off the marketplace known as the City of Dan. Bartholomew, it appears, did not know about that, which is a pity, but less of a pity than it might have been since this street has since been demolished, and the name perished with it. A source I found on the internet listed yet another Whitwickian city: the City of Hockley. What had become of the City of Hockley? I could find not the slightest trace of it.

I threw myself on the mercy of the Whitwick Historical Group, firmly enough established to have offices in the old station building (once served by trains to Loughborough via Shepshed and Snells Nook halt, and Shackerstone – change for Nuneaton and Burton – via Coalville, Hugglescote, and Heather & Ibstock) which are open to the public at certain times of the week. They sent me a book by a local historian, Eric Jarvis, called *City to City: a journey through Whitwick from the City of Dan to the City of Three Waters*. Jarvis tentatively concludes that the term 'City' was used for both in the biblical sense of the word. It's significant, he suggests, that the word 'town' occurs only eleven times in the Bible and 'village' four times, whereas 'city' appears more than a hundred times, bearing out the fact that in biblical times even the smallest pocket of population was called a city.

Whitwick, with its substantial churchgoing population, might have adopted that practice. The tribe of Dan in the Bible was famous for its wanderings; Whitwick's City of Dan was a place of lodging houses, which might explain that connection. The 'three waters' in the other city – where in fact there is only one – may reflect the fact that three streams come together to form the one that flows under the City of Three Waters bridge. As for the third of the cities of Whitwick, another local historian, Maureen Partridge, finds no evidence that a City of Hockley ever existed – though there is an unadopted road called Hockley off Castle Street. So this, it transpires, is a tale of two cities, rather than three.

CLEVEDON

CLEVEDON, urb. dist., seaside town and par., with ry. stas. G. W. R. and Weston, Clevedon and Portishead R., NW. Somerset... On the pier-head is a fixed light, seen 7m.; there is a rocket apparatus...

IN THE END, THERE was a reprieve. The elegant, delicate, almost ethereal pier has survived both philistine threats to its future and the attritions of wind and weather. Just after Clevedon celebrated the centenary of its construction in 1969, two spans collapsed, and the pier was threatened with closure. Even the local authority favoured knocking it down. Fortunately the final decision had to be taken by a known aesthete, Michael Heseltine, a minister in the newly established Department of the Environment; he said no. Instead it was lovingly, and expensively, repaired, a process that took the best part of twenty years. And now it's a Grade I protected structure, the only pier in the kingdom to qualify for that honour, and survives along with its battlemented tollhouse, a building which rather suggests a fear of armed attack from some envious seaside rival whose pier is less often praised – Weston-super-Mare, perhaps.

No such certain reprieve, though, for the hotel at the end of the pier, known as the Royal Pier Hotel, though the words 'Rock Hotel' are cut into the stonework. In 2007, the owners were set on demolishing it and replacing it with flats, a procedure shocking to English Heritage and the Victorian Society, but acceptable to Clevedon Town Council. It was still there as the autumn of 2007 turned to winter, but remained, its champions reported, in some jeopardy. There's another hotel at the pier head, the Campbells Landing across the road, but it is hardly the equal of the stately old Royal Pier; its garish livery seems decidedly unClevedonian.

Not that every visitor comes here for the pier alone, or even for the promenade with its fine Victorian bandstand. Others make the journey in search of favourite writers. George Gissing's novel *The Odd Women* opens in Clevedon, where the writer twice came for holidays. Dr Madden, who appears at the start of the book but is dead

by the end of Chapter I, has chosen to live here mainly for the town's literary associations: 'Tennyson he worshipped; he never passed Coleridge's cottage without bowing in spirit.' Subsequent visitors likewise. Yet the doctor should have known that Tennyson hardly set foot in Clevedon (and certainly didn't write 'Break, Break, Break' under Clevedon's influence, as people in Somerset sometimes allege: that came to him in his native Lincolnshire).

What linked him with Clevedon was his intense Cambridge friendship – love would be the more appropriate word – for his sister's fiancé, Arthur Hallam, whose family home was in Clevedon. Hallam's father was Henry Hallam, a celebrated historian; his mother, Julia, one of the grand Clevedon Eltons, who have left their mark all over the town. The family were no strangers to tragedy. Julia's brother, Sir Charles, a poet too, though hardly in the Tennyson class, lost two sons, aged twelve and fourteen, who were drowned while trying to cross from Birnbeck Island on the estuary to Weston-super-Mare.

Arthur Hallam, Tennyson's friend and also a poet, a feted star at both Eton and Cambridge, died at twenty-two, of a stroke, in 1833, while on holiday in Vienna. His father returned to their hotel to find his son dead on a sofa. Hallam is buried in the graveyard of Clevedon's 'old church', St Andrew's, a little out of the town, high above the sea. Tennyson was too upset to attend the funeral; it was many years before he felt able to come to Clevedon, which he finally did on his honeymoon with Emily Selwood. His great poem *In Memoriam*, was inspired by Hallam's death. The process of writing the work caused him much anguish and it took years to complete. ''Tis well,' he wrote in stanzas 18 and 19:

> 'Tis well; 'tis something; we may stand
> Where he in English earth is laid,
> And from his ashes may be made
> The violet of his native land.

'Tis little; but it looks in truth
  As if the quiet bones were blest
  Among familiar names to rest
And in the places of his youth.

The Danube to the Severn gave
  The darken'd heart that beat no more;
  They laid him by the pleasant shore,
And in the hearing of the wave.

As for Samuel Taylor Coleridge, that other subject of Dr Madden's reverence, there too the attachment was temporary and ambivalent. As a local historian Arthur L. Salmon admits in his *Literary Rambles in the West of England* (1906), it's not at all clear that Coleridge's cottage is the one that Coleridge lived in; and if he did, he wasn't there long. Having brought his bride Sara to the town he left on some pretext after only two months, repeatedly saying he meant to return but never doing so; eventually Sara joined him in Bristol and they started again, inland at Nether Stowey.

The town does have a sound claim to William Makepeace Thackeray. He often stayed with the Eltons at Clevedon Court, wrote part of *Henry Esmond* here – Clevedon masquerades in that book as Castlewood, Hampshire – and part of *Vanity Fair*; and after his wife drifted into madness he had a long involvement with Jane Octavia Elton, wife of his old university friend William Henry Brookfield, until her husband forbade her to meet him again. And Gissing, as well as using the location in *The Odd Women*, wrote a book called *Eve's Ransom* here, completed in twenty-five days. It was not, he said on reading it through at the end of his labours, quite as trashy as he'd supposed. Reviewers were not so kind. As John Betjeman noted in a television portrait of Clevedon – a piece which has a note running through it of something close to cruelty as he turns a patronising eye on old people ending their lives in Clevedon – the Manx poet and novelist T. E. Brown was immensely fond of the place. But who reads T. E. Brown now?

Jan Morris, I see, was born here; more surprisingly, it was where Sid Vicious went to school. Scenes which in Kazuo Ishiguro's novel *The Remains of the Day* occur in

Weymouth were transferred in the film version to Clevedon, though, to the mortification of Clevedon, episodes set in a grand hotel ballroom had to be filmed in mere Weston. When the film was shown in Clevedon, there were mutterings, or more, from the auditorium: 'It bain't Clevedon'; ''Tis another areal altogether'; 'Shame!' ('Areal' is Bristol Channel-speak for 'area': in these parts they frequently tack on a final 'l' which is recognized nowhere else.)

There are streets on the hills at Clevedon that aspire to be Bath, or perhaps a seaside North Oxford. 'Modes' – a word I thought had disappeared long ago from dress shops – are sold in Hill Road; there's a bookseller, and a centre for therapeutic massage called Rejuvenate. The word 'decorous' might have been specifically coined to describe the atmosphere here. It tells you something significant about the ambience of relentlessly civilized Clevedon that builders at work on a house in Hill Road had their radios tuned not to Radio 1 or 2 but to Radio 4 and John Humphrys.

CLYDEBANK

CLYDEBANK, town (police bur.)... on right bank of r. Clyde, 6¼m. NW. of Glasgow... is a most important industrial centre; contains shipbuilding yards, also chemical works and distilleries.

PEOPLE TALK ABOUT BOOM towns; they rarely talk about bust towns. But bust towns are what boom towns all too often become. Throughout history, natural selection caused some great towns and cities to atrophy and die. Nowadays, places in trouble are usually given succour: in this book, they include the Gipton estate in Leeds, and Lochgelly and Kinlochleven in Scotland. Yet huge sums spent in some stricken communities may not in the end pull them round: Grimethorpe, in the Yorkshire colliery belt close to Barnsley, is a poignant example of that. Few British towns, however, can have gone from boom to bust quite so dizzyingly and depressingly as Clydebank.

In 1873, there were 2,700 inhabitants in the place that became Clydebank; in 1880, 5,000: by 1913, 43,000. 'A little over a score of years ago,' said a local directory published in 1893, 'the new thriving and populous burgh of Clydebank was totally unknown to fame, in fact it did not then exist.' But by 1886, the year it achieved police burgh status, it was known as 'the risingest burgh'. It was shipbuilding which did most to create it and make its name known across the world. The brothers James and George Thomson, needing room to expand, moved here from Glasgow and named the new town Clydebank after their shipyard in Govan. Soon they ran into trouble, and their fate was effectively left in the hands of the Union Bank. The Sheffield manufacturers John Brown spotted an opportunity. They saw a boom in naval armaments coming, and in 1899 they bought out the Thomsons. Their order books became healthier, and in 1910 they were joined at Clydebank by the powerful Glasgow-based firm of William Beardmore. Both companies flourished, especially when there was war and rumour of war.

But Clydebank had a second front too, one more likely to prosper in times of peace. This was the Singer Manufacturing Company, producing sewing machines,

American in origin, international by ambition, which reached Glasgow in 1856 and before long was looking for room to expand. It picked a site at Kilbowie, on the edge of the burgeoning burgh of Clydebank. Here Singer built the largest factory of its kind in Scotland, with a vast ostentatious clock, reputed to be the second biggest in Scotland, to signal its presence, and before long there were more jobs at Singer than there were in the shipyards. Output swelled from 10,000 machines a year (produced at 80 per cent of the costs back in the US) to one million in 1906, by which time the name of the railway station that had started life as Kilbowie had been altered to Singer. The coat of arms of Clydebank incorporates a sewing machine. Places like these prided themselves on being part of the engine room of progressive industrial Britain. In accordance with its new status, Clydebank acquired a town hall in 1902, designed with a swagger which echoes the City Chambers in Glasgow, which in time was flanked by other prideful buildings, including a public library, funded as so many were in those times by Alexander Carnegie.

During these years Clydebank was at its peak. From the end of the First World War, the economies of the shipyards were becoming precarious (ship repair was the main source of profit). Clydebank was acquiring a reputation for political unrest, both from disputes at the shipyards and because of a rent strike that lasted for half a decade in the 1920s. If anything boomed in the inter-war years, it was unemployment. In 1932 the rate of those out of work topped 50 per cent. The yards that had launched the *Lusitania* in 1906 and the *Aquitania* in 1913 waited hungrily for new orders. John Brown's ran into such financial difficulties that work on the *Queen Mary*, for which the contract was signed in 1930, had to be suspended for a time. However, rearmament in the late 1930s averted potential disaster.

Yet where war was good for John Brown, it wasn't so hopeful for Singer. The First World War had brought a fall in production from more than one million models a year to fewer than 60,000. The cost of the Second World War, when the Singer workforce was largely switched to the making of armaments, was still more severe. And the town paid a brutal price for its dependence on shipbuilding and ship repair, becoming a prime target for German bombers. But its homes suffered even more than its industries. According to Angus Calder's book *The People's War*, all but seven of its 12,000 homes were damaged, and 35,000 of its 47,000 people made homeless – the most nearly universal damage, he says, inflicted on any town throughout Britain. More than 500 people were killed. The devastation of the nights of 13 and 14 February 1941 was even more terrible because most of the children evacuated from Clydebank in the early days of the war had found their way back again: only four out of ten evacuees were taken in by working-class households, and many of those in middle-class homes were unable to settle.

On the very eve of the war, John Brown's had launched the *Queen Elizabeth*; the king had missed the occasion because he was waiting in London to discover the outcome of Chamberlain's assignation at Munich. Thereafter the shipbuilder's one moment of glory was the commission to build its successor, the *QE2*, launched in September 1967, though even that was marred by Cunard's initial refusal to accept it. But by then the yard was irrevocably on the slide towards liquidation. The deal which created Upper Clyde Shipbuilders saved it from total extinction, but not for long. Having limped along on orders from the offshore oil industry, it finally closed in 2001.

By that time, too, Clydebank had also lost Singer. The company struggled in vain to hold its own against competition from mainland Europe but above all from Japan. Despite attempts to save it, which at one time involved the intervention of the British prime minister, James Callaghan, and the US president, Jimmy Carter, the works at Kilbowie shut down in 1980. In a fine local history compiled by a squad of academics under the editorship of John Hood and published by the now superseded Clydebank district council, one local woman remembers: 'I cried when they pulled down Singer's clock... you could see it from anywhere in Clydebank... I thought, Oh God! It was the only thing left... it came through the blitz untouched... it was a symbol of survival, and it meant so much to the people of Clydebank; I hate them for that.'

Other employers withdrew from Clydebank at about the same time. Once again, unemployment became what the place was famous for. The image of the late nineteenth-century's 'risingest' town had become one of dereliction and decay. Today, as you walk around it, it seems a disconsolate mix of past glory – the stretch of municipal buildings that survive on Dumbarton Road – and present, somewhat desperate aspiration. The site of the John Brown yard is now allocated for the building of upmarket flats – there is also to be a marina – with just one remnant of its great manufacturing days, the Titan crane, protected (which doesn't often happen with cranes) by a Grade I listing. It has been painstakingly restored and opened to visitors who can take a lift to the top and look down on the little stretch of the Clyde where so many world-renowned ships – whether built for peace or for war – were despatched to the oceans. But the shopping streets at the centre look beyond transformation.

Up the hill, on the way out of the town towards central Glasgow, where the Singer clock once dominated the proceedings, there's a business park, Clydebank College, and a determinedly glitzy regional shopping centre, the fifth busiest in the early 2000s in Scotland, according to statistics. What all these welcome and necessary elements lack is any feeling that this is specifically Clydebank. The crane in the dead shipyard complex retains that sense of continuing identity which is essential to make a community work. Something of that is needed at the Singer end too. I wonder what became of the clock?

COMPTON VERNEY

COMPTON VERNEY, par. and seat, S. Warwickshire, 2m. NW. of Kineton.

YOU MIGHT GUESS AS you approach the house down the curving drive, through the skilfully contrived gardens, that you are in the presence of Capability Brown; also of Robert Adam, who designed the elegant bridge and had a hand in creating the house on what was recognized as one of the finest of seventeenth-century estates. The house is now home to a stylish art gallery, set up by Sir Peter Moores, whose family fortunes were built on Littlewoods stores and football pools. The permanent exhibition reflects his own diverse tastes: Naples 1600–1800 (with some mouth-watering landscapes); Germany 1450–1600, especially carvings, with a haunting saint who has lost the right hand in which she held her symbol, so we cannot now know which saint she was; British portraits; objects from China; British folk art; and a collection accumulated by Enid Marx, in her day a celebrated designer, and Margaret Lambert. These are augmented with visiting exhibitions. The one in residence when I was there was called 'Opulence and Anxiety', which seemed entirely appropriate, since opulence and anxiety are two inescapable themes in the story of Compton Verney.

Moores rescued the house from the dereliction into which it had fallen after a series of short-lived proprietorships and a requisition for use by the War Office, which seems to have made a dreadful mess of this once cherished place. The Verneys, whose family portraits are still much in evidence under Sir Peter's stewardship, were one of the great aristocratic families of England: soldiers, statesmen, politicians, plotters, owners of vast estates; not the sort to feel at home with people who had made their money from commercial endeavour in the way the Moores family did. But the late years of the nineteenth century and especially the early years of the twentieth saw the old Verney opulence fading and anxiety on the march for this as for many such houses. The 19th baron, Willoughby de Broke, Richard Greville Verney, wrote a melancholy book, *The Passing Years*, published in 1924, which chronicled the twilight years of the age to which he felt he belonged: the great houses sold or rented to parvenus, or shut up and left to moulder, or even demolished; the pictures dispersed to hang on the walls of people too vulgar to appreciate them; the fine estates nurtured over the centuries, now presided over by self-satisfied nouveaux-riche chancers. He wrote about what he knew, for one fine estate to have suffered this humiliation – aristocratic knees forced to bow before mere plutocrats – was his own family's home at Compton Verney. Its social demotion began when his father rented it out to Sir Ernest Cassel, a man of matchless power in the City, and a friend of the king, but an emigré from Cologne with nothing to show in the way of breeding.

Then in 1921 Compton Verney was sold, and sold in a way that perfectly symbolized the general supersession of breeding by money. The new proprietor had made his fortune from soap. Joseph Watson's grandfather – also Joseph – had begun in the leather trade, but the next generation had diversified, first into tallow candles, then decisively into soap. From their works in Leeds, popularly known as Soapy Joe's, the Watsons sped their soaps, especially such popular brands as Nubolic and Matchless Cleaner, across the grimy terrains of northern England.

Their eminent rivals, the Levers, were unsettled enough by their challenge to resort to the traditional device of buying them out, which left Joseph Watson junior a very rich man indeed. At forty-eight, he was now perfectly placed to make his mark in society by acquiring those indisputable proofs of success – a palatial home, and a peerage. Watson had five splendid estates already, at Manton in Wiltshire, where his racehorses were in training, Offchurch in Warwickshire, Barlby in Yorkshire, Thorney in Cambridgeshire and Sudbourne in Suffolk; but none of these could signal as powerfully as acquiring this house did that he had arrived. The title he chose when awarded his peerage in the New Year Honours of 1922 (one of those that Lloyd George so shamelessly lavished on men with big money) was Lord Manton of Compton Verney: Manton, after his racing stables in Wiltshire, perhaps to commemorate his recent third in the Derby and first in the Grand Prix de Paris; Compton Verney as a reminder that – perhaps a still greater triumph – he owned an eagerly coveted house with 'Aristocracy' written all over it.

But rich as he was, he knew his neighbours regarded him as a mere upstart. That was a common anxiety which went with such opulence. One way to resolve it, one way to propel yourself up the social ladder and purge the stain of your humble origins was to take up hunting. Lord Willoughby de Broke, the one who wrote the brooding memoir, had followed his father and grandfather in taking on the Mastership of the Warwickshire Hunt. In his book, as quoted by David Cannadine in his masterly and wonderfully readable *The Decline and Fall of the British Aristocracy*, the disconsolate peer sets out the hierarchy of the society in which he grew up: large farmers at the foot of the scale; above, the lesser clergy; and then, rising through the ranks, Justices of the Peace, archdeacons, local MPs, the colonel of the yeomanry, the chairman of quarter sessions, the bishop, the agricultural landlords, and finally, behind only the Lord Lieutenant, the representative of the king in the county: the Master of Foxhounds.

But here too the old aristocratic families were feeling the pinch. Some had ruined themselves by persisting with the expense of a Mastership. Sir Ernest Cassel had sought to atone for his German origins by riding, somewhat unsteadily, to hounds. Watson, who knew rather more about how one should sit on a horse – he had hunted with the Bramham Moor while living in Yorkshire – enlisted with the Warwickshire Hunt even before he had moved into Compton Verney, which could be considered a fatal mistake. On 13 March 1922, while out for a day's exciting chase with the Warwickshire, Watson fell from his horse. His son, who was close behind him, thought he had broken his neck, but a medical examination established that he had died from a heart attack. He was just forty-nine. As the coroner sadly observed at the inquest, he had barely had time to enjoy his seat in the Lords, and he hadn't even moved into Compton Verney, which he was having refurbished. Rarely, as old established Warwickshire society no doubt said to itself – perhaps in some cases with satisfaction – had the old teaching that pride comes before a fall been more dramatically justified.

Watson was buried in his hunting clothes and one of his jockeys made a cross of flowers in racing colours to lie on the grave. He has left no mark on Compton Verney that I could see, though there is in a sector of the present-day gallery a time-exposure photograph taken at the house by Alathea, Lady Manton, his daughter-in-law. His son George sold the house in 1929 to a man named Samuel Lamb, who left when the army required it. For a time from the late 1950s the pride of the Verneys belonged to a night-club owner, who let it be used for filming. Thereafter it fell into the sorry state from which Peter Moores rescued it. Sir Peter drove up the curving approach as I left, looking pleased with himself, which is hardly surprising. He doesn't, so far as I know, go out hunting.

A B C D
E F G H
I J K L
M N O P
Q R S T
U V W XYZ

DEBATABLE LAND

DEBATABLE LAND, tract of country on the Border, between the rs. Esk and Sark. It was long the subject of contention between England and Scotland.

THE BORDER WHICH RUNS through the Debatable Land is that between England and Scotland. You cross it on the A7 between Longtown, the last town in England, and Canonbie, Scotland, tucked deep in its valley, away from the world's agitations. As Bartholomew says, the border wasn't always delineated with such certainty: indeed, it wasn't in any practical sense delineated at all. Anyway, in this indeterminate region, the great Reiver families – the very word reiver means plunderer – behaved as if borders between the nations did not exist, as if the writs of the kings of England and Scotland were of no consequence; the only power they recognized was their own. 'In a sense', George MacDonald Fraser, creator of Flashman, writes in his book, *The Steel Bonnets: the Story of the Anglo-Scottish Border Reivers*, 'it belongs in the same class as the Khyber Pass, the Badman's Territory, the Bombay Coast, or even Harlem, Soho and the Gorbals.'

Attempts were made from time to time to settle the border finally, sometimes by war and sometimes by diplomacy. After the wars of the 1540s, the English proposed a simple solution: most of this ground should be theirs. The Scots could hang on to Canonbie, but not to very much more. As a preliminary to this new division, it was agreed that anyone who wanted to would be free to rob, burn, plunder and kill within the debatable land without being found guilty of any crime. In 1551, Lord Maxwell, Warden of Scotland, adopted his own original solution: he devastated the whole area, leaving no building in place. But the land was good, and both sides still wanted it, so a fresh division took place, with the French ambassador called in to act as referee. Given the ancient links between Scotland and France, it was perhaps no surprise that his ruling was more generous to Scotland than to England.

Since then we've had a joint monarchy, an Act of Union, and good relations (on the whole) between England and Scotland. Though early in 2008 the Scottish National Party put in a claim for Berwick-on-Tweed (now in England) to be returned to the Scots, there's been no suggestion so far that should the SNP take Scotland to independence, the French ambassador or anyone else would be called on to renegotiate the line through the Debatable Land.

And yet in undebatably English Longtown you can pick up a hint of uncertainty. A taxi belonging to Joan's Cars of Longtown, I noticed, said on its side: Joan's Cars of Langtoun, as if to demonstrate their eagerness to appeal to Scottish customers too. The town bears the stamp of the Grahams – remembered on both sides of the border as the most ruthless and violent of all the ruthless and violent families who once created such mayhem and misery here. The church at Arthuret, just to the south of the town, and the heart of the parish to which Longtown belongs, is full of memorials to the Grahams and acknowledgements of their benefactions; the churchyard is full of them too, clustered close the door, outnumbering the Bells and the Armstrongs and Littles with whom they contended in life. The worst of their outrages led to their expulsion from the territory, with most of them packed off to Ireland, but they never disappeared: they simply seeped back when the crisis was over, often reappearing under the alias Maharg. (They might not have been pillars of scholarship, but they knew how to spell things backwards.) Subsequently, though, their reputation was for philanthropy, rather than slaughter and pillage. They shaped the town, built its hotel (the Graham Arms) and established it as a staging post and trading centre at the end of the long bridge over the fast-flowing Esk on the route between England and Scotland.

It might make sense, even so – both to reflect the history of this place, and to prepare for any serious move towards Scottish independence – to resurrect and refurbish the ditch between the two countries that is known as the Scots Dike. It is said to be lurking somewhere on the A7 behind the March Bank Hotel, though I could not find a way through to it. Prospects improve, however, if you take a modest left turning off the A7, at the point where the B7201 goes off to the east to investigate Canonbie, and follow it through Glenzierfoot and Fauldie till you reach Evertown, from where a more easily navigable road will carry you on to Milltown. Here you turn south near the telephone box past Glencroft and Croftside to a place called Crawe's Knowe. I stopped here to ask a local man for instructions, but these were delivered in such a rich brogue that I scarcely understood a word of them. I did, however, discover a narrow wood to the east with a ditch running through it, and here, I think, I had found what I was looking for.

I contemplated this meagre spot with amazement. Was this ignominious declivity something nations had struggled over, for which hundreds had fought and died? Surely all this demanded a better memorial? And a greater certainty – for where exactly you ought to stand to proclaim 'I am now in England' (or Scotland) is, one might say, debatable. Later, south of the border, I came across a book by Eric Robson, well known in the region as a writer and broadcaster, in which he complains that protests made by himself and a mate called Moffat about the obscurity of the line have consistently been ignored. His book also says that when the ditch was dug – apparently as a consensual act between England and Scotland – one party started at the western end and one at the eastern, and they failed, by 21 feet, to meet in the middle.

The term 'Debatable Land' – first used at least as far back as the fifteenth century, but familiar in popular use only after Sir Walter Scott, who so haunts my pages, adopted it – is not confined to the England–Scotland border. You can find land in dispute on the England–Wales border too, and all over the world the futures of debatable lands are still being resolved, sometimes by intricate diplomacy, sometimes by terrible, bloody battles. And the concept has been broadened into the realms of poetry and philosophy. Don't we, it is sometimes soulfully posited, all have some kind of debatable land in our lives, either between ourselves and others, or sometimes within ourselves? In July 2005, the British Association for Romantic Studies took as the theme for its biennial conference: 'Romanticism's Debatable Lands', invoking Lord Macaulay's description of history as a debatable land between reason and imagination. And on an even more existential scale, the spiritualist Robert Dale Owen, son of the social entrepreneur Robert Owen, who settled in the US and became a Congressman, published in 1872 a celebrated book called *The Debatable Land Between This World and the Next.*

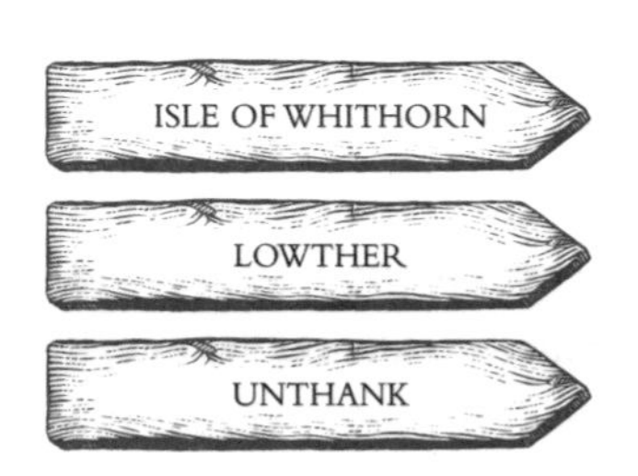

DEFIANCE PLATFORM

DEFIANCE PLATFORM, G.W.R., Cornwall, 1m. S of Saltash.

SAY 'DEFIANCE PLATFORM' AND what does it conjure up? Orator Hunt before Peterloo? Martin Luther King damning segregation, or Nelson Mandela destroying apartheid? Ian Paisley trumpeting 'no surrender' and certainly no deals with Sinn Fein? Or since we're so close to Plymouth, Drake daring the Spaniards to do their worst? Or perhaps something to do with the radical family Foot? In fact it was none of these: as Bartholomew correctly indicates, Defiance Platform was a kind of railway station, on the line from Plymouth to Cornwall.

But it is an odd kind of railway station. Look closely at the 1910 edition of *Bradshaw's Railway Guide*, and a picture begins to emerge. Certain mainline trains stop at Defiance Platform on, of all days, Sunday. On other days there's a regular service listed as 'Saltash to Plympton', though some of these trains in fact start at Defiance. One way to discover the answer is to take the train to Saltash as it crosses the Tamar by Brunel's iconic bridge, boldly marked with the date of its construction, 1859, and sidles around a tight bend into Saltash station. Walk up the main street, which like many main streets in the West Country is called Fore Street. At the top of Fore Street, take a left fork. When you enter St Stephen's Road, follow the sign for the community school and the church. If you pass a Spar shop on your left you are doing well. Where Weare Road wheels away past the community school, don't take it, though if you do you might meet a woman walking her dog who will warn you of your error and point you in another direction (though that too will turn out to be wrong).

Do not give up. 'In defeat, defiance', as Churchill once said. Go doggedly on down the metalled road, and where that becomes a track, take the road on your left until it runs down the hill and crosses the railway. There on your left, down a stairway which is sensibly always locked (a mainline express from London to Cornwall might otherwise gobble you up) you will see the remains of Defiance Platform.

Go on down the hill, and you can probably pick out the spot where HMS *Defiance* was moored at the quayside, to which the sailors might return on a Sunday at the end of their shore leave.

There are many names almost as odd and exotic as Defiance Platform which have vanished from the railway map, but which a website called Subterranea Britannica saves from oblivion. Bradford Adolphus Street. Chequerbent (two separate sites in its history, serving Hulton near Bolton). Glogue, on the Whitland line in Wales. Huskisson, serving a Liverpool dock and perpetuating the name of the politician William Huskisson killed at Parkside, near Newton-le-Willows, by the train making the inaugural journey on the Manchester to Liverpool railway. He must have been accident-prone, poor fellow; he came close to death years earlier, when he fell from a horse, on his honeymoon. Tennyson and his beloved friend Hallam were travelling on the train when this disaster occurred.

Other stations on the same line as Huskisson were called Canada and Herculaneum. And then, Monmouth Troy. Pitfodels Halt close to Aberdeen. Rosebush in Pembrokeshire. Salvation Army Halt, on the southern side of St Albans, close to the Army's printing works. Uralite Halt, on a line from Gravesend to Port Victoria, Isle of Grain. Others changed their names to something more salubrious. Norwood Junction, quite a serious railway station in south London suburbia, was originally Jolly Sailor. And Coulsdon North started its life as Stoat's Nest. 'Single to Stoat's Nest, please':

perhaps commuters in their bright new spec developer homes found making such a request at the ticket window a little demeaning.

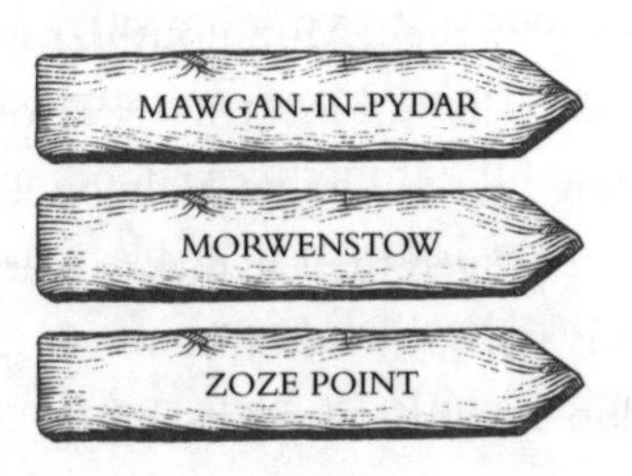

DEVIL'S QUOITS

DEVIL'S QUOITS, three large stones near Stanton Harcourt, Oxon. Supposed to be memorials of a battle between Britons and Saxons in 614.

OFF THE ROAD THAT runs south out of the improbably pretty village of Stanton Harcourt, where thatch and good stonework prevail, and Alexander Pope worked in his tower, translating Homer, and the Harcourt family lived in the manor house until they decamped to the splendours of Nuneham Courtenay, there's a set of stones called the Devil's Quoits, whose purpose, like that of Stonehenge, is by no means certain. You cannot now see them. The tract where they stood for centuries has become a landfill site, the property of the great conglomerate Hanson, and access is banned except by written permission. 'You won't be missing much', a longtime Stanton Harcourt resident reassured me when I failed to get in. The original site, he said, had been hopelessly messed about long before Hanson got there – during the war, when they built the airfield. (Churchill found it useful to have one there – so convenient for Blenheim.)

The present exclusion is not to last. Hanson is working with a team of experts to try to undo the damage done to the site and reinstate the stones in a way that befits what was once, some believe, as important a place as Avebury. The journalist Celia Haddon, who has taken a close interest in this territory, has said that when she first gained admittance back in 2000 the place was a chaotic mess in the middle of a huge extraction and waste site, but that two years later, she saw that work had begun to re-create the circle, using the original stones and supplementing them with others of like appearance; by 2005, some of the stones were standing again. That is no doubt a great improvement on the state to which this historic place had been reduced, but it won't of course restore the quoits as the Devil left them.

Still, there seem to be plenty of the Devil's other accoutrements scattered around the land. There are two other sets of his quoits in Pembrokeshire alone. Here, though, are some of the evil one's possessions from John Bartholomew's list – as ever, excluding his entries for Ireland and the Channel Islands: his Apronful in Wharfedale (a set of rocks); his Arrows, 'three monumental pillars of millstone grit' near Boroughbridge; his Beef Tub, a vast hollow near Moffat, Dumfriesshire, also known as the Marquess of Annandale's Beef Stand; his Bellows, a deep chasm on Asparagus Island, Cornwall, which also houses his Throat, a name that crops up too at Cromer Bay, Norfolk; his bridge, near Aberystwyth, served by a railway line; his Cauldron – an ancient circular structure on the Isle of Bute, or alternatively, a romantic chasm with cascade, on the river Lednock in Perthshire. Then there's his Causeway, from the Roman Wall to Longframlington (not to be confused, if you wish to avoid diabolical vengeance, with his Highway, across Bagshot Heath), and a Devil's Cave near the excellent little town of Kilconquhar, Fife, and a Devil's Den, a 'locality' near Hollingbourne, Kent.

You will find his Ditch in Cambridgeshire, Bartholomew says, and his Dyke north of Brighton, his Elbow in the Grampians south of Braemar, and his Garden ('hollows abounding in rare wild flowers') south-east of Radnor. His Jumps are a set of mounds close to Haslemere, Surrey, where he also left his Punch Bowl; his Limekiln, 'a remarkable chasm' on Lundy in the Bristol Channel, and his Mill, a waterfall on the boundaries of the counties of Perth and Kinross. Skipping nimbly over his Mother, since she is in Ireland, we come to his Pit, 'a remarkable hollow' near Cadgwith, Devil's Point and The Devil's Point, both in Aberdeenshire, and his Staircase – which crops up in my trip to Kinlochleven – above bloody Glencoe. (He must, to judge from this inventory, have spent a good deal of his time in Scotland.) Finally, there is Devil's Water, to be found in Northumberland, near the Durham boundary; it flows into the Tyne near Hexham.

The Devil, on this evidence, it has to be said, seems hugely to outrank God. Most of Bartholomew's entries starting with God, such as Godalming, Surrey, and Goddington and Godinton, Kent, have more to do with local bigwigs with names like Goda and Godhelm than they do with the deity. Even Godmanchester, for which I had hopes, proves to be derived from Godmund's chester, or fort. (Bartholomew says, by the way, that the name is pronounced Gum'sester.) Of the list of places beginning with God in Eilert Ekwall's *Concise Oxford Dictionary of English Place-Names*, only Godshill in

Hampshire, possibly, and Godstow in Oxfordshire certainly (home to a nunnery: the name means 'place dedicated to the service of God') seem to have any direct connection, though perhaps one might add Gad's Hill, home of Charles Dickens, to that.

Given this unholy imbalance, it's reassuring to find when you arrive at the letter S that Bartholomew has found not a single place named for Satan, whereas places named after saints run to more than eight pages.

DEVIZES

DEVIZES (pronounced Devī'zez), mun. bor. and mkt.-town...
N. Wilts, on the Kennet and Avon Canal, 25½m. NW. of Salisbury
by road and 86m. W of London...

GO, IF YOU CAN, on a Thursday. Thursday is market day; its market, after the end of its days as a fortified town clustered around its castle, was what Devizes was all about. (The name, so often misspelled outside Wiltshire, derives from the original '*castrum ad divisas*' – the castle at the point where three manors met.) Approach it from the north-east, on the exhilarating road that bounds over the downland from Beckhampton on the A4. The village to the left some five miles on, and worth dipping into, is Bishops Cannings, where in a sense Devizes began: it was the bishops of Salisbury who owned the manor here and who first established the castle and the town to support it. Soon the road runs down from the hill and you're into the town, past forbidding Le Marchant barracks, the last remnant of military Devizes, but latterly converted to flats. Follow this road past the church and the pond and the green, which we'll come to later, on to the crossroads by Roses the ironmongers (we will come to them later too). Then wheel right past Sainsbury's into New Park Street and leave the car on the car park at the Wharf, by the canal. Follow the canal to your left until it meets the main road, and turn left again into the town, brooding perhaps on the way on the unfortunate fate of the mighty classical building known in its better days as Devizes Assizes. The fashion for centralization doomed it long ago to redundancy, since when it has been unwanted for any use except nightclubs, casinos and other projects deemed in the light of its history too undignified for this location. Beyond is Wadworth's brewery, from where on occasion horse-drawn wagons still clatter out; and then you're in Northgate Street, which broadens out into a marketplace that is full of the sense of the town as it used to be.

The buses beetling in and out from Bromham and Rowde and Seend and Potterne and the Lavingtons, some serving such grand destinations as Swindon, Bath and

Salisbury, perpetuate the tradition of the countryside coming to town to trade, shop and to drink in the many and various inns and catch up with the news. The Bear Hotel on the western side, alongside the 1857 Corn Exchange with the obligatory figure of Ceres perched on its roof, has been there in various forms since the sixteenth century; the portrait painter Sir Thomas Lawrence, whose father was the landlord, grew up here, and the charismatic radical politician Henry 'Orator' Hunt ran off with a subsequent landlord's daughter. The main bar under its low beamed roof, where you can sink into a deep armchair under pictures of old hostelries and a tapestry titled *The Orchard* in which a disconsolate maiden toys with a tulip against a backdrop of foliage straight out of William Morris, is a most agreeable place on a cold Devizes morning. The shops in the marketplace are far fewer than they were formerly, outnumbered now by banks and estate agents, but the stalls in the open marketplace on a Thursday, like those in the indoor market several days of the week, sell much what they always did: great succulent Wiltshire hams, cheese, fresh vegetables, 'bacon misshapes' (only £1) and home-made chutneys and jams; supplemented these days by tapenades, banderillas and boretanne onions – for Devizes, despite appearances, moves with the times.

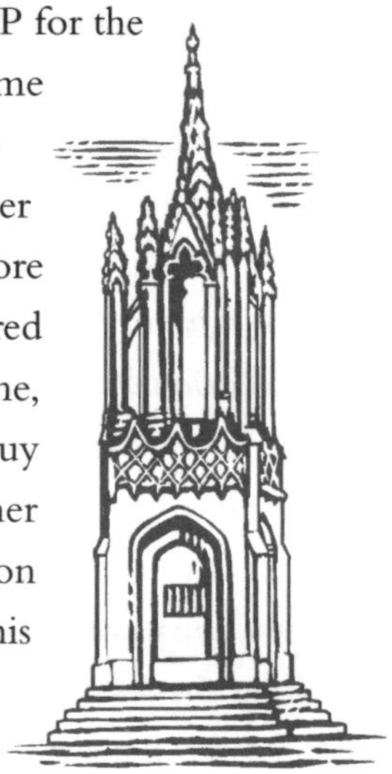

Almost lost on a Thursday in the midst of all these visiting attractions are the market cross and the fountain. The fountain, built by public subscription in 1879, bears a florid dedication to Thomas Sotheron Estcourt, MP for the town and, as the inscription proudly proclaims, the nation's Home Secretary twenty years earlier (though it understandably fails to point out that he lasted only three months in this office, after which his government fell). The market cross has a far more disturbing inscription, recording an Awful Event which occurred here in 1753, when a woman called Ruth Pierce from Potterne, who had agreed with three other women to club together to buy a sack of wheat, was accused by the others of not having paid her share. She vehemently denied it: let her, she said, be struck dead on the spot if what she maintained was untrue. She repeated this Awful Wish; at which point 'to the consternation and terror of the surrounding multitude' she instantly 'fell down dead and expired', and was found to have the disputed money clutched in her hand.

The inscription expresses the hope that this record may serve as a salutary warning against the danger of impiously invoking divine vengeance or of calling on the holy name of God to conceal the devices of falsehood and fraud. It cannot be said that this warning has entirely banished ungodly behaviour from the marketplace at Devizes. Until recently the place was plagued by platoons of tattooed, shaven-headed young men in vaguely military gear, with unlimited beer cans and snarly dogs, sometimes to the consternation and terror of the surrounding multitude. Happily the introduction of a bylaw seems to have dealt with them.

The imposing four-arched building at the south-eastern end of the marketplace is the old town hall (also known as the New Hall or Cheese Hall) of 1752, and behind it is the new town hall which superseded it half a century later – a sign, no doubt, of the high municipal aspirations of Devizes. It is still home to Devizes Town Council, which has mayors and ceremonial occasions and all the appropriate flummery, but in most respects, in these days of centralization, has little more executive power than a parish council. Just beyond are three places absolutely not to be missed: a small dark street of medieval houses, one of which has become a hat shop, called St John's Alley; and two impeccably local and irresistibly tempting shops: Giddings (an outcrop of Wadworth's) wine merchants, grocers and delicatessen providers, and D'Arcy Books, which is high on my list of the most enjoyable second-hand bookshops (and I know many) anywhere in the land, both for its stock and for the pleasure of browsing in its elegant rooms.

If you now take the road to the right of the 'new' town hall, you come to a path which leads past a medieval hall to a quiet enclave around the most distinguished of Devizes's churches, St John's. Its Norman tower has a hint of the military which comes from its original role as a garrison church. It was closed when I was last in Devizes, for health and safety reasons (there had been a disastrous fire here in September 2006) – but was reopened in good time for Christmas 2007. A path at the eastern end of the church takes you into Long Street, where grand houses mingle with modest ones in a wonderfully harmonious unplanned assembly. From here you can turn into Bridewell Street on the left, deviating at a roundabout to inspect Morris Lane (for one of the joys of Devizes is the minor streets you discover while trawling the main ones) and then pass up Hare and Hounds Street to the broad and generous green, at the far end of which is the pond on the road that comes in from the north, paraded by majestic swans and known as the Crammer. It is said that this was the place where local smugglers, caught by excise men trying to hide their illegal booty, claimed to be trying to fish the moon out of the water, though that's told of a whole host of places in Wiltshire and outside it.

The road back to town takes you to Roses, which began as a grocer's but somehow evolved into an ironmongers which – the essence of the charm of Devizes again – is like ironmongers' shops used to be, marvellously crammed with what you'd expect and what you might never have dreamed of, staffed with exemplary expertise and courtesy, and encouragingly holding its own against interloping chain competitors on the fringe of the town. From here you can walk down Sidmouth Street into the main shopping streets, and especially the traffic-free Brittox, steering your way around richly Wiltshire-accented clusters of people in for the day who have just bumped into each other.

Although the Palace cinema has somehow survived, and gigs take place in the Corn Exchange, and the Bear does a flourishing line in jazz nights, one can't help feeling that the young of Devizes find the place boring, and hanker perhaps for more glamorous Swindon. But in every other respect, certainly for those who have left restless youth behind, I think it's as sweet and endearing and satisfying a small town as any in England. And if you have time and the light has lasted, there is still more to savour. There's a road across the green signposted to Andover which will take you into the Vale of Pewsey, of which Bartholomew has no more to say than: 'separates Marlborough Downs from Salisbury Plain'. That's a little like saying the Forest of Bowland 'separates Blackburn from Preston' or that Exmoor 'separates the A361 from the sea'. All through the Vale there are captivating roads – the road that runs east from West Lavington and takes you through Urchfont and on towards Andover has a wonderful moment when it opens up to disclose the Marlborough Downs to the north and Salisbury Plain to the south – and byways leading to still largely unspoiled villages. Wilcot is perhaps the prettiest. Charlton, a turning off the main road near a pub called the Charlton Cat, was the birthplace of Stephen Duck, a thresher, whose poetry was taken up by people keen to discover such noble savages; whose eagerness to impress his new patrons drained his verse of its spontaneity but who nevertheless was considered a potential poet laureate; who became an ordained minister, and rector of Byfleet; and who in 1756 on his way to Charlton drowned himself in a pond behind the Black Lion pub in Reading. And then there are little Stert and Urchfont and sleepy Woodborough and... but it's better perhaps to pick some signpost at random and see where it leads you. Near Alton Barnes, below the white horse, there's a road north to Marlborough with a car park near the top of the hill from where you can walk a little way eastwards and see a great swathe of the vale laid out before you. Devizes is far too decorous to market itself as the Gateway to the Vale of Pewsey. But that is what you may make of it if you wish.

DOLBADARN CASTLE

DOLBADARN CASTLE, an ancient circular tower,
in co. and 8m. SE. of Carnarvon. Is situated under Snowdon,
on Llyn Peris at Llanberis.

DRIVE EAST OUT OF Llanberis and you may miss it; I did. But drive west to the town from the Llanberis Pass and suddenly it materializes before you, powerful and inescapable. It's called a castle, but today it is merely a tower.

Merely a tower? What is it about a tower suddenly perceived on a skyline which quickens the pulse and lifts the spirit? How can one explain the well-documented circumstance that some writer, setting eyes on a tower, soon finds a whole tale invading the imagination, perhaps a small sad romantic story, perhaps a substantial novel, even an epic? Thomas Hardy, who kept an eye out for towers, wrote a novel called *Two on a Tower*, based on Charborough Tower, which steals in and out of sight on the A35 as you drive west to Dorchester. The crime novelist P. D. James was inspired by another Dorset tower of which Hardy was fond, Clavell Tower, built in 1830 as an observatory and a folly, and sometimes known as the Tower of the Winds, near Kimmeridge Bay. 'All of a sudden,' she said in an interview, 'I had this dark picture of a woman being pushed over the top of the cliff, and that formed the story of *The Black Tower*.' But by 2004 the cliff on which it stood was so badly eroded that the Landmark Trust arranged for it to be dismantled and re-erected somewhere safer.

The rich and dangerously eccentric William Beckford had a monstrous fantasy tower constructed for him at Fonthill in Wiltshire, which collapsed not long after he left it. The builder, when dying, confessed to Beckford that the work had been so shoddily done that the edifice could not last. Beckford passed this on to the man to whom he had sold it, who dismissed it as nonsense. The tower then fell down, as predicted. He had a second built, mercifully to higher standards of craftsmanship, on the hills north of Bath, which is still there today. 'Mr Beckford', his builder complained, 'keeps shouting "higher".' The campanile in Venice so excited him that he ran all the way to the top. In his novel, *Vathek*, he imagines a tower with 11,000 stairs. A painting depicting the Tower of Babel was one of his most cherished possessions.

Other writers have felt that they wrote their best when enclosed in a tower: Alexander Pope worked through two summers translating Homer in an abandoned tower at Stanton Harcourt in Oxfordshire (see Devil's Quoits), almost all that was left of a once-famous house. His enthusiastic descriptions of his retreat were read with a certain scepticism by the Earl of Harcourt, who owned the place. 'Although his description be ludicrous and witty,' this nobleman wrote, 'it is in almost every particular incorrect, the situation of several buildings being exactly the reverse of that in which they stood, as is demonstrated by a still existing plan.'

The greatest adorer of towers, the writer most intent on writing one into his story whenever he could, was Thomas Love Peacock. In towers, his heroes and sometimes heroines pine and grow delicate, or work away at schemes for improving the world, or gaze from the topmost windows for visitors who never arrive. The towers he loves best are ruins. The tower at the south-western corner of Nightmare Abbey, Lincolnshire, 'a venerable family-mansion, in a highly picturesque state of semi-dilapidation', where disappointment in love preys deeply on the sensitive spirit of Scythrop Glowry, is 'ruinous and full of owls', that is to say, the kind of tower that Peacock most craves. As Mr Chainmail, in *Crotchet Castle*, dreamily contemplates the wall of a ruined castle, a vision wells up before him of an enchanting damsel, but by the time he has coasted the dry and bramble-grown moat, crossed the unguarded bridge, passed the unportcullised arch of the gateway, entered the court, ascertained the tower and ascended the broken stairs to stand on the ivied wall, she is, of course, gone.

In *Melincourt*, a novel in the course of which an orang-utan becomes a respected Tory MP, as one sometimes suspects they still do, the dramatis personae meet in what was formerly Rednose Abbey, but now, in the care of the moody and misanthropic

Mr Forester, has become Redrose Abbey. 'Your Redrose Abbey', observes Mr Fax, 'is a beautiful metamorphosis. I can scarcely believe that these are the mouldering walls of the pious fraternity of Rednose, which I contemplated two years ago.' 'The picturesque tourists', his host replies mournfully, 'will owe me no good-will for the metamorphosis, though I have endeavoured to leave them as much mould, mildew, and weather-stain as possible.' Much later they come on a ruined mansion – not in this case a tower, yet even so: 'There was an air of melancholy grandeur in its loneliness and desolation… The briers that choked the court; the weeds that grew from the fissures of the walls and on the ledges of the windows, the fractured glass, the half-fallen door, the silent and motionless clock, the steps worn by the tread of other years, the total silence of the scene of ancient hospitality, broken only by the voices of the rooks whose nests were in the elms, all carried back the mind to the years that were gone.'

Gryll Grange, location of the last of Peacock's novels, close to the New Forest, is near to a solitary round tower, on an eminence backed with a wood, which is taken to be a folly. One day Dr Theophilus Opimian, incumbent of Ashbrook-cum-Ferndale, out walking with stout stick and Newfoundland dog, finds a young man called Falconer installed there, who says he has acquired it and divided it into three rooms, one on each floor; one a dining room, the others dedicated to books and pictures. 'This building', the doctor reflects, 'might belong to the age of chivalry.' It is, however, in Hampshire, which for a novel by Peacock seems disappointingly tame. *Headlong Hall*, the first of the novels, is set in a far more romantic location, and one that Peacock especially loved, in the vale of Llanberis, Dolbadarn territory. Here Squire Headlong has gathered around him a crew of whom we'll learn more when we get to Tremadog later on in my book: Mr Foster, the perfectibilian, Mr Escot, the deteriorationist, Mr Jenkison, the statu-quo-ite, and the Reverend Doctor Gaster, who though neither a philosopher nor a man of taste has so impressed the squire with his dissertation on the art of stuffing a turkey that he's been allotted a place in this erudite company.

There is bound to be conversation – for great stretches of Peacock novels, there's little else – and soon, you may be certain, there will be a tower. Mr Milestone, a landscape architect eager to beautify everything that he can get his hands on, has arrived and set out for a walk with the squire. 'The object that most attracted Mr Milestone's admiration was a ruined tower on a projecting point of rock, almost totally overgrown with ivy. The ivy, Mr Milestone observed, required trimming and clearing in various parts; a little pointing and polishing was also necessary for the dilapidated walls: and the whole effect would be materially increased by a plantation of spruce fir, interspersed with cypress and juniper, the present broken and rugged ascent from the land side being first converted into a beautiful slope, which might be easily effected by blowing up a part of the rock with gunpowder, laying on a quantity of fine mould, and covering the whole with an elegant stratum of turf.'

Mercifully, Dolbadarn tower, though well within reach of such beautifiers, has never been Milestoned. You may park on a convenient lay-by and walk up a broken and rugged ascent, with the tower before you reassuringly ruined and adorned by bits of greenery growing out of the top. CADW, the official custodians of Wales's historic monuments (*cadw* is a Welsh word, meaning 'keep') have somewhat over-festooned it with notices, though no doubt these were required by health and safety rules. There are warnings of five kinds of misadventure which might befall you if you are not ultra-careful, with cartoons of unwary people in undignified postures to ram home the message.

It's a tower, even now, that seems to mean business, 40 feet high and 40 feet round, less romantic than rugged, with little to hold out hope that owls might frequent it at nightfall. And the backdrop is daunting: the high hills behind have been brutally hacked away by quarrying. 'A godsend to generations of water-colourists', says the *Shell Guide to North Wales*, which in view of the quarriers' depredations seems at first sight a shade surprising. Yet exhibited here is something which makes you see Dolbadarn in a different, more romantic, more Peacockesque light. It's a reproduction of a painting of the castle by Turner on a day of cloud but with sunlight touching the mountains – one of the very many such paintings he did on tours which in those days before picture postcards guaranteed him a good income. And here, as the caption says, is Dolbadarn, gloomy and isolated, set against a stark mountain landscape (no quarrying then) which 'perfectly evokes the artistic sublime'. There are lines of verse too, commemorating Owain Goch, imprisoned here for more than twenty years by his powerful younger brother, Llywelyn ap Gruffydd, last prince of Gwynnedd. In the valley, a tiny train with a red and yellow engine chugs and hoots its way back from Snowdon.

The reproduction of Turner's painting which is hung out at Dolbadarn is, inevitably, crude. But when later I went to Compton Verney, there it was in all its original glory. Which Dolbadarn should I remember: the one to which I climbed by its broken and rugged ascent, with the savage quarries behind it and the little train in the valley, or the Dolbadarn seen and commemorated and, in the way of these things, imaginatively romanticized, by an artist of genius?

DURHAM

DURHAM, capital of the co., mun. bor. and episcopal city and mkt.-town with ry. stas. L.N.E. … Durham is nearly surrounded by the r. Wear. The present fine cathedral, containing the tomb of the Venerable Bede (d.735) dates from 1093…

IN THE NORTH-EAST corner of Durham's sublime cathedral, close to the chapel of the nine altars and the shrine of St Cuthbert, you might catch sight of a modest plaque commemorating the death of three Townsends: his first wife, his son, and finally, almost as if a postscript, the Reverend George himself, prebendary of this cathedral, who was laid to rest on 23 November 1857. The tribute to his wife, whom he survived by twenty-two years, is far more lavish. He is seen away simply with a line from Ephesians 1:6: 'Accepted in the beloved'.

There's lot more than that to be said about Dr Townsend. Not as much as might have been said had he progressed, as many around him believed he deserved to, to the eminence of a bishopric. As it is, he's remembered, if he's remembered at all, for his years of service to the church and to scholarship, and for a number of books that were talked about in his day. Yet in 1850 Canon Townsend embarked on an adventure which, had it succeeded, would have brought about a revolutionary change in the history of the Christian religion, and established the conclusion that popes over three centuries, far from being infallible, had been mired in most grievous error.

I discovered George Townsend in a second-hand bookshop in the very agreeable town of Swaffham, Norfolk. On the shelf was a book of essays by Monsignor Ronald Knox, Catholic priest, academic theologian, satirist and unquenchable wit, called *Literary Distractions*. These mostly began as lectures delivered direct to an audience, and Knox started this one with a disclaimer. He had, he accepted, a reputation for fooling his readers – in his earlier *Essays in Satire* he'd adopted the very methods used by some who argued that Francis Bacon had written Shakespeare's plays to prove that the great poem *In Memoriam*, hitherto attributed to Alfred Lord Tennyson, was in fact the work of

Queen Victoria. This lecture, based on George Townsend's book, *Journal of a Tour in Italy in 1850*, was not, he insisted, another such invention; it was simply the authentic story, as he called it, of 'the man who tried to convert the pope'.

That the pope needed converting had been a settled conviction of Townsend's since an anti-Catholic tract he had written when a bright young man had caught the eye of one of the great Dunelm bishops, Shute Barrington. His reward was a prebendary stall at Durham Cathedral, which meant rather more than somewhere convenient to sit during services. It brought with it an income which, as one of his obituarists noted, saved him from being trapped in the round of a parochial ministry and gave him the freedom and ease he needed to think and write. The fruits of his reflection were a growing conviction that the Christian Church had come to the wrong decisions at the Council of Trent between 1545 and 1563, had consequently taken the road to perdition, and needed to be hauled off it; and that, the Archbishop of Canterbury having proved reluctant to take up the case, he, George, was the man to tackle this daunting assignment.

Accordingly he resolved to visit Pope Pius IX and convince him of the error of his and his Church's ways. He knew this would not be easy; indeed, respected friends had told him it was impossible. It was not then and never had been the practice of popes to grant interviews to any old Anglican canon who might be visiting Rome, especially if such canons had pre-announced their intentions to lecture them on their heresies. That he spoke not a word of French or Italian might have seemed a disadvantage, but fortunately his second wife, Charlotte, was fluent in both. Nor would George be distracted by any other consideration. 'I would appeal to him', he says in his account of his journey, 'to begin, and to commend with his great authority, the reconsideration of the past… The very attempt to gain admission to the Vatican would subject me, I well knew, to the charge of enthusiasm, fanaticism and folly…'

George was not only resolute: he was resourceful and well-connected. He enlisted the aid of the brilliant but notoriously unreliable Whig politician and lawyer Lord Brougham, Lord Chancellor until he exhausted his colleagues' patience, writer of some hopelessly undependable memoirs, and the man who did most to establish a fine resort at Cannes. Lord Brougham had to admit that even he did not know the pope personally, but he knew a number of intermediaries. That led to an introduction to the Archbishop of Paris, who duly produced a letter recommending him. Four weeks into their journey, the Townsends arrived in Italy, and on 25 April 1850 a letter reached George which offered a private audience with the pontiff on the very next day. He and his wife-translator were greeted with warm cordiality and invited to give their impressions of Italy, but at last they came to the meat of the matter, which was Dr Townsend's proposal that the pope should call a new Council to discuss the reunion of the Catholic and Anglican Churches – the canon's intention being that the deal should be done largely on Protestant terms. Quite how far he spelled it out to Pius IX is unclear: certainly a text which he left for the pope to read at his leisure failed to advance any specific proposal for renouncing the Council of Trent. Dr Townsend notes in the *Journal* that though they behaved with the utmost courtesy they at no time bowed their knees before His Holiness as other visitors did. The happy couple then left for Naples in the expectation that Pius IX would shortly summon them back. In this, though, they were disappointed, and on 27 May they set out for home.

The *Journal*, Knox notes, written a few months later, looks back on the outcome with something close to despair. But this was in the light of new evidence that the pope, far from feeling contrition when the Townsends had finished with him, issued what the canon calls 'an unscriptural, absurd and insolent' Bull, restoring the English hierarchy. (Before this, the Church in England had been under the general supervision of Vicars Apostolic: now, under the terms of the Bull, the country was divided into twelve episcopal sees with the Archbishop of Westminster in charge. Canon Townsend was not alone in his outrage at this impertinence: Queen Victoria herself condemned it as an infringement of her prerogative and 'in the highest degree, wrong'.)

The canon was also aware of a wave of predictions that Rome and Naples might soon be destroyed by fire, moving him to write: 'Oh, for that warning voice, which he who saw the Apocalypse heard cry in heaven, that I might be heard in my appeal to the Bishop of Rome when I say, Repent, Repent, rescind your additions to the religion of Jesus Christ.' Yet here, says Catholic Knox, the canon himself was in error. The conclusions of Councils cannot be repudiated and rescinded as if they were Acts of Parliament. A Council was in time assembled – the one which Alfred Austin of Ashford went to report – much as George had recommended, but the hoped-for *mea culpa* did not emerge.

No doubt, among the high pillars of Durham Cathedral under the rib-vaulted roof there were mutterings from time to time that amounted to 'told you so'. Certainly the canon's obituaries in the *Durham Chronicle* and *Durham Advertiser* found much to celebrate: such seminal works as *The Old and New Testament Chronologically Arranged* and *Accusations of History against the Church of Rome* – the work that had so enthused Bishop Barrington and which had since become 'a textbook and bulwark of antagonism in the Romish controversy' – as well as his spirited rebuttal of a book by Sir William Drummond which suggested the twelve apostles were really the twelve signs of the Zodiac, and even his stalwart work for the local Conservative cause. Against that, though, they felt bound to recall and deplore the aberration that had taken him off to Rome: 'We felt some distrust', the *Chronicle* remembered, 'and no small dismay, at the appearance of Dr Townsend's *Journal of a Tour in Italy*. In older days, the penalty of praemunire, we thought, might have been talked of.' Not language you'd find in a local paper these days.

'No doubt', they consoled themselves, 'it proceeded from the boundless charity of a most generous heart.' Yet for all his disappointment and sense of frustration, the canon remained imperturbable. He continued to sit and to worship in his prebendary stall. The stalls at Durham are labelled with the offices of their incumbents – Canon Major, Canon Honor, Cancellarius Spuae and so on – and I tried to deduce which one George might have sat in, and from which he would have risen, Sunday by Sunday, with difficulty in old age, for the singing of the Magnificat; but friendly attendants told me that the stalls of the time had been ripped out during some late Victorian refurbishment and these were mere modern replacements.

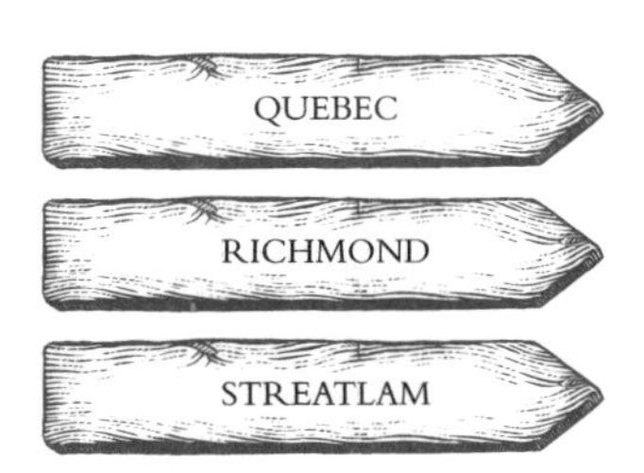

A B C D
E F G H
I J K L
M N O P
Q R S T
U V W X Y Z

EARDISLAND

EARDISLAND, par. and vil., Herefordshire, on r. Arrow 5m. W. of Leominster…

…which must not be confused, I was warned in Herefordshire, with:

EARDISLEY, par and vil. with ry. sta., G.W.R. and L.M.S., West Herefordsh., 5m. S. of Kington…

BUT I THINK THIS was bad advice. If you confuse them, you end up seeing them both, which is all the more rewarding. Eardisley is a long thin village on the busy route from Hereford to Kington. At the far end, going north, is Tram Square, home to the Tram Inn, which confronts across the square another hostelry called the New Strand whose notice boards boast not only food and drink but that glorious calling, the selling of second-hand books. The Tram Inn, it is somewhere explained, derives its name not from the trams themselves, which don't seem to have frequented the square, but from the horses that drew them, which used to be stabled here. Having established that, we can walk slowly and cautiously down the main road, examining on the way a fine congregation of black and white houses, some of them neat and regular, others sporting those saggy, wonky lines familiar in black and white buildings which sometimes cause the untutored to fear they could soon fall down. These are cosy, cottagey homesteads, which makes it all the more exhilarating to come at the end, by the church, upon what seems at first sight to be three noble mansions, surprisingly close, like great ships moored together in harbour. In fact, they are terraces, subdivided into separate cottages, and forming an eye-catching preface to the church, which is dedicated to St Mary, where just inside the door you will find a

quite astonishing twelfth-century font, intricately decorated with carvings of battlesome knights and figures out of Heaven and Hell, the first observed by an owl, the second with an attendant lion.

So Eardisley is worth seeing, but Eardisland even more so. Both are part of a tourist lure called the Black and White Trail, and you may, if you wish, deviate on the way to look at another constituent, Weobley, the largest of the villages on this route. Without any deviation, you will come to Pembridge, which also has many characterful black and white buildings but is blighted by the incessant traffic of the A44. Once Eardisley, I imagine, scored over Eardisland by being on the railway, with its own minor service from Kington and entertaining much more significant trains passing through on their way from Hereford to Hay and Brecon and Neath and Swansea. They, of course, ceased long ago, and nowadays it's Eardisland that looks the more sought after. There's another fine array of black and white (which in practice is often brown and white) and not just on the road through the village, for Eardisland, unlike Eardisley, has several byways to wander down where more good houses are lurking.

Better still, it has the river Arrow, here with a little stream as a companion, which adds to the charm of the place by the bubbling, plashing sounds it makes as it burbles over the stones. Two splendid old bridges carry you over them: there are houses ranged around the waterside with lovingly cared-for gardens, and when the *Shell Guide to Herefordshire* says that Eardisland 'just misses being one of the prettiest villages in the county', that tells you how good the others are. Having just come from Eardisley-on-the-A4411, which seemed to be suffering from some kind of mass infestation of motorway maintenance lorries, the peace of Eardisland seemed even more blessed. Look out, too, for the dovecote, open to public inspection at all reasonable hours, with an exhibition explaining how dovecotes worked.

You can reconstitute in your mind the village that used to be from the names of some of the houses: Shop Cottage, Shop House and Olde Shoppe House, the Old Post Office. No call for them now that Eardisland is, by the look of it, in the hands of people who probably know to the nearest foot how far it is to the nearest Waitrose. There are houses on the fringe of the village which do not have what it takes to make an estate agent salivate, but most of what you will see in Eardisland looks expensively paid for, privileged and blatantly middle class – and yes, you might even say, smug.

You shouldn't, though. The urge to live in places like these ought never to be disparaged. Any doubt about that might be dispelled by the exhibition I saw in the church of photographs by Kathleen Freeman, who with her husband runs the village tea rooms and guest shop, and whose book of pictures of Herefordshire, lent to me by a friend, I would have bought had the Freemans not been taking their annual holiday. Each picture representing the county had a poem printed alongside it. One of these was by that strange, sometimes demented and sadly unprivileged figure, John Clare. In a poem called 'Proposals for Building a Cottage', he wrote:

Beside a runnel build my shed
  Wi' stubbles coverd oer
Let broad oaks oer its chimney spread
  And grassplats grace the door

The door may open wi a string
  So that it closes tight
And locks too woud be wanted things
  To keep thieves out at night

A little garden, not too fine
  Inclose wi painted pails
And woodbines round the cot to twine
  Pind to the wall wi nails

Let hazels grow and spindling sedge
  Bent bowering over head
Dig old mans beard from woodland hedge
  To twine a summer shade

Beside the threshold sods provide
  And build a summer seat
Plant sweet briar bushes by its side
  And flowers that smelleth sweet

I love the sparrows ways to watch
  Upon the cotters sheds
So here and there pull out the thatch
  As they may hide their heads

And as the sweeping swallows stop
  Their flights along the green
Leave holes within the chimneytop
  To paste their nest between.

Stick shelves and cupboards round the hut
  In all the holes and nooks
Nor in the corner fail to put
  A cupboard for the books

Along the floor some sand Ill sift
  To make it fit to live in
And then Ill thank ye for the gift
  As something worth the giving

People who scoff, not always by reason of envy, at those who aspire to live among such picture-postcardy Birket Fostery properties as you find in Eardisland should hold their tongues in the face of that.

One might also, having left Eardisland, usefully go on to confuse it with such places as Shobdon, for its fantasy church, complete with a little enclave with separate chairs and a fireplace reserved for the Bateman family who created it. Lord Bateman vainly and vandalistically knocked down the original church, which must have been as fine as any early church in the county, but this is some recompense. And then, perhaps, a further daffy confusion might take one on to Kilpeck, for its Norman church and especially for the carvings around the south door, though that, I have to admit, is some distance away, back past Hereford.

EDWINSTOWE

EDWINSTOWE, par., vil. and ry. sta. L.N.E.,
N. Notts 4¼m. E. of Warsop…

THE E STOOD FOR Ebenezer, but he always preferred that his Ebenezer should not be used: he would rather be E. Cobham Brewer – the Reverend Dr E. Cobham Brewer, to whom we owe that learned and unfailingly entertaining reference book, *Brewer's Dictionary of Phrase and Fable*. Brewer was born in London and lived most of his life in the south of England, but after the death in 1878 of his wife of twenty-two years he moved in with his daughter Nellie and his son-in-law, the Reverend Henry Hayman, first at Ruddington, south of Nottingham, and then at the vicarage in the country village of Edwinstowe, on the edge of Sherwood Forest.

Here he lived in apparent contentment for a further thirteen years, preaching whenever invited to do so, lecturing likewise, gardening – his only vice, as he liked to say – entertaining and being entertained by his grandchildren, but above all copying or cutting out every snippet of information that took his fancy and putting them into books. Even in his eighties he would work until 3 or 4 in the morning and then be down for breakfast at 9 a.m. prompt. With his big bald head, his long grey beard and his kindly smile, he must have been a familiar sight as he made his way down Edwinstowe's narrow main street, until he died in March 1897 in his eighty-seventh year, and was buried in the churchyard of St Mary's, under a beech tree.

One of those grandchildren later recalled Brewer at work in his sitting room. The walls were covered in plain white paper on which he used to record in pencil his discoveries, and the names of those who visited him. 'My method', he once told a reporter, 'is very simple. I always read with paper and pencil at my side and jot down whatever I think may be useful to me… In fact the Phrase and Fable dictionaries and the other books of that class may be said to be merely different sections of one giant commonplace book.'

These other books ranged far beyond the territory of *Phrase and Fable*. One of his earliest and most successful was his *Guide to Science*, based on the practice he had adopted from his early years of writing down scientific questions that intrigued him, digging the answers out, and then adding them on the same page. This book sold a million copies, was translated into languages which ranged from French (at the specific request of the Emperor Napoleon III) to Greek (published in Smyrna in 1857). Some books dealt with history (*Great Central Points of Mediaeval and Modern History*; *The Historic Notebook: with an Appendix of Battles*), or subdivisions of history (*A Dictionary of Miracles*); others with literature (*Authors and Their Works; A Poetical Chronology*); one had a title in ancient Greek. They culminated, somewhat unexpectedly, in *Constance Naden and Hylo-idealism: a critical study* (1891).

That he isn't celebrated as he deserves perhaps reflects the fact that *Phrase and Fable* is now remembered where most of his other work is forgotten; also that, in any case, *Phrase and Fable* is sometimes snootily written off as if it were a mere accumulation of inconsequential trivia. And some of the treasured gobbets in the earliest editions are indeed relentlessly trivial. Does anyone now need to know – did anyone then – that Amine, the beautiful wife of Sidi Nouman, ate her rice not with a spoon but with a bodkin, carrying it to her mouth in infinitesimal proportions? Probably not. Though the reason for her behaviour is tasty enough: as her husband later discovered, she was a ghoul who feasted at night on the recently buried dead.

His *Reader's Handbook of Allusions, References, Plots and Stories, with three appendices* proceeds on its stately and all-encompassing way, from Aa'ron, a Moor, beloved by Tam'ora, queen of the Goths, and Aaron (St.), a British martyr of the city of Legions (Newport, in South Wales) to Zulzul, the sage whose life was saved in the form of a rat by Gedy, the youngest of the four sons of Corcud. It seems mean to complain about his occasional excesses. He is full of useful compendiums (patron saints, decisive battles, deaths from strange causes, persons eaten alive by mice and rats, precocious genius, extreme longevity). He has found a stack of errors in Shakespeare's plays. He knows who introduced some commonplace words into the language (the word 'starvation', he says, was first used by the Scottish lawyer and politician Henry Dundas), and he rescues words that have perhaps undeservedly fallen into disuse (London, he tells us, was once known as Sombragloomy).

He knows that salubrious Abingdon Street, near the Houses of Parliament, used to be called Dirty Lane; he knows (or he thinks he does: others think differently) that 'mad as a hatter' is a corruption of 'mad as an adder', and he knows that in saying 'By Jingo!' – though few people now still do – we're invoking a Basque Supreme Being. He enlivens his pages with copious quotations from his favourite writers, who clearly include Milton and Scott, and occasionally with jingles of his own composition. Sometimes he gets quite cross. He's affronted that Louis XIV of France, 'a man of mere ceremony and posture', who lost battle after battle, and brought his nation to absolute bankruptcy, was nicknamed the Great King: 'He was little in stature, little in mind, little in all moral and physical faculties; and *great* only in such littlenesses as posturing, dressing, ceremony and gourmandising.'

Brewer today is a whole light industry, as his publishers perpetuate his name in areas of which he could have known nothing – *Brewer's Politics* or *Brewer's Cinema*, for instance. But when in 2000 John Ayto and Ian Crofton produced the first edition of *Brewer's Dictionary of Modern Phrase and Fable*, excavating the origins of such wildly post-Brewer expressions as 'axis of evil' and 'yummy mummy', they were essentially doing what Brewer did in his paper-festooned sitting room at Edwinstowe all those years ago. They would never have got there without him.

Edwinstowe in those days was a rural community with a population in the mid nineteenth century of around a thousand, mostly employed on the estates of the great landed proprietors known as the Dukeries. You can get some picture of it as it was when Brewer lived there in *Kelly's Directory* for 1895, two years before he died: a large township, village and extensive parish on the river Maun, it says, with a railway in the course of construction, which will give it a station. Apart from St Mary's, with Mr Hayman as vicar (he was also vicar of Perlethorpe), the village had Wesleyan and Primitive Methodist chapels, and a library. There were several grocers, butchers, shoemakers, wheelwrights and general dealers to choose from, as well as the store of the Edwinstowe Co-operative Society Ltd, and a blacksmith, two hotels, at least three pubs, and a Post Office.

What drastically altered original Edwinstowe was partly the railway, which brought rather more trippers into the town than local opinion was happy with ('Edwinstowe:

Station for the Dukeries', it said on the platforms), but mainly the mining developments of the 1920s, when pits were sunk all over this territory. The village later looked back on 29 September 1925 as the day when everything changed: when the Bolsover Colliery Company started sinking its Thoresby pit, a process for which ancient forest trees had to be cleared.

Old and new communities were slow to mix. An elderly Edwinstowe resident, interviewed by Robert Waller for his book *The Dukeries Transformed*, recalled: 'Well, they didn't want to mix with us, really. They were they and we were us, and they tended to look down on us… It seemed almost as though High Street at Edwinstowe was a dividing line in the village at one time. The old side of the village was one side, and the new side, you know, the colliery side, was on the other side of the High Street and they just didn't like us in their shops. I can remember during the War… going into one of the shops at the top of High Street, it was Woodhead's actually, he owned a toffee shop then, and unless you were old village, he didn't want to serve you.'

Thoresby pit was still open in 2008, but there's little sense of social division now. Grand Edwinstowe House has gone, replaced by a Centre for Business Excellence, there's a spot called Trends Café, and the place seems mildly obsessed with Robin Hood and Maid Marian (sometimes spelled 'Marion'). There's a Robin Hood's Den (quality gifts) and a Robin Hood Plaice (fish and chips), a Robin Hood Corner, a Maid Marian Restaurant, and Maid Marion's Secrets (to judge by the windows when I was there, she seems to have had a thing for black underwear). Near the library there's a statue that depicts them together, as befits the place in which (it is said) they were married. I feared at first she was curtseying to him, but on closer inspection it looked as though they were simply caught in an old-fashioned troth-plighting posture. A plaque by the church announces the start (or finish) of Robin Hood Way, a 105-mile recreational path. The trippers still crowd into Edwinstowe High Street on their way to or from the forest.

I had rather supposed that the erudite Dr B. would have kept his distance from the Robin Hood story, which recent editions of Brewer have written off as mere legend. But not so. In his *Reader's Handbook of Allusions, References* and the rest (1892), he states as if it were established fact that 'Robin' was a man called Fitz Ooth, commonly assumed to be the Earl of Huntingdon, who was born at Locksley, Notts, in 1160. He lived a freebooter's life in Barnsdale, Yorkshire, in the Sherwood Forest and in Plompton Park, Cumberland; had a single female, Marian, in his entourage; and was bled to death on 12 November 1247, by a relative, the prioress of Kirkley's Nunnery, Yorkshire, at the age of eighty-seven. Could this apparently uncritical summary have had something to do with all those good years in Edwinstowe?

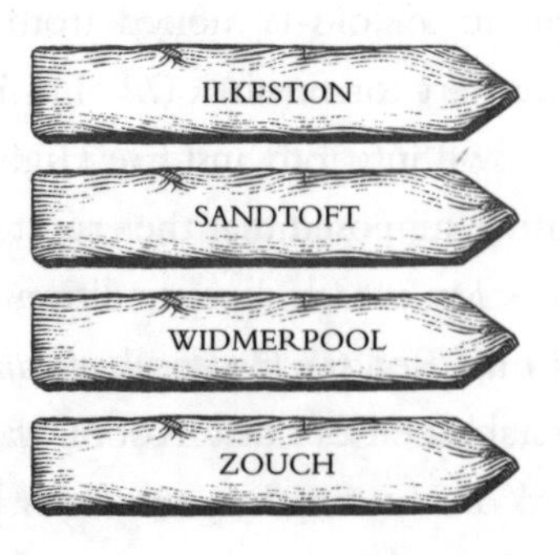

ENVILLE

ENVILLE, par. and vil., W. Staffs, on border of co., 3m. NW. of Stourbridge… In vicinty of vil. is E. Hall, seat.

A SATURDAY AFTERNOON IN late May. The car radio has been bringing news of England humiliating the once mighty West Indies. Here, on a cloudy day with occasional moments of drizzle, Enville CC of the Worcestershire League division III are enjoying themselves at the expense of visiting Belbroughton: in fewer than forty overs they have almost two hundred runs on the board for the loss of only four wickets, and the two visiting bowlers – as is often the case in club cricket, an eager young tyro at one end and a plumpish, slightly time-worn trundler, off a run of five paces, at the other – are being despatched to all parts of the ground. And what a ground! Set on one side of the Enville Hall estate, long the home of the earls of Stamford, it is broad and handsome, beautifully nurtured and ringed by fine trees, with soft hills outlined beyond.

There's an air of privilege here which is not what one might have expected in the Worcestershire league, division III. But this ground used to stage more glamorous matches than it ever does nowadays. In the days of the Rt Hon. George Harry Grey, 1827–83, Earl of Stamford and Warrington, president of the MCC in 1851, teams described as 'An England XI' used to play here, taking on teams led by the Earl. You can inspect some of the score sheets inside the pavilion. Here is the greatest of all such nineteenth-century eminences, W. G. Grace, at the head of a visiting XI matched against the Earl of Stamford and friends. Grace made 14 and 10. 'Grace found the place settings difficult to penetrate,' a recent secretary of Enville CC, recalling that day, exulted in the *Daily Mail*; but then the earl had a team of eighteen to deploy, who disposed of Grace and Co. by an innings and 40 runs. A team of eighteen, indeed, was quite modest: sometimes the earl took the field at the head of a team of twenty-two. He was out for a duck in the game against Grace, by the way.

Some of the participants in these games played for money – Grey would pay them £100 to be available for cricket from May until the end of September – while others were simply enthusiastic aristocrats. In one match, where an 'England XI' – one of whose players was Julius Caesar – were all out for 66, the home side included the Earl of Strathmore to open the batting (he made 0) and the Earl of Stamford himself (out this time for 4) as well as Lord Guernsey. As usual, the Earl of Stamford batted well down the order: in a team of twenty-two, one could go in fourteenth and still not be a tail-ender. And even those among the participants who didn't get paid still had the pleasure of playing on one of the best grounds in England. In 1867, the *Illustrated London News* rated Enville, for its size and ground condition, well above Lord's, and even suggested it had some claim to be the best cricket ground in the world.

These matches, which brought truly notable players – two Graces, G. F. as well as W. G., and Jupp, and at least two Lillywhites – to Enville were great local occasions, attracting crowds of 10,000 and more. Sometimes they were simply one element in wider festivities. In 1856, club records say, a three-day fete, including one of these matches, with a firework display to round it all off, brought in 80,000 people. The Enville estate was an even grander place in those days. The house, 'totally destroyed', the *County Express* reported, after a fire in 1904, was rebuilt, but the private racecourse has gone, and so has the glasshouse, a kind of mini-Crystal Palace, used by troops for target practice during the Second World War.

Crowds no longer flock as they did from the surrounding country when the cricket is on. The attendance in the half hour or so when I was there, discounting Enville players waiting to bat, the scoreboard staff and the ladies making the tea, numbered five. Worcestershire play some second XI matches here, but even those, I imagine, don't summon crowds in their thousands. A young man who was running the scoreboard was confident that Enville would make 250, and he didn't see Belbroughton matching that. I checked with the club later on to discover the outcome: they duly made their 250 and dismissed poor Belbroughton for 59 (Mark Heathcock, 6 for 16).

But at least the defeated Belbroughtonians would be able to tell their grandchildren that they'd played on a ground where W. G. Grace didn't do much better, and on a pitch once considered more than a match for Lord's. Even those who play on the grounds of other stately homes, such as those of the Gettys, can't better that.

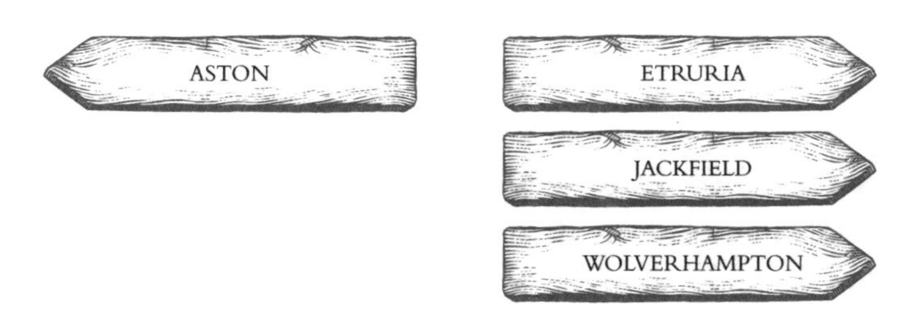

ETRURIA

ETRURIA, eccl. dist. and vil., with ry. sta. L.M.S., Stoke-upon-Trent par., and within bor. of Hanley, N. Staffs… is the seat of the earthenware manufactory erected by Josiah Wedgwood. E. Hall is now a commercial office.

STOKE-ON-TRENT IS one of the least loved of British cities. It's not really a city at all, simply a federation of towns whose centre is Hanley rather than Stoke. It's a utilitarian, jobbing kind of a place with few pretensions to art and none to glamour. All the more surprising, then, to find close together within its boundaries three places whose names evoke the highest traditions of European culture: Etruria, Dresden and Florence.

Etruria is the one that people have heard of. Josiah Wedgwood conceived it, as a place where he might re-create a culture he hugely admired. He chose a site on the banks of a canal, created by Joseph Brindley on a route which Wedgwood had helped to determine, establishing in 1769 an elegant factory combining an Ornamental Works with a Useful Works, which came a year later; to which he added a fine house for himself, Etruria Hall, and homes for his workforce in an industrial village long pre-dating Sir Titus Salt's exemplary Saltaire in Yorkshire. He commemorated the establishment of this new Etruria by firing a set of celebratory vases in the Etruscan style, which he decorated with the legend: *Artes Etruriae Renascuntur* (the Arts of Etruria are Reborn).

Surviving prints of Wedgwood's enterprise – the dappled canal under its sheltering trees, a barge drifting lazily past the handsome factory buildings – make it look idyllic. That was certainly how it seemed to the Revd W. Fernyhough, who in 1795 commended its creator in a poem: 'Such the true patriot, from whose gates each day/ A crowd of healthy workmen make their way/ Whose rare productions foreign courts demand/ And while they praise, enrich his native land./ View his Etruria, late a barren waste/ Now high in culture, and adorn'd with taste.'

The factories flourished; the workforce seemed largely content. Wedgwood was a kindly employer. Among the treats to which the employees looked forward all year was Trentham Thursday, when they could journey by barge from the landing stage at Etruria to the fine house and gardens at Trentham of the Marquess of Stafford, whose family's louring presence remains inescapable in this part of Staffordshire. Other, more permanent departures took place from here too, as machines began to take over work formerly done by men. In the 1840s, the Pottery Union set up a society to help unemployed Staffordshire men to emigrate to America and settle on land it had purchased in Wisconsin. All those wishing to go had to put down a stipulated payment and some were picked from the list by a lottery. Cheering crowds saw them off as they left Etruria to make their new lives in Pottersville. But Pottersville failed.

Before long, though, other enterprises were setting up in Etruria which were less conspicuously devoted to culture and taste than Wedgwood's. The Gas Light and Coke Company arrived early in the new century. In the 1840s the railway came, taking over the traffic that had formerly used the canal, steaming smokily through the parkland and interrupting the view from Etruria Hall. By then a plant had been established that developed by 1860 into the Shelton Bar Iron and Steel works. Though these might not have delighted the poet Fernyhough, some who saw them found them beautiful, especially at night. A subsequent poet, Charles Tomlinson, who lived as a child in Basford, overlooking Etruria, remembered, in a book published in 1985 called *Eden: Graphics and Poems*, the 'immense dazzling shafts of fire' that flared out to be mirrored in the waters of the canal: fire and water blended. He imagined the ghost of Wedgwood returning to this territory: 'The plan had been a factory and model cottages/ A seat and prospect for a gentleman/ But history blackened round him...'

Christina Speight of London W4 started her life, she said in a letter to the *Daily Telegraph* in July 2007, in Etruria. 'The whole city on a dark winter's night', she recalled, 'was unforgettable, with countless ovens belching out black smoke and flame, the miasma hanging like a pall over all. No wonder we used to say: Down towards the north of England/ Lies a dreadful pall of smoke./ Its awful name is Hanley, Longton/ Fenton, Burslem, Stoke.'

Wedgwood died in 1795, long before the blackening began. His company left Etruria for Barlaston in 1940, and in the mid 1960s, when so much worth saving was briskly knocked down, the factory was demolished. Only a curious roundhouse survives, in what is now the grounds of the *Stoke Sentinel* newspaper. The rest of Etruria's industry has similarly died away. The steelworks closed in 1978 and was later razed. All that remains today is the Etruria Industrial Museum, occupying what was once another thriving Etruria enterprise: Jesse and Henry B. Shirley's Etruscan Bone and Flint Mill, which still operates for visitors during the summer. The railway station serving once busy Etruria was closed in 2005. It was being used, protestors were told, by only twenty-two people a day.

Dresden, five miles from Etruria, hoped, its name suggests, to evoke high culture too. But the local businessmen of the Longton Freehold Land Society, who created it, had other less high-minded motives. The 1832 Reform Act had given the vote to owners of freeholds worth more than 40 shillings and houses worth at least £10 a year. The businessmen behind the Dresden project hoped to enhance the fortunes of the Liberal Party by creating homes which met these qualifications, and installing in them Liberal sympathizers and supporters of further reform, who would borrow the money they needed for purchase from building societies and, once established, would start delivering Liberal votes: a manoeuvre located, it might be said, at the respectable end of the political art form known as gerrymandering.

They bought land at a place then known as Spratslade, owned by the great lord of Trentham, the Duke of Sutherland, and then added two further areas to it. The street names, as so often in cities, tell the story of the place's origins. Some commemorate Liberal heroes both national (Russell, Cobden, but a shade more surprisingly, Peel) and local; others reflect the Sutherland connection (Dunrobin, where the Sutherlands were based in the Scottish Highlands; Lilleshall, the name of another Sutherland estate in Staffordshire). These streets would hardly swell the pride of the duke today; some look woebegone. The Dunrobin Arms, near the modern relief road which slices this part of the city off from old neighbours, looked when I was there to have taken its final call for last orders.

Yet Dresden has one artistic achievement that few British towns can match. It has produced a composer who wrote thirty-two symphonies, one of which (his first, which took eight years to complete) requires the services of a 200-strong orchestra, four brass bands and four choirs, making a total of around 1,000 musicians in all. Havergal Brian (1876–1972) – his parents named him William, but he adopted the name of a hymnodist he greatly admired, W. H. Havergal – wrote twenty-seven of his symphonies and four of his five operas after his seventy-second birthday, which is even more remarkable since during the 1930s and early 1940s, when hardly anyone played him, he produced little work at all. Estimates of his ability vary from ecstatic to aghast, but the fact that Sir Charles Mackerras became president of the Havergal Brian Society is enough to warn thoughtful people against writing him off.

And certainly, parts of Dresden, as you wander about in them, have a flavour which Florence – a brief episode off the A50 road out of Stoke, and once the site of a pit – seems to lack. Florence possesses a tennis and bowling club which claims to be the oldest such club in the city, and a Sutherland Institute, now a library. You will not find here even the mildest equivalent of the Ponte Vecchio or the Boboli Gardens. One might suppose that the choice of the name showed some intent to develop craft traditions in leather, ceramics and stationery. Not a bit of it. This was pure flattery. Florence was the name of one of the Duke of Sutherland's daughters.

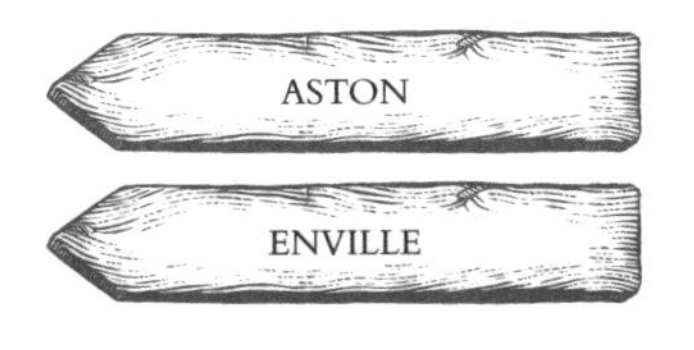

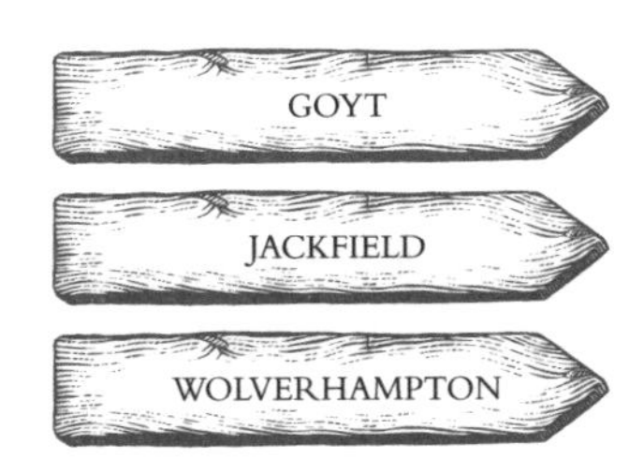

A B C D

E **F** G H

I J K L

M N O P

Q R S T

U V W XYZ

FOULNESS

FOULNESS, insular par. and vil., S. Essex, at mouth of r. Crouch, 7m. E. of Shoeburyness; 6,133 ac., pop. 460...

DRIVE TO THE VERY far end of the pleasant, if straggling, village of Great Wakering, Essex, and you come to the parish church of St Nicholas. To the right of this church a signpost indicating Foulness points down what looks like a placid country lane leading towards the sea. The countryside here cannot have changed very greatly over the centuries. Yet for three years at the start of the 1970s, it seemed destined for a startling transformation. Foulness (though the name its advocates intended to use was the more salubrious Maplin, after the sands to the south of the island) was designated as the site for a spanking modern airport with a seaport attached and perhaps an oil terminal too – with the inconvenient islanders, numbering two hundred or so, evicted and relocated, and their ancient island community largely obliterated.

A Commission set up by Labour and headed by a High Court judge, Sir Eustace Roskill, had rejected the Maplin option, recommending instead a site at Cublington, Buckinghamshire – one of three possible inland locations which it had shortlisted, the others being Nuthampstead in Hertfordshire and Thurleigh in Bedfordshire. The Conservative government which took over in June 1970 disagreed. It fastened instead on the dissenting report of a single Commission member, the celebrated planner Colin Buchanan, who had found all the inland sites unacceptable and advocated Foulness. That preference was backed by most of the newspapers and buoyed by the enthusiastic support of big City and business interests who thought they saw the chance of vast profits. Debates in the Commons and especially in the Lords produced little or no support for Cublington, and overwhelming endorsement of the choice for Foulness, a place regarded by most of those who contributed to these debates as one whose loss was of little consequence. Foulness, one Tory MP declared, 'seems to have been aptly named by our forebears'.

The island, in a sense, was paying a price for its isolation. Until the 1920s, it had always been a difficult place to get to. It was linked by a track across the Maplin Sands from Wakering Stairs to Fisherman's Head, between 5 and 6 miles to the north-east. This track was known as the Broomway because a line of upturned brooms had been placed along it, to signal the safest available route for travellers. Most of the island's provisions were brought by boat from Burnham-on-Crouch, across the estuary to the north.

What began to diminish the loneliness of Foulness was the establishment of artillery ranges at Shoeburyness in 1849, though it wasn't until after the First World War that the island became conveniently linked to the mainland. In 1915, a bridge and a road were planned across Havengore Island, a project completed in 1922. Now, there was even a bus service, and Foulness became a spot to which Essex car owners came for a day out at the weekend. The Second World War, however, reversed that process. The establishment of defence installations and research centres where secret work took place, culminating in the arrival of the Atomic Energy Authority in the 1950s, restricted access again, both for visitors and for those who lived on the island, and the population declined.

So when Edward Heath's government overthrew Roskill and plumped for Buchanan, the villagers of Foulness were not nearly so well equipped as those who lived close to the inland sites to resist imperious progress. What made things even more daunting was that though the Conservative government's case for Foulness was made mainly in terms of its environmental attractions – the sacrifice of a small slice of Essex to save desirable chunks of Home Counties England – the political arithmetic pointed just as strongly that way.

For the government to choose any of the three inland sites would threaten the party's electoral chances in Conservative-held marginal seats. The MPs for these seats banded together, calling themselves the Inland Group, and recruited others who hoped that building Maplin would reduce the noise and nuisance from which their constituents suffered around Heathrow and Gatwick. A government with a majority of thirty-one could not ignore such pressures. William Whitelaw, one of Heath's most senior ministers, was invited to open a new golf course in one of the threatened areas. As he raised his club to strike the inaugural ball, a man at his elbow, cunningly primed to do so, said to Whitelaw: 'Of course, you know that if the airport is built here, all this is going to be lost?'

The great man paused in mid-swing. 'Won't happen,' he said, 'too many marginals.'

The Defenders of Essex, the pressure group formed in the hope of averting Maplin, treasured the traditions and culture of Foulness Island: its twin villages of Churchend and Courtsend, its nineteenth-century church of St Mary the Virgin, its pub, its Crippses and Duckers and Rippingales, Beltons and Pottons and other established island families, its beaches and coastal paths and fishing, and particularly perhaps its abundant bird life – which the proponents of Maplin, if they troubled about it at all, thought of only in terms of the possible threat that Brent geese presented to incoming aircraft. But the objectors lacked the political clout of the Inland Group, and they could not command the kind of resources and influential connections that the inland protestors could muster (the treasurer of the resistance association at Cublington was a Rothschild). To add to their difficulties, Essex County Council, which was ready to sacrifice Foulness Island to avert the threat of having the airport elsewhere in the county, and the borough council in nearby Southend, both backed the project.

At Westminster, only three or four Members on the government side were willing to take up their case. Sir Bernard Braine, Conservative MP for South-East Essex, told the Commons: 'It has not been said before in this place, but Foulness is not the bleak, desolate place which the media have tried to portray.' In the Lords, Lady Stocks, who, exceptionally, had actually been there, told her fellow peers that Foulness Island was 'beautiful'. But few in the House were impressed. And in terms of political calculation, it was all too clear that Maplin would be easier to steer through Parliament than any inland venture, since so much of the area it would occupy was on the sands and under the sea, where the fear of losing marginal seats could not apply.

What saved the embattled islanders was the defeat of the Conservatives in the general election of February 1974. Anthony Crosland, the Labour politician who had set up the Roskill Commission, had denounced the choice of Foulness as soon as the Tories adopted it. His appointment as Environment Secretary in the new Wilson government ensured that it would be doomed. On 20 March, three weeks after Labour returned to office, he announced that he would not authorize any more work on Maplin.

In the light of that history, about which I had written a book at the time, I was keen to go back to Foulness and see what Crosland's decision had saved for the nation.

I failed. The placid country road out of Wakering brings you not to the bridge and road across Havengore Island but to Landwick Gate, a kind of block post – all high fences, barbed wire and strident notices warning of danger. I would not be allowed, a courteous security guard told me, to go beyond this point unless I'd been given clearance by QinetiQ.

This QinetiQ is an organization hived off from, but still acting under the authority of, the Ministry of Defence. Originally it was DERA – the government's Defence Evaluation and Research Agency – but under the guiding hand of its managing director, Sir John Chisholm, most of DERA was transferred to this separate entity. Though initially the government retained a 31 per cent share in QinetiQ, that was sold off in 2003 to the US private equity company Carlyle in a deal which was later condemned by the government watchdog, the National Audit Office, as a poor deal for taxpayers. Not so bad, though for Chisholm and his chief associate Graham Love, who are now multi-millionaires.

There used to be a convenient way of infiltrating this Essex QinetiQland. All you needed to do, it seems, was to ring the landlord of the island's only surviving pub, the George and Dragon, Churchend, and tell him you'd heard good reports of the place and would like to go for a drink there. He would then ask QinetiQ's permission to let you in. But when I phoned in the early months of 2008 to solicit this favour, a doleful voice told me it couldn't be done. The pub had gone out of business. There are still ways on to the island by boat or by crossing the sands, though the advice put out by the parish council sounds daunting, requiring the use of tide tables and detailed maps and satellite navigation.

I had heard there were open days every now and then, but my kindly security guard said he couldn't assist me there, as the office was being redecorated and all the paperwork had been taken away. In fact, as I later learned, they occur on the first Sunday of every month from April to October when between 12 and 4 you may look at selected parts of the island and visit its heritage centre. That represents an allocation of twenty-eight hours of standard visiting time in a year.

Having been repulsed at the Landwick Gate, I cannot report what the remaining islanders think of this curious sealed-off existence, though a book I found in Southend library, based on interviews with some of them by Johnnie Quarrell and published in 1998, mixes praise for the absence of crime with unease over some of the regulations. 'You feel so safe on Foulness,' one resident testified, 'you never have to lock your door.' But another complained that where once you could go round the island much as you wanted, this was no longer the case. Having set his nets overnight at Fisherman's Head he had turned up next morning to find access to them denied.

Still, at least I could feel reassured, as I drove back past Great Wakering church into civilian England, that, thanks to Labour's sinking of Maplin, the Brent geese have been spared from the planes, and the planes from the Brent geese.

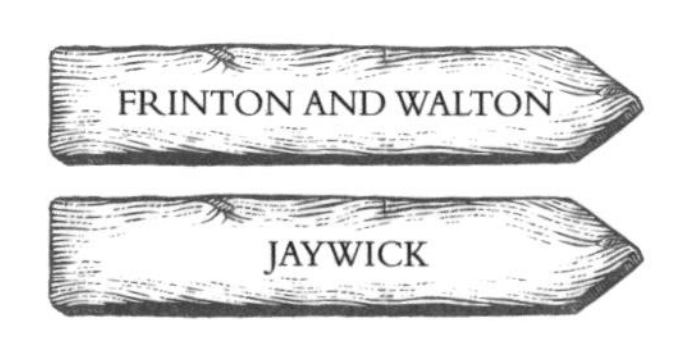

FRINTON AND WALTON

FRINTON AND WALTON, urb. dist. and par., Essex; see Frinton-on-Sea and Walton-on-the-Naze.

TOGETHER AS ALWAYS; FRINTON placed first, as usual. The once independent Walton district council was subsumed in the Frinton and Walton council that Bartholomew lists, though both are now subordinate to a district council named for the village and ancient hundred of Tendring. It's the Frinton and Walton swimming pool, too, rather than the other way round. So inferior did Frinton think Walton in 1904 that the two were involved in legal battles for custody of a road called Pole Barn Lane, one side of which was in Frinton and the other in Walton. Frinton complained that Walton's stewardship had reduced the road to a state unacceptable to decent Frintonians. Walton's fight back ended in the usual humiliation, the court finding for Frinton in terms which did not attempt to disguise its feeling that Walton was a slatternly poor relation.

Yet Walton was here before upstart Frinton. Once it was called Walton-le-Soken. *Soken*, or *soke*, denotes privilege: the privileges in this case enjoyed by the Dean and Chapter of St Paul's in London, who held the jurisdiction for this corner of Essex. But Walton shed its connection with privilege and became instead Walton-on-the-Naze. The Naze is not a river: it means a nose. The naze itself, at the very northern end of the town, with the sea to the east and a minor archipelago of islands out to the west – Horsey Island, Hedge-end Island, Skipper Island, with a forest of masts in a little harbour – is an enviable place to be on a fine April morning. Walton is walking its dogs, communing with neighbours, and waiting for the season to start. There are mazy paths through the dunes down to the water and looming above them a solemn mysterious tower, erected by the authorities of Trinity House in 1720, well before the Martello towers built to defy Napoleon began to appear on this coast.

That Walton is not what it was is true in two senses. There is less than there was, since some of it has been eaten up by the sea. The parish church vanished under the waves at the end of the eighteenth century. Even a sizeable chunk of the golf course of 1928, designed by the celebrated James Braid and claimed to be one of the most difficult links outside Scotland, has gone. There's a 'Save the Naze' campaign with a 'Save the Naze' shop in the town. Notices out on the Naze warn that cliffs are unstable and subject to slippage.

But it's not what it was in another way too. Since package tours were invented and people discovered Europe, a holiday at Walton no longer exerts the pull on East London that it did when the railway came here (insisting in the bossy way of the railways on calling the station Walton-on-Naze, dispensing with the definite article). Yet 'Walton is not what it was' is a lamentation that was probably heard in the town through much of the twentieth century. Meetings have been called from time to time to discuss its decline. An old Waltonian who had attended one recently told me the air had been full of nostalgia for the great days of the 1960s; yet he'd been to similar meetings in the 1960s when people reminisced in much the same terms about the glory days of the 1930s.

So perhaps it always had a feeling of second-best. Even the entrepreneur who began to develop it as a resort, a Colchester Quaker, Sargent Lay, chose Walton only because he could not get hold of the land he wanted at Clacton. In the late 1830s, a Hertfordshire man called John Warner tried to extend the town northwards on to the Naze, building a handsome terrace with a house for himself at the southernmost end. Thereafter Walton stagnated, until the arrival in the mid 1850s of an engineer called Peter Bruff, one of that bold and brave and frequently later bankrupt band, the British maritime entrepreneurs, who shored up the cliffs, built new terraces designed to attract the discerning gentry, created a pier, and brought in the railway. The railway determined a kind of coastal hierarchy – now overthrown. It ran to Walton; Clacton had to make do with a spur. If you wanted to get off at Frinton you had to ask. Then – the story of Walton's life – Bruff moved on to better things. He bought the land in Clacton that the Colchester Quaker had been unable to buy. The energy and ingenuity once devoted to Walton were Clacton's now.

The sands at Walton are beautiful. The pier is still there, sticking stubbornly far enough into the sea to service the boats that no longer generally call there. 'The Happiest Sound in All the World Is That of Children's Laughter' says a notice over the main doors. Another promises both an amusement arcade and 'Pirate Pete's soft play area' – a concept that must sound rather odd to students of piracy. The array of hotels that used to welcome visitors to Walton has been gravely reduced. Where once it ran to a branch of the International Stores, there are nowadays very few shops whose names you would have heard of; it's the kind of place where you are glad to see that they've got a Woolworth's. Walton has the unexcitingly restful air of a place where nothing much has been happening and nothing much is likely to happen. And it's full of reminders of its subordination to younger, more prosperous Frinton.

Where Walton is open to all, Frinton has gates. Coming from Walton, you rather expect that the gates will be stately, ceremonial affairs, of the kind which developers now attach to prestige private estates, designed for keeping the plebs at a decent distance. In fact it is merely the gates to the level crossing which cut Frinton off from the outside world. Yet even such mundane barriers help establish the feeling that Frinton and the people who live there are a cut above those on the rest of this coast. Almost since its beginnings Frinton has acquired a reputation for a toffee-nosed (or toffee-nazed) wish to exclude. There were ructions when it was first suggested that a fish and chip shop might open there: not only because fish and chips seemed to smack of trippers with downmarket accents in comic hats but because it was feared that fish and chips were the shape of hideously unFrintonian things to come. If Frinton were now to admit a fish and chip shop, it was tremblingly argued, then someone before very long might try to open a pub. And so they did – to make matters worse, adopting one of the town's oldest family stores. It is called the Lock and Barrel (what became of the Stock, I wonder?),

and a more demure and well-behaved pub I never saw in my life. Not that bad behaviour is entirely unknown in Frinton. A notice on the Spar supermarket announces: 'If there are any more than four youths outside this store, none of you will be served. Thank you.' That 'thank you' is very Frinton.

Frinton (I should say, Frinton-on-Sea; they are rather insistent on that), much more than Walton, was meticulously planned. It was mainly breathed into life by a man called Richard Powell Cooper, who took over from the Marine and General Land Building and Investment Company, which, having proposed the building of a new town, achieved next to nothing. The population of Frinton in 1891 was still only eighty-seven. Within five years Powell Cooper gave it a golf course, a tennis club and a grand hotel, and the beginnings of a main shopping street which became Connaught Avenue – the Bond Street of Frinton, as inhabitants liked to call it. The genteel aim of Powell Cooper and Frinton Urban Council, quite explicitly, was to create a place that was nothing at all like Clacton. In the 1920s a further large but wholly unClactonian extension was planned, but although building began it came to a halt and was then abandoned.

The curious thing about Frinton's long reputation for prim sobriety is that through the decade that followed it also became a fashionable centre for the not-always-morally-faultless rich and famous, drawn by the sea but also the sport – the golf and the tennis, especially. At the sea end of Connaught Avenue you come to the esplanade and the greensward, with its perfect lawns and decorous places to sit overlooking the sea. Somewhere near here, it is said, you could once see the Prince of Wales mowing his lawn. Mrs Simpson was reputed to turn up there too, when, as was so often the case, Mr Simpson was absent on business. You could even catch sight of Douglas Fairbanks, who used frequently to come to stay.

Walking down Winchester Road, Eton Road, Cambridge Road – they are largely interchangeable, but all full of houses which even those not imbued with the spirit of Frinton might secretly yearn to live in – it is easy to imagine Fairbanks vaulting off one of these balconies to pursue some low miscreant (from the Walton side of Pole Barn Lane, no doubt) along the greensward, past the tiny church of St Mary and up Connaught Avenue, just as far as the gates, but no further: for surely no great star of the movies would ever be caught running through Walton. In time, the Prince of Wales, having discovered France, ceased coming to Frinton, and the consequent loss of social cachet did for much of the rest of the town's celebrity trade. Here, too, once prized hotels, even the Grand, have shut their doors and undergone conversion into apartments. There is one house of cachet and distinction in Frinton, built by C. F. A. Voysey in the days of his eminence, on a sloping site at the corner of Second Avenue and Holland Road.

The old church – 'the smallest complete church in Essex', it announces – was superseded in 1929 by a bigger and less distinguished one just up the street. The writer Ursula Bloom is remembered in the churchyard. I have never knowingly read a book by Ursula Bloom but you have to admire a writer one of whose many pen names was Lozania Prole. Inside there are four stained glass windows created by William Morris to designs by Sir Edward Burne-Jones. The Ten Commandments, giving a list of things thou shall not do, are prominently displayed. You might have thought that none of that needed saying on this, the ultra-respectable side of that great social canyon, the Pole Barn Road; though I guess the adultery count in the days when celebrities flocked here used to be pretty high.

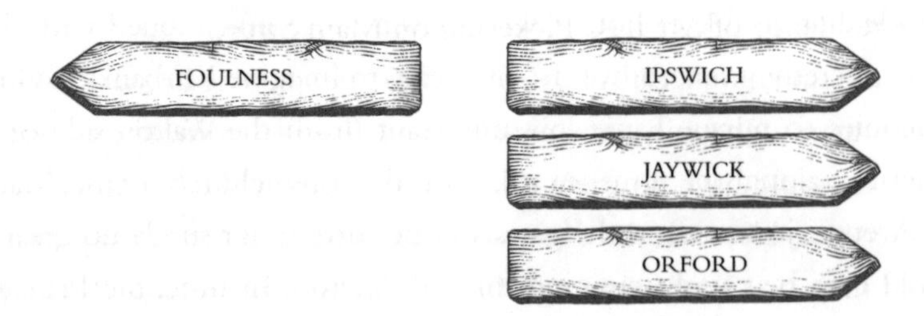

FRODSHAM

FRODSHAM, mkt.-town and par.… W. Cheshire, at confluence of rs. Weaver and Mersey, 10m. N.E. of Chester.

THE PARISH CHURCH OF St Laurence in Frodsham, Cheshire, Grade I listed, partly dating back to the Normans, is uphill and out of town. This explains why, in the centre of town, you will find what is now the Main Street Community Church but was formerly the Anglican church of St Dunstan; it belongs to that undervalued class of ecclesiastical architecture fondly known as 'tin tabernacles'.

This is not an unambiguous tin tabernacle now, but a hybrid, since like many of its breed it was subsequently extended and refurbished. What immediately catches your eye behind the main street market stalls is an enclosed porch stuck on to the front. At the back, a brick extension has almost doubled its size. But the essence of the community church is the item bought out of the manufacturer's catalogue in 1872. The belfry on top – which is one reason why it looks so immediately appealing – came from that era too.

Its introduction in this well-to-do market town was planned and executed with what now seems amazing speed. On 20 January 1872, the *Chester Chronicle* reported that plans were in hand for an 'iron church' – a more usual description than 'tin tabernacle' – in the centre of town. Mr Gwyer, the senior curate, had undertaken to raise the money, handsome promises had already come in, and the search had begun for a suitable site. On 9 March, the *Chronicle* was able to report that a piece of land had been found, adjoining the residence of Mr J. R. Pickering on Main Street.

By then, the tin church, capable of seating 250 people, was already awaiting delivery by the London firm (unhappily, unnamed by the *Chronicle*) from whose catalogue it had been plucked. It would have no pretensions to architectural beauty, the newspaper said, being as plain as possible, with the exception of a small turret to contain two bells. They hoped to hold their first service there in four weeks' time – on Easter Sunday. This they did, even though it wasn't quite finished, and so many came that some worshippers couldn't get in. And one of the two bells, it was discovered amid the celebrations, had disappeared from the turret; someone found it the following day, hanging in an oak tree some distance away.

The *Chronicle* was clear why the building was needed. Some worshippers had through age or infirmity or for some other reason been unable to manage the slog up the hill to St Laurence's. There may, however, have been a second imperative. On 20 January, the day the *Chronicle* announced the plans for St Dunstan's, the *Warrington Guardian* devoted two columns to the laying of a foundation stone for a Wesleyan chapel in the upper portion of Main Street. This was a much grander affair. A Runcorn man had put up £6,000, and the congregation had raised enough for a minister's house. Unlike plain-as-possible St Dunstan's, the chapel would be in the Gothic style with French ornamentation. Long speeches were made before tea was taken, including one from a visiting Methodist minister who insisted that their enterprise had not been conceived out of any sense of rivalry with neighbouring churches.

The fact that he found it necessary to make this point rather suggests that it had been, and the Runcorn benefactor had something of a reputation for this kind of ecclesiastical empire-building. It must surely have entered the heads of the progenitors of St Dunstan's that if the Wesleyans had a church at ground level, whereas Anglicans faced an ascent to St Laurence's, some of the faithful might possibly seep from one to the other.

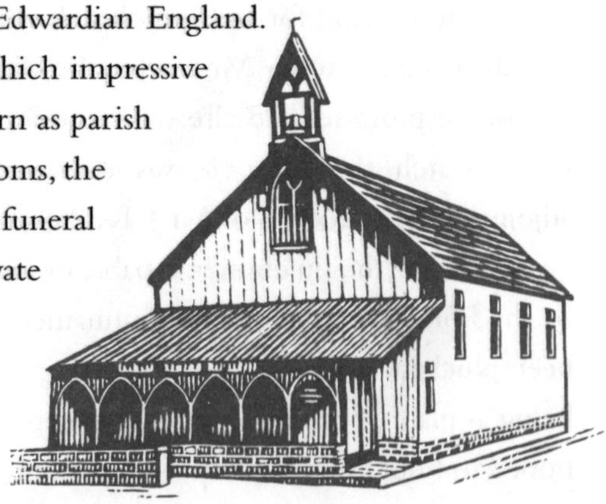

No one knows just how many tin tabernacles like Frodsham's sprang up in these islands in Victorian and Edwardian England. There must have been several hundred, of which impressive numbers survive. Some have since been reborn as parish halls, community centres, workshops, storerooms, the headquarters of all kinds of enterprise from funeral direction to local politics. Many are now private houses. They are copiously listed and pictured in a book called *Tin Tabernacles – Corrugated Iron Mission Halls, Churches & Chapels of Britain* by Ian Smith (who mildly exceeds his title, roping in some examples from places as distant as Iceland). Many have gone: some pulled down because the money had been found to build something grander, others removed in redevelopment schemes, still others destroyed by fire. Some have passed from mainstream churches to particular sects. Others have been guilefully adapted in the light of experience: one congregation in Suffolk grew so tired of the noise of the rain drumming on their corrugated iron roof that they had it removed and thatched it instead.

Some, when you set aside prejudice and give them a more than cursory glance, are quite beautiful, even more when you get inside them, as I did at the church of St Michael and All Angels, Hythe, which was built mainly for working-class families who had settled close to the Royal Military Canal, but was also a boon for those who could not face the stiff ascent (twenty-two steps) to Hythe's mighty parish church, St Leonard's. Church crawlers armed with standard reference books will rarely find them, but many are worth deviations on journeys: the one at Syre, on Strathnaver in Sunderland, for instance, a township which was the venue for the darkest events of the Highland clearances; or the Scottish Episcopal church of St Fillan, at Killin in Stirlingshire.

That Ian Smith's book specifies mission halls in its title is some indication of why this great outburst of cheap and immediate church-building occurred. Much of it was undertaken in the hope of bringing religion to communities springing up out of nowhere to serve new industrial enterprises, especially mining. The astonishing diversity of the Nonconformist movement, in which doctrinal differences frequently led to secessions and the start of new churches which needed homes of their own, was another boost for the off-the-shelf building industry, as was the impact of the great late nineteenth-century religious revivalists, most notably Evan Roberts of Loughor in Glamorgan. A table published in the *Western Mail* newspaper in January 1905, reprinted in Ian Smith's book, credits Roberts with over 70,000 conversions, with smaller communities like Abertillery Sixbells and Cwmtillery outscoring even Cardiff for conquests.

Manufacturers were ready and waiting. William Cooper of Old Kent Road, London SE, would do you a church 30 foot long and 20 foot wide for under £110 – or for only £77 10s if he merely delivered the pieces and the congregation erected it for themselves. J. C. Humphreys, based in the Borough, London SE, offered whole churches and chapels, some of them very substantial, but also slightly soiled galvanized corrugated iron roofing sheets which any labourer could easily fix.

These buildings might be basic – no pretensions to architectural beauty, as the *Chronicle* said of Frodsham – but could still be richly ornamented and glorified. A tin tabernacle built for their private use by the Pears family at Windlesham, Surrey, later part of a school, has stained glass windows one of which is based on Holman Hunt's *Light of the World*. Frodsham's church, which the Frodsham Evangelical Fellowship rescued from years of disuse and reopened in the early 1980s, has the unusual distinction of having been moved ten feet to the left, on rollers, because it was blocking the way to land on which developers wished to build houses. Since this land belonged to the church, the proceeds helped to pay for the church's extension.

The most beautiful of all the unconventional churches I saw on my travels, though, is not in Smith's book, presumably because it doesn't entirely fall under his remit. It stands at a place called Lambholm, across the bridge from the mainland on the road to South Ronaldsay, close to the famous wartime construction known as the Churchill Barrier – a line of concrete blocks designed to stop the entrance to Scapa Flow, with a causeway built across it. The Germans had penetrated the previous line of defence and sunk the *Royal Oak*, with the loss of more than 800 lives. The church was made by Italian prisoners of war out of two Nissen huts, with a graceful façade added across the front, under the direction of a man called Domenico Chiocchetti, who came back to be honoured by Orkney in 1960.

Nissen huts are named after a Major, later Colonel, Nissen, who devised them in 1916 in one of those brilliant pieces of wartime improvisation which carry over into the subsequent peace. They were designed to be bleakly practical, devoid of any attempt at architectural pretension, which is usually how you see them today, often as blots on a landscape. Their military progenitor could surely never have envisaged his humble invention having some part to play in anything as gorgeous as this.

A B C D

E F G H

I J K L

M N O P

Q R S T

U V W X Y Z

GATTON

GATTON, par. and ham., mid. Surrey, 2½m. NE. of Reigate...
In vicinity of ham. are the seats of G. Lodge, G. Park
and Upper G. Park.

AT THE HEART OF the former borough of Gatton, on the slopes of the North Downs, near Reigate, stands Gatton town hall. Around it are the buildings of the Royal Alexandra and Albert School, established in 1864 for the benefit of orphans but now classified as a voluntary aided comprehensive school for pupils aged between seven and sixteen, many of whom are boarders. The most important of these surrounding buildings is what has survived of a big house called Gatton Park, most of which was destroyed by fire in 1934. Its replacement is sadly drab, but, tacked on to the front is the great pillared portico, dating from 1891, of the previous house.

I first went to Gatton on the orders of the great Ian Nairn, who listed it in his *Sunday Times* column as one of the two dozen places around London which one had an absolute duty to rush off and look at. The Surrey volume of Pevsner's Buildings of England series was largely written by Nairn, and the entry on Gatton is unmistakably his. 'The portico', he says, 'consists of ten Corinthian columns wrapped around a projecting wing in temple fashion with a pediment above; the blank walls behind retain sober classical detail. The proportions are superb and the execution exquisite – in fact this is the best example in the country, though seventy years late, of what might be called Canova architecture, strictly classical forms handled with humanitarian C19 sensibility.'

Nearby is the church of St Andrew, kept locked, quite understandably, given the treasures inside it, which were brought home by Lord Monson, owner of Gatton Park, from his travels in France, Flanders and Germany in the 1830s. The Monsons later sold the place to the Colmans, makers of mustard: Sir Jeremiah Colman junior laid the foundations of the Gatton Park portico in 1891. The parklands around the estate had fallen on bad days, but are gradually being reclaimed and the grounds are now open on the first

Sunday of every month from February to October. There are regular tours of the property, on a Sunday, conducted by the volunteers who work on the project.

The particular joy of Gatton, though, is the town hall, erected in the mid eighteenth century and drastically different from almost any other town hall one has ever seen. It has none of the usual paraphernalia of civic self-celebration, having no walls, only steel columns at its corners, and is at most about 15 feet high. It was put there because the law required it. Until the Reform Act of 1832, Gatton was one of the rottenest of all rotten boroughs, perhaps third on a list headed by Old Sarum in Wiltshire, which in 1831 had just seven electors who returned two MPs. Gatton in its last days had twenty-three voters, who likewise sent two Members to Parliament, though in 1542, it's recorded, the electorate numbered just one. While happy with those arrangements, the framers of electoral law required that elections should be conducted in a suitable public place and not in someone's backyard. If you had MPs, you had to have a town hall in which they could be elected, which is why this strange little edifice was put up in Gatton.

In this it was not entirely alone. I came across another such building in Newport, a northern extension of Launceston in Cornwall. Built in 1829, only three years before Newport was disenfranchised, this was named the Temple of the Winds, but was customarily referred to as Newport town hall. Newport's brace of MPs had been chosen on this spot for 300 years; it was also used as a base for proclamations affecting monarchs, on such occasions as their jubilees or their deaths.

When I visited Newport there was nothing to see inside the town hall but an empty half-bottle of Stella. Gatton's town hall does better than that. It contains an urn with a grandiose, and considering the facts of the matter, wonderfully cynical inscription which Nairn includes in his book and translates as follows: 'When the lots have been drawn, the urn remains/ Let the well-being of the people be the supreme law/ The place of assembly of Gatton 1746/ Let evil deception be absent.' As they drew up their election returns, ready to announce them in this distinguished oddity, those who fixed them no doubt used to declare (as I like to think, over several large libations of port): 'The people of Gatton have spoken!' All twenty-three of them. Or in 1542, of course, all one.

GIPTON

GIPTON, ham., 2m. N of Leeds, W.R. Yorks.

BARTHOLOMEW CALLS IT A hamlet. His intelligence service has failed him here. By 1943 Gipton had long since ceased to be a hamlet on the fringes of the city and had become a pioneering council housing estate. For a while, it was the pride of the city of Leeds. Less so thereafter.

Leeds in the 1940s and 1950s, when my family moved there, was a great northern city. But the Leeds of those days is hardly recognizable now. The centre is seething, suppurating with money, bursting with stylish restaurants and bars and swish hotels. The streets on the city side of the river, which used to be dejected and dirty, have become a place to be seen in. Though it lacks one or two essential elements – notably, these past few seasons, a successful football team – it has the feel now of a great European city. That ought, on some convenient assumptions, to mean prosperity for all. The riches that accrue at the centre, that swell the pocket and purse of the opulent, we were constantly told in the heyday of Thatcherism, will in time trickle down to the whole community.

The enrichment of the richest duly took place. But where are the signs of trickle-down on the Gipton estate? On Sunday afternoons, making family visits, we used to catch the number 38 bus from Moortown in the north of the city to Whitkirk in the east on a route which took us through the Gipton estate. I found it depressing then. In the context of the transformation of living standards in the fifty years since, Gipton, together with the Seacroft estate created alongside it after the war, seems even more depressing in 2007. Two miles away, the tills have never been busier and the wine flows like water, but these two places fall in the bottom 3 per cent on the national index of deprivation. As an audit commissioned by Leeds Corporation concludes, the gap between the haves and the have-nots in the city grows ever wider. That's a process that

classically breeds resentment, disillusion, sometimes desperation, sometimes drugs and crime.

And yet there's abundant evidence as you walk around Gipton that it was created with the very best of intentions, as a garden city for families who had previously lived in such squalid slums that the council offered a free disinfection service for such furniture as they had brought with them. This was, as the *Manchester Guardian* reported, 'the most radical programme of slum clearance... that any housing committee in the country has so far prepared'. That it happened was due above all to two factors: Labour's victory in the local elections in November 1933; and the presence in the ranks of the new governing party of an Anglican priest from the East End of London, Charles Jenkinson, who established himself over the next few years as the most powerful and influential force in public housing anywhere in the land.

In his own childhood Jenkinson was forced to live with his grandmother because there was no room for him at home. For a time he acted as secretary to the 'red priest' of Thaxted, Conrad Noel, while campaigning for better conditions for agricultural workers. Although his lack of anything more than an elementary education was against him, he resolved to become a priest. Having served as a medical orderly in the First World War, he was given a place at Cambridge and went on to Ripon Hall, Oxford, and in 1923 he was ordained. He started as a curate in Barking. When the time came to have his own living, he asked for somewhere tough. He got his wish: he was sent to Holbeck, Leeds.

Housing conditions in Leeds were notorious. Some 30 per cent of the population, the Medical Officer of Health had testified, were living in housing unfit for human habitation. The only solution, said George Bernard Shaw, was to blow the whole place up. What made it worse was the very high proportion of back to back houses, some 72,000 across the city, which experts had long condemned as a serious health risk. The only way to remedy that, Jenkinson insisted, was through wholesale municipal action, and the only way to propel the municipality into action was to get on to the council and clamour for it. Which he did. As a councillor, it was he, along with allies from the churches across the city, who badgered the council into the revolutionary step of setting up a housing committee; and when that committee attempted to move with caution he attacked it with his usual vigour and bluntness. He was always better, even his friends contended, at talking than listening.

Jenkinson took on the chairmanship of the committee and summoning to his side a newly appointed director of housing from Manchester, R. H. Livett, went into battle. His ambitions for those he was going to rescue from the slums of the city had an echo about them of Baron Haussmann's great replanning of Paris. He wanted things done in style. The houses should be solidly built and given not just gardens but plenty of green space around them, with as many trees as there were houses. Wide boulevards cut through the new estate – some so wide as to look almost grotesque today, but that was to accommodate reservation space for the city's trams to speed through the middle.

The houses, Jenkinson said, must not be uniform: they would vary in size and style to reflect the socially mixed population he hoped to bring into Gipton. They would even include, one local newspaper wonderingly noted, a new kind of accommodation for municipal dwellings in Leeds, the one-bedroom flat. The main shopping centre at Coldcotes Circus would have forty shops, with subsidiary shopping parades scattered around the estate. Churches would be created, and schools with generous playing fields. He wanted in time to see a sports stadium built on York Road, on the edge of the Gipton estate. They should build it, he said, bigger than Wembley.

And no time should be wasted in bringing this brave new world into being: he wanted it all completed within two years. There was often fierce opposition and there were practical problems, which he underestimated. Some tenants were reluctant to go; the thought of losing familiar places and familiar faces filled them with apprehension. (Today's replanners of Gipton have found that too.) The first contractor went bankrupt. Yet Jenkinson was not be thwarted – even when it meant, as it eventually did, giving up his parish. The first house, allotted to Mrs and Mrs Frederick Jepson, formerly of Waterloo Place, York Road, was handed over on the first day of January 1935, fourteen months after the city council voted to go ahead with the project.

But his vision proved to be too euphoric. Fewer than half the shops planned for Coldcotes Circus ever appeared. There was never the promised profusion of trees. Not every tenant relocated from the city's slums settled into to their new surroundings as happily as their benefactors had wished. And the problems that were always bound to develop were compounded when, again for the best possible reasons, the city went on to build council estate after council estate across the east side of Leeds: Gipton, Halton Moor, Osmondthorpe, Seacroft, Whinmoor – all, despite Jenkinson's founding intentions, socially monolithic and destined for trouble.

What you sense for yourself in the streets is confirmed by statistics. Those the city keeps for the Gipton estate are marked by high levels of benefit dependency, low educational qualifications and minimal skills, high unemployment, low pay and deadbeat jobs for those who do find work; also, high levels of crime, especially burglary. One can now get such figures broken down to specific sectors, even specific streets, and the evidence shows that one section of the Gipton estate, behind the Amberton shopping parade, was rated, in the latest figures I saw, the nineteenth worst for crime anywhere in the country.

For all the hopes with which the estate was built, the standards of housing are often poor, made far worse in some cases by such persistent trashing – sometimes by vandals, quite often by tenants – that demolition becomes the only solution. It's notable, though, that the worst of the lot tend to be those that were built post-war; and that's where the present programme of clearance in Gipton and Seacroft is heavily concentrated.

If you want to see why, drive into the Seacroft estate down South Parkway – how alluring that name was designed to make it sound – and look at the wretched remnants of 1960s and 70s housing. Would Jenkinson have permitted it such shoddiness? These places looks almost as if they were built to be slums. This was housing for people who couldn't hope to do better, whose chances of ever buying a home of their own, as the price of houses exploded, would reduce from initially meagre to effectively nil: it is residual housing, obliterating all hope of establishing a socially mixed community. And to say that middle-class families were needed is not to elevate the needs of the middle class over the rest. Socially balanced housing makes for socially balanced communities. It gives greater hope to the schools. Good communities, as everyone knows, need good schools; yet equally, good schools need good communities, otherwise the best teachers will depart, and the children they leave behind will have even less chance in life than before.

If you waited for trickle-down to solve the problems of Gipton and other creations like it, you would wait for ever. Indeed, as one of the planners bitterly notes, the Thatcher years, which helped make the city richer, had quite the reverse effect on places like these. 'If you put three million out of work in eighteen months,' he says, 'what else would you expect?' In fact, the necessary work of repair and rehabilitation and some restoration of hope is left to public authorities, just as it was in Jenkinson's day. The prosperity of the centre will help pay for it, but how you deploy resources depends first on the strategic priorities that you set, and then above all on patience. It will take at least half a decade, the planners say, and possibly a whole one, before anyone can hope to use words like 'flourishing'about these estates.

Even so there are plenty of signs as you drive through Gipton and Seacroft that improvement is under way. Close to the Amberton shopping parade, in a sector that's an entire anthology of neglect – all potholed roads and crumbling pavements and boarded-up houses and derelict overgrown patches where houses have already been razed – a new enclave is taking shape, designed to produce a mix of social and paid-for, but 'affordable' housing, through devices such as shared equity with a target average price of £120,000. Six sites on the Gipton estate and two on the Seacroft were earmarked in the spring of 2007 for this treatment. Ideally, these places will begin to create a much richer social and cultural mix than exists on the estates today. One striking indication of that, in a multi-ethnic city, is the very low proportion of people in these estates from the ethnic minorities who nowadays throng the streets of Victorian suburbs next door such as Harehills.

Housing is only a part of it. The shopping centres of these estates are drab and inadequate. There's a Lidl supermarket close to the Ambertons, and Coldcotes Circus has a Co-op, and there's a decent parade of small shops on South Parkway, but the place badly needs a big supermarket that is more its own than the Asda out on the bypass, and, perhaps even more, the sort of lively local parades which not only fill shopping baskets but generate gossip and so companionship. Money, big money, scarce money, will have to be spent on schools, on social centres, on all kinds of health provision, and on new roads to enable people from these estates to get to those sectors of Leeds where the jobs are.

It is sad, but inescapably true – it has always been sad but inescapably true – that some communities reach a pitch of dejection from which they can never recover. Some of the old mining villages not so far away from Gipton are testimony to that. The vast sums expended to rescue places like Grimethorpe near Barnsley have failed to redeem their desperate sense of failure. What the next ten years will make of the Gipton and Seacroft estates, and Halton Moor, Whinmoor and Osmondthorpe too, is anyone's guess. If it all works, it will, as in Jenkinson's day, be because the resolution was there and the money was found to propel it. Anyone who – should that happy outcome occur – stands outside the smart shops of the Amberton shopping parade, and proudly proclaims, 'There you are, we told you, trickle-down works!' will deserve to be knocked on the head. If anyone then still resorts to that kind of practice in Gipton.

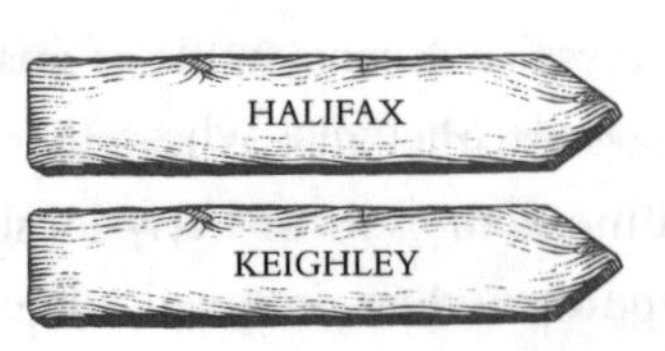

GOYT

GOYT r., Derbyshire and Cheshire. It rises in Derby and for some distance forms the boundary between the 2 cos., and flows W. to the Mersey at Stockport.

IT WAS NOT BARTHOLOMEW'S job to evoke and extol the sublime, but had that been so he would surely have furnished a richer commendation than this one of the landscape through which the Goyt flows on its journey to ominous Stockport. The Goyt valley lies close to the boundary of these two counties. You can reach it on weekdays on a byway which turns north from the twisting and hazardous road from Macclesfield to Buxton, just beyond a pub called the Cat and Fiddle, which Bartholomew says is reputed to be the highest licensed house in the country, though nowadays this accolade has passed to the Tan Hill Inn in Swaledale. On Sundays and Bank Holidays when the crowds are out and the road to the Cat and Fiddle is swarming with motorbikes, this byway is closed, and a long, though entertaining, diversion is necessary. Go early on a weekday morning, as I did on a brilliant sunny day in early July, and you may even get the luxurious sense of having it all to yourself.

In the heart of this valley under the wooded hills are two reservoirs, the Fernilee and its later neighbour the Errwood. Beneath their waters lie the remains of the hamlet of Goyts Bridge, one of a melancholy collection of villages across the country sacrificed over the years to meet the demands of thirsty cities. What people remembered when it was gone was its bridge and its stepping stones, but once there was a gunpowder factory here, where in 1909 three people died in an explosion.

What was lost on the ground, when these reservoirs were built to satisfy the people of Stockport, was modest compared with the toll that was taken by projects like Ladybower, outside Sheffield, where the villages of Derwent and Ashopton were lost, complete with a church whose spire used to re-emerge above the waters in times of drought. Young men were drowned while trying to swim to the spire, which had to be demolished to remove the temptation. The creation of Rutland Water, west of Stamford, obliterated a village called Nether Hambleton and most of Middle Hambleton and Normanton, though Normanton church was saved, and part of it has become a museum.

Such losses ought not to be too much mourned: the reservoirs for which they made room were overwhelmingly necessary, and the new landscapes that they created are often made more beautiful by the presence of water than they were before. But it wasn't only those places that disappeared under the water that they obliterated. Communities on the hills above them had to go too, for fear that they might pollute the water below. There's a poignant reminder of that in the woods above these Goyt Valley reservoirs, where amid the rhododendrons and azaleas for which they were famous, you may come across the remnants of Errwood Hall, once the home of the mighty Manchester mill-owning family who began as the Grimshaws but later celebrated their eminence by adding an E at the end. Stockport's chances of getting the land it needed may have been eased by the circumstance that the last of the Grimshawes had ceased to live in the hall in 1930.

In the North West Film Archive at Manchester Metropolitan University there's an amateur film showing some of what was submerged after Alderman Padmore of Stockport pressed the button which detonated the explosion to begin the construction process. Picturesque scenes follow, in which, led by the mayor (Councillor Penny) sporting his ceremonial chain, Stockport councillors, all hatted and scarved on a February day in 1932, arrive to inspect their council's grand creation, with a small contingent of the general public allowed to observe at a respectful distance. A light railway has been built, on which trains manoeuvre; a shepherd leads his incongruous flock through the devastation; a house still awaiting extinction is seen marooned amidst the workings. But the loss of Errwood Hall and its surrounding estate goes unrecorded.

There's a path from the Errwood car park which leads you up the hillside to a point where a signpost indicates a route to the hall; or perhaps better still, there's a pillared gateway on the right of the path which will take you there more directly. There is just enough left of the walls and stone floors and arches and crumbling steps to testify to its solid northern grandeur, reflecting the wealth and eminence of a family whose properties included not only the family mansion but farms and workers' houses and even a private coal mine. Standing here in the stillness it is easy to imagine how what is now a grassy track was once the grand drive to the principal door down which generations of Grimshaws and Grimshawes came happily home in appropriate style and comfort from their serious business enterprises in cities at home and abroad. Perhaps the most evocative spot on this hillside is the private cemetery where the Grimshaws and the closest of their servants were buried. Elizabeth Ann Bradock, died 1903, at nineteen. John Butler, for sixteen years the friend and faithful servant of Samuel Grimshaw, and captain of the yacht *Mariquita*, the family's boat. Irma Niorte, born in Bayonne, France, died at Errwood in 1882, aged twenty-seven: a governess for the Grimshawe children, perhaps.

The family had established a private school, to which they brought Dolores de Bergin, the daughter of an aristocratic Spanish family. When she died, at Lourdes in 1889, they built a shrine to her, close to the hall. And here, at the top of the burial ground, are Samuel himself, who died in 1883, and Jessie Mary Magdalen, his wife, who died ten years later; also – his name inscribed on the plinth – their little son Arthur, 'died in infancy'. It's a touching spot, on the top of a hill, where the only sounds to be heard are birdsong and the bubbling of a stream; so tranquil that you might almost imagine that what the hymnodist calls the crowded clangour of cities belonged to another world. And though much of it is the property nowadays of North West Water, one of those powerful companies which dominate everyday life quite as much as the Grimshaws once did, it is part of the Peak District National Park, and ours to wander in wherever and whenever we wish. The Grimshaws and Grimshawes had much to be grateful for; but so, here and now, do we.

GRIMSTHORPE

GRIMSTHORPE, ham., S. Lincolnshire, 3½m. NW. of Bourn… in vicinity is G. Castle, seat of the Earl of Ancaster.

HALFWAY BETWEEN STAMFORD AND Grantham on the A1 there's a turning eastwards for Bourne. If you take this road, shunning your chance to turn left for Scotland (one of four settlements of this name known to Bartholomew, which he lists ahead of the name of his native country) and persist for eight miles or so, you will see a signpost for Grimsthorpe Castle; and there, at the end of a long green drive is what Simon Jenkins, in his *England's Thousand Best Houses*, picks out as 'one of the great houses of England'.

It's all the better for being mildly eccentric. The Palladian front elevation, by Vanbrugh, is so extravagantly over-the-top that the rest of the building, a cheerful assemblage of different styles which, had Vanbrugh lived, he might have gone on to replace, comes as something of a relief. It incorporates King John's Tower, named after this much maligned monarch as his reward for permitting Gilbert de Gant, Earl of Lincoln, to build it, and finds a continuing use for some of the remnants of the Cistercian monastery called Vallis Dei – the valley of God – that was still in business here until another imperious king had it liquidated. The ancillary buildings include an orangerie to have tea in, and an adventure playground which is said to be a whole lot of fun, though I haven't tried it myself. The entire place is set in grounds so large you could build a sizeable town in them. There is also a lake, in whose beautiful, wide, peaceful, apparently unthreatening waters around which Grimsthorpe's visitors stroll in the sun, there drowned on 5 August 1778 one of the great hopes of English music.

Thomas Linley junior came from a musical family. His father, the son of a carpenter, was a composer and musical director. His sisters, Elizabeth Ann, Mary and Maria, were singers and actresses; Elizabeth, already a star at fourteen and repeatedly

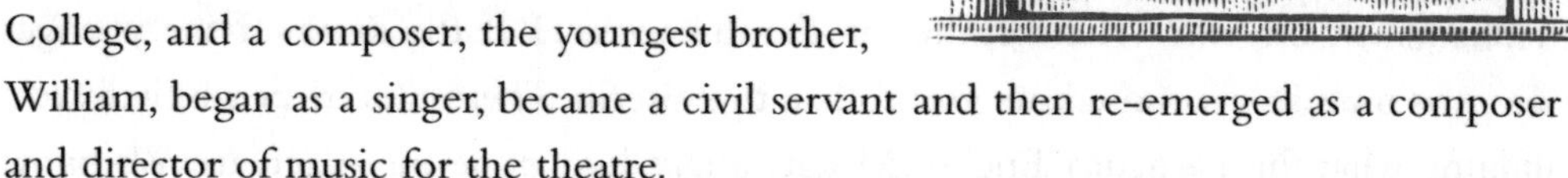

painted from that time on by Thomas Gainsborough (one of these portraits hangs in the Dulwich Gallery, London), eloped with the playwright Richard Brinsley Sheridan, and subsequently married him: not a good idea. Both Thomas Linleys, father and son, worked with Sheridan, supplying music for his play *The Duenna* and for his production of Shakespeare's *The Tempest*. Another brother, Samuel, was an accomplished oboist, but gave up music on deciding to join the Navy; yet another, Ozias, was organ fellow of Dulwich College, and a composer; the youngest brother, William, began as a singer, became a civil servant and then re-emerged as a composer and director of music for the theatre.

The younger Thomas outstripped them all. At the age of twelve he was sent to Italy to study with Pietro Nardini, a violinist and composer who had been a pupil of Tartini's. His fellow students included Mozart, who was four months older, and who said after Linley's death that his friend had been a true genius who, had he lived, would have become one of the great ornaments of the musical world. Inevitably, Linley would come to be described as England's Mozart, though that accolade was perhaps too often bestowed on musicians who showed exceptional talent early in life, since, like William Crotch, whom we will encounter in Norwich, they did not always maintain it. But Charles Burney, who saw them together in Italy, said Linley and Mozart were talked of in the same breath as the most promising geniuses of the age. There's enough of Linley's music on disc – some of it, poignantly, evoking fierce storms at sea – to suggest that he might in time have taken his place in the emaciated ranks of truly great English composers. He too was painted by Gainsborough, on three occasions; one portrait is at Dulwich.

The circumstances of his death are unclear. He was staying at Grimsthorpe Castle on a family holiday. He and others took a boat on to the lake; the boat, for some reason, capsized. The Annual Register for the year recorded: 'Mr Thomas Linley, a celebrated performer upon the violin, and eldest son of Mr Linley, one of the proprietors of Drury-lane Theatre, fell out of a boat into a lake belonging to his Grace the Duke of Ancaster, at Grimsthorpe in Lincolnshire, and was unfortunately drowned. He remained under water full forty minutes, so that every effort made to restore him to life proved ineffectual.' There is no suggestion that weather was unwontedly wild or that the party were risking their lives by venturing out in it. He was twenty-two. He was buried in the churchyard at Edenham, a little way south on the road to Bourne, where a plaque commemorates him as 'composer, violinist and childhood friend of Mozart, drowned at Grimsthorpe Castle and laid to rest in this church'.

This was only the first of a series of tragedies to afflict the family. His three sisters all died of consumption between 1784 and 1792, and Samuel followed in 1795. Some accounts say he drowned, like his brother, though others attribute his death to pleurisy. Their father, the older Thomas, died in the same year. But the death of the younger Thomas must be accounted the greater loss to posterity. There is no dependable way of judging what this particular English Mozart might have gone on to achieve. We know what Beethoven would have left us had he died at thirty-five like Mozart or at thirty-one like Schubert. But there's no way of judging what Mozart or Schubert might have bequeathed had they survived, like ageing, crotchety, deaf, but still gloriously productive Beethoven, who lived to be fifty-six.

Maybe, in terms of reputation, it helps sometimes to die young, as Linley did, and as did the brilliant young Spaniard, Juan Crisóstomo de Arriaga, who died in 1826. He was even younger than Linley – not yet twenty. But *The New Grove Dictionary of Music and Musicians*, the nearest thing we have in this context to biblical authority, says that Thomas's early death 'was one of the greatest losses that English music has suffered'. In that light, the lovely tranquil lake in the grounds of Grimsthorpe Castle on a sunny afternoon in late April suddenly looks a lot less benign.

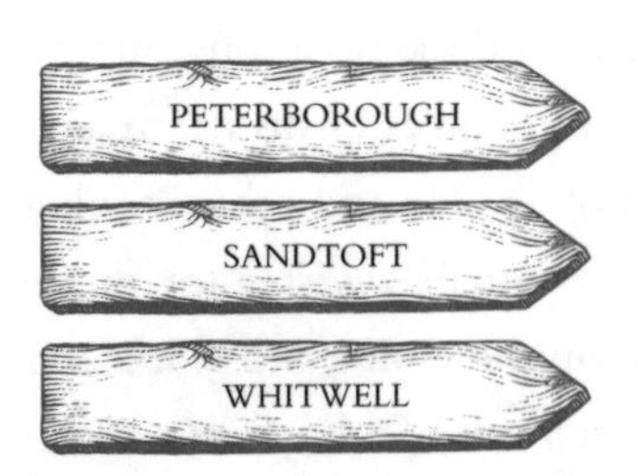

A B C D

E F G H

I J K L

M N O P

Q R S T

U V W XYZ

HALIFAX

HALIFAX, parl. and co. bor. and par., N. div. W.R. Yorks…
on r. Hebble, near its confluence with the Calder…
the town is a centre of the woollen and worsted mfrs.

FROM HULL, HELL AND Halifax, it used to be prayed, Good Lord, deliver us. Well, Hell, certainly, and Hull here and there quite possibly – but why Halifax? In most respects, this is a very agreeable place, a town where you're always conscious of the countryside close at hand, with a spectacular view as you leave the station of high hills and crags and woods and meadowland, interspersed with houses and one dramatic church. If this was a stage set, the audience would applaud when the curtain went up. And the views from the top looking down over the town are no less exciting. The view from Beacon Hill, Ian Nairn declared in one of his TV travelogues, was one of the most dramatic anywhere in Britain. A place full of character and hidden beauty, said John Betjeman, one whose skyline, all churches and chapels and mills and workshops, was never to be forgotten. I remember the first time I saw it: at night, in wartime, on an apprehensive railway journey from Wigan to Leeds, the blackout darkness redeemed by the lights of the trams as they sailed over the hills. 'Looks best when it's dark' some sceptic in Leeds remarked. A calumny, that; but only one of many carelessly inflicted on Halifax.

There's a striking town hall, by Charles Barry, who rebuilt the Palace of Westminster, and in Commercial Street, a cluster of exuberant, self-confident banks and views of mills and viaducts and a bridge commended by Pevsner as a twentieth-century triumph to rank with the Piece Hall, which to me is the best of Halifax: a square, and ranged around it more than 300 rooms where merchants used to sell cloth pieces handwoven in homes in the Calder Valley. Because it is on a slope, the top side of the square has two storeys, the bottom side three, and the two at the sides change from two to three halfway down. The sale of pieces ceased long ago. The place became a fruit and vegetable market, which also closed down, in 1973. Three years later it reopened with the rooms now occupied by shops and cafés and galleries and an information centre. It is all – the odd garish banner aside – extremely elegant and composed. Were this place in some favourite town in the south of England, thousands of tourists would come here, exclaiming 'oh, wow' as they captured it on their digital cameras. But such things rarely happen in Halifax.

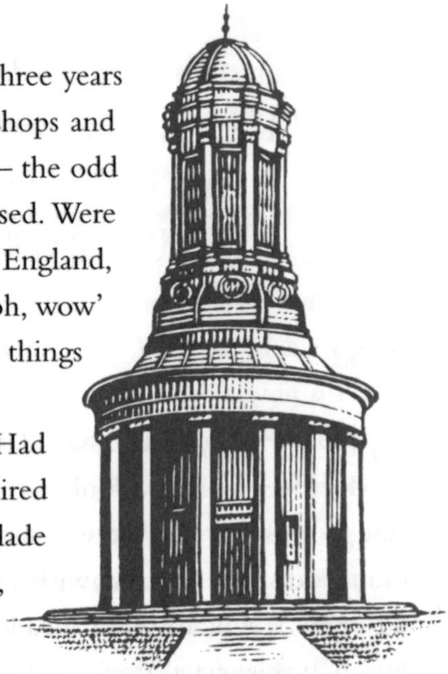

It might have had even more to boast about. Had things worked out differently, it might even have aspired to the status of a site of world importance – an accolade bestowed on Saltaire, 12 miles away to the north-east, beyond Bradford. Saltaire was the creation of the Victorian industrialist and philanthropist Titus Salt, who built a mighty mill, model houses to accommodate his workforce, imposing public halls, and a stately and opulent church for his Nonconformist fellow religionists. Salt was a benevolent despot: sometimes the benevolence was more to the fore, and sometimes the despotism. People who lived there had to subscribe to Salt's rules. 'No pawnshops, no pubs' says Pevsner at the end of his account of Saltaire. When I was there, a bar was about to open to which the owners had given the impertinent name: Don't Tell Titus.

Saltaire, conveniently pitched alongside the canal and later the railway, was the model which others followed. Yet a Halifax man called Colonel Edward Akroyd had the same notion before Titus Salt. A little way south of the centre of Halifax you can find a village called Copley. What is now the main part of Copley is strung along the Wakefield road on the Halifax side of the Calder and Hebble Navigation Canal. Akroyd's Copley, begun at the end of the 1840s, is down the hill, over the canal and then under the railway. There are two streets of Akroyd's houses, terraced, with a corner shop still trading on the corner of one of them; solid, decent houses, suggesting a kindly concern for his employees, but some of them built back to back, so that all but the front of one's house shared walls with the neighbours, with only vestigial front gardens and of course none at all at the back. This was a practice common in places like Leeds where the urgent imperious demands of new industry required houses to be run up quickly and cheaply, but reformers, including official committees concerned with public health, were already saying they ought to be banned.

The original estate at Copley comprised some 130 dwellings. Additional houses have been tacked on since Akroyd's day, but sympathetically. Also here is the playing field of the Old Rishworthians rugby club, and over the river, the church of St Stephen, built for Akroyd by W. H. Crossland, an architect who often crops up in these parts. The church is now closed, though it sometimes reopens for the funerals of old inhabitants.

Colonel Akroyd's motive for building these houses was a mix of generosity and self-interest. He was shocked and alarmed by rioting that broke out in the town in 1842, two years before he started work on his mill, and saw it as a reflection of the circumstances in which poor families had to live. Give them something better and discontent might be allayed. Akroyd's mill at Copley was a modest affair, set against Salt's, which matches the length of St Paul's Cathedral, and he had far fewer employees to build for. Had Copley been created on a bigger scale it would surely be better recognized now as Saltaire's precursor.

Later, he did indeed build on a larger scale, near his mill at Haley Hill, on the road from Halifax out to Queensbury. This second new community, which he named after himself – Akroydon, pronounced with a long A, as in A-team – is nowhere near the scale of Saltaire but is much more grandly ambitious than Copley. There's a square as its focal point with houses ranged around it and at the centre, what is described as 'a monument of Christian reverence for the emblem of the Cross and of loyalty to our sovereign lady Queen Victoria by Edward Akroyd, the founder of Akroydon, MDCCCLXXV, Fear God, honour the King'. Like Salt's at Saltaire, the houses here are graduated, some notably grander than others, with the initials of Akroyd's first householders inscribed over the most notable doors. As at Copley, he is mean with green space; not much at the front, little or nothing at all at the back – though some of the houses have been blessed with detached gardens and as the streets descend to the valley, there's a spread of allotments.

Akroyd clearly set out to be a model employer. He not only built well for his workers, he also equipped his new settlement with a school, shops, societies and sports clubs and burial and clothing funds; he helped those with redundant skills to retrain; he encouraged them to provide for old age, establishing the institution which became, and remained until pennies were almost irrelevant, the Yorkshire Penny Bank.

Back up the slope on the main road is Akroyd's own house, Bankfield, originally quite a modest affair, but aggrandized over the years: it now houses a museum of textile and regimental history, with an Akroyd Library attached – which turns out to be a standard branch library which, sadly, has no section devoted to Akroyd. He bought it in 1838 and four years later, during the riots which had moved him to start work on Copley, had to defend it against Chartist attack.

Below Bankfield, towards the foot of the hill down to Halifax, is his church, All Souls – built by Sir George Gilbert Scott, no less, who is said to have thought it the best of his churches. Outside is a statue of Akroyd, elegant, bearded, a scroll clutched in one hand, a discarded cloak at his feet. There are also emblematic scenes, disappointingly unexplained, in one of which someone who may or may not be Akroyd stands on a cart, looking as though he's delivering some kind of lecture. The church was closed for repairs when I was there. The Victorian Society was so concerned about its future that it put All Souls on the cover of its November 2007 magazine, noting that the Churches Conservation Trust was having to deal with the 'inexorable destruction' caused by Gilbert Scott's practice of alternating chemically incompatible substances, sandstone and limestone.

The great manufacturing families of Halifax were friends, but rivals. The Crossleys, who built Clough Mills, once a major carpet manufacturing centre, now rescued from debilitation and transformed into a complex for business, the arts and education, developed their own model settlement at West Hill Park. Francis Crossley also created a People's Park, designed by Joseph Paxton. Eager in the mid 1850s to give Halifax a new town hall to match its high aspirations, the Crossleys commissioned a design from the busy Bradford architects Lockwood and Mawson. Colonel Akroyd retaliated with a rival proposal, based on plans by George Gilbert Scott. A third contender appeared in the form of the borough engineer, but his scheme was thought inadequate. 'He is not a great architect,' the *Halifax Guardian* cruelly commented. 'If he were, he would not be the borough engineer and surveyor for the town of Halifax.'

The corporation committee charged with making the choice turned the problem over to Charles Barry, who, having rejected all three contenders, graciously agreed to take on the job himself, though he died a year later leaving his son E. M. Barry to finish the job. As for Akroyd, nobody could pretend that his legacy matches Salt's. He was a competent businessman, though his generosity reduced him in the end to near poverty: he died in November 1897 at St Leonard's in Sussex where he'd been living with only one valet for company. There was never a visionary moment in Akroyd's life to match that in Salt's when, visiting Liverpool, he came across unwanted stocks of alpaca, bought the lot, and began a whole new trend in the wool manufacturing industry. Akroyd's mills were never as majestic as Salt's and, in present-day terms, he hasn't got David Hockney, the star attraction nowadays of Saltaire. Yet he was a pioneer; a progenitor, at modest Copley, of the movement that led through Saltaire and Bournville and Port Sunlight to Ebenezer Howard's garden city at Letchworth. And Halifax may also pride itself on this: Salt, with the whole of the West Riding to choose from, made his home not in Saltaire or Bradford but at Crow Nest at Lightcliffe, which falls, more or less, in the Halifax sphere of influence. Clearly Sir Titus for one must have rated Halifax higher than Hull and certainly better than Hell.

But there's a footnote to that: Hell in this ancient formula is not quite what it seems. The saying is thought to derive from the testimony of beggars who found the local administrations of Hull and Halifax harsher than most – in the case of Halifax, because anyone caught stealing cloth was summarily hanged. (There's still a street just outside the centre of town called Gibbet Street, where the executions took place.) As for Hell, that most likely reflects the fact that just south of Copley is the small town of Elland. That name, as beggars railed against it over the years, became corrupted. Hell, in this case, is less other people than Elland.

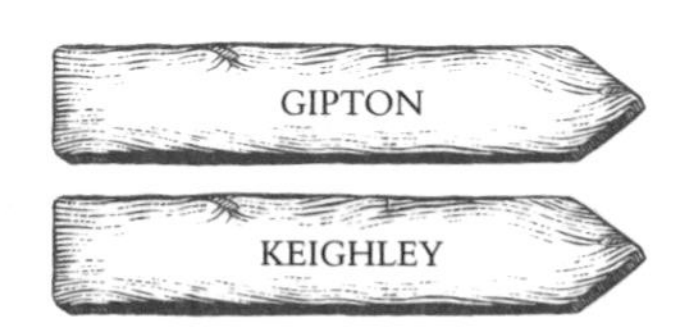

HAY-ON-WYE

HAY, urb. dist., mkt.-town, par. … E. Brecon, on r. Wye, 7m. NE. of Brecon and 20½m. NW. of Hereford…

HOW CAN WE KNOW, the philosopher Bishop Berkeley famously asked, that an object exists when we cannot see it? Similar questions apparently haunt some of those who assemble each summer for the literary festival in the Welsh border town nowadays known as Hay-on-Wye. The polemicist Christopher Hitchens, defender of George W. Bush and castigator of God, who had been performing at Hay at the 20th anniversary festival in the summer of 2007, was troubled by just such thoughts. There was something dreamlike about these occasions, he mused in the *Guardian*. 'To this very day, I think of Hay-on-Wye as a place standing at some slight angle to the rest of the known universe: perhaps a sort of Brigadoon that isn't really there for the rest of the twelvemonth.'

Alarmed by this suggestion, I went to check. And yes, there is still a Hay-on-Wye (or in its Welsh denomination, Y Gelli Gandryll) even when it is not being dreamily gazed on by Christopher Hitchens. One could not any longer call it a typical market town, since there's no denying that even out of festival time it is haunted by book lovers, searching its inescapable bookshops and quite often buying. And yet there's a good deal else to Hay which has nothing to do with reading. It has at its heart an ancient castle, to the remains of which is attached a later house. There are plenty of other shops to cater for needs that have nothing to do with literature: not now in the kind of profusion which existed a century or so ago, when Hay (not then Hay-on-Wye: life was simpler then) accommodated no fewer than fifteen grocers, twelve boot and shoemakers, six butchers and seven tailors. But it still has a far better range of practical everyday shops than Brigadoon; Brigadoon, if I remember, did not run to a Nepal Bazaar, or a Bedecked (trimmings and haberdashery), or an outfitters' shop called Golesworthy's, its windows stuffed with Barbours and stetson hats and boots of every description and its name inscribed in gold lettering on the pavement. And on Thursdays there are market stalls scattered around the town doing a lively trade. Of course I have no proof that any of this was still there once I'd driven away into Herefordshire, but my sympathies here are with Dr Johnson, who, on being told what Berkeley's theories implied, kicked a large stone and said: 'Sir, I refute him thus.'

Let us, however, ask an alternative question: not what festival-goers and the celebrity visitors whom they have flocked here to see make of Hay in season, but what Hay in season thinks of these privileged infiltrators? Do they even – as they step off the pavement to make way for the festival's stars and their entourages, busily debating the question: is Ian McEwan's latest a novel or a novella? – mutter under their breaths the suspicion that Christopher Hitchens and co. stand at some slight angle to the rest of the universe? The answer, I guess, is that they don't much care. They treat this annual event with a solid Welsh stoicism. The people of Hay, after all, have seen it all before. For it's evidently part of the town's traditions to have had its streets swamped at least once a year by often rowdy and even, I'm sorry to say, sometimes drunken strangers.

In the library – yes, they do have a library, as well as those myriad bookshops – I found a history of the town by a local man called Geoffrey Fairs. It's a history of The Hay, by the way, not of Hay-on-Wye: Fairs maintains that the imposition of this hyphen-infested name in 1947 had no historical justification. 'From earliest times', he writes, 'travelling showmen and cheapjacks set up their booths, with performing bears, two-headed sheep and the like, Aunt Sallys and coconut shies...' – to the detriment of the place, respectable folk concluded. The markets and fairs, it was complained in the reign of James I, were continually attended 'by all manner of dissolute and disorderly persons and notorious fellows, drunkards, rogues and vagabonds and such like, both men and women... in all ryotous [sic] kind of living...'; who, this protest continued, had become the cause of 'great offence annoyance and hindrance of your majesty's faithful subjects dwelling in or near the same town, to the manifest corruption of the inhabitants, who of late are growing to be of like disposition to the said and disordered persons…' There may well be those who becoming aware of the preaching in Hay of atheistical and republican sentiments, duly recorded next day in the columns of the sponsoring newspaper, the *Guardian*, feel much the same way about some of its twenty-first-century visitors.

One man who lived close to the town between 1866 and 1872, and who nowadays would be in mighty demand to speak at literary occasions well beyond Hay, records in his celebrated diaries similar feelings of apprehension tinged with disgust as the time of invasion arrives. The whole spectacle of Hay's hiring fairs – the source of these huge excitements, when men and women seeking employment paraded themselves in the streets hoping to catch the eyes of potential employers with the same kind of blatant hopefulness with which writers at festival lectures seek to sign and sell books – made Francis Kilvert of Clyro resolve to keep out of town as much as he could on these occasions. 'Hay Fair and a large one,' he recorded in April 1870. 'The roads thronged with men and droves of red white-faced cattle hustling and pattering to the Fair, an unusual number of men returning drunk.' Not that unusual, though, since the following night he noted: 'Last night the Swan was very quiet, marvellously quiet and peaceful. No noise, rowing or fighting whatever and no men as there sometimes are lying by the roadside all night drunk, cursing, muttering, maundering and vomiting.'

Behaviour at today's Hay festivals, I am told, comes somewhere between these two extremes. 'The great May hiring fair at Hay,' Kilvert writes disconsolately a year later, 'and squadrons of horse came charging into the town and battalions of foot tramping along the dusty roads to the town.' 'Hay Fair still going on,' says an entry for May 1872. 'To get out of the sight and sound of it I went up to the unfrequented path from Penllan to the Wern below Gwernfydden to look for bog beans.' Even now, believe it or not, there may be some in the town of Hay who'd prefer an afternoon searching out bog beans to an evening with Germaine Greer.

HELMSDALE

HELMSDALE, small spt., with ry. sta., L.M.S., Kildonan par., Sutherlandshire… It is a coastguard and lifeboat station and the head of the fishery dist., extending from Embo to Dunbeath.

THE A9 ROAD FROM Inverness to the north sweeps you through Helmsdale over a big bold modern bridge, superseding the earlier road where the river was crossed a little way into the valley by a bridge created by Telford in the service of the 1st Duke of Sutherland. That imperious nobleman had decreed that a village should be built here, as at Brora a little further down the coast, to create a fishing community where the crofters whom he and his agents had cleared out of the inland valleys might make more useful and prosperous lives by reinventing themselves as fisherfolk. The harbour created then, opened by the Duke and Duchess in 1816, was later improved and reopened under the patronage of a subsequent duke in August 1892.

Those who enjoy sustained and abject deference would treasure the account of that ceremony in a local newspaper. 'Helmsdale', it gushed, 'has not been seen in such gala-day attire since the memorable 16th of May 1871 when the railway to that place was formally opened. On that day, as on Saturday last, the Duke of Sutherland was the chief figure on the scene; and rightly so, as the Duke's money and influence was then, as they are now, the principal motive power in bringing about the improvements which called forth the popular rejoicings.'

A triumphal arch was erected at the south entrance to Telford's bridge, with a tower at each side surmounted by flagstaffs from which fluttered the union flag. In a long succession of speeches, due honour was done to the foresight and generosity of the Duke. The Duke replied in tones of apparent modesty, while taking his chance to mock the Land League, which had bravely championed land reform in the Highlands against magnates such as himself. He also expressed high disdain for those who championed home rule. Contrasting the lavish indulgence shown (he claimed) to the Irish with the stinting treatment the government gave the Scots, His Grace excluded from his strictures Protestant Ireland, 'a people whom the government proposes to put under the bloodthirsty tyranny of the Roman Catholics' (a voice: "Never!").'

Yet it has to be said that this autocrat and his agents and minions had done their work well. It's a good-looking place, with grid-pattern streets named, as so often with this family, after their various properties scattered about the kingdom: Sutherland Street, Stafford Street, Stittenham Street (his place in Yorkshire), Trentham and Lilleshall, his great estates in Staffordshire; also, Strathnaver Street, after the scene of some of his family's crueller clearances. That a street by the water was allowed to call itself Shore Street seems like a kind of concession.

The new bridge must gladden the heart of anyone driving the coastal road, and Helmsdale, no doubt, is proud of it. Yet in one sense it is regrettable. But for this bridge, there would still be a potent reminder that Helmsdale existed long before Sutherland or Telford or those who planned and built the upgraded A9. For one casualty of its construction was the loss of the surviving fragments of Helmsdale's fifteenth-century castle. Given this castle's history, one might have supposed that even a scrap of it might have been thought worth preserving. That history, as so often in Scotland, is full of the feuds of great families, Caithness versus Sutherland and the like, fought with the usual bloodsoaked determination. Few performers in that league surpasssed George, 4th Earl of Caithness. It was he, the world suspected, who had contrived an event at Helmsdale which, by the time it was over, had become the stuff of Greek tragedy.

At the earl's insistence, a woman called Isobel Sinclair, who had married into the Sutherland family, devised a triple murder which would give her son the Sutherland succession. Her purpose was to poison the 11th Earl of Sutherland, his countess, and their son. Accordingly she prepared a poisoned drink and gave it to the earl and countess, who swallowed it. But their son was not there when his parents downed the fatal dose, and before he could be found and offered his own death-dealing draught, Isobel Sinclair's own son appeared, looking thirsty. He was given the drink by unwitting servants and collapsed, and died even before his mother's intended victims. So the Sutherland heir survived. He was held a virtual prisoner by the Earl of Caithness, but was rescued, as it's proudly claimed in the museum of that cathedral city, by the brave men of Dornoch. Isobel, meanwhile, was seized, tried and sentenced to execution – but succeeded, on the night before it was due, in killing herself.

I first found this story in Groome's *Ordnance Gazetteer of Scotland*, a book I've commended already, and found it astonishing. Theses events took place in the year 1563: Shakespeare was three then, giving him plenty of time in the remaining fifty-three years of his life to hear the story and build it up into a bloodstained drama. I've seen it claimed that he did indeed know it and it helped him to formulate the plot of *Hamlet*. But that is hardly convincing. You'd have thought he would rather have envisaged it as the plot of a second Scottish tragedy, to go with *Macbeth*. Seeing that Shakespeare had overlooked it, how did it escape the attention of Gaetano Donizetti, never one to hang about when some melodramatic Scottish circumstance (*Lucia di Lammermoor, Maria Stuarda*) or even something suitably lurid from England (*Anna Bolena, Roberto Devereux*) swam into sight? It would have given him another multiple murder, to follow the burst of five slayings at the end of his *Lucrezia Borgia*, and, as with *Lucia* and *Anna Bolena*, a chance to write a mad scene. It could even, like *Lucia*, have offered a role for a ghost. Hordes of opera lovers might then have converged on Helmsdale, creating a general prosperity that even the Duke of Sutherland at his most philanthropic could never have dreamed of.

HIGH CROSS

HIGH CROSS, 4½m. SE. of Hinckley, S. Leicestershire. Is the crossing point of 2 Roman roads, viz. the Fosse and Watling Street. Site of a Roman station (Bennones).

YOU WOULD HARDLY THINK, standing here on the edge of the thunderous A5 trunk road, wondering whether your chance to cross it will come around this year or next, that this used to be one of the most important places in England: the junction, at the highest spot hereabouts, where two great roads, Watling Street and Fosse Way, intersected, with a Roman station nearby. The crossroads is staggered now; but it wasn't in those days. If two chariots met, which had priority? E. Cobham Brewer, following the antiquarian William Stukeley (not always a safe thing to do), says it was regarded as the centre of England, which, since borders have shifted over the years, is misleading. Its claim to have been the centre of Roman England seems a much safer bet.

A location with such a history ought to attract the epithet 'numinous', but even when you rack your imagination it's hard now to see it that way; mainly because of the traffic on what used to be Watling Street (today's A5) – this stretch of the old Fosse Way having long ago dwindled into roads of little importance. Watling Street had Thomas Telford to improve it and make it an important national highway once more. Fosse Way lacked such a champion, though in terms of Roman road-building achievement it too deserves to be marvelled at: 200 miles or so of almost unwavering straightness. You may read about all this on a notice board stationed just east of the High Cross junction, on Bumble Bee Lane.

Better account was taken of this now insignificant spot three centuries back. In 1712 the Earl of Denbigh and friends put up a stone pillar to mark it as the centre of Roman England. You will find it now close to a small car park between High Cross House and Tollgate Cottage, looking a little battered and with some of its Latin lettering eroded. Later generations have added their own names or initials. I found on Wikipedia translations of the two inscriptions, taken from a work called *The Mirror of Literature, Amusement and Instruction*, published in 1827. One, with boundless self-importance, declares: 'The noblemen and gentry, ornaments of the neighbouring counties of Warwick and Leicester, at the instances of the Right Honourable Basil, Earl of Denbigh, have caused this pillar to be erected in grateful as well as perpetual remembrance of Peace at last restored by her Majesty Queen Anne, in the year of our Lord, 1712.' And the other reads: 'If, traveller, you search for the footsteps of the ancient Romans, here you may behold them. For here their most celebrated ways, crossing one another, extend to the utmost boundaries of Britain; here the Vennones kept their quarters, and at the distance of one mile from hence, Claudius, a certain commander of a cohort, seems to have had a camp, towards the street, and towards the foss of a tomb.'

'The ground here is so high', says a guidebook of 1827, 'and the surrounding country so low and flat, that, it is said, fifty-seven churches may be seen from this spot by the help of a glass.' All this, let us be clear, is in Leicestershire, close to the intriguing hamlet of Wigston Parva (a deviation to which I would recommend). Anyone who ever succeeded in getting across the A5 would then be in Warwickshire.

HOUGHTON HALL

HOUGHTON HALL, NW. Norfolk, seat of the Marquess of Cholmondeley, 7½m. W. of Fakenham.

ROWS OF MODEL COTTAGES, drawn up on either side of the road like a guard of honour, usher you into the drive which will take you into the spacious grounds of Houghton Hall, once the home of Sir Robert Walpole, and subsequently, as you're constantly reminded here, the home of the Cholmondeley family. It's very grand indeed, a feast of high ostentation, announced by a fine Palladian frontage – echoing that at Grimsthorpe Castle, with a riot of roof-top activity featuring figures in classical postures. The interior too is full of self-glorification. 'I am a very great person,' Sir Robert seems to be telling us, 'and this is a very great house, built in my image, and furnished as I deserve.'

In the Stone Hall you will find a specific tribute to the eminence of Sir Robert, as no doubt ordained by Sir Robert himself: 'Robertus Walpole senatus Britannici princeps qui hasce aedes condidit incoluit illustravit' (Robert Walpole, chief of the senate of Britain, who founded, dwelt in and adorned these buildings). All this was paid for, at least in part, by the fruits of corruption, for which Walpole was famous and for which at one point he was (unjustly, perhaps, in this instance) locked up for six months in the Tower of London. His recent biographer, Edward Pearce, calls his life of Walpole, published in 2007: *The Great Man: Sir Robert Walpole, scoundrel, genius and Britain's first prime minster.* His justification would no doubt have been the sentiment later expressed by Thomas Babington Macaulay: 'That there are ten thousand thieves in London is a very melancholy fact. But, looked at in one point of view, it is a reason for exultation. For what other city could maintain ten thousand thieves? What must be the mass of wealth, where the fragments gleaned by lawless pilfering rise to so large an amount? St Kilda would not support a single pickpocket.'

The house, though, used to be even more magnificent, because it then housed Sir Robert's pictures, a collection which said to society: first, only a man of conspicuous wealth could have assembled so many exceptional works; and second, I may have a reputation as a mere country squire, as a shameless womanizer, a stupendous drinker and drunkard, as a waterspout of disgusting language – but see: I'm a man of high taste, after all. And he *was* a man of high taste, or at least a man who took good care to equip himself with the advice and guidance of men of high taste where the acquisition of pictures was concerned: the catalogue of what he possessed establishes that beyond question.

But where are they now? In the final room in your tour of Houghton, the great salon, before you go out on the balcony and admire Sir Robert's magnificent deer park, you will see a portrait of Catherine the Great, Empress of Russia. And if she looks pleased with herself, it's with some justification. For most of Sir Robert's collection ended up in her hands – and at a knockdown price: £45,000 at most, quite probably less. John Wilkes said the pictures should have been bought for the nation as the basis of a national art gallery. Josiah Wedgwood said their export was a mark of the nation's decline. Sir Robert's youngest son, Horace Walpole, author, letter-writer, all-purpose aesthete, creator of that fine Gothic excess, Strawberry Hill at Twickenham, appealed to King George III to intervene, but he would not. All that remained at Houghton after the sales were completed were the family portraits, which are there today. An exhibition staged at Kenwood House, London, and in Norwich in 1996 brought many of Walpole's pictures back from Russia to show us what had been lost: perhaps the best crop of Van Dycks ever assembled, Poussin, Rubens, Claude Lorrain, Guido Reni…

Some of the money Sir Robert – the Earl of Orford as he later became – spent so lavishly was money he hadn't got. The whole project at Houghton was reckless and he seems hardly to have troubled himself with what it was costing. His first intention had been to renovate the existing house on the site, but that was swept aside in the fervour of building new. A village that interfered with his plans was moved out of sight. Sir Robert's very fondness for Houghton had endangered Houghton, Horace Walpole moaned. He had made it 'much too magnificent'. The great man's death, in 1745, brought the awful reckoning. His debts amounted to more than £20,000 (something like £2.75 million today). His eldest son, also Robert, merely made matters worse by his own extravagant life, matched by that of his wife, who disported herself with various lovers in Italy. He began the sale of Sir Robert's treasures, which would later be accelerated. When he in turn died in 1751, he left grievous debts to his son George, George's mother having first helped herself to her share, and probably more than her share. George, as Horace lamented, came into his inheritance as 'the most ruined young man in England'. It was he who would preside over the sacking of Houghton.

Everyone thought George, 3rd Earl of Orford, extremely eccentric; many thought he was mad. On occasions he had, as was said in those days, to be 'placed under restraint'. The wise and considered historian of Norfolk, R. W. Ketton-Cremer, whose account of George I have followed here, says that by modern standards these detentions may not have been justified; but he does not seek to minimize the havoc that George created. The new earl wasn't one to consider with due alarm and sobriety the prospect of Houghton Hall deteriorating still further while the assembled temptations of racing, hunting, coursing, hawking, cock-fighting and bull-fighting were there for the taking. He could never resist a bet, however bizarre the occasion: he once raced five turkeys from Norwich to Mile End in London because it gave him the chance of a wager.

Some of the stories told about George are probably folklore, and cannot be proved, though given what can be proved, they don't sound all that unlikely. It was said he liked to parade around the county in a phaeton drawn by red deer. On one occasion, the deer came face to face with a pack of hounds and, not surprisingly, bolted. 'The fantastic procession,' says Ketton-Cremer, 'clattered through the main street of Newmarket, scattering all before it, until the stags bolted into the inn yard where they were habitually stabled and the ostlers closed the gates, just in time, against the pursuing hounds.'

Repeated attempts were made, by Horace especially, to tempt young George into respectability. Government posts were found for him, and the lord-lieutenancy of the county, and the command of the local militia. He performed his duties indifferently, or in some cases not at all. Like the young Henry in thrall to Falstaff, or in our own day, Paul Gascoigne, a footballer of near genius, constantly led astray by his friends, George was at his happiest, and most vulnerable, in the company of the gang that gathered about him. Some were his women, whom Horace called harpies, though even Horace had a soft spot for George's principal mistress, a woman called Patty Turk who had once been a maid at Houghton.

George's gang, to be sure, operated on a higher intellectual level than Gazza's: they produced poems (some quite obscene), and spent hours in philosophical speculation. But they also systematically drained what money he had. The first real crisis occurred in 1773 when, possibly because he had taken a remedy recommended to him by a groom when he was ill, George slid over the edge. Horace was called for, and coming to Houghton found its condition even more grievous than people had warned him. The rain had poured through the roof on to the two great staircases; a further £40,000 or so had been added to those debts George had inherited; and what Horace called 'a group of banditti' were encamped there. Recovering from his dementedness, George promised Horace – he was always adept at promising – to mend his ways and put the place, and his life, in order.

The following year was better. George and Patty spent much of it in a house in the village of Eriswell, between Brandon and Newmarket. Here he assembled a flotilla of boats, appointed himself its admiral, and took it on a watery tour of the fenland to Whittlesey Mere, a huge lake near Peterborough where sailing, racing and fishing were to be had. On the other hand, he ordered the voters of Castle Rising, a parliamentary seat he controlled, to return to the House of Commons a waiter to whom, it was thought, he owed money. The year 1777 saw another downward drift into irrationality; and 1778, another apparent but short-lived recovery. He would pay off all his debts, he promised Horace – but only on the condition that Horace, who because his nephew was childless, was George's likely heir, must renounce any claim to Houghton.

It was now that Horace learned of the impending sale of the pictures to Catherine, a plan which he denounced as 'the work of a madman, executed by rascals', these rascals being, again, George's greedy and villainous entourage. George also now gave up the office of Lord of the Bedchamber which he had fulfilled so fitfully for more than twenty-five years, and was sacked from the office of ranger of St James's and Hyde Parks. But that did not bother him: it gave him more time for his outside interests. He had now discovered ballooning, and took it up with his usual exuberance.

What finally halted his riotous progress was the unexpected death of Patty Turk. This left him distraught. Friends rescued him from the slum that Eriswell had become and took him to Houghton. But less than a month after Patty's death, he fell ill. Some accounts say he over-excited himself while watching greyhounds competing, fell from his saddle and died, but Ketton-Cremer, whom I unwaveringly trust, does not support this: he thinks that George died of grief. He left his estates, partially derelict and debt-ridden as they were, to long-suffering Uncle Horace, who became the 4th Earl of Orford.

A codicil attached to the will stipulated that after Horace's death, everything should go to the Cholmondeleys. Their stewardship in the early years was less than attentive; they preferred living in Cheshire. The house and estate deteriorated still further and attempts were made to sell it. Wellington came to look at it, but thought it too far from London. Friends of the Prince of Wales, later Edward VII, offered to buy it for him, but he preferred Sandringham. The Cholmondeleys returned in 1916, and Lady Cholmondeley – born Sybil Sassoon, into one of the richest families in the land – lovingly and knowledgeably reprieved and restored it. In the present disposition, an afternoon at Houghton Hall is almost as much about Sybil as it is about the various Walpoles.

I can understand why the Cholmondeleys, who continue to own it and open its doors and grounds to the inquisitive public, should be reluctant to admit that the home of Sir Robert Walpole was George's home too. Even so, I think the odd glimpse into his strange career would enliven the proceedings a little. There's a phaeton on show at Houghton, but sadly it cannot claim to be George's, the one that was pulled by stags. 'A light four-wheeled carriage with open sides and drawn by one or two horses', the caption says. 'This carriage was driven by Lord Cholmondeley's grandmother into the 1980s.' It's exhibited in the stables, a building by William Kent, which you come to before you enter the house. Perhaps that would also be the appropriate place for a modest mention of poor, infuriating, battened-on, boisterous, crazy George.

HUMBER

HUMBER, estuary of rs. Ouse and Trent, on E. coast of England, separating the cos. of Lincoln and York. It is 38m. long, from 1 to 7¼ m. broad, flows E. then SE. to the North Sea… Lights are at Spurn, Bull Sand, Grimsby, Middle Shoals and Killingholm.

INTO THIS MIGHTY RIVER there plunged with utter finality in 1640 the Reverend Andrew Marvell, father of the poet. I know this because I found it in one of the works of J. L. Carr, headmaster, novelist, publisher, mapmaker, collector in the tradition of E. Cobham Brewer of curious information and crammer of that information into books no more than five inches down and three and three quarters across, whom we shall meet at Kettering. In his *Welbourn's Dictionary of Prelates, Parsons, Vergers, Wardens, Sidesmen & Preachers, Sunday-School Teachers, Hermits, Ecclesiastical Flower-arrangers, Fifth Monarchy Men and False Prophets* – sometimes his titles threaten to become as long as his books – Carr writes as follows:

> **Mr Marvell**, (father of the poet), Minister at Winestead, The East Riding, mounted the gunwale of a sinking Humber ferry and, waving his walking-stick and cheerily crying, 'Ho for Heaven!' leapt into the tide.

This image – the storm clouds building, the boisterous waves overwhelming the boat, the sailors despairing, the good old man plunging joyfully into the fatal waters – lodged in my head as soon as I saw it and has haunted me ever since, though I fear the story here is slightly more vivid than it ought to be. Mr Marvell had in fact left the living at Winestead to be Master of the grammar school and Lecturer (which in this case means preacher) at Trinity Church, Hull, the finest church in that disparaged city and one of the biggest in England. The first known account of the tragedy occurs in *Gent's History of Hull*, published in 1735, which says: 'The Rev. Mr Andrew Marvell, Lecturer of Hull, sailing over the Humber in company with Madame Skinner of Thornton College and a young beautiful couple who were going to be wedded; a speedy Fate prevented the design'd happy union thro' a violent storm which overset the boat and put a period to all their lives, nor were there any remains of them or the vessel ever after found, tho' earnestly sought for on distant shores.'

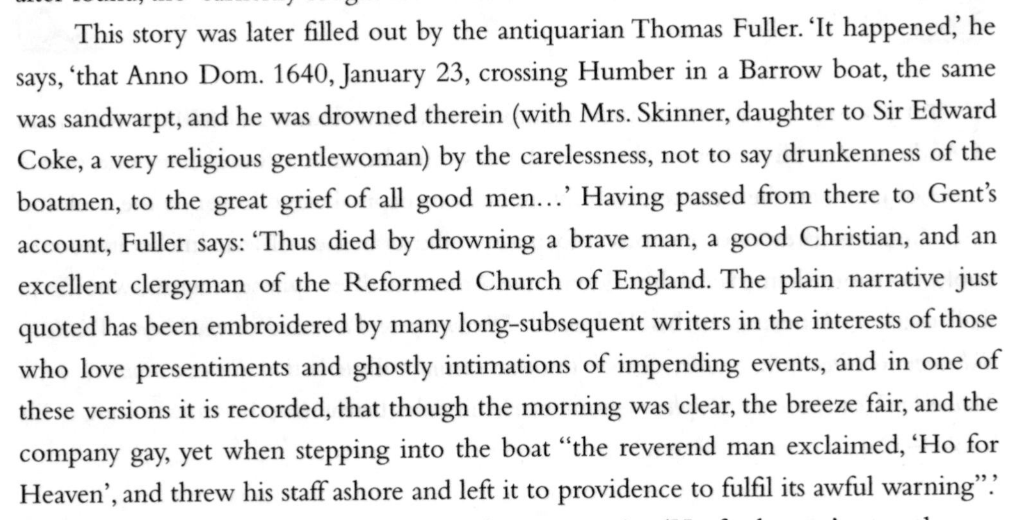

This story was later filled out by the antiquarian Thomas Fuller. 'It happened,' he says, 'that Anno Dom. 1640, January 23, crossing Humber in a Barrow boat, the same was sandwarpt, and he was drowned therein (with Mrs. Skinner, daughter to Sir Edward Coke, a very religious gentlewoman) by the carelessness, not to say drunkenness of the boatmen, to the great grief of all good men…' Having passed from there to Gent's account, Fuller says: 'Thus died by drowning a brave man, a good Christian, and an excellent clergyman of the Reformed Church of England. The plain narrative just quoted has been embroidered by many long-subsequent writers in the interests of those who love presentiments and ghostly intimations of impending events, and in one of these versions it is recorded, that though the morning was clear, the breeze fair, and the company gay, yet when stepping into the boat "the reverend man exclaimed, 'Ho for Heaven', and threw his staff ashore and left it to providence to fulfil its awful warning".'

There is some distinction, I suppose, between crying 'Ho for heaven' as you leap to your death over a gunwale and uttering the same sentiment in the anterior belief that this journey will be your last in this wicked world. I still imagine the Reverend Mr Marvell as a brave and cheerful soul, certain as he must have been that the world he was soon to enter would be a better and happier place than this one; yet I cannot help wondering whether the young beautiful couple on their way to their happy union would have been quite so joyous as he was as the sky grew darker, the storm welled up, the slovenly boatmen panicked, the vessel began to founder, and they found themselves suddenly and inescapably faced with a union with mortality.

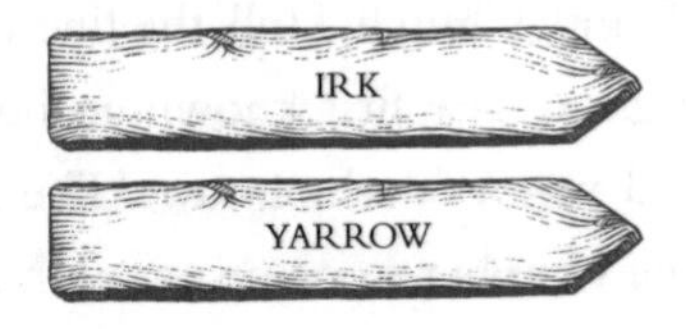

HUNTINGDON

HUNTINGDON, par., mun. bor., and co. town of Huntingdonshire... on left bank of r. Ouse (which connects it with the port of Lynn), 17½m. S. of Peterborough and 59m. N. of London... The Roman road, Ermine Street, passes through the town...

HUNTINGDON IS NO LONGER a county town, for Huntingdonshire is no longer a county, leaving the town as simply a minor ingredient in the rich mix that is Cambridgeshire. It feels today like a disappointed, because a diminished, place. But you can't diminish its history, which is full of epic occasions, especially in its parliamentary elections. Huntingdon has the distinction of being the first town in England known to have challenged a published election result with the fifteenth-century equivalent of the cry 'we wuz robbed'. (The sheriff, who was the returning officer, had announced the result on a show of hands: dissatisfied electors demanded a poll; the sheriff refused it and a petition was raised against him. Unhappily for the protestors, the right to demand a poll was not then established in law.) And how many other counties can claim to have given the country not just a prime minister but a head of state; an MP who campaigned for one of his predecessors to be murdered, and later on for his body to be disinterred and humiliated; and another who, before he met his death after choking on a fishbone, had advertised (though already a bigamist) for an Italian bride, who must, he insisted, be pregnant?

Most of these occasions have something to do with Oliver Cromwell. He was a Member of Parliament here as his father and various other relatives had been before him. Among his successors was a combative Presbyterian royalist called Colonel Silius Titus, a relentless scourge of anything popish and a bitter opponent of Cromwell, who was heavily involved in rebellions against the Commonwealth. It cannot be firmly established whether he also wrote a notorious pamphlet called *Killing No Murder*, advocating the assassination of Cromwell, but it's usually assumed that he had a hand in it. Indeed, some argue that one can tell it was Titus's work from its note of persistent sarcasm. Certainly the award of a coat of arms made to him after the Restoration declared that 'by his pen and practices against the usurper, he vigorously endeavoured the destruction of that tyrant and his government'. That Cromwell's body was removed from its hallowed place in Westminster Abbey, and his head cut off and displayed at Tyburn, was a product at least in part of the colonel's advocacy.

In the less turbulent times that followed, the elections in the town and county of Huntingdon, as across much of the country, were fixed by leading families. If you wanted to get elected here, your best course was to be well in with the Montagus or, better still, to be one of the family. By this means Ralph Montagu, later the 1st Duke of Montagu, a notorious conniver and plotter and a man who, one historian of the family says, 'combined uncommon rascality with all the marks of culture and good breeding', and whom Swift condemned as 'as arrant a knave as any of his time', became MP for the county in 1679, though this was as much to gain parliamentary immunity from prosecution as for any wider political purposes.

Montagu achieved the unusual distinction of being thrown off the Privy Council, and was judged by others fortunate not to be thrown into the Tower, a fate he helped to contrive for Thomas Osborne, Earl of Danby, whose impeachment for surreptitious dealings with foreign powers he had helped to ensure. Montagu was something of an expert on surreptitious dealings with foreign powers, since he was lucratively engaged in them also. His private life too was unscrupulous. His second wife was almost certainly mad, but very certainly rich. Having been warned that she had vowed to marry into royalty or not to marry at all, he masqueraded as the Emperor of China in order to win her hand, and her money. This Montagu, in sum, was that not unfamiliar parliamentary phenomenon, a highly respectable rogue. But another Montagu-related MP for the county was closer to being a rogue pure and simple. Indeed the *Oxford Dictionary of National Biography* categorizes him simply as 'traveller and criminal'. 'Edward Montagu, known as Wortley', as he was habitually styled, was the son, born in 1713, of another Edward Montagu (who, needless to say, was at one time MP for Huntingdonshire) and his far more famous wife Lady Mary Wortley Montagu, a celebrated beauty in her youth, later affected by smallpox but still much sought after by men, and quite often, it was widely believed, responsive. One pursuer whom she rejected was the poet Alexander Pope, who was only 4 foot 6 inches tall and misshapen, and whose addresses she was said to have laughed at: he got his revenge by publishing poisonous verses about her. Other pursuers had greater success. The marriage began to unravel, and she lived for much of the time abroad, until her husband died, when she returned to England. Her son Edward had lived for a while with his mother in Turkey. She was by common repute a neglectful parent. Sent to Westminster School, he twice ran away – he was found on the first occasion working in a London market as assistant to a fishmonger – and later disappeared again, to enlist in the Navy.

Montagu subsequently established a reputation as a serious scholar, reading a paper on earthquakes to the Royal Society (to which he was later elected) and publishing a book called *Reflections on the Rise and Fall of the Ancient Republics, Adapted to the present state of Great Britain*, though some alleged that most of it had been written by others. He was, however, better known, in the words of John Timbs, the Victorian compiler of anecdotal histories, as 'a rake, a beau and a debtor'. He was also a bigamist. In 1730 he married a woman 'of low degree', whom Isobel Grundy, in the *Oxford Dictionary of National Biography*, suggests may have been a washerwoman. He very soon left her – his long-suffering father had to make an allowance to her, as well as looking after two other women whom his son had misused – and set off for Spain, where it was thought he might enter a monastery. Thereafter he had a spell in a debtors' prison, fought, apparently bravely, in the war of the Austrian Succession, and became secretary to his kinsman John, Earl of Sandwich, a diplomat to whom Edward's skill in languages was invaluable.

In spite of this unentrancing CV, Edward became MP for Huntingdonshire in 1747. He might not have been an ideal candidate, but as a Montagu selected by fellow Montagus he was sure of success. Four years later, he bigamously married Elizabeth Ashe, leaving her after three months. The child that was later born to her was on some computations his fifth, most of them illegitimate. His parliamentary attendance seems to have been fitful ('as one of England's senators', says Timbs drily 'he does not appear to have distinguished himself') and his main occupations now were gambling and extortion. He had to escape the country in 1751, and for a time seems to have been up to no good in Paris. His service as MP for Huntingdon lasted seven years, whereafter his father found him a seat at Bossiney, Cornwall.

Later he travelled again. In Alexandria he met a woman called Caroline Dormer Feroe, and having persuaded her that her husband was dead, married her. When the news emerged that her husband was still alive, he insouciantly informed her that for quite other reasons their marriage had never been valid. By now he was reaching a pitch of eccentricity which seems to support the view that much of his weird behaviour was founded on serious mental instability. 'At a late period of his life,' says Timbs, 'he became enamoured of the dress and habits of Armenia, to which he conformed to the end of his life. He lived upon rice, and drank nothing but coffee, or sometimes a little claret, and it is said prayed to Mohammed with the unction of a true Mussulman.' He had even begun to assert that his true father was a Turkish sultan, though as Isobel Grundy points out, this was hardly likely, since he was already four when his mother first went to Turkey.

He had always been haunted by debt, and now there arose what looked like a problem but might, with luck, be converted into an opportunity. His father's will had excluded this errant son, but stated that should a son be born to Edward, the estates which had passed to his sister, Lady Bute, should revert to Edward's heir. Having no legitimate heir, he resolved to obtain one. An advertisement therefore appeared in a paper in Venice, where he was living, which read as follows: 'A gentleman who has filled two successive seats in Parliament, is nearly sixty years of age, lives in great splendour and hospitality, and from whom a considerable estate must pass away from him if he dies without issue, hath no objection to marry a widow or single lady, provided the party be of genteel birth, polite manners and is five or six months gone in her pregnancy.' But before any claimant could conclude a deal, he choked on a fishbone and died.

Since then, the parliamentary representation of Huntingdon has never been quite so exotic. For years after the 1832 Reform Act, the great families of the county continued to split the town and county seats between them; it is sometimes forgotten that, despite the reformers' success, this kind of dynastic politics persisted for much of the nineteenth century. In the final years of the twentieth, Huntingdon sent to the Commons a capable young Londoner who went on to become prime minister. No more apparently respectable politician, it seemed, sat nowadays on the green benches. And then Edwina Currie published her memoirs: but that is another story.

HURSTPIERPOINT

HURSTPIERPOINT, par., mkt.-town and seat, E. Sussex, on eminence, 8m. N. of Brighton…

THE BRITISH TEND TO be dwellers on the plain, so it is always gratifying to come across a town perched on a hill, like Petworth in the county of West Sussex, or Hurstpierpoint, which, by a narrow margin, is in East Sussex. Two old roads intersect here: one, the signposts announce, from Henfield and Albourne to Hassocks, Ditchling and Lewes, the other running north–south from Cuckfield to Brighton. The best way to come to it is from the west, off the old A23, which brings you in through a kind of prelude to Hurstpierpoint, called West Town, and then to the church, with clustered about it the most pleasing sequence of houses in the place.

The church itself is a big bold affair, with almost a hint of thuggishness, a replacement in 1845 for one that was considered too small. There was only room in that for a quarter of Hurstpierpoint's inhabitants, it was complained, 'whereby three quarters are deprived of the comforts and advantages of churchgoing'. Sir Charles Barry, no less, the architect of the modern Palace of Westminster, was called in to advise, with results strangely similar to those when he was consulted about a town hall for Halifax; that's to say, he ruled out all other canvassed solutions and ended up designing the building himself.

The road towards Lewes takes you over the crossroads and on to the middle of the old market town. The traffic through the centre is relentless, but because the street is so narrow, it has to stutter along, alternately claiming and ceding priority, so at least it is slow. The effect of this street is mysterious. There are fewer really good houses in Hurst (as it's usually called) than I had remembered, and it's mildly surprising to find that as many as eighty are listed as of architectural or historical importance. There are certainly few to celebrate in this principal street. So why does it seem so inviting? Part of that has to do with the intimate and companionable feel which comes from the buildings on either side crowding together, as if they had met for a gossip. The most striking episode is a big, bogus, aggressively gabled building of 1900 on the southern side called Cards Place. It's inscribed with the legend: *Ego autem et domus mea serviemus Domino* (My household and I shall be obedient to the Lord). The closer you get to this creation, the clumsier and uglier it looks, and its general condition, the result no doubt of years of fuming traffic, is shabby. Yet in an odd way it gives the whole street its character.

Hurst no longer, has the sense that it used to have of being a market town. I had always thought of it in the same way as Ashwell in Hertfordshire, as a town which ought not to think of itself as a village. But there's no denying that some of its old towny flavour has eroded over the years. The main street still has a fishmonger, but there's no old-fashioned family grocer or baker. The butcher's ('the finest meat only purveyed in this establishment'; 'fresh pies made on the premises') had just closed down when I went there in the autumn of 2007, though another one was still trading just around the corner. There are cashpoints here, but no longer the kind of bank where you can go in and chat to the counter staff and if necessary seek a session closeted with the manager. Some years ago Barclays were treating the town to a weepy melodrama. Lloyds was about to pull out, and Barclays had festooned itself with notices, which said in effect: Lloyds may have abandoned you – nay, betrayed you – O people of Hurstpierpoint, but you won't get that kind of behaviour from Barclays; Barclays is here to serve. And where is Barclays today? No longer in Hurstpierpoint. Disappointing, too, not to find this street packed with the kind of pubs you'd really like to go into. I picked out one (The Poacher) which was decent enough, but local websites seem unimpressed with most of the others. Perhaps that reflects the loss over the years, as charted in the tiny museum in the village centre, of the Oak and the Royall Oake, the Black Lion and the Old Lion, the Swan and the Lamb and the Sussex Arms. And probably quite a few others.

But if Hurstpierpoint seems diminished since its days as a market town, when it was not yet vulnerable to the consumer delights of bigger towns around it, there's much else to commend it, with fine open country all about, criss-crossed with footpaths, the green backdrop of the Downs to the south, and Brighton and Lewes and the sea just beyond. I like a place which, as this one does, treasures its history. In the library, I found a book called *Hurstpierpoint – Kind and Charitable* (that being an accolade once bestowed on it), edited by Ian Nelson for the Hurst History Study Group. It's a book one could happily sit and read all day on some sunny hillside just out of town. It's proud enough of the place to rebuke the Pevsner guide to Sussex – in this case, it would have been Pevsner's co-author, Ian Nairn, who wrote the offending words – for saying that the present large and prosperous church had replaced a 'sweet and villagey one'. A hundred and twenty years on, the book snorts, could anyone judge just how 'sweet and villagey' it had been.

The religious history of the place, quite aside from the alleged offence of knocking down sweet villagey churches, is full of turbulence. There used to be a nest of Quakers here, who were harried by an Anglican priest called Leonard Letchford. The Quakers, he proclaimed in a pamphlet, had a devil in ten particular forms. They were these:

1. An irreligious devil
2. A seducing and erroneous devil
3. A proud, supercilious, uncharitable, censorious devil
4. An uncivil, unmannerly devil
5. A covetous, fraudulent, sacrilegious devil
6. A rebellious, traitorous devil
7. An absurd, senseless, stoical devil
8. A trifling, peddling, ridiculous devil
9. An atheistical devil
10. A discontented, blundering devil

An *irreligious* devil? An *atheistical* devil? An *unmannerly* devil, even? Would this fiend stop at nothing? Letchford's death in 1673 was greeted by the Quakers with unQuakerlike pleasure. 'The said Leonard Letchford went to bed,' they recorded, 'but was found dead in the morning, and soe ended the wicked persecutor who was a constant persecutor of the people of God not onley for the tithe he claimed of them, but also tooke all other occasions to stirr up persecution against them and wrott a very false and lying pamphlet against them stuffed full of grosse abuses to render them unfitting to live upon the earth which was answered by Ambrose Rigge.'

There is also a history of Hurstpierpoint College – St John's – by its former head of history and archivist Peter King, from its founding by Nathaniel Woodard, alongside his schools at Lancing and Ardingly. Its first headmaster was Woodard's second in command, Edward Lowe. One of Lowe's trials was to have on his staff that extraordinary figure Sabine Baring-Gould, minister in a succession of Anglican livings and eventually squire-parson of Lewtrenchard, Devon, the writer of innumerable books including inventive biographies like that of Robert Stephen Hawker of Morwenstow, and sixteen volumes of the lives of the saints; the composer of many hymns including 'Onward Christian Soldiers' and 'Through the Night of Doubt and Sorrow'; a collector of folk songs, an intrepid traveller and kindly disher-out of advice to less hardened travellers, and the father of fifteen children with Grace, an illiterate mill girl whom he married after leaving the college to take holy orders and become the curate of Horbury, Yorkshire: the bride was sixteen. There's a famous tale of Baring-Gould at a party approaching a child and asking, 'And whose pretty child are you?' To which she tearfully replied: 'Yours, papa'.

Baring-Gould appears, unsurprisingly, to have been a difficult colleague, flamboyant, pushy and known for some reason (the shape of his nose? or perhaps it was some recondite reference to the tinker who plays Wall in Midsummer Night's Dream?) as Snout. He offended Lowe in ecclesiastical matters, especially by his taste for vestments and by his complaints about Hurstpierpoint's chapel practices. At one point, the carrying of the crucifix in procession at services was banned. In protest, Baring-Gould insisted on changing the refrain of his hymn 'Onward Christian Soldiers', from 'With the cross of Jesus marching on before' to 'With the cross of Jesus left behind the door'. He also demanded more money (understandably, since according to King, masters at Hurstpierpoint were wretchedly paid) and was told by Lowe, when he mused that he might join a monastery, to stop talking nonsense. But his versatility – he taught chemistry and music as well as Latin, French and German (he was fluent in other tongues too, including Danish, but the college had no call for that), produced school plays and contributed lavishly to the school magazine, the *Hurst-Johnian* – must have made up for his defects, and he stayed eight years before he succumbed to the lures of Horbury. I had read elsewhere that Baring-Gould used to teach at Hurstpierpoint with a pet bat perched on his shoulder. This allegation is omitted from the school history; further proof, perhaps, that living in Hurstpierpoint makes people Kind and Charitable.

A B C D

E F G H

I J K L

M N O P

Q R S T

U V W XYZ

ILKESTON

ILKESTON, mun. bor., mkt.-town and par… S. Derbyshire. At Ilkeston is a mineral spring.

IN THE SQUARE AT Ilkeston, perched on the top of the hill, looking over the market towards the church, is Ilkeston town hall, built in 1868 and equipped, as all good town halls should be, with the sort of balcony on to which, on election night, there ought to emerge the mayor, the returning officer, and the beaming candidate in whom the borough has just invested its future. It is probably just as well in this case that Ilkeston never elected to Parliament a man who, though he had almost everything else, yearned to represent it: Ernest Terah Hooley, entrepreneur, philanthropist, entertainer and inveterate chancer. Had he come out on the election night with two substantial officials, there must have been justified fears as to whether so small and frail a balcony could survive. Ilkeston was fortunate to be spared his election in another sense too: had he succeeded, the town might have joined the ranks of those which in the late nineteenth and early twentieth century had their Members taken away and clapped in jail.

Hooley says in his autobiography that Ilkeston was his birthplace, in 1860, but his birth certificate, a more neutral source in these matters, puts him down as a son of Sneinton, Notts, born a year earlier. His claims to have sprung from a long line of yeoman farmers are equally unreliable. His father ran a lace-making business at Nottingham, where the young Hooley initially joined him, becoming a partner at twenty-one. As a deacon, church organist, teetotaller and non-smoker, he seemed to ooze nonconformist respectability.

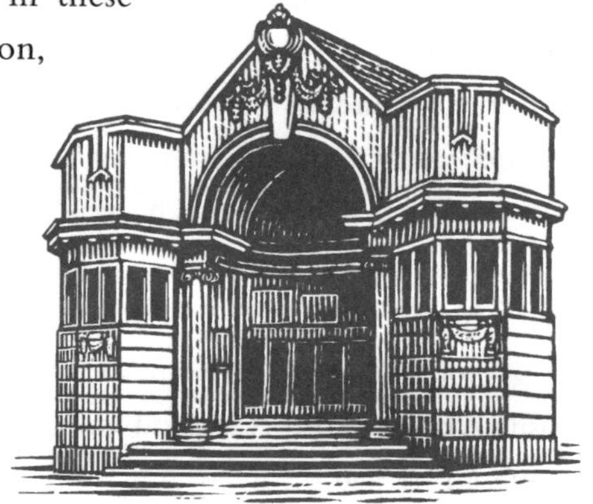

Yet by now he'd already discerned that there might be more to life than making lace in the Midlands. 'I wanted to deal in millions,' he later recalled. And you didn't do that, he had already deduced, by being excessively trustworthy.

Bursting the bounds of his father's business, he set up on his own account. 'My stock in trade', he later reflected, 'consisted of nothing but my own native wit.' That, and a shrewd eye for unexploited opportunities. He began to stalk and then to acquire manufacturing companies which seemed unaware of their commercial potential: at the peak of these operations, he claimed, he was buying a couple a week. He bought them with money he hadn't got, but soon would have. 'I could see the day dawning,' he would later recollect, 'when there would be millions of people waiting to drop millions of pounds into companies promoted by my humble self.' One acquisition bought cheap and sold dear, which would later become famous was Schweppes. And one future craze he profitably spotted was cycling: he collected the firms that made Raleigh, Humber, and Singer and Swift bicycles, and then, since bicycles would always need tyres, Dunlop – which would turn out to be his biggest success. He recouped the purchase price, as was his habitual practice, by floating the company – a process which usually went swimmingly because the company's prospects were boosted by the financial writers on newspapers he had in his pocket, along – he claimed – with some of their editors. After Dunlop came the purchase of the Trafford Park estate outside Manchester, snapped up while Manchester Corporation was pondering whether to buy it; he then sold it off profitably in lots.

Hooley was always eager to live in style. One demonstration of that was his early purchase of a substantial house called Risley Hall, on the Nottingham to Derby road, and its surrounding estate for £5,000 from a man called Fytche, who had bought it in the expectation that big money was to be made from mineral deposits beneath it. There were no such deposits; Fytche was forced to sell and Hooley was one of his principal creditors. Who had so gravely misled him about the wealth his purchase was likely to bring him? Fytche blamed a man who was known to be close to Hooley.

Hooley's growing financial success brought him social advancement. He mixed easily with the aristocracy, and not only with those – the notorious 'lords on the board' – whom he had on his payroll. He could always be relied on to come to the aid of a nob in need. The lavishness of his lifestyle quenched all doubts about his financial security. Not content with Risley Hall, he purchased a fine estate at Papworth, near Cambridge, where he owned the whole village apart from the church and rectory, and a spacious home in Mayfair. He bought a yacht, the *Verena*, from the Earl of Lonsdale; as he explained in his memoirs, 'Most newly-made millionaires buy a yacht at some time or another, and I was no exception.' He counted the Prince of Wales as a friend, and offered to buy Sandringham for him. He even tried to acquire the royal yacht *Britannia*, but royal advisers stepped in to stop it falling into the hands of a mere plutocrat.

The world observed and marvelled. Journalists graciously entertained at one of his fine addresses had scepticism swept straight out of their systems. 'Where one can do so without indelicacy', wrote one sucker in the *Illustrated Sporting & Dramatic News*, 'it is always satisfying to arrive at some sort of conclusion respecting the methods by which this or that man has attained an amount of success which marks him out from amongst his fellows. To account for the exceptional triumphs which have attended the career of Mr Ernest Terah Hooley would be by no means easy for anyone who had not enjoyed opportunities of seeing him both at work and at play. The tall, spare, well-knit form of the foremost figure in the realm of finance is one to command admiration and respect, with which (in the case of his intimates) is mingled an affection given to but few men to inspire.'

Hooley's admirers had been watching in awe as the great financier held court all week at his new London base, a floor of the Midland Grand Hotel at St Pancras, reserving weekends for his yacht or for one of his country houses – if not Risley or Papworth, where he entertained in such style (people talked in awe for weeks afterwards of the breakfasts served up to them), then Maddington House in Wiltshire, Anmer Hall in Norfolk (which he later sold cheap to the Prince of Wales), on the Countess of Warwick's Essex estates or Woodthorpe Grange in Nottinghamshire. What was the secret of his ascendancy? 'His sagacity', the man from the *Illustrated Sporting & Dramatic News* concluded, 'saves him from the pitfalls into which less skilful tacticians are continually stumbling.'

Soon some discreet and well-greased pulling of strings landed him the office of High Sheriff of Cambridgeshire; the bestowing of such an honour on a mere parvenu astounded and disgusted high Cambridge society, rather to his amusement. It could now surely be only a matter of time before his achievements were recognized in the traditional manner – by a knighthood, or perhaps more suitably, by a baronetcy: honours which, he let it be known, he not only deserved but would be happy to pay for. Yet he still had one further ambition: a strangely unglamorous one for a man who seemed already on top of the world. One of his interests was agriculture – he had pioneered new methods of farming across his estates and vowed to make Papworth the wonder of the agricultural world – and he felt it would be for the good of the country generally were he to be installed as Minister of Agriculture.

The first step on that ladder would have to be his election to Parliament; and though Ilkeston was a Liberal stronghold, he was sure that the town would vote Hooley, even if that meant voting Conservative. After all he had a reputation, transcending politics, for generous gifts to local institutions of every persuasion, some in money and some in kind (400 rabbits, for instance, for the use of local clergy), all of them flatteringly listed at regular intervals in the columns of the besottedly Tory *Ilkeston Pioneer*. Accordingly there was little doubt about the probable outcome when he presented himself at the Conservative Club in Regent Street (the building of which he had paid for) to seek the party nomination, which the party, of course, enthusiastically bestowed on him.

But unhappily, the sagacity which saved him from all those pitfalls into which lesser men sank was not quite as comprehensive as the *Illustrated Sporting & Dramatic News* had supposed. What awaited him was not the green benches of Westminster or the ministerial office or the Sir in front of his name, but bankruptcy, which put paid to the lot. Hooley had over-reached himself: he had won a series of dangerous court cases brought against him, but he could not satisfy clamorous creditors and in June 1898 declared himself bankrupt. His downfall (which of course would be only temporary) was all the result, he claimed, of old colleagues and jealous rivals plotting against him. 'Blackmailed right and left,' he later recorded, 'faced with unjustifiable claims totalling over £1,000,000, I took the only remedy that was open to me. I filed for petition and in doing so practically committed social suicide.'

It was political suicide too, and cost him his chance to fight Ilkeston: he resigned the candidacy in March 1900. The *Pioneer* could hardly hold back its tears; this was 'nothing less than a local calamity', it moaned. 'The stoppage of his princely gifts to local institutions and to the poor of the neighbourhood is a great loss, more especially to the old people who had the evenings of their lives to some extent illumined by his generous donations...' The *Daily Telegraph* went to see him at Papworth. 'Ask any questions you like,' he told the reporter expansively. '"You haven't then, Mr Hooley – forgive the bluntness of the question – feathered your own nest?" "I have not a penny piece in the world" was the reply. "Look, here are four mailbags of messages which back me," he said.' And had any been hostile? Just one, from a man called Grant. 'Hearty congratulations on your bankruptcy,' it read. 'Hope nothing left to you. God save the Queen.'

Still, the bankruptcy hearings in 1898 could be turned to his advantage. He used them to expose a whole string of dubious or clearly fraudulent practices on the part of those he had dealt with. A notable victim here was Earl De La Warr. Hooley told the hearing of payments amounting to £25,000 he had made to persuade this nobleman to grace the board of one of his companies. Next day he was back to report that the peer had offered him £1,000 to withdraw the statement he'd made to the court the previous day. What was more, he added, he had been stopped while walking through Catford by a man who had offered him a thousand sovereigns to retract another vastly embarrassing statement he had made about Lord Albemarle.

The earl and several associates were summoned to court to show cause why they should not be committed for contempt. De La Warr admitted having tried to get Hooley to change his statement, but was surprisingly acquitted, though he had to pay costs. Not so fortunate was another of Hooley's apparently respectable targets, Sir William Marriott, a former judge advocate-general. Sir William denied having taken money from Hooley to get him into the Carlton Club, but a cheque for £50,000 made out to Sir William said otherwise.

Nor did Hooley intend letting a mere bankruptcy disrupt his business career. There were new ventures as far afield as Newfoundland and Siberia, and others close to home of questionable legitimacy. In 1904 he was again appearing in court for attempted fraud, along with a business partner named Harry Lawson. Lawson was convicted; Hooley, represented by distinguished lawyers, was cleared. He now acquired another business partner, who was an even murkier figure than Lawson: Horatio Bottomley, who would come to be regarded as perhaps the greatest rogue of his age.

For a time Hooley remained a figure of much local consequence in Risley and in Papworth especially, where he built solid houses, staged big village suppers, and upset other local farmers by the generous wages he paid. A delegation turned up at the house to complain, but stayed on to be wooed over lunch with good wine and cigars.

Then, taking one chance too many landed him in trouble again, and this time with more lasting consequences. In 1911 he was committed to Brixton for contempt of court. The following year his previous luck in the courtroom failed him, and he was sentenced to a year in prison for making false declarations in a land transaction. By then, Papworth had gone. An auction of goods held at Papworth Hall in September 1911 was said to reveal 'opulence without much taste or discrimination'. There were stuffed heads of buffalo, bison, wild boar, moose, eland and antelope, and a library of 2,500 books, some with their pages uncut. The Hall became a centre for tuberculosis patients. Hooley hardly ever went back; except that, two decades on, he turned up one day, a faded, forgotten figure at the scene of his former glory, and sat silently in the library for a while.

His crowning disaster came in 1920, when he sought to exploit an upturn in the Lancashire cotton trade. Incurably optimistic, he thought this was going to be his early triumph with bicycles all over again. But his sale of the Jubilee Cotton Mills ended in a prosecution for fraud and a sentence of three years' penal servitude. 'I felt that my life had ended,' he says in the autobiography he wrote in 1924. He served his sentence in Parkhurst prison, where he encountered his old associate Bottomley.

Hooley was bankrupt again, this time to the tune of £686,000. The cost of his trial was met by relatives. 'I have been acclaimed', he recalled, the old swagger resurfacing now, 'as a prince of sportsmen, a pillar of the church, the friend of kings and noblemen, the greatest financier ever known, and last but not least, a sinister, dangerous personality who ought never to have been allowed at large.' He had also, he wryly added, been for a time the most popular man in England – though only for the money he had spent. Just one honour remained to him, and he put it on the title page of his book: *Hooley's Confessions*, by Ernest Terah Hooley, Squire of Risley.

He had always regarded Risley, even above Mayfair and Papworth, as the principal home for himself, his wife and their seven children. Here in his heyday there had been shooting parties and cricket festivals, featuring players as distinguished as those at Enville – Prince Ranjitsinhji was one – and a cellar 'of which the King of England might have been proud'. And here he felt in touch with his Derbyshire roots.

In the end, though, he lost even Risley. There was a third and final date with the bankruptcy courts in 1939, when he was eighty. He died in 1947 in a lodging house in Long Eaton, dependent for his survival on his children and local friends, not all of whom had ceased to like and even revere him during his tribulations. Hooley was a crook – not the worst by any means of his crook-ridden times, and no more culpable than some who escaped their deserts – and a rogue, yet even those who were called on to prosecute him saw his attractions. 'Hooley,' said Sir Norman Birkett QC after the Jubilee Cotton Mills trial, 'is a charming man… I can well understand how he got his money from susceptible people.'

The Tories, even without him to carry their flag, came within a thousand votes of capturing Ilkeston at the 1900 election, but thereafter it went back to its usual practice of producing solid Liberal majorities and then, from 1918, of electing Labour. Indeed, the Tories have never won the constituency. Yet who can deny that had his sins not caught up with him, this greatest of all financiers, prince of sportsmen, pillar of the Church, friend of kings and noblemen, most lavish of Ilkeston's benefactors – as in his best days he seemed to be – might have achieved the impossible?

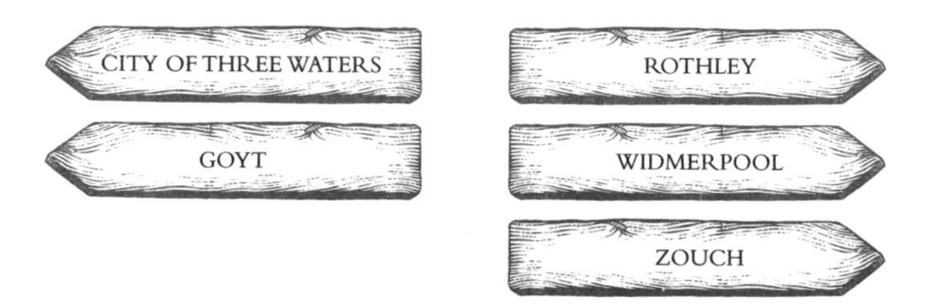

INVEREWE

INVEREWE HOUSE, seat, NW. Ross and Cromarty, on Loch Ewe, 1m. N. of Poolewe. The shootings embrace a deer-forest and extend to 13,000 ac.

THOUGH YOU ARE NOW almost as far north as Moscow – north of Riga and Tallinn and Leningrad – you may walk among tropical foliage in the gardens at Inverewe. The benign conditions which the Gulf Stream creates in this north-western corner of Scotland, and which climate change may one day destroy, enabled a man called Osgood Mackenzie to create a garden which otherwise might seem to defy the known facts. Not that its situation is perfect: it is subject to gales, and the garden had to be shaped to minimize damage from spray off the loch.

Mackenzie was twenty when he began. First came a house in the customary Scottish baronial style (it burned down in 1914: the present house is a less ostentatious replacement). Then came a walled garden, always the part of the grounds he most prized; and in time he devised the rest of the site of more than 100 acres which, since the death of his daughter Mairi, has been in the care of the National Trust for Scotland. You don't need to be a deep devotee of gardens to relish this one. Even those who can't without prompting tell a cotoneaster from a hibiscus, and who feel truly safe only with roses and daffodils, should not be deterred.

It's not just the wildly eclectic community of flower and tree and bush and shrub that makes it remarkable, though at any point here you may come upon imports from Italy or Austria, Australia or New Zealand, Sri Lanka, Mexico, Chile, the Falkland Islands and particularly Japan (which like the Americas, north and south, has its own special section); it is also the way that Mackenzie exploited the territory he had acquired. Because it is on a promontory, you may look out over one loch, then walk back through an area known as the Devil's Elbow and suddenly find yourself viewing what seems to be another – a bay known as Camas Glas.

Best of all, as you look across Loch Ewe from the terraced gardens, there seems to be a wonderful symmetry, fusing Mackenzie's creation with those of other hands, and of God. The terraces descend to the water; across the water, the levels ascend to a village (Poolewe), and then to low hills, and then on and upward to the mountains of Torridon and its deer forest. It's a spot to be cherished not just for itself but also for what may follow. Should you choose, there is Loch Maree, said to be one of the most lovely in Scotland, awaiting inspection, just beyond Poolewe village. The road which passes the gardens, the A832, having travelled west to Gairloch, turns south and then eastwards to run on its southern side to Kinlochewe and on to Achnasheen; or from Kinlochewe, you may take a different road to Loch Maree and then proceed, perhaps with a deviation to much-lauded Plockton, by way of the Kyle of Lochalsh to the Isle of Skye.

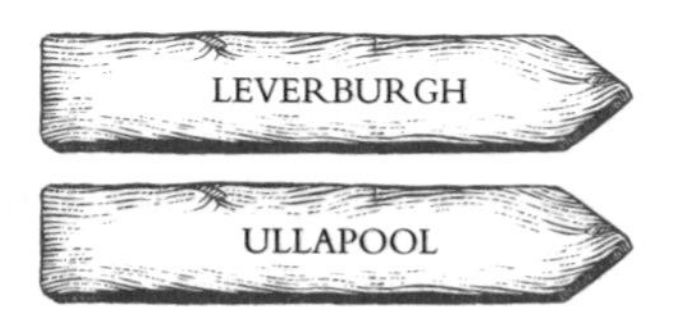

IPSWICH

IPSWICH, parl. and co. bor., seaport and co. town, with ry. sta., L.N.E., Suffolk, 12m. from the sea...

IPSWICH, LIKE NORWICH 43 miles to its north, has the distinction of being a county town. Both have football teams in what, less pretentiously, was once called the second division. Ipswich is a borough, but Norwich is a city. Ipswich has an MP; but Norwich has two. The population of Norwich, at 126,000, tops that of Ipswich (114,000). Norwich is home to the University of East Anglia; Ipswich, to Suffolk University Campus, a kind of academic outpost dependent on East Anglia and Essex. Ipswich has a parish church, but Norwich has two cathedrals. No prizes for guessing which of these places recently opened the biggest and best-looking library in East Anglia. So if Ipswich sometimes gives Norwich the kind of look that Esau gave Jacob, or Cain turned on Abel, that's not entirely surprising. Norwich, however, can assure itself that what Ipswich thinks doesn't matter.

These animosities between neighbouring towns are common in Britain and perhaps under-documented. They are well known in football – Oxford and Reading, Swindon and Bristol, and so on, though there they sometimes pale against feuds between two sides in a city: Celtic–Rangers in Glasgow, Everton–Liverpool, United and Wednesday in Sheffield, United and City in Manchester, Arsenal and Spurs in London. They are commonplace off the terraces too.

The polling company MORI was invited by the Banham Commission on local government, set up in 1992, to measure local opinion on the sort of new patterns of local administration that people would like to see. That included consideration of whether one authority might usefully merge with another. In the course of their investigations they asked respondents which of their neighbouring towns they most disliked, an exercise which showed that some of them not merely disliked but detested towns just down the road. In Essex, none of its neighbours liked Basildon much – though it also transpired that quite a few people in Basildon didn't like Basildon either. In Kent, Sevenoaks had no time for Swanley, and Swanley felt the same way about Sevenoaks. Much of Bedfordshire was distraught at the thought of Luton. Sometimes in such situations, shotgun marriages have nevertheless been ordered. Outside Hove town hall there used to be a notice listing the virtues of Hove, every one of which could be construed as saying: we aren't like Brighton. But now the two towns are one – a decision discreetly sweetened by the award of City status.

Since the two top towns of East Anglia are in separate counties and well away from each other, they didn't come into MORI's invigilation. But anecdotal evidence suggests that the two are not natural soulmates. When the makers of the board game Monopoly, in the course of creating different boards for separate parts of the nation (there is even one for Barnsley), came to do Ipswich, they found themselves faced with a very unusual request. There's a space on one corner of the Monopoly board which carries a picture of a minatory policeman who seems to have a whistle plugged into his mouth, with a caption that says: 'Go to jail.' You're required to do that directly, not passing Go and not collecting £200. Some ingenious people in Ipswich suggested varying this square. Instead of saying 'Go to jail', they maintained, it ought to say 'Go to Norwich'.

Monopoly is made and marketed nowadays not by John Waddington, Ltd, London and Leeds, as it always used to say on the label, under a cartoon of a dapper plutocrat flourishing a wad of pound notes, but by Winning Moves of Praed Street, Paddington, London. Early indications were that Winning Moves might agree to this wheeze. The *Daily Telegraph* quoted the company's spokesman, Graham Barnes, as saying: 'When we first got a few of the suggestions from people in Ipswich about their version, we didn't think anything of it. But, as we got more emails, we started to take it very seriously. Now it is very likely that the square will say: "Go to Norwich".'

Ipswich isn't a bad-looking place. The main street seemed lively and cheerful enough, and there are pleasant vistas down side streets: Dial Lane, Tower Street (part of it, anyway) and particularly Northgate Street, satisfyingly sealed off at the top by the Bethesda chapel. Best of all, it has a proper traditional square, of the kind that every county town should be equipped with. There's a town hall here, and the old Post Office,

and bars where you can sit outside, and on one side Lloyds Arcade, splendidly over the top, with glimpses through its arches of a subsidiary streets beyond. If only, I thought, observing this agreeable scene, someone were able to clone it, revise the result to meet local circumstances, and give it to poor traffic-battered Bedford.

Sure enough, I found Ipswich Monopoly on sale in the main street shops at £25, but too securely wrapped to offer an opportunity to peek at its pointing policeman. But Winning Moves told me that in the end they'd decided to drop the assault on Norwich. The stories in the national and local papers had no doubt served their public relations purpose. Meanwhile, since football is now the twenty-first-century British equivalent of the wars in which Italian cities used constantly to engage during the Middle Ages, fought for the most part by mercenaries who had little real connection with the places for which they turned out, Ipswich must simply take satisfaction from having finished, in the 2007–8 season as in the one before it, well ahead of Norwich for all Norwich's city status, cathedrals, more numerous population and brace of MPs.

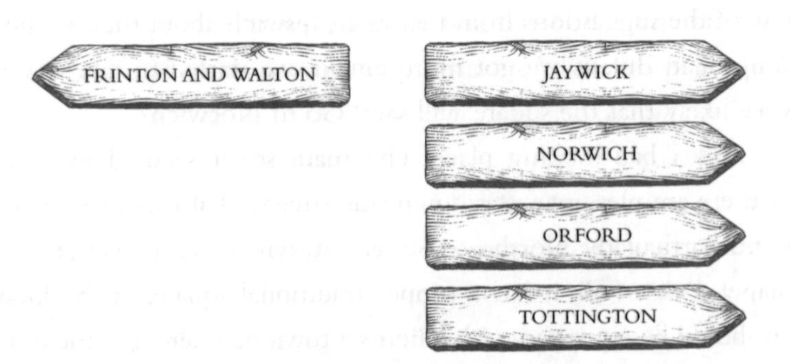

IRK

IRK, r., SE. Lancs, rises a little N. of Oldham and flows 10m.
SW. to the Irwell at Manchester.

A LITTLE N. OF Oldham: what discretion, what impeccable judgement Bartholomew shows in not saying quite where. Presumably he and his minions never tried to seek out the source. I did, and it isn't easy.

Most rivers have humble beginnings. Those of the Thames in a field near Kemble in Gloucestershire, for instance: who would guess that such a river would have its origins in this inglorious trickle? Yet one day it will flow past the Palace of Westminster and under Tower Bridge. No such luck for the Irk. Some authorities maintain that the origins of the Irk are to be found close to a place called Low Crompton, off the Rochdale road out of Oldham, beside a golf course. Others allege that its source can be found on the other side of the golf course, at a spot called Cowlishaw, no more than a mile away.

I went to Low Crompton first, and there on the edge of the golf course I found a field of llamas, augmented by the occasional cow, grazing peacefully in the drizzle. Approaching as close as I could without seeming to menace the llamas, I searched for any sign of an incipient river. None was visible. That left the Cowlishaw option, which seemed at first no more hopeful, and lacked even the saving grace of a consort of llamas. As I plodded dolefully onwards, two women with dogs and raised umbrellas kindly inquired if I was lost. Not exactly, I reassured them. I was here in search of the source of the Irk, but it seemed resolved to elude me. At the mention of this inconspicuous waterway a light came into their eyes. 'Ah, the Irk!' said one, with more nostalgia than I'd ever expected this river to generate. 'Used to flow through the end of our garden, but that got changed with all the building. Just go down the hill, turn through the narrow gate, and you'll see it. Full of disgusting rubbish! United Utilities ought to be doing something about it.' United Utilities are what we used to call the waterworks here.

And sure enough, close to the golf course, I discovered the source of the Irk, or something purporting to be the source of the Irk, sidling through a drain. Across the road, back towards Cowlishaw, a further ditch suggested that it might in better days have been the source of the Irk, but was empty now, and littered with rubbish (though I've seen worse). A river which had no corporeal presence even in a summer which had broken all records for rainfall was, I decided, no longer fit to be called a river. So the honour of being the Irk's place of conception should go to the drain.

But that, it seems, is the life story of the poor Irk. As the women with the dogs had explained, it had so often been rerouted, culverted, required to make way for the schemes of developers, that its course nowadays was different by far from the one that it enjoyed in its heyday. If it had a heyday, that is. Engels, inspecting the Irk, found it confirmed his worst fears about capitalism. The courts which led down to it – he was contemplating a later stage of its course, close to the heart of Manchester – contained what he called 'unqualifiedly the most horrible dwellings I have yet beheld'. Refuse, filth, disgusting crime and cholera are invoked. At the bottom of the district flowed, 'or rather stagnated', the Irk, 'a narrow, coal-black, foul-smelling stream, full of debris and refuse, which it deposits on the shallower right bank'.

There must be hundreds, perhaps even thousands, of rivers across the land as unfamous as this one, some even outpacing the Irk for the title of Britain's most squalid river, others pleasant to walk by, and still others that tempt one to spend hours on their banks, watching the fish zooming about in their dappled waters. Some, even the pretty ones, have names which alone are a powerful deterrent and would certainly jar if discovered in the works of a poet such as Wordsworth with a taste for hymning the joys of the Wye and the Severn or, as we'll discover later on in this book, Yarrow Water. The name Severn belongs on the tongue of a poet, just as the Irk, or what sound like its partners in grime, the Irt, or the Mite (there is also a Smite) do not. (Stevie Smith once wrote a poem in praise of the river Mimram, Hertfordshire, and the Irt, on close inspection, is in Cumbria, so it may have been praised at some point by one of the Lakeland poets.)

As well as two Dons, in Scotland and Yorkshire, both well known, there's a Sid and a Len and a Liza. Bartholomew is full of rivers I'd never heard of, and even more are to be found in Eilert Ekwall's *English River-Names* or on the internet. Alongside such current names as the Amber, the Gamber, the Bleng, the Gannet, the Gaunless and the Gwash, we find Keekle Beck, the Kendijack, the Loud, the Meavy, the Must, the Nar and the Nent, the Pang, Pant and Penk. Then there's the Quarme, and the Quinny (or Quenny), Snary Beck, the Tiddy, the Wissey and Yantlet Creek. Who outside its near neighbours had heard of the river Sense – at least until a woman using a Satnav senselessly drove her very expensive Mercedes into this river, and wrote it off? Ekwall lists others now given new names, or lost. The Cad has become the Ding. The Wooth is the Brit. But what has become of the Cunkel, the Difrod, the Dork, the Glangles, the Grivel, and the Thrackriveling?

The database of Scottish National Heritage uncovers a series of burns whose names exude varying degrees of allure. The Burn of Canny, The Burn of Durn, Shaggie Burn, Tarty Burn, Tifty Burn, the Burns of Colp, Monquhitter and Ludquharn; also one called Black Stank. The Water of Milk sounds appealing – I think of it also as the Water of Humankindness – but the Water of Bogie, less so. There's a river Cur in Argyll, and a Gloy in the central Highlands, and I see there's a loch near Dalmellington, Ayrshire, known as Loch Muck. Against that, there's the prospect held out by Bartholomew of one day seeing Loch Quoich, in Inverness-shire, which as he says 'receives the Quoich and gives out the Garry'.

Since this book does not cover Ireland, I'm precluded from mentioning, as Bartholomew does, the river Oily, a rivulet in south-west Donegal which flows into McSwyne's Bay, or, perhaps more enticing still, the Quagmire. Some of the names in England, as in Scotland, are so laconic one imagines they must have sprung from the first reactions of primitive man on coming across them. The Hiz, for instance, in Hertfordshire, the Pow close to Whitehaven, the Og in Wiltshire, or in Scotland, the Ba and even the river E, named perhaps on a day when Scottish winds were blowing so fiercely that those who discovered it hardly dared open their mouths.

Some rivers – the Teise (pronounced Tice) in Sussex is a notorious case – regularly force their way into the newspapers by flooding. My prey, the Irk, is rarely written about. In August 1953, part of a train from Manchester to Bury fell into the Irk after a collision: ten people were killed and fifty-eight injured. So even then, the publicity it earned was unwelcome. Yet one always needs to remember that even inconsequential rivers can sometimes leave their mark in the minds of millions. The Rubicon was an inconspicuous stream which no one really thought much about until Caesar crossed it, thus belligerently demonstrating to his superiors that he didn't intend to obey the rules and disband his army before returning to Rome. Now 'crossing the Rubicon' is part of the language – well, part of the language of cliché, anyway. So maybe the Irk's day will come. Yet having stood for a while, pensive, beside its feebly seeping waters, just out of Cowlishaw, in what had started as drizzle but was now heavy rain, I doubt if there's much chance at present of international fame for the Irk.

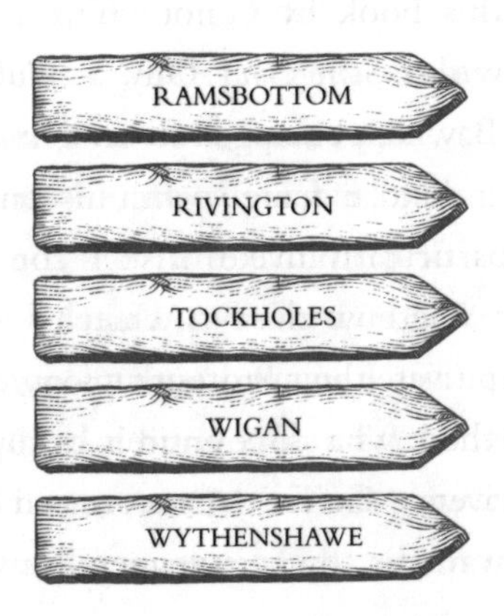

ISLE OF WHITHORN

ISLE OF WHITHORN, spt. vil., with pier, 3¼m. SE. of Whithorn, SE. Wigtownshire…

OUR LAND IS LOPSIDED. People underestimate the way that it tilts. Which is further west, Bristol or Edinburgh? Cardiff or Inverness? The answer in each case may not be the one you first thought of. The angle of the England–Scotland border is deceptive as well. The English city of Sunderland is some ten miles north of the Isle of Whithorn, one of the southernmost spots in Galloway.

This area between Wigtown Bay and Luce Bay is known as the Machars – a Scots Gaelic word meaning a low lying coastal plain. Wigtown is the chief town, though Whithorn is bigger and busier. Wigtown has the bay; and it has books, stocked in the nineteen bookshops which allow it to claim the title of Scotland's book town, although the bookshops on the day I was there were mostly deserted, and it's hardly in the same league as Hay-on-Wye. No longer a county town – the old Wigtownshire was abolished in the 1970s – Wigtown still has a county hall, where the more important meetings in the life of the town are held, along with the biggest occasions during book festivals. It is also – says a book by Gordon Fraser called *Wigtown and Whithorn: Historical and Descriptive Sketches, Stories and Anecdotes, Illustrative of the Racy Wit & Pawky Humour of the District* (1877), which belonged to my grandfather – a place which, to the contemplative and reflecting mind, is fraught with historical interest; frequently bloodstained.

What particularly makes it so is the fate, commemorated at various spots in the town, of the Wigtown martyrs, chief of whom were two women who, because they refused to repudiate their Protestant convictions, were taken out to the bay in 1685 and forcibly drowned. It's a story entirely devoid of racy and pawky humour. Their epitaph on the Wigtown Martyrs' Memorial, erected in 1858 at the top of Windyhill, the highest point in the town, is vengeful. It does not hold back from naming the guilty men. One face of it says: 'This monument has been erected in memory of the noble army of Martyrs in Galloway and other parts of Scotland, by whom, during the age of persecution our Religion and Liberties, as now established, were secured, and as a lesson to posterity never to lose or abuse those glorious privileges planted by their labours, rooted in their Sufferings, and watered by their blood.'

On the east side it says: 'Margaret Wilson, aged 18, daughter of a farmer in Glenvernock, and Margaret McLauchlan, aged 63, tenant in the farm of Drumjargon, both in this County, were drowned by sentence of the public authorities in the waters of Bladnoch, near this place, on the 11th May 1685, because they refused to forsake the principles of the Scottish Reformation, and to take the Government oath abjuring the right of the people to resist the tyranny of their rulers; also William Johnston, gardener; and John Milroy, chapman in Fintilloch; and Gilbert Walker, servant in Kirkala; all in this County, were summarily executed the same year and for the same cause.' The agents of the execution of the two women, 'the actors of this cruel crime', were Lagg, Strachan, Windram and Grahame. Lagg was the laird of Lagg, Grahame the sheriff, and Strachan a military captain. The most hated of these four men was Windram, who took charge of the execution. Up to the very last moment, both women were given their chance to recant. Both refused, according to local accounts, with something like joy. My grandfather's book contains this account by the eighteenth-century historian Robert Woodrow:

> This barbarous sentence was executed the foresaid day, May 11th, and the two women were brought from Wigton, with a numerous crowd of spectators to so extraordinary an execution. Major Windram with some soldiers guarded them to the place of execution. The old woman's stake was a good way in beyond the other, and she was first despatched, in order to terrify the other to a compliance with such oaths and conditions as they required. But in vain; for she adhered to her principles with an unshaken steadfastness. When the water was overflowing her fellow-martyr, some about Margaret Wilson asked her, what she thought of the

> other now struggling with the pangs of death. She answered, What do I see but Christ (in one of his members) wrestling there… When Margaret Wilson was at the stake she sang the 25th Psalm from verse 7th, downward a good way, and read the 8th Chapter to the Romans with a great deal of Cheerfulness, and then prayed. While at prayer, the water covered her; but before she was quite dead, they pulled her up, and held her out of the water till she was recovered, and able to speak, and then by Major Windram's orders she was asked, if she would pray for the King. She answered, 'she wished the salvation of all men, and the damnation of none'.
>
> One deeply affected with the death of the other and her case, said, 'Dear Margaret, say God save the King. Say God save the King!' She answered, in the greatest steadiness and composure, 'God save him, if he will, for it is his salvation I desire'. Whereupon some of her relations near by, desirous to have her life spared, if possible, called out to Major Windram, 'Sir, she hath said it, she hath said it'. Whereupon the major came near, and offered her the abjuration, charging her instantly to swear it, otherwise return to the water. Most deliberately she refused, and said, 'I will not, I am one of Christ's children, let me go'. Upon which she was thrust down again, into the water, where she finished her course with joy. She died a virgin-martyr about eighteen years of age…

Whithorn, eleven miles to the south, has a long and rambling main street, on the west side of which is St Ninian's Priory; Whithorn was the home of the saint and possibly his birthplace, which made it a place of pilgrimage. It developed a reputation for healing, like some kind of minor Gallovidian Lourdes. King James IV of Scotland (1473–1513) came here once every year, sometimes twice. On one occasion, being fearful for the health of his queen, he came all the way from Edinburgh on foot (a distance of 142.6 miles, according to the AA) accompanied by four Italian minstrels, who found the journey too much for them, and had to be carried home on horseback. The king, however, made it; the queen recovered, and St Ninian was allotted the credit. So overjoyed was the king that he then made a further pilgrimage, during which the queen was carried all the way on a litter. Seventeen horses, the king's treasurer recorded, were required to convey her wardrobe and luggage.

The nineteenth century was an age of improvement here. The old thatched hovels, the *Ordnance Gazetteer of Scotland* records, made way for good slated houses, while the streets were no longer grass-grown. A new town hall was built in 1885. My grandfather at this time was a well-regarded figure in Whithorn. Though he was born in Liverpool, this was his home town. He started work in a bank here at fourteen, was transferred to Edinburgh, sent back to Whithorn to gain some managerial experience and then promoted to head office, eventually becoming chief accountant. That meant living in Edinburgh, from where he published several standard books about banking, but he kept his links with Whithorn, where he published a great deal of poetry in the Scots language. He was one of a group of local bards who, as one of them put it in a poem in praise of my grandfather ('Charmed, genial bard of Galloway', it began) 'oft-times blithely did convene' in the town. In retirement he translated the fables of Jean La Fontaine into Scots. A list of notable citizens which I saw displayed in the town, headed by one of the first editors of *The Scotsman*, also includes local poets: Jeanie Donnan, James Cannon, John Fleming – and David McKie. How gratified he would have been to be remembered for his poetry rather than for his banking.

Still, the object of my pilgrimage now was neither Wigtown nor Whithorn but the Isle, a little way to the south. This was once a busy and quite important harbour. In a pub – the Steam Packet – there are pictures of passengers embarking on the *Countess of Galloway* bound for Liverpool. There are pictures too of the place *en fête* for an annual regatta (commodore: the Earl of Galloway). The summer drinks special at the Packet when I was there was

Pimm's No. 1, a concept quite unthinkable in the strict Presbyterian Isle of Whithorn half a century back, when my brother and I, on holiday in a dreadful hotel, were mocked in the street for our English accents. The place dwindled over the years into a fishing port, which it remains. On the edge of the village is St Ninian's Head, the point at which pilgrims used to complete their perilous journeys and give thanks in a chapel whose ruins still stand. Nearby there are two monuments to the crew of a fishing vessel, the *Solway Harvester*, lost with all hands off the Isle of Man in 2000.

Up here by the chapel ruins, with views across Wigtown Bay to the hills of Kirkcudbrightshire, I sat in the sun and tried to imagine the Isle as it was in the time of my grandfather: Presbyterian, stern and God-fearing, and by the lights of this age of Pimm's No. 1, oppressively primitive. There are clusters of modern housing, some seriously ugly, but the sense of unhurried calm and reflectiveness is, I guess, much as it was.

A group of north-country visitors in the pub were extolling the quiet beauty of the Isle. The young barman would have none of it. It's completely dead, he complained. So where did he go for an evening out? 'You can go to Newton Stewart,' he said, as he gloweringly polished a glass, 'but that's dead, too.'

The question one probably shouldn't ask, but I did, in a nearby shop, is: in what sense is the Isle of Whithorn an island? The fact is, it isn't. It used to be a part-time island, since high tides in those days cut it off from the rest of the peninsula, but once the causeway across the foreshore was built, in 1790, it ceased to be so. That seems to be true of many such places that claim to be islands. Since Scotland is said to have nearly 800 offshore islands it would take a very long time to disentangle those that deserve the name from those that do not. But it's clear that several places in England that say they are islands no longer are, and in some cases never were. Some like Holy Island on the Northumberland coast are part-time islands, cut off at times by the tide. Others, like Thanet, once severed from the mainland by the Wantsum Channel, were undeniably islands once but scarcely qualify now. Yet even a place as famously insular as the Isle of Portland was never really an island, linked as it was to the mainland by Chesil Beach. Athelney, Axholme, Ely, Grain, Oxney, Purbeck, Ramsey, Thorney in Cambridgeshire, Wedmore – all in some ways are suspect. Is Skye the island it was now that it's linked by a bridge? Is Sheppey?

Your genuine island is one like Lundy in the Bristol Channel or Caldey off the Pembrokeshire coast, or, on a bigger scale, Wight or Man, which requires you to reach it by boat. You can get to the Isle of Whithorn quite simply by catching one of Mr King's buses from pleasant, though unpulsating, Newton Stewart, which – family pride aside, and unless you are out for bright lights and high excitement and some outside chance of catching sight of celebrities – is an excursion I'd recommend.

ISLIP

ISLIP, par. and vil., with ry. sta., L.M.S., Oxon, on r. Ray, 6m. NNE. of Oxford by rail…

'IF ISLIP HAS ANY claim to fame,' says a leaflet I picked up in the church of St Nicholas, close to the village centre, 'it lies in the fact that it was the birthplace of St Edward the Confessor.' Exactly; and Islip, perched on its hill on the edge of that bleakly mysterious tract of land that is known as Otmoor, doesn't let you forget it. You can, if you wish, follow the Confessor's Walk, introduced to mark the millennium, around the village: a pleasant enough experience, but no one pretends that evidence exists that Edward himself ever walked it.

Still, a king who was also a saint: not many places can be said to have given birth to a hero of such dual distinction. There's a rudimentary picture of him in the church, recording the characteristically generous and pious gesture he made in bestowing his natal town of Islippe on the monks of Westminster. But maybe that isn't the only thing he is famous for giving away. From the eleventh century onwards, there were those who thought that, far from being a figure worthy of reverence (so much so that he was once his country's patron saint), Edward might have helped bring about a gross betrayal which, had we not been the people we were, might have eradicated our true national destiny.

By the end of the reign of William the Conqueror, the triumph of the Normans over the Saxons appeared complete. They ran the country, more authoritatively and thoroughly than the Saxon monarchs had done. They ordained its laws. They remodelled its institutions. The court and the centres of power below it spoke their language. The practices and traditions of the England that they had conquered were cast aside. And in time the legend evolved among those who wished to supplant their masters and assert the rights of the common people that the days of pre-Conquest England had been a golden age, faithful to the concept of liberty, but ruthlessly terminated by the tyrant invaders; to which poor put-upon England must one day return. The writings of Gerrard Winstanley, the leader of the Diggers who took over land at St George's Hill near Cobham in Surrey and declared their inalienable right to it, are full of rants against the Normans and dreams of the restitution of the rights that people enjoyed until the Normans arrived and stole them.

In *The True Levellers Standard Advanced: or, The State of Community Opened, and Presented to the Sons of Men*, Winstanley compared the Conquest to 'the Babylonish yoke laid upon Israel of old under Nebuchadnezzar'. The present 'Kings, Lords, Judges, Bayliffs, and violent, bitter people that are Free-holders', he says, are the true descendants of William, the Norman Bastard, 'who still are from that time to this day in pursuite of that victory, Imprisoning, Robbing, and killing the poor enslaved English Israelites'. In *An Appeal to the House of Commons, Desiring their Answer*, he says: 'The Norman laws William the Conqueror brought into England robbed the people of their land, and those very laws were written in the Norman and the French tongue.' 'Do not stand in awe of the Norman yoke,' he counsels his followers, 'seeing that it is broke': take possession of your own land, 'which the Norman power took from you, and hath kept from you for about 600 years'.

This would be classed today as the politics of the left, and later radicals took up the same theme, notably that great champion of the people's liberties, Tom Paine, who said of 1066: 'a French bastard arriving with armed banditti and establishing himself the King of England against the consent of the natives is in plain terms a very paltry rascally original and certainly has no divinity in it'. Thomas Jefferson set the liberties of the American people in the context of Saxon freedoms before the Norman yoke.

But the political right embraced the message too. The controversy between those who saw the Normans as saviours and those who gave thanks that the Conquest was never complete – exulting that the old culture survived, despite the invaders' ruthless attempts to eradicate it – boiled up in Victorian England. Without the Normans, Thomas Carlyle demanded, what would it have been? 'A gluttonous race of Jutes and Angles capable of no grand combinations, lumbering about in pot-bellied equanimity; not dreaming of heroic toil and silence and endurance such as leads to the high places of this universe, and the golden mountain tops where dwell the spirits of the dawn'. Or, as a twentieth-century historian would put it, 1066 was the moment when England 'emerged from the barbaric twilight into the full glamour and glory of the medieval noonday'.

Yet for many romantics of the right, as for Winstanley, the Saxon age embodied values that ought never to have been abandoned. The right of the people of England to determine their own destiny had before 1066, as they imagined, been sacrosanct, and ought to be sacrosanct now. Champions of self-government, and particularly of local self-government – hailed by *The Times* as 'the most distinctive peculiarity of our race', to be proudly contrasted with the subservience in which foreign rulers held their subject peoples – lauded the Saxon and condemned the Norman.

The historian Edward Augustus Freeman, one of Carlyle's antagonists in the battles over pot-bellied equanimity, described the Norman yoke so complained of by Winstanley and others as a merely ephemeral imposition incapable of disturbing the deep entrenchment in the psyche of England of its Saxon inheritance. It was only, he wrote, 'a temporary overthrow of our national being'. The fabled power of the Norman was evanescent. Before very long, 'England was England again'.

One essential piece of evidence would seem to support this theory of national continuity: the nature of the language we speak. Walter Scott, another great popularizer of the Saxon cause, famously pointed out the difference between the words we use for the meat that is placed on the table – beef, mutton, pork – and the words we use for the animals that provide it – cow, sheep, pig. The indigenous people of England produced; the Normans consumed.

In a masterly account of the evolution of the language we use today, *The Adventure of English* (2003), Melvyn Bragg analyses the sources from which it comes. Our everyday conversation, he says, is steeped in Old English. The Conquest was 'the greatest threat the English language has ever encountered'. After 1066, the new social order was spelled out in French: crown, throne, court, duke, baron, nobility, also peasant, authority and obedience, all derived from the Normans. In the law, words have come down to us – felony, warrant, judge, jury, justice – which we owe to them too. Few of the great men of power spoke English. 'If you believe', says Bragg, 'that words carry history and meaning often deeper than their daily purpose, then we see with the coming of the Normans an almighty shift of power. The words that regulated society and enforced the hierarchy, the words that made the laws, the words in which society engaged and enjoyed itself were, at the top, and pressing down relentlessly, Norman French. Latin stood firm for sacred and high secular purposes. English was a poor third in its own country.' And yet it was never crushed. It remained the speech of the people. Even under the yoke, it went on evolving.

So it could be said that on any analysis stopping short of the pot-bellied equanimity school, those who let the Conqueror in had a lot to answer for. That could mean Harold and his forces at Hastings, exhausted after their now half-remembered victory at Stamford Bridge. Or of course it could, I mused as I walked the Confessor trail, mean Edward.

The role of Islip's favourite son is at issue here. Edward the Confessor, son of Emma of Normandy, lived for his first twenty-five years in France. His continuing Norman connections were one of the counts against him that brought him into conflict with territorial chieftains like Godwine, Earl of Wessex. Whether or not he gave secret undertakings to his Norman kinsmen – perhaps even employing Harold as go-between – that William of Normandy should be his successor can never now be determined. The Normans, naturally, asserted that this was so; the Saxons, equally naturally, denied it. But suspicions must have persisted. Edward, of course, was a saint, and a miracle worker – capable of curing scrofula with his mere touch; even as one contemporary biographer claimed, 'like an angel'. Therefore, it must be presumed, he was a man of peace. His canonization was secured in 1161 in the reign of a king, Henry II, who sought to reconcile the Norman and Saxon traditions and to emphasize the continuity of his office. How better to do that than by celebrating the God-given king who (allegedly) had made William his heir?

In time, Edward's reputation as a king so attached to peace, and by extension, so weak, that he had no place in appeals on the eve of battle, led to his being supplanted as patron saint of his country by that wonderfully elusive but undeniably valiant figure, St George. 'Cry God for Harry, England and St George' stiffened the sinews at Harfleur. 'Cry God, for Harry, England, and St Edward the Confessor' might have led to the wrong result.

In March 2005 the Oxford historian Henrietta Leyser, who lives in Islip, came to the village hall to deliver a lecture to the Otmoor Archaeological and Historical Society in which she sought to assert the facts and dispel the myths about Islip's hero. Mrs Leyser is not a subscriber to the pot-bellied equanimity theory. Edward, she said, was the king and head of the richest and most sophisticated state of Western Europe. This was an age of prosperity: there were many people with money to spend – and the desire to be seen spending it. Indeed, that was one reason why England attracted Viking incursions. There was plenty to grab. That was why, on the death of Ethelred, father of Edward, Cnut took the throne, and with it, Ethelred's widow, Emma of Normandy.

What of the story of Edward's endorsement of William rather than Harold? Whatever the truth of that, Mrs Leyser argued, it was, at base, irrelevant, since according to English rules of succession, Edward had no authority to make such an offer. 'English kingship', she said, 'was elective; only a small group at any one time were eligible to make such a choice – usually the previous king's sons – but succession was not automatic, and however much influence the king might bring to bear, it was still, emphatically, not in his gift. The chief men of the country had to meet, to discuss and agree; only then came election and coronation.'

So whether Edward named William as his heir or whether, as others claimed, he settled on his deathbed for Harold was a matter, it seemed, of no significance. It was heartening after my morning in Islip to feel I could leave the place without a stain on his character.

IWERNE COURTNEY, OR SHROTON

IWERNE COURTNAY, OR SHROTON, par. and vil., N. Dorset, on r. Iwerne, 4½m. NW. of Blandford… pop. 417…

IWERNE COURTNEY, OR SHROTON? Shroton, or Iwerne Courtney? Why can't they or won't they make up their minds? Bartholomew, who uses the spelling 'Courtnay', seems to prefer the statelier name, since his entry for Shroton says: see Iwerne Courtnay. Yet if this was the balance of public opinion when Bartholomew's book was compiled, that's not the case now. My investigations suggest that Shroton (originally Sheriff's Town, which sounds more of a social match for Iwerne Courtney than Shroton could ever aspire to) is in the ascendant. The notice board in front of the church maintains a studied neutrality by not naming either claimant, though once inside, you're left in no doubt by a sign that says 'Welcome to St Mary's Shroton.' Other witnesses on this side of the argument are a banner which says 'St Mary's Shroton' and an invitation to join the next Alpha course in Shroton, and a wash drawing labelled as *St Mary's, Shroton, From The South*, 1565, donated by Robert Crew, 'who would like to be remembered as having made the highest score for Shroton cricket club up to 1934 and as having played for the MCC'.

The pub, which is called the Cricketers, is unconditionally Shroton too. Nearby I noted a promise that Dorset Moviola would be proudly presenting *The Inside Man* (15) in the Elizabeth Freake Hall in association with the Shroton Village Hall committee. Yet the hall itself sported a notice put up by the Iwerne Courtney and Stapleton Parish Council. One local writer has suggested that anyone who says Iwerne rather than Shroton must be a visitor. I asked the landlord of the Cricketers whether he would agree. He replied with the weary courtesy of someone who'd been asked that question on a thousand occasions before that he thought he probably did. For himself, the choice was no contest, since Shroton was so much simpler.

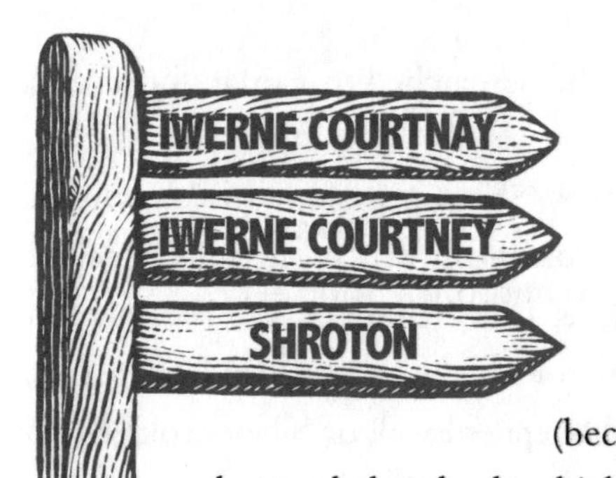

Let me not suggest that Iwerne Courtnay, Iwerne Courtney and Shroton have nothing of interest to offer apart from contentious nomenclature. The church was the scene of an epic encounter during the English Civil Wars when a kind of third force known as the Clubmen (because clubs were the only weapons they carried), who tended to back whichever side, Royalist or Parliamentarian, was doing worse in a given place at a given time, encamped on the hills across the main road from the village. In a book called *Highways and Byways in Dorset*, Sir Frederick Treves, a Dorchester surgeon, gives a patronising mock-kindly account of them. 'Every hamlet', he writes, 'mustered its lumbering quotum of red-faced countrymen; and a fine show they made when they gathered at the village cross, valiant with much ale, gay with ribbons and flags, wept over by wives and sweethearts, and hoarse with shouting, "For England and our homes…" Poor red-faced, clumsy patriots, they were doomed to do nothing but come to grief.'

Cromwell's forces came across several hundred of them (Treves thinks 2,000; Carlyle, in an edition of Cromwell's letters and speeches suggested 4,000) who had dug in close by on Hambledon Hill. The Parliamentarians attempted at first to negotiate, but in the manner of Sir William Courtenay at Bossenden Woods, a Mr Bravell, minister of Compton Abbas, a little way north, said he would pistol anyone who retreated. So Cromwell felt he had no choice left but to have them attacked, a task he entrusted to Desborow. Some Clubmen fled, some fell; 'they beat them from the woods', Cromwell reported to Fairfax, 'and did some dismal execution upon them; I believe killed not twelve of them, but cut very many'.

Many more were marched into the village and stowed in the church, where Cromwell made them confess that they were misguided. He was not, however, as vengeful as his reputation might have made them fear. 'We have taken about three hundred,' he wrote to Fairfax, 'many are poor silly creatures, whom if you please to let me send home, they promise to be very dutiful for time to come, and will be hanged before they come out again.' The ringleaders, though, who had taken Parliamentary soldiers prisoner and used them barbarously, would be despatched to Fairfax for him to decide their fate.

Let me also never suggest that Iwerne Courtney/Shroton is alone in this state of geographical indecision. Bartholomew lists plenty more, from which one might pick at random Campbelltown or Ardersier, Inverness-shire; Dairsiemuir or Osnaburgh, and Cellardyke or Nether Kilkenny, both Fife; Northmoor Green or Moorland, Somerset; Golant in Cornwall, which is also St Sampson, and Shepherdswell or Sibertswold, Kent. There's a pub in Dorset which calls itself the Sailor's Return, Chaldon Herring; but the barmaid said the Herring isn't so often invoked, and residents usually call it East Chaldon.

In some cases, one name has ousted another over the years. Tayport, across the river from Dundee or more precisely from Broughty Ferry, whose two fixed lights, Bartholomew tells us, can be seen at 12 miles and 10 miles, may also, he says, be addressed as Ferryport-on-Craig. The Hertfordshire village of Nasty used to have the alternative name of Munden Furnival, but as far as I can ascertain it is pure Nasty now. Hurstbourne Tarrant in Hampshire has likewise ceased to be known as Uphusband. Some confusion was caused by the railway companies, who, as we shall see when we get to Pontlottyn, were choosy, even pernickety, about the names they attached to their stations (which is why you have the strange circumstance that Clapham Junction is not in Clapham and Willesden Junction is not in Willesden). In Durham, the railway balked at Egglescliffe, insisting on Eaglescliff; on the Essex coast they insisted that Walton-on-the-Naze had to be Walton-on-Naze. Brooding on these matters after an excellent pint and pie at the Cricketers, I bade 'goodbye' to sweet Shroton, and 'au revoir' to Iwerne Courtnay or Courtney.

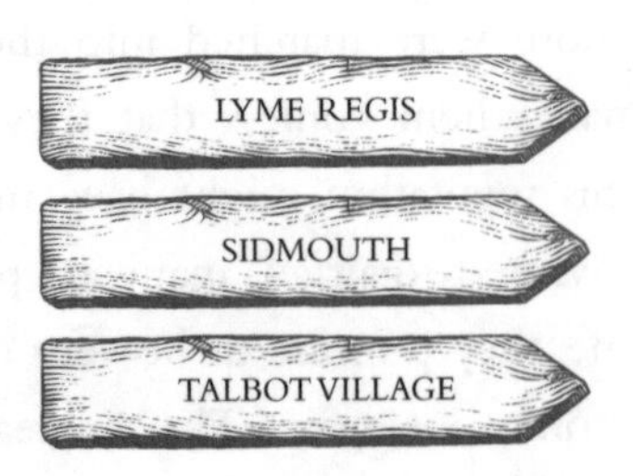

A B C D

E F G H

I J K L

M N O P

Q R S T

U V W X Y Z

JACKFIELD

JACKFIELD, eccl. dist, and vil., Broseley par., Salop…

A MILE OR SO FROM the visitor-rich streets of Ironbridge, in a riverside settlement called Jackfield, there's a pub called The Boat, over the door of which is the legend 'Unspoiled by progress'. This seems odd on the edge of a place which, more perhaps than anywhere else in Britain, exemplifies progress – once throbbing with industrial activity and now scattered with buildings and sites that celebrate what progress made us: the iron foundries of Coalbrookdale, the porcelain factories of Coalport, the canal and its linked inclined plane at the Hay, and the great iron bridge itself, a technological innovation which means as much in our history as any bridge of Telford or Brunel.

In a book called *The Iron Bridge: Symbol of the Industrial Revolution*, Neil Cossons, who used to run the modern Ironbridge complex, and the historian Barrie Trinder say of this bridge that it epitomizes not only the development of engineering science but a whole optimistic view of industrial society. For the age that followed, progress was something to be celebrated, almost as a matter of faith: it was the religion of manufacturing Britain.

Yet the claim of The Boat to be somewhere that's safe from progress suggests the erosion of that belief and that optimism. Progress here, as so often today, is seen as something detrimental, something that destroys. In the name of progress, lovely old buildings are extirpated, great landscapes scarred, even utterly spoiled, in the service of high-speed travel. Why can't they leave things alone? Why must everything always be changing? Why do *they* – that vague, undefined but always menacing 'they' – insist on taking our birthright?

Such a reaction is not always based on reasoned reflection but more on instinct, or the tug of the heart. It explains why we venerate Betjeman, above poets of broader range and talent. He's the one that wanted bombs to fall on progress-wracked Slough. He's the one who warned that planners – plansters, he calls them – have little regard for what we cherish. Less known than his invocation of friendly bombs, but even more characteristic, is a furious piece called 'The Planster's Vision':

> Cut down that timber! Bells, too many and strong,
>   Pouring their music through the branches bare,
>   From moon-white church-towers down the windy air
> Have pealed the centuries out with Evensong.
> Remove those cottages. A huddled throng!
>   Too many babies have been born in there,
>   Too many coffins, bumping down the stair,
> Carried the old their garden paths along.
>
> I have a Vision of the Future, chum,
>   The workers' flats in fields of soya beans
>   Tower up like silver pencils, score on score:
> And Surging Millions hear the Challenge come
>   From microphones in communal canteens
>   'No right! No wrong! All's perfect, evermore.'

And indeed, even here in this easy, gentle, unchallenging corner of Shropshire, industry at its most furious once created scenes that might have come out of hell – as in the roaring red flames in the painting by Philip James de Loutherbourg called *Coalbrookdale by Night* which hangs in the Science Museum in London. These were sights which some found majestically beautiful, and others, in the proper sense of the word, quite frightful. The bridge itself was an object of pride and pleasure when it was opened on New Year's Day 1781. The New Inn on the bank, now the Tontine Hotel, advertised itself as 'close to the Cast Iron Bridge, so universally admired, in the centre of most Romantic country'; yet there were those even then who complained that monkeying about with iron rather than simply building a conventional bridge was an expensive mistake. Indeed, the original plans were modified in the light of such objections. But the flames from the furnaces, the clamour that came from productive industry, were a price to be paid for progress which prosperous Victorian England (that part of the population, anyway, which would never be required to work there, among whom public debate was conducted) was happy to pay. Yet if the Great Exhibition was the crowning exemplification of the celebration of progress, a reaction against it was already evident as observers from Marx and Engels to Ruskin and Morris condemned the ruinous damage that some of this progress had brought.

Here's another aspect of progress to reflect on at Jackfield. One problem in building the iron bridge was that the sides of the Severn Gorge are notoriously unstable. A landslide at nearby Build was in 1773, eight years before the bridge was opened, was described as an earthquake. And Severn tides rise high and cause flooding, as is demonstrated by the record of previous flood levels which you'll find outside The Boat. Indeed, in 1957, before present protections were in place, part of Jackfield village was swept away. The highest tide on The Boat's indicator was 19 ft 6 ins in November 2000, but thanks to schemes of improvement – in other words, progress – no more of the village was lost.

Still, I can't deny that the thought of a pub unspoiled by progress, not marred by the sound of piped music or customers yacketing into their mobile phones, or the clamour of cars revving up in the car park, with its ancient dimness and darkness preserved from excessive abrasive light, was alluring. So I sought to visit The Boat, particularly in the hope of noting how it differed from the simulated nineteenth-century pub across the river in the re-created Victorian village at the Blists Hill site. I went there

first on a lunchtime in mid-November, a bleak kind of day with few people about: even the iron bridge had hardly any admirers. The Boat was shut. I went again in summer, on the night before a Bank Holiday, expecting the place to be buzzing as much as any location unspoiled by progress could manage. It was shut again. And this time a notice had been displayed. Sorry, it said, we are closed for refurbishment.

For *refurbishment*? Is not refurbishment a sub-division of progress? Would they need after all these years to block out these legend above the door? I shall have to go back yet again to see.

JACOB'S ISLAND

JACOB'S ISLAND, in met. bor. of Bermondsey, co. of London. In his *Oliver Twist* Dickens made this densely populated locality the scene of Bill Sykes's death

THE SCENE OF BILL Sikes's death? You would hardly think so to see it now. Not many villainous bullying murderers, desperate to escape their just deserts, fall to their deaths, hanged by the very rope they hoped would be their means of escape, on Jacob's Island nowadays. This tract of land just east of Tower Bridge on what used to be called the wrong side of the river is now, for the most part, relentlessly smart. The Thamesside warehouses – St George's, St Saviour's, Butlers, Scott's Sufferance, New Concordia, Java – are still there, but wholly transformed, some as shopping and restaurant complexes, and some as the sort of apartments which developers like to call 'stunning'. A fountain plays in the private gardens beneath the balconies of highly desirable, even more highly expensive, modern apartments. The bars by the river pulsate with chattering custom.

Those who drink and dine here, even those who live here, probably have little idea of what this place was like when Dickens invoked it in *Oliver Twist* or Henry Mayhew called it 'a peninsula set in sewers'. Even the evocation of the past in this place has a romantic ring to it: there's a Southwark Council plaque in Mill Street recording that most of the island's original buildings had gone by 1860, replaced by Victorian constructions many of which have now gone too. 'In the early nineteenth century,' it says, 'this area was a notorious rookery or slum. Dickens used it in his novel *Oliver Twist*. He set Fagin's den in one of the warehouses, and Bill Sykes met his grisly end in the ooze bed of Folly Ditch.'

This territory, perhaps more than any other in London, has gone from one socio-economic extreme to the other. People who live in Providence Square nowadays have every reason to be grateful to providence: those who, in Mayhew's day, lived in

Providence Buildings had every reason to curse it. What brings people here now, at work and at play, has a single uniting thread: affluence. What brought Charles Dickens, Charles Kingsley and Henry Mayhew here was the spectacle of misery and suffering. The worst, most crowded, most unsavoury and insanitary, most contaminated, most death-dealing tracts of housing in London were known as rookeries. The most famous was in St Giles, but that did not make it the worst. 'All have heard of the rookeries of St Giles', says Charles Knight's *London*, published in the early 1840s 'but less is known of Jacob's Island.'

If so, that was hardly the fault of Dickens or of Kingsley, who in *Alton Locke* (1850) describes the state of Jacob's Island in pages for which the reader will need a strong stomach. Yet Mayhew, pursuing fact, evokes this place in terms that are hardly less dreadful. He described it in a report for the *Morning Chronicle* on 24 September 1849, soon after a terrible epidemic of cholera had abated. 'Out of the 12,800 deaths which, within the last three months, have arisen from cholera,' he wrote, 'more than half occurred on the southern shores of the Thames; and to this awful number no localities contributed so largely as Lambeth, Southwark and Bermondsey, each, at the height of the disease, adding its hundred victims a week to the fearful catalogue of mortality. Anyone who has ventured a visit to the last-named of these places in particular, will not wonder at the ravages of the pestilence in this malarious quarter, for it is bounded on the north and east by filth and fever, and on the south and west by want, squalor, rags and pestilence. Here stands, as it were, the very capital of cholera... Jacob's Island – a patch of ground insulated by the common sewer...'

The striking peculiarity of the quarter, Mayhew wrote, consisted in the wooden galleries and sleeping rooms at the backs of the houses overhanging the turbid flood. They were built on piles, some extending so far out that they almost touched the houses opposite; 'and here, with the very stench of death arising through the boards, human beings sleep night after night, until the last sleep of all comes upon them years before its time'. Behind the houses, those whose properties ran to a yard had built pigsties. Cocks and hens scratched at the cinder heaps, looking for offal. Mayhew's guide was Dr Martin, from the Registrar's office. As they walked down George Row, the doctor recalled that a little while back he could see at the corner of London Street at least nine houses, in a group of perhaps a dozen, where one or two people were lying dead of the cholera. The narrow close courts beyond never saw the sun. In a street called The Folly, Dr Martin described the house of a barber who had somehow survived scarlet fever and two bouts of typhus. His child was dead from cholera; his wife had it now. It was a wonder, said Martin, that any of them was alive, for when the barber put his hand on the wall behind him it would be covered with the spoil of his neighbour's privy, sopping through the wall.

What followed in their progress through today's hyper-affluent island was even worse. 'As we passed along the reeking banks of the sewer, the sun shone upon a narrow slip of the water. In the bright light it appeared the colour of strong green tea, and positively looked as solid as black marble in the shadow – indeed, it was more like watery mud than muddy water; and yet we were assured this was the only water the wretched inhabitants had to drink. As we gazed in horror at it, we saw drains and sewers emptying their filthy contents into it; we saw a whole tier of doorless privies in the open road, common to men and women, built over it; we heard bucket after bucket of filth splash into it, and the limbs of the vagrant boys bathing in it seemed, by pure force of contrast, white as Parian marble… We saw a little child from one of the galleries opposite lower a tin can with a rope, to fill a large bucket that stood beside her…' Finally, they crossed a little shaky bridge into Providence Buildings, his 'peninsula set in sewers'. And here, in a garden no bigger than a tablecloth, they saw the round red head of a dahlia.

It is good that Southwark Council should remind those who live on, or simply frequent, Jacob's Island of Dickens's account of the place, but ideally they would have recommended a reading of Mayhew too. By the way, the authority ought to note (and Bartholomew should have done, too) that Dickens spells his villain Sikes, and not Sykes.

JAYWICK

JAY WICK, ham., E. Essex, 2½m. SW. of Clacton.

BARTHOLOMEW'S *GAZETTEER* LISTS SEVEN places called Paradise: one hamlet (in Somerset), five 'localities' (in Hertfordshire, Lancashire, Northumberland, Warwickshire and Worcestershire), and one 'place and seat' (in Gloucestershire). But people have different definitions of Paradise. They find it in places which others might consider wholly unparadisal. There is no better case that I know than Jaywick (as Bartholomew ought to have spelled it) on the coast of Essex just below Clacton. People say Clacton is vulgar, but compared with Jaywick it's positively effete. For a time the house agents' notices along the route try to persuade us we might still be in Clacton. Then they give up, and Jaywick begins.

This place was created for, and by, plotlanders (a word applied by planners to people who bought small plots of land which were sold off piecemeal). And maybe the first bits you see are not very different from many other such places that plotlanders took over in the years between the world wars. Some of their buildings have a slightly knockabout air, but there's little outrageous in the various Walks and Ways on either side of the road that bisects the settlement, with roads on the beach side all given names that reflect their superior station: *Sea* Pink Way and *Sea* Shell Way and *Sea* Holly Way where it's mere Pink Way, Shell Way and Holly Way on the less favoured side. The house names reflect the air of contentment which must have infected families who, until they came here, had lived all their lives in London's East End. Happy Days. Why Worry? Bodger's Rest. And then, as you come to the Slots of Fun Amusement Hall, everything changes and disbelief begins to set in.

Jaywick or, as it used to be called, Jaywick Sands, was created by a man called Frank Christopher Stedman, usually known as Foff. He began it in 1928, reclaiming some of the land which he then proceeded to sell to the better-off portions of largely impoverished London districts like Stepney, Poplar, East and West Ham. His prices seemed enticingly low, and a service of three coaches a day, six at weekends, made it easy to get to your cherished seaside retreat. At first he had planned for permanent occupation, but some of the technical difficulties at Jaywick, particularly the lack of main drainage, made him settle for holiday homes – ladies' and gentlemen's dressing rooms, together with a lounge and a reading room, some of his literature said: no more, in effect, than glorified beach huts.

Stedman is a difficult man to place. George Lansbury, the East End MP who founded and edited the *Daily Herald*, led (and was jailed for) the Poplar rates strike, and was briefly, almost by accident, leader of the Labour Party, was a friend and admirer. Jaywick, he declared on one visit, was a happy place: 'It has been a real joy and pleasure to see the good feeling among you,' he told the inhabitants. Most of his audience would have agreed: this was their community, and they liked, even loved it, in spite of what the rest of the world might say. And yet there were blots on this paradise. Stedman did not always deliver what he so generously promised. Where were such inducements, advertised in his brochures, as the bathing pool, the licensed club, the tennis courts, the sporting lake offering motor boat racing, water polo and water carnivals? Be patient, he told them, they're coming. Not paradise lost: more paradise postponed.

The Clacton Council was constantly after him too, often backing its complaints with the threat of recourse to the courts. One of the problems was that some of Stedman's families were living illicitly there all the year round. Stedman said he had made it clear that they must not do so, but the plotlanders claimed they had purchased on the basis that they'd be able to sleep there, which the council could well believe. Lord Justice Greer, called to adjudicate in a case in 1936, was no more impressed with Stedman than were the councillors and their officials. In their book *Arcadia for All: the Legacy of a Makeshift Landscape*, Dennis Hardy and Colin Ward report this exchange:

> *Lord Justice Greer*: Of course it should never have been made a building estate at all.
>
> *Mr Montgomery* [for Stedman]: That may be, my Lord.

Lord Justice Greer: I think it is perfectly scandalous.
Mr Montgomery: It may have been unfortunate. I have not a word to say on behalf of Mr Stedman.
Mr Beyfus [for the council]: Someone has said that the bungalow owners were poor people. In fact they were nothing of the kind. They were people who went there at weekends and took their cars with them.
Lord Justice Greer: Nobody with ample means would go and live in this marsh!

Yes, their paradise was in some senses a marsh. That was another of Stedman's miscalculations. The council had warned him when he began that the land was subject to flooding. He had chosen not to believe them. So when the homesteaders weren't fighting Stedman, they were fighting the sea. In 1948 there were storms which, according to the historian of Jaywick, Mary Lyons, tore the place apart, with some 2,000 people having to be evacuated and a bill for damage of around £100,000. The following year there were gales which swept the sea over the wall that the freeholders had erected in defence of their homes.

In the subsequent wave of recriminations, they sacked their committee and installed a tougher one, led by a man called Adrian Wolfe, a mosaics dealer from Chelsea who had owned one of Stedman's bungalows since 1932. Wolfe cajoled and bullied them into raising the money to build a superior fortification against the sea, which soon became known as Adrian's Wall. The local Tory MP came to open it in May 1951. But the floods of 31 January and 1 February 1953, which devastated so much of the Essex coast, were too powerful even for Adrian's Wall. They were thought to be the worst to affect this coast for 250 years, and though warning messages were despatched to alert the community, they did not get through until well past midnight. The wall survived, but the water, more than 2,000 gallons by one subsequent estimate, simply washed over it. Thirty-five people died: some were drowned in their beds; one man saw his artificial leg swept out to sea. The local policeman crawled all the way to Clacton to warn that Jaywick had suffered this disaster and was ordered to crawl straight back again to help out. Of some 600 buildings, around 400 were damaged, 250 of them seriously. Some who fled that night never came back.

In time the sea defences were strengthened again, though never enough for the freeholders, who suffered from further floods at the turn of the year in 1977–8 and 1982–3. They could never feel safe until the completion in 1988 of the West Clacton ('West Clacton' rather than Jaywick, note) sea defence scheme. Now a formidable fortification stands between the settlement and the sea – cutting off, by a savage irony, the view of the excellent beaches and the sea beyond which was partly why people settled here. Perhaps that is why it is nowadays Jaywick, rather than Jaywick Sands.

The damage was worst of all in the region beyond the Slots of Fun Amusement centre, where, as you wander through Jaywick, wonderment turns to disbelief. Here are juxtapositions of salubrious little houses, some sporting coach-lights, some equipped with burglar alarms, with derelict, boarded-up buildings or plots where hardly a trace of earlier buildings is left. The roads are pitted and puddled: abandoned and smashed-up cars are parked in front of abandoned and smashed-up buildings. What makes these scenes even more poignant is the naming of the roads: Alvis, Lancia, Fiat, Riley – and in the Grasslands estate beyond them, Lincoln, Napier, Buick, Lanchester, Daimler, Triumph: all named for the smartest, most fashionable cars bought by the rich and famous around the time this place was created. The main estate in this sector of Jaywick is called Brooklands, after the Surrey racetrack where world-famous drivers raced between 1907 and 1939. Stedman was a car fanatic and built his 'new town' to match. What you don't see, until you look at the map, is that the very shape of Brooklands reflects that addiction. It's designed in the form of a Daimler radiator.

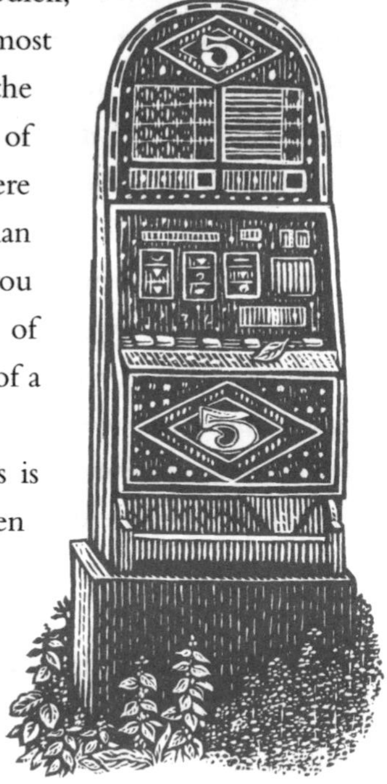

The single track road from the Slots of Fun onwards is squeezed, as it passes this strange procession of houses, between them and the wall, making it feel like some kind of trench. At the end, it gives way to Tower Park. If you climb the sea wall, you can see what awaits you there: a seemingly endless roofscape of caravans. The voice of the bingo caller echoes across the wastes like some kind of muezzin.

J. D. Salinger wrote a novel called *For Esme with Love and Squalor*, and this is a place of love and squalor, distressing to those who like order or who simply recoil from a landscape of wholesale mess – but loved, as Lansbury said, by those who have chosen to be here. And others have championed Jaywick too: Hardy and Ward, in *Arcadia For All*, quote an architecture critic, Sutherland Lyall: 'Not shanty town jerry building, but an indigenous British paradigm of the way twentieth-century "bricoleurs" respond directly to their exigent circumstances'. Certainly some of those who come and recoil forget that the instincts which brought people to Jaywick are much the same as those to which they responded themselves when they bought their own little place in Cornwall or France.

Jaywick even had champions in the government service. 'I found this extraordinary piece of shack development surprising and rather interesting in a way,' wrote a civil servant called P. J. F. Mansfield, holding his nose as he contemplated this indigenous British paradigm but retaining his liberal instincts, 'though it does leave one with a feeling of nausea about it all. There are many hundreds of wooden shacks erected without proper regard for the right use of materials or proper layout, but it is an inescapable fact that the colony does provide for many thousands of holiday-makers each year to enjoy a holiday by the sea, under living conditions of some independence... The Jaywick estate, though it is emphatically not a piece of development which should ever have been allowed to grow up in its present form, is there, and must be accepted...'

That kind of defence was invaluable when the Jaywick freeholders began an even more crucial fight than their battles with Stedman, who had died in 1963. In 1971, the local authorities sought to close Jaywick down – to eliminate it entirely, and replace it with something markedly more salubrious. And not just on the grounds of aesthetics. Medical evidence was submitted that the place was a health risk. The inspector who heard the inquiry disagreed. These people, he wrote, were worthy citizens, with a high degree of community organization, who should not be pushed around just because their houses were sub-standard. He censured the local authority for perpetuating Stedman's failure to bring them the water supply and the drainage for which Jaywick had then been waiting for half a century.

At the opening of the new century there was at last generous money for rehabilitating the place, with a scheme put forward by Tendring District Council winning a rural challenge competition. A new development on the road back to Clacton, past the Grasslands estate, came in for plaudits of a kind that original Jaywick would never have dreamed of receiving, for a group of wooden-clad three-storey houses which, faithful to Stedman's addiction, has been called Lotus Way. 'The project, with high insulation standards and solar power, has won a string of awards', the *Guardian* observed. Maybe; but at the risk of sounding curmudgeonly, I have to say that the look of this new creation is so passionless, so reserved, so austere, compared with the wild impromptu diversity of the settlement to which it's been added, that it seems like a kind of rebuke. And certainly, it is far removed from the dreams of twentieth-century 'bricoleurs' responding directly to their exigent circumstances by creating their own private paradigms and paradises.

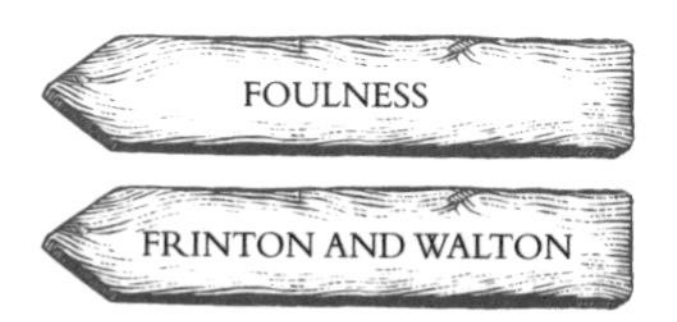

A B C D
E F G H
I J K L
M N O P
Q R S T
U V W XYZ

KEIGHLEY

KEIGHLEY (pronounced Keethley), mun. bor., mkt.-town and par., with ry. sta. L.M.S. (alt. 324 ft), N. div. W.R. Yorks, 9m. NW. of Bradford... Keighley communicates with Hull by the Leeds and Liverpool Canal.

THERE WASN'T A DAANYAAR food store next to Staples the butchers (quality meat from the Dales) when I used to walk every morning almost fifty years ago to report for duty at the *Keighley News* (Keighley, pronounced Keethley, as Bartholomew usefully warns us: even the regional news on TV sometimes gets it wrong) and there certainly weren't all these cheerful brown faces as the children spilled out from St Anne's Roman Catholic primary at teatime. Or, as they would say in Keighley, when the schools were 'loosing' the children. Keighley had its own modes of speech which seemed strange even coming from Leeds. 'The pictures are loosing' meant people were coming out of the cinema after the latest Cary Grant or James Cagney. The greeting to friends in the street was usually 'now then'.

This was all part of the sense that Keighley was Keighley and not merely part of somewhere else. As you walk along North Street, its grandest and most stylish thoroughfare, you can still catch the sense of the civic pride which suffused the place at the time it achieved its coveted borough status, in 1882. That has gone, of course, in local government reorganization. Keighley today is officially Keighley, Bradford: it's a mere dependency, compared with what it used to be.

One of Keighley's own subordinate villages is called Ingrow, and that seemed right, for Keighley seemed a curiously ingrown place. They used to say in the reporters' room that if you looked out of the window for five minutes or so, you'd see somebody passing by who was related to one of the *Keighley News* staff. 'That's my auntie!' one of the homegrown reporters would chirrup. That didn't apply to us graduate trainees who, in Keighley parlance, were merely 'off-coom'd -uns' (meaning people who had come from outside this territory). The great Keighley familes married each other and sons were given their mothers' surnames as forenames, which was why, in the course of a day, you might find yourself talking to a man called Brigg Smith and a man called Smith Brigg. (The town clerk redeemed this monotony: his name was Julius Caesar.)

The marriages page in the News – the *Keighley News and Bingley Chronicle*, as it was then – seemed to me to contain an amazingly high proportion of people from somewhere in Keighley wedding people from somewhere in Keighley. To encounter someone from Oakworth marrying into, say, Sheffield came as a culture shock. Mr Smith from Haworth, Miss Brigg from Riddlesden: that was the staple arrangement, with copious accounts of what the bride and her bridesmaids were wearing, and a final line which told you where they had gone on honeymoon; probably Filey, then (today it could be Phuket).

Even mighty Bradford in those days seemed in some ways parochial. We at the *Keighley News* served as a local news service for the Bradford evening paper, the *Telegraph and Argus*. The editor then was a big bold figure, still detectably Welsh, called O. B. Stokes. If you see O. B. in a corridor, I was warned by old hands, he will stop you, ask who you are, and then challenge you to write two words in shorthand: hospital and ambulance. (Stokes was a powerful figure on the local hospital board.) I duly met Stokes in a corridor and confessed I was the new graduate trainee. 'Got your note book?' he said. 'Let's see your shorthand. Write "hospital". Good. Now write…' Of course I had practised them both, so came away basking in his approval.

The Telegraph in Stokes's time was obsessively all about Bradford. It was mocked even in self-centred Keighley. Once on some dull news day we had a competition for the most characteristic headline that could ever appear in the *Telegraph*. 'Bradford man', read the winner, 'slightly injured in nuclear holocaust'.

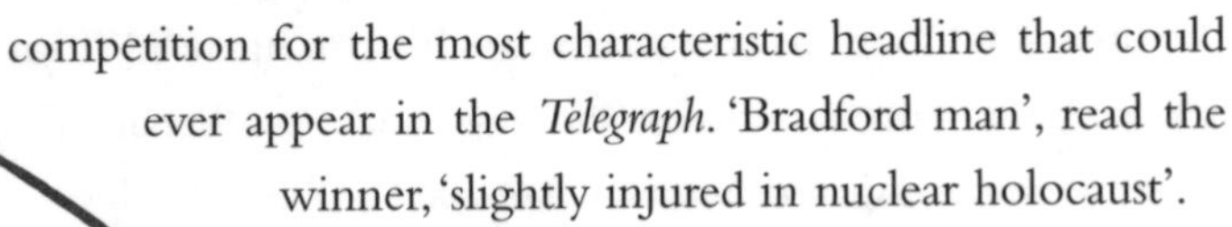

The *Keighley News* in those days had two hauntingly frequent items. Week after week, the headline came up on the inside pages: 'Septuagenarian sustains fatal fall'. Sometimes it was an octogenarian, and just now and then even a nonagenarian, but it gave you the feeling that at any given moment, somewhere in Keighley, a septuagenarian or one of his seniors would be terminally falling down. The word 'sustained' seemed an inescapable part of the formula. The other, in a town with a strong choral tradition, was a report of some recent performance of Handel's *Messiah*. ('Never "*The Messiah*", lad', I was warned soon after I joined; always, '*Messiah*'.) Week after week there would be a reverent notice in the *News* of the latest *Messiah* put on by some church or choral society. The formula, again, was always the same. 'A moving [or 'memorable': the adjective at least was varied from time to time] performance of Handel's *Messiah* was rendered at Ingrow Church…'

The editor of the *News* then was a man called Bill Black, who'd returned to his home town (where his father had long ago edited a rival weekly, the *Herald*, which the *News* had put out of business) after a long career as a senior sub-editor on papers all over England, including, for a while, London. Black was a kindly soul, but, like Stokes, was said to be frightening when angry. One day he marched fiercely into the reporters' room, without any word of greeting, and, producing a drawing pin and a sheet of paper, hammered them into the notice board. When he'd gone we crept tremblingly up to the notice board to see what it was we'd done wrong. The rebuke was terse but masterful. It said: 'Music is never rendered – only lard. WHB.'

In Keighley Library, which used to be an austere and disciplined place where noise was growled at and elderly people brought in their magnifying glasses to read the columns of our rival, the *Craven Herald and Pioneer*, a paper published in Skipton, I skimmed through some recent copies of today's *Keighley News*, which went tabloid (I'm sorry, compact) in March 2007. No *Messiah*s here, even in the run-up to Easter; hardly any marriage reports – hardly any marriage announcements, even, in the page of classified ads headed Births, Marriages and Deaths, and a quite surprising absence of fatal falls among septuagenarians. I found one nonagenarian death, which sure enough followed a fall downstairs. On the other hand, a Keighley septuagenarian was planning, though partially sighted, to take part in the London Marathon.

But then Keighley today is in every way different from Keighley yesterday, and not quite, I'm afraid, the 'spacious clean and friendly' place which seems in the context of gritty industrial Yorkshire to have rather surprised Dr Pevsner, whose *Yorkshire: the West Riding* in the Buildings of England series I bought from my meagre earnings in my days at the *Keighley News*. (It cost 10s 6d: you could get several half-decent lunches for that in Keighley in those days.) Apart from the best of North Street, the townscape has lost some of that sense of local cohesion and independence it used to have. Cavendish Street, named after the lordly Devonshire family who were big here once, as they were in so many places, with its arcaded shop fronts completed in 1883 and designed to impress 'off-coom'd-uns' as they ventured up from the railway station, used to be a stylish street with some of the choicest shops. Now the heart of Keighley shopping has moved elsewhere, into streets where you find the big names like Marks and Spencer, who though founded in Leeds rarely bothered with Yorkshire in those first post-war years; or into identikit shopping malls.

But the worst disaster is the square at the junction where Cavendish Street meets North Street. The dominant building here used to be the Mechanics Institute, a centre both for instruction and for entertainment. It was always a lively scene on a Friday night, and attenders would be disappointed if the evening finished without some call to the police. And this was not the only venue where part of the entertainment seemed to be a fight at the finish. I once told my *Keighley News* colleagues that I'd been on a Friday night to the cinema in Haworth, which, like so much in Haworth even then, was known as the Brontë. Was there a fight? they asked. Not that I saw, I said. They seemed to assume my evening must have been wasted. I also missed, though I gathered some vivid descriptions, an evening at the Mechanics which followed the arrest of a local policeman for stealing sheep. He had, if I remember, a Scottish name: McTavish perhaps or McDougall. When the police came to answer the usual Friday night summons the revellers greeted them with a chorus of a song that everyone knew, amended to begin with the line: 'Old McTavish had a farm...' Several arrests were made.

The Mechanics Institute, however, has gone: destroyed by fire in the 1960s. What is even worse is that this commanding site is occupied today by the Park Lane College, a real blot on the townscape. It must have looked plasticky when it was put there, and today it looks demeaningly tatty. Look first at the Keighley Library, funded by the great philanthropist Andrew Carnegie who had been persuaded to do so by an eminent son of Keighley called Sir Swire Smith; and then perhaps at the Temperance Institute (it's a

Wetherspoon's now): so much well preserved stone, so much natural dignity. Then look on Park Lane, and despair.

If you glanced out of the *Keighley News* windows now you wouldn't have the sense which I had at the end of the 1950s that, at a very rough guess, 96.7 per cent of the people who passed were British by origin: probably 80 per cent were West Riding, and as many as 70 per cent might be Keighley. There was in those days a sturdy contingent of Keighley Ukrainians, one of whose celebrations I was lucky enough to be sent to report on: their friendliness and their spirit sent me home in a glow. Now the Daanyaar shop and the children being loosed at St Anne's signal a multi-ethnicity here which the Keighley of the 1950s could not have imagined. It was still the case in the 2001 census that 89 per cent of the population was classified as white. The Indian/Pakistani/Bangladeshi contingent amounted to 9.2 per cent, placing Keighley 63rd on this test among British constituencies. But there have been troubles. The Keighley MP Ann Cryer has been castigated by some of the leaders of minority communities for various campaigns, which include repeated assaults on forced marriages. The BNP leader Nick Griffin picked this seat to fight in the 2005 election in the hope of exploiting tensions. He polled 4,240 votes, 9.4 per cent of the total.

The *Keighley News* has moved with the times. A Keighley man, it proudly reports on page one, has been selected to help promote non-violent means of resolving world conflicts: his name is Javed Bashir; he's thirty-seven, and a governor of the Holy Family Catholic school. More than 2,000 Keighley Muslims took part in a procession to honour the birthday of the prophet Muhammad… A column called 'Down Memory Lane', written by a former Keighley librarian, Ian Dewhirst, shows the top of Cavendish Street as it used to be and points out that every man in the frame is wearing either a substantial overcoat or a raincoat. That's the town I used to report in. 'Eheu fugaces!' As not many people would say in a down-to-earth place like Keighley.

KETTERING

KETTERING, mun. bor., par. and mkt.-town... Northants...
A centre of the boot and shoe trade.

EDWY THE ALL-FAIR, 'd. 959, aged 19 of excess. The coronation of this youthful satyr was delayed whilst the Archbishop of Canterbury dislodged him from bed where he was lying between his voluptuous sweetheart and her equally amorous mother...' Edgar the Peaceful, 'd. 975, aged 32, a handsome dwarf, who demonstrated his overlordship by having eight sub-kings row him up and down the Dee. His anti-crime measures (nostril-slitting, eye-gouging and ear-ripping) were horrifyingly effective. When an Andover ealderman, invited to provide his daughter as the royal guest's bedmate, substituted a housemaid, this poor girl, having given every satisfaction, was awarded her employer and his family as servants.' Which makes Cynewulf, King of Wessex, died 754, 'whilst entertaining a young woman from Merton' sound quite a dull old stick. And we haven't yet reached 1066.

How about Oliver Cromwell? 'After the Restoration his body was dug up and hung at Tyburn. His mummified head for many years was stored in an East Anglian parson's hat-box.' Or 'James II (Tom Otter) d. 1688 aged 68 of a cerebral haemorrhage... He was a brave, stubborn and swarthy man who misunderstood the mood of his countrymen. Besides a second wife of 15, he kept numerous plain mistresses who, after his conversion to popery, were explained by his brother, Charles, as penances imposed by priests...'

Or perhaps you would rather have figures from the US frontier? 'Nettie Cook Dramsdahl, aged 12 and resident in Beadle County, S. Dakota (a place highly thought of by this publisher) rose briefly to fame when, on August 28, 1884, a passing whirlwind lifted into the sky the farmhouse, her mother and the bookbox in which the child had sought refuge. At a height of 60 feet the house imploded, dropping these pioneer aviators amongst their surviving possessions – five dishes, a Singer sewing-machine, a stove lid, the house-dog attached to a wheel-spoke and that part of Nettie's doll which says, "Mamma! Mamma!"' 'Preacher Waddell, a licensed exhorter, looking into the grave whilst preaching a valedictory sermon at Central City, observed a rich vein of gold ore exposed by the sexton's spade. He instantly cried Amen, hurriedly helped to inter the coffin and then rode at speed to register several claims surrounding the burial yard. Many years later he hotly disputed this, declaring it "a damned Episcopalian lie".'

And then there are all those cricketers, peculiar umpires and cricket addicts, among them the Reverend Lord Frederick Beauclerk, D.D. 'This choleric man took his stand at the wicket wearing a scarlet sash and a white beaver and demonstrated his contempt for some bowlers by suspending a valuable gold watch from his middle stump. He is said to have been an unutterably dull preacher.'

We are in the presence here of a remarkable and completely original man who disinterred, wrote up, edited, illustrated, and published all this and much more in a series of tiny books (5 inches by 3¾) from a modest house on the outskirts of Kettering, Northants: every one immediately recognizable as the work of J. L. Carr, schoolmaster (latterly headmaster), historian, novelist, mapmaker, publishing entrepreneur and famous – in Kettering, certainly – eccentric, of 27 Mill Dale Road. He wrote and published bigger books too. His novel *A Month in the Country* sold thousands, and inspired a successful film. He wrote about the American frontier (*The Battle of Pollock's Crossing*) and India (*A Season in Sinji*) and football (*How Steeple Sinderby Wanderers Won the F. A. Cup*) and of course about teaching – his main job for much of his life – and publishing.

Yet his most characteristic output, in that there's nothing else like them, are the tiny books: erudite, witty, terse and as packed with oddness as he was. Some have dedications His *Welbourn's Dictionary of Prelates, Parsons, etc etc*, already invoked in this book in the context of Alexander Cruden of Aberdeen, has three: the first to King John, 'who interrupted matins in Lincoln Cathedral conducted by Bishop (later Saint) Hugh (q.v.), remarking sardonically that sermons on bad kings bored him'. Three more dedicatees are honoured in *Carr's Dictionary of Extra-ordinary English Cricketers*, including Abdul Aziz, known as Abdul the Damned who (he says) on witnessing English sailors playing cricket, exclaimed: 'Remarkable! But what needless exertion! Why do you not compel your slaves and concubines to perform it for you?'

'These books', he explains to the reader at the end of his *Dictionary of English Kings, Consorts, Pretenders, Usurpers, Unnatural Claimants & Royal Athelings*, 'hover between a greeting and a present… In cold bedrooms only one hand to the wrist need suffer exposure.' One fruit of his brevity is that it leaves you wanting more. About Gilbert Jessop, for instance, whose '1902 innings of 104 in 77 minutes when England, needing 200, were 48 for 5 can only be compared with Henry V's speech at Harfleur. His cricket career ended in 1916 when he was forgotten in a heat-treatment box.' Eh? One might not normally credit a tale like this – it sounds like dressing-room talk – but if Carr puts it into a book you have to pay attention. He could, though, be erratic. I found a misspelling of Headingley, Yorkshire's principal ground (and Carr was a Yorkshireman, from Wakefield, though over the years he transferred his allegiance to Northamptonshire). He isn't, as I noted in the case of the Reverend Mr Marvell, who drowned in the river Humber (see entry for Humber), always totally glued to the facts. He could also be difficult. 'Stubborn' is a word applied to him almost as much as 'eccentric'. In his life of Carr, whom he hugely admires, Byron Rogers never tries to disguise that, though perhaps he couldn't have done so, after what some of Carr's associates told him.

I went to Mill Dale Road to pay my respects to his memory, as many do. There's a plaque on the house, and a quince tree, a kind of J. L. Carr trademark, still in the garden. (His little books are nowadays published by his son and daughter-in-law, whose company is the Quince Tree Press.) As I noted down the words on the plaque, a woman from a neighbouring house marched up and asked me what I was doing. I explained. She said she had known Carr well (he died in 1994) and her husband had known him still better. And what was he like? She pondered. 'Well, we got on pretty well,' she said tentatively, and then, brightening, 'And, he was, you know, *very* eccentric.'

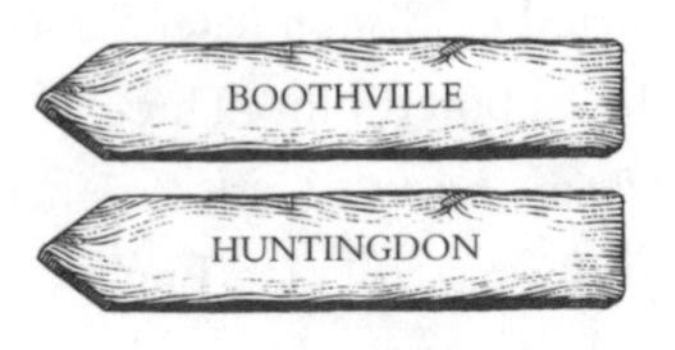

KINLOCHLEVEN

KINLOCHLEVEN, vil., at head of Loch Leven, N. Argyllshire, 7m. ENE. of Ballachulish… has large aluminium works. At end of jetty and on NW. corner of wharf are fixed red lights.

THERE'S NO ALUMINIUM WORKS any more, but the name of the village survives; which makes one doubly grateful that they decided to call it Kinlochleven, rather than, as some enthusiasts had suggested, Aluminiumville. Before the bridge was built at Ballachulish, travellers on the road north from Oban to Fort William had either to wait in protracted queues for the ferry or to engage on a long though picturesque excursion up one side of Loch Leven and down the other, which brought you midway to a very strange place. Tucked away at the end of this valley, a romantic lakeside framed by mountains, was this bleak, utilitarian place which the aluminium industry had created. Before that there was nothing here except two tiny settlements, Kinlochbeg and Kinlochmore, with shooting lodges and a few cottages, accessible only by the old military road built by General Wade (now part of one of Scotland's great walking trails, the West Highland Way from Milngavie on the fringe of Glasgow to Fort William).

What brought the industry here was, above all, the rain; then the possibilities of the mountain above the lakeside settlements, where abundant water could be trapped and stored and then precipitously despatched down the mountain to power the smelter. The North British Aluminium Company bought the Blackwater Valley on the lonely and treacherous Rannoch Moor, built what was then the biggest dam in Europe across the loch, and created a reservoir eight miles long. Down below, they built their industrial units and began to construct a village to house their workforce. These were pioneering enterprises: both technologies – the production of aluminium, and the use of hydroelectric power – had only just begun in Scotland. There were no adequate roads to service these projects. Some of the equipment could be brought by boat down Loch

Leven, but the shallowness of the loch made the use of large boats impossible. The only other route was across the mountains from the railway that crosses Rannoch Moor, through a territory known with good reason as the Devil's Staircase. The present roads around Loch Leven were built by prisoners of war after 1914.

The construction of this place was a vile and dangerous exercise, involving around 3,000 men over eight years. How many died in the process is not recorded: some were never identified. They were navvies, some from the Highlands, far more from Glasgow, many Irish, some from even further afield, moving from place to place in the frequently desperate search for work and wages. What they did might never have been documented but for the presence among them of a man from Donegal called Patrick MacGill, who in 1914 published a book called *Children of the Dead End*. Ostensibly the book is a novel, describing the life and hard times of a navvy called Dermod Flynn. Astonishingly, MacGill wrote some of the book in the Garden House of Windsor Castle, having been taken up by Canon Dalton, confidant of George V and father of a later Labour Chancellor of the Exchequer, and something of a talent-spotter of gifted, good-looking young men.

But the circumstances MacGill describes, from early life in an impoverished household with an illiterate father and many siblings (one of whom died because his parents had no money to call in a doctor), have clearly been lived through. Flynn offers himself, as MacGill had to do, at a hiring fair in County Tyrone; is picked out by a bullying master, assaults him and runs away; earns pitiful money doing casual jobs on farms, and then crosses to Scotland as so many of his contemporaries did, in the hope of making better money picking potatoes. Most of his earnings are sent home to his ever-demanding family, and finish up in the pocket of the landlord or else of the parish priest.

There are more children now to be fed, and Flynn (that's to say, MacGill) reflects bitterly on his fate: 'Why had my parents brought me into the world? I asked myself... At home I heard them say when a child was born to such and such a person that it was the will of God, just as if man and woman had nothing to do with the affair. I wished that I had never been born. My parents had sinned against me in bringing me into the world in which I had to fight for crumbs with the dogs of the gutter. And now they wanted money when I was hardly able to keep myself alive on what I earned.' He digs sheep drains on a moor in Argyllshire. Undeterred by seeing a man employed there cut in two by a ballast engine as he approaches to ask for a job, he finds work on the railways. Then he hears of the aluminium project at Kinlochleven.

The sequence which follows is perhaps the most vivid in the whole book. He describes the long slog, along with his friend Moleskin Joe, which brings them at last up the demanding road from the Bridge of Orchy through Glencoe. Here at night they suddenly hear the sound of exploding dynamite. '"The navvies on the night-shift, blastin' rocks at Kinlochleven!" cried Joe, jumping to his feet..."Hurrah! There's a good time comin', though we may never live to see it..."' (That, throughout their adventures together, is his constant, bittersweet refrain.) In the dawn, they see the outer line of derricks standing gaunt and motionless against the bald cliffs of Kinochleven: 'We sat on a rock, lit our pipes, and gazed on the Mecca of our hopes.'

Paradise, it is not. The conditions of work – at any time, but particularly in the course of a harsh winter – are appalling, too tough for some to survive; the conditions of leisure, such as it is, hardly less so. They drink and gamble and fight through nights in which rest, crammed three to a turbulent bed, is all but impossible. 'I know not', Flynn muses, 'whether drink and gambling are evils. I only know that they cheered many hours of my life, and caused me to forget the miseries of being'; likewise fighting, at which he proves to be very adept. Nobody ever washes, or changes clothes. Squalor is absolute. Men steal from each other and, gleefully, from the company. Deaths in the course of their labours are casual events. A man called Sandy MacDonald is clearly dying: so clearly that his workmates have a whip round to send him home to where he dreams of being – the Isle of Skye. One evening they give him the money. Next morning he is dead.

The men who are making Kinlochleven have no idea of what they're creating.

They are told what they have to do hour by hour, but never why they are doing it. 'Only when we completed the job, and returned to the town,' MacGill writes, 'did we learn from the newspapers that we had been employed on the construction of the biggest aluminium factory in the kingdom.' And later: 'We were men despised when we were most useful, rejected when we were not needed, and forgotten when our troubles weighed upon us heavily. We were the men sent out to fight the spirit of the wastes, rob it of all its primeval horrors, and batter down the barriers of its world-old defences. Where we were working a new town would spring up some day; it was already springing up, and then, if one of us walked there, "a man with no fixed address", he would be taken up and tried as a loiterer and vagrant.'

Eventually the job is completed, and the men are told with brutal abruptness that their services are no longer required. They tramp out of Kinlochleven, mostly with no idea where they are going. MacGill's description of the retreat from the valley is the most powerful thing in the book: 'We were an army of scarecrows, ragged, unkempt scarecrows of civilisation. We came down from Kinlochleven in the evening with the glow of the setting sun full in our faces, and never have I looked on an array of men such as we were... Some sang as they journeyed along. They sang about love, about drink, about women and gambling. Most of us joined in the singing...The sun paled out and hid behind a hump of the mountain... Still the mountain vomited out the human throng, and over all the darkness of the night settled slowly...'

The road down the side of the loch, no longer essential to anyone not concerned with the village of Kinlochleven, is now advertised as a 'scenic route'. The smelter closed in 2000, an event long expected: it was now too small to be viable. Its owners, Alcan, said to be the largest landowners in the Highlands, gave the place to the community. The old industrial plant was put to new uses: the former carbon house is now the Ice Factor, where you can learn and practise climbing and climbing on ice. A brewery has arisen behind it. Bright notices put up by the Kinlochleven Land Development Trust proclaim: Kinlochleven – a Highland village reborn. Its streets and shops still have the unmistakable air of a company village, although there is now no company. There's a little museum evoking the place's strange history. Small businesses have moved in, and the West Highland Way sustains a bed and breakfast trade.

As for MacGill, he abandoned his navvying, tried his hand as a journalist, did not take to the trade (there's a rich account in the book, ripely amusing but bitter, of his days among the cynics of Fleet Street) and drifted out of it, but was then taken up as some talented piece of rough by Canon Dalton and other grand people, and given the time and space he needed to write. Books of his poems appeared in 1912, and this near-autobiographical book two years later. But by then he had enlisted and gone out to fight at the front, which inspired further books and the script of a long-forgotten film called *Suspense*.

In the 1920s MacGill began a lecture tour in the United States, but his financial backing collapsed and he and his family found themselves stranded. They remained in America, MacGill continuing to write but with dwindling success: his wife Margaret, who also wrote, used to pretend that the royalties she was earning were his. His health failed and he died in Florida on 23 November 1963, the day after the assassination of President Kennedy. He deserves to be read alongside George Orwell, all the more because Orwell, writing of down and out days in London and Paris or the privations of life in Wigan, was never more than a visitor who would soon be taking the train back to London. MacGill was charting the world he came out of, the world that for years was the only one that he knew, and might never escape from.

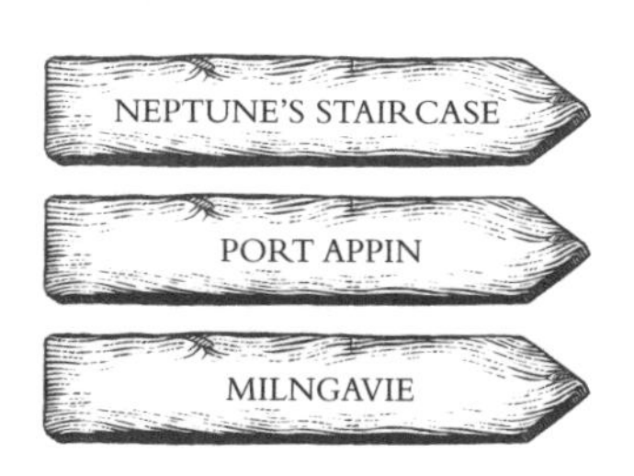

KNOCKIN

KNOCKIN, par., vil. and seat, Salop, 5½m. SE. of Oswestry...

TRAVELLERS MAY OCCASIONALLY COME on this place as they take a fairly insignificant road between Llanyblodwel, q.v., and Ruyton-XI-Towns, q.v. too (though for reasons which are overwhelmingly logical, but also opportunistic, it appears in this book under X). Those who have used this road before tend to do so again whenever they're in the area, even though they don't need to; first to make sure that the village still has a shop (it has; or at least, had when I was there in the summer of 2007); and second, to check that it's still called the Knockin Shop; which I'm happy to say it still was, and long may it remain so.

KNOWESIDE

KNOWESIDE, ry. sta., L.M.S., in co. of and 11m. SW. of Ayr.

THE FATE OF SISYPHUS, as described by Homer, might have been even ghastlier had the Judges of the Dead condemned him to carry out his allotted task on a stretch of the A719 between Ayr and Girvan. Sisyphus (a nasty piece of work, incidentally, who well deserved what he got) had offended Zeus by assuming he was the cleverer of the two. In Book 11 of the *Odyssey*, its hero sees him at work: 'I witnessed the tortures of Sisyphus, as he tackled his huge rock with both his hands. Leaning against it with his arms and thrusting with his legs, he would contrive to push the boulder uphill to the top. But every time, as he was going to send it toppling over the crest, its sheer weight turned it back, and the misbegotten rock came bounding down again to level ground. So once more he had to wrestle with the thing and push it up, while the sweat poured from his limbs and the dust rose high above his head.'

How bystanders must have mocked! Yet they would surely have had even more reason to do so had he been assigned to perform at a spot where it might have appeared that he was failing to push his rock down a hill, rather than up it. This spot near Knoweside on the A719, which is known as Croy Brae, or more popularly, for reasons we'll come to shortly, as the Electric Brae, has just this effect. When you're going up it, you think you are coming down; when you're coming down, you think you are going up. I made the mistake of approaching the Brae on foot – it's a tidy walk up from Dunure on the coast, where there's a ruined castle, but a cheerful one in my case, since a group of men whom I took to be Turkish were drinking white wine in the layby alongside the spot where these odd things occur, and they kindly gave me a glass. Well, a plastic cup; but still very welcome. And all the more cheerful because of the breathtaking view from this road across the sunlit sea to the Isle of Arran; you can also see Ailsa Craig, a celebrated rocky landmark which two people I met on my journey separately told me was known locally as Paddy's Milestone, though one of them immediately apologized for political incorrectness.

The wine-drinkers, who proved to be the owner of a B&B in Ayr and some of his visitors, had sensibly come in cars, since it is only when driving that you get the full whack of the Brae experience. Coach-drivers entertain their passengers to demonstrations of how to freewheel uphill and how to fail to freewheel going down, which is fun for the passengers, though less so for cars behind which simply want to get from Ayr to Girvan, or vice versa.

This place is now best known as the Electric Brae (a term not recognized by Bartholomew, who doesn't list Croy Brae either, and mentions Knoweside only for its station, now closed). The brae – people who thought they were experts used to affirm – had various electric or magnetic properties which caused these events to occur. As a notice on a cairn on the layby explains, smarter people later recognized that the true source of the mystery was a straightforward optical illusion, with the pitch of the field and hillside alongside the road tricking the eye and brain into error. There are said to be many similar phenomena around the world, though none in the United Kingdom is as celebrated as this one.

It's also a haunting metaphor for people who think they are making progress when in truth they are sliding downhill (or the other way around; but I guess that doesn't happen so often). There can be few who come here to see this sight who do not summon to mind some couple whom everyone except themselves can see are involved in a kind of Croy Brae relationship.

A B C D

E F G H

I J K **L**

M N O P

Q R S T

U V W XYZ

LAMBETH

LAMBETH, parl. and met. bor.… L. Palace (1197) has for centuries been the official residence of the archbishops of Canterbury… L. bridge crosses the river above the palace; between the bridge and Westminster bridge is the Albert Embankment…

CLOSE TO THE BRIDGE and palace, behind the Albert Embankment, in the faded indeterminate street that is still called Lambeth High Street, there's a little park, overshadowed by flats and the backs of imperious offices on the Embankment, whose origins can be deduced from the fact that gravestones are stacked around the perimeter. These grounds contained the borough's mortuary and the offices of its coroner. On the morning of Monday, 16 August 1926, an excited crowd assembled here, many children among them, to witness what they supposed would be a moment of history – the arrival of the remains of a great English popular hero: Horatio Herbert Kitchener, Field Marshal, 1st Earl Kitchener of Khartoum, victor of Omdurman, and the man who in a famous poster a decade before had told the young men of Britain that their country needed them. At the age of sixty-four, he had been called back in 1914 to be Secretary of State for War, taking over these duties from the Prime Minister, Herbert Asquith. His death, lost at sea off the Orkneys in June 1916, had been at the time and ever since a matter of mystery and suspicion, perhaps comparable to the speculation eighty years later over the death of Princess Diana. How had he died? Why had he died? Who was responsible? And who knew much more than they were saying?

It was clear that HMS *Hampshire*, on which he was crossing these waters, had struck a mine. But was that the whole of the story? His journey – on a mission to the Russian government – was meant to be secret. The route that the *Hampshire* was taking, which was not the route that had originally been planned, must have been mined with great precision. Could someone have tipped off the Germans that Kitchener was aboard? Had Sinn Fein been involved? Or – an even darker theory – could someone in the British government have been eager to get rid of him? He was known to have been at odds with Lloyd George. What made the event seem even more sinister was the immediate reaction of the authorities when the fate of the *Hampshire* was known. Local people, and even the Stromness lifeboat, which had sought to go to the aid of the *Hampshire*'s contingent, had been prevented from doing so. Why, unless there was something that had to be covered up? It was said there were secret papers on board which had to be protected. If so, it was clear that this imperative had cost additional lives.

Could anyone be sure that Kitchener had been lost with the rest? There were those who simply refused, then and for several years afterwards, to believe that their hero was dead. His sister, volubly, was among them. Some had come forward who were ready to swear that they'd seen the great soldier being smuggled away from the scene. Perhaps that was why would-be rescuers had been turned back? Others asserted that Kitchener had not been on the *Hampshire* at all; that the man who'd been seen aboard was a look-alike; that the government had decided to keep him in hiding while he formulated plans for the war, this being a subterfuge designed to lull the Germans into a false sense of security. One day he would re-emerge to accept the acclaim of the nation for having steered it to victory.

In 1926, nearly ten years on, these suspicions were far from allayed. And as the anniversary approached, a paper called the *Sunday Referee* revived them, parading them on page one week after week from November 1925 onwards in reports from a writer who called himself Frank Power, though his real name was Arthur Vectis Freeman. The agitation was fuelled by the continuing refusal of the authorities to agree to a public inquiry, by the unwillingness of Kitchener's official biographer to accept the version authorized by the government, and by the broad endorsement of the case Power was making in a book published by Walter H. Page, who had been the American ambassador in London at the time of the loss of *Hampshire*. First one thing, then another, Page noted, had been taken out of the hands of the Secretary of State for War. When he'd gone to Gallipoli, 'some persons' had predicted he would never come back. The field marshal was said to have remarked that the only reason he was going to Russia was because he had been ordered to do so. There seemed, in Page's view, to have been some feeling, even some hope, that he might not return from the mission; there was little sorrow evident when he was lost at sea.

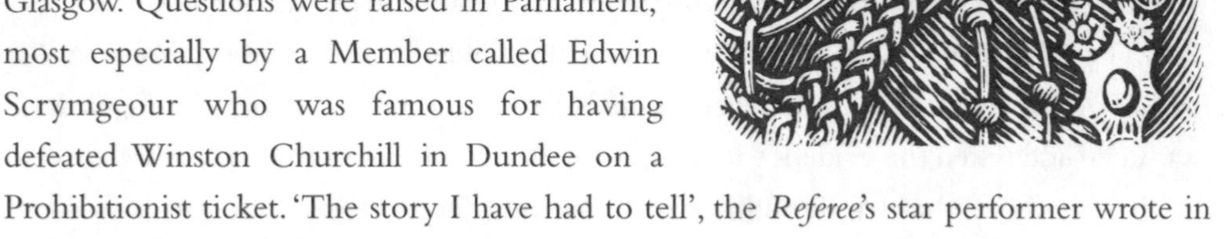

Week after week Power produced his remarkable revelations. In February 1926, he announced he had bought the pinnace in which Kitchener had been taken away from the *Hampshire*, and had put it on show in John Barker's department store. Soon after, Power reported that the enemy had managed to station a 'Teuton spy' on the *Hampshire*; then, that there had been 'orgies of dissipation' among the boat's officers. Power addressed packed meetings in London and Glasgow. Questions were raised in Parliament, most especially by a Member called Edwin Scrymgeour who was famous for having defeated Winston Churchill in Dundee on a Prohibitionist ticket. 'The story I have had to tell', the *Referee*'s star performer wrote in April, 'has been startling, and through no fault of mine, sensational in the extreme.'

Not, however, entirely consistent. Sometimes his theme was that Kitchener had not died on the *Hampshire*; next, the whole point of the accusations seemed to be that he had, but that those in power had done nothing to see he was found and properly honoured, and that the task of finding the body and bringing it home had by default fallen to him. (Home, in the sense that Kitchener had lived in England much of his life, though in fact he was Irish, born in Ballylongford in County Kerry.)

'I am going to bring Kitchener's remains back to England,' Power wrote, 'in a private yacht which is being lent to me for this purpose by persons who place honour before dishonour and truth before falsehood… I shall have Lord Kitchener's remains removed either to Westminster Abbey or to the great cathedral where he already lies in effigy.' In May he produced a letter from a survivor, a man named Sims, who testified that he'd seen Kitchener getting into a boat with officers who had escorted him to a place of safety. This boat, it appeared, was the one that Power had purchased, which had now left John Barker's in Kensington for the higher sea that was Oxford Street. The government was shaken enough to issue a statement denying his charges, but that, Power told the *Referee*'s readers, had been greeted on Orkney with 'derisive laughter'. During the summer, the flow of information seemed to abate. In one edition, Power wrote about the attractions of Orkney as a place for holidays. But excitement rose again when, on 1 August, the *Referee* reported that Power was in Norway and hoped to make an announcement of 'exceptional public interest' the following week.

Sure enough, in a space festooned with such statements as 'all rights reserved' and 'copyright throughout the world', Power duly delivered what appeared to be the goods. He had found the body of Kitchener in Norway, where it has been washed up by the sea. He had interviewed those who had found it (though in fact, if one read him closely, there was only one of them who said he had found it: the other merely asserted that what his friend was saying now was what he had said at the time).

The *Referee* endorsed all this with only the mildest visible tremor. 'We give Mr Frank Power's account of his discovery, as he believes, of Lord Kitchener's body. We have examined and tested the evidence he adduces with considerable care, and we are satisfied that it is so strong that we should not be doing our duty to the public to withhold it.' On 15 August, Power's reports soared to new heights of triumph. 'The case containing the elm coffin, in which the body was placed in the Norwegian graveside, and which was made by the admiralty's instructions ten years ago, is in a *chapelle ardente* adjoining the premises of Mr T. Hurry, undertaker, close to Waterloo station,' he wrote. The *Referee*, however, had begun on this crucial Sunday to worry about Mr Power. 'Mr Power', it said, 'has conveyed to London a coffin containing what be believes to be the remains of the late Lord Kitchener. He may be right – he may be wrong. The statement is made on his authority. We do not and never have accepted any responsibility for it.'

The coffin had reached Mr Hurry's establishment from Southampton on Friday night in a packing case which needed eight men to carry it. From there it would be conveyed to the mortuary, where the famous pathologist Sir Bernard Spilsbury would personally superintend its opening. On Monday, as the crowds waited eagerly for news that the body of Kitchener had indeed been retrieved, the coffin was opened and Sir Bernard and those around him peered inside. It was empty – except, reporters were told, for a quantity of tar which had been put in to simulate the weight of a body. The *South London Press* reported: '"There will not be an inquest. There was no body in the case." With those words, given on Monday by Mr J. Ingleby Oddie, the Lambeth coroner, another amazing episode has been added to the controversy concerning the body of Lord Kitchener…' Or, as the *Daily Mail* put it, under the headlines: 'Kitchener coffin fraud… no body… Home Office statement… end of a ghoulish trick…' : 'Crate, coffin and shell – all that there was beneath the Union Jack that was filmed in the streets of London and received with reverence by people in it – have been removed to the Lost Property Office of Scotland Yard.'

Two mysteries remained. One was Power: what had he thought he was doing? How could he ever have hoped to get away with it? The other puzzle was why the *Referee* had fallen for this imposture, and whether its reputation could ever recover. The following Sunday there was for once no news report on page one; only a squirming leader comment which claimed that when Power came to the paper they had not been prepared either to endorse or to reject what he had to say. He had been paid very little, and certainly not enough to cover his journey to Norway. It was now up to Power to prove his claims. Thereafter the *Referee* went back to reporting issues where the ground was unlikely to crumble under its feet: Mr Lansbury's latest outburst, and the *Referee*'s plan to end the coal strike.

Power, however, was not withdrawing a word. The explanation for what had occurred at Lambeth, he said, was simple, and entirely consistent with the cover-ups that had been practised over the years. The authorities, desperate to refute his revelations, had arranged for the box he had brought from Norway to be switched with another. He'd suspected a trick of this kind might be tried, so he had made a secret mark on his coffin to enable him to detect if they'd switched it. He demanded now that his property – the case containing the coffin allegedly containing Lord Kitchener – be promptly restored to him.

The unfortunate proprietor of the *chapelle ardente* at Waterloo, finding himself in the thick of events, vehemently denied that a switch could have been made. And in any case, investigative journalists were at work and quickly confirmed the true sequence of events. Power had bought the coffin in Kirkwall when he went to Orkney for the unveiling of a memorial to Lord Kitchener at Marwick Head, close to the spot where the *Hampshire* went down. On 27 June, he'd had it shipped to him at Newcastle. He had then gone to Norway, where he had staged a mock funeral in Stavanger and despatched an empty coffin to Bergen. The *Daily Mail* was able to plot every movement of the coffin thereafter until its fateful arrival in the parlour of Mr Hurry. There was furious public rage at Power, not least among those who'd believed him. One patriot demanded that he be shot. Yet in the way of these things his case was soon swept aside by other pressing events. What became of him thereafter I have not been able to trace. He simply seeped back into the obscurity from which he had sprung.

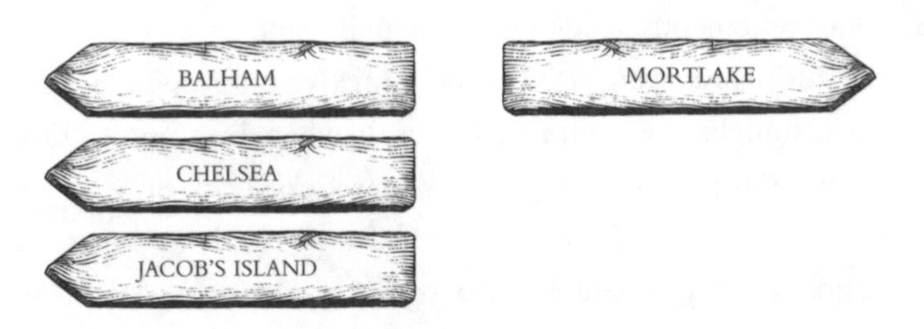

LEVERBURGH

LEVERBURGH, coast vil., adjoining Obe, S. Uist, Inverness-shire. Has fixed lights at various points of approach to harbour… [S. Uist was corrected in later editions to Harris.]

IT IS NOT UNUSUAL to find in Bartholomew places named after people. Several others occur in this book. Saltaire, as everyone knows, was named after Sir Titus Salt, Akroydon after Colonel Akroyd, Tremadog and Porthmadog after their founder William Madocks, and Talbot Village, which we shall come to soon, after two sisters called Talbot. The Chartist leader Feargus O'Connor, who created Snig's End, set up his first communal settlement at a place near Rickmansworth called Herringsgate. He renamed it O'Connorville, though later generations changed that to Heronsgate. Fleetwood on the Lancashire coast is named after its creator, a man then called Fleetwood, though in fact he was born a Hesketh and had turned himself into a Fleetwood by royal warrant. One south coast resort created by a man called Hotham narrowly escaped being named Hothampton, though the name it acquired instead, Bognor Regis, may have been less than ideal. But William Hesketh Lever, 1st Viscount Leverhulme, surpassed them all by having four places named after him: Lever Park, just outside Bolton; Leverville, in the Belgian Congo; the Lever Pacific Plantation, in the Solomon Islands, where he farmed coconuts; and Leverburgh, on the Isle of Harris.

Before Lever arrived, this spot was occupied by a few acattered settlements of no more than three or four houses, tiny, remote and battered by Hebridean weather. He was eager to change most of that. He arrived, as it were, on the rebound, having spent some five years trying to persuade Harris's northern neighbour, the Isle of Lewis, to reinvent itself as somewhere pulsatingly prosperous. Lever had first seen these islands in 1884, when he was thirty-three, having chosen them for the celebration of the tenth anniversary of his wedding to Elizabeth Hulme, to whom he was deeply devoted. He'd already by then built a sound business reputation. He began to work for his father, a wholesale grocer, and at twenty-one was a partner, on a then substantial £8,000 a year. But while managing his father's Wigan branch he spotted a grocer's shop which was up for sale, bought it, and started to build what by the time he first saw the Western Isles was the biggest wholesale grocery business in north-west England outside the great cities of Manchester and Liverpool.

He and his wife were so taken with the Hebrides that they thought for a moment of selling the business, buying an island and settling there. Lever, however, was far too restless a man for that, and instead he began to build an empire founded on soap. First at Warrington, then, when further expansion was urgent, in his purpose-built company village at Port Sunlight (see that entry) on the Wirral, he sold soap with an almost evangelical fervour. Unlike his competitors, he wrapped it, which customers liked, and branded and marketed it on an unprecedented scale. At first he bought his soap in from established manufacturers, but in time he found new and sudsier recipes, whereafter he sacked his suppliers and made his own. Punchy, pugnacious, just 5ft 5ins of boundless drive and ambition, Lever became a Liberal Member of Parliament in his party's landslide victory of 1906, a baronet (1911), a baron, choosing the name Leverhulme so that his designation would also honour his late wife (1917), and eventually a viscount (1922); and crucially, a very rich man indeed.

In 1918, at sixty-six, still mourning the death of Elizabeth five years earlier, he went back to the Hebrides, alerted by a report that Lewis was up for sale. He liked the look of Lewis, and bought it, making him the apparent master of 400,000 acres of land and the 30,000 people who lived on it. He bought it for himself, and from his own pocket, rather than through the company Lever Brothers, which he commanded. His purpose, he explained, was not to make money out of it; his concern was with the welfare of the people who lived there.

Like the agents of the Highland clearances, though a great deal more instinctively generous, Lever hoped he could bring the inhabitants to see what was best for them. To this lad from industrial Lancashire, the islands seemed impossibly backward. Previous proprietors – regarded on the island as despots quite as much as philanthropists – had begun developments, but nothing on the scale that Lever envisaged. The islanders' fatal failing, it seemed to him, was their addiction to crofting. Surveying the eerie, primitive landscape of the islands, enduring the unforgiving weather, he simply could not understand why they should want to live in the way they did, why they should see any future in trying to hack a living out of this intractable land, how they could be content with their crude black houses ('not fit for kaffirs', he said) when, by falling in with his plans, they could live dynamic and prosperous lives. He promised them – using these very words – 'wealth beyond the dreams of avarice': and the key to that would be fishing. There was already a fishing trade at Stornoway, the principal town of Lewis, but that too was hopelessly underdeveloped. He would rebuild and re-equip and open up trading links through the use of refrigerator ships. Lewis would become an industrialized paradise.

The new owner arrived on Lewis in June 1918 to be greeted with banners saying 'welcome to your island home'. He summoned a public meeting, where in his folksy way he described himself as a poor Lancastrian lad, a long way from home, but brimming with good intentions. With all the famous enthusiasm that some found infectious and others oppressive, he promised to harness science to create a brave new world of contented lives and high wages. Even air travel, which few on Lewis would ever have experienced, had a place in his glowing prospectus. He thought he had pleased his audience, and in some senses he had: they recognized a bossy man when they saw one, but Lever was rich, and liberal, and whatever his faults, looked likely to be an improvement on their previous owners.

Soon he was pushing ahead with his plans for a fishing revolution. The harbour was redesigned, new ships purchased, factories built, and an outlet created to sell what the island's waters produced, in the shape of a new chain of high street shops across Britain, to which he gave the name MacFisheries. Stornoway, he promised, would now be reshaped as a capital for his island, appropriate for its new industrial destiny. Its population would double, treble, even quadruple. New houses would be built, far better than anything seen here before, even matching Port Sunlight. New roads, new railways, an art gallery, a noble tower, a cultural life which would make it a centre of arts as much as of commerce: Stornoway, he proclaimed, would become a new Venice.

His advisers quailed as the aspirations multiplied, and warned him that some of his notions were fantasy. Lever was undeterred. In the shop at what's left of Leverburgh I found a fine account of these days entitled *The Soap Man: Lewis, Harris and Lord Leverhulme*, by Roger Hutchinson, which evokes the response of the people of Lewis: fascination mixed with deep scepticism. The almost unimaginable scale of Lever's vision, as Hutchinson says, would from any other source have seemed preposterous; 'issuing as it did from the multi-millionaire creator of Lever Brothers, its giddy immensity seemed almost seductive'.

It would end in tears. To Lever's astonishment, the poor people of Lewis rejected salvation. They preferred their own culture to that which Lever was eager to offer them. They did not want to relinquish their black houses to live on Lever's modern estates. They did not wish to abandon their crofts to work in his processing plants. One Lewis man, newly returned from the war, summed up a common feeling: you will find more happiness in our hovels, he told the great proprietor, than in castles throughout the land: 'You have bought the island – but you have not bought us, and we refuse to be the bondslaves of any one man.'

What made Lever's predicament worse was the impetus which the return of men from the war gave to the already established campaign for the land to be restored to the people. They believed that common land had been stolen from them to establish sheep farms. Land had always been scarce, and the influx of men back from the war made it scarcer. From March 1919, they began to seize land that they thought should be theirs by right; and in this, they had the sympathy, even perhaps the tacit support, of a Liberal government, since an earlier Liberal government, in Gladstone's day, had introduced legislation to establish crofting.

Even as great a landowner as the Duke of Sutherland was yielding some of his land to ex-servicemen. Yet Lever would not. He wanted to end the tradition of crofting; the break-up of farms would interfere with his schemes, and especially with his plans for milk production on Lewis. He threatened – if the raids did not cease – to drop all his projects outside Stornoway; he might even abandon Lewis completely. Protest meetings were held which condemned the raiders and called on Lever to stay. For a while, the raids stopped. Lever withdrew his threats and ordered that work be resumed. Then the raids broke out again, the government continued to press for farms to be subdivided and offered to crofters, and Lever's patience ran out. From now on the future was Harris; and on Harris, specifically Leverburgh.

Lewis and Harris are not separate islands. Intractable mountains rather than water keep them apart. Lever had bought Harris, along with St Kilda (then still inhabited) in 1919. If Lewis had been backward when he arrived there, Harris was more so. Its only detectable industry was the manufacture of tweed. Again, the agent of transformation was to be fishing; also possibly whaling. But his choice for the place that was to become his centre of operations astonished people who knew the island better than he did. Tarbert, in the north, today its principal town, seemed to them the obvious place to begin, with better communications and safer waters. But Lever dismissed all such doubts. If the fishermen of Harris could not cope with these waters, he would bring men from England who could. As for the hazards, he was willing to put a light on every rock on the Sound of Harris. (What joy that would have given to John Bartholomew!)

As he'd done on Lewis earlier, though with rather more caution this time, he called a general meeting to outline what he intended to do for the island. According to one account, Lever declared that Obbe – the name of the largest of the local settlements – was not an adequate designation for the town he intended to create there. Why not, he suggested, adopt a name commemorating some former owner: Port Macleod, or Port Devonshire? At which someone at the back of the hall shouted out: 'Name it after yourself.' 'Very well, if that is your wish,' Lever replied; and on 1 October 1920, Leverburgh was ushered into the world.

As ever, Lever wasted no time in starting to build. He hoped by the time the town was completed to have 10,000 people installed there. There was no talk of Venice this time, no promise of railways even, but industrial buildings, a water tower and houses, some imported from Norway, began to take shape. The land campaign which had thwarted him on Lewis was more modest on Harris, and easily quelled. There was less urgency here, since the hunger for land was less pressing, and where trouble occurred, he took the offenders to court, as he'd hesitated to do on Lewis, and saw them jailed. When the raiders resumed, men from Leverburgh marched on the farms they had seized and drove them out.

Lever's main offence, in the view of some of the islanders, was his importation of young women from England to work as secretaries. 'It is awful,' one local preacher complained, 'to see the harlots and concubines of Lever running about the streets of

Obbe.' But before long, disillusion began to creep in. Public buildings he had promised were not taking shape. He had plans to reform the production of tweed, but islanders objected that if these went through, the products that came off the island would no longer be Harris tweed.

The winter of 1923–4 was so cruel that staple products – fish, potatoes and peat – all failed. The islanders were put to work building roads. The first full fishing season at Leverburgh began the following summer. At the start it seemed full of promise, but the market for fish from Scotland was now declining, and by August returns were already diminishing. Lever was back in the Hebrides the following month, where one of his engagements, designed perhaps to show they had been forgiven, was to unveil a war memorial for the people of Lewis. Then, at seventy-three, he set out on a 15,000-mile journey which included a visit to Leverville in the Congo, where everything seemed much more serene than it had been in north-west Scotland. He was back in London in March 1925 and planning a visit to Harris in May.

But by then Lever was dead. He caught a chill which turned into pneumonia and died at his home in Hampstead on 7 May. His projects perished with him: Lever Brothers promptly abandoned them, and the new Lord Leverhulme could not afford to continue. Just as Stornoway was destined never to become the new Venice, so Leverburgh was doomed to be next to nothing at all. The port installations were sold and demolished. The whaling factory at Bunavoneadar showed no sign of succeeding.

If you go there today it is difficult to understand how a hard-headed business tycoon such as Lever undoubtedly was should ever have seen any future in Leverburgh. There are two roads from Tarbert, one heading west and the other, where my bus took me, through a territory on the eastern side even bleaker and more rockstrewn than Lewis. There is little left of his lordship's legacy: a few houses, some on a hill designed for his captains and managers, and decidedly better than anything that had preceded them; his water tower; and what used to be a public hall and is now the Leverhulme memorial school. There are several churches and a modern shop with a café and visitor centre where I sat for a while reading Roger Hutchinson's book while the rain battered at the windows. Up the road there's a quayside from which the car ferry leaves for the island of Berneray. To a visitor's eye, it's a bleak kind of place; but its older inhabitants are well aware of how much bleaker it would have been had Lever never arrived here. He is spoken of still with gratitude.

It is hard, as it always was, to make a decent living here; some dozen or so fishing boats continue to put out to sea, and crofting survives, but many are forced to leave the island to find work. The population is estimated 200 today. Yet the tendency which so frustrated Lord Lever – the preference for the traditional way of life of the Western Isles above the glitzier world they see every night on the television – seems to persist. In 1991, a company called Redland, later taken over by the French group Lafarge, proposed to reopen and greatly extend a quarry at Lingerbay on Harris, which objectors said would leave a scar six times the height of the cliffs of Dover. At first the proposal was welcomed by the Western Isles Council and by many people on Harris – 62 per cent, according to one survey. But soon there were second thoughts, and a further survey found 68 per cent were opposed. Thirteen years of controversy and litigation ensued before Lafarge sent a delegation to Harris to assess opinion. In April 2004 the company announced that it was withdrawing its plans. Once again, economic progress had been judged too high a price to pay for the desecration of the island, and the possible destruction by rich invaders of its chosen way of life.

I returned bumpily on the switchback road to Tarbert on a bus taking children from the Leverhulme school to the tiny scattered settlements of south Harris. I asked them what they knew of Lord Leverhulme. 'He made SOAP!' one cried gaily. Others talked of his death, which they gleefully attributed (wrongly) to something very nasty he'd picked up in Africa. But then: 'You feel him around you,' one boy contended, 'you feel that he's always there.' In what way? He couldn't tell me, but someone else could. 'He comes to haunt the school in the early hours on the night after Hallowe'en!' he shrilled, to general approval. But that, I think, was merely a tale designed to confuse one of those elderly interfering Sassenachs from whom the Western Isles have suffered from time to time.

LLANTHONY

LLANTHONY ABBEY, ruin, Monmouthshire, on r. Honddu, 8½m. N. of Abergavenny... Was built 1108–1115.

OFF THE PURPOSEFUL ROAD through the hills from Abergavenny to Hereford, close to the village of Llanvihangel Crucorney, there's a wandering lane which leads through Llanthony to Hay-on-Wye, following more or less the winding course of the river Honddu. This road is not built for speed. If you are harassed by vans driven by young men in baseball caps on their way to urgent repair jobs, pull into the side where you can, and wave them through. Otherwise you might miss the distracting attractions along the way: an inviting pub called the Queen's Head, south of Cwmyoy, with couples in the new-found leisure that comes with retirement sitting out in the October sun; a sudden compelling view to the east, as the road runs northward, of the village of Cwmyoy; a church (sited, it's said, at the foot of what once was a landslip); the hills rising out of a fan of forest; cottages tucked into coombs.

You will then come to a tiny place, not even a hamlet, which is nevertheless equipped with a Baptist chapel: one imagines the Sunday morning congregation coming down in best clothes and hats and bonnets from the hills. In due course, you come to an inn sign from which a contented monk invites you to patronize a twelfth-century bar.

This is Llanthony: the ruins of the priory (rather than abbey), with a house set among them which became a hotel and offers food and drink in what was once the undercroft. Ringed around are the high hills of the Black Mountains, green and brown and purple, sealing Llanthony off from the everyday world. Along the top of the hills to the east is Offa's Dyke and the English border. There's a tiny church dedicated to St David, which is kept open.

If you wonder what this place must have been like in the beginning, there's a vivid account in one of the histories written by the twelfth-century priest, historian and man of letters, Gerald of Wales, who knew the place well and arrived here with Baldwin, Archbishop of Canterbury, when he came to South Wales to recruit for the Third Crusade in 1188. 'In the deep vale of Ewias', Gerald wrote, 'which is shut in on all sides by a circle of lofty mountains and which is no more than three arrow-shots in width, there stands the abbey church of St John the Baptist... This church is constructed in the very spot where once there stood the humble chapel of Saint David, the archbishop, which was adorned with woodland moss and wreathed about with ivy. It is a site most suited to the practice of religion and better chosen for canonical discipline than that of any of the other monasteries in the whole Island of Britain.'

It is well chosen for the beauty of its location, too. The monastic orders were famously good at discovering delectable places and they rarely did better than here. Gerald certainly appreciated that: 'As they sit in their cloisters in this monastery, breathing in the fresh air, the monks gaze up at distant prospects which rise above their own lofty roof-tops, and there they see, as far as any eye can reach, mountain-peaks which rise to meet the sky and often enough herds of wild deer which are grazing on their summits.' Yet all has not been well, he concedes, with this once happy place. The English, always likely to come in for contumely in the pages of Gerald of Wales, are at fault again, he declares, both for neglect of this abbey and for creating a second Llanthony, close to Gloucester, which was named Llanthony Secunda – a daughter church which, Gerald complains, has odiously supplanted its mother. Still, there's satisfaction to be had in the fates which have overtaken those responsible for this decline. Prior William, the first to despoil the house of its herds and stores, was deposed and expelled by his monks; Prior Clement, who, though attached to the place, could not enforce discipline, allowing his monks to plunder the house and commit other outrages, died of a paralytic stroke; while Prior Roger, the worst of the lot, who quite brazenly stole all he could, stripped the church of its books, its ornaments and its charters, suffered paralysis, just like Clement, and died a lingering death.

The buildings that Gerald saw were superseded in time by those whose quite substantial ruins are there today. Some of the years that followed were good and fruitful; others were bad and even deplorable, with the priory reduced in status to a mere cell long before Henry VIII closed it down. After that the land became farmland, with what was spared of the priory in the midst of it. And then in 1807 there erupted into this sheltered pool of tranquillity the poet Walter Savage Landor, who planned to redeem the community by refurbishing the priory, establishing a farm run on progressive lines, and beautifying it by planting thousands of trees.

Few nowadays could, if challenged, recite more than a couple of lines of Landor, but there's one piece that remains quite famous:

> I strove with none, for none was worth my strife;
> Nature I loved and, next to Nature, Art:
> I warm'd both hands before the fire of life;
> It sinks, and I am ready to depart.

These words, written around the time of his seventy-fifth birthday, were entitled 'Dying Speech of an Old Philosopher'. They may have been true of the old philosopher: they were scarcely true of Landor. His was a life of strife: when things were going well, he was generous, open-hearted, a foe to injustice and a friend to those in need, kind to women, children and animals. Nevertheless, from his earliest youth, he had been possessed by a tempestuous temper. At seven, he shocked a friend of the same age, who never forgot what she saw and heard, by his insolence to his mother. At Rugby School, seething over an imagined slight, he so insulted the headmaster that he had to leave to avoid expulsion. At Trinity College, Oxford, he fired a gun at the window of a fellow undergraduate who had riled him, not least by parading his Tory views (Landor's sympathies then were republican). For this and other offences he was rusticated – that is, sent down, not finally but for a while; his pride ensured that he never went back.

He quarrelled with his father, left home and said he would never return. He settled in Wales, where he got a young woman from Tenby with child: both she and their daughter are thought to have died soon afterwards. A family friend then reconciled him with his father, who settled his debts and, dying in 1802, left him the money which enabled him to purchase Llanthony. There is no doubt that his intentions were good: he meant to do his best both for his new estates and for those who worked on them. But he wasn't cut out for this kind of day-to-day management, and after a year he took off for Spain to fight against Napoleon, leaving his properties in the hands of lawyers – first Mr Gabell and then Mr Gabb – who failed to look after them. He quarrelled with both these gentlemen and later denounced them in one of his tart little poems:

> If the devil, a mighty old omnibus driver
> Saw an omnibus driving downhill to a river
> And saved any couple to share his own cab
> I really do think 'twould be Gabell & Gabb.

He quarrelled with neighbours and tenants and local farmers, with the civic authorities and with the Church, which had challenged his plans to rebuild the priory and obstructed his scheme to establish a local school. His attempts to build a house for himself and the wife he married in 1811 – she was Swiss, and regarded as beautiful, but was far from rich – were marred, he claimed, by local villainy: his building materials were stolen, and the trees he planted uprooted. He took to denouncing the Welsh in venomous terms as idle, drunken and feckless. What a dereliction it had been on the part of Caesar, he said, not to have exterminated them!

And his debts were mounting, to a point where he had to accept he could not go on. The Landors moved to Jersey; then (despite his stated dislike of the French) to France; then to Lake Como, from where he was expelled for uttering rude sentiments about the Italians; and from there on to Florence: here he was briefly expelled for his unconstrained views, though soon readmitted. But here too he quarrelled violently with his wife, left her, and came back to Britain – where before long he was once again involved in litigation which left him close to poverty.

He did not, however, return to Llanthony. In his absence the estate had remained in the hands of his brothers, who seem to have managed it better than he did, though Francis Kilvert, curate of Clyro, who visited it with his vicar, Mr Venables, in the spring of 1870, was upset by the irreverent conduct of other visitors. 'What was our horror on entering the enclosure', he wrote, 'to see two tourists with staves and shoulder belts all complete postured among the ruins in an attitude of admiration, one of them of course discoursing learnedly to his gaping companion and pointing out objects of interest with his stick. If there is one thing more hateful than another, it is being told what to admire and having objects pointed out to one with a stick. Of all noxious animals too the most noxious is a tourist. And of all tourists the most vulgar, illbred, offensive and loathsome is the British tourist.'

Kilvert and his vicar were not, of course, tourists. They had arrived not only in search of a holy place but to visit a settlement established by an Anglican lay reader called Joseph Leycester Lyne, who now called himself Father Ignatius. He had come to these parts in the hope of establishing an Anglican monastery – a project vehemently discouraged by higher authority – on the old site at Llanthony, which he thought he could rescue from its spiritual decline. The use of a building within the priory as a hotel had particularly upset him. Since the Landors refused to let him acquire it, he had found a site just up the road at Capel-y-ffin, where, despite all discouragement, he created an institution he named Llanthony Tertia. Kilvert was rather impressed with Father Ignatius, though he found him excitable and too much obsessed with a single idea, and somewhat otherworldly perhaps: 'I could not persuade him that my name was not Venables.' After Lyne's death in 1908, the monastery declined and the last of the monks decamped to Caldey Island, off Tenby. Llanthony Tertia came into the possession of a spectacular saint-cum-sinner, the artist, writer and uninhibited sexual experimenter Eric Gill; Llanthony Prima, however, was still in the hands of the Landor family a century after the poet's death.

I left this glorious place reluctantly and resumed my journey northwards on a road whose 16 miles towards Hay seem even more erratic and minor than that from Llanvihangel Crucorney. Capel-y-ffin has a chapel that looks like a cottage and a cottage that looks a bit like a pub. North of here, the country turns severe and rugged, and suddenly you find yourself driving high up on a hillside with vast views over the valley below. From there the road eases down into Hay.

I thought I heard on this journey an echo of the plea that was made to me at Abbeycwmhir much earlier in my travels: 'Don't please tell the whole world about us, or everyone might want to come.' The ancient road retains its magic – at least out of season – only because it is lightly used, on a weekday out of season at least. Walking or pony trekking, or perhaps if you're strong enough for the hills, a modest unassertive bicycle, are far better ways to invade Llanthony in its blissfully beautiful setting. Those who have that choice of locomotion should take it. Not all of us, at our age, can.

LLANWRDA

LLANWRDA, par. and vil., with ry. sta., G.W. and L.M.S. rs., E. Carmarthenshire…

IN THE EARLY DAYS of the railways, entrepreneurs who wanted to take their new service into a town often found they were unable to do so. Maybe local landowners would not permit the railway to cross their territory; maybe the engineering challenge was beyond their wit to resolve; maybe providing a station a mile or two out of town was simply cheaper. For whatever reason, they used to resort to putting the station a little way out and calling it after the road that led into the town. Thus, Wantage Road was a station two and a half miles out of Wantage (but linked by a steam tramway); Lyndhurst Road was two and a half miles from Lyndhurst and St Columb Road a similar distance from St Columb Major, while Ticehurst Road was nearly three from Ticehurst; which was why, no doubt after having to cope with the fulminations of the footsore, they eventually changed the name to Stonegate. Bodmin Road (now known as Bodmin Parkway), as travellers to Cornwall nowadays have cause to know, is three miles by bus from Bodmin, though in earlier days there was a rail link into the town.

The most daring resort to this kind of deception, though, vastly outdistancing any of these, was Lampeter Road station in Carmarthenshire. The Vale of Towy railway, opened in 1858 to link Llandovery with Llandeilo (as it still does, as part of the Heart of Wales railway, Shrewsbury to Swansea), built a station at Llanwrda, which, presumably because few people outside Llanwrda had ever heard of Llanwrda, they decided to call Lampeter Road.

And there was indeed a road from Llanwrda which would take you north to Lampeter. But what the unforewarned traveller would discover on alighting at Lampeter Road was that the distance between these two places was 16 miles. True they are mostly enjoyable miles if you're driving, especially when you get north of the

Tafarn Jem pub and a glorious valley opens up to the west. (The view coming back from Lampeter to Llanwrda is if anything even better.) 'Some of the finest valley and mountain scenery in South Wales,' says the *Shell Guide to South-West Wales*. They were punctuated, too, by wayside hostelries to refresh and reinvigorate those who found themselves having to walk the whole way. They would not, even so, have thanked the railway company for its duplicity.

There's a kind of shrine to the Vale of Towy railway at Llanwrda, across the main road from the present-day station which honestly and unreservedly bears the name of the village. It's kept by a man called Richard Rees, who's devoted part of his house and most of his garden to it. There is a station sign for Llangadog, and part of an old station platform, and a wheel from a signal box, and a London and North West Railway notice threatening fines of 40 shillings, BY ORDER, if you don't shut its gates behind you. It was gratifying to know, I said to Richard Rees, that the railway had repented in time of its naughtiness and ceased to pretend that the station here had anything much to do with Lampeter. But that hadn't been the only factor, he said. A rival company had taken its line – a line that used to run from Carmarthen to Aberystwyth – right into Lampeter, so clearly they had a superior claim to the name of the town.

The last passenger train on the Mid Wales line left Lampeter station in 1964, but the Heart of Wales line survives, and Llanwrda station with it, which, seeing how few people use it, is something of a miracle. It has often been threatened. Some attribute its escape to a kindly official concern for people who, in an area where roads are often indirect and difficult, would have no other way of getting to their jobs or colleges in centres like Swansea and Shrewsbury. Others say that what saved it from the Beeching process was the number of marginal parliamentary seats strung along the line.

Lampeter is now a university town, as it keeps reminding you. What was once a college established in 1822 to improve the education of Anglican clergy in Wales, began after the Second World War to admit students other than those intending to enter the Church, and in 1971 it became part of the collection of universities which make up the University of Wales. It's hardly Oxford or Cambridge, but it's said there is a charm about it which makes its graduates keep coming back. I arrived in the little town on a summer evening to a general honking of motor horns incongruously recalling the streets around the Arc de Triomphe in Paris in the mid 1950s, before the use of horns was banned and the traffic had to learn to behave itself. But this turned out merely to be local youth having fun, and after a while they swerved and screeched off elsewhere, leaving Lampeter to the kind of easy, if never exactly cloistered, calm to which university towns always used to aspire.

Since I went to Lampeter, I think I have found a challenger to its supremacy in the railway impertinence league. Tulloch, on the West Highland line, used to represent itself as the station for Kingussie, 30 miles away – and in another company's territory.

LLANYBLODWEL

LLANYBLODWELL, par. and vil., Salop... on r. Tanat,
5½m. SW. of Oswestry.

THAT MOST ADMIRABLE, DECENT and – one cannot avoid the word in his case – *nicest* of Conservative politicians, John Biffen, who died in August 2007, was for many years the Member for Oswestry, later renamed North Shropshire. In the midst of his constituency he had a house in the village of Llanyblodwel (as it's now usually spelled). If the border here were not so erratic and arbitrary, it might have been, as its name suggests, in Wales, but no: Llanyblodwel is English, and Salopian.

Biffen was once, for a rather uneasy season, a member of Margaret Thatcher's Cabinet, but she sacked him for being, as her spokesman put it, 'semi-detached'; which is only to say that he was never encamped, as she and her faithful friends seemed mostly to be, in the realms of Utter Certainty. Sometimes, in the middle of some foaming parliamentary argument in which gobbets of conventional wisdom were being traded across the floor, Biffen would remark with his usual diffident courtesy that what he'd been hearing did not quite square with the wisdom of the taproom bar at Llanyblodwel.

So intriguing did this contention become that one day I drove up to Llanyblodwel and settled myself in the bar of its pub, the Horseshoe Inn, in the hope of discovering what manner of wisdom this might be. There was in fact no taproom in the Horseshoe, but when I pointed this out, John Biffen said that what he meant was the wisdom of the bar that would have been a taproom bar had the Horseshoe had one. This seemed an unimportant deception. I listened diligently all lunchtime in the hope of enlightenment, but the conversation, naturally in these parts, was virtually all about farming, and was peppered with concepts to do with agriculture and the economics of agriculture which whirled uselessly around my urban head and fell to the floor uncomprehended. The only political strand to the conversation was the general denigration of the Ministry of Agriculture, Fisheries and Food.

In the autumn of 2007, just after Biffen's death, I returned for the purposes of this book to the Horseshoe to see if the wisdom of Llanyblodwel had waxed or waned over the decade. Its denizens, I assumed, wouldn't now be able to spend so much time slagging off MAFF, since that institution no longer existed, but it would not be surprising to find they were equally scornful of its governmental successor, DEFRA. The obvious way to approach Llanyblodwel for those coming from London is to take the A5 and turn off westward, perhaps through the village of Knockin, which is also in this book. But the obvious routes are not always the best ones. It's more satisfying to take the Welshpool road and turn off after two or three miles on to a B road that eases its way through the hills as it heads north-west.

At about the point when the B road crosses the border, you will see on the left an endearingly shaggy hill with an eye-catching monument perched on the top. This is the Rodney's Pillar, erected in honour of the naval commander Sir George Brydges Rodney in 1781/2 after he had inflicted a humiliating defeat on the French. The original inscription (in Welsh) read: 'The highest pillars will fall, The strongest towers will decay, But the fame of Sir George Brydges Rodney shall increase continually, And his good name shall never be obliterated.' Casual visitors to the sight might assume from this that Rodney was some kind of local hero, but in fact he had no connection with the area and probably never saw the monument. The quality of the county of Montgomery seems to have chosen to honour him because his successful ships were built partly of oak from the local Breidden woods.

Those who climb to the top to see it are rewarded, it's said, by spectacular views back towards Shropshire and out into Wales. But I had no time for such indulgence. Llanyblodwel called – though first, I would take a road that proved to be even more enjoyable west of the Pillar than before it, to a place across the border from Biffen's village called Llansantffraid; or as Bartholomew lists it:

LLANSANTFFRAID YN MECHAN dist.,
Llansantffraid par., Montgomeryshire.

Llansantffraid is famous for its football team, which, though it plays in a lower league than Swansea or Wrexham, let alone Cardiff City, qualified in 1996, as winners of the Welsh Cup, for a place in the UEFA cup, then a top European competition. Llansantffraid was drawn against a team called Ruch Chorzow – fourteen times, supporters were warned, the champions of Poland, and boasting five internationals. So great was the attention this encounter attracted that there seemed little prospect of accommodating everybody who wanted to come in the Llansantffraid ground, so the home tie was switched to Wrexham, where the village side held the formidable Poles to a 1–1 draw; after which they travelled to Poland, and lost 5–nil.

They played in several more such competitions thereafter, latterly in the mighty Champions League. But by then an offer of sponsorship which no cash-strapped club could have resisted had caused them to change the club's name to that of its sponsors. They were now Total Network Solutions. I had always hoped to get to one of their home games to ascertain how the crowd now saluted them. Did the cry go up, 'Come on, you Solutions'? But then the Total Network Solutions company fell into the hands of BT, the sponsorship ended, and the team reappeared as The New Saints, cleverly keeping the same initials.

In the light of their record, perhaps the nearest thing in real life to the novel by J. L. Carr of Kettering, *How Steeple Sinderby Wanderers Won the F.A. Cup*, I'd expected the village to be festooned with signs pointing the way to its heroes' ground. There were none. So I asked at a shop. 'Where will I find your famous football team?' I inquired. 'Not round here,' said the shop assistant morosely. 'They've gone to Oswestry.' Gone to Oswestry? But Oswestry is in England. 'Do you mean,' I expostulated, 'that you've lost them to *England*?' The woman eyed me pityingly. 'They never had many players from round here,' she said.

I found the football ground. The Bernabéu it is not. It's a decent non-league venue with a big stand under a corrugated green roof behind one goal, a dapper one on one touchline, and a curious high, narrow contraption, again with green corrugation, on the other. A partly undecipherable notice at one end of the ground said the next match would be sponsored by some people called Ashton from the Trederwen caravan park, but that could have been there for some time. A newspaper I bought in the shop

carried the happy news that after a poor start to the 2007–8 season the Saints had now won seven games in a row and soared to second place in the Welsh Premier League. But if my shop assistant was any guide, that will not have set off much general dancing in the streets of Llansantffraid.

And so to Llanyblodwel, the object of this pilgrimage. It is best approached from the east, down a narrow road which nicely signals that you're entering someone else's territory, past a school and a schoolmaster's house in a distinctively curious style which is all explained when you reach the church. The road divides: right for the church, left for the pub. There has been a church here for centuries, but the one you see today is essentially the work of a highly original, perhaps eccentric and usefully rich vicar called John Parker, who was in charge here from 1845 to 1860.

The church when he took it over was in a poor state. Don't worry, he told his parishioners: I can improve it. It is doubtful whether they knew very much about what he intended, and it certainly wasn't agreed in detail with them, for the church that he
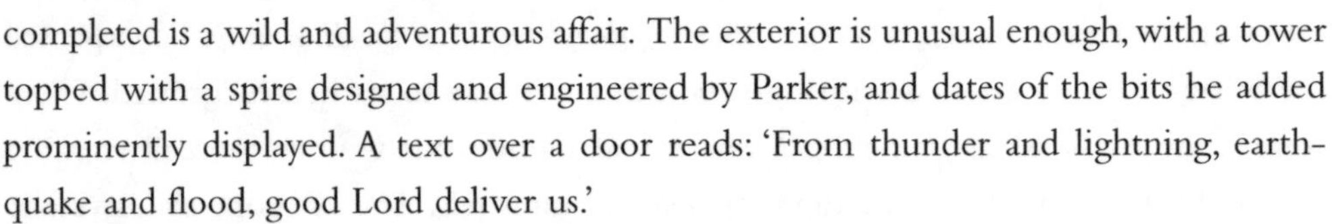
completed is a wild and adventurous affair. The exterior is unusual enough, with a tower topped with a spire designed and engineered by Parker, and dates of the bits he added prominently displayed. A text over a door reads: 'From thunder and lightning, earthquake and flood, good Lord deliver us.'

The interior, though, is a riot. 'What I love to see', a parishioner told me 'is, people come through the door, and they just sort of stagger back when they see it.' Everything that can be decorated is decorated exuberantly. Parker refrained from painting murals all over the walls, though he might well have done so, since he was an enthusiastic painter; instead he posted biblical texts from Isaiah and from Timothy, adding the Ten Commandments behind what today is an unexpectedly simple altar. The pillars are coloured so garishly that they make you remember Gaudi: there's something of the same feeling that they're really works of confectionery. It's a dazzling performance, ideal for occasional visitors, though my parishioner friend confided that she sometimes wished she was able to worship in something a little simpler. No doubts can persist once you've seen this place about who built the school and the schoolmaster's house you saw on the way here: that was Parker too.

Finally down the hill and across the sparkling Tanat to that other fount of wisdom – in this case earthly – the Horseshoe. But the door would not budge when I tried it. Though it was 1 o'clock, no cars were parked in the precincts. The landlady, hearing my struggles with her front door, came out to apologize. Like many country pubs, she said, this one's lunchtime trade had declined to a point where it wasn't any longer worth opening on weekdays. It wasn't just the beer and the pie I'd be missing, I moaned: it was the world-famous conversation. Yes, she missed that too, she said. She'd always enjoyed it; there were so many characters…

One could, of course, come back of an evening, but I sense that the clientele then would be younger, more lively, noisier, and less likely than the old lunchtime congregation to exchange the kind of wise words that used to instruct and enlighten the casual visitor. John Biffen left the Commons at the 1997 election and went to the Lords. It looks as though the wisdom of the bar which isn't the taproom at Llanyblodwel may not have survived that departure for long.

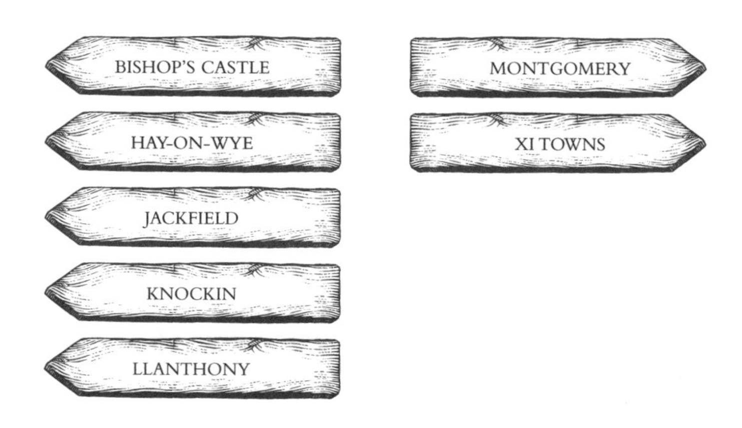

LOCHGELLY

LOCHGELLY, town (police bur.)… with ry. sta., L.N.E., Fife, ½m. NW. of Loch Gelly… Between the town and the loch (9 ft. deep) is the seat of L. House.

WHEN LOCHGELLY GETS INTO the newspapers – as it does in most years – it's because its houses are cheap, which immediately suggests that most people do not want to live there. In 2006, a survey by Halifax Estate Agents made it the only town in Britain to have average prices below £100,000. In 2007 they had rocketed up to £105,000, nearly twice what they'd been in 2004 (£60,000), but that still made it cheaper than anywhere else. That's a poignant contrast with Cupar, the county town of Fife until 1975, and on recent statistics, its boom town, since people who could no longer afford St Andrews settled on Cupar as second-best; which meant that people who would once have hoped to get into Cupar now had to look for somewhere else.

So since it's Affordabilityville, why not Lochgelly? Why not inspect the local house agents' windows? Easier said than done: you don't find many house agents' windows in Lochgelly. I found only one, which as often in Scotland works in tandem with a solicitors' business. Offers of over £45,000 were invited for an upper flat in a block of four with views over parkland and countryside; and offers of over £63,000 for a ground-floor flat in South Street, two beds. There are rather more agents, all with Lochgelly houses to offer, down the road in Cowdenbeath, which, compared with Lochgelly, is a thriving metropolis. Once, it's alleged, people used to call it the Chicago of Fife.

Yet Lochgelly has the longer history of the two. In the 1790s its population was given as 342, making it the ninth biggest location in all the Kingdom of Fife: that of Cowdenbeath was nil. By 1841 Lochgelly scored 770, Cowdenbeath 127. It was said at the end of the century that the countryside between the two places was one vast prairie of heather, all but impassable to those who tried to get through in summer. But both places grew as the mining industry multiplied. 'The headquarters till 1798 of a gang of notorious Gypsies,' says Groome's *Ordnance Gazetteer of Scotland*, 'it dates mostly from modern times, and owes its rapid rise in prosperity and population to the extensive collieries and ironworks of the Lochgelly Coal and Iron Company (1850). It has a post office, with money order, savings bank and railway telegraph departments, a branch of the Union Bank, a hotel, a police station, a public water supply, a gasworks, a music hall, a floral and horticultural society (1871), a Co-operative store (1892), a Good Templars' Lodge (1871), a masonic lodge, and curling, bowling, cricket and bicycle clubs.' As for nearby Loch Gelly, Groome made that sound more desirable still: 'measures 5¾ by 3½ furlongs, and is wooded and beautiful on the northern bank...', though elsewhere it was 'bleak and tame'. At its north-west corner stood Lochgelly House, seat of the Earl of Minto.

By 1911, Lochgelly had over 9,000 people, Cowdenbeath, pulling ahead, had 14,000. Yet Lochgelly was a harder, harsher place than Groome made it sound, certainly when Jennie Lee – the Labour politician who married Nye Bevan, brought the Open University into the world and became Minister for the Arts – was growing up there. This was the place where they made that odious instrument of correction, the tawse.

Then, in the 1980s, the pit shut down and the jobs went with it. As you can see in Lochgelly today, what rose with the mining industry also sank with it. A blight fell upon the place. It had, of course, known sad times before. Stop a moment outside the church of St Serf (he's a popular dedicatee for churches in Fife, where he preached and founded churches; also known as Servanus, he's the subject of many pretty legends, few of them credible). There is a war memorial here which more than most brings home how the war affected such communities: some 270 men and women from this little town died in First World War, others were feared dead: they include one Italian. The Second World War claimed 76. But the loss of the pits was a tragedy too in its own way; it left little hope that Lochgelly's best days, such as they were, could ever return.

The sense of a once-proud place, a place that felt to some extent in charge of its destiny, is still evident today in Lochgelly: you can sense it in the town hall (now a local services centre) and even more in the decently ostentatious Co-op building of 1909–10, complete with a clock tower, of which the Co-op today has only a part. There's a statement of affluence here which is lost almost everywhere else. The saddest sight is the east end of Main Street, most of it shuttered up, shops where Lochgelly spent its never limitless riches left useless as the money dried up. Lloyds TSB is still here, and a Chinese takeaway, and Fife Butchers has relocated around the corner, but Hutt's Leather Suites is no more, and Hutt's Discount Leather centre ('huge range of leather suites under £949'), and Body Language are gone. Here and there, there are signs of revival. The Miners' Welfare and War Memorial Institute was being refurbished when I was there – a project paid for, a notice board said, by a cast list that included the European Regional Development Fund, the Heritage Lottery Fund, Historic Scotland, Fife Council, Communities Scotland, the Coalfields Regeneration Trust, the Robertson Trust, the Architectural Heritage Fund, and the Heritage Building Preservation Trust; so you can't say nobody's trying. The institute opened in 1925, with a party to which the coal owners did not deign to invite the miners and their families. So with admirable truculence they stormed the place and helped themselves to the feast that had been prepared for their betters.

What, then, might tempt one into Lochgelly – apart from the fact that the houses here cost about what you'd pay for a flowerbed in Fulham? There's the Loch Gelly centre where according to Glen Pride's excellent survey, *The Kingdom of Fife*, 'multi-activities (entertainment, leisure, art) are articulated in utilitarian brutalism'. There are frequent trains to Edinburgh, and if you've the patience to go by a convoluted route, for Kirkcaldy; and buses to Dunfermline every ten minutes. There's Loch Gelly right on the doorstep and Loch Ore, a man-made affair of 125 hectares, the biggest in Fife, close by, and, if you've got a car, and money for petrol, it's not far to the coast of the Firth of Forth and the pretty, varied villages of the East Neuk of Fife: Elie, St Monan's Pittenweem, Anstruther and its strange appendage Cellardyke, and Crail, and so through to St Andrews.

But Lochgelly is also – and this ought to settle the matter – only two miles from Central Park, home of Cowdenbeath football club of the Scottish second division: 'the Blue Brazils' as they call them round here. In the season 1992–3, this outfit achieved the wrong kind of record by going thirty-eight games on their home ground without a win. I went to see them one Saturday in the season 1998–9. They were playing at home to Livingston in the Scottish Cup. Unusually for a league club, they were kicking off at 1.30, and the surrounds of the pitch were hung with old tyres. This, supporters explained, was because the ground was used for stock-car racing, and the owner had told the football club to be out of the way in time for the evening's racing to start.

The crowd would, I suppose, have numbered around 150. I stood at the rail with a sweet-natured old man who had worked down the pit for most of his life. Through most of the game he talked gently and reflectively about his life's experience, but now and then he broke off to address to the Cowdenbeath side, who were being thrashed, some of the filthiest language I have ever heard in a public place. 'Tis a wee hoor you are,' he admonished the team's left back (also I think its captain) after some hideous blunder; the only time I have heard that said on a football ground, though most of his language was a great deal more lurid than that. The referee injured himself, and a long lacuna followed as the appeal was broadcast for some qualified person to run the line while a linesman took over as referee. This intermission was so lengthy that, to the huge delight of my ex-miner friend, the chance of the owner getting his way on the starting time for the stock cars dwindled away to nothing. So infectious was his joy at this outcome that it dispersed my own frustration at having to miss the end of the game to catch a train back to London.

I returned to look at the ground in the 2006–7 season and little had changed. They still had the tyres, and the admission charges posted over the gates were about what you'd pay to watch AFC Wimbledon in the English Ryman League premier division – where the crowds, by the way, are roughly ten times the size of those they get nowadays at Cowdenbeath. Still, to go there and see the game played at this simple, unsophisticated level, with not a single overpaid 'star' import from Latvia, is enough to restore one's faith in the game, and should be considered a clinching reason for moving soon to Lochgelly, before the word gets around and everyone wants to.

LOWTHER

LOWTHER, par. and vil., Westmorland, in NW. of co. on r. Lowther… 4m. S. of Penrith… L. Castle, seat of the Earl of Lonsdale, is in vicinity of vil. The par. also contains the vil. of L. Newtown…

YOU COME ROUND THE corner of a road through rural Cumbria and suddenly you are confronted with what looks like a bit of Bath; an episode of Georgian townscape that has somehow broken loose from its moorings and drifted 260 miles northwards to wash up incongruously here: elegant, though curiously scaled-down crescents, built in reddish stone, lovingly kept and superintended – a memorable sight, but grotesquely out of place in this countryside.

A traveller in 1802 through the ancient county of Westmorland, which with Cumberland makes up the Cumbria of today, was suitably astonished: 'Stopped near the new village of Lowther to smile at the fantastic incongruity of its plan which exhibits the grandest features of city architecture, the Circus, the Crescent and the Square upon the mean scale of a peasant's cottage. These groups of houses were built for labourers of Lord Lowther but from their desolate deserted appearance it should seem that no sufficient encouragement has been held out to their inhabitants to continue in them.' This was Richard Warner, in his *Tour Through the Northern Counties of England and the Borders of Scotland*. The Lord Lowther who created the circus and crescents was the most remarkable, ruthless and powerful of the ruthless and powerful lot of them: Sir James (1736–1802), subsequently Earl of Lonsdale, but best known to the world, with good reason, as Wicked Jimmy.

These Lowthers had some cause to regard themselves as the uncrowned kings of Cumbria. Indeed, according to the Liberal MP Sir Wilfrid Lawson, whose own first parliamentary aspirations had been crushed in West Cumberland by the family's power, a man who entered a local grocer's shop and announced that William IV was dead was asked if the king had sons. None, said the visitor. 'Then', said the grocer, 'likely Lord Lowther will be king.'

The family had been installed in Cumbria since the thirteenth century, since when branches of the family had spread all over the north of England and into the Midlands and even the south. Down the hill from this mini-Bath is an essay by one of Wicked Jimmy's predecessors in creating a decidedly urban country village: Lowther New Town, built the previous century (1683–4) to replace an earlier settlement which stood in the way of plans to aggrandize the Lowthers' estate. They also hoped it might sustain a carpet manufacturing industry, but that failed. Where the later village at the top of the hill is all uniformity, interrupted today only by a Sky dish in one front garden, the earlier one is full of careful social gradations.

The land and property empire that Sir John Lowther I (1582–1637) inherited was split three ways on his death. Sir John II, MP for Westmorland and sheriff of Cumberland (the Lowthers always liked to have a big intrusive finger in both these pies) inherited most of it, apart from an estate at St Bees on the coast, which included vestigial Whitehaven; that went to the second son, Christopher. A third son took the estate at Swillington, Yorkshire. It was Jimmy's unique good fortune, and everyone else's ill luck, that, because of a series of family deaths which left no successors, the two great Lowther estates came back together to form his power base.

The village that bears their name was always the heart of the Lowther empire. The original castle had been built to replace Lowther Hall, which Sir John Lowther IV in the late seventeenth century had first beautified, then demolished. But it survived for only eighteen years before fire destroyed much of it. The next few incumbents lived in the parts that still stood and left the rest as it was. Even the mighty Sir James, though he planned to build something vainglorious, never got round to doing so. He lived in one wing and left the rest to moulder. He had plenty of other homes to go to, of course.

Five years after acquiring Lowther at the age of fourteen, Jimmy came into his second fine inheritance: that of the Whitehaven line that Christopher had begun. His predecessors here had served Jimmy's interests well. Christopher, who inherited it from Sir John Lowther I, had been busy in St Bees long before his father died, developing the natural advantages that it offered, which were coal, salt and the bleak haven called Whitehaven.

His heir, the active though gout-ridden John, began to develop the first planned town to be built in Britain since the Middle Ages. The haven was so far expanded that in 1681 it was designated a port; with Sir John thereafter exploiting opportunities to develop trade with America. Ingenious new techniques were introduced in his coal mines. His second son (his elder brother had been disinherited) had made it the biggest coal port in England except for Newcastle, and the second port of England overall, with a lucrative trade with Ireland as well as with America, especially in tobacco. The Lowther mines, meanwhile, were being radically extended under the sea. Along with all that, Jimmy could count a fine estate at Maulds Meaburn near Appleby in Westmorland, and an opulent London home in Carlton House Terrace. Before he was twenty-one, this Lowther, as the Duke of Newcastle confided to George II, was the richest of all the king's subjects. And by marrying, tactically rather than amorously, the daughter of George III's prime minister, the Earl of Bute, he was able to add a bulging dowry that included several coal mines in Yorkshire.

The defence of Lowther interests demanded a powerful presence in Parliament, and the Lowthers had never been slouches in seeing to that. The family had a talent for political and especially for electoral manipulation perhaps unmatched until the rise of Tammany Hall. A remarkable book called *The Lowther Family* by Hugh Owen counts fifty-two Lowthers who have sat in the Commons, to which you can add at least a score more of MPs married to Lowther daughters and Lowther mothers of MP sons, plus a formidable contingent who sat in the Lords.

Jimmy's predecessors had been determined to keep most of the representation of Cumbria under Lowther control. They had undisputed charge of both Cumberland seats from 1727, and Jimmy's predecessor Henry also controlled one of two seats in Westmorland, where he installed his brother. At Appleby he had reached a convenient agreement with the Earl of Thanet. He would choose one of the two MPs while the earl chose the other. But having most of the Cumbrian seats was not enough for Jimmy; he wanted the lot. He even applied his methods to Surrey, where he added Haslemere to the clutch of seats he controlled by bringing miners down from his northern estates and installing them in houses, which gave them the right to vote.

You can catch him at his worst in Carlisle, where the right to vote belonged to all freemen. So, in 1785, he manipulated the sudden creation of enough new Lowtherite freemen to guarantee him a majority. Among the willing accomplices whom he involved in these procedures was the young Scottish lawyer James Boswell, who thought he had been promised – as a reward for his services – the recordership of the town and a seat in Parliament. Perhaps he had; but when he dared to inquire when his rewards would arrive, Jimmy told him contemptuously that he would not get either.

The MPs he installed were known as his 'ninepins' (there were nine at their peak) and the price they paid for preferment was absolute unquestioning loyalty. No political party ever issued its three-line whips with so stern a countenance and so fearful a sense of menace. The ninepins knew not to answer back. Indeed, it was said that in Jimmy's presence it was best not to speak at all, unless specifically invited to do so by him. The one conspicuous exception to this tyrannical regime was the young William Pitt, whom James installed at Appleby in 1781. Pitt was never bullied as the rest of them were, but as soon as he could he broke free from Lowther's clutches and went off to represent Cambridge University.

Preoccupied as he was with defending his interests in London, Jimmy's taste for tyranny was evident locally, too. Burgeoning Whitehaven learned it must not offend him. He seems to have taken to life at Whitehaven more than to life at Lowther. While Lowther Castle was left to deteriorate, the family mansion at Whitehaven, Flatt Hall, was refurbished as Whitehaven Castle. Designs were commissioned from Robert Adam, though not, Hugh Owen says, ever paid for. Jimmy's subject people, here as elsewhere, were required at all times to bow to his will. At one election, angry that Whitehaven voters had failed to fulfil his instructions, he threatened to ruin the town by shutting down its collieries. Persuaded to drop this, he began to boycott his castle. The voters responded by giving him the results he wanted at the following election. Their reward was a massive feast for all freeholders.

But he exercised no such benevolence as an employer. When faced with legal action over subsidence caused by one of his pits, he sulkily responded by closing the pit. In 1780, a group of actors asked him if they might reopen a disused theatre in Roper Street. Getting no reply, they rashly assumed that this meant acquiescence, an error for which he had the manager and leading actor thrown into jail. Now and then, it is good to discover, the town dared to rebel. There were riots against him in 1782, as there would be in 1790 in Carlisle over his electoral malpractices, where they reached such a pitch that his house was destroyed.

The essential meanness of this very rich man was never better displayed than in his treatment of his agent, John Wordsworth, the poet's father. The Wordsworths lived at the back of a house belonging to Jimmy at Cockermouth; he kept the front for himself. When their father died, his children discovered that Jimmy owed John Wordsworth the then very substantial sum of £4,000, which he refused to pay. Six years of litigation followed, during which William came to regard Lowther with loathing. Indeed, it may have been this that made the young poet a radical. The prompt repayment of the money by Jimmy's successor, who also found the poet remunerative work as distributor of stamps for Westmorland, might then explain his emergence as a seething reactionary and a writer of poisonous tracts against the Lowthers' troublesome neighbour, the brilliant but erratic lawyer politician Henry Brougham, who had dared to challenge their monopoly on parliamentary seats in Westmorland.

Though a brute to his political allies and dependants, a brute to his tenants, famously quarrelsome (he fought two duels and threatened more), regarded by some as demonstrably mad, and as celebrated for his meanness as for his riches, Jimmy did have some redeeming features. He built those odd Georgian crescents at Lowther, and a linen factory to provide work for their tenants. And though some said his heart must be made of granite, the affair of his mistress Betsy Lewes seemed to suggest the opposite. His marriage to the Bute heiress had ended in separation after fifteen years, so he could regard himself as a free man. One night in the early 1770s, stopping at an inn on his journey from Cumberland to London, he met a barmaid whose charms, according to an account in *Town and Country Magazine*, 'were heightened in his opinion by an agreeable though modest leer'. (The magazine printed a cartoon of the couple, reproduced in Hugh Owen's book: her advertised charm seems a little elusive.)

On his way back to Cumberland he stayed at the same inn again, and made suggestions which, the magazine told its readers, 'began to stagger her virtue'. Initially she seems to have temporized, not least because she was engaged to a farmer's boy called Smithson, but rich and powerful Sir James spirited her away. 'Here', says the *Town and*

Country, 'we shall drop the curtain for a while, and suppose our hero as happy as the gratification of his most voluptuous wishes could make him.'

It became an enduring relationship. At first he still saw other women, but gradually Betsy became his only companion. In 1796 he set her up in some style in a village called Northington near Winchester, but three months later she died. The earl was distraught. For several weeks he kept her in an open coffin in one of the principal rooms, despite the inescapable evidence that her body had started to putrefy. It was still there a month later as he repeatedly found reasons to put off the funeral. The power of love, it appeared, had been enough to move even the icy heart of Wicked Jimmy.

Yet even these events can be seen in a different light. This was also a case of Jimmy thwarted. He had got what he wanted, in the shape of the still-alluring Betsy, and now her death had cheated him out of it. A man of his wealth and power was not used to being treated so dismissively – even by destiny; even by God.

He died in 1802, rich in honours. In 1784, Pitt had rewarded him for his earlier patronage by making him Earl of Lonsdale, Viscount Lonsdale and Viscount Lowther, Baron Lowther of Lowther, Baron of the Barony of Kendal and Baron of the Barony of Burgh. Yet even this great panoply of adornments was not enough: when eight years later Pitt refused him a dukedom, he withdrew his support for the government. The cause of his death was put down as mortification of the bowels. He was not widely mourned. *The Times* could not bring itself to compose and print an approving obituary. His heir and godson, William, dutifully erected a memorial to him, at the same time furnishing Lowther church with memorials to two other Lowthers whom Jimmy, according to family tradition, should have honoured, but hadn't. You have to admire the discretion of whoever wrote the tribute on the memorial: he knew how to gild the bully. It may have helped that the words are in Latin.

His decent successor William replaced the shattered castle, building a new one straight out of dreamland – a Gothic fantasy, porticoed and towered and battlemented and turreted, the exuberant work of the twenty-five-year-old Robert Smirke – and now all the more romantic because it is a ruin. The best way to see it is to come up the hill from the handsome village of Askham, and suddenly it is there before you, a haunting, even heartbreaking sight. Its windows are gone, bricked up or gaping. You can walk

through the meadows, quite close to it, but bright yellow danger signs warn the curious to keep a safe distance while operations continue – not, so far, to re-create this stricken place, but to save it from further collapse.

A glowing account in a guidebook of 1851 especially commended the southern front, with paths which led to a terrace, 'below which the river Lowther pursues its devious course, 'twixt flowery meads, stately trees, sometimes hiding its pellucid waters beneath the umbrageous foliage which skirts its banks, and anon peeping through the matted branches in the full glow of picturesque beauty. From the great tower there is an extensive and panoramic view of the surrounding country, with the lofty Skiddaw, Helvellyn, and many other distant mountains, rearing their towering heads to the skies, and a promenade on a terrace on a still summer's evening, under a clear blue sky, is a rich treat to an admirer of the works of the Almighty.'

Skiddaw is lofty still, and the waters of the Lowther pellucid, and the Lowther estate all around has been impeccably, efficiently and productively kept. But what had become, in the days after Jimmy's tyranny, the glory of the almighty Lowthers, is now no more than a shell.

LYDIARD PARK

LYDIARD PARK, seat of Lord Bolingbroke,
4m. W. Swindon, Wilts.

ONCE SWINDON WAS A market town, on a hill. But what made it famous was what then arrived in the valley: a railway works, and a new town designed to serve it. At the end of the twentieth century, the works was gone, replaced by a shopping complex called the Great Western Designer Outlet Village. Yet something of the old order survives; notably, on top of a building called the Hooter House, the industrial muezzin that used to summon Swindon to work. At 5 a.m., it told the workman to rise from his bed and hustle towards the works. It sounded again to tell him when he had only fifteen minutes left to get there on time. Its most insistent call, at 6, told those who had got up late or had lagged on the way that they now were facing trouble. And at the end of the day it signalled to the workforce its moment of liberation, and told the housewives of Swindon to get their kettles on ready for their men's return. But three and a half miles away to the west of Swindon, it invaded the peace of some who needed no such summoning: the high-born Bolingbroke family, who owned the fine house at Lydiard Tregoze. One day in the winter of 1872–3, Henry St John, 5th Viscount Bolingbroke, long infuriated by this daily impertinence, resolved to have the hooter silenced.

This was not the first time the viscount had made such a protest. He had several times complained to the local management, but though they responded courteously they declined to bow to his will. They had, after all, a works to run and a sleepy-eyed workforce to be wakened, and the gods of productivity told them the hooter could not be spared. So this time the viscount resolved to go to the top. He despatched a memorandum to James Stansfeld, MP, president of the local government board. Three times in the early morning, he wrote, and at several other points during the day, the

Great Western Railway's steam trumpet gave forth a loud, piercing, roaring noise, breaking on his mansion house with great power and force, affecting his health, impairing his enjoyment of his estate and reducing projected rents should he try to let it. In the circumstances, he respectfully submitted, though the hooter could be classed as a boon, a necessity even, to New Swindon's workforce, the licence to use it ought to be cancelled.

Writing that 'respectfully' must have caused him a twinge or two, for the viscount belonged to a family of very high consequence, in its own eyes at least. You get a strong sense of that from the church at Lydiard, most of all from the triptych erected by Sir John St John, 1st Baronet, in the 1630s, honouring his parents with the help of a genealogical table tracing their origins back to the Conquest. The same pride was evident in his monument to his own immediate family, depicting his two wives and his thirteen children arrayed in homage around an effigy of himself. This work was commissioned, not by his grieving family and friends after his death, but by Sir John, giving him fourteen years to enjoy it before he expired in 1648.

For all their high pretensions, few of these Bolingbrokes contributed much to the life of the nation. Only Henry St John, 1st Viscount, the eighteenth-century Tory politician and philosopher, figures in today's history books. And for much of the time, it has to be said, they set a poor example to the common people of Wiltshire. The 1st Viscount's father killed a man in a brawl. The 1st Viscount himself was a notable roué (women and wine particularly) who, having backed the wrong side, had to flee to France to escape his impeachment, which led to his being stripped of his viscountcy. His nephew Frederick St John, known to the world as 'Bully', was famously foul to his wife, Lady Diana Spencer. 'Much the same as mad when drunk,' it was said of him, 'and that is generally.' He ran up vast debts at the gaming table, imperilling the future of Lydiard. By the 1820s the place was in a state of serious disrepair, and throughout the nineteenth century the house had to be mortgaged. The assault on the hooter came from a household all too publicly not what it had been. Nevertheless, when this latterday Henry complained to a government minister he expected his words to be listened to.

New Swindon fought back. 'I trust he will reconsider the matter and make a small sacrifice for the workmen; it would show a spirit of nobleness, and that which becomes a gentleman, in obliging the British workmen and more lowly born,' a lowly born workman, signing himself 'One who has Whistled at the Plough', wrote to Swindon's newspaper, the *Advertiser*. At first, the voice of the aristocrat prevailed. After taking more than a year to consider the matter, Mr Stansfeld and colleagues cancelled the licence.

Once, that would have been the end of the matter. But industrial Swindon would not bow down. The *Advertiser* published a richly sarcastic leader contrasting the number of beneficiaries of the hooter – perhaps 10,000 – with the number of aggrieved complainants – one. A protest meeting early in 1875, hugely attended, carried a resolution to reinstate it. The Great Western Railway reacted by installing a brand new hooter. The viscount retired, defeated: the future had beaten the past. And the hooter continued to hoot until the works closed in 1986.

The 5th Viscount died in 1899, though his widow lived on until 1940. By then the house was abandoned; children roamed at will through its ruined, echoing rooms. A hutted camp, first for POWs, then for the local homeless, was erected on the viscount's lush estate. Swindon Corporation bought the place and opened the house to the public in 1955. Now families parade through the gardens and down to the lake. School parties tramp through the bedrooms. On the front lawn, lads who have discarded their shirts thump a football around. After a tour of the premises, children from Lethbridge Road primary school sent thank-you letters to their imaginary hostess, which were put on display in the house. 'Dear Lady Bolingbroke,' wrote Isabel Rowe, 'thank you for letting us, common folk, have a look at the grounds.' Isabel got the Bolingbroke message all right. But the common people won in the end.

LYME REGIS

LYME REGIS, mun. bor., spt., watering-place and par., on Lyme Bay… It is a coastguard and lifeboat sta. On the inner pier-head is a fixed light, visible 4m.

LYME IS ONE OF those watering-places (that delightful and sadly outdated description) that crops up a good deal in novels. A flibbertigibbet tumbles off its pier, the Cobb, in Jane Austen's *Persuasion*. The French Lieutenant's Woman (unforgettable Meryl Streep in the film of John Fowles's novel) broods enigmatically at the same photogenic venue. But it's also a famous name in natural history. Mary Anning, as commemorated in the Lyme museum of which Fowles was for some time the hon. curator, was active here, discovering the fossil skeleton of an icthyosaurus, now in the Natural History Museum; to which she in time added the first plesiosaurus and the first pterodactyl. But long before this, Lyme had an irreplaceable status in the nation's history, as the last place in England to be invaded. This took place in 1685, in Monmouth's rebellion against James II, which is remembered now as an epic exercise in utter futility, rewarded by bloody retribution.

On the death of his father, Charles II (but make that, perhaps, his reputed father: there were suspicions that he had resulted from his mother's affair with Colonel Robert Sidney), James Scott, Duke of Monmouth, believed he had a better claim to the throne than Charles's brother James, not least because James was a Catholic. Monmouth, though he proclaimed himself the legitimate son of the king, had not been accepted as such – but better a Protestant bastard, some may have thought, than a man born in holy wedlock who was a papist.

Monmouth had been living in exile in Holland, but now he saw his chance to return, and the place he picked from the map for the launch of his enterprise was devotedly Protestant Lyme. In this, to judge from the greeting he got from the town, he was largely right; but his welcome party did not include the mayor, who sneaked off to Exeter to rally an opposition. The story of his forces' arrival on what from then on has always been called Monmouth Beach, is told with his customary vividness, wit and verve by the master of narrative history, Lord Macaulay.

> On the morning of the eleventh of June, the Helderenbergh, accompanied by two smaller vessels, appeared off the port of Lyme. That town is a small knot of steep and narrow alleys, lying on a coast wild, rocky, and beaten by a stormy sea. The place was then chiefly remarkable for a pier which, in the days of the Plantagenets, had been constructed of stones, unhewn and uncemented. This ancient work, known by the name of the Cob, enclosed the only haven where, in a space of many miles, the fisherman could take refuge from the tempests of the Channel.
>
> The appearance of the three ships, foreign built and without colours, perplexed the inhabitants of Lyme; and the uneasiness increased when it was found that the Customhouse officers, who had gone on board according to usage, did not return. The town's people repaired to the cliffs, and gazed long and anxiously, but could find no solution of the mystery. At length seven boats put off from the largest of the strange vessels, and rowed to the shore. From these boats landed about eighty men, well armed and appointed…
>
> Monmouth commanded silence, kneeled down on the shore, thanked God for having preserved the friends of liberty and pure religion from the perils of the sea, and implored the divine blessing

> on what was yet to be done by land. He then drew his sword and led his men over the cliffs into the town.

Crowds had gathered, and as Monmouth's presence and the purpose of his invasion became clear to them, 'the enthusiasm of the populace burst through all restraints. The little town was in an uproar with men running to and fro, and shouting "A Monmouth! A Monmouth! the Protestant religion!" Meanwhile the ensign of the adventurers, a blue flag, was set up in the market place.' A declaration was read from the town cross, the language of which disturbed the historian. It was not only badly written, but 'libellously contentious', he says. On the other hand, 'Disgraceful as this manifesto was to those who put it forth, it was not unskilfully framed for the purpose of stimulating the passions of the vulgar.'

The townspeople having been roused, the rebels made off for Axminster, where they met the forces the mayor of Lyme had alerted, headed by the 2nd Duke of Albemarle, who was powerless to stop them and ordered a retreat. Here Monmouth, in Macaulay's view, made his first big mistake. He accepted advice from his close counsellor and confidant Robert Ferguson, who appears to have been the Donald Rumsfeld of these proceedings: even more disastrous than Rumsfeld, perhaps, in Macaulay's reckoning ('at once unprincipled and brainsick... with this man's knavery was strangely mingled an eccentric vanity which resembled madness') and made not for Exeter, which he might have taken unchallenged, but for Taunton, where they proclaimed him king. James could hardly have called himself King James without confusing the ill-informed, so he had himself hailed as King Monmouth.

Lyme in greeting them may have repeated 'A Monmouth! A Monmouth! the Protestant religion!'; but what did his forces shout as they stormed up the beach? An account which I read long ago and has stuck in my mind ever since says their war cry was rather different: 'No Prelacy! No Erastianism!'. If that's so, it was hardly surprising that the invasion failed. Just try running up that steep shingle beach in the general direction of the car park, the powerboat club and the bowling green, howling at the top of your voice 'No Prelacy! No Erastianism!' and you'll see what I mean. The only slogan I know that's remotely as cumbersome is the one attributed to the Bodmin rebels who rose in defence of the traditional Latin prayer book in 1549, whose cry is said to have been: 'Kill the gentlemen and we will have the Six Articles up again and ceremonies as they were in King Henry's time.' Rather takes your breath away, doesn't it?

The expedition, anyway, was soon in serious trouble and the forces of King James finished it off at the battle of Sedgemoor on 6 July 1685. Monmouth was discovered afterwards cowering in a ditch, and when taken to London begged cringingly for his life, even promising to turn Catholic. Nevertheless, his adherents continued to believe in him. His public execution followed – a botched affair; despite the Duke's entreaties that he should do a better job than he'd done on a previous outing, the executioner made five attempts to remove Monmouth's head before lopping it off with a knife. Yet his men would still not accept their leader was dead, a common delusion when famous figures have died: men like King Arthur and Nero and Charlemagne and Barbarossa, Harold (who it was said was not killed at Hastings but decamped and lived as a hermit near Chester), Richard II (sneaked off and lived in the Hebrides), and Billy the Kid; also the so-called Sir William Courtenay of Bossenden Woods, and Lord Kitchener, who may or may not have died off Marwick Head – and Elvis Presley: most of them people of rather more lasting consequence than James, Duke of Monmouth.

A B C D

E F G H

I J K L

M N O P

Q R S T

U V W XYZ

MACHYNLLETH

MACHYNLLETH (pronounced Ma-hun'-tleth), mkt.-town, par. and urb. dist., with ry. sta., G.W. and Corris Rs., Montgomeryshire, on r. Dovey, 20¾m. NE. of Aberystwyth by rail… pop. 1870…

WHEN THE WELSH ASSEMBLY was planned, one or two other towns were bold or foolhardy enough to challenge the capital, Cardiff, for the right to house it. One of these was Machynlleth. Those who need to know how to pronounce this name should take advice from the Welsh. To my untutored ears, as to Bartholomew's, it sounds a bit like Ma-hun-thleth. But if you're booking a ticket at an English railway station, don't ask for Ma-hun-thleth. Outside Paddington, all you are likely to get is a funny look; or, as I did at the booking office at Wimbledon station, a withering glare and this rebuke: 'Oh, you must mean Mar-chin-leth'.

And yet there's a lot to be said for making Machynlleth the chief town of Wales. It has a small population (around 2,200 now), but so has Vaduz in Liechtenstein. It is on the main road and railway that run west to east through the middle of Wales. Although it is proud of its ancientness, just up the road it has a Centre for Alternative Technology, begun in an abandoned quarry in 1970, and fully attuned to the urgent environmentalist agenda of the twenty-first century.

But more than that, it's an entirely distinctive and exceptionally flavoursome town. When you're in Machynlleth, you never suspect for one moment that you might be somewhere else. It is full of good Welsh history, and not least of knees unbowed to the English. It lays claim to, and venerates, Owain Glyndwr. He led the rising against the English that erupted in Wales in 1400. Though technically it was sparked by a land dispute, it owed its passion to poverty and the desperation that comes from poverty. Also to the calendar-millenarian opinion taught that the world was likely to end in 1400.

But it had a nationalist feeling to it as well. He had been sent by God, Glyndwr told his followers, to liberate them from English bondage. They responded by proclaiming him Prince of Wales. Some of gentrified Wales was aghast, but by no means all of it: Glyndwr had his adherents there too, clergy as well as laity. It no doubt helped that he took the view expounded by Gerald of Wales that the English had robbed the Welsh Church of its independence, and he planned to restore it. At first it seemed that Henry IV had the matter in hand. Glyndwr was driven back to take refuge in the mountains. But in 1401 his forces rallied, and in the following year they succeeded in turning back the English tide. In his rebellion of 1403, Henry Hotspur made common cause with Glyndwr. Though Hotspur was killed at the battle of Shrewsbury, Glyndwr continued to prosper, capturing the castles of Aberystwyth and Harlech and gaining effective command of much of Wales.

In 1404 he held a parliament in Machynlleth, where, according to some accounts, he was crowned Prince of Wales in the presence of representatives from France, Scotland and Castile. Yet the following year saw Glyndwr in decline, despite French assistance, and in 1408–9 both Harlech and Aberystwyth were lost. In 1412 he was offered a pardon, but made no reply; by 1413 he had disappeared entirely. No one knows where or when he died, but his monuments, and the sense that he made this town the national centre of Wales, are still there in Machynlleth.

The little town stands on a hill, encased by hills, at the end of the Dovey estuary, at the point where the roads from Aberystwyth, Newtown and Dolgellau join, all in their scenic and twisty ways principal highways of this part of Wales. Everything meets at this junction, where the scene is brilliantly completed by a clock tower of 1873, replacing the old market cross, erected by the inhabitants of the town and district to mark the coming of age of Viscount Castlereagh, son of the Marquess of Londonderry – the Londonderrys having bought the best house in town, Plas Machynlleth. Their successors presented

house and grounds to the town at the end of the Second World War, 'for their perpetual use and enjoyment'. Near the house, now a Celtic cultural centre, is a memorial stone to Glyndwr.

You have only to look at the clock tower and try to delete this elegant fantasy, with its dragons and angels and spikes and narrow indentations for archers to fire though, a creation right out of Disneyland long before Disney, to see how much it gives a sense of place to the town. Ahead, down broad Maengwyn Street, there is a lively open market and a building called Parliament House, commemorating the honour that Owain did to Machynlleth, though the one that you see today is not the building his parliament met in. Six or seven inns survive of two dozen or more which this place sustained in the mid nineteenth century. Balked in its ambition to take its place with London, Paris and Athens as a national capital, plucky Machynlleth went on to bid for city status, along with nearby Newtown and Aberystwyth, in the millennium year, but was disappointed again. Just too small, no doubt – though it's bigger than St David's.

The natural capital city for Wales, of course, is in England. Even by rail, more so by road, to get from somewhere like Ynys Mon (Anglesey) to the present capital, Cardiff, is a long and weary struggle. Either by road or rail, though, there's excellent access from both the north and south to once-Welsh Shrewsbury. Had the Welsh, having captured it, not had to hand it back to the English, it could have served the principality very well. It just goes to show that questions like these are best not decided by battles.

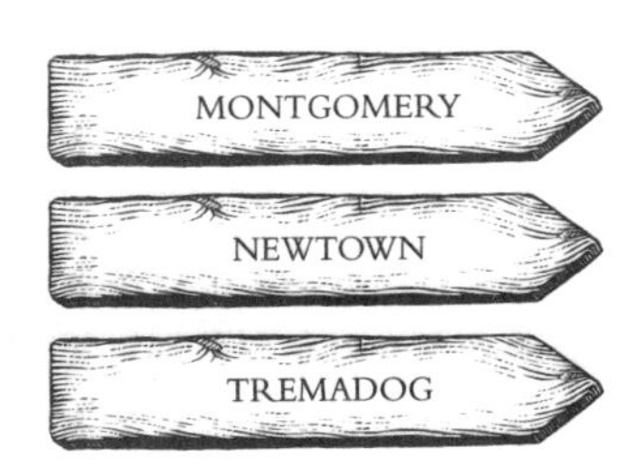

MARKET HARBOROUGH

MARKET HARBOROUGH, urb dist., par. and mkt.-town...
Leicestershire, on r. Welland and Union Canal, 16m. SE.
of Leicester...

FROM THE POST OFFICE here, G. K. Chesterton, essayist, novelist, biographer, poet, literary critic and unstinting enthusiast for good food, good drink, England and Roman Catholicism, having set out one morning to deliver a lecture, despatched the following message by telegram to his patient wife, who no doubt barely flinched on receiving it, since by then she was well accustomed to the great man's absent-mindedness: 'Am in Market Harborough. Where ought I to be?'

MARSTON, SOUTH

MARSTON, SOUTH, par. and vil., Wilts, 3½m.
NE. of Swindon.

HIS GRAVE IS CONSPICUOUS in the churchyard, on the left as you go through the gate, under a towering tree: Alfred Williams, the Hammerman poet. If you've heard of South Marston, off the Swindon to Shrivenham road in the north-eastern corner of Wiltshire, that is probably because you know the sad story of Williams's life, and possibly even one of his books, or a poem or two.

Williams was born and lived in this quiet place for most of his life, and for all the anguish he suffered here, called it 'a sweet and rare village'. Much of the place that he knew is still there – the four houses he lived in at various times, the church, the Carriers Arms, the house which was once a shop, kept in his day by Daniel Lewis, a dissenting minister, who could not bear to press the indigent for their debts and was thus eventually ruined. But all that is now augmented by a decorous contingent of desirable late twentieth-century residences. If you edit out the drone of planes and occasional shouts from the sports field, it's a calm and even somnolent place. It is something of an event when the bus to Swindon appears for a journey down a main road that takes passengers past PC World, Poundstretcher, Sainsbury's, Pets at Home, Toys 'R' Us, WH Smith, Argos, Curry's – places where working people will nowadays spend far more in one afternoon, even in real terms, than Williams ever saw in a year.

He was born on 6 February 1877, the fifth child, and fourth son, of a father who in time abandoned the family, leaving his wife to cope with eight children under twelve. From the age of eight Alfred worked half-time on a farm to eke out the family's income. At eleven, he packed up school for good and worked on the land full-time. At fifteen, like his brothers Edgar and Henry and most of the lads in this territory, he went to work for the railway. He was strong enough to find work in the 'hellish heat and clamour' of the railway forge. Over the years his journeys to and from work became a familiar sight in the area. 'I recall him', one villager told Leonard Clark, whose fine and moving life of Alfred Williams was published in 1945, 'passing by the windows of my house in Stratton St Margaret village, from the railway works in which he worked for so many years, a tall spare figure with no redundancy of body, nothing extra, hardly enough maybe to challenge life; upright as a dart, active, cheery, kind, courteous of disposition, with a mind which took broad sweeps and sailed uncharted seas.' Others were not so charitable. He was somehow suspiciously different. One sympathizer, a man called Henry Byett, recalled that Williams, 'was considered mad by those villagers to whom animals were just animals, either of value or pests according to their type. One said, "I see'd Alfie Williams t'other night walking on Poor Meadow wi' 'is 'ands behind 'im and gawkin' up at the sky for all the world like a b— lunatic."'

The forge was a tough, exhausting workplace for any man, but for Williams that life was coupled with an epic course of self-education. He would wake at four and read by an oil light until it was time to walk to the works. He would even read on his way. He would read through his dinner hour, and read again for a while when the day had ended to give himself things to think about on his journey back to South Marston. Then he would read until midnight. He embarked on a correspondence course in English Literature with Ruskin Hall (later Ruskin College), Oxford. Finding his books full of Latin quotations he started to learn the language. He also taught himself Greek, French and mathematics. He would mark some Greek word he was trying to master on the toe of his boot to consult from time to time through the day. He even wrote Greek characters on the wall above his furnace until management put a stop to it.

That did not make him a popular figure among his workmates. Like Frank Owen in Robert Tressell's account of Hastings housepainters, *The Ragged Trousered Philanthropists*, he was mocked for his scholarly ways. But even his scoffing workmates were much to be preferred to the managers. The book he published at the end of his life at the forge, *Life in a Railway Factory*, is full of instances of insensitive, degrading, contemptuous treatment of working men by those set in authority over them. Tressell saw socialism as the only hope for the kind of men he was working with. Williams was never a socialist; in fact he became in time a denouncer of socialism, and worked on a

book warning workpeople against it. He was, by nature, conservative; but the thoughtlessly bruising way in which working men were used stirred him to anger.

He left the factory after more than twenty years' employment in September 1914. He could not take any more the grinding toll of his labour. He could not bear being cut off all day from the countryside. The only redeeming aspect of the railway works was the chance now and again to escape to a meadow of flowers behind a long fence at its northern edge, where rosebay flourished, and delicate toadflax, bright golden ragwort, wild mignonette, yellow melilot, ox-eye daisies, mayweed, small willow-herb, meadowsweet, ladies' bedstraw, tansy, yarrow and cinquefoil. The Hammerman's famous strength was eroding. His doctor had told him the smoke of the factory had ruined his digestive system; also he wanted to write, to add to the verse and the pictures of village life he had published already. He had to go from door to door selling his book *A Wiltshire Village*, published in 1912, and its successor – which Clark thought his masterpiece – *Villages of the White Horse*. The first book, about South Marston, upset the village, and most of all the farmers, of whom Williams had harsh words to say. The vicar, who had bought a copy to give to the village reading room as well as one for himself, declared it too disgusting to read, denounced it from his pulpit, recovered the book he had put in the reading room and publicly burned both copies.

But if Williams's life at the works had been hard, his life thereafter was more arduous still. He and his wife lived on the edge of penury. She was Mary Peck, from Hungerford. She had jilted a former lover to marry him in 1903 – he was twenty-six, she was twenty-three. Having left the railway's employment, he was able to publish *Life in a Railway Factory* in 1915, which he had finished in just twelve weeks, writing each night after work. Its judgements on the way the works was organized and run were unsparing. Reviewers unconnected with the industry praised it abundantly. But the

Great Western Railway's own magazine was offended. The book, it conceded, was 'interesting'; but the man who had written it had never been cut out for his job. 'It is well', it said, 'to bear in mind the oblique mentality of the writer, due largely to the uncongenial environment. He detested the factory simply because it was a factory…' But even this spat did not help sell copies. Six years after its publication, only about a dozen had sold in Swindon.

The Williamses were doing their best to live on five shillings a week. Their chief sources of income were their cottage garden – though even here their hopes were constantly blighted by pest and frost – and his work collecting rates for the parish council. His admirers in the literary world of London tried to get him a pension, but the word came back that at thirty-seven he was too young. The prime minister, Herbert Asquith, who thought he deserved one, opened a subscription fund and offered to start it with £150.

What eventually rescued him from his downward drift and depression was, curiously, the war. He volunteered, and by some weird misjudgement, was considered fit to serve. He was posted in time to India, which he came to love with passion. He would like to have stayed there for good: 'what's to come back to in England', he wrote to Mary, 'except you'. But Mary wrote back from South Marston with news that their home, Dryden Cottage, was about to be sold. Williams returned to England in 1919, and he and Mary set about building a house on a plot of land near the church, left to him by his mother. To find the materials to build with, they had to dismantle, brick by laborious brick, a ruined house by the canal, and then the abandoned walls of the lock, wheeling their supplies in barrowloads back to their chosen site, sometimes working until midnight. For the building, they had the expert help of a mason, but he was seventy-two, and far from biddable. In time, though, the house was ready. They called it Ranikhet, after an Indian hill station where Alfred had served, and moved in to begin what was meant to be their new life.

But as ever, little went well for them. The garden brought in only a pitiful income. Alfred trudged the streets trying to sell his books, but the admiration they commanded in some of the salons of London was barely echoed in Wiltshire. At one point their plight was so desperate that he considered going back to the railway works. Yet now he was teaching himself Sanskrit. He completed a book of Sanskrit tales and cycled to Oxford, 54 miles there and back, to show them to Basil Blackwell. The book was published in 1930. The new prime minister, Ramsay MacDonald, was impressed enough to promise to seek a pension for Williams: in the meantime, he sent a cheque for £50, drawn on his personal account.

Leonard Clark's history of Alfred Williams's final days is like something out of the novels of George Gissing: the struggle of a man whose poverty was due at least in part to his stubborn integrity. A book of his collected poems was published, but so full of errors that he tried to have it withdrawn. He wrote an industrial novel: no takers. Then a version of the Sanskrit *Panchatantra*: no takers again. His reputation was fading. At South Marston, the weather blighted his crops. He felt the village had turned against him, even that they were persecuting him. He knew he needed to leave Ranikhet and find some healthier spot, but money would not permit it.

Then Mary fell ill. Cancer was diagnosed. An operation was unsuccessful. 'I shall have nobody in the world when she is gone,' he said. He cycled every morning and evening to Swindon to see her in hospital. On 9 April 1930, visiting his good blind friend Lou Robins on his way to the Victoria hospital, he suddenly became agitated, moaning and weeping and crying out at the fate of his wife. When he reached the hospital, they told him Mary was worse. Next day, neighbours, troubled at not having seen him, went to the house to investigate. Getting no answer, they climbed in through a window and found him dead on his bed. His heart had failed. Mary was brought back from hospital to watch from a window as the funeral procession passed on its way to the church. His total resources were found to be £69, £50 of which was the gift from Ramsay MacDonald. Told of Alfred's death, MacDonald arranged an immediate grant for Mary; but the money was never paid, for she died at the end of May.

His three first homes in South Marston – Cambria Cottage, Rose Cottage and Dryden Cottage – all have plaques on their walls in his honour. Ranikhet is almost hidden by high hedges, but its name can still be seen carved into the stone. 'In loving memory', says the graveyard inscription, 'of Alfred Owen Williams, poet and author, died April 9 1930 aged 53 years; also in loving memory of Mary Maria Williams, his dear wife, died May 27 1930 aged 50 years.' Then, below, a little eroded, and difficult to read in the shadow of the high tree, brave and defiant lines from his poem 'The Testament':

> I will sing my song triumphantly.
> I will finish my race,
> I will work my task.

MARWICK HEAD

MARWICK HEAD, Birsay Bay, mainland, Orkney; crowned by the Kitchener memorial cairn.

ON THE CLIFF TOP close to the tidal island called the Brough of Birsay, on the north-eastern corner of the mainland of Orkney, the scene of the first important settlement on the island, a tower (it is more than a cairn) commemorates Lord Kitchener, lost in the sinking in 1916 of the *Hampshire*, doomed by a German mine, with 667 men aboard, of whom only 12 survived. Frank Power, the journalist who (see Lambeth) first argued that Kitchener had not died but had been smuggled away to safety, and then claimed to have done what those in authority had failed to do by finding Kitchener's body and bringing it back to Britain, was present at the ceremony in 1926. The inscription says: 'This tower was raised by the people of Orkney in memory of Field Marshal Earl Kitchener of Khartoum on that corner of his country, which he had served so faithfully, nearest to the place where he died on duty. He and his staff perished, along with the officers and nearly all of the men of the HMS *Hampshire*, on the 5th June 1916.'

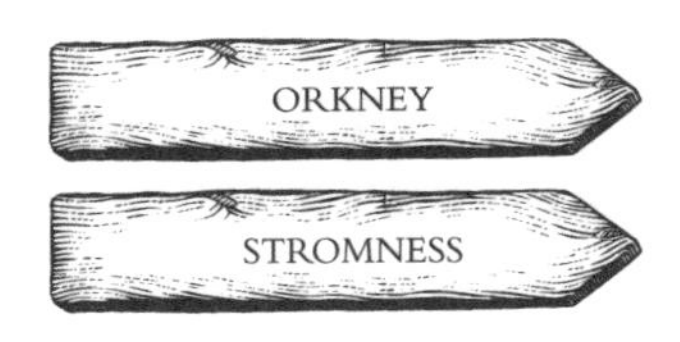

MARYLEBONE

MARYLEBONE, parl. bor. and name of a L.N.E. terminus, in NW. of London… see also St Marylebone.

THE GREAT HECTOR BERLIOZ wrote an early part of his wonderful *Memoirs* – his prose is almost as vivid and rompish as his music, full of the iconoclastic exuberance that shocked his musical masters – in a house in Osnaburgh Street, east of Regent's Park. On 10 April 1848, having begun to record how his father had demanded that he give up music and take up medicine, he abruptly put down his pen, left the house and strode purposefully southwards to Kennington Park on the other side of the Thames. Characteristically, he apologizes to his readers for this break in transmission. 'Here I pause for a moment', he says, 'before taking up the story of my Parisian life and the relentless struggle in which I became involved almost from the moment of arriving there, and which I have not ceased to carry on, against men, ideas and things. The reader will perhaps grant me a breathing-space. Besides, today, the 10th of April, the two hundred thousand English Chartists are to hold their demonstration. In a few hours, maybe, England will be engulfed like the rest of Europe and this refuge too will have failed me. I shall go out and see how this issue is decided.'

You can almost hear the sigh of relief when he gets back. '8pm. Your Chartist is a very decent sort of revolutionary. Everything went off satisfactorily. The cannon, those eloquent orators and formidable logicians whose arguments appealed so powerfully to the masses, were in the chair. They were not required to utter a word, their presence being enough to persuade everybody of the inexpediency of revolution, and the Chartists dispersed in perfect order. My poor friends, you know as much about starting a riot as the Italians about writing a symphony. The Irish are doubtless the same, to judge from O'Connell's injunction, "Agitate, agitate, but never act."'

His next sentence is dated 12 July. He's been too busy to write any more, he says, and now he is returning to 'the country which is still called France', which is, after all, his country. 'Farewell England!' he says, graciously taking leave of it.

I could find no trace in today's Osnaburgh Street of the house where he was writing, nor of anything else that was there in those days. In a feast of demolition in the mid 1930s, nearly all that remained of Osnaburgh Street was obliterated, including both Berlioz's lodging and the house in which the Fabian Society was founded. Only the parish church of St Mary Magdalene has been allowed to survive, along with the house next door which looks to have been the vicarage. A chunk of the original street is replaced today by a clunking edifice, described at the time it first appeared as 'a magnificent building of modern, economical and luxurious flats', called the White House. Having started life as a block of apartments it then had a club attached to extend its services to non-residents, and so evolved into a hotel. It is big, bold and dashing and has probably featured on several occasions in TV productions set in the 1930s. I can picture Hercule Poirot emerging from it, accompanied by his immensely tedious sidekick, Captain Hastings. A treat if you like that sort of building, which I don't think I do.

As for the rest of the street, impressive operations were under way when I was there to knock much of it down, including much of what had been erected with pride in the 1930s. A grievous loss to British architecture? I doubt it. At the top of the street, still intact, is a square, and before it a crossroads from which one may contemplate a pub called the Queen and Artichoke: how did those two get together? The square, which is Munster Square, has a small park and a playground, a good calm place where one might sit on a summer day enjoying Hector's memoirs.

This is a man who, had he not been a great composer (some purists dispute that, but what's good enough for Sir Colin Davis is good enough for me), could have been a great writer, and this is beyond argument a great book. Such a privilege, until the final, despairing pages, to spend hour after hour in the company of this wild, crazy, headstrong, imperious, frustrating, frustrated genius, with his huge unstaunchable passions (Shakespeare, Beethoven, the English actress Harriet Smithson who, against all the odds, became, for a time, his wife). Like the roving gangs in the Abruzzi who crop up in his *Harold in Italy*, Berlioz is a brigand. At one point he imagines his muse: 'an armed virago, bounding barefoot over the wild rocks, hair streaming to the winds, dark cloak flashing with gaudy trinkets or dreaming to the roar of the elements, terrifying the women with her baleful glance and maddening the men, but not to love'.

He is constantly at war with philistines of every kind: people who cannot see that Beethoven was the greatest musical genius who ever lived; people who cannot accept that free spirits like Berlioz must never be straitjacketed by ancient, indefensible rules, administered by chilly pedants; his enemy the conductor Habeneck, for example, who tries to sabotage the premiere of his *Requiem*. At a point in the score which Berlioz regards as the fulcrum of his whole work, Habeneck lays down his baton and takes a pinch of snuff. The composer, lurking behind him, springs forward and conducts the crucial passage himself.

He reports for duty with provincial orchestras only to find that the instruments for which his works are scored are simply not available. His tour of Europe in 1843 is blighted by the absence of ophicleides, a now obsolete keyed brass instrument. Mannheim: the orchestra has no ophicleide; an adapted valve trombone has to be used. Weimar: no cor anglais, no ophicleide; its part is played by a 'tolerably powerful' bombardon. Leipzig: the cor anglais is hopelessly out of tune. The ophicleide, 'or rather the abject brass object masquerading under that name', has to be banished. Brunswick: you can't find an ophicleide in Brunswick, and no cor anglais is available either. Hamburg: a decent ophicleide, but the cor anglais player has to be dropped. Berlin: 'there is no ophicleide at the Berlin Opera... they replace it not with a bass tuba but with a second bass trombone. The effect... is disastrous...' Hanover: 'there is no ophicleide... the cor anglais is badly out of tune'. He is not safe even in Paris. In 1833 he's unable to start a performance of his *Symphonie Fantastique* because only five violins, two violas, four cellos and one trombone have turned up.

So, forward to 1848, with Berlioz leaving our shores. But what is this? Just four days after saying goodbye to England, he's in London again. 'I have come back. Paris is burying her dead. The pavements used for the barricades have been replaced – to be torn up again, perhaps, tomorrow... Surrounded', he soliloquizes, 'by this ghastly confusion of justice and injustice, good and evil, truth and falsehood, hearing a language spoken whose words are perverted from their normal meaning, what is to prevent one from going completely mad? I shall go on with my autobiography. I have nothing better to do, and scrutinizing the past will take my mind off the present.' How very apposite. Thinking about Hector Berlioz and his excursion to Kennington has helped me take my mind off poor dreary, charmless Osnaburgh Street.

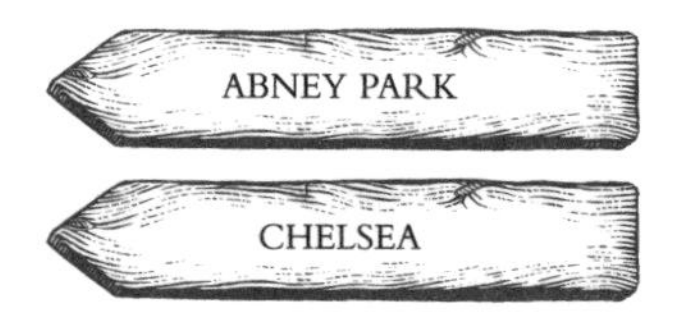

MAWGAN-IN-PYDAR

MAWGAN IN PYDER, par. and vil., Cornwall, 3m. NW. of St. Columb Major; 5524 ac., pop. 745... 2m. NW. of vil. is M. Porth, coastguard sta. At the vil. is Lanherne Nunnery.

THE 556 WESTERN GREYHOUND bus from Newquay to Padstow – it's a lovely ride, and St Mawgan (St Mawgan-in-Pydar is the usual designation these days) deserves to be spared your car – comes in down a narrow, winding, mysterious lane and deposits you in the heart of the village: church on one side of the road, pub on the other, and a joyful bubbling stream by the stop. A minor road on the pub side leads you down to the village shop (cream teas and lunches a speciality) and the river Menahyl which flows through and enlivens this Vale of Lanherne. It feels like a place that has scarcely left the nineteenth century, let alone come to terms with the noisy, thrusting, headline-infested twenty-first.

St Mawgan seems to have been an abbot in Pembrokeshire – an area then known, the church guidebook unexpectedly says, as Dementia – who along with his comrades St Brioc and St Cadoc migrated to Cornwall, and established here a monastery dedicated to St Hernan, from whom the valley derives its name. St Cadoc settled down as a hermit on the hill above the village, close to what is now Newquay airport. St Mawgan preferred to stay in the valley. The first church here was dedicated to this saint, though later, on the edict of Rome, which did not recognize Celtic saints, it was rededicated to St Nicholas. Now Mawgan has it back again, and quite right too. With its fifteenth-century tower and twin east windows, his church, reached through a Victorian lychgate, is an immediately endearing sight. The 'lan' in the name Lanherne denotes a graveyard, and the graveyard here seems, even as graveyards go, unusually reflective and tranquil. Both inside and outside the church there are poignant reminders that this was a seafaring parish: here, says one memorial in the graveyard, lie ten bodies – nine men are named, along with 'Jemmy'; perhaps the ship's boy? – who drifted ashore in a boat, frozen to death, at Tregurrian Beach in this parish, on Sunday, 13 December 1846. Nowadays rescue operations at sea are often conducted from the nearby RAF station, which gets the name of St Mawgan's into the news.

Up the hill behind the graveyard one comes to an ancient stone wall, decorated with religious emblems. This shields what Bartholomew calls the nunnery, though it's more often now called a convent, and the Roman Catholic church of St Joseph and St Anne – home, as a notice explains, to a Carmelite community of Franciscans of the Immaculate Friars and Contemplative Sisters. While I stood admiring this wall, an aged car stopped beside me, and its driver, one of the friars, wished me good morning and told me something of the place's history, not omitting to point out that the church of St Mawgan had once been a Catholic church too.

Buses from Newquay to Padstow call here once an hour; you need at least that to get acquainted with St Mawgan-in-Pydar especially if you intend to call at the Falcon Inn, where one may sit outside in a secluded garden. A little way on towards Padstow, there's a Japanese garden and bonsai nursery, a community hall which records that this was Cornwall's best kept village in 2006, a Methodist chapel, and rows of pretty cottages. And that's about it; but it needs no more. I was there on a brisk but benign morning in February: the village is no doubt rather less tranquil at the height of the season when motorists are busy looking for somewhere to park, and the shop is doing a lively trade in cream teas and lunches, and perhaps the flights out of the airport just up the hill may be more intrusive. The fact that the church appears in some episodes of *Miss Marple* must have boosted the place's tourist appeal. But choose the date and time of your visit with care, and St Mawgan-in-Pydar may seem to you like the Carmelite order it houses – contemplative and immaculate.

MIDDLESBROUGH

MIDDLESBROUGH, parl. and co. bor., par. and r. port… on right bank of Tees estuary, 3m. E. of Stockton and connected with Port Clarence by a transporter bridge… is the principal seat of the English iron trade…

THIS IS WHERE IT all started. Leave the railway station (once compared with St Pancras, somewhat extravagantly) and turn, not south into the centre of town, but north towards the transporter bridge past an immensely self-satisfied one-time branch of the National Provincial Bank of 1872. Keep on until you come to a road leading up to a square, where nothing remains but a chunky red block with a tower. This is the old town hall of 1846, the centre of the Middlesbrough that began to grow out of nowhere in the 1830s; more recently it became the Under the Clock Community Centre, but now – it is nothing.

In 1801, Middlesbrough was just four houses containing twenty-five people. In 1829, their numbers had swelled to forty. Twelve years later, the population was over 5,000. What transformed it was the creation of a port for the shipment of coal to the Stockton and Darlington railway by a group of Darlington Quaker businessmen, chief among them, as was so often the case in Darlingtonian enterprises, one of the Pease family – Joseph. Off this square, in the beginning, ran North Street, West Street, South Street and East Street. Close by – and still there, because it's protected, though it's in a very poor state – is the Custom House, Greek Revival, 1837, home of the Middlesbrough Exchange Association until 1886 when the Custom House was established, as a mark of the town's burgeoning trade.

This area is known nowadays as St Hilda's, after a church demolished in 1959 (but at least it survived long enough for L. S. Lowry to paint it). The whole place feels abandoned, with weeds growing out of pavements where important municipal feet once trod, though the oddest sight is a patch of postwar semis, some spick and span and fitted with burglar alarms, some – even in the same pair – empty and boarded up. In a book which I treasure called *Victorian Cities*, published in 1963, the historian Asa Briggs called it a tragedy that in an age of deliberate new town-building, this fascinating example of nineteenth-century town planning had been all but destroyed. It looks even more desolate now.

The new Middlesbrough soon vastly outgrew the expectations of its Quaker creators, though it was they who effectively determined its future by persuading two entrepreneurs, Henry Bolckow and John Vaughan, close friends who married two sisters and set up home next door to each other, to settle here and open a foundry and iron mill. No town in Victorian England grew faster. By 1851, the population was over 7,000; by 1861, 19,000; by 1871, 56,000; twenty years on, over 75,000; and by 1901, above 91,000. From 1853, the old town hall on the hill was reduced to a mere police station.

Men wanting work, far outnumbering women, had flooded into the place with all that this always implied in terms of crime and fighting and drunkenness. A noble army of churches tried as best they could, but too often unavailingly, to inculcate decency and religious observance into this swarming mass. Yet nothing could stem the town's commercial success. 'Ironopolis', people called it. In time, the town even had a team called Middlesbrough Ironopolis in the football league.

Though a son of distant Mecklenbergh, Bolckow became the borough's first mayor, and in 1868 was elected, unopposed, as its first MP, continuing to represent it until his death in 1878, when 10,000 people came to his funeral. Bolckow's statue stands in what once was a hallowed quarter of Middlesbrough, the square which held its exchange. Today, it is a much less dignified spot than such an influential figure deserves: a bypass has now been slapped across it and the old exchange building has gone.

The prestige space in Middlesbrough now is Victoria Square, where a statue of John Vaughan shares pride of place with that of a Conservative, Sir Samuel Alexander Sadler, the first Tory MP for the town, in front of the new town hall that was opened in 1887 by the Prince of Wales. The Prince, no doubt hoping to flatter the people of Middlesbrough, confessed to its dignitaries as they worked their way through many courses and copious drink that he'd feared he was coming to somewhere smoky; to which, according to press reports, the Conservative mayor, a shipbuilder, Major Dixon, replied fearlessly in terms which, as Asa Briggs says, catch the spirit of mid-Victorian

Middlesbrough: 'His Royal Highness owned he had expected to see a smoky town. It is one, and if there is one thing more than another that Middlesbrough can be said to be proud of, it is the smoke (cheers and laughter). The smoke is an indication of plenty of work (applause), an indication of prosperous times (cheers) – an indication that all classes of workpeople are being employed, that there is little necessity for charity (cheers) and that even those in the humblest station are in a position free from want (cheers). Therefore we are proud of our smoke.'

There were times, though, when the leading men of new Middlesbrough – their local patriotism transcending mere political differences at moments like these – must have feared that the smoke might not last. The great days of iron were over; the town was now entrusting its fortunes to steel. In the years after Bolckow's death, the place was losing momentum. The better off were finding pleasanter places to live. Men like Bolckow and Vaughan had, as their riches accrued, moved away from the smoke to fine houses outside the town, but had still remained part of its governance. A later generation of industrial moguls was far less involved.

In spite of Mayor Dixon's confidence, under the glittering chandeliers and in the general glow of a royal presence, that even the humblest were strangers to want, life for many was hard. Much of the housing run up in the boom days to meet an urgent demand was barely fit to be lived in. Death rates were high, and a council committed to the religion of thrift would not inflict the cost of necessary improvement on the ratepayers.

On a ceremonial visit Gladstone had talked of Middlesbrough as 'a modern Hercules'. There is less to wonder at now. The one truly eye-catching achievement of twentieth-century Middlesbrough was the transporter bridge, opened in 1911 by Prince Arthur of Connaught. There are pictures of the occasion in a waiting room by the bridge. The scene is all serious hats and official horses, except that Arthur, who looks a jolly old cove, is smiling and bald in their midst.

The Liberal progressives who founded Middlesbrough and presided over its boom years would find it surprising and probably saddening today. It has failed to fulfil their dreams. Old industries have declined and folded, especially in days when severe and unsentimental economic doctrines helped deepen the desuetude of places like this. Manufacturing employment fell by more than a third in the 1980s. In September 2007 a report from the Office of National Statistics found that Middlehaven, the sector of Middlesbrough where the adventure began, had the lowest life expectancy of any council area in England or Wales, fifty-five: that was more than thirty years less than the place at the top of the pile, a 1990s estate in Didcot, Oxfordshire. Another government survey placed it last, jointly with Blackburn, in a table of fifty-six towns and cities ranked for their economic progress. When in 2002 the town came to choose a new mayor, it plumped heavily for a man called Ray Mallon, whose tough law and order commitments had earned him the nickname Robocop.

The focus of local pride and enthusiasm since the 1990s has been Middlesbrough FC, run by a chairman called Steve Gibson. The youngest councillor ever elected in Middlesbrough (at twenty-one) when he won the tough Park End ward, where he came from, Gibson was exactly the kind of young and talented entrepreneur who might once have aspired to run the town, but he settled instead for running its football. Where once the crowd used to flock to the less than elegant Ayresome Park to watch homegrown stars like George Hardwick, who captained England after the Second World War, and the gifted inside forward Wilf Mannion, now they go to watch expensive imports with names far more strange and exotic than Bolckow's performing at the glitzy Riverside Stadium.

In 2007 the collection of buildings around Victoria Square – the town hall, the back of the Empire theatre, the library, the 1980s law courts, the sadly dim and inadequate line of shops on the western side – were augmented by a dashing new

Institute of Modern Art, designed by a Rotterdam architect, Erick van Egeraat, which extends the original square. It is all the more welcome in Middlesbrough because the town is so light on beauty or fantasy; though pleasingly one can see the occasional bus with a destination blind on the front that says it is heading for Norman Conquest.

MIDDLESEX

MIDDLESEX, an inland co. adjoining London. It formerly included a great part of the Metropolis, but that area was severed from it by the Local Government Act of 1888. … there is no co. town nor is there a co. constabulary, the whole co. being served by the metropolitan police. The appearance of the country is generally flat…

THE APPEARANCE OF MIDDLESEX may in Bartholomew's judgement have been generally flat, yet even a flat appearance is better than none at all. Aside from some curiously anomalous postal addresses, this county no longer exists. When the little county of Rutland was threatened with extinction by the local government reforms of the 1970s, proud Rutlanders – well, some of them, anyway – pledged themselves to defend it 'to the last rut'. They failed, but at least they fought. When Middlesex faced extinction in the reforms which led to the creation of the Greater London Council in 1965, no one marched and few even muttered. There was no great fuming in Feltham, no rancour in Ruislip, no high dudgeon in Harlington, Hayes, Hounslow or Harrow. No exceptional wrath was reported from Rickmansworth. Mill Hill was all mute acquiescence, Staines as supine as Sunbury, and no consuming grief gripped Greenford. Northolt knuckled obediently under, Cranford caved in.

No Middle Saxons demonstrated, banners waving and brass bands blaring, through the doomed county town, since, as Bartholomew says, Middlesex didn't have one – it never had. The nearest equivalent was Brentford, the polling place for parliamentary elections. That bold bad eighteenth-century aristocrat John Wilmot, Earl of Rochester, who regularly rode up from Bath, used to say that the devil entered into him as he came into Brentford. But that did not mean that he found temptation in Brentford itself; only that when he passed through the town he knew he was nearing the centre of sin and shame that was London.

Before 1888, Middlesex was larger and meatier. It stretched eastwards as far as the edge of the city of London: what is now known as Petticoat Lane but is legally Middlesex Street was right on the border. The London home of the monarch, the place which housed the imperial Parliament, the Abbey where so many great Britons are buried, all were in Middlesex. Middlesex had a regiment, and an often formidable county cricket team, which gave England the Hearnes and Hendren and B. J. T. Bosanquet, who invented the googly, and in the 1940s those kings of the middle order, Bill Edrich and Denis Compton. The chronicling of its past takes up twelve volumes of the *Victoria County History*, three more than Sussex, four more than Lancashire. Great battles have been fought on Middlesex territory: Barnet, in 1471, where York routed Lancaster and the Earl of Warwick met with his just deserts; Turnham Green in 1642 when King Charles I was turned back from entering London. It has been the site of momentous political battles too: the voters of Middlesex sent John Wilkes to the Commons, and when he was rejected there, returned him three times more. Its highways and byways are explored in elderly books as lovingly as those of Surrey, Essex or Kent.

Yet it never had their sense of identity. Even the county's own historians say so. 'Among all the counties of England', according to a book called *Memorials of Old Middlesex*, edited by J. Tavenor-Perry and published in 1909, 'there is, perhaps, not one which seems to possess less individuality or that is less known as a territorial entity, than the one which contains the great capital of the British Empire.' And why? Always, you get the same answer. 'As the light of Mercury is lost in the blaze of the Sun's glory', says Tavenor-Perry, 'so the dazzle of London has obscured Middlesex.' The monster which lay at its door grew inexorably, swallowing up old towns and suburbs, and encompassing ancient villages in its colony, Metroland. Even after the sad extirpation of much of the county in 1888, it still had a royal palace (Hampton Court), and a public school which over the years had produced seven prime ministers, one of them Churchill and another, Baldwin, who on reaching 10 Downing Street said his aim was to included in his Cabinet as many Harrovians as possible. It still had the model estate of Bedford Park, spectacular industrial buildings along the Great West Road, and Lord's, Wembley and Twickenham for international sport. Heathrow, when Bartholomew published, was still only Heath Row, a hamlet 4 miles north-west of Hounslow; it would grow, before the extinction of Middlesex, into one of the world's great airports.

All lost now and largely, it seems, unmourned. 'Breathes there a man', mused Sir Walter Scott, 'with soul so dead that never to himself hath said "this is my own, my native land"?' That's not how most of Middlesex's inhabitants felt in its dying days. I was born in Mill Hill, Middlesex. Do I feel even the slightest frisson if I set foot in Mill Hill now? Not a trace. Just possibly an earlier generation of Middlesex men might have stirred themselves to fight for their county against a government that took the decision which Harold Wilson's did in 1964 to surrender Staines and Sunbury, Laleham and Shepperton, on the northern banks of the Thames to its ancient rival, mere transpontine Surrey. Yet even on lapsed Middlesex territory like the racecourse at Kempton Park, one wouldn't be wise to bet on it.

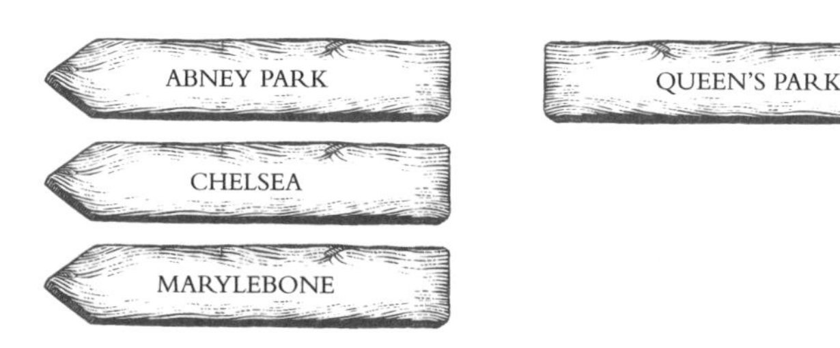

MILNGAVIE

MILNGAVIE (popularly Milguy), par. and town (police bur.)...
Dunbartonshire, on Allander Water, 7m. NW. of Glasgow...

THE ROAD FROM BEARSDEN to Milngavie takes you uneventfully from one douce upmarket suburb of outer Glasgow to another. You would not in most conceivable circumstances go there expecting excitement. Yet this was not always the case. Once, eager children craned round to catch sight of a private zoo on the western side. While on the other, even more irresistibly, there hung from overhead girders a construction which looked to the young William Black like one 'of the spaceships in which heroes like Flash Gordon or Dan Dare hurtled into space to thwart the evil plans of Ming the Merciless or the Mekon of Mekonta.' This object, glamorous and mysterious, though sadly, always motionless, was the Bennie railplane, which Black recalls in a brief but enlightening history published by East Dunbartonshire library service.

George Bennie was born in Glasgow, the son of an engineer. From his youth he was an inventor. The first news of his plans for a railplane emerged in 1921, when he was just short of thirty. He was granted a patent two years later, but four years passed before he was able to muster the funds to proceed. A company was formed to work on the project, and plans were displayed in its offices, attracting the attention of some of those who attended the British Association for the Advancement of Science meeting at Glasgow in 1928. There's a picture of his model in Black's account, showing it suspended over a train made up of what look like toy carriages.

It was not as if Bennie's notion of monorail travel was fantastical or bizarre: Wuppertal in Germany had operated a system since 1898. But Bennie believed his design was better than any before it. The London & North Eastern Railway (LNER), which had sidings off the Glasgow to Milngavie line at Burnbrae, was impressed enough to let him build a test track above them. You can see where the sidings were on waste ground close to a building which is now the headquarters of Kelvin Timber on the road into Milngavie. The first journeys were made in the summer of 1930. There's a photograph in Black's book of LNER officials sitting comfortably in the superior armchairs which Waring and Gillow had supplied for the car. Some of those who were early aboard were reporters, and they wrote with enthusiasm of their experience. True, they conceded, the conveyance was noisy, but only for a moment or two at the start. By mid-July, the public was able to sample it and they too were impressed. By now there was talk of a Bennie railplane route linking Glasgow with Edinburgh. Speeds of up to 150 mph would be possible, the inventor claimed, and the service would be safer and cleaner than conventional travel.

Now, international visitors took the road to Milngavie, while at home, Blackpool was showing interest in a railplane link with Southport. Bennie saw other glamorous possibilities. Why not Manchester–Liverpool? Or central London to Croydon airport? Even more ambitious plans were discussed: a combined railplane and seaplane route linking London with Paris and Brussels at speeds which rivals could only dream of; a fast link from central London to a new London airport, at Folkestone. Bennie must have supposed at this stage that he was set to make his name and his fortune. It only needed some big player to bite. The relevant authorities, though, consistently failed to sign up.

The early momentum began to flag. Bennie cast around for investors, and failed to find them. His own funds were exhausted. Even that did not erode his confidence in the visionary creation that still intrigued every new traveller who came upon it, suspended, waiting and ready, over the sidings near the Milngavie Road. It took the onset of war to cool his evangelizing fervour. Yet as late as 1950,

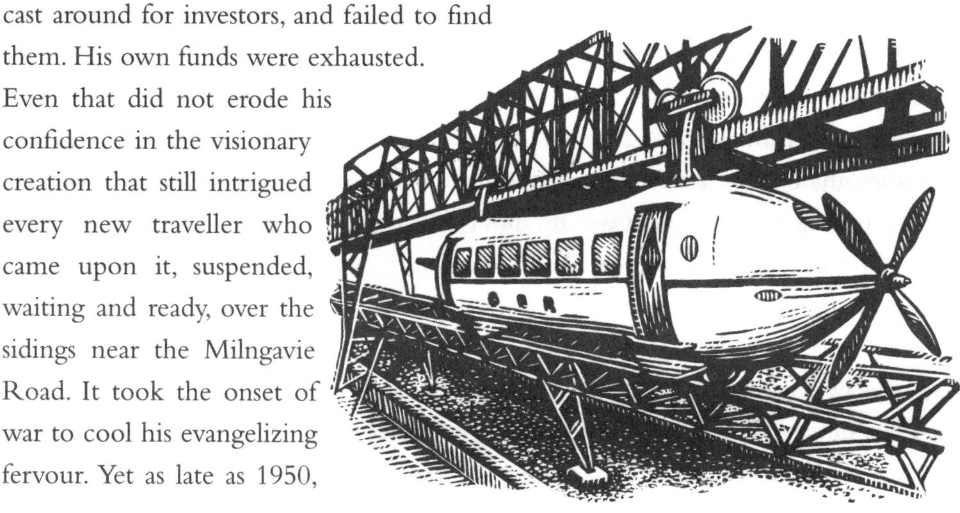

says Black, Bennie was proposing a railplane link between Baghdad and Damascus, and investigating possible openings at Amsterdam and Los Angeles. But by now, to almost all eyes but his, the operation at Milngavie was doomed. The track was disintegrating, and in 1956 what was left of it was dismantled. Bennie died in a residential home at Epsom the following year. Apart from a plaque commemorating the railplane, unveiled at the Kelvin Timber works in 1990, few today will ever have had cause to hear of him.

It is easy to write off Bennie as one of those obsessive enthusiasts who get an idea into their heads and can't get it out again, persisting in their self-belief long after the rest of the world has written them off. And maybe that's fair in this case. Yet operating where he did, he might well have been aware of others who, having persisted despite all discouragement with equal stubbornness, were in the end proved right. Twenty miles to the west of Milngavie is the pleasant Clydeside town of Helensburgh, where on the waterfront you will find a needle commemorating perhaps its most famous son. Henry Bell came to Helensburgh to run a hotel; his wife was in charge of the public baths. Bell believed it would be possible to power boats by steam. From 1800 he submitted plans to the government showing how this might be done. They were ignored.

Horatio Nelson supported him: 'If you do not accept Mr Bell's scheme,' he warned the House of Lords, 'other nations will, and in the end vex every vein in this empire.' That made no difference. As early as 1800, says a Victorian guidebook, 'he suggested the principle to the British government, but was treated as a visionary'; as if visionaries were mere dreamers instead of – sometimes, at least – people ahead of their age. Like Bennie, Bell was a man whom indifference and rejection could not deter. In 1812 he produced a prototype, the Comet, which he successfully launched on the Clyde. This boat was the first of its kind in regular service and, though rival claims have been made, is persuasively argued to be the precursor of steamboats, great and small, on rivers and oceans around the world.

His Comet was later sent north to run between Oban and Fort William, but was wrecked off Oban in 1820. Its replacement, the Comet II, sank in 1825 off Gourock after a collision: sixty-two of the eighty on board lost their lives. Yet his reputation survives, not least for his persistence when others had doubts. Despite Bell's triumph and

Bennie's folly the two had something crucial in common. The Bennies who innovate only to fail are no less essential to patterns of progress than the Bells who persist and succeed.

MONTGOMERY

MONTGOMERY, mun. bor., par. and co. town of Montgomeryshire, with ry. sta., G.W.R., 6¼ m. S. of Welshpool by rail… pop. 918…

IT DOESN'T TAKE LONG to get the hang of it. You can take most of it in if you stand at the crossroads, dodging the occasional car speeding through at a pace which is quite out of character in slow-moving Montgomery, look up and down the main road, then turn east to the church of St Nicholas or west to the Georgian square. If action, excitement and adventure are what you pine for, keep well clear. If you want a place of quiet natural beauty, augmented by quite a few pleasing man-made adornments, Montgomery is sublime. Henry III built a castle here in 1223 to guard a ford on the Severn against Welsh misconduct. Much of the town looks Georgian, though sometimes Georgian frontages conceal older buildings behind. The whole place is defiantly out of date. Almost all of this scene must essentially have been created by the end of the eighteenth century. The church, as John Betjeman noted, largely escaped the Victorian clamour for improvement: 'unspoiled by progress', it could credibly say of itself, echoing the pub at Jackfield.

It's suffused with the legacy of the Herbert family, who came from Chirbury, a mile or two to the east on the far side of Offa's Dyke. George Herbert, metaphysical poet, rector of Bemerton and briefly MP for Montgomery (though certainly not a man you'd back to win an election now), may have been born in the castle. His parents' tomb is in the south transept. The rood loft looks magnificent. 'In later years', says a guide to the church, 'it has been used as a place to sing from especially at Christmas time.' But access is no longer permitted for reasons of health and safety.

I was there on a summer day. People were sitting out in the sun in front of a pub in the square, exuding contentment. At the top of the square is the old town hall; behind it, a black and white hotel, the Dragon, which looks authentic until you get close to it. Down a side road near the town hall, you will find the museum in what was once a pub called The Bell and later, a bakehouse, a butcher's and slaughterer's, a temperance hotel, and a general stores. It's simple and robustly old-fashioned, and there to tell a local story without gadgets or much interaction. Clocks made in Montgomery, ancient photographs, bills from Davies the butcher and Powell the grocer, a Band of Hope hymnal, a cobbler's price list, a cricket team picture; also a poem written by William Mitchell after the theft of some pigwash:

> Oh, Montgomery, oh Montgomery,
> You have some awful prigs.
> Where would you find another place
> Where they would rob the pigs?

An odd definition of prig, perhaps, but it gave him his rhyme. Some of the most fascinating material comes from an old workhouse in Forden. They did their best, says the caption about those who superintended it (just in case visitors start to suspect that the place was run by sadists; which on some of the evidence here, they very well might). There's a terrible but perhaps not uncharacteristic workhouse tale of Elizabeth Austen being examined as to who had fathered her child and saying it was Mr Henshaw the steward, and Henshaw soon after being found dead.

And then, across Arthur Street, another of the ingredients which makes Montgomery so gloriously unhomogenized and such an exceptional treat: Bunner's, the ironmonger's shop, taking its name from the family that acquired it in 1891 and is still behind the counter today. The ground floor is a warren of rooms crammed with every kind of device you ever saw in an ironmonger's, and others you could not have imagined. Downstairs there are even more, with cluttered arrays of netting fasteners and 1½ inch ovals and springheads, of which you may buy just a handful, instead of being required, as is customary nowadays, to come out with a bag of fifty even if you need only two. And high above the town there's King Henry's castle, or what little was left after the Parliamentarians had finished with it. It is quite a serious slog up the hill to get there, but the view from the summit is a more than adequate recompense.

On my bus out of Montgomery I fell into conversation with a woman who said she lived there. 'You're lucky,' I said. 'Do you know,' she said, 'I grew up in this town, and by the time I was fourteen my one great aim in life was to get right out of the place and never come back.' But twenty years on, she did come back, and thought it wasn't so bad. Next time round she quite liked it. The time after that she was looking in house agents' windows. Perhaps you have to grow older to be ready for Montgomery, but once you've reached that stage in life which others think of as crinkly, but you might by then call mellow, you may find that there are very few places you'd rather be. I certainly did.

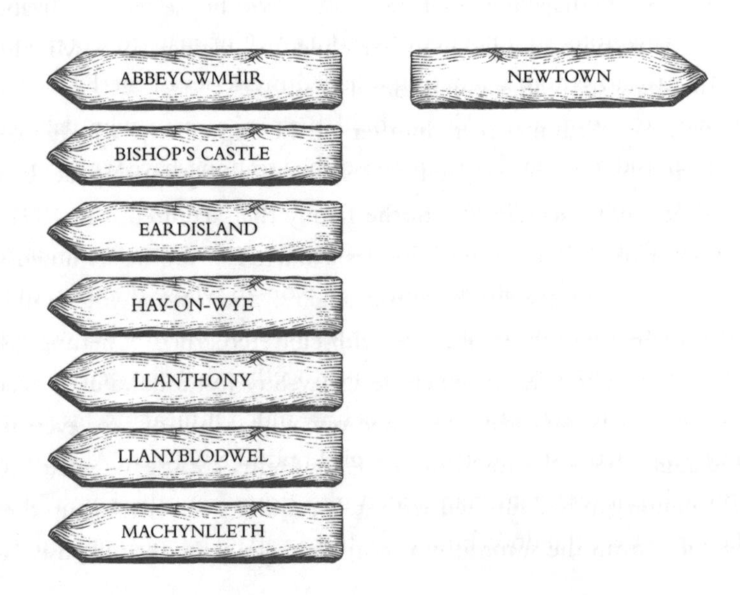

MORTLAKE

MORTLAKE, par. in mun. bor. of Barnes, and large vil., with ry. sta., S.R. N. Surrey, on r. Thames, 1½m. NE. of Richmond… The University boat-race finishes here.

A LARGE VILLAGE IN Bartholomew's estimation; a drab London suburb, overshadowed by more glamorous and pricier Richmond and Kew, in mine, Mortlake, none the less, has its mysteries, of which the most intriguing can be found at the back of a graveyard between the main road and the railway. An Anglican church dedicated to St Mary the Virgin is prominent on Mortlake High Street, but it's the Catholic church of St Mary Magdalen, tucked away behind it, that accommodates the mystery, which is this: what on earth is a demonstratively Islamic tomb doing in this Catholic churchyard? And even when you've discovered that the tomb is the last resting place of Sir Richard Burton – adventurer, traveller, master of disguise and, it sometimes seemed to his contemporaries, of every language spoken by man, penetrator of places hitherto considered too dangerous or impenetrable for any Christian to enter, poet, writer, translator, and a man to whom many of the fabled mysteries of the East were open – a second, subsidiary question arises. Why would Burton, as man who dabbled in many religions but as far as the world was aware subscribed to none, have wished his last resting place to be in a Catholic churchyard?

The key to all this is Burton's wife, Isabel – until she married, an Arundell of Wardour, born into a leading Catholic family – a woman whose devotion to Burton, for all his legendary angers and his inconstancy, was exceeded only by her devotion to God and her Church. They chose the site at Mortlake together: Isabel eagerly, Burton perhaps resigned to this last location because he knew how much it meant to his wife. It was she who designed perhaps the strangest sight in all London SW14: an Arab tent, complete with ropes though not tent pegs, transcribed into stone from the Forest of Dean, with Christ on the Cross over the door, but below this a parade of crescents and pointed stars

– once gilded, but the weather has done for that – as if to assert a mixed allegiance. The Catholic authorities agreed to the crescents, but insisted on having them placed below the Cross, for fear that otherwise Islam might have seemed superior. There's a stone open book with dedications to Sir Richard and Lady Burton and a poem, also cut into stone, by Justin Huntly McCarthy that begins: 'Farewell, dear friend, dead hero! The great life/ Is ended, the great perils, the great joys…' and proceeds in much the same vein to a further, final 'farewell'. You cannot pass through the door of the tent to reach Richard and Isabel, but you can go round to the back of the edifice, where by climbing a rusty ladder you may peer through a window and discern in the gloom the couple's twin tombs, with various symbolic emblems of the East scattered about them.

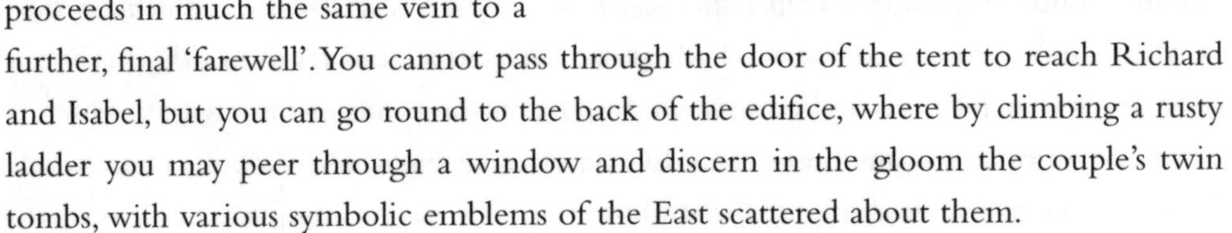

Though he made this self-denying concession to Isabel, Burton was still, through his final days of ill-health in Trieste, where he held the undemanding post of British consul, and even on the morning of the day that he died – 20 October 1890 – unconverted. The battle (see Ventnor) that would later take place over the laying to rest of Burton's friend Swinburne, whom his family claimed for the Church while his friends proclaimed his lasting irreligion, had a kind of pre-echo here. Isabel firmly assured the undertaker that Sir Richard was a Catholic. That had certainly never been true before. There may have been a death-bed conversion: more likely, though, it was posthumous.

Burton's early biographer Thomas Wright, whose book was published in 1906, dismisses Isabel's testimony. He sees it as part of the widow's attempt, filled out in her own life of Burton (1893), to redesign him, as it were, in her own image. Wright's account of the final moments make Burton's reception into the Catholic Church sound completely spurious. Burton's breathing, he says,

> became laboured, and after a brief struggle for air he cried, 'I am dying, I am dead.' Lady Burton held him in her arms, but he got heavier, and presently became insensible. Dr Baker applied an electric battery to the heart, and Lady Burton kneeling at the bedside, and holding her husband's hand, prayed her 'heart out to God to keep his soul there (though he might be dead in appearance) till the priest arrived.' But it was in vain. The priest, a Slavonian, named Pietro Martelani, came in about half-past six. We may regret what followed, but no one would judge harshly the actions of an agonised woman. Pity for human suffering must drown all other feelings. The priest looked at the dead but warm body and asked whether there was still any life. That the heart and pulse had ceased to beat, Lady Burton herself afterwards admitted to her relations, but deceiving herself with the belief that life still continued in the brain, she cried: 'He is alive, but I beseech you, lose not a moment, for the soul is passing away.'
>
> 'If,' said the Priest, 'he is a Protestant, he cannot receive the Holy Sacrament in this way.'
>
> Lady Burton having declared that her husband 'had abjured the heresy and belonged to the Catholic Church,' the priest at once administered 'the last comforts'.
>
> It was certainly a kind of consolation to the poor lady to feel that her husband had not departed unhouselled; but it is equally evident that her mind had given way…

Wright says that later, 'when her mind had regained its equilibrium', she gave an account of these events to one of Burton's family. 'To a Protestant, Dick's reception into the Holy Church must seem meaningless and void. He was dead before extreme unction was administered; and my sole idea was to satisfy myself that he and I would be buried according to the Catholic rites and lie together above ground in the Catholic cemetery. He was not strictly received, for he was dead, and the formula Si es capax, &c., saved the priest's face and satisfied the church.' His family were fervent Protestants, and their anger was unassuaged. In 1896, the year of Isabel's death, his niece, Georgiana M. Stisted, published a life of Burton which did not spare his widow. 'The terrible shock of so fatal a termination to what seemed an attack of little consequence', she wrote, on the basis of evidence supplied by Burton's doctor, who was there,

> would have daunted most Romanists desirous of effecting a death-bed conversion. It did not daunt Isabel. No sooner did she perceive that her husband's life was in danger, than she sent messengers in every direction for a priest. Mercifully, even the first to arrive, a man of peasant extraction, who had just been appointed to the parish, came too late to molest one then far beyond the reach of human folly and superstition. But Isabel had been too well trained by the Society of Jesus not see that a chance yet remained of glorifying her Church – a heaven-sent chance which was not to be lost. Her husband's body was not yet cold, and who could tell for certain whether some spark of life yet lingered in that inanimate form? The doctor declared that no doubt existed regarding the decease, but doctors are often mistaken. So, hardly had the priest crossed the threshold than she flung herself at his feet, and implored him to administer Extreme Unction. The father, who seems to have belonged to the ordinary type of country-bred ecclesiastic so common abroad, and who probably in the whole course of his life had never before availed himself of so startling a method of enrolling a new convert, demurred. There had been no profession of faith, he urged, there could be none now; for – and he hardly liked to pronounce the cruel words – Burton was dead. But Isabel would listen to no arguments, would take no refusal; she remained weeping and wailing on the floor, until at last, to terminate a disagreeable scene, which most likely would have ended in hysterics, he consented to perform the rite. Rome took

> formal possession of Richard Burton's corpse, and pretended, moreover, with insufferable insolence, to take under her protection his soul... After the necessary interval had elapsed, Burton's funeral took place in the largest church in Trieste, and was made the excuse for an ecclesiastical triumph of a faith he had always loathed.

But Isabel had offended, even outraged, far more than Burton's Protestant kinsfolk. As soon as her husband died she burned whole books of his writings: journals, diaries, and the text on which he was working of a version of the *Arabian Nights* to be called *The Scented Garden*. Throughout his life Burton had been fascinated by sexual practices, especially in the communities to which he came on his travels. Already he had published a version of the *Arabian Nights* translated from a French text, which he called *The Perfumed Garden*; but for this book he had gone back to the original, and included material which to every good Catholic then, and indeed to many today, was shameless pornography. Knowing that they risked prosecution under the Obscene Publications Act of 1851, he and his collaborator Forster Fitzgerald Arbuthnot (with whom he produced the best-known English version of the *Kama Sutra*) had set up an organization called the Kama Shastra Society, calculating that if such works were circulated only to subscribers, they would be safe.

More than 1,500 enthusiasts had subscribed to *The Scented Garden* and soon they began to ask what had become of the work they had paid for. Isabel claimed to her friends that her husband had appeared to her in a vision, telling her the book should be destroyed. That was not, however, the explanation she gave in defending her conduct in a letter to the *Morning Post* in June 1891. She had feared, she explained, that of the 1,500 men who had subscribed, no more than fifteen would read it in the scholarly spirit which Burton intended, while the other 1,485 would read it 'for filth's sake'. In the same cause there was tossed on to the bonfire Burton's translation of Catullus. But perhaps the saddest casualty of them all was the great man's journals, the very breadth of whose revelations – according to yet another biographer of the day, they were 'full of the secret thoughts and apologia of this rare genius' – had ensured their destruction.

Isabel had been diagnosed with cancer eight years before Burton died; even so, she lived on for six years without him. They lie side by side in their mausoleum at an address that could hardly be more removed from the Meccas and Medinas which his writings opened up to the world. Mortlake: a name, I used to think as a child, of fearful foreboding, a place inextricably linked with death. But Eilert Ekwall, supreme authority on these matters, says there is no such connection, and the name means either a stream full of young salmon, or something to do with someone called Morta.

MORWENSTOW

MORWENSTOW, coast par. and vil., Cornwall, 6m. N. of Bude...

THERE'S A BUS OUT of Bude, on occasions, which will take you the six miles to Morwenstow, though by roads so erratic and devious, roads where the very notion that a bus should attempt to penetrate them might once have been laughed at in taverns, that you'll doubt at times if you're ever going to get there. Eventually we stopped at an open plain before an inviting pub: the Bush Inn ('13th century free house'). 'Is this Morwenstow?' I asked the driver in some disbelief, and he insisted it was; though even that needs to be qualified, since Morwenstow is essentially an agglomeration of small settlements clustered together close to the thrillingly jagged North Cornwall coast, of which this spot by the pub is just one, properly known as Crosstown.

You need to look beyond, down a lane that approaches the sea, for the essence of Morwenstow, which is the church: and definitively, the church of the legendary Reverend Robert Stephen Hawker, still wonderingly remembered both for the facts of his life and for the encrustations of fiction which accumulated about it, many of them the confections of another quite extraordinary West Country clergyman, the Reverend Sabine Baring-Gould. I don't think they ever met, but they certainly corresponded, sometimes cordially, at other times with some acrimony. There was, for instance, a heated dispute between them about the saints Morwenna and Modwenna, which Hawker shut down by saying that the sources of *his* information were supernatural. In a sense, though, Baring-Gould had the last word – by writing the life of Hawker, which he published in 1876, thus denying Hawker, who had died the previous year, any right of reply; even, as it transpired, a supernatural one.

Yet the truth of his life, as rescued from Baring-Gould's embroideries by Piers

Brendon in *Hawker of Morwenstow: portrait of a Victorian eccentric* (1975) is strange enough: a solitary, difficult, superstitious, depressive, troublesome, frequently turbulent priest-cum-plotter-cum-mystic, as odd as the forms of dress he affected; hats like nobody else's, blue jersey, knee-high seaboots, rarely a clerical collar, and an absolute boycott of black, which he shunned even for funeral services. He seems to have had an unquenchable taste for extremes. He married, first, at nineteen, a woman of forty-one (Baring-Gould says she was his godmother and that his motive was to raise enough money to get him to Oxford: Brendon says that both these statements are wrong) and then, at sixty-one, a second wife who was twenty.

He was famous in youth for his practical jokes, and remained, to the end, a prankster: it was probably as a joke – though you can never be sure with Hawker – that he once excommunicated his cat. His likes and dislikes were celebrated: he could not abide a beard, he distrusted false teeth, he claimed to hate everything American; he despised Plymouth Brethren ('as a general principle no Plymouth person can speak a true word'); he deplored the prospect of electoral reform, which meant extending the franchise, as he believed, to those who would only misuse it; he had all his writing paper tailored to his requirements by De la Rue, the high-class stationers, so that if a letter arrived from Hawker the recipient would know at once who it was from; he spent a fortune on tea and was addicted to cream and tobacco.

But his fame rested most of all on his ministry, on the poetry, and to some extent on his fondness for opium. The poetry had begun early in life. While still at school he published a work called *Tendrils*, under the pseudonym Reuben. At Oxford in 1827 he carried off the hotly competed-for Newdigate Prize with a poem about Pompeii. His most famous work of all was a patriotic Cornish ballad with the refrain: 'And shall Trelawny die? (Here's twenty thousand Cornish men shall know the reason why)', a work of such rollicking fervour that it was usually attributed to either Anon., or Trad.; and indeed the famous refrain was probably borrowed. What is usually now regarded as his greatest production was *The Quest of the Sangraal*, published in 1864 and probably opium-driven, which Longfellow thought was better than Tennyson's treatment of the same Holy Grail theme. Even more notably, so did Tennyson.

As a priest, Brendon shows, Hawker famously cared for his flock, many of whom lived in cruel poverty, even though he constantly quarrelled with them, for their wickednesses, their drunkenness, their cruelty to animals, their fornication (bizarrely, he blamed their addiction to extra-marital sex on John Wesley, whom he called 'the father of English fornication'). He was the first vicar for a hundred years to live in the parish – a previous appointee had declared the place 'unfit for my residence' and left it in the hands of a curate. Hawker signalled his long-term commitment to Morwenstow by pulling down the wreck that the vicarage had become and building a new one, grander than it needed to be, designing a roof that incorporated echoes of the towers of the churches that he knew best. He remodelled the church, eliminating the gallery and the old box pews with their places reserved for the privileged: Baring-Gould asserts, though he cannot be trusted, that when one farmer objected to losing his pew, Hawker fetched an axe and smashed it to pieces.

And though, unlike Baring-Gould, he was nowhere near rich enough to qualify as a squarson (the familiar Victorian combination of parson and squire), he battled for his people in practical terms as well as spiritual. It was he who raised the money to build a bridge at a spot which had often been flooded: he met most of the cost himself, though the king was persuaded to contribute £20. He provided them with a school, and a house for the schoolmaster. And tucked away in this isolated, often desolate, still inaccessible place (the railway did not reach Bude until 1898, thirteen years after Hawker's death), in the company – for most of the time – of people with whom he could rarely feel comfortable, he wrote, and smoked as he wrote: carols for Christmas, and a form of service, soon copied elsewhere, designed to rescue the celebrations at harvest-end from their pagan associations; and verses for stricken families to engrave on Morwenstow tombstones. This one, perhaps:

> To the memory of Eliza, daughter of William and Mary Hoar of
> Woodford in this parish who departed this life April 22nd 1860
> aged 14 years.
>
> Afflictions sore long time I bore
> All medicine was in vain
> For God did please by death to seize,

> And ease me of my pain.
> Grieve not my friends that I am gone
> Where oft I wish'd to be:
> My griefs are gone, my joys increased,
> So do not weep for me.

There was much to weep for in Morwenstow: mean, pinched lives, gruelling illnesses, early deaths – and the constant toll of the sea. Hawker lived in fear of that urgent knock on the door which would summon him to some shipwreck on the perilous coast. He hated the funeral services such deaths required him to take and would have escaped them had he known how. There used to be in the graveyard the figurehead of one of the ships that was wrecked here, the *Caledonia*. But the weather over the years had eroded and effaced it, and when I was there in the spring of 2007 it had been removed for refurbishment, to be re-erected, for its greater safety, within the church, with a replica placed in the churchyard.

The reputation of Parson Hawker spread. People used to come to Morwenstow in the hope of catching sight of this strange figure in his curious garb. He deplored their invasions but, as Piers Brendon says, he played up to them. It's the legend of Hawker which draws people to Morwenstow now, as it drew me. There are signatures in the visitors' book in the church from 'pilgrims', as it likes to call them, from Canada, Argentina, New Zealand, Mexico, South Carolina. Hawker died in 1875 in Plymouth, where he had gone for treatment, old, complaining and fearful, and dismayed by what he saw as the Anglican drift from old practices and old certainties. A few hours before his death he was received into the Catholic Church. Purple was worn at his funeral because of his hatred of black. He was buried in Plymouth rather than in Morwenstow, the community to which, sometimes joyfully and sometimes in anguish, he had given his life.

You can walk out today on the cliff path high above the Atlantic, exhilarating in sunshine but still forbidding and bleak when the weather turns rough, and discover the simple hut where he wrote and brooded and got his fix from the opium. You can sit on the bench where he sat and gaze out at the same sight he saw, unchanged, over the vertiginous cliff and out to the limitless sea. The next land west of here, as Hawker knew, in this place of an isolation he said that he hated but which he had sought, is Labrador.

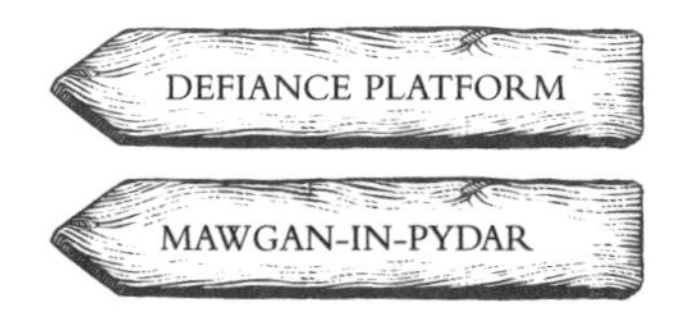

A B C D

E F G H

I J K L

M **N** O P

Q R S T

U V W XYZ

NEATH

NEATH, mun. bor., mkt.-town, par. and r. port, with ry. stas... Glamorgan, on r. Neath or Nedd... near the town are the ruins of a castle burnt in 1231. NEATH ABBEY, ry. sta. G.W.R., Glamorgan, at ruins of Neath Abbey (founded 1130), ½m. S. of Neath.

IN A BROAD AND once entirely beautiful Glamorganshire valley of river, mountain and forest there has grown up over the centuries the dogged and rather dull industrial town of Neath, which, through no fault of its own, scarcely does justice to its well-favoured location. On a road that runs west out of the town, near a rather grand Tesco, and closer still to a Cantonese takeaway and a fish shop and Monastery Motors, a minor road will take you to the spot which Cistercian monks in the twelfth century specifically chose because it was 'far from the concourse of men'. As you can see from the ruins, the abbey was a majestic affair, and later its site was shared with a handsome house, whose ruins also survive.

There used to be in these abbey precincts a copper smelting works and a casting workshop, but these have been cleared away, and the ruins stand there now unattended and largely unexplained. The abbey in its great days was surrounded by granges, or farms, worked by the monks, which later passed into private hands.

One of these, until then known as Cwrt Etberne, was acquired by a prominent local figure called Sir John Herbert, who changed the name to Cwrt Herbert and in the first decade of the seventeenth century built a fine house for himself and his family. Here, in 1794, a remarkable soldier, adventurer, diplomat, dandy, gambler and fighter of duels called Rees Howell Gronow was born, who in 1830 inherited both his father's wealth and his Neath Abbey estate. The house has gone, replaced in the 1960s by a private housing estate where the street names reflect the abbey connections: Benedict Close, Friars Close, Monk's Close, Nidum Close (Nidum being the Roman version of Neath). There is nothing that I could find to commemorate Captain Gronow.

And that is scarcely surprising, since the environs of Neath were hardly the place he'd have wanted to settle in. Where the Cistercians had yearned to escape the concourse of men, Gronow was always eager to throw himself head-first into it. His memoirs, which emerged spasmodically between 1861 and 1866, are as recklessly unstructured as the rest of his life, hurtling from battlefield to gaming table to gossipy triviality and back again, and written from memory, not from notes made at the time.

He fought, when not long out of Eton, in the Peninsular War and then at Waterloo, of which battle he gives vivid, authentic and blood-stained accounts, with friends and comrades dying around him. Later, as much to dodge his creditors (at one point before he inherited he had been imprisoned for debt) as for any positive reason, he lived in Paris, which gave him a ringside view of the 1848 uprising which forced out King Louis Philippe and the 1851 coup in which Louis-Napoleon Bonaparte seized unconditional power. Both here and on his return to London, he constantly encountered the rich and famous and gives sharply observed accounts of them.

Of Balzac, he wrote: 'the great enchanter was one of the oiliest and commonest looking mortals I ever beheld... the only striking feature in that Friar Tuck countenance was his eye; dark, flashing, wicked, full of sarcasm and unholy fire'. While Dumas, he related, on being told that his actress wife, from whom he was estranged, was living in poverty, he immediately promised to double her annuity: but since he never paid that annuity, it amounted, Gronow says, to twice nothing. Of the poet Samuel Rogers, whom he regarded with a kind of horrified fascination, he says: 'His intonations were very much those one fancies a ghost would use if forced by some magic spell to give utterance to sounds. The mild venom of every word was a remarkable trait in his conversation. One might have compared the old poet to one of those velvety caterpillars that crawl gently and quietly over the skin, but leave an irritating blister behind.' My favourite of all Gronow's tales is about Lord Westmorland, who, representing his country at the court of Louis XVIII, and required by diplomatic protocol to speak his hosts' language, attempts to say that he wished to do something but couldn't: 'Je voudrais, si je coudrais, mais je ne cannais pas.'

He's a snob (though he also complains against snobs) as well as a dandy, obsessed with what he calls 'the upper ten thousand', though eager to chart their failings. His unbounded adulation of Wellington becomes cloying; what he says about Louis-Napoleon is unsettlingly sycophantic. But he's too sharp and honest an observer to pretend that all is right with the rule of the privileged. Though he condemns the turbulence and bloodshed of revolutionary Paris, he understands what drives its participants to do what they've done: this is a desperate and impoverished population, living in misery and squalor, who 'wildly expected to lessen their sufferings and improve their conditions by acts of violence'. 'No one', he concludes, 'had attempted to ameliorate their condition; it was not dreamt that, by the judicious expenditure of money, these people might be made good citizens, and enabled to throw off the yoke of crime and misery.'

This serves as a reminder that, despite his privileged background and the excesses of his behaviour, Gronow's politics were Liberal rather than Tory. In the first General Election after the Reform Act, he won Stafford, a town which also at one stage elected Richard Brinsley Sheridan (of whose insouciant conduct as Member for Stafford, and his genius for charming his way out of sticky situations, he gives a hilarious account). With characteristic candour he explains how he won the seat: having earlier lost his chance of a seat at Grimsby by his failure to bribe the electors (this, he explains, was because he'd been banned from doing so by his sponsor, the Earl of Yarborough) he set out at Stafford 'to bribe every man, woman and child in that ancient borough'. He lost the seat three years later, apparently by letting himself be outbribed.

Conspicuous absentees from his memoirs are his wives and children: neglected in life as well as in literature, one might say, for on his death it became painfully clear that he'd signally failed to provide for his second wife and their four children. Neath and Cwrt Herbert don't get much of a mention either, apart from his recollection of escorting the poet Southey on a tour of the district in 1801. I have two versions of his memoirs: one, found in a second-hand bookshop in Tunbridge Wells, lightly edited by John Raymond, who retains the inconsequential sequences of the original; the other compiled by Christopher Summerville for Ravenhall Books, which is generous with explanatory notes and tidily rearranges the book by themes – though that mildly reduces the pleasant sense which you get in the Raymond edition of sitting with Gronow, perhaps in the window of one of his clubs, as the histories and anecdotes tumble torrentially out of him.

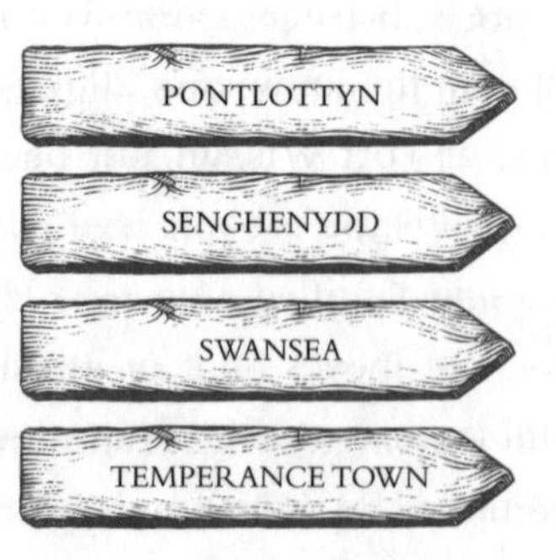

NEPTUNE'S STAIRCASE

NEPTUNE'S STAIRCASE, a series of 8 locks on the Caledonian Canal, between Banavie and Corpach, Inverness-shire.

THE CALEDONIAN CANAL IS in essence a chain of natural lochs linked by the work of man. The lochs account for some 38 miles of its progress from the Moray Firth to Loch Linnhe; the rest we owe to the great Thomas Telford. Built between 1810 and 1822, it was, quite exceptionally for those days, funded entirely by the state: mercifully for everybody concerned, no PFIs were involved. Yet those who believe that nothing that fails to attract private money is really worth doing might be heartened by the story of the canal, in that by the time it was finished it was already seen as something of a disaster. The technology of shipbuilding had evolved so much in the years of its construction that by the time it was finished it proved too shallow for some of the boats that would have wanted to use it. Indeed, in the 1840s there were those who favoured closing it down. In terms of engineering achievement, though, this was an epic enterprise, not least at Corpach at the westward end, where its course had to be cut through rock. And just short of Corpach, there's a chain of locks which, for the time it was built, was also remarkable – namely the sequence at Banavie near Fort William known as Neptune's staircase.

You can get to Banavie on the West Highland railway. The train I caught started at Glasgow, though in the summer of 2007 Scotrail was still running a sleeper service from Euston arriving at Fort William just before 10 the next morning. It's useful on the journey to take with you a book now published as *Victorian Travel on the West Highland Line*, though originally titled *Mountain, Moor and Loch*. Although it describes the line as it was in 1894, and spends a lot of its time musing on sights to be seen south of the border, it is still an informative companion as you rattle north. The west of Scotland, it says, is 'torn to tatters' by lochs, some of them mainland sheets of water, some far-reaching arms of the Atlantic. From Helensburgh, where I joined the train, the panorama of landscape that passes before the carriage window is, says this guide, changing almost every minute, into more and more bewitching visions of infinite variety. From Helensburgh to Ardlui, the route is dominated by lochs; beyond Ardlui, by a bewildering maze of stupendous crags; onwards from there, one comes to the great moor of Rannoch, which has no parallel in Britain – 'a morass, yet one of the most picturesque parts of the route, a place of infinite solitude, a spectacle never to be erased from the memory of the dweller in big cities'; while thereafter the line combines all the kinds of landscape for which the journey has now prepared you.

The book is punctuated by stories, many of them as you'd expect in Scotland quite bloody, about the places you see along the line and quite a few that you don't – including, for instance, an account of the Appin murder about which I learned at Port Appin. Corrour, perhaps the strangest place of them all, has more allure now than the book prepares one for. Corrour Lodge, says the book, is said to dispute with the Cat and Fiddle pub near Buxton the claim to be the highest position of any habitation in the United Kingdom. What is the point of Corrour? There's a station, but nothing that I could see for a railway to serve: not even a made-up road. The only point of having the station seemed to be to serve the station. Yet quite a few people got on or off there. The secret of its attraction now, I later discovered, is that it features in a scene in the 1996 film *Trainspotting*: it's to Corrour that Renton, Spud, Sickboy and Tommy go out for their day in the mountains.

Rannoch Moor ends at Luibruaridh (trying saying 'Lebruary') where there are views of Ben Nevis. Almost three hours out of Helensburgh, almost three and three quarters out of Glasgow, and twelve and a half for those on the sleeper, the train runs westward into Fort William.

After all that rugged empty Highland scenery it's a shock suddenly to see a wall with a sign that says 'Argos'.

From here the train journeys gently on to Mallaig. A traveller who often uses it told me this was the most beautiful stretch of the journey, but pilgrims who've come for Telford's masterpiece are denied that pleasure. The train stops at Banavie, and as soon as you leave the station you see the chain of locks nicely stacked up before you, carrying the shimmering water up the hill towards Inverness. This isn't by any means the greatest sequence of locks anywhere on a British canal. Tardebigge in Worcestershire, so some refugees from the English Midlands running a café just down the road from Banavie proudly assured me, is the top of them all, with thirty-six locks in just over two miles. The Caen Hill flight series west of Devizes has twenty-nine, sixteen of them in a straight line, taking boats up 237 ft in two and a half miles. The Giant's Staircase on the Chesterfield canal has twenty-two locks in a single mile. But Telford's sequence is earlier than any of these, and none, surely, can match the all-encompassing majesty of its setting. To the west, the waters of Loch Linnhe stretch away towards the sea; and beside you is Ben Nevis, still capped by snow on this warm summer morning.

Three more hours on the gently sojourning train took me back to Helensburgh. 'To see a sunset on Rannoch Moor', my Victorian guidebook told me, 'is as essential as to see Loch Lomond by moonlight.' That can't be done by rail in mid June, when it gets dark so late, especially in Scotland; but with a little judicious balancing of tables of sunrise and sunset with the Scotrail timetable, it might not be beyond practicality. Some day, perhaps, I'll try.

NEW BRIGHTON

NEW BRIGHTON, ward of Wallasey co. bor. ... at NE. corner of the Wirral peninsula, 4m. N. of Birkenhead... New Brighton is a much frequented watering-place, with excellent bathing.

HALF PAST TEN ON a flawless morning in mid July, and the sea front of Bartholomew's 'much frequented watering-place' was deserted. Few were strolling; no one was bathing, excellently or otherwise. Even some of the wind turbines scattered about the water were conformingly flaccid. It tells you something significant about what has become of New Brighton that it used to be known as the Blackpool of Liverpool. Why should that great city, whose glamorous skyline is so close at hand across the water, have needed a substitute Blackpool when the real one was attainable only 50 miles or so up the Lancashire coast? Because Liverpudlians could cross here so cheaply and easily over the Mersey by ferry, and even if they'd had cars, which most of them didn't, it was quite a traipse to Blackpool then. Blackpool was for special occasions, perhaps for a holiday week. New Brighton was always there for a jolly day out.

That hadn't been its founder's intention. James Atherton, a Liverpool merchant who in 1830 bought much of the land New Brighton now occupies, until then sand hills and heathland, had envisaged an elegant watering-place, of the kind you so often see in prints of that period with dainty ladies with parasols descending from suitable carriages. That's why it was named after Brighton in distant Sussex, a watering-place fit for prince regents. By the time the diarist Francis Kilvert came in 1872 ambitions had started to shift. He makes it sound enticing. 'The Mersey', he notes, 'was gay and almost crowded with vessels of all sorts moving up and down the river, ships, barques, brigs, brigantines, schooners, cutters, colliers, tugs, steamboats, lighters, "flats", everything from the huge emigrant liner steamship with four masts to the tiny sailing and rowing boat... At New Brighton there are beautiful sands stretching for miles along the coast and the woods wave green down to the salt water's edge. The sands were covered with middle class Liverpool folks and children out for a holiday, digging in the sand, riding on horses and donkeys, having their photographs taken, and enjoying themselves generally.' The catering, though, was not to his taste: 'we tried to get luncheon upon the splendid pier, but they brought us some carrion which they called beef and which we immediately returned to them with thanks, leaving the place in disgust.'

By the end of the century, it must have been clear that Blackpool was more the model than Brighton, especially when you saw New Brighton Tower, built in 1896 when the place had really caught on, just after Blackpool's, which meant they could ascertain Blackpool's dimensions and ensure that theirs was that little bit higher; also, that the ballroom was as grand as any in Blackpool and hopefully grander. Through the 1930s, 40s and 50s, people flocked to a place that is now remembered with deep nostalgic affection. By the end of the 1950s, however, they had got the habit of flocking to somewhere else; perhaps Blackpool, perhaps somewhere further, perhaps even Abroad. New Brighton could never hope to become New Benidorm.

So New Brighton began to fade. Where is everybody, I asked a man at work on the beach, who sighed and said there should be people around by dinnertime. (It's still dinnertime in these parts, rather than lunchtime.) They turn up at the end of the morning, he said, and leave their cars in the car parks, which are free – no money for New Brighton there; and they wander down to the beach, and they eat the food they've brought with them, and drink the drinks they've brought with them, and after a while they depart, leaving behind them their wrappers and cartons and boxes and empty cans and bottles and sometimes their barbecue gear for New Brighton to clean up and dispose of. And the terrible thing, you know (he said) is that you can't really blame them. There are so few attractions left in New Brighton that there's nothing much else they can do.

That slightly defames New Brighton, but if you look at the public maps on the sea front you can see what he meant. There's still the beach and the prom and the lighthouse to see and Fort Perch Rock (to which we'll come in a moment); but interspersed on the map with these surviving gems are the old attractions which have not survived. They include the site of the former tower, which had to be shortened at the end of the First World War because the top was in such a bad state of repair, had become an acknowledged eyesore by the late 1960s and failed to see out that decade because of a ruinous fire; and the site of the former pier, built in the 1860s, removed in the 1980s; also the site where the ferry used to come in, no longer needed once you could use the Mersey tunnel, though that's less romantic as a way to drift home in the evening sunshine after a lazy day on the coast. To these one could add the site of the former open air swimming pool, the vacancies left by the closure of many of its grandest hotels, and the space which was once the home of its football league club: founded in around 1890 as New Brighton Tower FC, entered division two of the League in 1898, became one of the longest-serving inhabitants of the old division three north, but having finished in bottom place in 1951 failed to be re-elected, and drifted into oblivion.

So it's hardly surprising that past glories rather than present ones are celebrated on New Brighton websites. 'This place', says one contributor, 'was absolutely jumping with life 50 years ago' (that's to say, in the middle 1950s). 'The Tower, the Tower Ballroom, the ferries, the pier, the open air swimming pool, loads of night clubs and dance halls... all of them now gone.' The reminiscences of returning natives are the most poignant, but some who've remained in New Brighton sound equally dispossessed. 'I remember the real New Brighton,' writes one. 'To watch the way it has been felled is sad.' 'Remember the Beatles at the Tower Ballroom (just after their return from Hamburg)', another recalls. 'They were really good, but we didn't like to admit it because they came from "over the water".'

Fort Perch Rock, a solid dominant presence at the eastern end of the beach, was built, along with the lighthouse, in 1830, to protect the approaches to Liverpool. It remained in military occupation until after the Second World War (during which it was cutely camouflaged to fool incursive pilots into thinking they were looking down on a tea garden), and was finally sold off to a private owner in 1959. The fortress, I was delighted to see as I wandered the beach in search of distractions, is nowadays home to an art and memorabilia exhibition. 'Meet Elvis and the Beatles' it invited me. But although a big notice displayed on the roof said 'Open', the place was shut, its great implacable doors firmly locked against visitors.

The man on the beach wasn't surprised. 'You're not the first person who's asked me that,' he said when I pointed out this discrepancy. A man used to turn up and sit outside ready to open up if anyone came, but this summer (the notorious summer of 2007) had been so wretched that he seemed to have given up hope. Across the promenade was the Bright Spot, which held out the promise of amusement arcades, ice cream, and doughnuts; but the Bright Spot was still shuttered up. It was good to see the Floral Pavilion was still in business, though not a single attraction was promised on its notice boards; however, the man on the beach said they'd certainly be doing a pantomime.

New Brighton hasn't given up fighting. A few years ago the photographer Martin Parr inflamed the town by publishing a book of pictures of New Brighton life which objectors said made too much of the place's creaky old people and disparaged its working-class holidaymakers. He called it *The Last Resort*. A redevelopment scheme, featuring a new theatre, a multiplex cinema, upmarket flats, cafés and bars, and a supermarket which, whatever happens, is not going to be as big as Morrison's initially wanted, has been trying to find a way through the planning system. At the western end of the promenade there's a figure of a gesturing clown welcoming you to New Brighton – put up, the man on the beach complained, at an utterly ludicrous cost. The clown continued to wave as I left, with the same gummy optimism. I bade him a fond goodbye, while muttering under my breath: I'm afraid you've got quite a fight on your hands here, sonny.

NEWTOWN

NEWTOWN AND LLANLLWCHAIARN, urb. dist. and par.,
with ry. sta., G.W.R., on r. Severn...
Tre-Newydd is the Welsh name of the town.

A NEW TOWN, THAT is, in the reign of Edward I, who created it. Later it grew rich on wool, and specifically the manufacture of blankets; it was also the birthplace of the radical industrialist and social entrepreneur Robert Owen, whom it amply commemorates. It seems at first sight a staid kind of place, but like many towns of which that is said, it is not as staid as it looks.

It was here in December 2004 that the police moved in and arrested a squadron of Father Christmases who were brawling and fighting around the town at the end of a charity fun run. It was thought that the exercise might have invoked a certain amount of drinking as well as a lot of running. CS gas and batons had to be used. PC Gareth Slaymaker was reported as saying that many of the participants were still wearing their Santa Claus outfits – a strict requirement if those on the run were to get their achievement into the *Guinness Book of Records*. Five men were arrested, and police said a number of other Santas had been interviewed.

Oxford – home of lost causes. Newtown – home of sloshed Clauses.

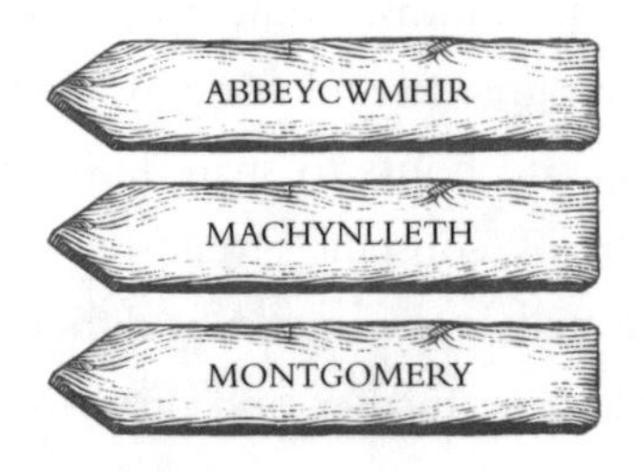

NORWICH

NORWICH, parl. and co. bor., par., city, co. town of Norfolk and co. in itself, with ry. stas.... The cathedral was founded in 1096... Norwich returns 2 members to Parliament...

ACROSS THE RIVER WENSUM from the centre of Norwich, over the Fye bridge, in an area colloquially known as Over-the-Water, you come to a pleasant lattice of streets which make up the parish of St George's, Colgate. Here, one morning in 1777, a master weaver called Paul was passing a house in a street which no longer exists, Green's Lane, when he heard the sound of music. Mr Paul was displeased. The house belonged to his master carpenter, Michael Crotch, who had failed to come in for work, pleading illness. Infuriated by this apparent deceit, he entered the house and marched into the room, expecting to find the defaulter at the keyboard. What he saw amazed him. An older boy was pumping the organ while his younger brother, a boy of no more than two, was producing the music. Their father, who had built the organ, was, as he'd claimed, ill in bed.

For a tiny child to be playing with such proficiency seemed to Mr Paul almost beyond belief. He was so astonished that he went out into the street and summoned neighbours, who gathered around as the boy continued to play. Before long, quite a crowd had accumulated, too many to cram into the Crotches' house. Some had to be turned away and asked to come back later. Next day, at least a hundred people appeared and stayed to marvel. The following day – as the musicologist Charles Burney, who went to observe the boy at the age of two years, eight months, would record in a paper read to the Royal Society – the numbers were even greater, and Mr and Mrs Crotch were forced to limit his exhibitions to certain days and hours to spare him fatigue, and to 'exempt themselves from the inconvenience of constant attention of the curious multitude'. The child, though prodigiously gifted, was sometimes difficult. He would break away from the keyboard, refusing to play any further, and draw in chalk on the

floor, sketching horses, churches, ships and animals, 'in his rude and wild manner' with his left hand.

So began the strange career of William Crotch, the Norwich child prodigy, inevitably tagged, like Thomas Linley who drowned at Grimsthorpe, 'the English Mozart'. As news of the prodigy travelled beyond Norwich, more expert assessors arrived, and they were astonished too. Around two or three, it appeared, the child had been able to pick out the National Anthem, and then to add to the tune his own improvised harmonies. If you played some other tune to him, he could play it back from memory. Challenged to transpose the music into a different key, he did so, Burney reported, 'with great archness'.

The implications, especially the financial implications, of these inundations of visitors were not lost on William's mother, who decided to put him on show, advertising him as Master Crotch, the self-taught musical child, aged three. At three and a half he was taken to London where he was introduced to J. C. Bach, the Duke of Clarence (later William IV), the Prince Regent, and eventually to George III himself. In 1780 and 1781 he was sent to parade his talents in Birmingham, Manchester, York, Newcastle, Edinburgh, Glasgow and Aberdeen. There were signs, which his mother seems to have ignored, that all was not well with the boy: he was sometimes perverse and truculent. But the crowds continued to come.

He was tutored at Cambridge, not yet as a university student, but by university teachers. On Sundays he played the organ at several churches, sometimes performing six times a day. His other talents were blossoming too, especially his painting, but a life in music remained his clear destination. At eleven he published an oratorio setting: *The Captivity of Judah* and at fourteen he was appointed organist of Christ Church cathedral at Oxford. At twenty-one he was professor of music at the university, a post he continued to occupy for fifty years. But he wasn't *the* English Mozart, or even *an* English Mozart, and his talents as a composer failed to develop. Later, aware that his early promise had not been fulfilled, he looked back with resentment on the way he had been exploited, on the pains and humiliations of this almost freakshow existence.

He began as an Oxford professor to acquire a reputation as a reactionary, pedantically devoted to the traditional rules, regarding anything written after the age of Bach and Handel as the fruits of a time of decline. Haydn, Mozart, Beethoven: they were all very well, but they showed a sharp falling off since these masters. Sir John Stainer would blame Crotch's crabbed approach to music since Bach and Handel for blighting several composing careers, especially that of Frederick Ouseley, another 'English Mozart' in youth whose talent, like Crotch's own, seemed to dry up. The hymnodist H. J. Gauntlett, who put the music to Mrs Alexander's words in the Christmas hymn 'Once in Royal David's City', was another unsparing critic. Crotch still composed when he could – his oratorio *Palestine* was widely acclaimed, and is still sometimes sung in cathedrals, as are some of the many anthems he wrote for Christ Church cathedral; but teaching had largely taken over his life.

In 1822 he was appointed first principal of the Royal Academy of Music, but this unexpectedly proved to be a disaster. Complaints were made by another student that Crotch had kissed a pretty young woman whose work had pleased him. A resolution was passed by the Academy's ruling authorities: 'the committee having received a report of the manner in which the harmony lessons in the female department were conducted by Dr Crotch which was extremely unsatisfactory, they resolved that his future attendance on the female students should henceforth be dispensed with'. Crotch resigned and left the Academy. He was fifty-six.

Thereafter, it was all downhill. His health was fitful and he repeatedly sprained his ankles. He destroyed many of his papers and letters, though using the rest to compile his memoirs. His judgements on latterday music became still more severe – more crotchety, one might say. Music less than a century old should be wholly excluded from church services, he argued. 'Few productions of the present day', he predicted, 'will ever become fit for divine service.'

In time, Crotch and his wife Martha, both ailing, were taken in by their son, a headmaster at Taunton. It was there that he died, on 29 December 1847, at the dinner table – 'though', as it was reported, 'he remained sitting upright at the table even after he had died'. A stone tablet put up at the church of St Peter and St Paul, Bishop's Hull, close to Taunton, gave a glowing account of his last years, describing how he exhibited, 'in a life of remarkable serenity and happiness, though not without its periods of natural sorrow, the fruits of the Spirit: Love, Joy and Peace'. If he had indeed achieved this happiness and serenity, then he must at last have transcended the blighting of his youth and the sad fading of his precocious talent.

In Crotch's case, the fate of the infant genius had been foreseen. 'Into what the present prodigy may mature is not easy to predict' Charles Burney, who had observed him so closely and carefully in the little house over the water at Norwich, had warned in his report to the Royal Society: 'Premature powers in music have as often surprised by becoming stationary as by advancing rapidly to the summit of excellence.' Even Thomas Linley, had he lived, might have failed to fulfil his promise. Society glories in, and celebrates, these early, inexplicable flowerings – in music, in painting, in books, and especially perhaps in sport. It should also watch them with apprehension, even perhaps with fear.

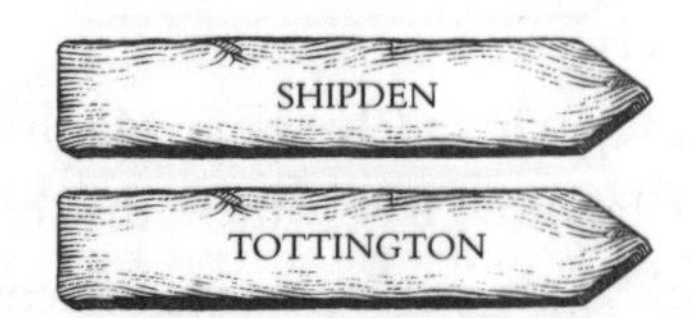

NOWHERESVILLE

AN UNSPECIFIED PART OF northern Scotland, not listed by Bartholomew, but mentioned in a BBC weather forecast in February 2007. Met Office man Tomasz Schafernaker predicted bad weather for a mountainous area of northern Scotland, but indicated that few would get wet since very few people lived there, and described it as 'Nowheresville'. After complaints to the Corporation from Nowheresville (where perhaps more people lived than he thought) and elsewhere, Schafernaker was forced to apologize.

Also by extension: *Schafernakersville*, a doghouse.

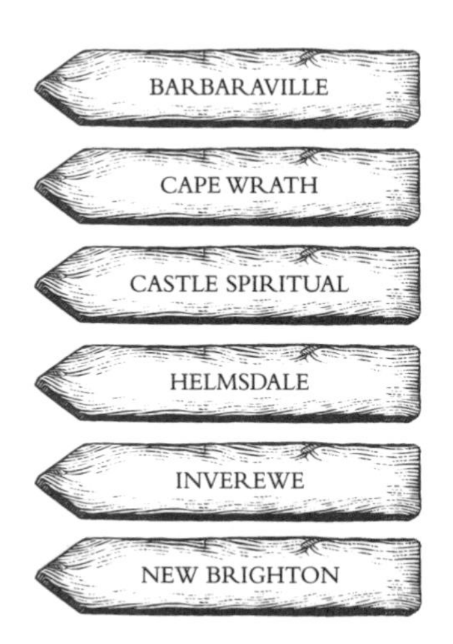

A B C D

E F G H

I J K L

M N **O** P

Q R S T

U V W X Y Z

ORFORD

ORFORD, fishing vil. and par., E. Suffolk, on r. Ore, 5m. SW. of Aldeburgh… there is a coastguard station. ORFORD NESS, promontory, on coast of Suffolk, at N. extremity of Hollesley Bay, 2½m. SE. of Orford. On the Ness is a lighthouse 99 ft. high with a five-seconds white flashing light seen 15m.; in the same tower is a fixed light (red and green sectors) visible 12m.

As BARTHOLOMEW'S DESIGNATION MAY imply, Orford is less famous than Aldeburgh – and that was a judgement arrived at long before Aldeburgh was famous for Benjamin Britten. And it's not, thank goodness, on absolutely everyone's route map, like Southwold. The story of this fishing vil. and par. at the end of the B1084 out of Woodbridge is simply told: the church, the castle, the square, the lighthouse, the harbour; and beyond the harbour, Orford Ness, the curse and the blessing of Orford.

The church (St Bartholomew's) is a stately affair which used to be even statelier: one end of it is now a mere roofless remnant of the church as originally built. You can see from the size of it now, let alone the size of it then, that Orford was a place of importance: a port of real consequence in the reign of the first Elizabeth. It has a claim to Benjamin Britten too. Several of his works – *Noye's Fludde*, the three *Church Parables*: *Curlew River*, *The Burning Fiery Furnace*, *The Prodigal Son*, were first performed here. On the walls of that part of the church which survives there are paintings by Emmeline Rope (1856–1940) – the Ropes were a dominant family in this part of Suffolk – and very good they are too. Another talented painter who came here was Turner.

The castle was built for Henry II. What survives is the keep, by common consent one of the finest in England. Sir Arthur Churchman, the local MP, having made a lot of money out of cigarettes, bought it in 1928 and presented it to the nation. The Orford Town Trust repaired it and opened it to the public two years later; from then it passed to the drably named organization that looked after great buildings then, the Ministry of Works. Now it is in the care of English Heritage. There are two halls in the tower, one above the other. The climb to the top is well worth the effort for the view of the little town and its green surroundings, the Ness beyond, and the sea.

The little square at the heart of the town was once a marketplace, and is now, thanks to visitations on Saturdays, a marketplace once more. There are two or three shops, and two or three pubs, all of which look inviting. On the road from the church to the sea there are decorous cottages, very pretty but not, I imagine, cheap. Though they know they are there to be photographed, they don't shout at you, 'Just look at me!' as some such terraces do in frequented villages. Down a road much favoured by parties of squawking, waddling ducks, past another good-looking pub called the Jolly Sailor, the scene at the end, on the waterfront, like most on the way, is all the more prepossessing because it isn't making great heaving efforts to be prepossessing. Boat trips around the bay are discreetly advertised: there's an hour-long ride on the *Regardless* to Havergate Island and the bird reserve; and had I come a day later I could have treated myself to a four-hour ride, with brunch, on the *Lady Florence*.

Beyond are Bartholomew's lights, and the spit, 10 miles long, that is Orford Ness – the curse of Orford, in that it ruined the place as a port by cutting it off from the sea, reducing the once busy port to no more than a fishing village – the blessing, in that it saved it from the fate of places like Dunwich, some 15 miles up this coast, or such lately threatened places as Happisburgh on the east coast of Norfolk. The sea, by creating this long line of shingle on the Orford shoreline, protected it from the sea. It's also a celebrated nature reserve, to which you can go by ferryboat.

But the Ness is also a place of mystery for other, unnatural reasons. It was long a forbidden territory in the hands of the Ministry of Defence. Radar systems were pioneered here: a big American project in the 1960s called Cobra Mist particularly intrigued the local community, and fed speculation that UFOs had been active in this tucked-away part of England. All kinds of belligerent device were tested here, from conventional bombs right up to nuclear weaponry, in buildings which local people called the pagodas, since that was what they roughly resembled.

The writer W. G. Sebald went there on one of the journeys he records in his compelling book *The Rings of Saturn*. The local man who ferried him over to the old MoD site said local people still avoided the area; even fishermen preferred not to go there 'because they could not stand the god-forsaken loneliness of that outpost in the middle of nowhere'. He felt the same way himself: 'With every step that I took, the emptiness within and the emptiness without grew even greater and the silence more profound'.

Stories of ghastly events and unreported disasters, more terrible even than anything in the works of Britten, haunt this part of the Suffolk coast. It was said that an entire company of the Royal Engineers had perished in 1919 at Shingle Street, at the southern end of the Ness, the victims of an experiment with biological weapons designed to make whole regions uninhabitable. As Sebald says, when the records were finally opened after a silence of seventy-three years, there was no confirmation of any of this: but perhaps it had been suppressed?

It feels odd as you walk back through Orford's ordered tranquillity (at least, that's how it seems out of season) to reflect on what is officially recognized as having been practised out on the Ness – let alone on what might have been plotted and practised and, even now, never admitted. But that kind of unease doesn't persist for long. There's a kind of reassuring sanity about historic Orford which is wonderfully therapeutic. The castle is eight centuries old; the surviving parts of the church have been there for five. In that context, whatever occurred on the Ness was merely a transient episode.

ORKNEY

ORKNEY, insular co. of Scotland, separated from Caithness by the Pentland Firth (6½m. to 8m. broad)… the Orkneys are divided into 3 groups – the South Isles; Pomona or Mainland, the largest island of the Orkneys… and the North Isles. … The islands were annexed to Norway in the latter part of the 9th century, and in 1468 were attached to Scotland as a pledge for the dowry of the Princess of Denmark, who married James III…

YOU DON'T HAVE TO be on the Orkney mainland for long to bump into the Orcadian family Laing. There's a plaque at the heart of the principal street of the principal town, Kirkwall, commemorating the birthplace of Malcolm Laing, historian, and his brother Samuel, philanthropist, agricultural pioneer, travel writer and above all, translator of Norse epics in a place whose Norse links remain abundantly evident. The big tree in front of the house was planted by Robert, their father. There's a memorial to Malcolm across the way in that rich and spirited building, St Magnus Cathedral. And just out of town is Papdale, the house where the brothers grew up. The green fields over which they looked out towards the grey rooftops of Kirkwall are playing fields now, and the house is an education centre.

Much less is said on the island, though, of a second Samuel Laing, son of the translator, who grew up here too. Local patriotism in this fiercely independent and self-contained place ranks the brothers first, since they made their lives and their names here. The younger Samuel, who through no fault of his own failed to be born on Orkney, though he came to represent it in Parliament, lived most of his life in London, where he became one of the most remarkable figures of Victorian England, and in a characteristically Victorian way. Like George Grove, who was famous then as a formidable engineer though he's chiefly remembered now as a musicologist, or Henry Cole, to whom we owe all kinds of boons from the Albert Hall to the Christmas card, he involved himself in a great array of differing and even discordant activities, and succeeded in most if not all of them.

Though with proper Orcadian pride he sometimes referred to himself as a son of Orkney, the younger Samuel is thought to have been born in Edinburgh on 12

December 1812 – though some Orkney historians dispute this date. His mother died when he was one. His father, dissatisfied with the standards of local schools, had him educated at Houghton-le-Spring in Durham, breaking the Orcadian link but enabling him to go on to St John's College, Cambridge, when only fourteen. By finishing second in the mathematical tripos, he achieved the rank of 'Second Wrangler' – meaning that he had the second best mark of the lot – and at twenty-one, in March 1834, was elected a fellow.

So he could have made a fine academic career; but he turned away from this to take up the law and was called to the bar in 1837. Then he switched again, taking up a post as Private Secretary to the Liberal President of the Board of Trade, Henry Labouchere. That began a connection with the rapidly expanding railway industry which lasted throughout his life. In 1840 he was appointed Counsel to the Board of Trade's Rail Road Commissioners. The Liberal defeat a year later cost him his job with Labouchere, but led to a much more important political connection, with Labouchere's successor, the young and ambitious Conservative, William Ewart Gladstone. Together, they worked out the shape of the 1844 Railway Act, a necessary response to the runaway explosion of railway creation.

There is no way of knowing how much Laing suggested to Gladstone and how much Gladstone suggested to Laing, but one innovation with which Laing is usually credited is the introduction of 'parliamentary tickets', a scheme which required the railway companies to run at least one train a day in each direction, stopping at every station and charging a fare of no more than a penny a mile. That was both benevolence and good business. It opened up railway travel to many who otherwise could not have afforded it, and third-class travel tripled over the next thirty years.

Laing left the public service, first to take up posts in the City and then in 1848 to join the industry he had previously tried to police, becoming chairman of the London Brighton and South Coast railway. By spotting the potential of cheap excursions, he brought Londoners to the seaside in unprecedented numbers and achieved a near doubling of the company's traffic within five years. The year 1852 saw him chairing the company that brought the Crystal Palace to Sydenham, and opening up yet another career as a politician, defeating a fellow Liberal, James Loch, a long-serving agent of the Dukes of Sutherland, to become MP for Wick Burghs, which included Kirkwall as well as the mainland towns of Wick, Dingwall and Dornoch.

Though Laing lost his seat in 1857, he regained it two years later, in time to become Financial Secretary to the Treasury under the wing of Gladstone, now a Liberal and Chancellor of the Exchequer. He had been in the post a little more than a year when Lord Palmerston hauled him out of the Commons to serve for four years in India. There, as Finance Minister, he was instrumental in reconstructing the ramshackle finances of the Raj, reducing government spending by £5 million in his first year and £2 million in the next. This interlude probably cost him his chance of further progress in government, however. He had two more spells in the Commons – again for Wick Burghs from 1865 until 1868, and finally as MP for Orkney from 1873 to 1885 – but he was never given office again. Nevertheless he had a decisive influence on Disraeli's extension of the franchise in 1867, when he moved an amendment, and persuaded Conservatives to back him in that amendment, taking reform well beyond what had at first been proposed. Its effect was to remove one Member from all boroughs whose electorate was under 10,000 instead of just from those of under 7,000 as the Bill stipulated. As many as seventy-two Conservatives backed him against the government, contributing to an outcome which Asa Briggs, in his book *Victorian People*, judges to be 'far more democratic than Disraeli, or, indeed, most of his opponents, had ever intended'. Laing moved steadily further away from his party's mainstream during his long parliamentary incumbency; in his last days at Westminster he emerged as a courteous but forceful critic of Gladstone, and especially as a champion of the Empire.

Although his recall to government never came, his services were still in fierce demand everywhere else. In his absence, the London Brighton and South Coast railway had opened up too many branchlines which were never likely to pay for themselves, had run into deep financial trouble, and wanted him back. He resumed the chairmanship, restored the company's fortunes, and stayed in the job until he was eighty-one. Elsewhere in the City, he and a partner founded a trust fund designed to give small investors a chance in the market by spreading their investments over a range of stocks.

And then, in what might have been his years of retirement, Laing emerged in a new and utterly different role: as writer, historian, philosopher, kind-of-theologian, and popularizer of science. If you ask in the excellent Orkney Archive at Kirkwall, they will bring you a high pile of books by Laing, whose diversity is quite astonishing. *Prehistoric Remains of Caithness*, (some of which he'd discovered himself) with additional notes by Thomas Huxley, no less. *A Sporting Quixote*, or, *The Life and Adventures of the Honble. Augustus Fitzmuddle, afterwards Earl of Muddleton* – this being a frothy two-volume comic novel which now and then breaks off from its narrative to treat the reader to disquisitions on such subjects as the oratorical talents of Bright, Disraeli and Gladstone. *A Modern Science and Modern Thought* (1885); *A Modern Zoroastrian* (1887); *Problems of the Future and Other Essays* (1889); *Human Origins* (1892 – the year he was eighty).

Amidst all his other preoccupations, writing and research had always appealed to him. Back in 1842 he had won the Atlas Prize Essay) written in 1842, but published two years later) for an examination of what he described as a 'deep-seated organic malady' blighting the nation. Both Karl Marx and J. S. Mill quoted this work, and commended it. The evidence he adduced was drawn from previously published material, notably the reports of the diligent committees of inquiry which were one of the glories of Victorian Britain. What chiefly concerned him was the wilful neglect of the poor – the 'intolerable mass of misery' that was the inescapable lot of the labouring classes and even more of those who could not find work. Despite what it suited the well-to-do to assume, while the rich had been getting richer, the poor, he found, had become still poorer.

Nor was it, as some who wrote and spoke on these matters found it convenient to pretend, the fault of those who were suffering. 'The criminality, sufferings and moral degradation of the poorer classes', Laing wrote, 'are for the most part occasioned by the pressure of circumstances, over which they have no control, and which have plunged a large proportion of our population into a state which renders anything approaching to decent and comfortable existence a moral impossibility.' Laing was outraged both because all this was unjust, but also because it was inefficient. The adoption of better employment practices in the Cornish mines, he noted, had pushed up their productivity.

There could, he concluded, be no effective remedies without a greater commitment to equity (though some of the notions he examined for achieving that greater equity, including a further widening of the franchise, he reluctantly discarded as utopian and impractical). 'The more enlightened economists', he asserted, 'have, indeed themselves come to see, that even on their own principles the mere absolute amount of wealth in a nation signifies little compared with the far more important question of its distribution. The economical writers of the continent have long since recognized this truth and abandoned the path pursued by the English school of political economy, as one that leads to false and partial results.'

And what if nothing was done? Then, he could see no alternative other than 'a violent and bloody revolution, shattering the whole existing framework of society to pieces, or a permanent degradation of the population to a state of abject and heart-broken resignation to misery which almost reduces the human being to the level with the brute.' Marx, who quoted him, welcomed the prospect of revolution. But Laing, who feared it, contended that with awareness, common sense and generosity, it might yet be averted.

But specific measures alone would not reverse the process. The malaise went deeper than that. At its heart was the worship of Mammon, the elevation of money above all other values. Whole sections of Laing's analysis could have been lifted and marched direct into battle more than century later against some of the economic doctrines of Thatcherism, and especially against the cosy, convenient theory that the benefits enjoyed by the richest class in society will automatically 'trickle down' to the rest. But what in his judgement was needed most of all was a change of heart and a transformation of attitudes; a way of seeing things which recognized that life was about something more than material wealth, and that there were higher things to aspire to than growing rich and having people see you grow rich. The essential precondition for that, he warned, was a return to religion. Not the formal religion identified, as he put it, 'with cant, narrowness, insincerity and hostility to the truth', but religion in the sense of commitment to higher, less obsessively material, more spiritual values.

Turn from there, from a young man's disgust and anger, to the books Laing wrote in tranquil old age, and the contrast provides an account not just of how one man has altered, but also, I think, of how a whole world has changed, above all through the agency of Charles Darwin, Alfred Russel Wallace and Charles Lyell. These later books are largely designed to explain the revolutionary discoveries of science to people for whom science is not their natural language. He is writing, he says, not for the scientifically trained, but for the open-minded, open-eyed, ordinary citizen. And the young man who believed that remedies were impossible without a return to religion is now, though not quite an atheist – he's perhaps too mellow for that – certainly a resolute non-believer. He has read and understood his Darwin, Wallace and Lyell and what he says, very urgently, is that there can be no health in perpetuating delusion. It's curious in this context to compare him with his almost exact contemporary Philip Gosse, whom we shall meet at St Marychurch, who so desperately fought off the menace he saw to religion in the teachings of Darwin and Wallace, at the very time when Laing was abandoning his previous beliefs in the light of this stunning evidence.

The other remarkable feature of these late books is Laing's overflowing contentment. Of course, he has enjoyed a particularly privileged and comfortable life, born into a prosperous, well-regarded family, endowed with exceptional talent and, just as important, exceptional energy, and blessed for most of his life with good health. But what gives him the deepest satisfaction is the feeling that his labours – his frequently mighty labours – have not been in vain. From his innovations designed to bring railway travel within the reach of all but the very poorest to the books which have brought understanding and enlightenment for those who otherwise found much of scientific writing intimidatingly abstruse, he feels he has been of service. And indeed he has.

Just as, to his regret, he had not been born on Orkney, he did not die there. He died in August 1897, at Sydenham in south London, and was buried in Brighton: almost as far from Orkney as you can go in these islands.

A B C D

E F G H

I J K L

M N O **P**

Q R S T

U V W XYZ

PEACEHAVEN

PEACEHAVEN, seaside garden city, E. Sussex, adjoining Newhaven, and 6½m. E. of Brighton…

'SEASIDE GARDEN CITY', BARTHOLOMEW's designation, is one way of looking at it, which would have delighted its founder. There are others: 'As unpleasant an example of maritime suburbia as can be found,' says W .S. Mitchell, in the *Shell Guide to East Sussex*. And in Nikolaus Pevsner's Buildings of England series: 'What is one to say? Peacehaven has been called a rash on the countryside. It is that, and there is no worse in England… Peacehaven derives its name from the end of the First World War. Whose haven was it? Whose haven is it? Small plots (or stands), yet nothing semi-detached, let alone in terraces. Every man in his own house, if only a few feet from the neighbours!' – though the exasperation there sounds rather more like Ian Nairn, who co-wrote the book with Pevsner.

Another, earlier verdict, though even more savage, comes from Virginia Woolf, who lived close by in Rodmell (where in 1941 she drowned herself in the Ouse) in 1925: 'Would it much affect us, we ask ourselves, if a sea monster erected its horrid head off the coast of Sussex and licked up the entire population of Peacehaven and then sank to the bottom of the sea? Should we mourn them, or wish their resurrection? No; for none of the qualities for which we love our kind and respect its misfortunes are here revealed; all for which we despise and suspect it are here displayed. All that is cheap and greedy and meretricious, that is to say, has here come to the surface, and lies like a sore, expressed in gimcrack red houses and raw roads and meaningless decorations…'

Whose haven was it? That is easily answered: it was a haven for men who'd survived the war. Early streets were named for events which many who came here might have preferred not to remember, like Loos and Mons (those names were dropped long ago). A man from Darlington called Charles William Neville created it. The land was divided up on a relentless grid system and sold piecemeal, sometimes for buyers to build what they pleased, sometimes with Neville's Peacehaven Estate Company as builder. Bungalows were a popular choice. When I saw it first in the 1950s many corner sites were empty and overgrown, and some of the streets petered out as though they had lost their purpose. These sites cost more, so no one had bought them.

At the start it was called New Anzac-on-Sea, a name which came first in a competition, designed to honour war heroes from Australia and New Zealand; but that choice failed to command a universal acclaim, and Neville resorted to Peacehaven, the most numerous choice among competitors. It was advertised, especially in the *Daily Mail*, and thousands came down to Sussex dreaming of a new life. As the place began to grow, the claims made for it became ever more boastful. Peacehaven was 'rapidly becoming a seaside resort of the first magnitude... acknowledged to be the greatest seaside town planning and land development enterprise yet undertaken in this country.' Acknowledged by whom? That wasn't stated. By Neville for one; but also by those who had bought into his fine new utopia, 'our garden city by the sea', as it was hailed in volume 1, number 1 of the *Peacehaven Post*.

Whatever its aesthetic failings, the first of those who came to the haven adored it. Even more than the plotlanders whom we met at Jaywick, they thought they'd arrived in heaven. *The Peacehaven Post* measured it up against Paradise, and Paradise came off worse. Elysium was also invoked. The *Post* itself, something Jaywick culture could never have matched, was one of the advertised joys of living there. 'In the pages of the *Peacehaven Post*,' its founding editor trilled, 'we propose from time to time to tell the story of these old-world beauty spots that knew the ancient woad-stained Britons, that saw the Saxons and knew the Norman Conquest, and have survived, almost unchanged, to become the happy haunts of the people of an England upon the dominions of whose sovereign the sun never sets.'

But mere prose could hardly do justice to such a creation. Poetry – well verse, anyway – was called for:

> On noble heights swept by the ocean breeze;
> Where eye can take its fill e'en to the brim,

Of downland glories, mighty banks and leas;
Mid eerie cries of seagulls as they trim
Their wings to kiss the crested wave below,
Seek ye such gifts as Nature doth bestow?
They are here! Peacehaven.

Subsequent editions plotted the growth of this ideal community. The first baby had been born here: Master John Wagstaff, a fine sturdy example of what the future population would be. Sites for shops were being clamoured for. Mr Parker was now in full stride in his bright little emporium, the Optima Stores, which was becoming as much a household word in Peacehaven as Harrods in London; but for needs not yet met, there were handy buses to Newhaven. Anyone hoping to sell (though the tone of the *Post* suggested this was impossible) might be gratified to learn that properties were changing hands for four times the original price. Those who stayed and hoped to expand might effectively add a room to their bungalows by investing in Pascall's Patent Double Oven.

All human life was there in the *Post*. The Peacehaven Pic-Chicks, with Uncle Merrydown, were there for the children, and Ann X was on hand for the ladies, with prizes awarded each month for the best 'brain wave' submitted. There were tables to show the times of high tides and of trains to London Bridge and Victoria, and literary competitions, challenging readers to make a better acrostic than the one the editors had devised: Pure Exhilarating Air Cutely Erected Homes Amid Vast Expansive Nature; and jokes with a Peacehaven flavour, and Peacehaven Prunings, which were gardening notes, by Q. Cumber.

'It would be interesting… to publish a list of notable people in art, literature, politics and other walks of life who are potential residents,' the first number had mused, and perhaps the first editor qualified under that heading. He was George Henry Powell, who for years had been part of a music hall act with his brother Felix. Together they'd written (words by George, using the pseudonym 'George Asaf', and music by Felix) one of the most famous songs of the age, a staple of British morale in the war: 'Pack up your troubles in your old kit bag (and smile, smile, smile)'. Before long, George Powell gave way as editor to the paper's cartoonist, Gordon Volk, son of Magnus Volk who created the electric seaside railway in Brighton. The good news, however, continued unabated, though this was hardly surprising, since Volk was on Charles Neville's payroll.

A new feature, 'Peering Through the Peacehaven Periscope,' by the Peacehaven Perceiver, revealed that a milkman would soon be making deliveries. A hotel was planned, and a golf course, and a philharmonic and dramatic society, and a literary, scientific and debating society. A bank would be opened; a place had been picked for a church. True, not everything promised by Neville had yet appeared – roads and drains which should have been ready in the early days of the idyll were still missing twenty years later and did not arrive until the 1950s – but that kind of negative news was not allowed to disfigure the *Post*. The prospect of a hotel stirred it to new heights of rapture. A site had been chosen – and in Phyllis Avenue, a location which could not have been bettered. Plans were being laid for its opening, with bonfires of such dimensions that they'd be seen in France. A dance hall would be created next to the hotel and named Lureland – a name bestowed on the Peacehaven area by a London journalist called George Sims who had settled there. His enthusiasm too was fanned by the founder's money.

It's often said that nothing stirs up a spirit of patriotism like an external threat, and Peacehaven had one of those too, the antagonist being the very newspaper in which in the early days its joys had been chiefly advertised. Neville was determined to stage something very spectacular to celebrate the opening of his hotel. Having heard that the Dutch air ace Anthony Fokker was coming to England for a gliding competition at Lewes organized by the *Daily Mail*, Neville offered him £1,000 to come to Peacehaven first. The *Mail* was outraged. The *Post*, in return, was magnificent in its disdain. 'While every other London and southern provincial newspaper gave to Peacehaven the credit for being the first to introduce a gliding exhibition as a public spectacle in this country,' it thundered, 'the *Daily Mail* sought to lead its readers to believe that Mr Fokker was in England wholly and solely in connection with an international gliding competition held later in the month.' The *Mail* had made no mention of the fact that the great airman, 'together with two gliders and his staff of mechanics, was brought to England by the directors of Peacehaven estates, and engaged at an enormous fee, to entertain Peacehaven's guests and residents and to establish for Peacehaven another record!' The day of the opening, 10 October 1922 – 'the day of days in the annals of our Garden City' – was marked by a celebratory issue. 'Every new undertaking has its critics' the *Post* reported. 'They came – a feeble insignificant minority among the host of friends and supporters – to carp but they stayed to admire and praise.'

Yet some troubles in life cannot be packed up into kit bags or even allayed by downland glories, mighty banks and leas, and the eerie cries of seagulls trimming their wings to kiss crested waves. In a piece he wrote for the *Independent on Sunday*, the journalist and author Charles Nevin unravelled the fate of one of Peacehaven's early celebrities, Felix Powell. Powell, like so many others here (though not his brother and lyricist George, who was a pacifist), had fought in the First World War. As he grew older he pinned his peacetime hopes on a musical he had written called *Rubicund Castle*, which was staged at the Pavilion Theatre, Peacehaven, with correspondents despatched from Fleet Street – attracted no doubt by the fame of his Old Kit Bag – to attend the occasion. West End producers were said to be hovering. For some time, nothing came of it, and when it was finally bought it was drastically altered and given a different name: *Primrose Times*. Only the music survived intact. A London enthusiast was ready to stage this revised concoction, but before he could do so, he was arrested and convicted for fraud.

The disappointment this brought to Felix Powell hardened into despair. One morning in February 1942, while on Home Guard duty at the Lureland Hall, he sent out his colleague on a confected errand and then shot himself in the chest with a service rifle. He left two notes, one apologizing to the Home Guard, the other saying: 'for some time I have not been able to work, and can see no other way out'. He was sixty-three. 'Felix', his brother George told the inquest, 'suffered mentally with frustration at not being able to find an outlet for his exceptional gifts as a musician and composer of light music.' The verdict was suicide while the balance of his mind was disturbed.

Today, Peacehaven is a solidly conventional place, briskly tidied up, its shackier elements replaced by the kind of buildings you would find in most of the urban seaside settlements that have occupied this part of the Sussex coast: formally ugly rather than informally ugly. The echoes of war have gone from the street names in favour of softer concepts such as Sussex towns and villages. The Pavilion Theatre, where the premiere of

Rubicund Castle stirred such hopes, became a cinema and burned down in 1940. Neville's hotel somehow survived until the late 1980s: Neville himself died in 1960. As for the *Peacehaven Post*, later renamed the *Downland Post*, that ceased publication in 1928.

The shops are still strung along the dreary main street where you catch the bus back to Brighton; there's also a shopping precinct, the Meridian Centre – Peacehaven is the place where the meridian line meets the south coast and leaves Britain – but this isn't much of a lureland. Yet there's still the downland, within easy reach once you are out of the maritime sprawl; and of course there is still the sea, which no one has managed to spoil.

PETERBOROUGH

PETERBOROUGH, mun. bor. and city in Soke of Peterborough, NE. Northants... the cathedral is a noble edifice. Peterborough is an important railway centre. The L.N.E. has here large locomotive shops.

WALK WESTWARDS FROM PETERBOROUGH'S majestic cathedral and you come to what used to be called the Market Place but is now – the markets having been banished – Cathedral Square. Before you, across the square, is the 1671 Guildhall, also, in a more modest way, quite a noble edifice, and beyond that the parish church of St John the Baptist. It's a sequence sure to give pleasure to every lover of townscape. And then, crammed up against the defenceless church, there's what in this context looks like some kind of deliberate insult: a building perpetrated in 1964 on the site of the former Corn Exchange by the Norwich Union Insurance Company. Not only does this demean its distinguished surroundings; it also bears a heavy responsibility for causing the rift which led their co-founder John Betjeman to withdraw from the editorship of that matchless twentieth-century series of topographical books, the *Shell Guides* to British counties.

There had been skirmishes before as Shell flinched from some of the judgements passed by contributors on the places they visited. An assault on the local administration of Worcester for what it had allowed to be done to the city, the work of James Lees-Milne, was one cause of contention. Peterborough was another.

The city's status has always been ambivalent. It belongs to the Soke of Peterborough; but who does the Soke belong to? A soke is defined as a district under a particular jurisdiction, suggesting a degree of independence from the counties around it, and recognizing that the place enjoys certain privileges, including the right to hold its own courts. This soke comprises some thirty parishes. The *Shell* book that caused the trouble, by Juliet Smith, first published in 1968, describes itself as a guide to Northamptonshire and the Soke of Peterborough, as if they were separate entities. For a time Peterborough was part of Huntingdonshire, but that county no longer exists; today it is included in Cambridgeshire.

According to research by Chris Mawson, available on his website, Juliet Smith – in private life, Lady Juliet Smith, which makes her sound more formidable – concluded, as any sane and sentient person must, that the Norwich Union building was a disaster. That Peterborough, as a cathedral town, had so little to offer aside from its cathedral made this injury even more unforgivable. So she said as much. This was not well received at the headquarters of Shell. The *Shell Guides* had been jointly devised in 1933 by Betjeman and his friend Jack Beddington, who as publicity director of Shell thought he could persuade the organization to put up some money. An enlightened Shell board agreed.

For years, Shell had tried to be patient, which was not always easy, especially when Betjeman's chosen writers regularly complained of clumsy, clodhopping petrol stations defacing otherwise pretty villages – not a sentiment with which this company was likely to agree. Worcester, lashed by Lees-Milne, was far from the only town to have words with Shell. Llandrindod Wells was unhappy about the account of the town in David Verey's book on Mid Wales, with its reference (too harsh, in my view) to red brick buildings of peculiar hideousness, its judgement that the place was 'pretty dead now all the year round', and the final dismissive sentence: 'Round every corner one expects to find the sea; but there is no sea, only rain.'

The company was anxious not to offend the powerful Norwich Union – and concerned enough to urge Betjeman to modify such a crushing verdict on what it had done to Peterborough. Betjeman refused, and in the ensuing altercations broke his connection with Shell. The *Guide* as published says merely: 'The fifteenth-century parish church of St John, by the seventeenth-century Guildhall, with its fine proportions and high arcades, is overshadowed by an office block.'

The *Shell Guides* continued after Betjeman's departure under John Piper, but the company's enthusiasm waned still further and the postwar series was never completed. Juliet Smith's account of Peterborough, though written before it attained the size it is now, seems to me just about right, glorying in the cathedral – 'one of the most impressive buildings of its date in Europe' – but finding the place as a whole unprepossessing. One defect is that there's simply not enough in the historic centre to leaven what's happened since: first, the expansion which came with the railway (taken through Peterborough because the mighty Burghley family banned it from Stamford) and then the postwar creation which its designers called Greater Peterborough, to accommodate London overspill.

It's a place – less so than Swindon or Slough, but still conspicuously – which tends to attract some measure of obloquy. Mark Haddon followed his novel about Asperger's syndrome, *The Curious Incident of the Dog in the Night-Time*, with another called *A Spot of Bother*, which he set in Peterborough, although he had never been there. It's an evocation of a place that is achingly boring. 'Humdrum' was the word which one critic chose to sum up its ambience. 'It is, for heaven's sake', the critic added, as if this were QED, 'set in Peterborough.' The book seems to imply that the city can be summed up by the fact that people like George and Jean Hall, its chief characters, want to live there: a couple who, until everything starts to crumble, and George thinks he is terminally ill and begins to drink on a scale which makes his family fear he's becoming the soak of Peterborough, lead drably conventional lives with their Jacques Loussier CDs, their prints on the wall, their *Daily Telegraph*s and their Scrabble. After he'd written the book, Haddon did visit Peterborough, and told the *Observer* it was even worse than he'd thought.

When a train on which I was travelling north stopped at Peterborough station, a man across the aisle began furiously to denounce the city and all its works. Yet at the end of his diatribe he noted a single redeeming feature. He had once, he said, stayed in the Great Northern Hotel, which you can see from the station, and found there to his delight a statue of one of his greatest heroes, Duke Ellington. It was almost as if he were saying – for this one good work, let even Sodom be spared. So when I was next in Peterborough I went to the hotel – not easily done; you have somehow to find a way across an intractable ring road – and asked at the reception desk if I might see their Duke Ellington. 'I'm sorry, but you can't any more,' the receptionist told me. 'It used to be in the garden; but they got rid of it.'

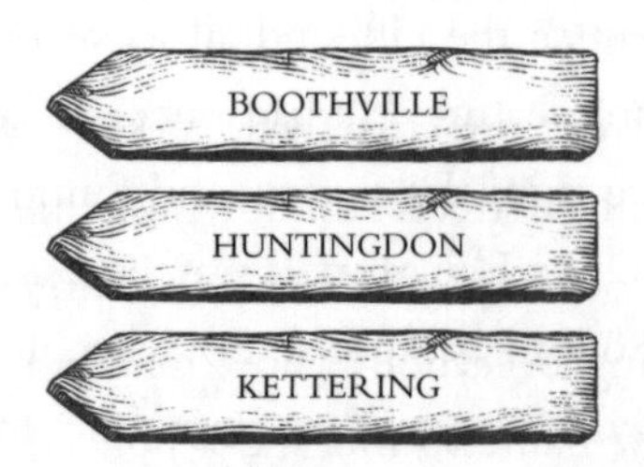

PONTLOTTYN

PONTLOTTYN, vil., with ry. sta., G.W.R. (alt. 832 ft.), Gelligaer par., Glamorgan…

ON THE RAILWAY LINE that runs north out of Cardiff through Caerphilly and Ystrad Mynach to the head of the Rhymney Valley, there's a station with the unimpeachable name of Pontlottyn. It's a name that was dredged from history books to serve a settlement developed in haste to house workers at a new colliery, in a spot that had no particular name but was loosely classed as Lower Rhymney. According to local legend, or at least according to a group of drinkers with whom I once fell in at a pub at Ystrad Mynach long after closing time, it was only when the railway came that the name Pontlottyn was plumped for. When officials of the railway company that was planning the line visited the vicinity to decide where to site the station, they asked local people what the place was called, and were told, to their horror, that it was known locally as Sodom and Gomorrah.

Their consternation must have been wonderful to behold. These were not words they would have wished, in those days, to see inscribed in any public location and they certainly did not want them displayed on their station. (This would have happened some time in the 1850s; the line was opened in 1858.) Pontlottyn, which might mean 'the bridge of the poor man', but might equally be a corruption of the name of a Roman bridge that used to exist in these parts, represented an appeal to antiquity. No one could quarrel with that.

Pontlottyn today is a long continuous street, punctuated by terraces, with the hills above it and the river and railway below. Tributary streets run down the hillside but they are few and don't go far. There's a scatter of shops (Kebabs and Burgers; Brides of Elegance; a hardware store; Con Minoli & Sons, 'everybody's bookmakers'), a sweet little parish church dedicated to St Tyfaelog, a new name to me, and a police station (1915) in a huddle with a magistrates' court (1923), both of which look fairly wretched. The railway line is a straight single track operated by tinny diesels, and the station is a brick hut – all very plain and utilitarian. It was therefore all the more pleasing – when a train for Cardiff came in – to see that one of its carriages bore the name 'Myfanwy'.

That the police station and magistrates' court, poignantly placed just across the road from Reform Street, loom so large in the village reflects the fact that from its beginnings the forces of law and order were kept busy here. This was a hard-drinking, hard-fighting, hard-feuding place with its poor Welsh and poor Irish inhabitants constantly at odds with each other and, from time to time, killing each other. Indeed, says a local historian Marion Evans in her book *A Portrait of Rhymney*, so unruly was this community that the Bute Terrace area gained the name Sodom and the Chapel Street quarter became known as Gomorrah. So the testimony of the drinkers in Ystrad Mynach, which I feared might be a case of the natives attempting to pull the wool over the innocent eyes of a reporter from London, a practice by no means unusual in journalism at home and abroad, did at least have an element of truth.

Yet there are two other communities known to me where the official name is Sodom, one of which is listed by Bartholomew as a locality in Malmesbury rural district, Wiltshire. It just about registers on a road that runs west out of Wootton Bassett, though unless you pay close attention you may motor on into Dauntsey without spotting it. Its main manifestation is a solid and quite substantial house which proudly proclaims itself to be Sodom Hall; which no doubt would elide after a drink or two in one of the local pubs into Sod 'em all. Long ago this was one of two Wiltshire Sodoms, the other being an episode in the village of West Lavington on the road from Devizes south to Stonehenge. The Ordnance Survey indicates the presence of yet another, somewhere near Caersws in what used to be Flintshire.

Sadly, Sodom's traditional partner in crime appears to go unrepresented in Britain. John Bartholomew moves direct from 'Gometra' – '*(pronounced Gom'etra), isl., Kilninian and Kilmore par., Argyllshire, on W. side of Ulva Island, pop. 33. Is a fishing station*' – to Gomshall, '*vil., seat and ry. sta. (G. and Shere), S.R., W. Surrey*' – as if there were no Gomorrah.

PORT APPIN

PORT APPIN, vil., N. Argyllshire, on E. shore of Loch Linnhe, 2½m. SW. Appin and opposite the N. extremity of Lismoreis.; pop. 73...

REASONS TO VISIT PORT Appin: 1) To see Port Appin. 2) To cross the water to the island of Lismore. 3) The one that moved me to go there, and made me glad I had done so: to gaze upon Castle Stalker, serene, reserved, apparently unapproachable, housed on its tiny island out in the loch.

In fact you don't need to go to Port Appin to see Castle Stalker. Let me put that more forcibly: you can't even see it from there. But you do get luscious views of it at intervals on the byroad which takes you from the A828 Connel Bridge to Ballachulish road into the village. Alternatively, you may stay on the A828 and use the official viewpoint, just north of the turn to Port Appin, where there's a café, a shop and a car park. If you do that, however, you will see the exactly the same view of the castle as everyone else and take exactly the same photographs as everyone else.

Still, wherever you stop, the view of the castle is captivating: the lonely tower in the broad and tranquil loch with the mountains massed behind, with an aura of sweetness about it for all its solemnity and the bloody events that have happened there. It was built in the fifteenth century, possibly by Sir John Stewart, Lord of Lorn. Stewart was murdered during his wedding service at Dunstaffnage, near Oban. He had come there to marry his mistress to legitimize their son Dugald. A man called Alan MacCoul was armed and awaiting him outside the church. Yet Stewart managed to get through the service before he died, and his son became the First Chief of Appin. At the battle of Stalc, close to Castle Stalker, in 1468, Dugald took his revenge on Alan MacCoul. Dugald in turn was killed in a skirmish with the MacDonalds some thirty years later.

The Stewarts and their feuding adversaries had begun as they meant to go on. In 1520 a party of Campbells murdered Sir Alexander Stewart of Invernahyle as he fished in the waters around Castle Stalker, in return for which his son, an infant when his father was slain, killed nine Campbells some twenty-five years later. The Campbells turned the Stewarts out of the castle in 1620; the Stewarts reclaimed it in 1689 when the Campbells were ordered to forfeit it, only for the Stewarts to lose it again when they finished on the losing side at the battle of Dunkeld. In 1745, the Campbells took the side of the government against that not very bonny figure, Bonnie Prince Charlie, and fought the Stewarts off.

Some time in the following century the castle was abandoned and fell into dereliction. In 1908 a Stewart recaptured it by the simple twentieth-century device of buying it. Yet sudden death continued to stalk this family: his successor at Castle Stalker, who was governor of Sarawak, was murdered by a Dyak. In 1965, Lt Col. D. R. Stewart Allward bought, rebuilt and restored it, doing much of the work himself. He died in 1991, but the castle remained in the family. It is not quite as unapproachable as it looks: it opens on specified days through the summer, and visits may be made by arrangement. Yet seen from the lane to Port Appin it is so mysterious and solitary that perhaps to go around it would break the spell; better to contemplate it wistfully, at a distance.

From Port Appin you may take a ferry to Lismore. The crossing takes roughly ten minutes. If you want to go there by car, you must take a boat out of Oban. But bicycles can be hired in Port Appin – they are carried free on the boat – if you wish to explore the whole island, which is one mile across but ten miles long, and shaped a bit like a crocodile. There are recommended flora and fauna, and places where you may have tea, and what's left of the cathedral, the base until the sixteenth century of the bishops of Argyll. Later, no doubt to the dismay of some of its Presbyterians, the island became the home of a Roman Catholic seminary.

And then there's Port Appin itself, which seemed a pleasant and cheerful place when I was there, with shops and two hotels (one of them, to judge by the menus displayed outside, disconcertingly expensive) and craft shops. Also – though oddly there's no word of this in lighthouse-besotted Bartholomew – there's a lighthouse here, which, one night in 2001, was painted pink with white spots; some said by vandals, but others said by protestors of a satirical bent alarmed by reports that a replacement lighthouse was planned. Go early or late in the year to Port Appin, though: it is said to be Trippersville in high summer.

You won't be long in the village before you are acquainted with the story of the Appin Murder, an event that furnished part of the plot for R. L. Stevenson's *Kidnapped*. But to taste the full horror of the event you need to press on to Ballachulish. Here in 1752 a Stewart called James of the Glen was hanged for the murder – of which he was almost certainly guiltless – of Campbell of Gilmore, a government agent. In the highest traditions of jurisprudence, the jury were mostly Campbells, and so was the judge. After a dignified speech in which he asserted his innocence, he climbed (it was reported) 30 feet up a ladder to the gibbet, singing Psalm 35, verse 11, which condemns false witnesses. 'Let them be ashamed and brought to confusion together that rejoice at mine hurt: let them be clothed with shame and dishonour that magnify themselves against me,' it goes on to plead in verse 26. In accordance with the sentence, the body was left to swing for seven years, during the course of which it disintegrated. A monument to James of the Glen – 'executed on this spot 8 November 1752 for a crime of which he was not guilty' – stands close to Ballachulish bridge where the lorries pound across on their urgent missions. To that extent, I suppose, the agents of his death have indeed been clothed in shame and dishonour, just as the psalmist advocated, though it's taken quite a long time.

PORTSDOWN

PORTSDOWN, in SE. of Hants, extending E. and W. nearly 7m. between Havant and Fareham… on its summit is a monument to Lord Nelson.

On the range of hills above Portsmouth known as Portsdown, there's a line of suitably grim-looking red-brick forts put up between 1865 and 1871 at the behest of Lord Palmerston to defend Portsmouth Harbour, the Spithead, and the Isle of Wight. There are others on the waterfront, and some in the sea, forming a protective chain around Portsmouth, but up on this hill, there are five: Fort Wallington at the western end of the line above Fareham, then Fort Nelson and Fort Southwick, with Fort Widley and Fort Purbeck at the eastern end towards Havant. To the untutored eye there is not much difference between them. But because of what happened there one autumn day in 1910, Fort Widley has a fame, or a notoriety, that the others can't match.

On Monday, 5 September of that year, shortly after noon, a group of men on horseback passing the fort spotted something they found alarming. It was Percy Hamilton, a civilian, who saw the figure first and pointed him out to his companions, Captain Horace de Courcy Martelli, the officer commanding the forts, and Lieutenant Salmond. A man was inspecting the building, making notes, and apparently sketching it. It couldn't be said that his behaviour was furtive: he was wearing an eye-catching Panama hat. But this was a time when the apprehension of war with the Germans was growing, and a touch of spy fever had broken out, fed by the excitable novels of a writer called William Le Queux, whose *Spies of the Kaiser*, as he explained, was only written as fiction because he feared that if it was written as fact – which it was – he might face prosecution.

The officers on Portsdown were moved by the thought: you can't be too careful. So they accosted the man and asked him what he was up to. The accent, and the fractured English of his response, confirmed their fears. The captain, as the senior officer, took the man's notebook, which was found to contain nine drawings of fortifications – he had been to other defences around Portsmouth too – with notes on positions of guns and searchlights, details of distances, and diagrams suggesting the likely lines of fire of defensive artillery.

Leaving his book with the captain, the man set off towards the nearby village of Widley. The officers, concluding he was unlikely to come and ask for his notebooks back, followed him, and stopped him again at Fort Purbrook, where Lieutenant Salmond arrested him. His name was Lieutenant Siegfried Helm, an engineer officer of the 21st battalion of the Nassau Regiment of the German army.

Plainly, it was decided, the man had been up to no good. There were serious doubts over what proscribed offence he ought to be charged with, but the officers and the police agreed that he certainly ought to be charged, and Helm was packed off to Winchester Prison. Proceedings began at the magistrates' court at Fareham on 15 September, when Helm was charged with being outside certain fortresses without the permission of His Majesty's government, taking plans and sketches thereof, and intending to communicate them to a foreign state, to wit, the empire of Germany.

The case of Lieutenant Helm was by now being seen as a serious matter. Initially, there had been doubts; even the *Southern Daily Echo*, headlining its story of the arrest, 'Sensational Occurrence at Portsmouth', had been unsure that Fort Widley had any serious secrets for spies to reveal to the empire of Germany. The fortifications, indeed, had become a bit of a joke on Portsdown. They were locally known as Palmerston's Folly. It was customarily said – and still is, by some – that they'd been built the wrong way around, facing north towards the country rather than south, out to sea. 'The facts that the forts have been dismantled', the newspaper said with commendable balance, 'and were stated in Parliament to be useless for the purposes for which they were erected makes the possession of such sketches a matter of little import, but the making of sketches in this way is regarded as an infraction of the law.'

Yet now the courtroom at Fareham was packed, with a posse of journalists down from London, and the German newspapers also following the case vigilantly. They didn't doubt that Helm had behaved unwisely, but some thought they smelt something suspicious here. Two English officers, Captain Bernard Trench and 1st Lieutenant

Vivian Brandon, were being held in Germany on suspicion of spying, and the seizing of Lieutenant Helm looked to them like retaliation. It could not have even occurred to Helm, the *Kreuz Zeitung* declared, that he was doing anything that was forbidden, for the tumbledown condition of the completely antiquated fortification could not escape the practised eye of an engineer such as Helm, who had clearly identified the Fort as a place that had been abandoned long ago.

Keenest of all to see the prosecution succeeding was man called Vernon Kell. In the course of 1909, the Liberal government had become so impressed by the extent of public excitement over rumours of German spies that it felt it had to take action. An organization called the Secret Service Bureau was launched under the dual leadership of Kell and Captain Mansfield Cumming, with Kell heading the counter-espionage section, which in time would evolve into MI5, and Cumming the foreign section, which became MI6.

Kell was a worried man. His organization had been set up for an initial two years only, and so far it had not a single scalp to its name. It seems probable that the press interest in the hearing at Fareham had been whipped up by Kell in the hope that the case of Lieutenant Helm might save his and his unit's jobs. Moreover, just as the German press had suspected, the Director of British Naval Intelligence had been badgering Kell to mount some kind of eye-catching retort to the arrests of Trench and Brandon.

It must have been a disappointment for Kell that the charges were now to proceed on the grounds that what Helm had done was a misdemeanour, rather than that more serious class of offence, a felony. The press, however, got what they'd come for: a sizzling story. The prosecution had produced as a witness a bubbly twenty-year-old woman called Hannah Wodehouse, who, having made friends with an earlier German visitor, a Lieutenant Wohlfahrt, had agreed to keep a friendly eye on Lieutenant Helm when he came to England.

It was she who had found him lodgings, for which he expressed his gratitude, though mildly complaining that the only other residents were very old ladies of forty-five to seventy. There were also far from unfounded suspicions that the friendship she had promised had gone rather further than that. Indeed, she told Kell that she had seduced the lieutenant in the hope of confirming her suspicion that he was one of these much talked-about German spies. So disturbing did she find her conversations with Helm that while he continued his prowlings around Portsmouth's defence installations she went off to Eastney Barracks and reported them to an officer. But before she could talk to Kell, she informed the court, she'd been interviewed by a man who said he had come from the War Office, though in fact he was a reporter: '*that* reporter', she said, creating a frisson in court by pointing out a man on the press bench, who instantly jumped up to deny it.

Helm was sent for trial and in October appeared at Winchester Assizes. That the case was no longer regarded as merely trivial was demonstrated by the firepower on either side. The government was represented by one of the biggest legal guns of the day, Rufus Isaacs, who had just joined the government as Attorney-General. Even so, the proceedings, were – to Kell's disappointment – low-key. The prosecution's chief aim, said Isaacs, had been to establish the right to try foreign nationals under the Official Secrets Act, and that had now been confirmed. In the circumstances, he would not press for serious punishment, so long as Helm was suitably contrite. Mr Travers Humphreys for the defence assured the court that Helm had expressed a sincere and profound regret. Binding him over, Mr Justice Bankes said that though the case involved no more than a misdemeanour, the matter was still a serious one, and in many cases would have had to be punished severely. Fortunately for Helm, this was not, in Bankes's judgment, necessary here and Helm was discharged. He and his father left by train for London, failing to recognize a man who travelled up in the same carriage. This was Kell, hoping to overhear something to his advantage, but in that he was disappointed again.

That might have been the end of the Fort Widley affair – but it wasn't. Alarm at the German threat continued to mount – Germans or people merely assumed to be German were being attacked in the streets of south London – and suspicions of German spying continued to accumulate; to a point where the following year the War Minister Lord Haldane, who until then had always resisted such a conclusion, was persuaded that legislation was necessary to deal with the German espionage effort. In making his case before Parliament, he picked out three instances which in his view demonstrated the need for a new and much tougher Official Secrets Act: and the one which he seemed to think was the gravest was that of Lieutenant Helm. This man, he said, had run away when challenged (that was untrue), and though the case had attracted great attention, the authorities' means of proving his motive had been found to be extremely inadequate.

Publicity over Lieutenant Helm probably saved Kell and his unit from being closed down. It is impossible, says Thomas Boghardt in a book which, echoing William Le Queux, he called *Spies of the Kaiser* (2004), to say how Kell's unit would have fared without the Helm case, but the Secret Service Bureau's probationary period of two years would then have expired without Kell having anything to show for his efforts, and it is not entirely inconceivable that Kell's contract might not have been renewed. After Helm's conviction, however, the question of a possible dissolution of the counter-espionage Bureau was not raised again.

The 1911 Official Secrets Act, superseding the much looser provisions of the previous legislation of 1889, survived well into the twentieth century. It produced in its day a string of sensational cases. Among those which followed the Second World War, Klaus Fuchs, a scientist who passed secret information on atomic weaponry to the Russians, was jailed for fourteen years in 1950. In 1961, a group known as the Portland Five were convicted of espionage for the Russians. One of them, who called himself Gordon Lonsdale, jailed for twenty-five years, was found to be a Russian called Konon Molody; two others, known as Peter and Helen Kroger, jailed for twenty years, also had stolen identities. The remaining two, Henry Houghton and Ethel Gee, were sentenced to fifteen years: they married on their release.

In the same year, 1961, a KGB agent, George Blake, was given the longest custodial sentence ever handed out by a British court: forty-two years. Sent to Wormwood Scrubs, he escaped and settled in Moscow. In 1982 Geoffrey Prime, who worked for GCHQ, was found to have been passing information to the KGB, and was jailed for thirty-five years. Two years later, an MI5 man, Michael Bettaney, was sentenced to twenty-three years for passing sensitive material to the Russians. But not every case went the government's way. In 1985, a civil servant, Clive Ponting, was tried on charges of having passed secret information on the Falklands war to a Labour MP. He claimed to have acted in the public interest, and though the judge instructed the jury that the public interest was whatever the government of the day said it was, the jury acquitted Ponting. That was enough to convince those in government that the law inspired by the case of Lieutenant Helm was no longer adequate. The result was the Official Secrets Act of 1989, which specifically precludes a public interest defence.

Fort Widley, meanwhile, went through several transformations, becoming a barracks, and a civil defence headquarters. At one point a modest nuclear bunker to serve the city of Portsmouth was dug out beneath it. Eventually it became what it is now: an indoor equestrian centre, operated by the Peter Ashley Activity Centre, which also runs events at Fort Purbrook. It opens at specified times to visitors, among the most assiduous of whom are students of the paranormal, since the place has a reputation for ghosts. When I went, notebook in hand, like Lieutenant Helm almost a century earlier, to take a snoop around, I was greeted by the caretaker, a man called Len Smith who has looked after Fort Widley for fifteen years. He told me he didn't really believe in ghosts, and yet on various occasions the closed circuit TV (which had helped him spot me) had shown up a figure lurking outside the main gate: a man with a squashy hat and a turned-up collar whom he took to be someone military. Others too had seen this man on the screen, but whenever anyone went out to look for him, no one was there. Also, he said, if a car approached while the man was standing there, he immediately vanished.

But if there's a ghost, who is it? It is tempting to think that it might be Lieutenant Helm. But I think one can say with some confidence that it can't be, since we know that on that fateful excursion in 1910, the lieutenant was wearing a Panama hat.

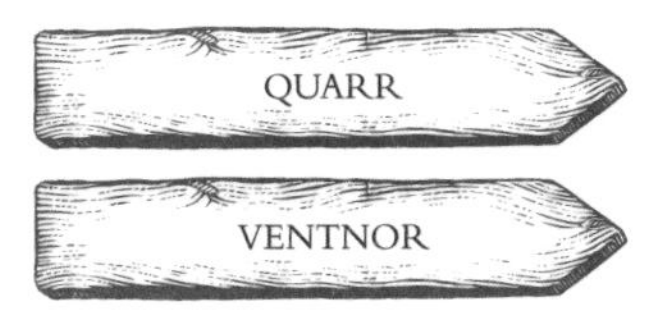

PORT SUNLIGHT

PORT SUNLIGHT, comprising the vil. and soapworks of Unilever Ltd., in bor. of Bebington, 3m. SSE. of Birkenhead, NW. Cheshire…

THOUGH HE WAS ALSO the author of Leverburgh, Lever Park under Rivington Pike in Lancashire, Leverville in the Congo and the Lever Pacific Plantation in the Solomon Islands, the most famous place that William Hesketh Lever, 1st Viscount Leverhulme, created was named not after himself but after his soap. His rise on a tide of soap to his eventual eminence has already been recounted (in Leverburgh), but especially if you have been to Leverburgh, the scene of one of his conspicuous failures, you need to come to Port Sunlight on the Wirral to catch him in the days of his greatest success.

All his landmarks establish Lever as an eminent twentieth-century benevolent despot, but there's no doubting when you look at Port Sunlight the breadth and generosity of his intentions. He had grown up at one of the better addresses in Bolton, but he was always uneasily aware of the squalor in which less fortunate Boltonians were expected to live. It distressed him, not just because he found it indecent, but because he came to believe that a happy, prosperous, well-housed workforce was more likely to be a productive workforce, more likely to honour the values of thrift, self-help and sobriety, less likely to be persuaded – as he knew that the poor and oppressed in some countries had ominously come to believe, that their only hope of salvation lay in revolution. All that is expressed in the homes that he built at Port Sunlight.

Before he came this was marshland, but he could not mistake its potential: a big enough tract of reclaimable land – 56 acres at first, but much more later – waiting to be transformed by the Lever touch. The first sod was cut – his wife Elizabeth, as always, was given that honour – in March 1888. By the following year his factory was complete, and the earliest houses were occupied. Soon a shop was added, and a public hall named after Gladstone, one of his heroes, who came to open it. Port Sunlight made Lever the heir

of Akroyd in Halifax, Salt at Saltaire and Cadbury in Bournville, and the precursor of Ebenezer Howard, who created the most famous of British garden cities at Letchworth in Hertfordshire. Letchworth is devised on a grander scale than Port Sunlight, but the great green swathe at the heart of the place, and the ceremonial boulevard interspersed with monuments which you find at Letchworth, were there in Port Sunlight before. The houses, 900 in all by the time that Lever had finished, though all in the same convention, are pleasingly different. The earliest subscribe to the Arts and Crafts tradition, but essentially the style is English nostalgic, with something of the cosy cottagey roses-around-the-door feel of a painting by Myles Birket Foster. Later the repertoire grew more varied, with hints of Dutch and Flemish creeping into the mix.

Lever's houses were far above the standard which most who worked in comparable jobs anywhere else in the land could have dreamed of, and the rents he charged were affordably pitched at around a fifth to a quarter of average earnings. In many respects Lever was a model employer as well as a model landlord: as a politician – a Liberal MP from 1906 to 1909 – he campaigned for a shortening of the working week; and he defended the role of trade unions, even arguing that a certain amount of industrial unrest was no bad thing, since it showed that a workforce had aspirations. But some found the expectation that those he employed and housed should conform to his will too high a price to pay for the comfort he offered them. 'No man of an independent turn of mind', said one trade union official, 'can breathe for long the atmosphere of Port Sunlight… The profit-sharing system not only enslaves and degrades the workers, it tends to make them servile and sycophantic.'

Port Sunlight had to wait until 1922 for the neo-classical temple which now stands at the head of its central boulevard. The Lady Lever Art Gallery was created nine years after the death of its dedicatee, and it's clear as soon as you enter it that it's his taste, not hers, which is represented here. The rotunda you come to first is a kind of anthology of his enthusiasms. The statues and busts are those of his heroes: Gladstone, John Bright (with the legend below him: 'be just and fear not'), Charles James Fox by Joseph Nollekens, Walter Scott, with his dog Maida, by William Scoular (a classic Tory, Scott – but not all Lever's heroes were Liberals). Napoleon is there in abundance. The emperor Hadrian crops up twice; Caligula is here too, though presumably not to suggest any sense of ideological kinship. Naked ladies with serpents writhing around them seem to have held a special place in his heart. Disconcertingly, one comes at one point across Oliver Cromwell and Charles I displayed on either side of a fireplace.

The pictures, not all of them here when the gallery was established, are a curious blend: some wonderful, quite a few mediocre, some cloyingly sentimental, one or two downright awful. To its credit, the gallery doesn't try to disguise the shortfalls in Lever's taste, and it is entirely clear that some of the magnate's purchases have less to do with aesthetics than with the selling of soap. He bought Reynolds and Romney, Turner and Constable, Alma-Tadema, Holman Hunt, Burne-Jones and Millais, but he also bought *The Wedding Morning*, by John Henry Frederick Bacon, 1892, of which he endearingly said it was only a moderate picture, but very suitable for a soap advertisement.

Millais' *Bubbles*, one of the most celebrated of pictures in this genre, was bought by his rivals Pears, who for promotional purposes had some of their soap smuggled into its foreground. But Lever was just as happy as they were to acquire a picture partly, or even entirely, because of what he took to be its potential for flogging his products. Some artists were surprised to find their work used in this way. A few were driven to protest. W. P. Frith, a painter of some consequence, who created such crowd-packed epics as *Ramsgate Sands*, *Derby Day*, and *The Railway Station*, was displeased to find that a painting which, to point home his moral he had called *Vanitas Vanitatum, Omnia Vanitas* (vanity of vanities, all is vanity) had now been renamed *The New Frock* and equipped with the strikingly different message: 'Sunlight Soap, and so clean.'

But Lever dismissed such quibblings. It was, he said, his property, and so he could do what he liked with it. As it happened, Frith might well have feared something worse: when Bacon's *The Wedding Morning* was used in Lever's advertisements, bars of soap had been painted in at various points in the picture. What a mercy, one thinks wandering around this gallery, that he never had a chance to acquire, and similarly revise and ornament, Botticelli's *The Birth of Venus*, where a bar of Sunlight soap could easily have been introduced into the goddess's hand where now a lock of hair is positioned to preserve her modesty. David's picture of the assassination of Marat might have been equally vulnerable, since that murder took place when Marat was in the bath. Lever's taste, we're assured, improved as he grew older, so when, as he liked to do, he bought whole collections, he didn't prune out the ones that had no commercial potential. But that doesn't detract from the individuality of the collection. The children on my bus out of Leverburgh had talked of being aware of the soap king's presence in their school. That was just how I felt in the Lady Lever gallery.

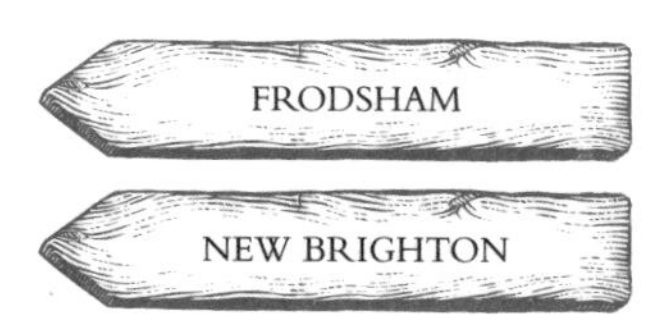

POVERTY BOTTOM

POVERTY BOTTOM, locality, East Sussex,
in Newhaven rural dist.

I CAME TO POVERTY Bottom by way of Terrible Down, which is just outside Halland on a minor road to Lewes. Destitution Road in north-west Scotland, I had already discovered when visiting Ullapool, refers not as I first expected to the mean nature of the territory but to the desperate poverty of the 1840s which the road was built to redeem. Did Poverty Bottom, I wondered, refer to the general indigence of the population in this inconspicuous fold tucked away in the Sussex Downs? Unhappily, the standard authority, *The Place-Names of Sussex* by A. Mawer and F. M. Stenton with J. E. B. Gover, is silent on this point, as is Judith Glover in her *Sussex Place-Names* (1997). Neither recognizes the existence of Poverty Bottom. They do, however, know why the Down got its terrible name; and amazingly, it's a euphemism. The original name – Tordhill or even Turdhill, probably relating to one whose unfortunate name was Robert Atte Turdehelle – implied a place of excrement. That understandably modulated over the years until it arrived at Tyrryble. And then, by the time local people started to write it down, it eased into Terrible.

Judith Glover says there used be local legends relating the name to a particularly dreadful battle, where warriors waded up their knees in the blood of their foes. One theory says that the victims were the straggling survivors of Henry III's defeat by Simon de Montfort at the battle of Lewes. But there's no substantiation for that. In fact, there's very little to Terrible Down: a notice on the side of the road says Terrible Down Farm, and another, just Terrible Down. There's certainly no road sign at either end of the settlement to say: 'Welcome to Terrible Down, please drive slowly through our village, abstaining from wholesale slaughter'. And before you have taken breath you're already in Shortgate. Bartholomew, for the record, doesn't known about Terrible Down, though he does know about Terrible Bay, which is in the south-east of Sark in the Channel Islands.

Happily, when I at last discovered the road to Poverty Bottom, which debouches unheralded from the Newhaven–Seaford road just outside Seaford, I asked a man who was cutting his hedge close to the ancient church of St Andrew, Bishopstone, if he knew where Poverty Bottom was – which he did – and how it might have come by its unprepossessing name – which he did too. 'It's because the ground is so poor,' he said. 'Nothing grows there. There's nothing there but a pumping station'. There was no sign at the end of the lane he had told me to follow to confirm that this was Poverty Bottom, but sure enough the pumping station was there. So, too, were two or three healthy-looking hayricks in a field a stone's throw away. Maybe the productive capacity of Poverty Bottom is not quite as mean as it's painted, any more than there's anything overtly terrible to be found at Terrible Down.

A B C D
E F G H
I J K L
M N O P
Q R S T
U V W XYZ

QUARR ABBEY

QUARR ABBEY, ruined abbey, founded in 1132,
Isle of Wight, on the coast, 1½m. W. of Ryde. Adjacent is Quarr A.
House, occupied by Benedictine monks.

IN FACT THERE ARE two Quarr Abbeys on the north shore of the island. If you take a path that runs west from the parish church at Binstead, you will come to a point where you see them both: the ruins of the old one in front of you, and beyond, above the trees, the imperious tower of the new one. The old abbey, destroyed by one state assault on the monasteries: the new one, strangely enough, born in effect of another.

Quarr began, as its name implies, with a quarry, producing stone of such reputation that Winchester Cathedral, Lewes Priory, Romsey Abbey and Chichester Cathedral all imported it. In the twelfth century, the Norman magnate Baldwin de Redvers, Earl of Devon, brought monks from Savigny in Normandy here to establish an abbey. These were Savignacs, grey monks – not Cistercians, who were white monks; but within a few years the orders had come together. These were turbulent times both for the island and sometimes too for the house. The frequent French assaults on the Isle of Wight forced the abbots of Quarr into the unwanted role of defenders of the island, though defences were sometimes inadequate; one of the worst incursions, in 1377, largely destroyed the town of Newport, now the capital of the island, and obliterated nearby Newtown altogether. Greater calm and stability returned in the following century. Life was still hard, for these were times of poverty for the monastery and indeed for the island, though given the kind of defiantly unascetic practices which developed in some of the richer religious houses, that was perhaps a kind of blessing for Quarr.

That did not save it from Henry VIII's assaults in the mid sixteenth century. The last abbot, William Ripon, did his best to ingratiate himself with Henry and Thomas Cromwell, but in July 1536 the axe fell on Quarr, as it did in time on them all. The offence for which it was condemned was, technically, a failure to show an income of more than £200. The house had not been thriving and in its final days it had only ten monks. The church continued in use for a time, but all the rest of the property was turned over to the Recorder of Southampton, to be dispersed among favoured persons, particularly those in Thomas Cromwell's employment. Some of the local aristocracy were aghast when they learned who was benefiting. 'So now', one complained, 'you may see the great abbey of Quarr, founded by Baldwin of Redvers, come down to the posterity of a merchant of Newport. *O tempora, o mores.*'

Some of the walls remain, and even parts of one of the main monastic buildings, alongside a house whose stone was plainly cannibalized from the abbey. The ruins stand unprotected and unpatrolled, between the track out of Binstead and the sea. Suddenly, as I contemplated these ancient walls, there appeared beyond them, majestic and incongruous, a huge twenty-first-century Isle of Wight ferry, five centuries divorced from this scene, followed by a small boat with two bright red sails.

That was the first Quarr Abbey. The second owed its creation to laws passed by the French after the Revolution, when monasteries were seized and dissolved. In 1833, a man in his late twenties called Dom Prosper Guéranger established a Benedictine community at Solesmes, east of Cambrai, over which he presided for forty years. But such institutions remained subjects of suspicion and hostility, and the passing of the Law of Associations in 1901 made some fear for its future. The abbot installed there in 1890 had already been looking for somewhere safe to transfer to, and he picked out a Palladian mansion called Appuldurcombe on Wight. The house is still there, but a landmine in the Second World War reduced it to a ruin. In Ian Smith's book *Tin Tabernacles* (see Frodsham), there are pictures of the tin church of St Peter and St Paul which the monks put up in woods near the house. As that suggests, Appuldurcombe was never more than a temporary billet. Though the house was offered to them, they could not have afforded to buy it, and they settled instead for a place of their own alongside the ruins of the first Quarr Abbey, around the former home of the Cochrane family, Quarr Abbey House.

The house alone was far too small for the monks' requirements. They would have to create their own buildings within its grounds. That task was entrusted to a monk of the order, Paul Bellot, who had trained as an architect, only to settle instead for the monastic life – possibly, it was suggested, because the girl he wanted to marry had chosen instead to become a Carmelite nun.

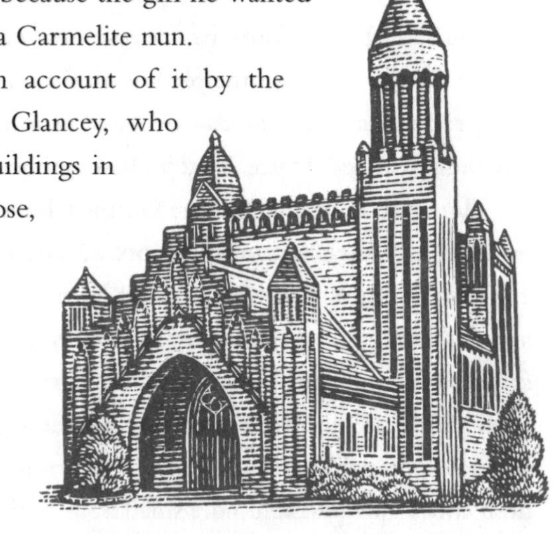

I went to Quarr after reading an account of it by the *Guardian* architectural critic Jonathan Glancey, who called it one of the most remarkable buildings in the country, and added: 'Bellot, I suppose, was the Gaudi of the Isle of Wight.' Those who doubted this, he added provocatively, should go and see it for themselves. With Glancey, as with Ian Nairn (see Bedford) before him, if he orders you to go and look at a building, you'd better go. Bellot had worked in Spain, and his tower is enthrallingly and spectacularly Moorish. But what strikes one first about his interior is its extreme simplicity. Gaudi, in this sense, it quite dramatically isn't. One's surprise is partly the product of years of visiting Catholic churches across the Continent, and being overwhelmed by the richness of their decoration, by their shrines, their icons and their candles and their general attempts to create an aura of sanctity. Here, because it's a monastery, there is nothing of that: just a hugely ingenious, passionate exploitation of brick and the skilful perspectives that come from the juxtaposition of arches as you look up below the high roof towards the altar.

As a visitor you do not get very far into the building. The dimensions of the nave are severely limited, as if to say, you are here to observe, rather than to directly participate. Visitors are encouraged to come to the services that punctuate the monks' day, but their place is at a reverent distance from the bold, high and spacious monks' choir and sanctuary where holy mysteries are proceeded with. We cannot forget we are interlopers.

Bellot's ambitions, his determination to build as no one had quite done before, made his project all the more difficult because the work had to be done by an Isle of Wight workforce with limited experience of his methods and his materials: the hard Belgian bricks they were required to use were the objects of some resentment. He fell out with the contractors and refused to accept the reasons they gave for delays: 'Let me tell you straight', he wrote to them somewhat unmonastically, 'that your talk about bad weather having impeded the progress of the works seems to me to be nothing but blarney.' On 12 October 1912, the day set for the consecration of the high altar, the work was still not quite finished. It was March 1914 before the place was complete as we see it.

Unexpectedly, the community for which it was built only remained for eight years. In 1922 a more accommodating political climate in France made it possible for Quarr's French monks to return to Solesmes, where the buildings they had vacated some twenty years earlier had been preserved. The new abbey survived their departure, at first with a small community of monks who had turned down the chance to go home, and then from 1930 on with English recruits. The new Quarr had even then not yet been granted the status of abbey: in that sense it was only in 1936 that one could validly say that a new abbey now existed alongside the old one. The first English abbot of Quarr took office in the mid 1960s.

Meanwhile money is at last being spent on what's left of the original abbey. There is, by the way, one further unusual feature at Quarr, at the point where the path from Binstead comes to the ruins: a gate where those who have the courage to do so can display any poem they've written, an invitation which, from pensioners through to primary children, is eagerly taken up.

QUEBEC

QUEBEC, vil., in co. and 6m. W. of Durham…

THERE ISN'T MUCH LEFT of Quebec. Quebec, County Durham that is, not its rather larger Canadian counterpart. On one side of the main road through the village there are rows of drab but serviceable cottages, and a pub called the Hamsteels Inn, and at the far end as you come in from Durham, the church of St John the Baptist, Hamsteels – that name again, not Quebec. On the other side, only a few houses remain, set back from the street. There are one or two more on the road that leads south down the hill, past the site where Hamsteels Colliery used to be and on to Esh Winning, another characteristic Durham mining village, whose name simply means a place near Esh where coal was won. Quebec's colliery closed in 1952. 'When it shut', said a man I met who was old enough to remember it happening, 'most of this place went with it. There were a lot of colliery houses down here and when the pit went, that was the end of them too.'

Coal created Quebec, and the end of coal has more or less done for it. But why was it called Quebec? It has never been a substantial place: this isn't one of those cases like Boston or Washington where a great transatlantic community across the Atlantic lifted its name from a rather more modest settlement back in Britain. The fields here were enclosed in 1759, the year in which – in one of the battles which determined the outcome of the Seven Years War – the British captured Quebec from the French in an encounter on the Heights of Abraham which cost both General Wolfe and the French commander, the Marquis de Montcalm, their lives.

In Canada, it's around 500 miles from Quebec City to Toronto. In Durham, Quebec to Toronto is more like 15 miles. Toronto – this name too is a celebration of British armed power – is another old mining village, not far out of Bishop Auckland, which housed the workforce of a colliery mostly known as Newton Cap but sometimes as Toronto. And five miles or so south-west of Quebec is another diminished place – much of it, having no further purpose once the pit had gone out of business, demolished shortly before the Second World War – that takes its name from another famous British victory: Inkerman, where in 1854 the British and French together defeated the Imperial Russian army.

There are names like these all over Durham, most of which are logged and unravelled on an entertaining and erudite website (www.northeastengland.talktalk.net) – some of them chosen by landlords, others by colliery companies, all trying to confect an air of prestige. Durham has no monopoly of such celebrity names, some pre-dating more famous places, others named after them. Bartholomew lists ten Californias, seven New Englands, four New Yorks, three New Zealands, two Floridas and two Marylands, though sadly no Massachusetts, Oklahoma or Texas, and I see there's another Quebec, in Sussex. But Durham seems to have them in greater profusion than anywhere else. There's a Canada – yes, a whole Canada – near Chester-le-Street, a Philadelphia on the A182 near Houghton-le-Spring (where a neighbouring settlement is known as Success) and a Bloemfontein near Stanley, as well as a Vigo in honour of a naval victory of 1702, and a Portobello near Birtley to commemorate a similar triumph nearly forty years later. There's Heights of Alma, near Stanley too, named like Inkerman after a battle in the Crimean War.

Other names here have established themselves almost by accident, sometimes, it seems, even out of the anguish of men who found themselves forced to live there. Pity Me sounds like a cry of despair from people who had to live and work there, and some sources say that's what it is, but it may be a demotic corruption of the somewhat upmarket Petit Mere; just as Bearpark, a few miles east of Quebec, has evolved from the classier Beaurepair. Some think that No Place, between Beamish and Stanley, was what its early inhabitants said about it – no place to live; but it may have developed over the years from Near Place. (When in 1983, the website says, an attempt was made to rename the place Co-operative Villas, people who lived there rebelled.) There is also, according to Victor Watts in his *Dictionary of County Durham Place-Names*, a spot in the county called Seldom Seen, and another called Linger and Die. Dabble Duck, an industrial estate close to Shildon, was once the Dabble Duck Pit, so called because it was so wet to work in.

Henry Thorold, who travelled the county for his *Shell Guide to County Durham*, comes to one of these stricken pit villages, Wheatley Hill, and describes it as 'tragic'. That's too grave a word for Quebec but it's certainly sad. Yet the slow eradication of places like these is also a form of revival. I walked the five miles from here to Inkerman down a pleasant road which took me past the old Cornsay Colliery and the Hedleyhope Fell Nature Reserve before surging exhilaratingly over the top of the moors and easing me down to Inkerman. As I walked the first two or three miles a wind farm whirled away on the hill above me, as if to say, forget your coal and the men who spent their lives deep down in the dark, hacking it out, winning it for you: this is how we get our energy now. No one who has visited sites of great mining disasters such as Senghenydd – the worst of them all, which we will come to soon – can wholly mourn the loss of the mining industry.

Walking through countryside that the loss of the pits has redeemed, one thinks too of the grief that was felt over the blighting of lovely valleys here, in South Wales, in Yorkshire, everywhere where the collieries came, as summed up in the title of Richard Llewellyn's novel *How Green Was My Valley*. Now, on the road from Quebec to Inkerman, the valley is green again.

QUEEN'S PARK

QUEEN'S PARK (West Kilburn), ry. sta., L.M.S. and London Electric, in NW. of London, 1¾m. E. of Willesden Junction.

HERE BARTHOLOMEW HAS BEEN misled. Queen's Park, east of Willesden Junction, is no mere railway station. The station is just an addendum to a fine Victorian estate, built by a company founded by an illiterate man who started his working life as a birdscarer; home for a time to a charismatic Congregationalist minister who, sadly, is now remembered only as the one twentieth-century politician ever to be expelled from the Commons on the grounds of insanity; and the origin of the most famous football club ever to come out of a place called Droop Street.

The estate was the work, and admirable work it was too, of an organization called the Artizans', Labourers' and General Dwellings Company (ALGDC). William Austin, the former birdscarer who began it, had progressed through the ranks of labourers to become a contractor and developer. This was the second of his company's estates – the first, named after Lord Shaftesbury who was the company's president, was established over the water on Battersea Fields. The site picked out for Queen's Park was part of an area then known as Chelsea Detached. Once almost entirely pasture land with a single fine house in the midst of it, it had been enlivened over the past seventy years by the coming of the Grand Union canal, the opening of one of London's great cemeteries, Kensal Green, and the building of the railway out of Paddington.

Here, on 80 acres, the company engaged to build what it called a new city, with homes for 16,000 working people. By then, Austin had gone, forced out by fellow directors. 'I was too honest for them,' he said. And maybe he was; for just as Queen's Park was taking shape, it was found that the company secretary, a man called Swindlehurst, had been living up to the first part of his name by helping himself to some of its money. Along with the company's chairman, Dr John Baxter Langley, he was sentenced in

October 1877 to eighteen months' imprisonment for defrauding the company's shareholders. An estate agent, Edward Saffrey, found to have colluded with them, was jailed for twelve months.

These houses were once disdained. In a book called *Portrait of a London Borough*, published in 1953, Basil Green said of them: 'Interesting examples of Victorian pseudo-Gothic architecture, squat, ugly, and built of greyish-green brick, they are certainly not attractive by modern standards, but the streets are wide and clean…' 'Reeks of Victorian paternalism,' pronounced another disparager. But I think they are wholly delightful. As they had to be, given the clientele the company was hoping to serve, they are modest in size and pretension, and most of them took many years to be parted from outside lavatories, but compared with much of the working-class housing being run up in London at the time, not least in the streets of Kensal New Town nearby, they must have seemed to those who acquired them like little palaces.

Much loving care has gone into their design. Though the style of the streets is consistent, the houses themselves are varied. Patterns are picked out in variegated brick. Some have little peaked hoods over adjoining front doors. Some have fantastical turrets, even mini-towers: the rent fixed for these – topping a sliding scale from 7s 6d a week for a fourth-class house to 11 shillings for a first-class – was 16s. The history of the place is charted in *Artizans and Avenues: A History of the Queen's Park Estate*, by Erica McDonald and David J. Smith, with evocative drawings by Martin Bannon, which I found in the Queen's Park library. It's as much a model for this kind of history as Queen's Park was for this kind of working-class housing, and what follows here is largely based on their account.

The main streets running from north to south, down almost to the Harrow Road were designated avenues: First Avenue in the east through to Sixth in the west, with Fifth and Sixth the longest and grandest. The subordinate streets, mostly east–west, were originally given letters to match these numbers: A Street, B Street and so on. Later they were promoted to fully fledged names of their own, but with initial letters preserved: A became Alperton Street, O, Oliphant, and P, Peach. Some bear famous names like Galton and Huxley; others are more obscure. I assumed that the sadly flat and morose name of Droop must have been picked up from a street name preceding Queen's Park; it seemed somewhat unlikely, for instance, that anyone should have wished to commemorate here the London barrister H. R. Droop, inventor of a method for allotting seats under proportional representation. But no, this Droop was one of two directors of the ALGDC to be honoured in this fashion, and now he's the only one, since the street named after the other has gone.

The company was choosy about who might be permitted to rent its properties and enjoy its library and reading rooms and the public hall that was added in 1882. They wanted to keep it tidy and respectable. Like Titus Salt at Saltaire they enforced the rule: no pubs, no pawnbrokers. No smoking or drinking was permitted in the public hall. They had built for honest, sober and preferably God-fearing working folk, and they seem on the whole to have got what they wanted. The 1881 census found railway porters and clerks, carpenters and plasterers, laundresses and dressmakers living here; later on, postmen and policemen were prevalent. The social reformer Charles Booth, carrying out an audit of London housing, found the inhabitants to be 'keen Congregationalists' who flocked to their chapel to hear the preaching of their minister, Mr Forster. 'The Congregational Church', say McDonald and Smith, 'was so much a focal point of the community that there was a special tram stop outside on Sunday mornings, marked "Tram Stop during Divine Service".'

The chapel's reputation had first been established by Mr Forster's predecessor, the Reverend Charles Leach. Leach was later to move to Bradford in a job swap with Forster, and stood successfully for Parliament as a radical Liberal at Colne Valley in the two elections of 1910. Though by then over seventy, he volunteered to serve as a chaplain at the front in the First World War. What he saw then brought on a breakdown from which he never recovered. In August 1916 the Speaker moved that his seat be forfeited under the terms of the Lunacy (Vacation of Seats) Act 1886 – the only such parliamentary eviction of the century.

The relative serenity of the early days did not last. Contemplating the substandard housing of North Westminster in the 1960s, the council concluded that most of it should be demolished, though it found that the Queen's Park estate was 'a possible exception in some respects', and might be refurbished rather than being razed. In the 1960s and 70s, say McDonald and Smith, the estate 'hit an all-time low'. In 1970, work began on a large contiguous estate, known as the Mozart. The area had existing streets named after both Mozart and Beethoven, and the planners expanded that theme in naming their tower blocks after Tallis, Farnaby, Boyce, Lawes and the lesser known Redford alongside Onslow and Quilter. But the new estate, as it turned out, seemed scarcely to be suffused in the spirit of the English madrigal. In a book called *Utopia on Trial: Vision and Reality in Planned Housing*, the geographer Alice Coleman rated the Mozart among the worst estates in the country for vandalism, graffiti, poor housing and social conditions; and that blight infected Queen's Park, with crime and vandalism proliferating.

Latterly that has altered. Young upwardly mobile couples who would once have aspired to get into some favoured spot like the Brackenbury estate at Hammersmith have discovered Queen's Park and bought improvable houses here. It doesn't seem, to judge from the mixture of faces to be seen in the playground of the school in Droop Street, to have changed the area into a well-to-do, yuppyish, ghetto. But with conservation area status established, and some of the houses, especially the turreted ones, individually listed for protection, and with two-bedroomed apartments on the market for half a million, it looks as though the worst times are over. Whether room remains for the Artizan company's railway porters and clerks, carpenters and plasterers, laundresses and dress-makers, postmen and policemen is another story.

And then there is Droop Street, the southernmost edge of the Queen's Park estate, its south side now occupied by excellent blocks of flats – Yorke, Rosenberg and Mardall – not attempting in any way to mimic what the 1870s built, but honouring its scale and its atmosphere. The school, built in 1875 on the corner of Third Avenue and what had been D Street (now Queen's Park Primary School but at that time the Droop Street Board School) was where Queen's Park Rangers began, as a team of Droop Street Old Boys. The team at that time was called St Jude's, after their headquarters, but in time they merged with a local side called Christchurch Rangers and QPR was born.

They played at the start on a local recreation ground, and through years in the Southern League were peripatetic, shifting from venue to venue, being asked to leave one of them for allegedly lowering the tone of the neighbourhood. They were founder members of the third division in 1920 and eventually settled down at a ground they had taken over from a defunct amateur side at Loftus Road, Shepherd's Bush, though twice flirting with a new address at the old White City athletics ground. They went on to sign glamorous, crowd-pleasing players like Rodney Marsh and Stan Bowles, and in 1992–3, when the premiership competition began, finished fifth, but were relegated three years later and have not been back since.

The young men of Droop Street School who started the club could hardly have envisaged achieving such heights. Even less could they have imagined the clashes which followed the appointment of Gianni Paladini as a director which culminated in the prosecution of seven men for allegedly holding him in the chief executive's office and ordering him at gunpoint to resign. All were acquitted. Soon after, a boardroom coup found him installed as chairman. It has also to be said that having narrowly escaped relegation from the old second division (now the Championship) the previous season, the team were once again struggling in 2007–8, and looked for a time likely candidates for relegation. There seemed to be, let us say, something Droopy about their performances. Then in December 2007 the club was taken over by the family of the billionaire Lakshmi Mittal, rated the fifth richest man in the country, and supporters began to hope that their club might have found its answer to Roman Abramovich, who had spent such vast sums on Chelsea. Would London W12 now begin to see the kind of spectacular signings that London SW6 had grown used to? If that happens, perhaps Rangers should change their name from Queen's Park to Chelsea Detached.

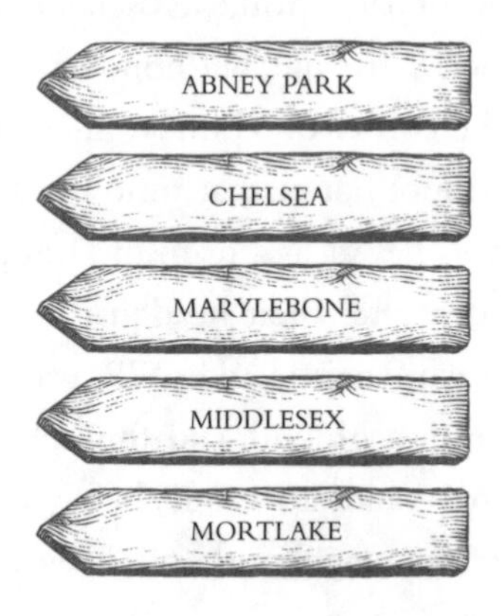

A B C D

E F G H

I J K L

M N O P

Q **R** S T

U V W XYZ

RAMSBOTTOM

RAMSBOTTOM, urb. dist., mfr. town and par., with ry. sta., L.M.S., SE. Lancs, on r. Irwell, 4m. N. of Bury… has paper-mills, calico-printing, cotton, woollen, slipper-mfrs. etc.

AT THE NORTHERNMOST TIP of the Manchester conurbation, at the point where that great urban agglomeration at last gives way to the moors, there's a pleasant and flavoursome little town called Ramsbottom. After the thunder of Manchester, one comes to a place like this, still a town of hill and river, with a sense of liberation. There are high hills above it, crowned with a monument to the great Lancastrian prime minister Robert Peel. Ramsbottom's appears to have been the second dedicated to this statesman, who died after falling from a horse in Hyde Park in 1850. It was beaten by just one day by neighbouring Bury, though that in a sense was just, since Peel was born in Bury, whereas Ramsbottom was merely the place where the family established its cloth-printing business in 1783.

The road that runs through the centre takes you north towards the old mill towns of Blackburn and Burnley, south towards manufacturing Bolton. It meets, at the marketplace, still very much the hub of the town, a road which runs down the hill and over the busy river Irwell. At the foot of this hill is the station, so well preserved and so smartly maintained that old cynics like me may immediately suspect it is in the care not of the grand official railways which like to knock down good stations and replace them with squalid huts, but of a very small one, operated by volunteers. And so it is: this is the old East Lancashire railway, Manchester to Bury, Ramsbottom, Rawtenstall and Bacup, closed to passengers in 1972 and to freight in 1980, but resurrected in 1987 to run from Bury and Ramsbottom to Rawtenstall. Beyond it is a sight to bring joy to the corporate heart of my old friend Bartholomew: a still-working paper mill.

Next to lights, which so gladden his heart whenever he meets one on pier or promontory, few places grab the Bartholomevian imagination quite like a paper mill. His pages are peppered with paper mills. Other mills – cotton, woollen, calico-printing – come and go, but he seems to seize on a paper mill like a dog on a bone. The sector of Lancashire around Bury was specially blessed with paper mills, most of which have now gone, even the famous ones – the East Lancashire, for instance, built in 1860 on a site of 15.5 hectares in Radcliffe, still talking of expansion in the late 1990s, demolished in 2002. In its greatest days, this industry had a workforce of over 100,000, more than 250 mills, and a total annual output of 4 million tonnes. By the end of 2007 only sixty-one mills remained, with a workforce of 12,600. Many have gone out of business, others have merged and been strenuously modernized as the industry found itself eaten away by the competition of cheaper foreign producers.

Little Ramsbottom, though, still has two. One is Stubbins Mill, in the village of Stubbins at the northern end of the town, now operated by Georgia-Pacific BG Ltd. This was once a calico print works, and later the base for a manufacturer of paper window blinds, but the first straightforward paper produced there did not roll out until 1911. The mill at the bottom of Bridge Street, now operated by an owner called Mondi, is a place of greater antiquity, where paper has been produced since 1857. Some of the old plant survives. There's a tall tapering chimney which you see as you come down Bridge Street, which must have been a prominent local landmark for well over a century, and a house which now serves as offices, though the changing nature of paper technology means that some of the other buildings are new. On the other side of the bridge, close to a pub called the Good Samaritan, there's another mill which failed to make the twenty-first century, its windows broken, its former purpose unspecified, a reminder of how many such essential components of industrial Britain now belong only to post-industrial Britain.

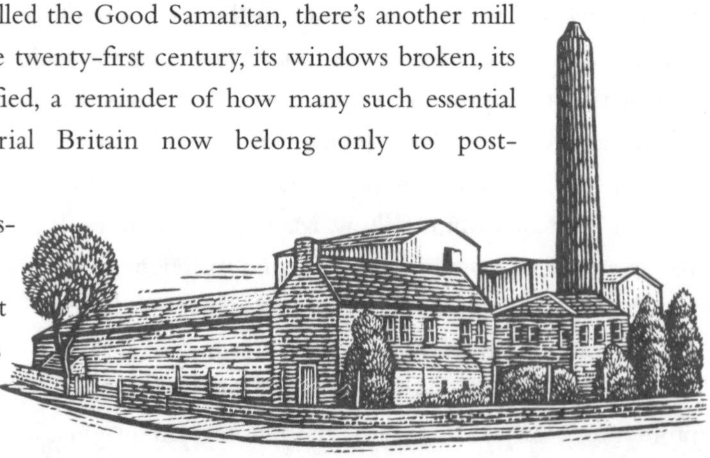

The town of Ramsbottom was shaped not so much by the Peels but by two Scottish brothers called Grant. The house they owned in the marketplace is now a hotel, the Grant Arms. They built a church for Ramsbottom's Scottish Presbyterians, which they later gave to its Anglicans. There used to be a Grant tower as well as a Peel one, but it fell down in the 1940s. It is said – how truly I do not know – that the Cheeryble brothers in Dickens's *Nicholas Nickleby* were modelled on the Grants. If true, that is high praise, for as E. Cobham Brewer (of Edwinstowe) wrote: they are 'the incarnations of all that is warm-hearted, generous, benevolent and kind'. Although I know this is impossible, I used to think that some of the aspects of Josiah Bounderby in the same author's *Hard Times* (though not of course his invented hard childhood) must have been modelled on the mutton-chopped former pedagogue and straight-out-of-the-catalogue right-wing Tory MP Dr Rhodes Boyson; and Boyson, I discovered after my visit, has Ramsbottom connections too, having been a teacher in the town. In a rather wandering Commons debate in March 1994 he gave this rather wandering account of his time there:

> *Sir Rhodes Boyson*: Those pupils, some of whom are still my friends, were the most awkward characters that I had ever met, and their big concern was to get out of school. The headmaster's job was similar to mine – to get them to a technical college three miles away, driving there in the morning, returning in the afternoon. I was allowed a full curriculum, anything that I wanted as long as those pupils did not return to school. They nearly drove me out of teaching. After my first two months I decided that I could not control one of them.
>
> That year the first snow came in November to Ramsbottom, from where Albert came and was eaten by the lion. At that time, his was the only name on the honours board of that school. I had to teach the class in a laboratory and the gas and water taps added to the excitement. I blew the whistle for the class to come in but nobody appeared and when I went out the pupils were pointing not to the Archangel Gabriel, but to the second-floor roof on which was a boy whom I called 'C', and he was the most difficult

> boy in the class. They said, 'What are you going to do about him, sir?' Fortunately I had been trained in the navy and I climbed the drainpipe all the way. This is all public knowledge because I have written it up. I got hold of the boy and brought him down, kicking him as we came. There was no corporal punishment, of course. When we got to the bottom there was a great cheer and the class said, 'Good old sir. That was good, sir.' They ran in like a set of whippets and I had no more trouble with them. One must pay attention to great philosophy, but one must also be sure that one can climb the rigging.

Maybe this was the secret of Dr Boyson's success, such as it was. As I know because I worked there for several years, one certainly hears some peculiar things in the Commons at night. He was wrong about Albert and the lion, though: his surname may have been Ramsbottom, but there's no indication in the sacred text that Albert came from this town of Peel and paper mill.

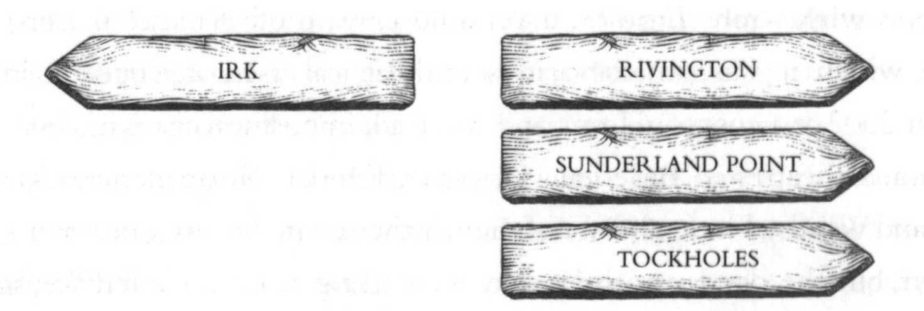

RICHMOND

RICHMOND, mun. bor., par., and mkt.-town, with ry. sta. L.N.E., N.R. Yorks, on r. Swale, 15m. SW. of Darlington… the castle (1071), now a ruin, occupies the summit of a cliff overlooking the river.

RICHMOND, A MILE OR two off the A1 but having nothing in common with the angry urgency of that powerful road, has almost every ingredient that makes a fine county town, except one. There's a big sloping cobbled marketplace with a church in the middle (though most of this church is now a military museum), and an unexplained obelisk, and an eighteenth-century town hall and a nineteenth-century market hall, and alongside the usual Edinburgh Woollen Mills and the rest there are shops with old family names on their façades which you wouldn't see everywhere else. Interspersed with these is the sort of abundant collection of hotels and pubs, great and small, which used to be the essence of market day. Enticing streets radiate off the square in every direction, some formal and stately, others, like Newbiggin, with its good little square and its Unicorn pub and mysterious gates at the end beyond a very odd church, easy and intimate. Presiding over it all is the eleventh-century castle, with a walkway around it from which you look down, a long way down, on the bubbling Swale, which has the town more or less surrounded. There's all the particular drama here that you find in a town full of abrupt changes of level.

Walk a little way out of the centre and fresh pleasures appear. The resurrected Theatre Royal of 1788 was built by Samuel Butler (not the one who wrote *Hudibras* or even the one who wrote *Erewhon*: a versatile crew, these Samuel Butlers). Closed in 1848, after which it was put to various untheatrical uses, it reopened in 1963, was upgraded in 2002 at a cost of £1.6m, and was back in business again in 2003. This Butler also established theatres in Beverley, Harrogate, Kendal, Northallerton, Ripon, Thirsk, Ulverston and Whitby, but few if any of them survive. The theatre offers tours every hour on the hour, but the day I was there they were using it for a conference, so I couldn't get in. There's also a Richmond museum, but that opens only in summer, so I couldn't get into that either. It is close to Frenchgate, just out of the centre, a good serious street climbing a hill, perhaps the best street of the lot.

All this ideal county town lacks is a county. It used to be part of the North Riding of Yorkshire, but it wasn't even the capital (that distinction went to Northallerton). On the other hand, there was Richmondshire – a survival from an age before the county system existed, when a 'shire' meant a sizeable tract with its own institutions. The most famous, apart from this one, among sub-county shires whose names are still in popular currency are Hallamshire in South Yorkshire, and Hexhamshire and Norhamshire (around Norham and Cornhill-on-Tweed), both in Northumberland. Others are still remembered and occasionally used. One was Allertonshire, around Northallerton. Canon Townsend, the Protestant from Durham who went to Rome in the hope of converting the pope, wrote a work called *A Charge to the Clergy of the Peculiar of North Allerton and Allertonshire*, which complained among other things of too much bowing and scraping in services, for which Edward Pusey rebuked him. The name is still much employed in the area: there's an Allertonshire School and an Allertonshire Civic Society. There was also, some sources say, a Riponshire.

On a website maintained by Simon Dew I found a comprehensive list of these old local fiefdoms. In Lancashire, there were Blackburnshire, Leylandshire, West Derbyshire (named from West Derby in Liverpool; nothing to do with the county of Derby), and Salfordshire, which covered much of what is now Greater Manchester. Cornwall had Wivelshire, Triggshire, Powdershire and Pydershire, all of which in the interests of euphony should be swiftly revived. Besides its Norhamshire and its Hexhamshire, Northumbria had an Islandshire, a Bedlingtonshire and a Bamburghshire. Cumbria had Applebyshire and Carlisleshire, and Yorkshire besides its Richmond, Hallam and Allerton, had Howdenshire, Hullshire, Coxwoldshire and Cravenshire. Winchcombeshire, another name that persisted when most of the rest were fading, was partly in Gloucestershire and partly in Worcestershire, which county also harboured a Halfshire.

There were three on the Scottish border: Yetholmshire, Coldinghamshire and one that's a match for those fanciful names in Cornwall: Bunkleshire. Other sources mention a Craikshire, around Crayke, near Easingwold, which was once in Durham but was later transferred to Yorkshire, and a Tynemouthshire. There is also a Wilpshire in Lancashire, near Blackburn, but 'shire' in this case simply meant an estate.

Richmondshire, though, has had a kind of reprieve: created in 1974, the district administration here is called Richmondshire. It commands an exceptionally desirable territory, including much of Swaledale and Wensleydale and such places as Hawes, Leyburn and Reeth. When I was there in 2007, the Richmond constituency had for the best part of twenty years been represented in Parliament by the former Conservative leader, William Hague, who won it in a by-election in 1989 in the final years of Margaret Thatcher, at a time when his party was losing most of the seats it defended. Then he went on wed Ffion and to write a bestselling life of William Pitt. All this and lovely Richmond too: what a fortunate man!

RIVINGTON

RIVINGTON, par. and vil., mid. Lancs… the vil.
overlooks a reservoir of the Liverpoool water supply…
In vicinity is R. Hall, seat. R. Pike, 1,191 ft. high,
now included in a public park.

PANTING AND GASPING FROM the effort of my ascent, I stood at the top of Rivington Pike by the landmark tower and began to note down what I could see. To the east, not a lot: only hills with a line of masts, some barely visible in the mist. To the south, the fanciful roof of the Reebok stadium, home of Bolton Wanderers FC, its pylon-like struts linked by a web which looks as if it was woven by a huge metal spider. The town close below is Horwich, an unfanciful place except that, with the whole world to choose from, it has twin-towned itself with Crowborough, Sussex. To the west, a great expanse of open land, interrupted by urgent roads, their characteristic roarings and screechings mercifully inaudible here. Surprising here at the top of Lancashire to see how green this countryside is, when I'd imagined inspecting a scene most of which had been built over.

And to the north – but at this point a group of men came labouring up the hill, one of them carrying what I thought at first was a small grey poodle unable to manage the gradient, but which proved to be one of those cuddly microphones broadcasters use for interviews. A man with a TV camera joined them. The expert they were planning to interview – for the Manchester Channel, they said – was a regular slogger up to the top of the pike, and while they assembled their gear he told me what I might have been able to see had the weather been kinder. Merseyside to the west, and the sea, and northwards, the Deepdale ground at Preston, where Tom Finney once played, to join Bolton's ground in my collection. A Victorian guidebook I picked up later was even more optimistic about the prospects on a clear day from Rivington Pike: Manchester and Bolton, it said, were hidden by higher ground, but Warrington, St Helens, the glitter of the waters at the mouth of the Mersey, Wigan's ironworks though not Wigan itself, the hills of North Wales 'in dimmest outline', even on an exceptional day the Isle of Man – all were there if you looked for them.

I came to the pike for these views, which I was brought to see as a child. ('Have you been here before?' one of the TV crew asked me. 'Yes, just once,' I said, 'more than 60 years ago.') But here again, as at Leverburgh and Port Sunlight, I found myself in the posthumous presence of William Hesketh Lever, the 1st Viscount Leverhulme. There are gates at the Horwich end of the road to Rivington – Lever Park Road – commemorating his generosity. Having bought the estate, some 2,000 acres of it, complete with Rivington Hall and its two great barns, from a man called John William Crompton in 1899, he gave most of it to the people of Bolton, where he was born, to be their perpetual playground, though reserving a little slice of it for himself.

As ever, he had his way with the place he'd acquired, remodelling the barns, establishing an open-air zoo, and creating beside the reservoirs a model of the ruins of Liverpool Castle. Liverpool Corporation, which against expectations had declined to purchase the land when Crompton put it on the market, soon decided they wanted it after all, to safeguard their reservoirs. The parliamentary committee which examined their demands recognized the importance of protecting the water supply but was anxious to ensure that the people of Bolton should not be deprived of what Lever had promised them. Accordingly, a deal was done under which Liverpool would own the land but would be required to maintain it as a park for Boltonians. Mr Lever (as he still was) should be allowed to keep the bungalow he had built there and the land around it. Some litigation followed before the terms of the deal were settled: it's some indication of the weightiness of these proceedings that Lever was represented by, among others, the future Liberal prime minister, Herbert Asquith, and the corporation by, among others, a future Tory Lord Chancellor, F. E. Smith.

So although the land became Liverpool's, Lever has left his mark on it. On the slope leading up to the pike, he created terraced gardens, with a zigzag path up which he used to encourage perspiring house guests. It's easier, though, if you're making this trip to leave the terrace gardens until later, walking down through them after the pike rather than climbing up through them. I began by walking almost to Rivington Hall, where I took advice from a man with a backpack on his way down. 'I know this may sound ridiculous,' he said, 'but all I can say is, turn right when you get to the hall and just keep going up.' Which I did, taking a cut through the pinetum, and I found the top of the pike with no trouble at all.

The tower at the summit, which is said to contain a single room with a cellar beneath it, was once a favourite place to shelter from the rain and gales but is now too unsafe to be entered. It had nothing to do with Lever. Stern and uncommunicative – there is nothing to tell you why it is there – it was put up by a previous proprietor, a man called John Andrews, in 1733. It used to have this date inscribed on it, but that bit of the building was lost when the tower fell into a dereliction severe enough for Liverpool Corporation to propose its removal. Fortunately such an outcry arose that Liverpool stayed its hand. Some such landmark is always welcome at the end of a stringent climb, since it somehow adds to one's sense of achievement in getting there, and anyway Rivington Pike had long been a cherished feature of the mid-Lancashire skyline; its disappearance would have seemed like the death of a good old friend.

A little below is a tall gaunt building, with something Scottish about it, called the Pigeon Tower, put there in 1910 by Lever. As you descend through his terraces, there are other places, gazebos and loggias, where visitors could sit, recover their breath and admire the view, all now closed because they are dangerous. There's an air of romantic ruin about the place. The terraces are overgrown, and some of the steps uncertain.

The two bungalows that Lever lived in have gone. The first, on 8 July 1913, an evening when the soap king and his wife were out dining with friends (the king and queen, as it happened), was burned down by suffragettes. Lady Lever died just eighteen days later. It was quickly replaced by a second. Both were modest affairs, designed for practical use and the entertainment of friends rather than for the greater glory of Lever. Not that Lever was indifferent to having his doings celebrated. The completion of his plan for the park was marked in 1911 by a feast at Rivington Hall, where toasts to the king, the queen, the Prince of Wales, the royal family generally, and the trade and commerce of Liverpool and Bolton and Birkenhead and Bootle and Chorley were all proposed by Sir W. H. Lever, Bt, leaving the toast to Lever Park to be proposed by T. P. O'Connor, MP.

The appeal of Rivington Pike owes more to nature than to Lever, though as at Port Sunlight, you get a strong sense of him here. Would any twenty-first-century Lever, I wonder, reward his home town in quite the same way? Perhaps the equivalent now would be to buy up the Reebok stadium, and promise the people of Bolton a regular stake in European football, ensured by expensive signings from Real Madrid or Barcelona, exercising their costly skills below its metal mesh and under the benign surveillance of Rivington Pike.

ROTHBURY

ROTHBURY, small town and par., with ry. sta. , L.N.E. (alt. 290 ft.), Northumberland, on r. Coquet, 11m. SW. of Alnwick, and 13m. N. of Scots Gap ry. sta…

WHEN I FIRST SAW Rothbury some time in the 1970s it looked like a place that was having the substance sucked out of it. Not so long before, people in this small market town could have gone to their beds at night happy in the knowledge that much of what happened in Rothbury was determined in Rothbury. It was then, as it had been for almost a century, the headquarters of the Rothbury rural district council, presiding over the fortunes of some 5,000 people scattered across 167,000 acres of a beautiful stretch of Northumberland.

The town had good shopping streets, with recognizably Rothbury names over their doors; a railway station, with several trains a day which would steam you gently to Morpeth, for connections with Newcastle and places of even higher significance; and a racecourse which, while never exactly famous, was a settled name on the racing calendar. It had a choice of hotels, some in the 1950s boasting of their modernity – the Station Hotel could promise its clientele electricity throughout,' cooking by the '"Aga" principle', and 'Vi-Spring mattresses in all rooms' – and a choice of churches, its own cottage hospital, a literary and scientific institute, a police station, and most other accoutrements of a well-appointed, self-contained market town.

But the era of a Ford or Morris outside most front doors, and then of a nightly introduction through television to the joys which existed, the thirsts which might be satisfied, in greater places than this at home and abroad, began to reduce a once independent town to a mere fiefdom. The last train was waved out of Rothbury station in 1952. The racecourse was lost in April 1965 after a life of more than two centuries when the Horserace Betting Levy Board, in London, resolved to discontinue financial support. In April 1974 Rothbury surrendered its independence to a new and mightier

district council based 12 miles away at Alnwick. Some treasured old names had by now disappeared from the main shopping street, and over the years most shops down the hill in Bridge Street have gone. The cottage hospital ceased to offer maternity services or consultant clinics; only convalescent and geriatric care survived.

None of that detracted from Rothbury's natural attractions, however. Whatever else might suffer decline, nothing could spoil its glorious setting beside the sparkling Coquet under the Simonside hills, or the great tract of land to the west that became the Northumberland National Park, or the view of the wooded hills surrounding the fine house at Cragside (*seat of Lord Armstrong*, Bartholomew tells us, *1m. E. Rothbury*), sealing it off to the east. The main street, too, is all the more distinguished because, west of the Newcastle Hotel, it continues its journey on two separate levels: the higher level serving the shops, the lower for the through road, relegating the traffic to the subsidiary status which it deserves. Trees shield the upper carriageway from the lower.

For all that, in the early 1970s, Rothbury had the sense of a place diminished, with no other likely prognosis but further decline. It had owed its best years to Cragside, the creation of the spectacularly rich armaments king, William (later, Lord) Armstrong.

The Armstrongs were an old and unscrupulous border family; as feared as the Grahams, it was said, which was very feared indeed. William Armstrong's forebears would from time to time have ravaged the area. He had come to Rothbury first as a child – a sickly child, for much of the time, happiest perhaps when he could come here to fish. As a rich and lethal manufacturer he took a holiday here (his first for sixteen years) and thought it might make a good place to escape to. The house he built in 1863 was a modest affair, but six years later he called in the celebrated architect Richard Norman Shaw and asked him to expand it.

Shaw was the expert, but Armstrong certainly knew what he wanted and regarded himself, not unreasonably, as Cragside's creator. 'I spent the whole of my spare time', he wrote to a friend, 'planning the transformation of that bleak Northumbrian moor into an earthly paradise. You must admit that I've made it almost as famous as my guns.' The process took fifteen years, and consumed what for almost anyone else would have been a phenomenal sum of money, but the happy (in Armstrong's terms) disposition of nations to go to war would easily pay for that. Technological expertise, the regular practice of devising solutions that had eluded previous engineers, had accounted for his success as a manufacturer. These skills were put to good use at Cragside, which became the first house in England, possibly in the world, to be powered by hydroelectricity.

When I drove into Rothbury at the start of the 1970s the house and its lavish grounds were opened only occasionally. But the family gave up the house in 1972, and in 1977 it passed to the National Trust. Houses like these reflect the nature of those who built them. Cragside reflects very powerfully Armstrong's restless ingenuity and his imperiousness, yet I left it without the sense of closer acquaintance that often comes out of such places. Formidable though he was, you don't get the aura of what he was like which you do with, say, Lever in his art gallery, or with the Boweses in the elegant County Durham chateau that they built at Barnard Castle – now the Bowes Museum.

There's a rather cold portrait of Armstrong by G. F. Watts which greets you in the hall at Cragside, and others beyond by his favourite portraitist Mary Waller which, even more perhaps than the fortune he made out of trading in death, prejudiced me against him. He looks – as he does to some degree in other portraits as well – chillingly like the odious lawyer Tulkinghorn, as played by Charles Dance in the BBC's *Bleak House*.

A genius, one account says of Armstrong: he was generally a mild-mannered man who did not smoke, drank only moderately, and hated swearing; he liked children, but was himself childless; a Liberal who broke with Gladstone over Irish Home Rule and stood as a Liberal Unionist in Newcastle in 1886, but for all his wealth and power was defeated. He was a hard employer, requiring ten hours a day, six days a week from his workers, and opposing legislation to shorten the working day. His domestic staff at Cragside must have had a tough time too. They were spared some standard hardships by his ingenuity – he installed a hydraulic lift in the 1870s to ease the task of bringing coal from the basement up to the second floor – but a notice strictly forbidding either 'thronging' or holding unnecessary conversation in the kitchen suggests something generally sterner.

Some of the pictures that hang on the walls of Cragside are mediocre or worse. The dining room has a huge and ghastly work by one John Robert Dicksee, but it isn't clear that this was one of his purchases rather than a later addition. But perhaps the most astonishing sight in the whole of one's progress through Cragside comes right at the end, in a vast ceramic fireplace by W. R. Lethaby, who I slightly suspect must have been joking. There are six miles of scenic drive, with appropriate stopping places, around the grounds to help you recover if you've found the house as overpowering as I did.

But it's all a big bonus for Rothbury. Few small towns that have suffered, as so many have done, from the steady seeping away of their *raison d'être* have an asset like this on their doorstep. The building of Cragside brought that fresh employment, initially for its construction, then for its services, which most of all made today's Rothbury; and the National Trust, by opening the doors throughout the year to the public, has now done the same all over again. That Rothbury has kept the shops that it has, while new gifts and craft shops and galleries have joined them, that the butcher is offering ostrich, crocodile, kangaroo and wild boar steak, that Tully's of Rothbury trade in 'interesting teas and infusions', that several of the old hotels have survived and new ones have opened up, that one of this latter class, the Tavistock @ The Coquetvale, on the other side of the river, boasts a restaurant called the Italia, must have something to do with the Cragside factor. When Cragside had to be closed for a time in 2007 for refurbishment – ironically, the chief problem was the wretched state of its electrical system: some 30 miles of replacement wiring needed to be installed – it was a sharp though temporary blow to the town.

The presence of Cragside close by might also have been a contributory factor on the great occasion, excitedly reported by the *Northumberland Gazette* when Prince Charles came to Rothbury in November 2006 to unveil a plaque marking the official reopening of its Jubilee Institute. Local people had raised more than £500,000 to renovate the hall, first opened in 1887 to commemorate Queen Victoria's fifty years in the job. He thought it, he said, a remarkable achievement to have brought this marvellous hall back to life. After this he visited Rothbury House, once a distinguished hotel, now headquarters of the Royal Air Force Association, and also the family butcher's that sells ostrich and kangaroo meat. Camilla, the *Gazette* reported, 'looked radiant in a green coat with a patterned scarf'.

None of this is to suggest that Rothbury would be utterly dead without Armstrong and the National Trust. The cottage hospital duly closed, though not until 2007, by which time there was a spanking new one across the river. It still has its own police station. It's a centre of Northumberland culture, with a folk festival every July. The celebrated folk musician Kathryn Tickell, who teaches music here, says the Coquet valley is full of Northumbrian music, and that its musicians not only sustain old traditions but help in a wider sense to preserve its history; they know every field, who farms it and who formerly farmed it, and thus keep alive its connections.

Yet Rothbury's old right to determine how its affairs were run may now be eroded still further. On my way to the town in July 2007 I bought a regional newspaper which reported a decision just taken in London. A review of local government had considered two possible options for the county's future. One, supported by Alnwick district council (the authority responsible for Rothbury since the mid 1970s) and by the three other neighbouring districts of Berwick, Castle Morpeth and Tynedale, advocated two new councils, one for the rural north and west of Northumberland, the other for the urban south-east. That proposal was broadly supported by public opinion: a countywide referendum in 2004 found 56 per cent in favour and 44 per cent against, and a poll by ICM at the end of 2006 suggested that two thirds of Northumberland now supported it. The alternative, backed by the county council, was a single authority controlling the whole of Northumberland: this had the support of a wide swathe of business and industry. The review, the newspaper told me, had not yet settled the matter, but the Secretary of State for Communities was (treasure this choice of word, a favourite of bureaucracies) '*minded*' to approve the single-state solution. Petitions were planned, and the district councils were saying they would go to law to overturn the decision. We shall see.

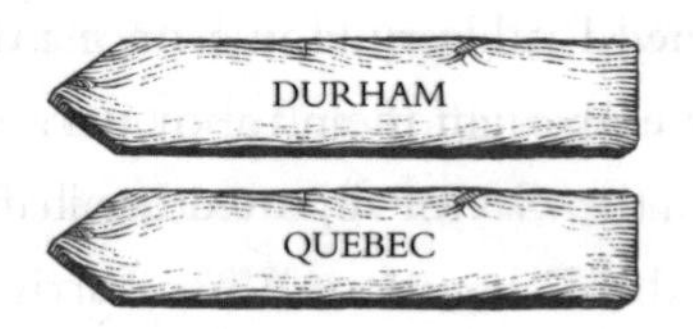

ROTHLEY

ROTHLEY, par. and vil.… Leicestershire…
R. Temple was the birthplace of Lord Macaulay.

IN THE SUMMER OF 2007, the village of Rothley became indelibly famous as the home of Gerry and Kate McCann and their missing daughter Madeleine. But before that its main claim to fame was the one that Bartholomew recognizes. This was birthplace of the unparalleled master of narrative history, by whose standards all subsequent practitioners of the art, through to today's Simon Schamas and David Starkeys, are judged; also a Liberal Member of Parliament, Cabinet Minister – first as Secretary at War and later as Paymaster-General – a member of the Supreme Council of India, a formidable and feared essayist and critic, and a poet whose work thousands of schoolchildren were ordered to learn by heart, and which, to their amazement, they richly enjoyed. The house in which Thomas Babington Macaulay was born – it belonged to his uncle, Thomas Babington, MP – is now a hotel, the Rothley Court, and is better known for its links with the Templars than as the place where that astonishing organ, Macaulay's brain, first woke to the world on 23 October 1800; it is also the place where the cricketer Mike Gatting had a fling with a barmaid which, although he denied what the tabloids claimed, led to his removal from the England captaincy.

The Templars came here in 1231, built a chapel, and made it a major centre of the movement. After the dissolution of the monasteries it became the private chapel of the Babington family, whose monuments are interspersed with those of the Templars. In 1893 the family sold it to some people called Merrtens, who enlarged and improved it. The revival of the Templar connection followed its acquisition by a man called Clive Wormleighton, a senior figure in the order who bought the place in 1959 and turned it into a hotel. The people who run it now are happy to let visitors other than guests look at the chapel. You get to it through a door in the dining room. When I arrived, the room was full of late breakfasters, who endured with stoic restraint my blundering efforts to discover the door, which was lurking behind the Corn Flakes and Weetabix.

You don't get any sense of the great historian here, only of his relatives, and especially Thomas Babington, who was married to Jean, the sister of young Thomas Macaulay's father, Zachary. Babington worked in this house with his old Cambridge friend William Wilberforce on legislation to abolish the slave trade. They were joined in this enterprise by Zachary, who had a particular expertise in this matter, since at one time he had worked as an overseer on a slave plantation, and was later Governor of Sierra Leone, a settlement set up for freed slaves.

That so little is made of the historian is in one sense right. Zachary and Jean often came to stay with her brother, and it was on one of these visits that the future historian was born. But he never lived here: he grew up and remained for much of his life in London, especially Clapham, which in days when telephone numbers included the abbreviated names of exchanges had an exchange named after him: MAC. Anyone in London who dialled 622 was dialling Macaulay.

His exceptional gifts were evident early in life. Both his use of language and his feats of memory were recognized as phenomenal. It was said that when asked at four by a kindly person how he was feeling after coffee had been spilled on his legs, the child replied: 'Thank you, madam, the agony is abated.' He talked very well, but he also talked a very great deal: some despaired of ever interrupting his flow once he was in full spate. He wrote with restless energy and rare fluency on a dizzying array of subjects, with power and authority. He exalted his heroes and damned those whom for various reasons he despised. Being reviewed by Macaulay must for a rotten poet like Robert Montgomery have seemed like a date with a firing squad.

And what he wrote changed opinions. The most famous case is Macaulay's review of a book which Gladstone, then thirty, published in 1839, entitled *The State in its Relations with the Church*. If you want to get a taste of Macaulay as critic and essayist rather than in his most famous role as historian, this is a good place to start. Gladstone was then, as Macaulay calls him, 'the rising hope of those stern and unbending Tories who follow, reluctantly and mutinously, a leader whose experience and eloquence are indispensable to them, but whose cautious temper and moderate opinions they abhor' (he means Robert Peel).

Gladstone's thesis, roughly simplified, was that since religion was the greatest of all human values, its teachings should colour every decision in every other context. Macaulay begins his account with what at first sight might have been taken for courtesy, albeit of a somewhat patronizing variety. But already there's a sting in it. He praises Gladstone's intellect, but regrets that he hasn't here fully employed it. The young man writes as he thinks, with a kind of 'dim magnificence': his language is grave and majestic, yet vague and uncertain. The meat of the question is this: has he proved his case that the propagation of religious truth is one of the principal ends of government?

From this point on, Macaulay takes poor Gladstone to pieces, not only with extraordinary forensic power, but also with scalding wit. It's commonplace to observe that he wrote in magnificent cadences; what's not always recognized is his command of humour and his skill at prising out the logical flaws at the heart of an argument. Here is Gladstone:

> Why, then, we now come to ask, should the governing body in a state profess a religion? First, because it is composed of individual *men*; and they, being appointed to act in a definite moral capacity, must sanctify their acts done in that capacity by the offices of religion; inasmuch as the acts cannot otherwise be acceptable to God, or anything but sinful and punishable in themselves. And whenever we turn our face away from God in our conduct, we are living atheistically... In fulfilment, then, of his obligations as an individual, the statesman must be a worshipping man. But his acts are public – the powers and instruments with which he works are public – acting under and by the authority of the law, he moves at his word ten thousand subject arms; and because such energies are thus essentially public, and wholly out of the range of mere individual agency; they must be sanctified not only by the private personal prayers and piety of those who fill public situations, but also by public acts of the men composing the public body. They must offer prayer and praise in their public and collective character

> – in that character wherein they constitute the organ of the nation, and wield its collective force. Wherever there is a reasoning agency there is a moral duty and responsibility involved in it. The governors are reasoning agents for the nation, in their conjoint acts as such. And therefore there must be attached to this agency, as that without which none of our responsibilities can be met, a religion. And this religion must be that of the conscience of the governor, or none.

In a passage of almost surrealist humour Macaulay explores the implications of what Gladstone has said:

> No combination can be formed for any purpose of mutual help, for trade, for public works, for the relief of the sick or the poor, for the promotion of art or science, unless the members of the combination agree in their theological opinions. Take any such combination at random, the London and Birmingham Railway Company for example, and observe to what consequences Mr. Gladstone's arguments inevitably lead. Why should the Directors of the Railway Company, in their collective capacity, profess a religion? First, because the direction is composed of individual men appointed to act in a definite moral capacity, bound to look carefully to the property, the limbs, and the lives of their fellow-creatures, bound to act diligently for their constituents, bound to govern their servants with humanity and justice, bound to fulfil with fidelity many important contracts. They must, therefore, sanctify their acts by the offices of religion, or these acts will be sinful and punishable in themselves. In fulfilment, then, of his obligations as an individual, the Director of the London and Birmingham Railway Company must be a worshipping man. But his acts are public. He acts for a body. He moves at his word ten

> thousand subject arms. And because these energies are out of the range of his mere individual agency, they must be sanctified by public acts of devotion. The Railway Directors must offer prayer and praise in their public and collective character, in that character wherewith they constitute the organ of the Company, and wield its collective power. Wherever there is a reasoning agency, there is moral responsibility. The Directors are reasoning agents for the Company, and therefore there must be attached to this agency, as that without which none of our responsibilities can be met, a religion. And this religion must be that of the conscience of the Director himself, or none. There must be public worship and a test. No Jew, no Socinian, no Presbyterian, no Catholic, no Quaker, must be permitted to be the organ of the Company, and to wield its collected force.

What a way, as we'd say nowadays, to run a railway! This is ridicule, but justified ridicule, since Gladstone's case is ridiculous. Sometimes in Macaulay there is an unpleasant air of bullying. The formidable intellect marshals a great clunking fist. But Gladstone was certainly shaken by this review, and some biographers claim that his brooding on it began the re-evaluation of his whole philosophical outlook, which led to his abandonment of Conservatism and his conversion to the Liberal Party which one day he would take three times into government.

Even besotted admirers and enjoyers of Macaulay like me must writhe at his imperfections. He could clearly be a very difficult man. He found it tedious to have to listen to lesser opinions. His conversation could be domineering. The celebrated wit Sydney Smith contended that Macaulay had become more agreeable since his spell in India: 'his enemies might have said before (though I never did so) that he talked rather too much; but now he has occasional flashes of silence that make his conversation perfectly delightful'.

He wasn't over-equipped with self-doubt. Lord Melbourne, who made him Secretary at War in 1839, is reputed to have said of him: 'I wish I was as cocksure of anything as Tom Macaulay is of everything' (though it may have been Thomas Carlyle who said it). He was stubborn enough to persist in demonstrable error. He had somehow confused William Penn, the good man who founded Pennsylvania, with a dubious courtier in the reign of James II who was said to have sold prisoners from the Monmouth rebellion to be slaves in the West Indies, and then with a Nevil Penn who was a Jacobite agent. Though friends of Macaulay pleaded with him to re-examine the facts and repent of his error, he resolutely refused to do so. (There is a technical term for this brand of scholarly stubbornness: *mumpsimus* – based on the legend of a priest who persisted in preferring this word to *sumpsimus* ('we have received') in the Mass.)

His view on the politics of his time became encrusted. A champion of the 1832 Reform Act – he had made his parliamentary reputation with a speech commending reform even though the seat he represented would be swept away by it – Macaulay was to be found later in life recoiling in horror from the prospect of a general extension of the franchise: not because he was ill-disposed towards the poor and uneducated, but because he so feared the quality of the government which a universal franchise was likely in his judgement to produce. His views on India, where he worked as an administrator, seem similarly intolerable now: confident as he was that since the Whig revolution of 1688 his own country was a model for the rest of the world, he believed that the best thing that England could do for the people of India was to make them English too.

There were other charges made against him at the time. Matthew Arnold, shaking his wise old head over the *Lays of Ancient Rome*, said that no man who failed to detect 'the ring of false metal' in Macaulay's verse could be considered a competent judge of poetry. But that was part of a wider indictment: Macaulay's deepest fault on Arnold's assessment was his lack of any detectable spirituality. The man was an eloquent philistine.

There's a word not much in use nowadays: rodomontade, which means a kind of bragging or blustering, and here and there even the best of Macaulay has a dangerous hint of it. But read him with the necessary scepticism at the back of your mind and the language will sweep you along and leave you, even if not convinced, still exhilarated. Best to think of him as an incomparable teller of stories, while remembering that as with many great storytellers, not every word of what he is saying is necessarily true.

This man who came out of Rothley was both a great writer and a great man. And although his relationship with the place was intermittent, he liked, his biographer George Otto Trevelyan says, to spend part of the summer and autumn here, 'in the valley that separates the flat unattractive country round Leicester from the wild and beautiful scenery of Charnwood Forest'. 'The stately trees,' he writes, 'the grounds, half park and half meadow; the cattle grazing up to the very windows; the hall, with its stone pavement rather below than above the level of the soil, hung with armour rude and rusty enough to dispel the suspicion of its having passed through a collector's hands; the low ceilings; the dark oak wainscot, carved after primitive designs, that covered every inch of wall in bedroom and corridor; the general air which the whole interior presented of having been put to rights at the date of the Armada and left alone ever since; – all this antiquity contrasted quaintly, but prettily enough, with the youth and gaiety that lit up every corner of the ever-crowded though comfortable mansion…' And certainly, Rothley must have been part of him; for when in 1857 the Queen, on the advice of Lord Palmerston, made him a baron, the title he chose was Baron Macaulay of Rothley.

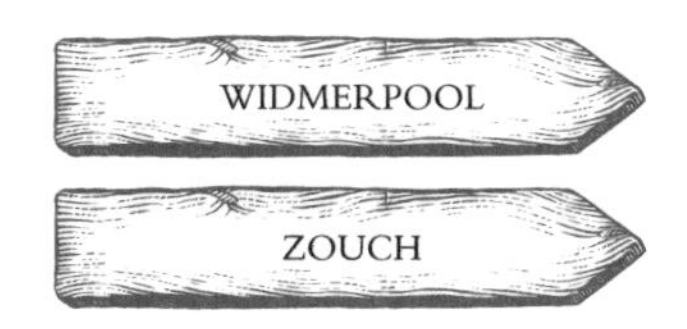

A B C D

E F G H

I J K L

M N O P

Q R **S** T

U V W XYZ

ST ELVIS

ST ELVIS, par., in W. of Pembrokeshire, on N. side of St Bride's Bay, 4m. E. of St. David's; 440 ac., pop.10.

THERE ARE HUNDREDS OF places in Britain named after saints. St John tops the list, with St Mary second and the rest a long way behind. Some of the most famous saints score meagrely – St Matthew is named only three times in Bartholomew, in each case in a Scottish city – while others less often spoken of do very well: why, for instance, are there so many St Leonardses? There seems to be no consistent theme about these attachments. St Helens in Lancashire – a tough and not sensationally beautiful Lancashire town famous for glass and its rugby league team – has little in common with St Helens, Isle of Wight, tidily gathered around its pretty green, with its pub and its cricket pitch and its excellent second-hand bookshop. What's pleasing is the number of saints you have probably never heard of who get their local commemorations: in Cornwall, especially, but far from exclusively. St Decuman, for example, was wholly unknown to me – I have never heard anyone, however old-fashioned, exclaim: 'By St Decuman!' – but he has an ecclesiastical district in Somerset, complete, as Bartholomew characteristically notes, with a paper mill.

St Erney (Cornwall), St Fink (near Blairgowrie), St Fittick (near Aberdeen), St Pinnock (Cornwall again), St Quivox (Ayrshire), St Trillo (near Llandudno), St Veep (yet another in Cornwall) and St Vigean (near Arbroath) all get their moments of glory. There are two St Mungo's (in Dumfries and Glasgow), one of which used to be called Abermilk, and a place in Kent, usually known as Blean, which is officially the parish of St Cosmus and St Damian in the Blean. But perhaps the least expected name on the list is that to be found on the coast of Pembrokeshire: St Elvis.

St Elvis, who flourished, as they say, in the eleventh century, and whose chief distinction seems to have been that he baptized St David, has a Farm on the upland and a Rock on the edge of the sea on the southern side of the harbour at Solva, close to St David's, overlooking St Bride's Bay. Boats once set out for this harbour bearing people who hoped to make new and more prosperous lives in America. Fishing persists, but most of the boats in the harbour now are there for pleasure. It's a great place for walking in all directions. There used to be a church on St Elvis's hillside, dedicated not to him but to St Teilo, another one who doesn't often get mentioned, but that fell down long ago. There is also a cromlech here, a place of pagan burial preceding even St Elvis.

Surely nobody, you might suppose, would think there was any connection between St Elvis the eleventh-century saint, and the man who gave the world 'Blue Suede Shoes' and 'Jailhouse Rock'. That is where you'd be wrong. It is held by some people in Wales that Elvis was Welsh. Start with his name. 'Elvis' is the name of this Pembrokeshire saint (though in fact the saint himself appears to have been Irish); and Presley – could not that derive from the Preseli hills in this county? The 'King' had a father called Vernon (a Welsh name) and a mother called Gladys, and you can't get much Welsher than Gladys. His twin who died had the very Welsh middle name, Garon. There are even those who think they were linked in sainthood. True, the appellation sometimes given to modern Elvis – St Elvis – is usually joky. But claims been made of miracles occurring at Graceland. I have also discovered an account of a paper by a learned professor who argued that Elvis, like Princess Diana, was a kind of secular saint, feeding in an irreligious age much the same passions as religious saints once inspired; filling, as you might say, a saint-sized hole in our psyches. People today have their favourite rock stars, whom they venerate and even set up shrines to much as those of earlier days did with St Christopher or St Catherine.

It may be that this eagerness to claim modern Elvis for Wales is retaliation against Scotland, where it's been argued that his family was inherently Scottish. It's surprising though, when, thirty years after his death, the cult of Elvis shows no sign of fading, that this spot in beautiful Pembrokeshire seems not to have attracted the faithful in any great numbers. It is good to see unsullied places like this left unexploited. Even so, if I were the Pembrokeshire tourist board, I'd think it was worth a punt.

ST MARYCHURCH

ST MARY CHURCH, town and par., Devon, on Babbicombe Bay, in mun. bor., Torquay…

ON A ROAD, MANOR Road, south-west out of St Marychurch, now part of the sprawl of Torbay, is a house which has known much misery. Today it is Sandhurst Court, transformed from a hotel into a residential home, and so augmented over the years that one can only just discern the house that was there originally, in the days of the misery. It was then plain Sandhurst, the home of the very distinguished naturalist Philip Gosse, and his motherless son, Edmund. *Father and Son*, Edmund's account of his tense and troubled relationship with his father – 'the record of a struggle between two temperaments, two consciences and almost two epochs', which came out in 1907, a century or so before Dave Eggers and others made stories of miserable childhoods the vogue subdivision of publishing they are today – is one of the most haunting and painful books of Edwardian England; and yet, not quite what it seems.

Gosse the father was by inclination and training a scientist; but also a religious fundamentalist, adhering to a tendency almost more austere than the rigorously self-denying sect known as the Plymouth Brethren. His wife Emily, a writer of religious tracts, was hardly less dauntingly committed than he was. Even so, she was a comforting presence to Edmund until, in the spring of 1856, when he was six, he overheard a whispered conversation between his parents and knew that something dreadful had happened. She had cancer. Her treatment at the hands of a dubious experimenter called Dr Fell did her no good and inflicted great suffering, which she bore with a fortitude that came of knowing that what had overtaken her must be God's will. She died at home in Islington in February 1857, and was buried in Abney Park cemetery.

Thus Edmund, as he recounts in *Father and Son*, was left in the sole care of his affectionate and well-intentioned, but stern, dogmatic and sometimes tyrannical father.

Seven months after Emily's death, Philip, as if on an impulse (though of course he prayed about it too) took a house on the Devon coast, the place where he was happiest, or at least most himself. In those days, much of this coast was still wild and a wonderful spot for both Philip and Edmund to explore and collect specimens.

Edmund Gosse wrote in *Father and Son*:

> Half a century ago, in many parts of Devonshire and Cornwall, where the limestone at the water's edge is wrought into crevices and hollows, the tide-line was, like Keats' Grecian vase, 'a still unravished bride of quietness'… All this is long over, and done with… The fairy paradise has been violated, the exquisite product of centuries of natural selection has been crushed under the rough paw of well-meaning, idle-minded curiosity. That my Father, himself so reverent, so conservative, had by the popularity of his books acquired the direct responsibility for a calamity that he had never anticipated became clear enough to himself and cost him great chagrin. No one will see again on the shore of England what I saw in my early childhood, the submarine vision of dark rocks, speckled and starred with an infinite variety of colour, and streamed over by silken flags of royal crimson and purple…

The once pleasant walks along the cliff top at Oddicombe had been extinguished too:

> In these twentieth-century days, a careful municipality has studded the down with rustic seats and has shut its dangers out with railings, has cut a winding carriage-drive round the curves of the cove down to the shore, and has planted sausage-laurels at intervals in clearings made for that aesthetic purpose. When I last saw the place, thus smartened and secured, with its hair in curl-papers and its feet in patent-leathers, I turned from it in anger and disgust, and

> could almost have wept... What man could do to make wild beauty ineffectual, tame and empty, has been amply performed at Oddicombe.

What he found on his return to St Marychurch village, with its narrow pavements and its shop windows full of trifles, was scarcely more acceptable. But at least The Room had gone. The Room was the meeting place where, very soon after he reached St Marychurch, Philip Gosse began to preside, Edmund unwillingly accompanying him. Here he preached to what Edmund Gosse's biographer, Ann Thwaite, describes as a group of simple, rustic souls with no formal adherence to any national religious body. He does not seem to have gone back to look at the house, though that would have been full of bad memories too: his failure to please his father, however much he might try; his grievous sense of inadequacy; his awareness that pleasures which others enjoyed were denied to him (Christmas pudding was banned from the house as 'idolatrous confectionery', though servants were allowed it, and fed him some surreptitiously). The house at St Marychurch in these pages is from the start a kind of prison, which soon becomes worse, in that what his father had expected to be the culmination of his life's work proved to be a disaster.

Like so many with one foot in science and one in religion, Philip Gosse was deeply distressed by the teachings of Darwin. How could it be – surely, it could not be – that the sort of evidence that he, as a scientist, diligently collected was being used to disprove what the Bible taught? At about the time he and his son moved to Devon, Philip Gosse was completing a work which he hoped would put all such conflict to rest by reconciling the teachings of both. The book that would work this miracle was called *Omphalos* – a word meaning the navel; a stone at Delphi called Omphalos was believed to mark the centre of the world. Edmund Gosse sums up his father's thesis like this: 'It was, very briefly, that there had been no gradual modification of the surface of the earth, or slow development of organic forms, but that when the catastrophic act of creation took place, the world presented, instantly, the structural appearance of a planet on which life had long existed.' A hasty press and public assumed that what Gosse was saying was essentially: God made the fossils as fossils.

'Never', says the son, 'was a book cast upon the waters with greater anticipation of success than was this curious, this obstinate, this fanatical volume.' Yet in the event, Christians mocked it no less than atheists. Even friends and admirers were sharply critical. Charles Kingsley said it had made him doubt the very Creation. The lonely widower had nowhere to turn for immediate consolation. Even God could not heal this wound. Sometimes Philip was angry with God; but sometimes he saw it as merited punishment, though for what he could not be sure. 'It was *Omphalos* as much as Emily's death', says Ann Thwaite, 'that hardened Philip's heart and drove him into rigid patterns of fanaticism and fear.' The tensions between father and son sometimes developed now into confrontations: the older man's implacable will and certainty challenged by a son who wanted the liberation of being allowed to think for himself.

I walked up the main street of St Marychurch, Fore Street, which climbs the hill to an Anglican church with a Roman Catholic church at its shoulder, wondering what father and son would make of it now. The church of St Mary the Virgin was advertising Toddler Time and a Sunday Club to which children of any age could come for fun, games, crafts, music and worship. An institution called Funky Fridays offered, for 50p, music, games, fun, sport, and 'woteva u want'. For those over ten, something called Rafters offered 'a look at the world and what's happening in it'. How Philip Gosse would have recoiled: not least when he saw that worship came last in the list of attractions offered at the Sunday Club. And the Fore Street shops – where there's plenty of room nowadays to stop and look at the windows, since, with the traffic exiled, the narrow pavements of which Edmund complained are no longer a hazard – are full of what Philip Gosse would have seen as appeals to base and unworthy desires.

And then, in one of the windows, I saw a yacht. The image from *Father and Son* that for years had lodged in my mind, seeming to capture the turning point in Edmund's childhood, his first taste of freedom, was a yacht in a Fore Street window. I remembered how the boy, passing the window often, began to covet the yacht, and finally mustered the courage to tell his father he wanted it; how his father rebukefully told him that what he should seek in life was not what he selfishly wanted, but what God wanted for him; how he told him to pray to God for guidance in this matter; and how the boy a day or so later came to his father and said: 'God wants me to have the yacht.' How that night, the boy locked the door of his bedroom to keep his father away. Here in this window was just such a yacht, with three masts and twenty-two sails, possibly even grander than the one which had drawn young Edmund. And the name of the shop which offered this huge temptation was one that would have confirmed every fear and prejudice in the heart and mind of the father: Sheer Indulgence.

Yet when I went back to the book, I could not find the yacht or the prayer or the subsequent purchase. This irresistible, climactic image belongs not to the book but to a television version by Dennis Potter. What Potter had done was to take one of the crucial events in the father and son relationship and transmute it. In the book, the boy wants to go to a party at the Browns, and his father says they must pray together and lay the matter before the Lord. 'As I knelt, feeling very small, by the immense bulk of my Father, there gushed through my veins like a wine', Edmund recalls fifty years later, 'a determination to rebel.' In the book, the prayers being completed, his father asks with smiling confidence what ruling the Lord has given and Edmund replies: 'The Lord says I may go the Browns.' Certainly this incident was a turning point. But there wasn't a yacht.

What right, I stormed to myself, had Dennis Potter, master of his craft though he was, to interpose himself between me and Gosse's account? Yet *Father and Son*, as I say, is not quite what it seems. Originally, Edmund had published a reverent account of his father, revealing little of their difficult relationship. Publishers urged him to revisit the territory and dwell more on himself and his memories of his childhood. *Father and Son*, the most successful book of his life, was the result. But there's little doubt that he embroidered it, and inflated his sufferings; no doubt in the hope of greater enrichment some of the present-day laureates of childhood agony mix fact and fiction too. As Ann Thwaite establishes in her biography, all Gosse's books were blighted by errors; a critic called John Churton Collins devoted himself to tracing and exposing them on a scale which seriously dented the writer's reputation. But what we see in *Father and Son* is less carelessness than confection. His claim in the Preface that it truly reflects what occurred is plainly unsound. Indeed, Thwaite suggested, in a piece she wrote to mark the centenary of *Father and Son*, that a bookshop which classified it under fiction was not so wide of the mark.

Perhaps we ought not to worry too much when dividing lines such as these are crossed. I've seen Orwell's *Down and Out in Paris and London* and *The Road to Wigan Pier*, parts of which are confected too, on the fiction shelves in big bookshops. Works of such power and insight ought to be read, however much the sometimes flat truth of events are improved on. If that's the licence we gladly extend to Orwell, we should also extend it to Gosse; and, however much he filled me with false delight at finding the yacht in the window of Sheer Indulgence, to Potter as well.

SANDTOFT

SANDTOFT, ham., Lincolnshire, 3½m. NW. of Epworth.
S. Grove and S. Grange are seats.

IN A FIELD NOT far from a motorway in northernmost Lincolnshire a stately vehicle makes its slow, majestic way around a circuit. Children, and not only children, watch it with curiosity, having never seen one before. For while buses persist, and trams are resurrected, the trolleybus, once hailed as the super-conveyance of the future, destined to sweep away the obsolete tram, has perished almost as if it had never been.

The trolleybus was a kind of free-range tram. Like the tram, it needed overhead wires, but it did not require the predestined grooves of a tramway. It could veer about from side to side of the carriageway. It could even, in its stately way, swerve. You will never see one plying its trade on the road nowadays. They cannot, unlike ancient buses, be wheeled out for exhibition days because they depend on overhead power. Yet in one barely accessible spot in Lincolnshire – there is no public transport, though sometimes on open days you can get there by special bus from Doncaster – you may still taste the delights of trolleybus travel.

Most of them stand day by day, motionless in their distinctive liveries, in sheds. There's the blue of Bradford, whose coat of arms bears the motto: *Labor omnia vincit*: work conquers all, and the yellow of Bournemouth (*Pulchritudo et salubritas*), easily outshining the dingy yellow-brown of Maidstone; and the orange and green of a Glasgow trolleybus whose destination blind says it is heading for Clarkston, and the blue and cream of Rotherham, where the trolleybuses had double backwheels, and the post-war green of Cardiff, which, as you can see from another exhibit, used grey through the Second World War. Also, in particular profusion here, the dark red of Reading, very much a trolleybus town.

The occasional foreigner has been admitted, too: a dishy French number, blue and

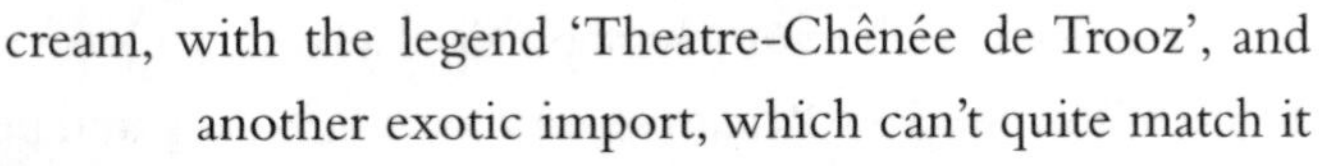

cream, with the legend 'Theatre-Chênée de Trooz', and another exotic import, which can't quite match it for looks, from Porto. Across the circuit they've re-created the trolleybus age with simulated shops of those days, their windows packed with nostalgic mementoes at even more nostalgic prices. Quite a serious camera for 52s 6d, which is £2.62 in present-day money. A typewriter for £7.10s (what a thrill it was to own a typewriter in those trolleybus times, before word processors were dreamed of). A Kenneth McKellar record (remember records?). In Dorothy's Toyshop, a *Bimbo Annual* for 1968, and a penguin driving a railway train, and a tortoise leading a string of minor tortoises. The café is full of mementoes of times when the trolleybus was a fact of everyday life. The inventor of the trolleybus is properly honoured: Ernst Werner von Siemens, who started operations in Charlottenburg, Berlin, in 1882; though his notion must have taken some while to catch on since elsewhere we are told that the first commercial service was opened in Dresden in 1901 – it ran a distance of just four kilometres and closed a mere three years later.

Never mind: other later routes achieved much greater longevity. Here are some of them now, sailing around the Sandtoft circuit. As you watch them, they seem to be gliding, though when you're aboard they are bumpy, and you have to wait now and then while the overhead points are adjusted to let you proceed. They give you an old penny as you come in through the gates, which will pay for one journey. The choice on the day I was there was between a Maidstone trolleybus heading for Loose, a red London Transport item which claimed on the front to be a 604 Kingston–Malden–Wimbledon, though the destination blind on the back said something quite different, and a route 24 from Bradford to Crossflatts, just outside Bingley, which I chose to remember old times. Bradford, which has a fine contingent of hills, was a trolleybus town, while neighbouring Leeds stuck to its trams. It travelled now on the plain, with a kind of bumpy serenity.

There's a fascinating chart on display which plots the trolleybus populations of a string of towns across Britain – some starting slowly and building up a steady collection; others, like Leeds, flirting briefly and dropping out. In 1927, Bradford had nineteen of these creatures and Leeds fourteen. Twelve years later, the year of the war, Bradford had 135 and Leeds none. By 1953, Bradford's total was 204, a figure matched by Newcastle, with Manchester, Wolverhampton and Nottingham catching up fast. Such population explosions in the trolleybus community often reflected the scrapping of trams, as in Cardiff, which paraded its very first trolley in March 1942 for the run between Wood Street and Clarence Road.

The lifespan of the trolleybus – the time between the trolleybus as the gleaming future and the trolleybus as the archaic past – was quite brief. Soon, like the final tram, the final trolleybus was being dressed up for its ultimate journey. The last one in London, advertising Ronuk, and Grey's cigarettes, ran out of Fulwell depot in March 1962. The ceremonial tour which closed down the service in Nottingham was staged in 1966, failing by just a year to reach the fortieth anniversary of the first one. Bradford persisted until 1972. Yet that ancient survival the tram continued to run for many years afterwards on the sea front at Blackpool, and in time new tramway services were being invented. 'Whatever is this?' death-doomed trolleybuses must have said to themselves. 'It must be the dinosaur making a comeback.'

One thing you discover at Sandtoft is that there are still trolleybus people, true believers, who have not yet abandoned hope that the trolley will rise again. It may, they will tell you, have vanished in Britain, but enlightened authorities elsewhere in the world have these things in better perspective. Why, Rome has rechargeable trolleybuses which don't depend on overhead wires (though those sound like electric buses to me: the whole point about the trolleybus was that it needed a 'trolley', a term that derived from the interaction of a trolley-wheel with overhead wires). Quito, a friend who has been there tells me, has a smart new trolleybus fleet.

Aficionados simply can't understand why the case for the trolleybus commands so little attention in Britain. There's another exhibit at Sandtoft designed to demonstrate public acclaim for trolleybus travel: a petition drawn up in Marseilles headed: 'Moi, je préfère le trolleybus', saluting its power, its economy, the silence in which it progresses, its comfort, its longevity, and what we'd now call its greenness. Letters appear now and then in the *Daily Telegraph*, making the case for the trolleybus to return. 'Ken Livingstone's Transport for London', one such letter complained, 'resolutely shows indifference to trolleybuses, opting instead for environmental tokenism by experimenting with unproven technology, such as fuel-cell buses.' 'The truth is out,' crowed another. 'Too many of Britain's new tram schemes have proved to be expensive ways of moving less than expected numbers of people… The only advantage the tram has over improved buses is that it is electrically propelled. But an improved bus service could be worked by electric trolleybuses for a similar overall cost to diesel.' True, both these letters came from Irvine Bell, of Lytham St Anne's; but Sandtoft, where, on the day I visited, there seemed to be more devoted believers present than casual visitors, shows that Bell is by no means the only one who wants to ring out that message.

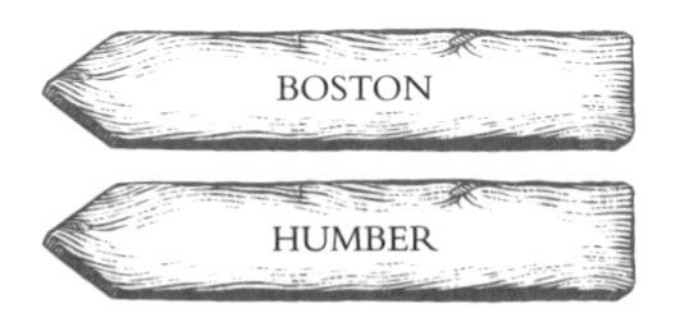

SENGHENYDD

SENGHENYDD, vil., E. Glamorganshire,
11m. NNW. Cardiff…

DRIVING NORTH OUT OF Cardiff on my way to Pontlottyn, I saw a sign pointing to Senghenydd. An old memory stirred. Something very important had happened there, something very terrible, something on the scale of great British disasters comparable with Aberfan in 1966. But what? I turned off my road and went into the village to ask. It's a characteristic pit village: long stone terraces, their windows picked out in red. I stopped at a shop called Cavanna's in the main street, Commercial Street, where the family that runs it found me an album they had compiled, which told the story of what had occurred in Senghenydd – not once, as they explained to me, but twice.

On 14 October 1913, at ten past eight in the morning, the peace of this valley west of Caerphilly was shattered by two huge explosions, loud enough to be heard in Cardiff. People in Senghenydd understood at once where it had happened: at the Universal Colliery. They guessed too what it meant. Some had been there twelve years earlier, when at 5 a.m. on 24 May 1901, 'an awesome report' was heard; a 'roaring cloud of dust and smoke' billowed over the colliery, and the pit stage was blown up into the air. Eighty-one men on the night shift had been trapped by the explosion: just one was rescued and sixty-three of the dead came from the village.

This was not the greatest disaster this sector of Wales had suffered: in 1894, 290 had died at the Albion colliery in Cilfynydd, a couple of miles away on the other side of the mountain. Yet in May 1901, fifty-four wives were widowed; more than 200 children lost their fathers. The colliery magnate Sir William Thomas Lewis, who had left school at thirteen, worked his way up through the industry, and set up the Universal Steam Coal Company to exploit the Senghenydd seams, and who was already hated in these valleys for his tyrannical rule and hostility to the unions, was in France when it happened. He declined to cut short his holiday but asked for progress reports every four hours. What had earned him his knighthood was his service on a Royal Commission on safety in the mines.

The report of an official inquiry – disputed by the coal-owners – found that the violent force of the explosion was attributable to trails of coal dust that had fallen from overloaded and inadequate wagons. But the company had not breached any statutory duty and there was no prosecution. Senghenydd, or at least its survivors, went back to work. The Universal Colliery was the essence of Senghenydd. There had been little here before its creation. Until the railway that was needed to service the mine came here in 1894, it lacked, like Ponlottyn, even a name. Senghenydd, unearthed from history books, was chosen, of course, by Lewis.

And then, in 1913, another, graver disaster overwhelmed it. The workforce had expanded since 1901 and the population of the village with it, from about 3,000 in 1901 to some 6,000 now. 'How the poor live', said the local medical officer of health after an inspection in 1904, 'is a puzzling question, and how these people can live in these dark dismal chambers where scarcely a glean [sic] of sunshine enters the precincts is a mystery.' The answer, of course, was that they lived as they did because there was no other choice.

This time the day shift was in progress: 945 men were underground in the two pits that made up the colliery. It took months for the bodies to be recovered, and some were never identified. But the final count showed that 440 men had died – 439 of them miners, the other, one of the rescuers. This was the worst disaster on land in the history of the pits. Four of the victims were in their sixties; one was seventy-two. Eleven were sixteen, four were fifteen and eight were only fourteen years old. More than 300 came from the village, and most of the rest lived close by in the valley. More than 200 women were widowed. One household lost three sons. Forty-six families lost more than one member. A boy called David Jones lost his father, grandfather, two brothers, two brothers-in-law and two uncles. A father died clasping the hand of his dying fourteen-year-old son with the body of another son, aged sixteen, a few yards away. The families of those who had died faced a future of poverty. As ever on these occasions, there were stories of lucky escapes. Miners who were members of the

Salvation Army band had swapped shifts because of a concert: they survived to play at the funerals of their comrades.

Sir William Thomas Lewis had grown even greater and grander over these twelve years. He was now Lord Merthyr of Senghenydd. At the time of the second disaster he was in Scotland, but this time he came. The king said he would have come too, but for the wedding of Prince Arthur of Connaught to the Duchess of Fife. Their wedding presents were put on show and the proceeds sent to Senghenydd. But the Home Secretary came, on the king's instructions, and the Labour politician Keir Hardie arrived too and said the disaster would not have occurred had the Coal Mines Regulation Act of 1908 been observed.

On the main weekend of the funerals – though it took six weeks before all the dead were buried – the valley was said to be inundated by a flood of mournful black. Some 15,000 people gathered at the pithead. After two months of pressure, the Home Office ordered an official inquiry, which found, as most in Senghenydd expected, that – just as had been the case twelve years before – the explosion had been magnified because of trails of coal dust that should have been eliminated or dampened.

What followed dismayed and disgusted not only the miners and their union but the mining inspectorate too. The manager of the colliery was tried on seventeen charges, acquitted on nine, and fined £25 for the rest. Magistrates in Caerphilly threw out all the charges against the company, but on being told to convict by the King's Bench in London, fined it £25. William Hyatt, who survived – and never again worked underground, becoming instead a pawnbroker's assistant before signing up for the First World War – recalled that his father had said there was always more fuss if a horse was killed underground than if a man was killed. Men came cheap; the company had to buy horses.

For a time the Senghenydd disaster was an event of national moment, but its notoriety quickly faded. The huge slaughter of the First World War must have made the loss of 440 lives seem a relatively minor affair; unless you lived in Senghenydd where almost every name on the list of the dead came, if not from your own household, then from a family you knew or knew about. Yet even in the village there was until quite recently no official list of the names of the dead. No memorial was erected until 1981, when the old pit wheel was set up, with a memorial plaque, beside the school that now occupies the site of the colliery.

Two books tell the story: one a chronicle of the village's history by a one-time local headmaster, J. Basil Phillips, and a book more directly concerned with the two disasters, and listing the victims – *The Valley of the Shadow*, by John H. Brown. Neither is now in print. In the community centre, I met Henry Evans, eighty-five years old, a miner and the son of a miner, who was lovingly superintending a small crop of exhibits: much more could be done, he told me, were there money to pay for it.

The Universal Colliery closed, very suddenly, in 1928. When the men turned up for work they were told: 'Get down the pit. Get your tools. You're finished.' Some went to work at the Windsor Colliery down the road, which over the years has had its fatal accidents too, though never on the scale of Senghenydd. Its victims have been commemorated only recently with a memorial behind the Windsor Hotel. Lord Merthyr died the following year. It was said, and was no doubt true, that the tragedy at the Universal had been a heavy grief to him. After years of deterioration the remains of the Universal Colliery were declared to be dangerous and blown up by the Royal Engineers.

Today there are no deep-pit coal mines left in Wales. Many old miners mourn the loss of their industry: many fought hard, bitterly and largely in vain, to save it. But Henry Evans, acquainted as few are today with the griefs of Senghenydd, talked of its going with something close to delight.

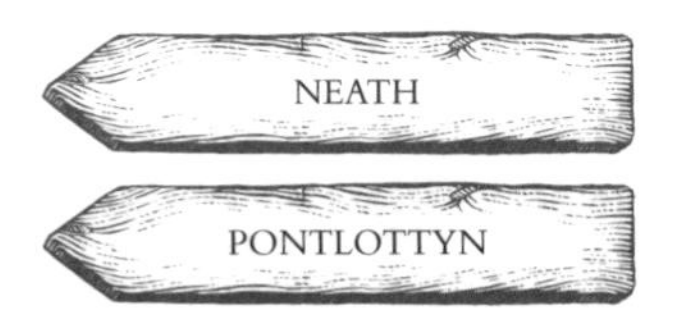

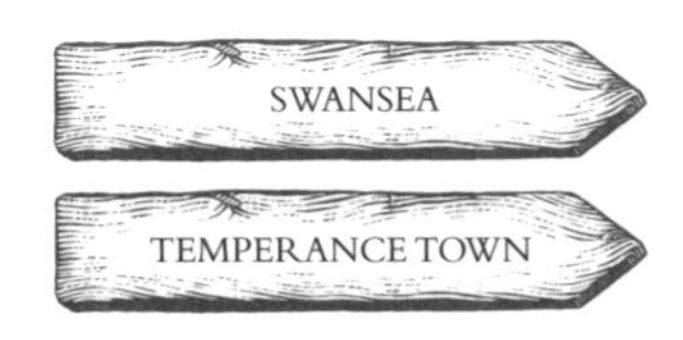

SHIPDEN

SHIPDEN, submerged town in Cromer Bay, Norfolk.
Was destroyed in the reign of Henry IV.

SOME OF THE PLACES Bartholomew lists are a struggle to get to: Hawker's Morwenstow, or Cape Wrath. Others, like Tottington in the war zone of Norfolk, can be entered only with written permission. But on p. 616 of his book he's inserted a place that no one has been able to visit for something like 700 years. People sometimes say it's still there and you'd see it if only the waters could be persuaded to part. A steamer is reputed to have struck the submerged church of St Peter's, Shipden, in 1888, but since then it has been no kind of hazard to shipping. The best one can do is to take the train to the North Norfolk coastal resort of Cromer and look out to sea, for which I'll give some general directions later. Even if you cannot spot Shipden, you'll have made the acquaintance of Cromer, so your day will not have been wasted.

Cromer still has one of its stations – there used to be two. The train comes in from Norwich on a line so rurally peaceful and inoffensive that one fears for its future, and sidles into the station, from where it's a few moments' walk past the Regency Fish and Chip restaurant and Breakers Amusements and BB's Fun Palace into the centre of town. Cromer still has one big central hotel, the gloriously ebullient and self-satisfied Hotel de Paris, where one can well imagine carriages arriving and downloading persons of quality into the welcoming care of uniformed flunkeys, trained obsequiously to observe what a pleasure it is to have them back for another year.

There used to be many more such hotels, but the decline of the old-fashioned English seaside holiday gradually did for them. A guide to *Lost Cromer* by Del Styan, available from the town's museum, chronicles some of their disappearances: the site of the Marlborough is now occupied by a filling station; Tucker's, demolished in 1970, has been replaced by a shopping arcade; the Imperial became a bedding shop; most of the

Melbourne was obliterated, though some of it has survived as a social club, restaurant and nightclub; and the imposing Royal Links was destroyed by a fire at the end of the 1940s. All belonged to a time when Cromer, once a simple fishing village, had established itself as favoured resort for the well-to-do: the great banking families took their holidays here; Evelyn Baring, who was born here, chose to be ennobled as the 1st Earl of Cromer; a lordly friend of the Prince of Wales constructed the golf course; and the Empress of Austria was spotted in the street by Compton Mackenzie.

By the early 1900s there were maundering complaints that the place was on a slippery slope to perdition. 'Cromer' moaned W. A. Dutt in *The Norfolk and Suffolk Coast*, published in 1909, 'has become commonplace; and although it still boasts that the nigger minstrel and the peripatetic conjuror are not to be seen on its beach, the theatrical performance of "popular pieces from the London theatres", its variety entertainments and Sunday concerts, and its char-a-bancs and brakes have brought it down to the level of other watering-places, to which it could once justly claim to be in many ways superior.' A *Daily Telegraph* journalist, Clement Scott, who called this stretch of the coast 'Poppyland', also said that he much preferred past Cromer to present Cromer, adding that he did not even dare contemplate future Cromer. It does not seem to have entered his head that by popularizing the place, as he undoubtedly did, he might have been contributing to the very change in its nature he so much feared.

If Dutt and Scott, those two disconsolate monosyllables, were unhappy about the place then, their grief would be even greater today. It can't be described overall as classy. Yet despite the opening burst of amusement arcades on the way from the train, I think it is fair to say that on a sliding scale from dauntingly demure (1) to strutting, whooping, football-sloganeering, Asbo-flaunting, bare-chested (both sexes) vulgarity (10), it still scores little more than 2.25. It is mercifully light on gewgaws.

The church in the centre of town is high and vast and seems so totally out of scale with the place that one might suppose it had taken refuge here after expulsion from somewhere much grander. There are monuments to various Wyndhams and Windhams, who intermarried, and to Noel-Buxtons, and to Mary Rust, dead at thirty-eight: 'What is your life?' her memorial mourns. 'It is even a vapour that appeareth for a little time and then vanisheth away.' (But her husband Benjamin lived almost twice as long: his vapour persisted until he was seventy-three.) There are bookshops and galleries and an improbably pretty town hall of 1890, now occupied by accountants. The little museum, with its emphasis on the nautical, is well-regarded. Henry Blogg, a Cromer man, is accounted one of the heroes of British lifeboat history. There is also a lighthouse, which Bartholomew does not mention, presumably because it is technically in the next parish, Overstrand, but *Kelly's Directory* for 1933 says it was visible 23 miles.

Two miles south-west of the town is a fine house called Felbrigg Hall, long the home of the Wyndham/Windhams. Like so many great houses, it must have been a devil to heat, and therefore frequently deathly cold. According to Simon Jenkins in *England's Thousand Best Houses*, a visitor in 1953 found that the family spent most of the day in the library, squatting on the few chairs that were not piled high with books. It was later acquired by the excellent Norfolk historian R.W. Ketton-Cremer, who, having warned that after his death it might become a cats' home, left it instead to the National Trust.

That is enough about Cromer, which for my purposes is merely the gateway to submarine Shipden. The most you can do nowadays is gaze out to sea from the jetty, but how far, and in what direction, is not always agreed. As grumpy old Dutt observes, its position is variously put anywhere from 400 yards from the shore east of the old jetty to half a mile westward. Best to scan the entire horizon: that will guarantee that your eye has passed over it.

Shipden, before it succumbed to the ocean, was far more important than Cromer, which was then its mere acolyte. But as Shipden submerged, so Cromer grew and prospered at its expense. There is little to help us re-create the lives that were lived in Shipden. I imagine its early fourteenth-century nobility and gentry – I gather it may have boasted a baron or two – communing in anxious twos and threes beneath the spire of St Peter's, deploring the likely fate of the town in language replete with words like 'eftsoons' and 'Gramercy' and 'gipsires', which one finds in inordinate use in Edward Bulwer Lytton's late medieval novel *The Last of the Barons*. Still, at least by disappearing below the waves it was saved, and is now free for ever, from the threat of nigger minstrels, peripatetic conjurors, theatrical performances of popular pieces from London, variety entertainments, Sunday concerts, char-a-bancs, brakes, strutting, whooping, football-sloganeering, Asbo-flaunting, bare-chested (both sexes) day trippers, and all other perpetual demeaners of watering-places.

SIDMOUTH

SIDMOUTH, urb. dist., par., watering-place and mkt.-town... Devon, at mouth of r. Sid, 16m. SE. of Exeter by road... Sidmouth is a lifeboat station. In the centre of the promenade is a fixed light visible 8m....

SUNK DEEP IN A deckchair on the sea front at Sidmouth, Devon, a year or two back, I began to reflect that there are essentially two kinds of English seaside resort: Sidmouth, and all the rest. The rest, of course, have a huge diversity: the high and the low, the grey and the garish, the cosy and the cosmopolitan, the piered and unpiered. But no resort I know gives one quite the same sense that one gets in the sun at Sidmouth that basically all's right with the world.

This therapy is worked in a modest space. The length of the esplanade, running between the red mudstone rocks which close it off at each end like a pair of exotic bookends, is less than a mile. Behind, a thicket of gentle wandering streets stretch back for perhaps half a mile. At the very heart of the town, occupying a site framed by Regency terraces and the parish church of St Giles and St Nicholas, for which I imagine salivating developers might gladly pay Abramovichian sums, are the grounds of the Sidmouth Cricket, Tennis, Croquet and Hockey Club (Visitors Welcome). The cricket, with its attached pavilion, may be the grandest, but the other games too are played with appropriate decorum, their participants all dressed in whites. Sidmouth, they seem to be saying, is a place where we do things properly.

Sadly, in a place that changes so little, the Fortfield Hotel, at midwicket or coverpoint from the cricket ground depending on which end's being bowled from, was all shuttered up when I went back to Sidmouth in the summer of 2007 and may have gone by the time that these words appear. Still, that's the exception. In so many other seaside towns outside the premier league, once-celebrated hotels with names like the Queen's and the Grand are now mere blocks of apartments. But Sidmouth's are still on parade, and as smartly turned out as they ever were: the Royal York; the Kingswood, on the site of what was once the hot and cold brine baths; the Bedford, which began as a library; the gorgeous many-balconied Belmont, a private house until 1921; and the heavy, stately Victoria, the only one to be purpose-built, which looks like the sort of place where once you might have expected to meet a man who had recently been on a shooting party with Edward VII.

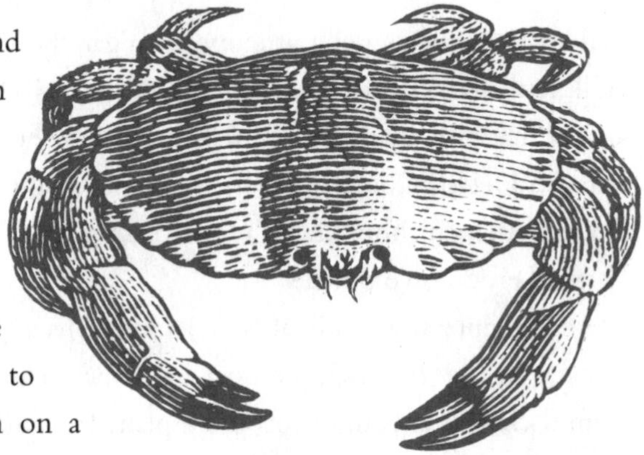

Small though it is, almost all you'd expect in a self-respecting resort is packed into Sidmouth. Here is a sequence of floreate public gardens, named after the Duke of Connnaught, third son of the Queen-Empress, who opened it in his 85th year; complete with a bandstand where, if you're lucky, the Ottery Silver band or some local equivalent may be playing; the parks and the putting greens, the family picnics, the solid citizens nodding off in their deckchairs (80p per session, £1.40 a day) behind their *Daily Telegraphs*; the market selling newly caught crabs and lobsters; the little boats with names like *White Lightning* and *Bella*; the ice cream parlours where you can choose from a range of flavours from Branscombe Blackberry to Cullompton Clotted Cream and Harcombe Honeycomb and, in a neat inversion, Beer Ginger; the lobster pots; and the Charles Vance repertory theatre company for yet one more summer.

There is even the odd opportunity for such old curmudgeons as might visit to complain that Sidmouth is not what it was: no elderly men reading the *Daily Mail* in their deckchairs with improvised hats made of handkerchiefs; no rather younger men, fully dressed except for socks and shoes, with their trousers rolled up, paddling at the very edge of the water. But miraculously Fields, Sidmouth's department store, founded 1809, which boasts on its shopping bags of 'service as it used to be' – and lives up to it – is still there, not yet absorbed into Debenhams, or carved up, as such old family emporia so often are, into burger restaurants and card shops.

Though Sidmouth doesn't flaunt its self-restraint, in the manner of Frinton, there's nothing garish or strident, except perhaps for the early afternoon sun. (They do say that things occasionally get a little more vulgar, though not indecently so, during the annual folk festivals.) I've long had a sense of guilt about finding this town so endearing. Isn't it just that little bit smug and self-satisfied? (There is even one street in the town named Elysian Fields.) Could it not be, for some people's tastes, unforgivably middle class? That John Betjeman should have adored it may alone be enough to condemn it now in the eyes of progressive people.

Yet since the death of Roy Jenkins I have put aside my doubts on this score. In a tribute in the *Telegraph*, the novelist Robert Harris said the great man had recalled for him a chance encounter on the esplanade at Sidmouth with the famously rough and ready Transport and General Workers' Union leader and subsequent Labour Foreign Secretary, Ernest Bevin. 'I'm 'ere on 'oliday with Flo,' Bevin had told him. If Sidmouth wasn't even in those allegedly stuck-up times too snooty for Bevin, all allegations of snootiness are struck from the record. And just to show that Sidmouth moves with the times without ever seeming to do so, here's a newspaper report from the summer of 2004: 'A man who jumped off a 400 ft cliff after a lovers' tiff was recovering in hospital yesterday after his life was saved by a tree… Brian Watts, 66… had been visiting with his male partner.' In *Sidmouth*? Who would ever have thought it?

SNIG'S END

SNIGS END, ham., in co. and 7m. NW. of Gloucester.

WHO SNIG WAS IS a matter of irresolvable mystery. But observant travellers may just about succeed in detecting his End as the A417 out of Gloucester approaches the Malvern Hills. It is somehow interspersed with a place called Corse and another called Staunton. There's no road sign to confirm that you have arrived here. The evidence to look out for is a big pub on the western side of the road called the Prince of Wales. Snig's End (the Ordnance Survey spelling) is at this point scattered about you.

Little happened here between the departure of Snig and the arrival of the charismatic, headstrong, and in the view of most who tried to work with him, seriously impossible, Irish Chartist leader Feargus O'Connor. Everyone recognized his passion and his matchless power to excite and to move an audience; but neither was there any mistaking his monstrous egotism, swollen by the adulation in which his supporters drenched him.

His pre-eminence in the movement was built partly on his oratory but even more on the success of his newspaper, the *Northern Star*, which became the movement's most popular and vehement voice. It grew rapidly from its launch to sell – by February 1838 – some 10,000 copies a week, well ahead of any provincial rival. Others within the Chartist leadership saw him as a malevolent influence and did their frustrated best to tame him. One was James Bronterre O'Brien (buried, as I noted, at Abney Park); another, William Lovett, said of him: 'I regard Feargus O'Connor as the chief marplot of our movement, a man who, by his personal conduct joined to his malignant influence in the *Northern Star*, has been the blight of democracy from the first moment he opened his mouth as its professed advocate. By his trickery and deceit, he got the aid of the working classes to establish an organ to promulgate their principles, which he soon converted into an instrument for destroying everything intellectual and moral in our movement… By his constant appeals to the selfishness, vanity, and mere animal propensities of man, he succeeded in calling up a spirit of hate, intolerance and brute feeling, previously unknown among Reformers.'

On being released from jail – most of the senior Chartists were imprisoned at some time or another – O'Connor had furnished Lovett with a poem he had composed, which he wanted him to recite. It ran:

O'Connor is our chosen chief
He's champion of the Charter;
Our Saviour suffered like a thief
Because he preached the Charter.

It was in the *Star* that O'Connor began to preach his doctrines of common land ownership, advocating the purchase of 20,000 acres to be distributed among 5,000 families on the fair shares basis of four acres apiece. Not only would this create unparalleled opportunities for working-class families: it would also lead, through the use of methods formulated by Feargus, to a revolution in British agricultural production.

As always, his colleagues in the leadership tried to dissuade their followers from falling in behind this militant Pied Piper. Marx and Engels objected too, on the grounds that the land would be privately owned. But O'Connor's drive and eloquence swept the opposition away, and in 1845 a conference in London agreed to the setting up of a Chartist Co-operative Land Society. The place chosen for the first of these settlements was Herringsgate (or Heronsgate – the name it uses today) near Rickmansworth in Hertfordshire. O'Connor characteristically renamed it O'Connorville.

Despite his high ambitions, O'Connor was never able to promise that every Chartist household which chose to take part in his schemes would soon have its house and four acres. All were invited to subscribe, but the allocation was made by ballot. It was, they were led to believe, only a matter of waiting, though; as the early schemes began to flourish, money would be generated to pay for their successors.

With O'Connorville taking shape, he found a second site at Carpenders Park near Watford, then a third at Lowbands in Worcestershire. The houses, as Alice Mary Hadfield says in her book *The Chartist Land Company*, were mostly bungalows built to a standard pattern, probably of O'Connor's devising: 'on all the estates today, the shape is instantly recognizable, the centre brought forward under a flattened gable, a little ornament cut under the peak, a chimney at each end of the roof-tree, and the roof steeply sloping down at the back to the working rooms behind the living quarters.'

Snig's End, the fourth of these settlements, dates from 1847, perhaps the most successful year of O'Connor's life, though in some ways the precursor of his later decline and fall. This was the year which saw him elected as a Chartist MP for Nottingham. His National Co-operative Land Company – the original designation, as a specifically Chartist organization had now been dropped – had 600 branches across the country and deployed a team of proselytizing agents. As well as Snig's End, he established at this time a site at Minster Lovell in Oxfordshire, to which he gave the name Charterville. And as plans developed for the great Chartist demonstration at Kennington the following year, O'Connor picked out Snig's End as his place to brood and plan. It was also here, he decreed, that the ceremonial cart should be built which would carry the monster Chartist petition to Parliament.

Yet 1848, the year in which so much Chartist hope was invested, would turn horribly sour on them. 'We are 4 million or more,' O'Connor had claimed in the *Northern Star* (the total population then was 19 million), upping that a few sentences later to 4.8 million. Six million, he claimed, had put their names to the Chartist petition: more sober supporters said 3 million, but when the names were scrutinized it emerged that the total was under 2 million, and some of the entries were bogus; the one, for instance, that read 'Victoria Rex'.

But, as Hector Berlioz discovered (see Marylebone), Kennington on 10 April hardly reflected that level of commitment. The movement had envisaged it as the precursor of a radical, even revolutionary, transformation of the established political order. Indeed, digesting the news from elsewhere in Europe in this 'year of revolutions', O'Connor had drafted a constitution for a British Republic: no prizes for guessing whom he had put down as president.

In the event, however, Kennington was a failure, indeed, a fiasco. The crowd which assembled, forecast to number hundreds of thousands, was somewhere between 25,000 and 125,000 – the more hostile to the Chartists you were, the lower your estimate. The attempt to carry the Charter in triumphal procession from Kennington to Westminster using the Snig's End cart was easily thwarted by the authorities: in the end, it was taken there in a cab. And when the blame was allotted, much of it fell on O'Connor. His excesses, said Richard Cobden, had retarded rather than advanced the cause of reform.

By now hard questions were being asked about O'Connor's conduct of the land operation, a process which seemed to combine autocracy with incompetence. At Westminster, where, for all his reputation for eloquence and persuasiveness, O'Connor had made little impact, a committee was set up to investigate the affairs of his company and the bank he had created alongside it. The evidence put before it, and especially O'Connor's own testimony, began to suggest that a man who had never been wholly stable might now be drifting not just into drink – that was all too obvious – but even into insanity. The committee was disturbed by the evidence it had accumulated. The houses O'Connor had built were safe and solid enough, but the company was dangerously rickety. This was a verdict endorsed by some who had moved to his settlements, and by many others who had put up money but still had nothing to show for it.

People who had moved to O'Connorville, Snig's End and the rest – hoping to own their own properties – were still paying rent and finding their protests ignored, partly because of O'Connor's autocracy and partly because of the muddle in which the company's affairs were transacted. As the parliamentary committee discovered, some of the accounts were inexplicable – though they accepted that, far from milking the Chartist estates, O'Connor had put his own money in, and lost it.

The expectation of prosperity in which these pioneers had taken up residence had swiftly begun to evaporate. When O'Connor sued the *Nottingham Journal*, which had accused him of failing to honour various undertakings, some of his householders turned up to testify on the paper's behalf. Some, declaring they had been lured there by false promises, refused to pay rent. Others, who did pay their rents, demanded that those who didn't should be expelled. Meanwhile, some of the host communities into which

O'Connor had injected his settlements had begun to complain that the cost to the poor rates of having to sustain so many indigent newcomers was greater than they could bear.

The whole enterprise was now beyond saving. In 1851, at the instigation of tenants at Snig's End and Lowbands, a Bill to wind up the company was brought before Parliament. In February the following year, O'Connor was summoned to appear before the Master in Chancery. He failed to comply, pleading illness. That he was now quite seriously mentally ill was no longer deniable. He disappeared for a while to the United States, but on his return created embarrassing scenes in the Commons. That led to his admission to an institution for the insane at Chiswick, from which he was rescued in time by his sister.

There's a poignant account of O'Connor in his broken state in the final years of his life, wandering through Covent Garden, 'a huge, white-headed, vacuous-eyed man, looking at the fruits and flowers, occasionally taking up a flower, smelling it, and putting it down with a smile of infantile satisfaction'. He died in August 1855, at the age of fifty-nine. A crowd of some 50,000, remembering the days of his ascendancy, followed his coffin to Kensal Green cemetery. In their book *The Common People 1746–1946*, G. D. H. Cole and Raymond Postgate record how the faithful stood motionless in the rain while a Chartist called William Jones 'pronounced the funeral oration both of his leader and of his movement'. Most of the estates were sold off by auction, and prospered far better in their new capitalist mode than they had ever done under O'Connor's rule.

For all that, O'Connor has left his imprint on this corner of Gloucestershire. What is now the Prince of Wales pub, Corse, was O'Connor's village school, the showpiece of his estate. A plan of 1853 shows eighty-one houses in a series of groups, of which the most conspicuous today is School Crescent (so called although it isn't strictly speaking a crescent) on the opposite side of the road. The houses here and elsewhere through Corse and Staunton – mostly brick, though a few are stone – are immediately recognizable as Chartist creations, not least because of the emblems – four joined crescents – cut into their exteriors, and there's no doubt when you see them that O'Connor built these places lovingly and well.

Today they look cared for and prosperous. Most have been adapted to suit a more affluent clientele. The place has a curious mixture of Chartist allegiances and allegiances to an establishment order that men such as O'Connor had longed to eradicate. The pub, O'Connor's creation, is named after the Prince of Wales and carries the arms and the characteristic feathers and the motto '*Ich Dien*'. The road by the pub, Prince Crescent, leads to late twentieth- and early twenty-first-century developments where Chartist names such as Henry Cullingham (O'Connor's local lieutenant) and Lovett (his adversary) mingle with royal allusions. Alongside Sovereign Chase when I was there developers were creating a new estate to be called Chartist Piece.

That name might sound like an appeal to an era which now seems remote and even – having dwindled to nothing – reassuringly harmless, despite the apprehension they caused as the crowds mustered at Kennington in 1848. But the Chartists, for all their dissensions and immediate disappointments, can't be dismissed as quaintly irrelevant. Of all the demands they made, there is only one – annual parliaments – which isn't now part of our established political order.

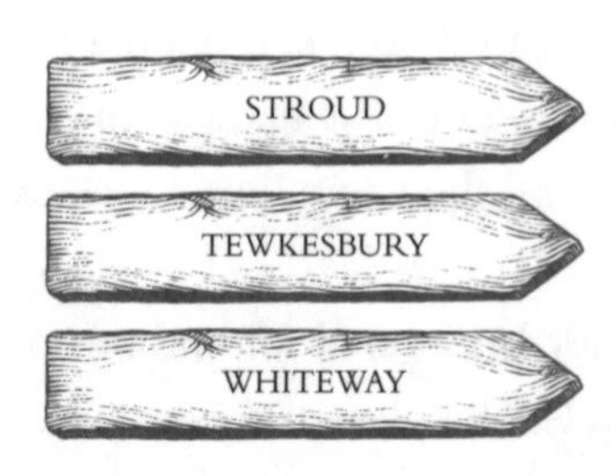

STEEPLE ASHTON

STEEPLE ASHTON, par. and vil., Wilts…
3m E. of Trowbridge.

ARE THERE PRETTIER VILLAGES in England than Steeple Ashton? Certainly. In Wiltshire, even? A few. But many of those are listed in all the guidebooks; what are more to be treasured are the gems come across by accident, while avoiding the obvious roads on a journey to somewhere else. Steeple Ashton is one of those. Few villages that I know have more character, and fewer still blend so much disharmony into something quite so harmonious. And certainly very few have such an exhilarating church.

It's the size of St Mary's, which tells you that Steeple Ashton was once a place of greater importance than it is now. This was a wool town. Some authorities say, though others don't, that 'Steeple' is a corruption of 'staple'. The interior is high, light and airy. Pevsner judges it to be even finer than the exterior. But that could be because he's an academic analyst rather than a mere pleasure-seeker, and what will thrill and delight pleasure-seeking church-crawlers here is the wild, exuberant, rip-roaring roof, all spikes and pinnacles, so zany and so fanciful that you might almost think that the architect was high on LSD. A rowdy collection of gargoyles adds to the sense of fantasy.

It stands proudly on the north flank of Church Street, a street which goes around three sides of a square with the High Street providing the fourth, just waiting to be admired. It once had a spire, but a storm disposed of that in 1670 and they didn't bother replacing it. It is not this book's purpose to provide detailed descriptions of churches: take Pevsner and Simon Jenkins's *England's Thousand Best Churches* if you want to know what to look out for. But I always search in such places for memorials which tell you something about the people (though in most cases, sadly, only the most important people) who lived there, in the hope of uncovering something tantalizing and mysterious.

And here is one such case: John Hynes de la Beche, died 1803 at thirty-eight, in 'Franfort' on the Maine. He was the son of Thomas and Helen Beach. Why, then, the de la Beche? Particularly when he died in Frankfurt, not France. His father Thomas, I imagine, would be the Hon. T. Beach, sometime Attorney-General and Chief Justice of Jamaica, who died in 1774 at fifty-eight, and his wife Helen who died three years before, at thity-eight – also memorialized here. Nearby is a tribute to Anne, wife of the Revd Wm Wainhouse and daughter of William Beech of Keevil who died in the twenty-second year of her age in 1771. It seems that she might have welcomed this fate. 'Rest, virtuous spirit!' the inscription commands; 'to thy latent grief/ Death, on thy slumbers stealing, brought relief./ Thy youthful Days, in silent sufferings past,/ Heav'n repaid with Smiles and Peace at last.' Below is the figure of a disconsolate maiden in charge of an urn. Did Anne and the Reverend William know when they married that it might not be for long? Imaginative people plot whole novels from details like these.

Where the exterior has its gargoyles, fierce and grotesque, the walls inside are populated with figures whose faces are much like those you might still encounter out in the street, apparently straining to hold up the pillars above them. One on the north side has his back and upraised arms braced against the wall as if the effort is almost beyond him. How envious he must feel of another, across on the southern wall, who seems to be doing his bit with nonchalant ease.

Away from the church you are more aware of the Longs – though they're well represented among the memorials too – than the Beaches or Beeches, or de la Beches. The pub is called the Longs Arms. It is modern enough to play piped music, but ancient enough to choose to treat its customers to 'Magic Moments' by Perry Como, a chart-topper in 1954 or thereabouts. The Longs were one of the dominant Wiltshire families and active in national politics too.

Walter Long, an MP for most of the period 1885 to 1921, when he was made a viscount, represented in turn North Wiltshire, Devizes, Liverpool West Derby, Bristol South, South Dublin, The Strand (that's the Strand in London, not the road of that name in this village) and Westminster St George's. He was leader of the Budget Protest League which sought to vanquish Lloyd George when that radical Welshman assaulted aristocratic privilege, and was seriously considered for the leadership of the Conservative Party after the resignation of Arthur Balfour. In an excellent book called *The Liberals in Power*, Colin Cross says of him: 'Long was a country squire of ancient lineage and hot temper. For years he had been at pains to keep in contact with the less-articulate members of his order on the Conservative back benches, and he now emerged as the representative of historic Toryism.' His main opponent was Austen Chamberlain, with whom he was on such bad terms that they came close to a fist fight after Balfour resigned. Then Andrew Bonar Law emerged as a compromise candidate, and Long and Chamberlain agreed to withdraw.

You may sit outside the Longs Arms and savour the view up to the triangular green, where there's a pound with a firmly padlocked wooden door and a grille which enabled malefactors to gaze out while their mockers gazed in. Here and throughout the village there are houses of every shape and size, some lavish or even magnificent, some austere, some cosily cottagey. It is quite an upmarket village, much of it fairly expensive and with something of a reputation in less privileged villages for being a trifle snobby. But it's still characteristically Wiltshire, and though they could of course be major-generals who'd moved in retirement from Aldershot, it was gratifying to see in the summer of 2007 that Steeple Ashton's church wardens were a Mr Dray and a Mr Plum. Do not miss, at the northern end of the village, one of its rare bits of dereliction: three crumbling petrol pumps, abandoned at least a decade ago. It may be the influence of that psychedelic church roof, but they irresistibly remind me of Dorothy and Toto's three friends in *The Wizard of Oz*.

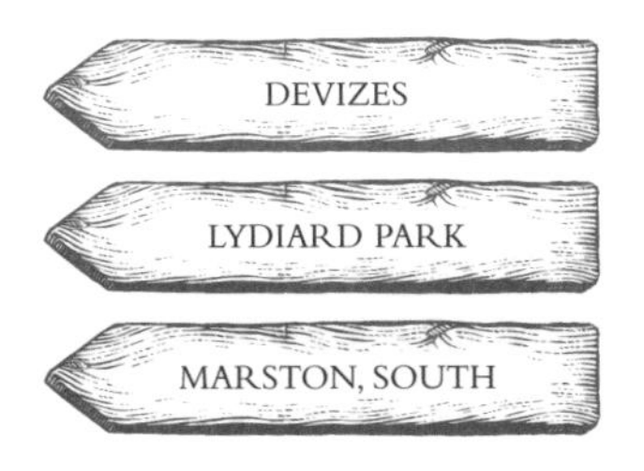

STREATLAM

STREATLAM AND STAINTON, par., Durham, 2½m. NE. of Barnard Castle... In vicinity is S. Castle, a seat.

STREATLAM CASTLE HAS GONE: the Bowes-Lyon family, never short of other fine houses to occupy, sold it in 1922. Most of the house was demolished in 1927 and what remained was destroyed in a Territorial Army training exercise in 1959. All that remains is the pair of gatehouses which you pass on the road from Bishop Auckland to Barnard Castle, and even they are not the originals, but Victorian re-creations. The ancient castle went long before, replaced by the house in 1718. Perhaps the family simply grew tired of the place; but perhaps they were also influenced by its grim associations.

In January 1777 Mary Eleanor Bowes, the young and beautiful widow of the 9th Earl of Strathmore, married her second husband. There's a portrait of him in the Bowes Museum at Barnard Castle. He doesn't merely look evil; he looks as though he revels in being evil. It is not the work, one may safely conclude, of a friend; but even apparently balanced accounts of Captain Andrew Robinson Stoney suggest that it scarcely does him any injustice.

The Earl of Strathmore, twelve years older than Mary Eleanor, died in 1776. She married him on her eighteenth birthday, having concluded shortly before the deed was done that those who had tried to deter her were right, and this was a big mistake. They had nine years together, in which time she produced five children. It was not a successful marriage: his family disliked and distrusted her, and she felt the same about them. She consoled herself with writing, with botanical studies, and with adventures. His last letter to her offered forgiveness for her 'liberties and follies', which included an open affair with a man called James Graham. He counselled her, too, to abandon her 'extreme rage for literary fame'. After his death, Mary Eleanor attracted a long queue of suitors, attracted by her beauty and her money: some were driven to rapture over her face and particularly over her breasts; others over her properties. On the death of her father, when she was only eleven, she had inherited the castles of Hylton, now a ruin in the suburbs of Sunderland, Gibside, now part of Gateshead, and Streatlam, in a glorious tract of County Durham, along with houses in Grosvenor Square and Chelsea.

It seemed for a time that the queue to capture this wonderful lady was headed by a lawyer called George Gray. Last in the line, on any rational judgement, ought to have been Andrew Robinson Stoney, an Irish soldier, adventurer, and inveterate waster whose main occupations at the time he set his sights on her seem to have been gambling, cockfighting, days at the races, and lounging about in London clubs. But while no match for the lady or for his various competitors in terms of breeding or money, he was, according to Jesse Foot, a doctor who became close to him and wrote an account of him on which every subsequent assessment has had to depend, more than their equal in determination and low cunning.

Suborned by Stoney, who seems despite all his deep-down nastiness to have been something of a charmer, some friends and associates of the countess spoke well of him to her. She also seems to have been influenced by the words of a fortune-teller – again, it's suggested, prompted by Stoney – whose studies revealed that Mary Eleanor was fated to marry a young Irishman whom she had only recently met. What tilted the case in his favour was the appearance in one of the London newspapers, the *Morning Post*, of a series of libellous stories about her. She became so alarmed by these calumnies that she vowed that anyone who could save her from them would deserve her heart and hand. Stoney promised to do so. According to some accounts – though Ralph Arnold, who in 1957 published a book called *The Unhappy Countess and her Grandson John Bowes*, remained unconvinced – this was a pledge he was uniquely positioned to keep since the stories placed in the *Post* had all come from him. Letters appeared, which were certainly written by him, defending the lady's honour, and a duel was staged, in which the editor of the *Post* was reported to have been worsted. The campaign ceased: the countess, abandoning Gray, by whom she was pregnant, committed herself to Stoney, who now took possession not just of the widow but, as he thought in the light of the laws then prevailing, of her castles and rich estates as well. Also, because of provisions in the will of her father, he took her name; from now on he would be known as Andrew Robinson Stoney Bowes.

This marriage, in January 1777, wasn't his first. Stoney's previous bride was a rich young woman called Hannah Newton. According to Jesse Foot, Hannah's friends believed her husband had tortured her, locking her in her closet on a diet of one egg a day, and at one point pushing her down the stairs. Some of her friends suspected that her death must have been his doing. He found consolation for her loss in her fortune and her estate. By this ill-advised match, some people now feared, the Countess of Strathmore was inviting a similar fate. But in this case, an early death would not have given him what he was after. The land and property he'd imagined would now be his were, he discovered, not his after all.

Gray, when marriage to Mary Eleanor appeared to be imminent, had drawn up a kind of prenuptial agreement that ensured that her assets would still belong to the countess rather than to her husband. The same provisions now applied to Stoney. He was always in need of money, particularly as he was eager to become MP for Newcastle – an ambition in which he failed shortly after the marriage, but succeeded three years later. But when he tried to sell off Gibside Forest, he found that it was not his to sell.

From then on, his only recourse was to force the lady to comply with his wishes. He made her sell off her fine London houses. He banned her from leaving the castle or associating with her friends. He would trap her hair in a chest and confine her to a lying position until she gave way to what were decorously termed his 'diabolical wishes'; he also paraded his mistresses in front of his wife. He impregnated the wet nurse whom the Countess had hired on the birth of their son William in 1782, and raped a nursery maid. At one stage he abducted one of the daughters of the Countess's marriage to the Earl of Strathmore and took her to Paris, but was forced by the courts to return her. To ensure his wife's subservience, it was also said against him (though again Ralph Arnold is not convinced) that he made her write a book, the contents of which he dictated to her, recounting her promiscuities and general wickedness. Should she go on giving trouble, he warned her, he would see that the book was published. As an additional precaution, he insured her life, for a year or two at the most. 'He had a devil in him', his biographer Jesse Foot concludes, 'that would have amazed ordinary villains.'

Six years of this regime, according to Foot, had reduced Mary Eleanor to a deep state of wretchedness; indeed, she was gradually dying because of his cruelty. She had made repeated attempts to escape, but servants betrayed her, earning fat rewards from her husband. But now an incorruptible personal maid helped her get free, and they hid up in London. Stoney Bowes used the law to get her back. She begged the court to protect her against his ill-treatment. He retorted by fulfilling his threat to publish her book of 'confessions'. The court was unpersuaded, and appointed a constable to guard her.

The story of what happened next is disputed, though it's clear on all accounts that Stoney acted with great ruthlessness and cruelty. Mary Eleanor and her maid had found a safe refuge in Holborn. But when the Countess went shopping in Oxford Street, agents of her husband entered the shop. The constable deputed to safeguard her said he would take her to the magistrates' court, where she would receive protection; instead, he directed the coach to Highgate Hill, where Bowes was waiting. As they headed north for Streatlam, where he planned to imprison her once more, Bowes tried to force her to sign papers agreeing to resume the marriage and halt the proceedings she had begun in the ecclesiastical court for its termination.

When, after many hours, they reached Streatlam Castle, she still had not signed. Producing a pistol, he told her to say her prayers, as he intended to kill her. She refused, and told him to fire. Word got about in the district that the Countess was being held in the castle against her will, and a body of colliers employed in the Strathmore pits attempted to rescue her, while the courts in London sent emissaries charged to bring her back to the capital. Streatlam, Bowes concluded, was no longer safe. He then embarked on a nightmare journey which took them through Cumbria and Durham until, in the village of Neasham, just outside Darlington, a valiant constable called Christopher Smith caught up with them. Bowes said he would blow the constable's brains out if he tried to intervene. Smith ignored him, seized the Countess, and carried her off to safety.

She divorced him and that seems to have been the last that she ever saw of him. He was brought to court, where the judge at one hearing spoke of 'as daring an outrage as ever was committed in a civilised country'. At a subsequent hearing, the judge told him: 'the crime... does appear to be of as atrocious and daring a nature as ever appeared in a court of justice'. He was fined £300 and sentenced to three years in jail. But imprisonment barely curbed him. 'Meanness, villainy and hypocrisy', says the anecdotal historian, John Timbs, in his three-volume work, *Abbeys, Castles and Ancient Halls of England and Wales: their legendary lore and popular history*, where I first encountered this story, 'marked the further course of Bowes – his law affairs and his seductions forming the business of his life. But the details of his prison life are too disgusting for profitable perusal. During his later years he was an habitual drunkard.' His reputation for debt became so remarkable that it gave the language an expression still used today: stony broke.

From the apartments (shared with his latest mistress) in which he was permitted to serve his sentence, Bowes continued to publish allegations against the Countess, ranging from claims that she'd tried to assassinate him through to complaints of neglect of her children to charges of depraved misbehaviour with one of her footmen and a gardener at Gibside. He still sought to prevent their divorce and achieve the invalidation of the prenuptial agreement that had denied him the Countess's fortune – a cause for which he had the support of many respectable men, the otherwise censorious Dr Foot among them. They would not have defended his general conduct, but were shocked by any suggestion that a wife's possessions should not pass as of right to her husband. The evidence on both sides, as various courts struggled to sort out these matters, must have been among the most lurid heard in any courtroom in Georgian London.

Bowes outlived his Countess. She died at Cosham near Portsmouth in 1800 and was buried in the dress she had worn for her marriage to the Earl of Strathmore, in Westminster Abbey. He died in 1810 and was buried much less grandly, at the church of St George, The Borough. Jesse Foot fashioned this memorably comprehensive epitaph for him: 'To sum up his character in a few words, he was cowardly, insidious, hypocritical, tyrannic, mean, violent, selfish, deceitful, jealous, revengeful, inhuman and savage, without a single countervailing quality. Let us hope when he departed, that never before nor since there never was, nor ever will be, taking him for all in all, his parallel.'

She, I think one might safely conclude, wasn't perfect either: spoiled, irresponsible, more than a bit of a flibbertigibbet. He, one can say with all appropriate caution, even without accepting every deleterious word of Jesse Foot's indictment, was, as the picture at Barnard Castle suggests, not a very nice man.

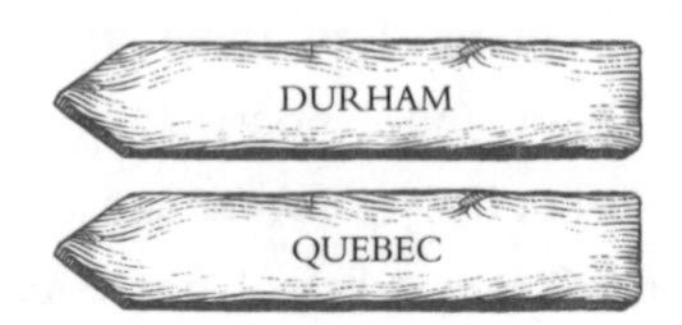

STROMNESS

STROMNESS, mkt. and spt.-town, police bur. and par. in SW. of Pomona, Orkney, 14m. W. of Kirkwall…

WALK SOUTH OUT OF Stromness, second town of the Orkney Islands, and you'll come on your right a to mean little passageway with a street sign that boldly proclaims: Khyber Pass. Just beyond, there's a street that runs parallel with the Pass which a sign on the front of Stromness Library suggests is the proud possessor of a second remarkable street name. Could this, I thought as I grabbed my camera, be the only place in the kingdom whose public library is situated in Hell Hole Road?

It wasn't until I was warned against this vulgar error by an Orcadian and examined my photograph with the aid of a magnifying glass that I spotted, lurking between the big, bold, confident capital letters of 'Hell' and 'Hole', a meagre, insignificant, snivelling lower case letter 'i'. This is not, after all, Hell Hole Road, but Hellihole Road, so-called on the indisputable grounds that it leads to a district called Hellihole. Such deception! And practised on the front of that repository of wisdom and truth, a public library! Clearly the racy wit and pawky humour on which – as I found on my expedition to the Isle of Whithorn – south-west Scotland prides itself, extends to these austere and unfanciful northern fastnesses too.

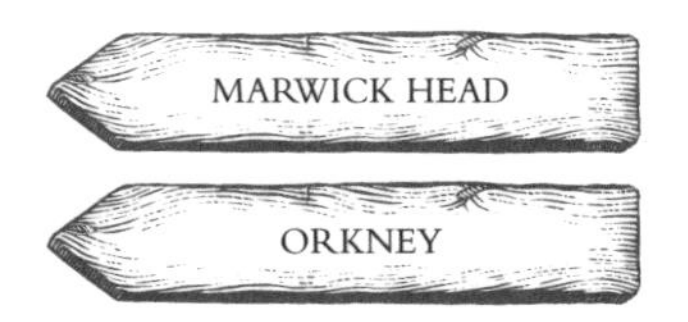

STROUD

STROUD (pronounced Strowd), urb. dist., par. and mkt.-town, with ry. sta., G.W.R. and (Cheapside) L.M.S., Glos., on the Thames and Severn Canal, adjacent to the Frome and the Slade…

THEY ARE PROUD, INDEPENDENT people in Stroud. Its local politics turned green long before that was fashionable. Activists installed themselves in a tree in the hope of preventing redevelopment long before that tactic began to spread. It's a shame they didn't do more of that kind of thing, because, though some of the greater excesses that had been planned were struck out, it looks as though the 1960s destroyed quite a lot of old Stroud – ancient houses and narrow alleys were swept away, some to make room for a bypass only part of which was then built. And proud independent Stroud was the very last place in England to adopt the same time of day as the rest of the country.

Before the railways came, towns took their time from nature rather than from metropolitan practice. Edinburgh was twelve minutes behind London and in Glasgow, further west, they were seventeen behind. The time in Bath was ten minutes behind that in London: for a while, its station clock, obedient to the instructions of the Great Western Railway, told the time that applied in Paddington while the other clocks stuck to the time in Bath. The clock on Tom Tower at Christ Church, Oxford, used to have two minute hands, one telling London's time and the other, Oxford's.

Gradually the rule of the railways came to prevail and local deviations faded away. Not, however, in Stroud, although it had two railway stations, the present one (then known as Russell Street) on the GWR and another, Cheapside, on the Nailsworth to Stonehouse service of the London, Midland and Scottish. It remained a defiant eight minutes fifty seconds out of kilter with Greenwich. It took the initiative of a local clockmaker to ease the town into harmonization. He displayed in his King Street window a fine clock which told London time in open rebellion against the prevailing chronological wisdom of Stroud. Gradually, the rest of the town succumbed.

Stroud is surrounded by places which throb with affluence. You cannot go far without some encounter with four by fours and jodhpurs and green wellington boots. Ultra-sought-after Bisley, home of the novelist Jilly Cooper, is only five miles away. Some people you see in the streets of Stroud have Bisley written all over them. I came across a notice which said that the high street of Stroud was originally part of the king's highway to Bisley. Why the king in these pre-Cooper days should have been going to Bisley was not explained.

Yet this is a town without any great airs or graces. Since it's set on sharp Cotswold slopes, you could hardly say it was flat, but some find it featureless: 'There isn't much to keep the tourist in Stroud' sniffs Anthony West in his *Shell Guide to Gloucestershire*. It doesn't sport the profusion of public clocks that you see in some towns: they have to be searched for, not an easy business, since when you wander through Stroud you always seem to be going uphill. A disobligingly named and appropriately unlovely shopping precinct called the Merrywalks Centre has a prominent clock which was two hours out when I was there in the spring of 2007: even if the recent change to British Summer Time accounted for a one-hour discrepancy, it could hardly explain the second.

There is no town hall clock because there is no town hall. The old one, which was once a market building, is now a volunteer centre, and clockless, and since the place lost its former status as a borough and later, as the capital of an urban district, a converted shop has served as its municipal headquarters. But as some compensation for that, the nearest equivalent to a genuine town hall clock, close to the Stroud Subscription Rooms, the most eminent building in town, had four clockfaces all of which were telling the truth. The church, however, to which one's supposed to turn for comfort and guidance in times of perplexity, was, I am sorry to say, also guilty of propagating falsehoods. Yet the one above the Soap 'n' Suds launderette was impeccable.

If you're looking for certainty, though, the best place to go is the library, for there you will find the original truth-telling – well, London truth-telling, anyway – clock of 1858, which Robert Bragg put in his King Street window to coax truculent Stroud into chronological compliance. This told me not only what the time was all over Britain, but also that if I didn't move on in a hurry I would miss my timetabled bus through improbably pretty Painswick (where the church clock was correct) and so on to Tewkesbury. On my route out of Stroud, a poster partly concealed in a tree invited me to vote for Roger Knapman, Conservative, although, as I happened to know, it was now ten years since he'd last fought the seat for the Tories and he'd long ago defected to UKIP. So perhaps the sense of other-timeliness has not yet entirely departed from Stroud.

SUNDERLAND POINT

SUNDERLAND POINT, locality, Lancs.
in Lancaster rural dist.

IT WOULD SEEM LIKE a rather taxing journey if it led to a mere 'locality'. You drive west out of the city of Lancaster, then south along the estuary of its river, the Lune. Diminishing roads take you to the village of Overton, where you find a still more tenuous road whose destination seems to be nowhere. This final stage is a tidal road, coated in mud and punctuated by warnings of what may await the unwary should they misjudge the tide, which twice daily cuts the place off from Overton.

Sunderland means separated land, and the place lives up to this designation: a huge empty landscape and seascape, just a huddle of houses awaiting you on the shore side, and boats of all shapes and sizes and provenances parked on the sand – here a trim yacht, there a green encrusted hulk which will surely never take to the sea again – but with not a hint when I arrived there on a bleak and ferociously windy November morning that life still existed here on the edge of the world. A sign outside one of the houses clanked as it swung in the wind, irresistibly recalling the scene in David Lean's film of *Great Expectations* when Pip and Mr Pocket wait on a stormy night in a waterside inn for the moment when Abel Magwitch can make his escape from capture and perhaps execution, and the swaying and clanking of the inn sign seems like an omen that they will not succeed.

Yet this desolate place was once a thriving port; and later still, a place where holidaymakers arrived across the sand in high excitement, no doubt envying those lucky enough to live there. They came to the Ship Hotel – later, after it lost its licence, the Temperance Hotel, and later still, Temperance Farm; they spent their money in shops that long ago ceased to be shops, and frequented two pubs, both now private houses. The Cunliffe family came here summer by summer, as one of them, Hugh, remembers in a little book in praise of the place called *The Story of Sunderland Point from the Early Days to Modern Times* which I found in Lancaster Library, and some of them played in the annual cricket match between the two groups of houses along the shore: First Terrace v Second Terrace. People still come here in summer, though not in such numbers, among them painters, attracted on bleak days as well as sunnier ones by the austerity of the scene and the sometimes eerie light on the water, and birdwatchers.

The port was created, as so many were, by a single entrepreneur, a Quaker called Robert Lawson, in the reign of William and Mary. He furnished it with a warehouse, an equipment and repair works, a blockmaker's shop, and a smithy. For a time it established a lively trade principally with the Baltic, but also with the West Indies, specifically buoyed by the traffic in slaves. Signs direct you from First Terrace to the grave of a sadly short-lived resident who came here with his master in 1736, one, it is thought, of some forty former slaves who arrived in this area, and known only as Sambo. He very soon died, and was buried here. The port did not flourish for long. As Lancaster's grew, Sunderland's trade reduced. When Glasson Dock was developed across the estuary, Sunderland was virtually finished: people called it Cape Famine. In 1728 Lawson went bankrupt – a particular blow in the case of a Quaker, for Quaker congregations believed that a man's default on a debt defiled the tradition that the word of a Christian is always to be trusted.

In time, as I wandered on the lonely edge of the place, there emerged from one of the well-kept houses a very old car, containing a very old lady, driving it very slowly as if from a sense of jeopardy, on the muddy trackway leading towards civilization. There were other signs too that life does not wholly freeze into immobility here when the winter comes. There were services in the mission room advertised, and an evening programme of 'Desert Island Discs', chosen by the vicar. There is still farming here, and fishing. But arriving in such a place at such a time, one feels like an intruder. Sadly beautiful though it was, I felt a sense of relief as I drove back across the sands to reassuringly everyday Overton.

SUTTON-UNDER-WHITESTONECLIFFE

SUTTON-UNDER-WHITESTONE CLIFFE, par. and vil., N.R. Yorks… 4m. E. of Thirsk.

THE A170 FROM SCARBOROUGH passes through Helmsley and heads off for Thirsk, where it expires. On the way there is a precipitous drop to take it from the top of the moors down to the valley. Travelling west, you engage low gear and proceed with caution, though also perhaps with complacency as you watch the eastbound traffic labouring up the bank, possibly, as on the day I was there, having to skirt some monstrous lorry which has failed the ascent and now has a tributary column of seething cars accumulating behind it.

At the top of this hill is the Sutton Bank Visitor Centre, whose massive car park testifies to the popularity of this place in summer. I was there in November, when the car park was utterly empty. That meant I might have had, more or less to myself, all the advertised walks to Nettle Dale and the Hambleton Hills, to the White Horse of Kilburn and to Kilburn Woods ('wander in a woodland wonderland'), and the tracks across to the abbey ruins of Byland and Rievaulx. On the other hand, November has a habit of staging fogs, and the penalty I paid for my empty car park was the loss of the promised views of crag and cliff and forest and valley; also of a mysterious lake called Gormire (five miles' walk, allow three to four hours), which is said to be bottomless and to have no river entering it, and to offer a glorious panorama of the Vale of York; all, on this day, invisible.

At the foot of the hill, however, impeccably visible, I found the routine village that Bartholomew calls Sutton-under-Whitestone Cliffe. A number of would-be authorities, from Wikipedia to one of the local pubs, claim that the name of this village is the longest in England, and I came there expecting to find the place full of boastful celebrations of this achievement. I found none. And having pondered for a

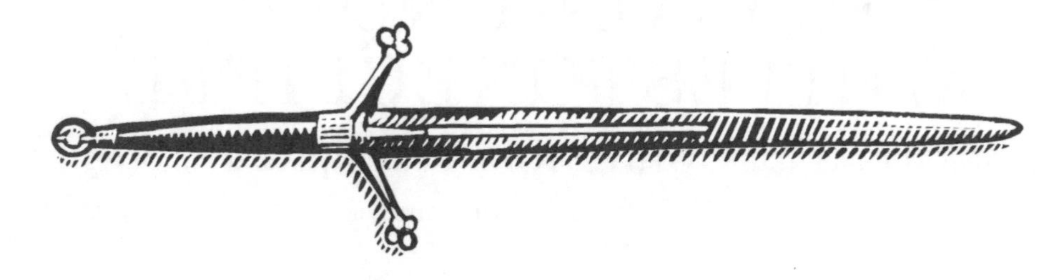

moment or two, I thought I knew why.

Count the number of letters in Sutton-under-Whitestone Cliffe and you'll find there are twenty-seven. But even that is uncertain: an 1890 gazetteer spells it without the concluding 'e', which egalitarians may think really has no right to belong in the name of a village that shelters under a cliff. Next, it is not at all clear that the cliff, or cliffe, really belongs in the letter count. Though some sources tack it on with a third hyphen, Bartholomew (see above) makes it separate. Even more significantly, the place name signs at either end of the village dispense with all hyphens and other unnatural aids, and call it simply 'Sutton under Whitestonecliffe': three distinct words. Clearly, for Sutton – which seems to be what most local people call it – to assert any form of primacy over the rest of England would earn it the permanent enmity of other communities with a better right to this high distinction. Indeed, surveying the territory, with its hills and streams and mysterious forests, it is easy to imagine the rallying here of a kind of coalition of the aggrieved, desperate to contest with Sutton a reputation it does not truly deserve.

Since the claim has been advanced only in the context of England, the village might be safe from the threat of invasion by fierce lowland hordes, arrayed with kilt and sporran and armed with dirk and claymore and the even more frightful bagpipe, advancing towards them down the A1 from the village of Hunterfield and Arniston Engine, Midlothian. But the border would be no kind of protection from the wrath of two Northumberland settlements, near neighbours in the Kielder Valley, a region once famed for its harshness, where the cry 'A Ridley! A Ridley!' was enough to affright most decent inhabitants even before Margaret Thatcher gave Nicholas Ridley a job in her Cabinet. These are Blakehopeburnhaugh, eighteen letters without any artificial additives, and Cottonshopeburnfoot, which thinks itself better still at nineteen.

Even here, Sutton might hope to be spared their united fury, since these two nurse their own rivalry. Blakehopeburnhaugh has the endorsement of the *Guinness Book of Records*, but only because the Ordnance Survey insists on amputating the foot from the other place, making it not so much 19 as 15 and 4. Yet certainly Suttonians might have feared finding one or other of these antagonists, if not both, encamped in the west, hiding up, say, in the Belmoor Plantation close to Hag House, and handily placed to sneak out for the odd surreptitious pint in the Carpenters Arms at Felixkirk.

And if it's conceded that places whose names are, like Sutton's, made up of three or four separate words, are also contenders for the title, then the spirit of rebellion would surely be hot and strong in East Anglia, where a place called Horsham St Faith with Newton St Faith could lay claim to 31 letters – and if Saint were to be fully spelled out in each case, 37. Perhaps those who mustered under the flag of St Faith might engage in a tactical alliance with a force from Wiggenhall St Mary the Virgin, their pauldrons, mamelieres and cuirasses glinting evilly as they marched northwards though the Lincolnshire sun towards their assigned positions in Hags Wood, near Hagg Hall, close to Rievaulx.

Even more feared perhaps than these men of East Anglia would be others raised in the north: a muster perhaps from North Leverton with Habblesthorpe, between Retford and Gainsborough, and others with claims to press from within the very same county as Sutton: a contingent from Airyhome with Hawthorpe and Baxton Howe (34 letters, though the population there when Bartholomew counted was only 26), Allerton Mauleverer with Hopperton (31), and possibly Havercroft with Cold Hiendley, near Barnsley taking up their positions at Hagmoor, near Thirkleby Barugh, just off the A19: such a daunting sight they would make, with their pikes, spontoons and martels-de-fer clenched in their gritty northern working-class hands, backed up by an artillery force armed with arquebuses, blunderbusses and dags.

And who might this be, arriving from the far south in a convoy of four by fours equipped with rocket launchers and ground-to-air missiles which have cost a small fortune in Reading? It's a force whose sophisticated technology Sutton should fear the most: the men of Sulhampstead Banister Upper End, near Reading, not so far from the Duke of Wellington's home at Stratfield Saye, making common cause just this once with those of Sulhampstead Banister Lower End, each scoring a cool 28 letters, under their fabled commander, Lieutenant-General Erne-Erle-Plunkett-Drax, and his trusty henchman, Brigadier-General Twistleton-Wykeham-Fiennes.

These insurgents might, some believe, decide in the light of this engagement to unite their communities permanently under the name Sulhampstead-Banister-Upper-End-with-Sulhampstead-Banister-Lower-End, making a count of 60 letters, which even the two united St Faiths could not match. No wonder, when you see things this way, that Sutton-under-Whitestone Cliffe is keeping so quiet.

SWANSEA

SWANSEA, parl. and co. bor., spt. and par. ... Gower Peninsula, Glamorgan, at mouth of r. Tawe, at its entrance into Swansea Bay, Bristol Channel... Swansea is called by the Welsh Abertawe from its position at the mouth of the Tawe... At the head of the West Pier is a fixed red light...

REMARKING THAT, DESPITE THE song, 'We'll keep a welcome in the hillsides, we'll keep a welcome in the vales', a Welsh welcome can be barbed, Dr Dannie Abse, in his memoir *Intermittent Journals*, recounts the following: 'Some years back I received a letter from a Mr E. Howard Harries (now no longer in this world, may his soul rest in peace). It read, "Our chairman, Mr Vernon Watkins, has arranged for you to visit us in Swansea. As Secretary of our Poetry Society, I need to tell you that we expect an audience of about eighty people. I trust you will not read too long as really the audience would much prefer to hear my poems about the Gower coast. Yours truly, E. Howard Harries, esquire." '

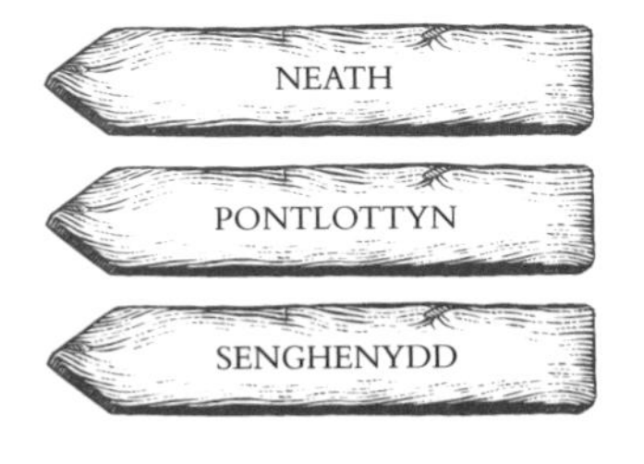

A B C D

E F G H

I J K L

M N O P

Q R S **T**

U V W X Y Z

TALBOT VILLAGE

TALBOT VILLAGE, eccl. dist., SE. Dorset,
2m. NW. of Bournemouth…

AT SOME DARK MOMENT in the 1840s, a contingent of poor and jobless men and their families congregated outside the plush home on Bournemouth East Cliff of Sir George Talbot, Bt, also of Grosvenor Square and Mickleham, Surrey, clamouring for food and employment. What Sir George made of this demonstration, with which his equally affluent neighbours were also visited, is unrecorded, but it made a deep impact on his two spinster daughters, Marianne and Georgina. 'All around the neighbourhood', Marianne recorded, 'the distress and suffering of the poor was dreadful. The people used to come in crowds, calling out, "Give us work; we are starving!" Men, women and children came in alarming numbers, with spades and sticks, under the windows – and the few sovereigns given away did more harm than good.' Georgina was the younger of the two, but she seems to have been the more passionate and spirited, and it was she who resolved that something ought to be done to bring relief to these stricken people – though not, she agreed with her sister, merely by dishing out sovereigns.

The death of their father in 1850 gave the sisters, then in their middle fifties, the money they needed to furnish some practical remedy, and they used it to buy a swathe of land north-west of the town, to employ the poor to clear it, and to set about the creation of homes and farmsteads designed to offer both succour and useful employment. Known at first simply as 'the village', the community consisted of sturdy, mildly rustic homes, based on the pattern book of John Claudius Loudon (1783–1843), each with three good bedrooms, two living rooms, a good sized kitchen, but also a well and a pigsty.

Rents were kept low. Householders were expected to undertake specified work, but lodgers must not be taken, and no trading was to be done except the selling of poultry, eggs and bacon. You come to it now on the A3049 close to the College roundabout, just across the road from the university. Some of the houses are visible from the road, but to get a full sense of the place you need to take a track through the woods which leads to the Talbots' school, opened in 1862 to take sixty-eight children, and greatly extended since. The schoolhouse, says an inscription, was built by G. C. Talbot – that's Georgina – in 1862, and endowed by M. A. Talbot in 1873: that is Marianne. The houses are scattered through the woods with space around them generous enough to have given the new arrivals a feeling of living in luxury.

Not everything went according to plan, however. Part of the problem was the background and lifestyle of some of the people the sisters were anxious to rescue. The Wallisdown area, from which many of them had come, was notorious for its smugglers and poachers. That made them somewhat unsuitable candidates for the respectably conventional life the Talbots envisaged for them, and must have upset their neighbours. 'The outset of this village', Georgina would later say (as recorded by Marianne), 'was anything but encouraging or cheerful. The first inhabitants were unused to any restraints; the women, many of them lax in their behaviour; the surrounding gentlemen and clergy having no sympathy with improvements and amelioration for the lower classes.' Nearly thirty years after Talbot Village housed its first arrivals, the school's headmaster complained of 'a large percentage of dullards, owing to low habits and the home influence of parents, a low standard of morality, poverty, and lack of boots'.

And no doubt they found some of the rules imposed on them by the Talbots unwelcomely strict. No cats and dogs were allowed in their homes. No limits were placed on religious allegiance, but all were required to love God, to honour the Ten Commandments, and to honour the queen. By the time the sisters came to build their almshouses, additional rules were added, presumably based on malpractices they had observed among previous denizens. Only persons of good character and sobriety would be considered. Those who might prove to be quarrelsome or otherwise troublesome must be excluded. No inmate was to 'lay out offensive matter' or hang clothes to dry in front of the almshouses. Most telling of all, perhaps, was an absolute ban on any applicant who came from over the county boundary in Hampshire.

Though their motives were essentially philanthropic, one can't help getting the feeling, as one wanders through Talbot Village, that the sisters, devoted as they were to the glory of God, kept a little place in their hearts for the glory of the Talbot family too. 'Laus Deo 1862' (Praise be to God) it says on the almshouses. 'These almshouses were built and endowed by Georgina Charlotte Talbot.' One financial endowment she offered the school stipulated that it should continue only 'so long as the portrait of Georgina Charlotte Talbot shall be hung in the schoolroom and the inscription kept'.

It seems curious in both contexts that it took the sisters so long to build a church for their new community: St Mark's was dedicated only in 1870, twenty years after the project began. The sisters are buried in its extensive graveyard. Georgina, the younger, died first, in February 1870, shortly before the church was due to be consecrated. She was buried, as she'd ordained, in its churchyard, with a gravestone designed according to her instructions with an Ionic cross. The text, now eroded, records that Georgina 'came from an ancient race and possessed in herself the nobility of mind which delighted in the happiness of her fellow creatures'. Marianne has a less ostentatious grave with another large cross, enclosed by box hedges, recording that, in the further fifteen years left to her, she 'munificently completed' her sister's work.

The fields around Talbot Village have in recent years filled up with houses which lap around the little estate. Many more are planned – far more than some village residents favour. That some of the new developments use the name Talbot Village seems to them, as it does to me, to dilute the original concept; though it's clear when you visit Talbot Village now that the people who live there are hardly the victims of poverty and starvation for whom the village was originally built.

Unhappily, though, the recent history of the community has been tainted with criminality, though this time not by the needy and desperate but by well-heeled professional men. In February 2004, three construction industry professionals were jailed for defrauding the village trust of £3.5 million. Guy Peter Pound, an architect, described as the dominant conspirator, was sentenced to three years in prison; the Attorney-General appealed on the grounds that this was too lenient and the Court of Appeal doubled the sentence to six. Two others, both surveyors, were given suspended sentences, confirmed by the Court of Appeal. All were ordered to pay compensation. Though it's good to see that the Serious Fraud Office sometimes wins its cases, it's sad that such a venal offence should have occurred in the place that these virtuous Christian sisters created.

TATTENHOE

TATTENHOE, par. Bucks, 2m. W. of Bletchley;
647 ac., pop. 27.

'IF YOU'D COME HERE in 1965,' Tom Humble told me, when at last I had steered my uncertain way through the serpentine brick-built avenues of what is Tattenhoe now to the segregated enclave of what Tattenhoe used to be, 'you'd never have found us. There was no road at all in those days. There were sheep grazing on the fields, and you had to find a way through them to reach the church door.' That was still very much the picture when Bruce Watkin came here fifteen years later while compiling the new edition of the *Shell Guide to Buckinghamshire*, published in 1981. 'Only 3 km from Bletchley,' he wrote, 'but feels the most remote place in the county. It is still, as Betjeman and Piper [compilers of the previous edition of the *Guide*] said in 1948, "what Bucks must have been like in Cowper's day." A medieval church sits in yew and scrub and the over-grown fishponds of a long-gone mansion, connected with the outside world by a muddy track across flat fields past still remote cottages...'

There were three farms here, sustaining the twenty-seven inhabitants whom Bartholomew recorded in 1943, on a site which in medieval times had been a whole village. The church of St Giles, conveniently close to the manor house for the benefit of the Staffords, a kind of subsidiary branch line of the Dukes of Buckingham, was built around 1540, making use of some materials pillaged from nearby Snelshall Priory after the dissolution of the monasteries, as you can see today at the base of the font and in the door lintels. What became of the medieval village is not yet established, but it may well have been that the Staffords, in the insouciant way of many such aristocrats, simply found it was in their way and got rid of it. If so, their hubris was duly rewarded. The family fell on hard times and were forced to abandon the place, and though the estate was sold on, the house crumbled over the years into nothing.

You can still very easily see where it stood, on a kind of moated peninsula just beyond the church.

Little else survived after that. By 1831, the population here was only thirteen. Greater places than this suffered the same kind of fate: Quarrendon, near Aylesbury in the south of the county (population sixty-five, says Bartholomew), was once, according to the first *Shell Guide to Buckinghamshire* (1936), one of the political centres of Elizabethan England, where a tournament was held every year in the queen's honour; but little remains there now. Tattenhoe (sometimes Tottenhoe then) seems to have experienced some kind of revival, for the census of 1861 found sixty-four people here. But by the end of the century, that figure had fallen back again, to 16. That left little continuing role for the church of St Giles, inaccessible on its muddy track among the overgrown fishponds. 'Now disused', Bruce Watkin noted bleakly in 1981 – though here he was wrong, as church records suggest it was never abandoned. It was closed up in winter, when it would have been unbearably cold, but reopened each summer and was even from time to time honoured by visits from bishops of Oxford. One old attender recalls the bishop arriving over the fields in the summer of 1949 dressed in his full regalia in a farm cart drawn by a horse.

And then ancient Tattenhoe acquired a new neighbour. There used to be a village not far away which is listed like this in Bartholomew: '*Milton Keynes, par. and vil., Bucks, on r. Ousel, 3½ m. SW. of Newport Pagnell; 1909 ac., pop 192*'. (Its 'Keynes' in those days was pronounced like the great economist: 'Kanes'.) Today, that Milton Keynes is simply a minor fragment of a very much bigger one: the new town designated in 1967, a project covering more than 30 square miles of largely rural England, its population already in the early years of the new century around 170,000, much the same as Swindon's. In a sense the new Milton Keynes was the death of old Tattenhoe: it finished the farms and it finished all farm employment. 'Twenty-eight thousand acres, 50 farms, 250 farmworkers, all lost,' Tom Humble recalled. He was one of the casualties. He had been a farm manager, but now, at forty-five, he found himself out of a job – and given the great tides of brick and concrete and tarmac spreading across the territory, with no chance of like employment on offer. He went to work for a bank.

Tom Humble has watched Milton Keynes grow from almost nothing, and that process is not done yet. Just beyond the two Tattenhoes, ancient and modern, there's a huge new estate under construction on strict ecological principles: Tattenhoe Park, filling the last grid square of the MK master plan. Already a city in all but name – its legitimate aspirations to that status have been brusquely denied to it – it is destined by 2011 to accommodate some 215,000 people, not far short of the population of Southampton.

But it won't advance any further on St Giles and the manor house site and the moat and the overgrown fishponds. One outrider of the red-brick army of Milton Keynes is stationed beyond the car park, visible as you leave the church; and at the back, where some of the old farmhouses still stand, a new estate laps up to them. The sense of the remote and romantic which the *Shell Guide* evoked is lost and cannot be re-created; but at least that which has survived until now is sacrosanct, ring-fenced, as planners say, against any further encroachment.

The onward march of Milton Keynes has succeeded as nothing else could have done in bringing St Giles fully back to life. For a while the church had been open only for Evensong on Sundays in summer. When the weather was good they kept the doors open, so that the sounds of the country could be heard in the background: from time to time, an interested sheep would put its head around the door. Harvest festival services here had the added dimension of the sound of the harvest still being gathered outside. Then, from the mid 1990s special occasions, Christmas and Easter, were celebrated here too. Since 1999 there have been services every Sunday throughout the year.

An ecumenical group, which until this time had met in a shopping centre, asked if they could meet in the church instead, and that developed into a pattern of regular Sunday services, sometimes conducted by Anglicans, sometimes by Baptists or Methodists, and sometimes – as on the day I was there, Remembrance Sunday 2007 – by a minister of the United Reformed Church; each service flavoured by the allegiance of whoever might be conducting it, but with far less difference in practice from one to the next than denominational tradition might have suggested. The various liturgies, Alison Drury points out – she chairs the council which runs the Watling Valley Ecumenical Partnership, to which this church belongs – aren't so far apart as non-churchgoers might suppose. And Tom Humble, who read one of the lessons on Remembrance Day, is a Roman Catholic.

It's a tiny church – it would seat perhaps thirty with ease, but forty would crowd it – and in the early days of its unpredicted renaissance it was in a very poor state. You could see the sky through the roof. There was no power supply – candles were used to light it – and no heating. 'Come wrapped up warmly', winter visitors used to be warned. Now there's light and heating; the fine old pews – the box pews reserved for the farmers, the open pews for their underlings – have been polished to a warm brown glow. 'A small, mean building', a guidebook called *Magna Britannia* called it in 1806. I wish *Magna Britannia* could have been there to see it, sparkling and burnished and decked out with flowers, on Remembrance Day.

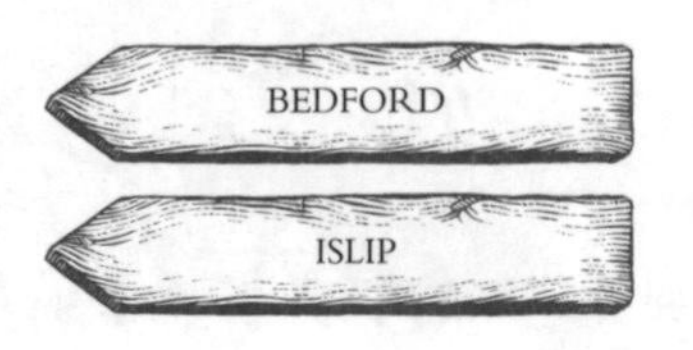

TEMPERANCE TOWN

TEMPERANCE TOWN, locality,
Glamorgan in Cardiff co. bor.

FEW WHO WAIT AT Cardiff bus station to begin their journeys to Llanrumney and Pantmawr (via Rhiwbina), St Fagan, St Mellons, Lllandaff, Lisvane or Lantwit Major know the history of the ground upon which they stand. This was once useless land, with no way across it, which disappeared under spring floods. Then the city authorities decided to alter the course of the river Taff, and some time in the 1850s a teetotal market gardener called Jacob Scott Matthews saw an opportunity to reclaim the land and use it to build a model community: a group of close-packed houses set out on a tight grid of streets with, as its centrepiece, symbolizing his purpose, a temperance hall, to be sited on the principal street – Wood Street, named after Colonel Wood, from whom he had leased the land. No outlets, it was strictly stipulated, would be allowed for the sale of the ales and spirituous liquors which damaged and diminished the lives of the working class.

There were other settlements scattered across the land devoted to the temperance cause: some created by people and organizations pledged to temperance or even teetotalism (not the same thing: temperance allowed beer and wine in moderation, where teetotalism did not allow them at all), and others by philanthropists like Sir Titus Salt at Saltaire who simply wished their beneficiaries to live in decent sobriety. Curiously, even Brian Harrison's hugely well-researched *Drink and the Victorians*, where I expected to find a comprehensive catalogue of them, finds no space to list all such settlements. Some foundered before they began. In March 1864, the *Temperance Star* announced that the Alliance National Land, Building and Investment Company, which had sprung from the temperance movement, had purchased an estate at Oxford where it intended to found a model community devoid of public houses. The land, it enthused, was peculiarly suited for a 'practical prohibition experiment', in that it was bounded on three sides by college properties where further building was never likely to follow. But those who eagerly scanned the *Temperance Star* through the rest of the year and thereafter for news of progress found none.

Such exemplary garden suburbs as Saltaire and Lever's Port Sunlight and Merton Park, developed by John Innes on the fringes of Wimbledon, contained no pubs. Ebenezer Howard's pioneering garden suburb at Letchworth, Hertfordshire, had a pub, the Skittles Inn, where you could not buy beer. But none took on, as this one in Cardiff did, a name which so unequivocally proclaimed its allegiance to temperance.

The trouble was that in practice this allegiance didn't last long. The people who settled in Matthews's crowded streets did not share his distaste for strong drink. They did not have to go far to find it elsewhere in Cardiff; and despite repeated raids and subsequent prosecutions, they cheerfully brewed it at home. In 1861, eleven years after the town had begun to take shape, the chief superintendent of police told the watch committee that in a city containing 131 brothels and 39 beer houses known to be brothels, Temperance Town was the worst spot of all – a reputation court records were said to confirm. By now, civilized opinion tended to call it a slum. Less than fifty years on, the city fathers had had enough of Temperance Town. In 1896, Cardiff's town hall committee agreed to acquire it and raze it, to create a useful space for civic purposes between the town hall and station and Cardiff Arms Park. Ratepayers were assured that, far from costing them money, this would generate useful income: new properties built there would bring in fat enough revenues to offset the cost of rehousing those that the clearance was going to displace.

So Matthews's dream-become-nightmare was more or less swept away. There is no trace left of Eisteddfod Street, Raven Street, or especially of Gough Street, which seems to have been the brothel capital of Temperance Town. Away, too, went the church of that not over-celebrated figure, St Dyfrig. As for the emblematic Temperance Hall, that had succumbed much earlier, converted into another institution tending to shock the respectable: a music hall. Park Street and Havelock

Street are the only survivors of the little world which Matthews devised in the name of the public good. The rest today is as forgotten as he is.

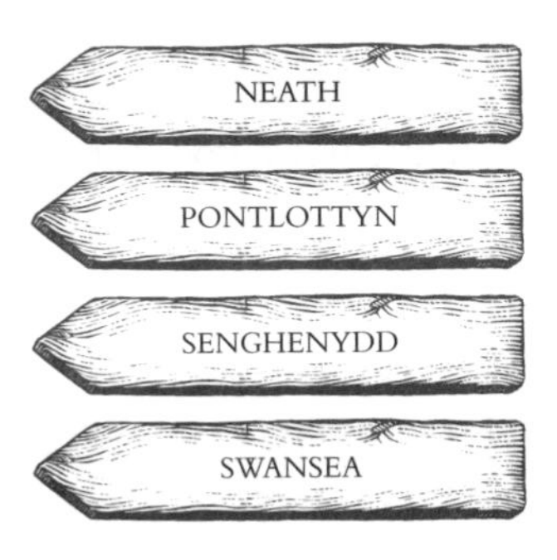

TENTERDEN

TENTERDEN, mun. bor., mkt.-town, par. and ry. stas.
(T. Town and T. St Michael's), Kent and East Sussex R., Kent, 7m.
ESE. of Cranbrook and 8½m. NNW. of Rye…
It is surrounded by hop plantations.

HOW HAS IT COME about that the Weald of Kent contains such a cluster of satisfying small towns and villages: Biddenden, Brenchley, Goudhurst, Cranbrook and Tenterden, places that, were there a national gallery of Britain's best-looking townships, would all be sure of a space? Goudhurst, with its hillside high street linking two squares – the one at the top with the glorious church, the big old-fashioned hotel and the cheerfully eccentric Church House, and the one at the foot, with pub, oast house and pond – is the more exciting, but Tenterden boasts of being the 'Jewel of the Weald', which does not seem unduly pushy when you see its exceptional high street: a kind of serene accidental anthology of domestic building, brick and tile hung, wood-boarded, Tudor to the present day; comfortable and elegant private houses interrupted by flavoursome shops and antique dealers. There are trees everywhere, a fine splash of green on each side of the road that runs south-west towards Hastings, and at the back the mighty tower of the church of St Mildred presiding benignly over it all.

How did it happen? One part of the answer is money: these were prosperous places, their fortunes made out of industry. Tenterden, Cranbrook and Goudhurst would hardly be taken for industrial towns today, but their money was made from wool and iron: also in Tenterden's case from the sea, since before the coastline took on its present shape what is now the inland settlement of Smallhythe was a port. Yet even that doesn't explain why so much of this townscape is harmonious, more harmonious than skilled planners and architects often contrive – yet here all achieved by impulse and improvisation and evolution.

But there's something more that Tenterden has to offer – assuming you've plenty of time. It's a gateway to one of the loveliest buildings in England: Bodiam Castle, some

ten miles away over the county border in Sussex. There are other ways of getting to Bodiam, but to go there by road denies you the drama and the mounting sense of expectation that you get on the slow chugging train out of Tenterden town as the castle begins to reveal itself. The Kent and East Sussex Railway (originally, the Rother Valley Railway) opened in 1900, running from what was then called Tenterden station, though it wasn't in Tenterden, to Robertsbridge, Sussex. The present-day terminus for its steam revival services was reached three years later, after which the line was further extended to join the London to Ashford line at Headcorn. This was the first of many light railways built by the pioneer Colonel Stephens: Holman Fred Stephens, son of one pre-Raphaelite artist, F. G. Stephens, and godson of a more famous one, Holman Hunt. No such railways were permitted until 1896, when Parliament approved legislation to make it simpler and cheaper to bring railways to rural areas which until then had largely been denied them, both for reasons of cost and because to establish a railway you needed a specific Act of Parliament.

With light railways, some of which were really no more than tramways, the standards that had to be met were less demanding, solutions had to be cheap and cheerful since money was always tight, and the enterprises, even some of Stephens's, were often short-lived. The shortcomings of such operations are well demonstrated by the history of the Kent and East Sussex Railway. Though Tenterden Town station is close to the centre of Tenterden, Rolvenden (the original Tenterden terminus) is two miles from the village of Rolvenden, Wittersham Road is three miles from Wittersham village, Northiam is a mile or so from the place whose name it has borrowed, and it isn't until you reach the end of the line, at Bodiam, that passengers can feel confident of truly having arrived at the place that they booked for.

It was always a struggle for the Kent and East Sussex to make ends meet, but the rise of the motor car, bus and van hit the railway hard, and from 1928 onwards it made no profit. The last passenger train on the line ran in January 1954 and the line was finally closed in 1961. But in 1973/4 a group of local enthusiasts resolved to revive it as a tourist attraction, first only as far as Wittersham, but then on to Northiam and finally through to Bodiam.

Despite some perilous moments, when it looked as though they might run out of money, their trains – some steam, some 'heritage diesel', a concept I'd never encountered before – were still running most days through the summer of 2007 with less frequent journeys in winter. The 10½ mile trip to Bodiam takes around forty-five minutes. This is partly due to level crossings: each time we approached one, the train had to stop; a uniformed figure descended to open the level crossing; the train, having crossed, stopped again; the uniformed figure closed the crossing, and off, for a while, we went. Drivers meanwhile fumed in queues, no doubt cursing this amateur operation. Yet aboard, none of that matters; to travel as slowly as this, so slowly that now and again you feel that if you wound down the window you'd be able to pick the blackberries off passing bushes, gives one a feeling of luxury. Time, and along with time, the relentless press of the world, cease to matter.

Beyond Northiam, though, a sense of occasion develops, a purposeful chuffing builds up and the sound of the wheels on the rails becomes almost urgent. Even the mournful call that the engine emits when the driver sees a sign saying 'Whistle' – which is more of a hoot, but perhaps rather suggests an animal's cry of pain – begins to sound businesslike. One must watch out here for a windmill on top of a hill to the right of the train and a pylon marching towards the track across the low meadows. Very soon, there is just a glimpse of distant towers; and then, rising majestically out of its wreath of trees, there is the fourteenth-century castle. The train at this point holds its direction, as if humbly fearful of coming too close to such a superior place. But gradually it edges towards it, to put you down at a still respectful but not very taxing distance from the gate to the castle grounds.

And the views as you reach the castle are even more magnificent than the ones you get from the train. What you've not quite seen from the railway is the way that, though its walls are so powerful and resolute, it seems almost to float like something out of a fantasy over the dark green waters of its capacious moat. Little is left of the barbican, but the gatehouse is much as it was when the Victorian antiquary and topographer John Timbs described it in his book *Abbeys, Castles and Ancient Halls of England and Wales*: 'The gateway is a majestic structure, composed of two flanking towers, defended by numerous oiletts for arrows, embattled parapets, and deep machicolations, whence stones and other missiles could be hurled on the heads of an attacking force.'

Built in the late fourteenth century, it passed from privileged owner to privileged owner until in the seventeenth century it fell into neglect. 'Bodiam', says Timbs, 'has gradually crumbled before the power of rain, frost, and storm; still, even now, above two hundred years after its ruin, enough remains to show the substantial manner in which the feudal lords of the time of the Black Prince raised their mansions.' There are pictures in the visitor centre of the building fallen away into ruin, its walls thick with ivy. Thomas Love Peacock, that devotee of battered romantic towers, would have wanted to leave it like that, as no doubt would the owls that used to frequent it: there are roosting poles along the railway line, in what used to be hop fields, put there to tempt the owls that have fled to return.

But the castle found a white knight – or much better than any mere knight, a marquess – to rescue it. George Nathaniel Curzon, one-time Governor-General of India, Foreign Secretary, contender for the Conservative leadership, which he might have won had he not been a lord, came upon it when he was Warden of the Cinque Ports, and longed to buy it. The then owner, Lord Ashcombe, refused, but on Ashcombe's death, Curzon, who earlier had saved Tattershall Castle in Lincolnshire from being demolished and shipped to the USA, got what he wanted.

Until I went to Bodiam, I had always thought of Curzon as a chilly figure, a man who established a reputation for being a 'very superior person', at home with those of his class but with few others. There are many unflattering stories told about him: that when someone persuaded him to get on a bus, he barked at the conductor 'The Ritz!' presumably on the assumption that this unfamiliar conveyance was some working-class equivalent of a cab; that when Stanley Baldwin, son of a mere Worcestershire manufacturer, beat him for the Tory leadership, he dismissed him as 'a man of the utmost insignificance'; that in wartime, seeing soldiers stripped off for bathing, he remarked that he'd never known before that the working classes had such white skins.

Not many of these tales are true. They circulated because they seemed to chime with his image. A. J. P. Taylor, no flatterer of the nobility, said that Curzon invented some of these stories himself.

The fact that he saved both the Lincolnshire castle and this one, and left them on his death to the National Trust for even the plebs to enjoy, suggests something better. And what most of all makes one warm to him is the extract you can read on a wall in the visitor centre from a memoir by his American second wife, Grace:

> As we approached the hill leading down to Bodiam the chauffeur was told to drive very slowly while George looked for an opening he remembered between the trees by the roadside. Suddenly he told the chauffeur to stop and we got out; and turning to me, he said, 'Now give me your hand and climb up this bank, with your eyes closed, and don't open them until I tell you!' He helped me up the bank and then said 'Now look!' I have that picture in my heart for all time...

They drove into the grounds and spent an hour or more there, 'while George, more excited than I have ever seen him before, described what he hoped to do to restore Bodiam to its original magnificence, so that its beauty might last forever'. Even a very superior person deserves to be warmed to for that.

TEWKESBURY

TEWKESBURY, mun. bor., par. and mkt.-town, with ry. sta., L.M.S., Glos, on r. Avon at its confluence with the Severn, 8m. NW. of Cheltenham... Tewkesbury is famous for its fine parish church and the remains of the monastery founded in 715...

ONE MORNING IN THE early 1870s two men walked down from the Malvern Hills into the abbey town of Tewkesbury. They were a curiously assorted pair. One was the fifty-five-year-old Master of Balliol, Benjamin Jowett, the son of a Peckham furrier, who had risen to be one of the most distinguished academic figures of Victorian England. A rhyme circulating in the college of which he was Master and soon well beyond it, had him saying: 'First come I. My name is J–w–tt./ There's no knowledge, but I know it./ I am the master of this college./ What I don't know, isn't knowledge.' The other was Matthew Knight, the nineteen-year-old son of a college servant, in whom Jowett had detected such promise that he included him in one of the reading parties he held for undergraduates at his vacation retreats in Malvern, Wensleydale and Pitlochry. But this, as Knight would one day recall, had been an uneasy occasion. For some time they had been walking in silence. Eventually Knight summoned his courage to venture: 'I believe there are more dogs than people in the streets this morning!'; to which the Master replied: 'If you have nothing more sensible to observe, you had better be silent.'

It must have been some consolation to Knight that Jowett, though in many ways a kindly man, was never slow to issue this kind of crushing rebuke to those who with some whimpering irrelevance disturbed his train of thought. The journalist and biographer J. A. Spender, in an article recalling Balliol in the 1880s, said of Jowett: 'During the whole four years I was up I scarcely passed a term without being invited to a solitary meal with him, either breakfast or dinner. The time passed in almost complete silence. Now and again I used to venture an embarrassed remark, but as likely as not the reply would be, "You wouldn't have said that if you had stopped to think" and after that, silence more glacial still he dismissed me with a brief "good morning".'

Even the reading parties were sometimes a torment. 'The master', another of his Balliol pupils wrote, 'is good-humoured and comes out with very good stories, about one per hour; but, oh! such terrible pauses and silences between! I too am becoming quite taciturn and sit for ten minutes without uttering.' The historian Sir George Trevelyan recalled an evening when Jowett came to call on his father, Sir Charles. Thomas Macaulay was also present, and long and fervent conversation ensued on matters such as civil service reform. But Jowett, throughout, said not a word.

It was not that he did not enjoy or value conversation. He was known at times, especially when in the presence of the poet Swinburne, to become almost overflowingly voluble. This too was an odd alliance: the apparently austere Master happily closeted with the wild and extravagant Swinburne (once one of his pupils, though characteristically he never completed his course) rattling away in a wholly uninhibited fashion. Swinburne could say what he liked to Jowett. 'Another howler, Master!' he chortled, perusing some work of Jowett's. 'Thank you, Algernon, thank you,' was the unrebukeful reply. 'Gaiety', Swinburne wrote, was natural to Jowett's temperament. He even liked jokes – though his own, perhaps, rather than other people's. Once he asked a student what words the young man supposed were written over the gateway to hell. Interrupting his stuttering answer, the Master furnished his own: 'Ici on parle français,' he said.

But Jowett could not sparkle in unsympathetic company. In the presence of strangers or flamboyant celebrities he faded into the background. Matthew Knight, recalling that awkward moment in Tewkesbury, said that on other occasions he and Jowett had talked of everything under the sun. 'He endeavoured to arouse my interest in the most varied topics. The educational process was the more effective because he expected me to understand all of which he spoke, and so compelled me to use my mind to the utmost of my power.' But using one's mind to the utmost of its power also meant, on Jowett's analysis, knowing when not to make pointless small talk.

One needs to distinguish between silence and mere taciturnity. William of Nassau, Prince of Orange, the man we now think of as William the Silent, of whom the American historian John Lothrop Motley wrote, 'As long as he lived, he was the guiding-star of a whole brave nation, and when he died the little children cried in the streets', has been mistranslated. He was taciturn rather than silent. In her fine biography,

C. V. Wedgwood explains that in his days as a troubled but loyal servant of King Philip of Spain, William was 'fortunately, good at hiding his feelings; sly, his enemies called him, "*schluwe*" in Dutch. Grandiosely rendered into Latin as "taciturnus" it came back absurdly into all the languages of western Europe as "silent". The surname earned during these next years – William the Silent – could hardly have been more unsuited to this affable young man, yet it was not without truth, even in its mistranslated form, for these were the years of suppressed and divided feelings.'

William Beckford, the rich and richly eccentric builder of Fonthill Tower and author of *Vathek*, would invite guests to dinner, dine and wine them lavishly, but not join them at the table. Leslie Stephen, joint editor of the original *Dictionary of National Biography* and father of Virginia Woolf, was famous for his 'formidable silences': 'alpine in their desolation' said Edmund Gosse. It was often hard to prise more than a word or two out of Calvin Coolidge, much lauded at the time but now rated as one of the worst of American presidents. A woman sitting in silence beside him at a dinner party confessed that she'd taken a bet that she would manage to get at least three words out of him. 'You lose,' he replied. He rarely gave a press interview. It is said that one reporter, admitted to his presence on the strict condition that his questions would be submitted in writing first, read them out one by one, only on every occasion to get the reply: 'No comment'. As he made his disconsolate way out of the room the president called him back. 'Oh, and by the way,' said Coolidge, 'don't forget that is all off the record.'

That may be legend, but if so, it became a legend because it seemed to embody Coolidge's way of behaving. His departure from office was no exception. In 1927, he appeared before the press to announce: 'I do not choose to run for the presidency in 1928.' (That's eleven words.) Besieged with further questions, he waved them away with this supplementary answer: 'There will be nothing more from this office today.' (That's nine.) Yet friends attested that in his favourite company, Calvin could gush like a geyser.

The enemy in these cases is usually extraneous talk, rather than talk per se, in line with Wittgenstein's edict: 'Whereof one cannot speak, thereof one must be silent.' Enoch Powell, asked by a Commons barber how he would like his hair cut, is reported to have replied, 'In silence'. Only in rare cases outside religious orders committed to silence does the practice of holding one's tongue and expecting others to do so grow rigid and unconditional. In *The Rings of Saturn*, W. G. Sebald reprints a newspaper cutting about a wealthy Suffolk man who had left his vast estate to his housekeeper in return for her obedient silences. 'Mrs Florence Barnes (57)', the paper reported, 'employed by Le Strange in 1955 as housekeeper and cook on condition that she dined with him in silence every day, said that Le Strange had, in the course of time, become a virtual recluse, but she refused to give any details of the Major's eccentric way of life. Asked about her inheritance, she said that, beyond wanting to buy a bungalow in Beccles for herself and her sister, she had no idea what to do with it.'

At Tewkesbury, Jowett and Knight apparently parted: Jowett was heading for Clifton. Perhaps they had a good lunch, if with minimal conversation. Since the summer of 2007, this town has been chiefly famous for being flooded, always a menacing possibility at a spot where two rivers meet. The summer floods were written about as if they were some unheralded visitation, but when I was there in March 2007 there were floods the like of which – so a man on a bus informed me – had not been seen in the town for the best part of sixty years. It was hard to judge from my riverside walk which were floods and which was the genuine river on which boat trips in summer were advertised.

It was disconcerting for an old fan of Tewkesbury to find, on a day in the town in the summer of 2007, that the famous inn in the centre, the Royal Hop Pole Hotel, mentioned in Dickens, was shut down and boarded up; but happily the pub chain J. D. Wetherspoon reopened it the following spring. As with many old coaching towns, this one's population of pubs has been gravely reduced over the years, but plenty remain, and the one I chose, the Nottingham Arms, was infectiously cheerful. A little way down the road was another dead pub, the Wheatsheaf, reborn as a second-hand bookshop. If pubs are to close, let them all become second-hand bookshops.

As for Jowett, when he died at seventy-six in 1893 he remembered Matthew Knight in his will; but Knight himself was dead two years later, at forty-one. The rest, as they say, was silence.

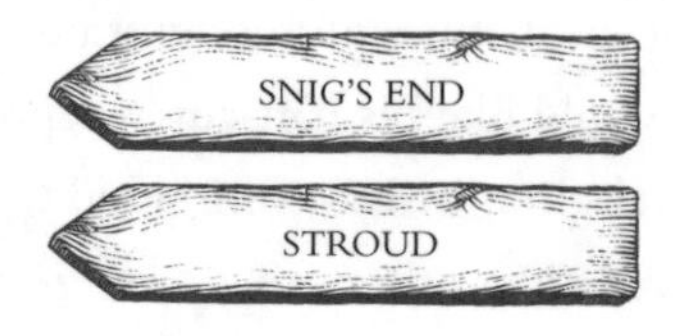

TOCKHOLES

TOCKHOLES, par., NE. Lancs, 3m. SSW. of Blackburn...

J. L. CARR (WHOM we met at Kettering) says in his *Welbourn's Dictionary of Prelates, Parsons, Vergers, Wardens, Sidesmen & Preachers, Sunday-School Teachers, Hermits, Ecclesiastical Flower-arrangers, Fifth Monarchy Men and False Prophets*: 'The Vicar of Tock-hole (Lancs), c.1847, customarily aroused sermon-dozers by bawling, "Wakken oop! Ye'll ha' time enuff t'doaze i'Hell".'

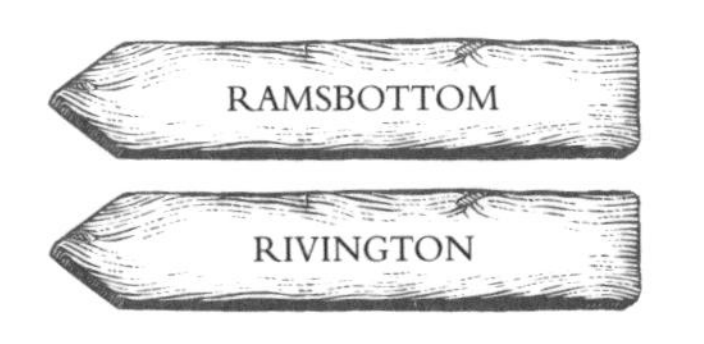

TONBRIDGE

TONBRIDGE, urb. dist., mkt.-town and par., with ry. sta. S.R., Kent, on r. Medway, 29½m. SE. of London, by rail and 4m. N. of Tunbridge Wells... It has the ruins of a castle.

THROUGH THE WINDOWS OF a train from the Kent coast to London, just beyond Tonbridge, I saw a man walking through fields at twilight. Instinctively I looked for his dog. If people walk in the fields close to a town when the light is departing, it is usually at the insistence of a dog. But there was no dog. He was walking alone. It could have been that he knew a short cut to get him into the town before nightfall; yet his walk, head bowed, hands thrust deep into pockets, was pensive rather than purposeful, and he wore the kind of boots which belong on a serious walk. That he found himself out in the fields at such a late hour, I concluded, was no accident. He was walking at twilight for the pleasure of walking at twilight.

Twilight is the time between sunset and darkness. There's another twilight: the lightening of the sky immediately before dawn. But the word as we overwhelmingly use it today belongs to the evening. It's the time when the light is dying, not being born. In metaphor, too, our twilight years come at the end of our lives, not the beginning; *Götterdämmerung*, the twilight of the gods, is the moment when an old regime is ending, not when a new one is burgeoning. It's a time not of hope and expectation but of introspection and melancholy, and a kind of contemplation, however unintended, of death. Also, in past times, it was a moment for fear; for twilight would swiftly be followed by surrender to a darkness so all-enveloping that nowadays one can scarcely imagine it. There's a Collect in the Prayer Book which used to bewilder me when it was read at school: 'Lighten our darkness, we beseech thee, O Lord; and by thy great mercy defend us from all perils and dangers of this night...' In what sense, I used to wonder, was night so perilous, when darkness could be dispersed on most occasions by a simple flick of a switch close at hand? Even out of doors, for people living in cities, the sky was never entirely dark because of the neon glow which suffused the sky once the blackout regulations of war were finally lifted. 'Light pollution' it is sometimes called nowadays. But in times when some strange noise in the house, or the street, or the surrounding fields, meant that candles had to be found and anxiously lit, the dangers and perils of night must have seemed inescapably real.

Even now, the melancholy of twilight persists. Yet it is, in a sense, a sweet, almost luxurious melancholy. We know this nightly death is not final. No need to rage against the dying of the light. Here, the sure and certain hope of resurrection which the funeral service promises is truly sure and certain. Light and life will return on schedule tomorrow.

This mood is often caught in literature, high and low. Gray's *Elegy* is the essence of twilight reflectiveness, which at least in part is why it is so much remembered and loved. The lowing herd winds, as it still does today, o'er the lea. The ploughman homeward plods his weary way, and leaves the world to darkness, and to Gray… No other hour would have inspired the meditation that follows.

Popular songs of Victorian England captured the same sense of twilight reflection: 'Just a song at twilight, when the lights are low, And the flick'ring shadows softly come and go…' by G. Clifton Bingham, 1884, to a melody by James L. Molloy. I find 'twilight' a touchingly evocative word. The French and Italians call this time *crépuscule*, and the word 'crepuscular' has entered the English language. To me, it's an ugly word, curled up, suggesting creeping, and even pus, though others think it is beautiful. When the great American jazz composer Thelonious Monk, worrying over the health of his wife, wrote a composition called 'Twilight with Nellie', his rich and glamorous patron, the Baroness Pannonica de Koenigswarter (a Rothschild from Britain who married a French diplomat, was divorced from him, and had settled in New York, where she befriended, to put it mildly, various talented jazz musicians) persuaded him that the French 'crépuscule' would suit it better, and the sometimes intractable Monk dutifully complied. He shouldn't have.

On my train up from Kent I had envied the freedom of the man I saw from my window to walk in these fields at twilight. At the same time of year, I went back to Kent to try to see for myself what he would have seen and even perhaps to feel what he would have felt. I was blessed, though it had not been forecast, with a glorious day in November: the sun had shone with conspicuous valour all day long, and the first sense of evening chill saw it barely diminished. As it settled ever lower on the horizon, the sense of its power seemed to grow rather than lessen: pitched where it was its directness felt like a kind of assault. 'The horizontal light of evening', Aldous Huxley says in an essay on 'Country Ecstasies' in a book called *Texts & Pretexts,* 'causes the world to shine, with such an unusual, such a goldenly improbable radiance, that, looking, we are startled out of our usual purblind complacency…'

Of course this sun was doomed, but it went out in glory, sinking from a sky of red and blue clouds with below, even more dramatic perhaps because less expected, a broad streak somewhere between yellow and green. The lights were coming on in nearby houses. Here and there, where once there would have been a profusion, some wisps of smoke curled up from chimneys; television screens flickered, much as open fires would have done half a century earlier. Birds had begun their dusk chorus, a kind of modest reprise of the exuberant celebrations with which they would have welcomed the dawn. And the trains from Kent to London glided through on their embankment, those running east into Tonbridge carrying their first contingents of London workers making their weary way back to the station car parks and so to home: some in the lighted carriages with heads turned to survey the landscape, others with heads lost behind newspapers, still others with heads bowed in sleep.

The passage in a familiar book that now came to mind as I stood in my twilight field in Kent was not from *The Golden Treasury* but from chapter five of *The Wind in the Willows*, which is called 'Dulce Domum', as Rat, journeying with Mole through fields where sheep huddle together in the frosty air, comes to a village, which Mole, fearing trouble, is disposed to avoid.

> The rapid nightfall of mid-December had quite beset the little village as they approached it on soft feet over a first thin fall of powdery snow. Little was visible but the squares of a dusky orange-red on either side of the street, where the firelight or lamplight of each cottage overflowed through the casements into the dark world without. Most of the low latticed windows were innocent of blinds, and to the lookers-in from outside, the inmates, gathered round the tea-table, absorbed in handiwork, or talking with laughter and gesture, had each that happy grace which is the last thing the skilled actor shall capture – the natural grace which goes with perfect unconsciousness of observation…

The man I saw from my train heading for home through the fields may have returned to a much less tranquil scene than this soft, sentimental one – full of raucous headlines of world disasters and an evening to follow of reality television or the flickering screen of a computer. Yet the event of twilight, the final slow, sad dissolving of some magnificent sky, the knowledge that by the time the world has grown dark one will have gained the safety of home, still wraps one round in a sense of comfort and security, as it must have done even in times so distant that we have no record.

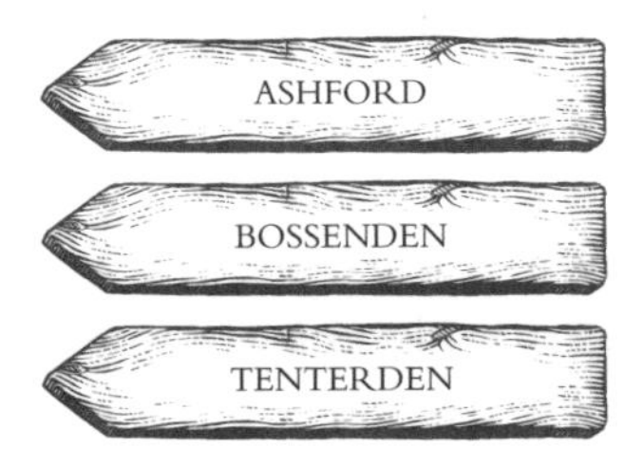

TOTTINGTON

TOTTINGTON, par. and vil., Norfolk,
3½m. SSW. of Watton; 3,244 ac., pop. 200...

A TURN WEST OFF the road from East Dereham to Thetford, inviting you to travel to Thompson, will bring you to Tottington war memorial. It stands at a junction, in a spot which is plainly not Tottington, and not really anywhere – just an arbitrary break in the woods. It remembers the men of Tottington who fell in the First World War: fifteen of them, including a Bone, a Flatt and a Worby, along with forty-five who returned: among these are a second Worby, and four spared Tuddenhams.

If you wonder why it is here and not in Tottington, that's because for all practical purposes there isn't a Tottington, which is why there's a sign to say that the lane that leaves the main road at this junction is closed one mile ahead. This was one of a cluster of villages which effectively went to war in the 1940s and never came back. Tottington, Stanford, Langford, Buckenham Tofts, West Tofts and Sturston (though Sturston had almost died anyway: Bartholomew puts its population at twenty-seven) were places where villagers were called on to make their personal sacrifice in the cause of the war by being ejected – only to find, when the war was over, that their ejection was permanent. All were subsumed for the indefinite future in a creation called Stanta – the Stanford Training Area.

Had this been good agricultural land, producing in profusion crops that were good for the war effort, they might have been spared, but the judgement was that the land here was poor and therefore dispensable. Imber in Wiltshire and Tyneham in Dorset, which met the same fate, became *causes célèbres*, yet the legion of the dispossessed here in the Thetford Forest was more numerous than either of them. Even communities around them, unrequired by the War Department, were lost in the process: just count the number of signposts in the surviving village of Thompson which announce that the roads now go nowhere. Or listen in the small hours at night to the sounds of artillery: 'We hear them at night', says a man in a neighbouring village, 'and we think, what's up, and we wonder where they'll be going.' The answer not so long ago was Iraq.

If you walk down the lane towards where Tottington used to be you come to the signs for the Peddars Way, an ancient track from Ixworth in Suffolk past Swaffham to the coast at Hunstanton. This isn't the route the original peddars (people who travelled on foot) would have used: that's been diverted to take it around Stanta. On the other side of the path the way was lightly barred – the gates look to belong to the world of agriculture rather than that of military security – but it was certainly clear that you had to keep out. On the other side of the area at West Tofts, though, where notices warned of a danger zone, the prohibition seemed oddly ambiguous. But even if you defied them, there would not be much left to see of the villages that used to be here: little more than their churches, still cared for by the military. In certain prearranged circumstances they'll escort visitors in, even though there is not the slightest likelihood that the ancient pattern of matins, communion and evensong will ever resume.

Tottington's church is St Andrew's – 'forlorn inside a chain-link fence, but the corrugated iron covering the windows was removed in 1993–4 and the roofs reclad in steel', according to the latest updated edition of Pevsner. West Tofts has a church that was partly rebuilt by A. N. W. Pugin and after his death by his son E. W. Pugin, for the Reverend Augustus Sutton, rector from 1849, one of the Sutton family of nearby Lynford Hall; it did have stained glass by the leading manufacturers, Hardman and Co., though that's now in store. Richard Muir, who was taken around the area while researching a book called *The Lost Villages of Britain*, found Tottington, 'rising ghostlike from the heath', the most appealing.

This is what happened to Tottington and the rest. As early as the summer of 1941 the land agent to Lord Walsingham, who owned the village, was unofficially warned that land might be required because of urgent military necessity, though strict secrecy was enjoined, and observed. Officially the process that led to the great ejection began in March 1942, when a committee was set to work to pick out suitable sites for field firing. Some 18,000 acres in the Thetford Forest, affecting between 750 and 800 people, were swiftly identified, much of it in the Tottington sector. Lord Walsingham, a peer and a former military man, was expected to be sympathetic to the government's case.

An open-air public meeting was called and the people of Tottington were told they had to be out of their homes and off their farmland in four weeks' time, on 19 July. A history of these events by Hilda and Edmund Perry estimates that there were 220 people living in Tottington then, in thirty-nine houses, and that some thirty of these were occupied by men who had served in the First World War, or by their widows. They were promised that everything possible would be done to protect their property, their churches and other places of local importance. *The Eastern Daily Press*, reporting this meeting, said the speech by the senior military commander charged with breaking the news was applauded, though in her book Hilda Perry (*née* Worby), one of those who was there to listen, denies this.

Lord Walsingham told the meeting he was proud to live among people who had reacted in the understanding manner that they had done – though according to Hilda Perry some villagers thought that he had sold them out. It was also made clear, and confirmed in correspondence between Lord Walsingham and Sir John Anderson, on behalf of the government, that when the war was won, their land and homes would be given back to them. The War Minister told protesting MPs, who were defending the interests of these and other requisitioned areas, that every possible alternative had been considered but rejected 'for cogent reasons'.

So belongings were loaded on to vans and carried to neighbouring villages. (At one of these, Merton, presumably in the hope of assuaging grief, a Tottington Terrace was built to house the evicted.) The army moved in behind them and, according to the Perrys, immediately began a process of destruction which continued for the rest of the war and beyond. Some who were allowed to go back later that year found belongings they'd left behind had been removed or destroyed and gardens crushed by vehicles. The harvest was brought in that autumn by schoolboys from Repton and Norwich Grammar School.

By the time that peace was declared, a convenient opinion had developed in Whitehall that these villages were in such poor condition that their old inhabitants would scarcely wish to go back, while the press were briefed that with ammunition everywhere, the places were far too dangerous for habitation. Bitter complaints in

Parliament and protests from the County Council brought the promise of a local inquiry, which took place in Thetford in January 1948. The inquiry not only upheld the retention of the land that the army had taken but approved the War Department's demand for more. This meant that some of those dispossessed in 1942 were now dispossessed again. The land was finally taken by compulsory purchase in 1950, with compensation restricted to the prices that had prevailed twelve years before.

I found on a website a vivid account of Tottington today by Simon Knott. He came to St Andrew's church along what had once been the village street, noting where the rectory had stood, and the pub. The only houses now were mock-up buildings – of the kind that Imber on Salisbury Plain has too, built for soldiers to practise hand to hand encounters in hostile territory. He was also able to see for himself St Andrew's Langford ('lovely – a soft little towerless church') and St Mary West Tofts ('a small medieval church transformed by Augustus Welby Pugin into a vast Gothic palace of worship' and still sometimes used for services) and All Saints Stanford. The church at Buckenham Tofts, like that at Sturston, had gone by the time the army moved in. His visits left him sad rather than outraged. Many of the houses the villagers vacated had after all been substandard, and the ones to which they were moved were distinctly better.

There's no point in pretending that traditional communities could ever be re-created here; should the lands be freed they would more likely be used to provide the kind of could-be-anywhere commuter villages now ranged around Thetford and Swaffham. Throughout the county's history villages have flourished and fallen away. That too is sanctified by tradition.

TREMADOG

TREMADOC [nowadays spelled Tremadog], small town, Carnarvonshire, under Yr-allt-wen (The White Cliff), 4½m. NE. of Criccieth…

DRIVE NORTH-WESTWARD ON the road that struggles through Porthmadog on its way towards Caernarfon and you come face to face with a high white cliff, and arrayed before it an elegant parade of early nineteenth-century buildings: a hotel called the Royal Madoc Arms and what was once the town hall and dancing hall, all tucked so tightly under the cliff that it's hard not to feel some sense of impending disaster. The cliff blocks the way: the road to the left goes on to Caernarfon, the road to the right to Beddgelert and Snowdon, and the town is so clotted with traffic that many who pass through it probably don't take it in.

Who, then, was Madog, who appears to have given his name both to the coastal resort of Porthmadog and to this model town? Madog was a Welsh prince, who's reputed to have discovered America long before Columbus. But these places have nothing to with him. Their creator was a man of exceptional energy, talent, imagination and the kind of courage which people call foolhardy when things go wrong: William Alexander Madocks, MP for Boston, Lincs. Without his vision, his resolution, his money, his constant activity when he was there and his ceaseless

bombardment of agents and subordinates when he was not, none of this would have happened. At the time the towns were called, in his honour and at his insistence, Porthmadoc and Tremadoc – Madocks's port, Madocks's town. It's a sign of the unjust neglect into which Madocks has fallen that officialdom preferred to invoke instead, on a spurious basis, the name of a much more celebrated, and more patently Welsh figure in the history of the principality.

Madocks was born in London to a Denbighshire family. His father was a Chancery barrister and one-time MP for Westbury, Wiltshire. He sent his son to Charterhouse school, which seems to have expelled him, but in spite of this he went on to Christ Church and then to All Souls, whose fellowships are a mark of high academic distinction. Throughout his life, Wales pulled him one way, London another. He was eager to make his name in politics – and, specifically, radical politics: his early hero was Charles James Fox, his early mentor, the turbulent radical Major John Cartwright, advocate of annual parliaments, full male suffrage and the secret ballot. Elected for Boston in 1802, he supported Catholic emancipation and parliamentary reform, boldly condemned the misbehaviour of royal dukes, and unsuccessfully sought to impeach Spencer Perceval and Castlereagh for electoral bribery.

But he was eager, too, to leave his mark on a part of Wales of which he was especially fond, and his father's will, which specified that some of the money he left must be used to acquire freehold property, gave him the start he needed. The whole area around the Traeth Mawr – the Great Sands – which takes in the estuaries of the Dwyryd and Glaslyn, seemed to him to teem with potential. He set out to reclaim a thousand acres of land which at high tide became a vast lake, and to safeguard it from the sea by a great embankment. Running across this embankment would be a road to a place called Porth Dinllaen, providing a safe and swift route for trade and travel, linking the principal towns of newly united England and Ireland. He would also at the end of the embankment construct a coaching and market town: Tremadoc, whose principal streets would be London Street and Dublin Street.

This wholesale amendment of what nature had given this part of North Wales upset some who watched Madocks's plans taking shape; among them, Thomas Love Peacock, then living at Maentwrog in the vale of Ffestiniog. In his first novel,

Headlong Hall, three philosophers – Mr Foster the perfectibilian, Mr Escot the deteriorationist and Mr Jenkison the statu-quo-ite, who briefly appeared in my account of Dolbadarn – walk out to inspect the work at Tremadoc. Leaving Beddgelert they proceed through the sublimely romantic pass of Aberglaslyn to the edge of Traeth Mawr, where they behold the sea in all its magnificence. Another five miles brings them to the embankment, not yet quite completed, designed to banish the sea.

'The tide', Peacock writes, 'was now ebbing: it had filled the vast basin within, forming a lake about five miles in length and more than one in breadth. As they looked upwards with their backs to the open sea, they beheld a scene which no other in this country can parallel, and which the admirers of the magnificence of nature will ever remember with regret, whatever consolation may be derived from the probable utility of the works which have excluded the waters from this ancient receptacle. Vast rocks and precipices, intersected with little torrents, formed the barrier on the left: on the right, the triple summit of Moëlwyn reared its majestic boundary: in the depth was the sea of mountains, the wild and stormy outline of the Snowdonian chain, with the giant Wyddfa towering in the midst. The mountain-frame remains unchanged, unchangeable; but the liquid mirror it enclosed is gone.'

Being characters in a Peacock novel, they debate the implications all the way home. Mr Foster the perfectibilian is happy that the advantages outweigh the disadvantages; Mr Jenkison the statu-quo-ite finds them happily balanced; and Mr Escot the deteriorationist, the nearest to Peacock's own way of thinking, laments the manufactories which have suddenly sprung up, 'like fungous excrescences, in the bosom of these wild and desolate scenes', filling him with horror and amazement.

The project, town and embankment, took several years to complete, but at last in the summer of 1811 the embankment was finished, an event Madocks celebrated with a huge party, complete with ox roast and Eisteddfod, to which everyone was invited, though invitations to the ball in his fine new town hall, the focal point of Tremadoc, had to be rationed, since the building was simply too small. In all other senses the day was a triumph. 'We congratulate the public at large on the completion of a work which stands unrivalled in the history of the world,' trilled the *North Wales Gazette*.

The euphoria did not last long. The building of Madocks's embankment cost him a fortune he had not got: the money kept running out, and creditors circled. During the following year, high tides and great storms breached it and the cost of repair left him virtually bankrupt. There was even a plague of toads. For several years, he had to curb his ambitions, yet to the end of his life Madocks was incurably eager to be the agent of progress. In 1820, he launched himself into his second great epic project: the one that created Porthmadoc. What had set him thinking here was the impressive development of the slate industry some 12 miles away in that gaunt and uncanny place, Blaenau Ffestiniog. A railway bringing slate to the coast; a fine harbour to take it out to sea – here was another way to promote the prosperity of the region (as well, no doubt, as his own). Madocks's legacy is not altogether what he would have wished. Ambitious competitors saw to it that the main route to Ireland would not after all lie over Traeth Mawr and on to Porth Dinllaen, but through Holyhead. But he left us today's Porthmadog, and best of all, he left us Tremadog.

Driving north towards Caernarfon, you come to Porthmadog first. It's a bright and busy resort town, murdered by traffic, and a place that more people crawl through than stop to savour. The harbour is pleasant enough, with a fine congregation of yachts; there are steam trains, a heritage enterprise now, out to Blaenau Ffestiniog on the line that Madocks devised; and the view across to Snowdon is acclaimed by people who've seen more of that country than I have as one of the best of its kind in Wales. But there's nothing especially distinctive about the town. You don't feel at every corner 'Madocks was here', as you do at Tremadog.

The hotel and the old town hall – the ground floor is now a shop – look out on a decorous square, with two inns, good houses, and three or four shops, one of which boasts postcards of romantic Welsh scenery, but none when I was there to remember Tremadog by. There's a beautiful church, St Mary's, a little way down the road to Porthmadog, said to be one of the earliest Gothic Revival churches in Wales. It was heavily under repair, so I could not get in, but the signs outside referred to a '*former* church project' and it has now been restored as offices and a community meeting room. There's a brass plaque in the church commemorating Madocks, and a marble one to John Williams, the indefatigable guardian and promoter of Madocks's interests during his frequent absences. On the edge of the town is the dissenters' chapel, built for Calvinistic Methodists, a fine affair, but fallen on bad days. Madocks scandalized some in the neighbourhood by building the chapel first and the church only afterwards; he sought to placate his critics by saying that the chapel was built on sand.

If you take the road that runs south towards Snowdon you will come upon another of Madocks's ingenious innovations, his once busy manufactory, one of the first woollen mills in North Wales, powered by water, for which he required a stone dam across the valley. The building is now abandoned, and though it looks well worth saving, the expense, people here will tell you, would be daunting because its use as tannery and laundry has left the ground so polluted. Further on you will find the house that Madocks built for himself: Tan-Yr-Allt, to which he invited his fine friends from London (much more, as was mordantly noted in the locality, than from Wales); notably Shelley who first appeared here with his new wife, looking for somewhere to live. He was nineteen; she was sixteen. Shelley's visits ceased after intruders attempted to kill him – or so he said: some cynics suggested this was a stunt to enable the Shelleys to escape their creditors. Tan-Yr-Allt, having been at one time abandoned, has blossomed since 2002 into a decidedly classy but still, on my brief acquaintance, very friendly hotel, with ravishing views over the town and the estuary.

The whole of the sequence has Madocks's mark on it. Throughout his involvement with this place, he pestered those who looked after it in his absence with instructions on how to proceed. The most put-upon recipient was his agent, John Williams, who deserves to be ranked just a pace behind him as Tremadog's creator. 'This letter', says one of Madocks's missives, 'you will find contains my general sentiments, and you should keep it, and read it often.' Many of these despatches, which have fortunately been preserved, were detailed instructions on building: which materials should be used, which windows should be selected, the heights and widths and depths and elevations he favoured. The town privy, he stipulated, must be built in the form of an old broken tower.

There was also meticulous guidance on the farming practices which he favoured or wished to prohibit, for along with his other callings in life he saw himself as an agricultural reformer. There were endless instructions, too, on how to prepare for his visits and the entertainments he required to be staged. Life here was full of Madocks-inspired attractions, both for those invited to his lavish house parties at Tan-Yr-Allt and for the neighbourhood generally. There were plays (Madocks himself had a taste for writing and appearing in theatricals), and concerts ('where is the harper?' he writes to Williams. 'I must have two [underlined] if not three [underlined] harpers for Easter Sunday and Monday. Send two fiddlers'). There were race meetings. But a fair with which he hoped to make a particular splash was a fiasco: his determination to ensure that his minions had every possible eventuality covered in this case failed. Humiliatingly, the innkeeper ran out of ale.

'We do not hesitate to predict that future ages will hail the day that gave birth to the enterprising William Alexander Madocks Esquire,' the *North Wales Gazette* had exulted on the completion of the embankment. The embankment was only the start of the enterprise, and the tourist traffic on this part of the coast is certainly a testimony to his foresight and resolution. 'His zest for life and amateurish inability to recognize both his and its limitations were part of the secret of the eventual success of his plans,' says his excellent biographer, Elisabeth Beazley. Yet walking around the area which Madocks did so much to contrive, the ingenious innovator of whom one is most aware is less Madocks than Clough Williams-Ellis, who created the Italianate village Portmeirion, a little south-east down the coast – a tourist honeypot even before the mystifying TV series, *The Prisoner*, attracted whole new contingents of reverent pilgrims here in the 1960s. Coaches bound for Portmeirion help clog the streets of Porthmadog.

Madocks died, on his way home from a rare family holiday, in Paris in September 1828 in a house in the Faubourg St Honoré. Reports of his death were initially disbelieved; as with the alleged attempt on the life of Shelley, it was thought they might be inventions, a device to fend off creditors. Some believed he was still alive, living in some other part of Wales in secure obscurity. Others feared he might have killed himself, as a brother had done. Official records, however, suggest he was truly dead, and buried in the Père Lachaise cemetery on the outskirts of Paris, though his name does not appear on the list I was given there of celebrities interred in its precincts. He deserves more attention and honour than he's been given in Paris; he deserves, far more, on the Gwynedd coast he did so much to transform, to be rescued from his present neglect.

A B C D

E F G H

I J K L

M N O P

Q R S T

U V W X Y Z

ULLAPOOL

ULLAPOOL, par., vil., and coastguard sta. … Ross and Cromarty, vil. on Loch Broom, 32m. NW. Garve ry. sta. with which there is coach connection…

THERE WERE ONLY ONE or two coaches parked up in Ullapool when I was there one morning in June, and the size of the coach parks indicates that it isn't like that in the height of summer. But chanced on just out of high season, Ullapool is a delight: low houses, interspersed with shops and cafés, clustered along the busy harbour, big boats putting out towards the sea, high hills across the loch, and as you climb the hill from Shore Street towards the edge of the town, well-appointed grid pattern streets, some unexpectedly spacious, and one at least (Market Street) defying you not to wander down and explore it.

It's not that any one building particularly invites you to come and admire it, but together they compose a satisfying portion of townscape. This is clearly a planned town. And who planned it? There's a clue in the name of one of the principal streets: Pulteney Street. That's a name more associated with Bath than with Ross and Cromarty. Sir William Pulteney was Thomas Telford's great patron. Telford has been here. He was called in by the instigators of Ullapool, the British Fisheries Society, who created this place at the end of the eighteenth century, along with Tobermory on Mull and Lochbay on Skye, more than a century before William Hesketh Lever appointed himself to bring prosperity to Lewis and Harris through fishing. Alongside his great canals and bridges, Telford, a Scot from the borders, built churches all over Scotland. One of them, completed in 1829, was in Ullapool, a few streets back from the harbour. It is now a museum, though the pulpit and galleries have been retained.

I came to Ullapool in search of a location called Destitution Road, which I knew to be in this district: the museum, I was assured, would know all about it. And here, sure enough, I found an album full of accounts of the desolate times which led to the building of Destitution Road, south-west of here through Dundonnel and westward along the south side of Little Loch Broom towards Gruinard Bay. Other roads in the area were destitution roads too, and a bridge at Kinlochewe, on the road between here and Garve, was known as Hunger Bridge, but the principal Destitution Road was this one.

The villain was the potato, imported into this territory in response to the poverty, deprivation and worklessness which had always been found here. That made the area even more vulnerable when the potato failed, as it too often did. Famine was only avoided, or eased, by charitable operations based in Glasgow. But nothing before had matched the severity of what occurred here in the 1840s. There were more mouths to feed than before – the population of the Highlands rose from 270,000 in 1755 to 420,000 in 1841 – with steamships arriving from Ireland, bringing in hired hands to work on the harvest, undercutting the meagre wages of those who lived there. And because landlords required so much land for their sheep, there was less to grow crops on.

Road-building schemes brought relief to these stricken places from time to time, but the cost of building the Caledonian Canal left less money for them. An official report summed up the suffering succinctly. 'Those who are habitually and entirely fed on potatoes (are placed up) upon the extreme verge of subsistence, and when they are deprived of their accustomed food there is nothing cheaper to which they can resort. They have already reached the lowest point of the descending scale, and there is nothing beyond but starvation and beggary.'

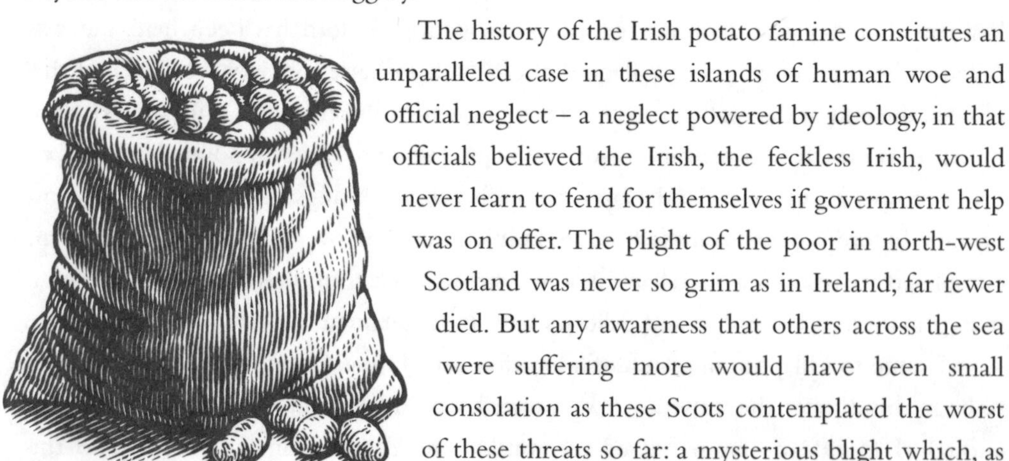

The history of the Irish potato famine constitutes an unparalleled case in these islands of human woe and official neglect – a neglect powered by ideology, in that officials believed the Irish, the feckless Irish, would never learn to fend for themselves if government help was on offer. The plight of the poor in north-west Scotland was never so grim as in Ireland; far fewer died. But any awareness that others across the sea were suffering more would have been small consolation as these Scots contemplated the worst of these threats so far: a mysterious blight which, as the *Inverness Courier* put it in August 1846, 'alike baffles all cure and prevention'.

The government in London took the view that this was a local problem and therefore should be dealt with locally. An official minute echoed much that officials had said about Ireland. 'Governments cannot encourage the expectation that by any direct system of pecuniary assistance, they can relieve the proprietors from the obligation which rests upon them, or take on themselves the charge of providing for the wants of the people.' But the landlords said they did not have the means to cope. The churches clamoured for action and gave what practical help they could manage, but the problems steadily worsened. 'Local distress', wrote Charles Trevelyan (the same Trevelyan who came to be vilified for his handling of the famine in Ireland), 'cannot be relieved by… national funds without great abuse and evils, tending to… an entire disorganization of society.'

In 1847 there were riots throughout the north. Officials below the rank of great men like Trevelyan, who were more ready to respond to suffering than their superior's ideology permitted him to be, reported that men had been so much weakened by the lack of food that work could no longer be got out of them. The following year was hardly better. But now desperation had reached a point where plans were made to create employment. Roads would be built in a region drastically short of them. The government was ready to meet one third of the cost of building a road from Loch Broom towards Gairloch; a third would have to be raised from the reluctant proprietors; the final third would fall on the general rates. In all, four roads would be built, covering 40 miles.

As so often in this territory, it demanded a degree of coercion to persuade highlanders to abandon their commitment to cultivating the land and do instead what authority required of them. To get any kind of job you had to prove you were destitute. From then on, you could only get relief if you worked on the road-building schemes and abandoned all other employment. So weary and desperate men, working in atrocious conditions, began to furnish the roads we speed down today. It's a place of great bleakness, this, though also of great beauty, the sweetly picturesque conjoined with the sinister – nowhere more perhaps than when, with destitutional rocks and forbidding crags behind you, you look across Gruinard Bay to Gruinard Island, dreamlike amidst the vivid blue water, and yet for years so blighted by anthrax that no one was permitted to go there. In 1942 sixty to eighty sheep were taken to the island and a bomb full of anthrax spores was let loose, which killed them all. The intention was that the effect would be temporary. The spores would disappear and the island would be accessible as before. But that did not happen. It took a four-year operation before the government could announce in 1990 that the island, after almost fifty years, was at last decontaminated. It remains uninhabited.

As they worked, the men who built Destitution Road did not give thanks as they might have been expected to do for the intervention that had at last found them work and a little money. Who, after all, would benefit from these roads, bringing ease of access and communication where before it was near impossible? Why, the proprietors; few who had laboured to build them would ever use them.

All this I found recorded in Telford's church in Ullapool, in a compilation called *The Potato Famine in the Highlands 1846–9,* text and research by Henry Noble, newspaper research by Marjory Gordon, the product of a community programme created with the help of the Manpower Services Commission: a telling reminder that finding good paid work in the Highlands is still a struggle today. Ullapool itself is a neat and civilized place nowadays, very different from the early days when life was rough and its future was far from assured. In 1808 one eminent figure described it as 'a nest of wickedness' where enforced idleness led to vice: which kinds of vice he didn't specify, but heavy drinking must have been one of them.

Now the tourist trade which throngs its summer streets helps keep it buoyant. Yet it seemed in the summer of 2007 that the future of this excellent little museum was uncertain. Notices posted around it warned that because money was short it might not survive much longer. The loss of the museum would surely threaten the church that houses it too. Were they to go, cultural destitution would not be too strong a term to describe it.

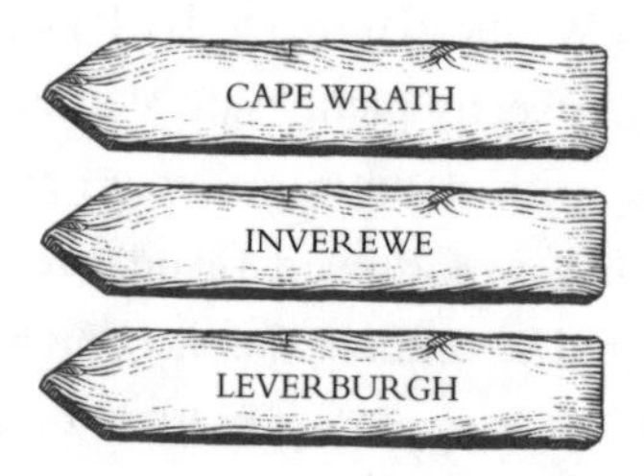

UNTHANK

UNTHANK, ham., Cumberland, 5m. NW. of Penrith.

THIS IS NOT THE only Unthank in what used to be Cumberland: there's a second, also close to Penrith, and a third just outside Dalston. How do the postal authorities cope? These coincidences sometimes occur: there are two places in Cornwall called Carnkie, one of which rhymes it with 'tie' and the other with 'tea', but that's not much help in deciding where to deliver a letter. Anglesey (Ynys Mon) has two Glan-yr-Afons. Such confusions happen even more often with road names. Oxford used to have two roads named after Pitt, but being a place of scholarship, it cleverly changed one to Chatham.

There's an Unthank in Northumberland too, Bartholomew says, 6½ miles from Rothbury, population 15; also elsewhere in Northumberland there's an Unthank Hall, near Haltwhistle. The name occurs again in a hamlet north-west of Barnard Castle. Nor is the name entirely confined to the north: there's a Newtown Unthank 7 miles west of Leicester. What is the meaning of all this apparent thanklessness? The answers in such matters are usually to be found in the pages of Eilert Ekwall's *Concise Oxford Dictionary of English Place-Names*. Ekwall has fewer Unthanks than Bartholomew, though he says he knows of other instances in Cumbria, Northumberland and North Yorkshire besides the ones he lists. The name derives, he explains, from an Old English word meaning a squatters' farm; or in the case of Unthank Hall, presumably, a squatters' Hall, which argues an even greater level of squatter ambition.

The Unthank 5 miles north-west of Penrith, the only one I visited, doesn't look as though it's a haunt of squatters today, and perhaps the others don't either. But without going around knocking officiously on every door, one cannot rule out the possibility that some dedicated preserver of Unthankian traditions is still in surreptitious residence somewhere.

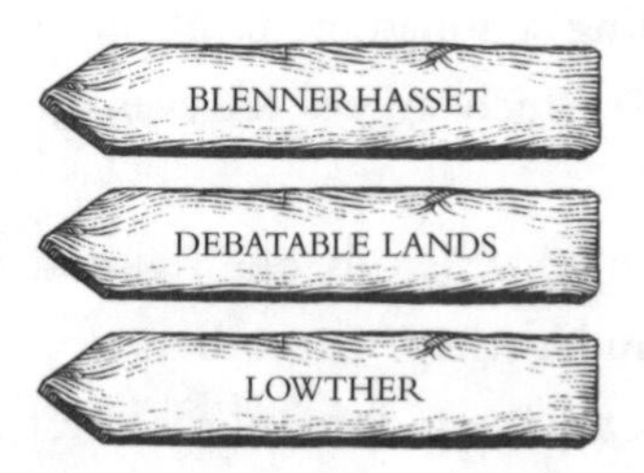

UPPER UPHAM

UPHAM, Upper and Lower, 2 adjacent hams., Wilts,
6m. NE. of Marlborough…

NOT FAR OUT OF the good-looking village of Aldbourne on the Hungerford–Swindon road there's a byroad surging exhilaratingly over the Downs that leads into Upper Upham. This tract of land was once Aldbourne Chase, good hunting territory, which brought John of Gaunt here. The manor house belonged for a time to the Goddards, a powerful Wiltshire family who owned much of the old town in Swindon. Later it fell into dereliction, but was saved and refurbished and had one of its fireplaces praised by Sir Nikolaus Pevsner. Also, up here on the breezy hills, is a cluster of modern houses grouped around a green, and an unexpected petrol pump, reinforcing the feeling you're now miles from anywhere; and a farm at whose gate a mysterious notice says:

> PARENTS
> CAN BE DANGEROUS
> PLEASE INSTRUCT CHIDREN TO

Instruct them not to eradicate the vital words in notices, possibly.

South from the road is a track, once a road, that leads down the hill. The wind as I walked down was blowing the trees, the bushes, the grass, bringing to mind the beautiful word 'sussuration'. Abundant birdsong and the voices of cattle raised in what sounded like protest filled the spring air. At the foot of the hill was the wood that is gathered around what was once the village of Snap: a place of just enough mystery to make dead Snap seem even more of a lure than still-alive Upper Upham. Snap: *locality, Wilts, in Ramsbury rural dist.*, Bartholomew says, apparently unaware it had perished at least three decades before.

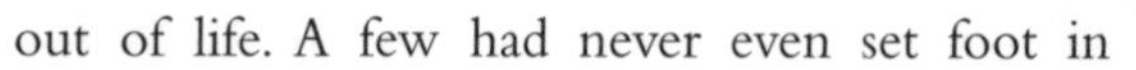

There is little left now but stray heaps of stones. Yet this was once quite a substantial village – rather more than a mere locality – families lived in simple cottages, working on the land or perhaps in service, not expecting much out of life. A few had never even set foot in Aldbourne, less than 3 miles away. Others did not stay long. My wife's grandmother was born here in 1873, in the thirty-seventh year of Victoria and the fifth of Gladstone's first administration. By the time she was seven, the family had moved to East Garston, near Lambourn in Berkshire, then to the small town of Lambourn itself, and after that back to Aldbourne. By then, in a period of agricultural downturn, Snap was falling into decline. For a time, the farm was unoccupied. In the 1890s, an optimist bought it; he didn't stay. Then it was empty again – until a butcher from Ramsbury, Henry Wilson, bought it, as he had other local farmland, in 1905, as a suitable spot for sheep.

What happened then became a subject of fierce debate. In 1913, a *Daily Mirror* reporter visited Snap and described a scene of dereliction and desolation. Some months later, the radical Liberal MP for Cricklade in the north of the county, Richard Cornthwaite Lambert, launched a public attack on the Wilson family (Henry had died in 1909 but his sons were still in control), whom he accused of deliberately running down employment in Snap and driving its population away in their lust to make money out of their sheep. Two of Henry Wilson's sons sued Lambert for slander, but despite a hostile summing-up from the judge, the jury cleared him.

The charge that the Wilsons had indulged in a kind of Wiltshire clearances persisted. In a book called *The Oldest Road: An Exploration of the Ridgeway*, published in 1975, the *Guardian* journalist J. R. L. Anderson wrote: 'There is no village any longer, only the ghost of a place that was deliberately abandoned in the last century to make more room for sheep. The Highland Clearances in Scotland are described in all the history books; the dispossession of a few inarticulate peasants in Wiltshire was not on a sufficient scale to pull the heartstrings.'

The safest course in trying to discern the history of this part of England is to turn to the writings of Kenneth Watts, an exemplary local historian who in 1989 published a book called *Snap: the history, depopulation and destruction of a Wiltshire village*. Watts in effect blames not Henry Wilson but Robert Peel for the downfall of Snap. The fate of Snap, he says, was decided as early as 1846, by the repeal of the Corn Laws. Through the rest of the nineteenth century circumstances conspired against it. The 1870s saw harvests ruined by heavy rainfall. It suffered too from the arrival in Britain of American grain, and years of persistent agricultural depression. By the time Henry Wilson arrived, the population had already dwindled away. The decision to turn the land over from arable to pasture made sense in the circumstances, especially as the land here had always been poor. The cottages, Watts establishes, were tiny, and only one room deep. And although the well at Snap had also provided the water for Upper Upham, shortage of water here could have been a factor in the place's decline.

Carefully and with sympathy, Watts traces the families who lived in the village and the kind of lives they endured. The lot of labourers who lived in such places was certainly not to be envied. His account is a sad story of almost unrelieved poverty and persecution for much of at least six hundred years. But Wiltshire-based Watts does not see the story of Snap as visiting Anderson did, through a romantic mist.

By the start of the First World War the story of Snap was over. The army used it for training exercises and the brick and stone remnants of its cottages were carried away for building elsewhere. Some accounts say the farmhouse at Snap survived until the 1930s, but so little is left of the place today that one could easily walk through these woods without ever knowing of the Ebsworths and Bateses and Coxheads who made their hard lives here. Except that some 25 years ago, children from Toothill school, Swindon set up a little memorial on the bend of the lane where the well used to be: 'In memory of the people of Snap.'

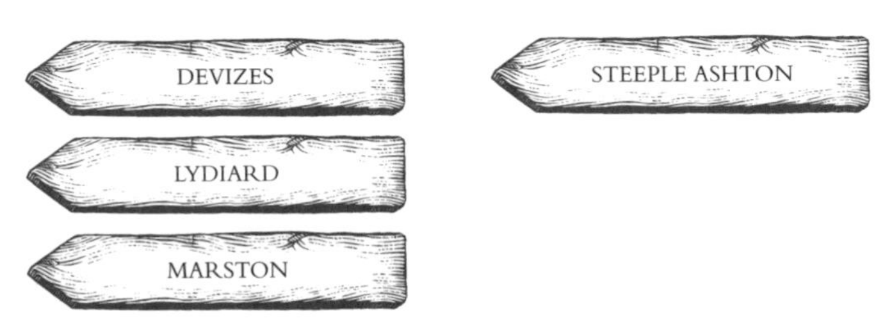

A B C D

E F G H

I J K L

M N O P

Q R S T

U V W X Y Z

VENTNOR

VENTNOR, urb. dist., watering-pl., coastguard sta. and par. …
Isle of Wight, on SE. coast, 11m. S. of Ryde
and 90m. SW. of London…

'THE ISLE OF WIGHT', wrote the much-read though not always accurate Victorian compiler of books about places of interest and their antiquities, John Timbs, 'may be said to contain, within a small compass, all the most pleasing and picturesque features of Great Britain. In beautiful and sublime scenery, much of it of a kind peculiar to itself, this gem of the ocean is surpassed by few spots on the globe.' And among the most favoured spots in this paradise is the south-eastern coastal resort of Ventnor, blessed with a sub-tropical climate and said by its admirers to give you the sense that you're holidaying abroad; an impression confirmed by those who, arriving at Ventnor sea front, have switched on their mobile phones to be greeted with the message: Welcome to France. As you wander its streets it seems a place of unusual tranquillity. But that has not always been so, and least of all perhaps in the spring of 1909, when the moment came to bury the poet Algernon Charles Swinburne.

Bonchurch has now become a virtual suburb of Ventnor, though in fact it was well established before Ventnor began to blossom. Admirers of Swinburne still come to the village each year, and no doubt find it just as pleasing as the Swinburnes did when Algernon's father, the admiral, first saw the house they acquired there, East Dene. John Keats, who visited the place in 1819, wrote to his sister: 'Bonchurch… is a very delightful place as I can see by the cottages, all romantic – covered with creepers and honeysuckles with roses and eglantines peeping in at the windows. Fit abodes for the people I guess live in them, romantic old maids fond of novels, or soldiers' widows with a pretty jointure.'

It is still an almost preposterously pretty village, full of sweet model cottages drowning in foliage, and an exemplary duck pond populated by exemplary ducks,

presented to the people of Bonchurch by the doctor-turned-novelist Horace de Vere Stacpoole in memory of his first wife. As I walked through the village, I saw, tending a cottage garden, a man with a heavy beard poignantly reminiscent of pictures of Swinburne. Signposts marshal you towards the old church down a lane, past East Dene where Swinburne's family lived, and then past a house, now a hotel, where Dickens stayed while writing *David Copperfield*. Breaking off on occasion for picnics with the Swinburnes, he described the area as 'only to be equalled on the Genoese shore of the Mediterranean Sea', though sometimes he complained that the place made him feel sleepy. Karl Marx was a visitor here too, taking holidays in a house on the road into Ventnor.

Ventnor and particularly Bonchurch were, and still are, fiercely respectable, which was not often said about Swinburne. He had never since early youth been willing to have his freedom to act as he chose confined by his family traditions. Though the poet had some reputation for his wild and louche behaviour, the full truth about his excesses was confined – until more candid books were written much later – to a well-informed few. This led to a crisis when the poet Alfred Lord Tennyson died, aged and full of honours, in 1892. Who should succeed him as Poet Laureate? Queen Victoria, whose views were never to be disregarded, wondered if Mr Swinburne might be suitable. Her prime minister, Gladstone, was apprehensive. He knew more about Swinburne than she did. Swinburne's sexual alignment was always a matter of some dispute, but he was certainly deeply interested in practices of which Victoria was thought to know little. His novel *Lesbia Brandon*, which dealt with incest and flagellation as well as lesbian love, had been suppressed and would not appear until those licentious years, the 1950s.

Swinburne was said by some people who knew him well to have so much enjoyed being beaten at Eton that he retained a taste for flogging and being flogged. He used to receive a ready supply of pornographic material from his famously dissolute friend, the radical MP, Richard Monckton Milnes. He witnessed flagellation in brothels. The celebrated American writer Ralph Waldo Emerson called him a leper and a sodomite. 'I kept my temper,' Swinburne assured Edmund Gosse, 'I preserved my equanimity.' But how, asked Gosse, had Swinburne replied? ' "I called him", replied Swinburne in his chanting voice, "a wrinkled and toothless baboon who, first hoisted into notoriety on the shoulders of Carlyle, now spits and sputters on a filthier platform of his own finding and fouling."'

His *Poems and Ballads* of 1866 had to be withdrawn by his publishers after threats of prosecution for obscene libel. His drinking scandalized Edmund Gosse, who claimed that if Swinburne saw a bottle of wine at dinner he would pounce on it like a snake on a mongoose. Visiting an old friend called Nichol, a professor at the University of Glasgow, he became so hopelessly drunk that Nichol locked him into his room, whereupon the poet began to rattle the doors and yell: 'Oh my God! And he is a petulant provincial pedagogue, and I a poet of European reputation!'

Not all of this would have reached Gladstone's ears, but he certainly knew the poet to be an unrepentant atheist. He may even have known of the fantasies Swinburne had written about Queen Victoria, picturing her happily enwrapped in the lecherous embraces of such figures as one of her earlier prime ministers, Robert Peel, while another imagined her being displaced in a *coup d'état* by Prince Albert. In the event, the selection of a Laureate was deferred and deferred again, until three years later (as reported in this Gazetteer's entry on Ashford) the Marquess of Salisbury entrusted the post to the famously respectable, but otherwise wholly unsuitable, Alfred Austin.

Algernon's wild outbursts of passion abated in time. He lived for his last thirty years in a house at the bottom of Putney Hill, which he shared with the solicitor, poet, critic and writer of many books, Theodore Watts-Dunton. Swinburne's mother paid Watts-Dunton £200 a year for his services as a kind of fair-but-firm prefect charged with curbing the poet's excesses. They lived in apparently happy amity in their gloomy-looking house, with Watts-Dunton dishing out Swinburne's pocket money, just enough to enable him to have one drink before lunchtime at the Rose and Crown in what is now known as Wimbledon Village, but not enough to enable him to buy any more. Swinburne walked up the hill to Wimbledon Common most days, and liked to chat to the nursemaids wheeling their prams on the Common, and to utter little cries of admiration as he peered at their babies; one of whom grew up to be Robert Graves.

This curious relationship even survived the dangerous moment when Watts-Dunton, who was seventy-three, abruptly announced his intention to marry a woman called Clara Reich, who was twenty-one. Happily, when she moved in she got along very well with the sometimes difficult poet. Under Watts-Dunton's tutelage Swinburne became quite restrained, and began to amend his views, expressing his admiration for Queen Victoria, championing the Boer War, and even becoming a bit of a prude, condemning the kind of licentious writing that was then getting into print.

His relationship with his family over the years had been fitful. Sometimes, in moments of trouble, he returned to the family home, only to leave it again when the horizon was clearer. But when the news of his death – of a fever, brought on by having gone out on a cold spring day without an overcoat – became known, the surviving members of Swinburne's family immediately laid claim to the body, demanding that he be buried in the church of St Boniface, Bonchurch, alongside his siblings.

There are, confusingly, two churches at Bonchurch, both called St Boniface's. Some people look in a graveyard down a steep hill close to the sea for his tomb, as I did. Fortunately I was redirected to the other, newer church of St Boniface, built because the old one was considered too small, up the hill, where I found the family grave containing Algernon and his siblings Alice, Edward and Isabel close to the gate. This church was built with the help of Swinburne money, which also contributed to the cost of buying the land and providing the school, the schoolhouse, the stained glass windows and the rectory. So although he had maintained only sporadic contact with his family, they wanted him to have a formal Church of England burial there, an insistence that affronted many of Swinburne's London friends, and especially Watts-Dunton, who wrote in thunderous terms to the Rector of Bonchurch, forbidding any such notion.

It was, then, in the grounds of the new church of St Boniface that there assembled on 15 April 1909 – a day when, according to the *Ventnor Advertiser*, the sun shone with golden splendour and genial warmth – two rival parties ready to see the poet committed to the earth: the Swinburne family party and their friends and adherents; and the representatives of the friends of the poet, some of whom were adamant that Swinburne had expressly forbidden any kind of religious ceremony. Watts-Dunton, who as Swinburne's carer spoke on these matters with undoubted authority, was ill, but despatched his feisty young wife with strict instructions not to permit any religious malarkey.

Swinburne's sister Isabel had planned the service, but she also was too ill to come and had charged her cousin, Mrs Disney Leith, to see that her wishes were honoured. Mrs Disney Leith, who was a published poet and novelist, had become friendly with Swinburne after her husband died; they had even shared in their letters memories not just of their schooldays but specifically of schoolday flagellation. She deputed the supervisory role that Isabel had given her to her son, who with Sir John Swinburne had been to see the rector, the Reverend Mr J. Floyd Andrewes, to insist on a full religious ceremony.

But the family mourners, arriving in the expectation that this would take place, were greeted at the church gate by the rector, who proceeded to read a formal announcement. Late the previous evening, he said, he had received a telegram from the dead man's executor, Mr Watts-Dunton, stating that the burial service planned by the family must not take place. The text of this telegram later got into the newspapers. It had, Watts-Dunton wrote, been Swinburne's express wish not to have the burial service read over his grave. Mourners should gather around the grave in silence, throw flowers into it, and disperse: nothing more.

Poor perplexed Mr Andrewes was pulled two ways. As rector of the place where Swinburne had spent the earliest and some of the happiest days of his life, he had felt it his bounden duty to pay the utmost respect to one who – whatever his later thoughts might have been – had been a baptized member of the Anglican Church, and who wanted his resting-place to be in the beautiful churchyard which his father, the admiral, had been chiefly instrumental in securing for the people of Bonchurch. And yet, he felt the wishes of the dead must be complied with, and that it would be a mockery to read the traditional service over a man who desired to keep himself free from all outward religious forms and ceremonies, in death as in life.

The occasion was bound to be tense, and soon there was trouble. As the rector started to read the opening sentences of the funeral service, what reporters called 'vociferous interruptions' began. Clara Watts-Dunton, the *Advertiser* reported, started forward, apparently in protest, but was held back by Colonel Leith. There was further contention as the rector closed the service by saying: 'Although no formal religious service is desired over his grave, yet we do now commit his body to mother earth, earth to earth, dust to dust, ashes to ashes', which inescapably sounded like part of a formal service.

'The birds singing around him', the *Advertiser* reported, 'were his only choristers, the wind sighing in the trees and the sob of the waves as they broke on the rugged shore near at hand that he knew and loved so well were his only requiem.' But they weren't the last sound to be heard. The controversy was taken up in the newspapers, with Mrs Watts-Dunton confirming that she would have staged her protest had Colonel Leith not prevented her. Mr Andrewes was roughly condemned for disregarding the dead poet's wishes and flouting the promise he'd made to Watts-Dunton, while Watts-Dunton's party was accused of fabricating the claim that Swinburne had sought to ban all religious content. Meanwhile in Canterbury Cathedral, the vice-dean, Canon Mason, preached a sermon, perhaps reflecting the view of a great many Anglicans, that Swinburne was not a fit person to be accorded a Christian burial. 'There is no more deadly poison than the portrayal of corrupt passion in glowing and artistic language,' the canon declared.

It helped to restore the peace of mind of the rector that Watts-Dunton himself later wrote to him saying that the threat of a beautiful occasion degenerating into a ghastly failure had been averted by Mr Andrewes' delicacy and tact. Later Thomas Hardy came to visit the grave, and sitting by it, wrote his poem, 'A Singer Asleep', which begins:

> In this fair niche above the unslumbering sea,
> That sentrys up and down, all night, all day,
> From cove to promontory, from ness to bay,
> The Fates have fitly bidden that he should be
> Pillowed eternally...

And ends:

> I leave him, while the daylight gleam declines
> Upon the capes and chines.

VERNEY JUNCTION

VERNEY JUNCTION, ry. sta. L.M.S. and Met., and G.C. Jt R., in co. and 4¾m. SE. of Buckingham.

LIKE STATIONS THAT CALL themselves 'Somewhere' Road (see Llanwrda), you need to be careful of railway stations that call themselves 'Somewhere' Junction. Clapham Junction, the most famous in England, isn't in Clapham, and Willesden Junction isn't in Willesden. They should have been Battersea Junction and Harlesden Junction, but the railways wanted classier names (which is also the reason that the south London station once known as Jolly Sailor is now Norwood Junction). The name of the junction was often used to signify not where you were but where you were changing for. Llandudno Junction is where you changed for the spur to Llandudno.

But Verney Junction is odder still. There wasn't ever a place called Verney, and today there isn't a junction either. Until 1868, this had been the sort of unremarkable spot that people sometimes describe as being in the middle of nowhere. Now it found itself elevated to the status of western terminus of the Metropolitan line, which ran out of Baker Street through the suburbs of Metroland, past Aylesbury, stopping at Waddesdon Manor (alight for the Rothschild family), and Quainton Road and Grandborough Road – though if you changed at Quainton Road you could take a further train to the hilltop Oxfordshire village of Brill, with its famous windmill. Here, too, was the so-called Universities line, some of the westbound trains on their 77-mile journey from Cambridge heading for Oxford, while others would take you to Buckingham, Brackley and Banbury.

I travelled once or twice from Oxford to Cambridge, looking with awe at the distinguished heads of my fellow passengers, freighted, as I imagined, with all the superior scholarship they were carrying towards the fens. The great Master of

Balliol, Jowett (see Tewkesbury), I told myself, could have travelled this way; Dr Spooner, who lived until the 1920s, must surely have done so, telling the college lodge before he left: I am taking the crane to Tramebridge. Maybe such titans of our own day as Maurice Bowra of Wadham or Isaiah Berlin might possibly be on board, though probably they would travel first class, denying us mere students the joy of their conversation. It was always a very slow journey, often made worse by having to change at Bletchley, now swallowed up in Milton Keynes but then an independent township.

For some reason I once attempted the journey back from Cambridge on Sunday, not something anyone untroubled by masochistic impulses would ever do twice. An effortless rain fell ceaselessly from a leaden sky. Nothing was open on Bletchley station, a dispiriting place at the best of times, and nothing seemed to be open in Bletchley. It was hard to determine which was the greater penance: to mooch about on the station or to mooch about in the sullen, deserted streets of the town. The risers on the stairs of the station accommodated advertisements for a product called Virol, which, as its name – derived from the Latin *vir*, meaning strength – implied, was supposed to boost one's energy and resolution. Maybe the only hope of redeeming Bletchley, I morosely concluded long before my rescuing train arrived, was a massive injection of this allegedly inspiriting substance.

The line closed in 1967, by which time many making the journey had decided that even going through London was better than this. But without the line we would not have had Verney Junction. Though possibly strangers to Virol, the boards of the two great railways, the London and North Western and the Great Western, had emboldened themselves in the 1860s to a create a station uniting these lines. Such a serious station required a serious name; the nearest hamlet, a mile or two distant, would hardly do. With no ringingly resplendent place name available, they named it after a man: Sir Harry Verney, Bt.

Sir Harry was big in railways – he was chairman of the Aylesbury and Buckinghamshire Railway Company – and generally big in Buckinghamshire, where the Verneys had been one of the dominant families since the Middle Ages. Born in 1801, he succeeded to the baronetcy in 1826, married nine years later, but was widowed in 1856. A year later he was married again, to a woman called Parthenope, the older and less beautiful sister of Florence Nightingale. He had started by courting Florence, but, like most of her suitors, without success. The switch from one of the sisters to the other caused much speculation. It was even said he had written his proposal, but addressed it simply: 'Miss Nightingale'; and since Parthenope was the older sister, the letter by the convention which then governed these things came accidentally to her.

There had been Verney MPs in the Commons since the reign of Edward VI, and like many aristocratic families the Verneys didn't intend to let the 1832 Reform Act make any difference to that. Sir Harry, a Liberal, took the Buckingham seat in the new reformed Commons from 1832 until 1841 when he stood down, returned in 1857, and remained in the Commons with two brief breaks until 1880. So by 1868, when the new station opened, Verney was a name that people would recognize, and that would, in the view of the railways, give their new station the necessary cachet – which, for a while, it did. But today Verney Junction is no more than an inconspicuous, unmemorable hamlet on a minor road near the small town of Winslow. There's a pub called, inescapably, the Verney Arms, and a cluster of houses built for railway workers, and a track which leads down to a railway notice where it crosses the line which says: 'Stop Look Listen'. You needn't bother. No trains have run here since the 1960s. Vestiges of two platforms and remnants of track remain, but it's overgrown, with trees sprouting out of it.

John Betjeman came here when he made his television film *Metroland*. 'The houses of Metroland', he mused, gazing soulfully out over the abandoned track at the end of his journey from Baker Street, 'never got as far as Verney Junction. Grass triumphs, and I must say I'm rather glad.' The name, for all that it's lost its original purpose, survives, announced on boards at each end of the hamlet. But the curious thing is this: the name which Sir Harry Verney gave to the station was not the one he was born with. He was born a Calvert, and changed his name, as so frequently happened in Victorian England, to get his hands on a legacy. But for that, the settlement known as Verney Junction (though there is no junction) would be Calvert Junction; and the nearest pub to the junction that isn't would be the Calvert Arms.

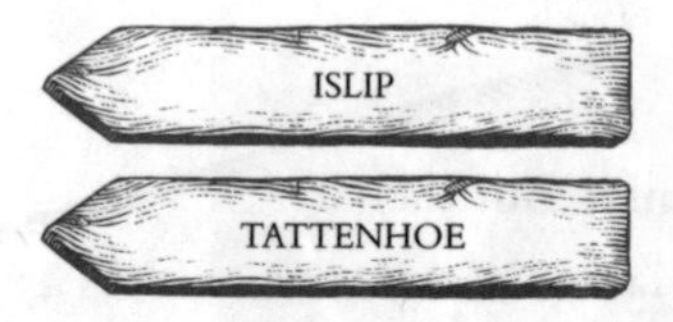

A B C D

E F G H

I J K L

M N O P

Q R S T

U V W X Y Z

WHITEWAY

WHITEWAY, locality, Glos., in Stroud rural dist.

IT ISN'T OFTEN THAT one quarrels with Bartholomew's judgements but this one is very odd. Whiteway a mere 'locality'? And this in a book published in the 1940s, some fifty years after the colony came into being? Perhaps he didn't like anarchists. In fact it's a quite remarkable place, a place of high aspirations, with more than a sniff of scandal, and turbulent enough to have been infested for a time with government spies.

The easiest way to find it is to take the B4070 between Birdlip and Stroud. There's a prettier route if you turn off the A417 Cirencester to Gloucester road and treat yourself to a quick inspection of the pleasant hillside village of Syde, but progress beyond is perilous without a degree in advanced navigation. Still, one way or another you can come to the village as now constituted down a bosky byroad. Though the wood of the houses built by its pioneers is now largely replaced by brick, there's enough of the flavour of the original settlement down the narrow lanes off the main road to give you some sense of the Whiteway colony when the first of its settlers came to establish it.

Their adventure began in Croydon, where in 1894 a group of young socialists associated with an organization preaching the doctrines of Tolstoy, the Croydon Brotherhood Church, met in a house in Tamworth Road to plot the creation of a colony run on the lines which their prophet advocated. One was Nellie Shaw, who wrote the first published account of the Whiteway experience, *A Colony on the Cotswolds*. The site they chose was at Purleigh in Essex, but in the way of such small idealistic sects, dissension quickly set in, as some of the colony sought to prevent the admission of two new adherents, which others said was totally inconsistent with the spirit of Tolstoyan anarchism. The inclusionists, having lost, decided to go elsewhere and start afresh, leaving the exclusionist tendency to manage without them, which they did for only three years.

The defectors – having prowled through sites across Gloucestershire – finally picked out Whiteway, bought the land, and in 1888 began to build; though first they signalled their commitment to goods in common by sticking the title deeds on a pitchfork and holding them over a fire until they were burnt to cinders. Nellie Shaw's book describes the early years in ecstatic terms. They were making 'a splendid attempt to create a little Utopia in the midst of a capitalistic world'; or as Joseph Burtt, another of the Whiteway pioneers, says in a foreword to Nellie's account: 'If our feet were down in the potato trenches, our heads were in the stars. We felt we were gods.' They took their rules of life directly from Tolstoy: hard work was one; an unorthodox sexual morality was another. Chastity, or failing that, abstinence, was the ideal – neither, subsequent records suggest, often achieved. Marriage was not recommended; free unions – which could be as firm and binding, their advocates believed, as any formalized marriage – were always to be preferred.

Nellie Shaw's book does not try to disguise the difficulty of those opening years. The first winter was cruel, though the second was kinder. There were raging ideological disputes, sometimes occasioned by new recruits with differing ideas from the founders'. A visiting Tolstoyan rebuked them for using money. There was tension with a rival community established nearby at Sheepscombe, which might have ended in court had the disputants been ready to recognize courtrooms.

There was trouble, too, with more conventional neighbours. Malcolm Muggeridge, who came from Croydon, was related to one of the early activists and who at that stage admired the Croydon pioneers, recounted the case of a local farmer who exploited their known distaste for the property laws by filching part of their land. To go to the law was unthinkable. The only alternative seemed to be physical force, to which they were also opposed – except that their doctrines held that in certain circumstances a principle could be breached on individual occasions without being wholly discarded. So they seized the farmer and threw him over a hedge.

Year by year, the place and its practices were evolving. The initially strict communistic principles began to droop and by 1902 'mild socialism' rather than communism was the formula, with even a developing taste for individualism. Nellie Shaw was one of its advocates: 'To those who may still be inclined to look on us as renegades because we gave up the communal living,' she would later write, 'I venture to say that the present is the better way; more calculated to develop character and initiative; indeed, far more honest and independent.' A bakery was established, which flourished: it was privately owned. Gates and fences and walls began to appear between properties. Primitive buildings were modernized; eventually they had running water, and electricity. There were even those who began to adopt more conventional forms of dress, in a place where clothing had once been considered optional, though others continued to wear what they chose. Some clad themselves in the fashion of ancient Greece.

Not surprisingly, the Whiteway colony remained a constant source of local gossip, speculation and wonder, with curious sightseers, as Nellie Shaw complains, coming to gawp at weekends. There was lipsmacking talk in the pubs of Gloucester and Cheltenham of reckless promiscuity, the swapping of wives and people prancing about in the nude. Officialdom was taking an interest too. In 1999 the National Archives opened its files on Whiteway, revealing the agitation of the local police and the Home Office over the dangerous politics thought to be practised in the colony and perhaps even more over what was seen as rampant immorality. Messages flew back and forth warning of danger. Police spies operating in the community reported that well-known anarchist agitators had arrived from abroad and were preaching their revolutionary doctrines there.

Nearly all the colonists, it was fearfully noted, now had radio sets and were using them to keep in touch with the outside world. One man had practically completed the construction of 'a transmitting set (wireless)'. In July 1925 the chief constable, who had long had them under surveillance, warned the Home Office of the double threat the colonists posed to his county and to the country. 'As can be seen from the attached dossiers,' he wrote, 'in many cases their morals are absolutely rotten. Many are in touch with subversive political movements… I have no hesitation in saying that politically the colony is potentially dangerous and that, during periods of internal unrest, and diplomatic tension with other countries, and so forth, the majority of the colony would give active assistance in every possible way to the enemies of this country.' They had openly boasted, he said, of having sheltered deserters and men trying to escape military service during the war.

The Special Branch of New Scotland Yard appeared to be less excited. According to a Home Office memo written a few months after the chief constable's blast, they did not accept that the colonists were plotting red revolution, but thought they were merely 'a group of faddists' (a reflection perhaps of their tastes for vegetarianism and the learning of Esperanto). The Home Office's Mr Newsam, however, veered towards the chief constable's interpretation, and urged his superiors to consider whether steps might be taken to disperse the colonists. Many were aliens who had lived in this country for many years. A man called Kleber Claux (sometimes spelled Klaux), for instance, was clearly an undesirable person. Unhappily, a decision had been taken in 1919 not to deport him.

Claux was one of the stars of the dossier to which the chief constable had alluded, in which the cases of fifty-six residents and some sixty regular or occasional visitors – all named, as well as numbered – were investigated. Some were singled out for their immorality, some for their frightening political views, and some were condemned for both. The man who had built the wireless set, a red-hot socialist, conscientious objector and deserter, had made a study of chemicals and was 'conversant with explosives'. His daughter, described as pretty, and accomplished on the violin, was at nineteen living with a fellow fiddler, forty-five years old, who had been having sex with girls of sixteen or seventeen.

Number 10 on the list was 'a dangerous Bolshevist' who had once been jailed for ten years for possessing explosives. He had also flown a black flag (an anarchist symbol). Number 16, an American Jewess, born in Russia, was cohabiting with Number 44 (who claimed they were married); she was an extreme Bolshevist and a very dangerous woman but unpopular in the community. Number 24, who had been in Winchester prison, had once been described by a member of Cornwall Constabulary as 'morally filthy and a danger to young persons'. Number 26, who spoke six languages and was taking instruction in the Mohammedan faith, had intercourse with any young girl he could get hold of. The baker, though a public school product, had a conviction for indecent exposure: young girls frequently visited his shop.

Number 41, a Czech, once of the Foreign Legion, author of several books, had, the spy reported, formerly lived with Nellie Shaw, and now lived off her, having begun other relationships, which he justified by arguing that a woman had to sin before she could be saved: 'he seems to turn the head of all women, young and old'. Nellie herself was 'an extreme Bolshevik and a very dangerous woman'.

As for visitors, they included Morgan Philips Price, three times an unsuccessful Labour candidate for Gloucester, described as 'one of the most dangerous men in the land'. (He would later serve for twenty-four years as Labour member for Gloucestershire constituencies.) One woman visitor, a friend of number 41,was in the informant's view 'the most dangerous person I have ever met' and a personal friend of the Plymouth anarchist James Tochatti. On and on these pages of testimony go, most of them full of trepidation, though here and there someone is found to be harmless, like the two regular women visitors, also friends of number 41, who shared a London flat: 'they did not appear', says the spy,'to have sufficient brains to be dangerous on their own initiative.'

Identifying undesirables was one thing: dealing with them quite another.'Manners have they none,' says one note attached to the file, 'and their customs are beastly. But though the colony is unpleasant and a possible source of trouble there is no way of bricking it up altogether.' The Home Secretary, William Joynson-Hicks, by reputation no liberal, reluctantly concurred. 'I should like to see this outrageous community dispersed. But action could lead to agitation and... an even greater concentration of undesirables. I think our plans will have to be made with great circumspection with the break-up of the colony as the ultimate object.' Sir Leonard Dunning, one of His Majesty's Inspectors of Constabulary, who was then in his mid-sixties, was sent to investigate. He had found the place 'a plague spot on morality', he reported in October 1925. In his view, the real attraction of Whiteway, both for its permanent residents and for some of its visitors, was 'promiscuous fornication'. Clearing the aliens out of the colony would not break it up, but it would at least get rid of some of the worst elements. 'I think', he recommended,'that the law should be strained to its furthest point to make its existence difficult.'

After further talks with two of the chief constable's spies, Dunning submitted another memo, regretting that in his concern for the place's standards of morality he had perhaps underestimated the dangers of the community as 'a centre for revolutionary propaganda'. The original founders had merely intended to create a communal life free from the laws which governed the rest of us. The aliens who had joined them during the war had boiled this up into active hostility to the state. Soon, though, he was back to sexual activity. As with politics, the new arrivals had exceeded the intentions of the founders, and free love was now being practised on a scale which upset even some old inhabitants: 'indeed, promiscuous fornication seems to be a prominent feature of the life of the place – and its worst feature is the early age at which both boys and girls are said to begin sexual intercourse…' Here again, aliens had aggravated the evil.

The new year brought no relief. A number of arrivals from France, Bulgaria and even China were expected daily. Newsam had drawn up an augmented list of people who if possible should be deported. But none of this would be easy. Number 41 was a particular problem, in that he had been described as harmless by Lord Haldane, a former War Minister, who had even allowed this alien to dedicate one of his books to him. Number 26 had once been served with a deportation order, but this had been rescinded after representations on his behalf by the Labour politician Philip Snowden. Yet Gloucestershire police regarded him as a desperate man and an extreme Bolshevik. In April, Dunning was forced back into recommending that a better way to proceed might be to stir up a local agitation against the colonists, whom at present people tended to see merely as cranks rather than as menaces to society… But then the excitement faded. The locals were not stirred up. There was not enough money to maintain a close surveillance of Whiteway. However politically and morally wretched these people's lives might be, authority was forced to conclude, there was nothing that could be done to repair them.

Certainly there's no sign of suspicion, let alone of hostility, in this quarter of Gloucestershire now. It's a quiet and settled place, with a strong community life even though the original concept of communal living faded long ago. The simple, well-kept colony hall of 1925 is busy and handsome in the way that tin churches are often handsome. There's a colony swimming pool and a regular Eric and Geoffrey Quiz Night. The bakery has revived; also, when I was there, there was a strange kind of shop offering an old stag's head, part of it missing, a red Gilbert Scott-type phone box, a muddy bike, a mass of fitments of indeterminate purpose, and a a hugely various collection of books – from *Once Aboard the Lugger* by A. S. M. Hutchinson to *The Complete Guide to Letterwriting*.

The dwellings now are mostly fairly conventional, and they have to be bought at prices which few anarchists of the age of the Croydon pioneers could have afforded. Here and there you can spot a survival of the spirit of earlier times. A house which used to be called The Old Pavilion now calls itself Freedom. A black flag flew in one garden, and a man with the kind of long black beard that you used to see in cartoons depicting anarchists (though disappointingly he did not also wear a cloak and carry a bomb) emerged from a wooden hut. But what struck me most was how eager the people I met in the street were to talk about Whiteway, 2007, and to say how much they delighted in living there. When she finished her book in 1935, Nellie Shaw was depressed by the way the vision of those who had stood with their feet in potato trenches but their heads in the stars had been dissipated. The ideological wrangles – could an anarchist community really settle disputes by majority voting? and if not, how were they to be resolved? – dismayed her. Some of the new arrivals seemed to her to have little in common with the founding Whiteway ideal. All of which must be truer now.

Even so, I think it's a place to cherish, both for its particular brand of communal individuality, and for its very eccentricity; for as John Stuart Mill maintained: 'Eccentricity has always abounded when and where strength of character has abounded; and the amount of eccentricity in a society has generally been proportional to the amount of genius, mental vigour, and courage which it contained.'

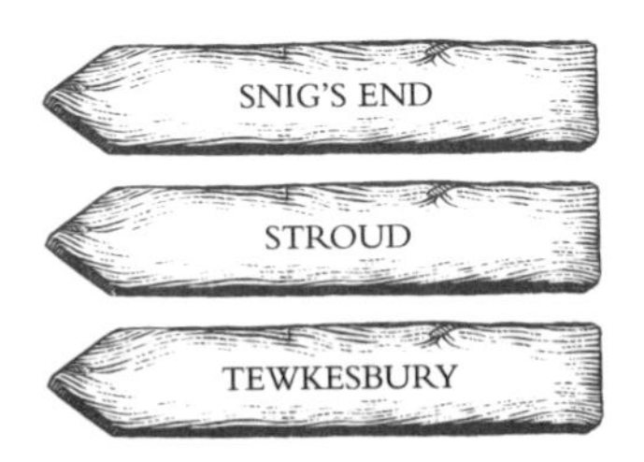

WHITWELL

WHITWELL, parish, Rutland, 4½m
East of Oakham; 629 acres, pop. 84.

AT EACH END OF the tiny village of Whitwell, a brief interruption on the A606 from Stamford to Oakham through the restored county of Rutland – the smallest in England, yet as full of places worth exploring as some many times its size – there's a road sign that sometimes breeds disbelief among motorists speeding through. Whitwell, it says, twinned with Paris. And yes, that isn't Bartholomew's Paris, *locality, West Riding of Yorkshire, near Huddersfield*, or Paris, *Worcestershire, ¼m. SW. of Ashton, Underhill*, but world-famous Paris, France. What's more, the road signs bear the imprimatur of Rutland County Council, so it must be rather more than some local spoof.

Like many good ideas dreamed up in Whitwell, this one began in the Noel Arms, where regulars were discussing the popularity of twinning and specifically the lust of local authorities big and small to find somewhere delightful to twin with. Sadly, no record was kept of their debate, but words like 'junket' may well have been used. One of the villages in the vicinity – bigger than Whitwell, but then most of them are – had recently got itself twinned, and the air at the Noel Arms was tainted with envy. Why should Whitwell be left behind? Spirits were roused, as well as consumed, and a consensus began to emerge that the village should find somewhere inviting to twin with on the other side of the Channel. At which point some hitherto mute, inglorious Whitwellian Hampden seems to have said: what about Paris? If the city fathers of Paris knew about Whitwell, perched as it is on the edge of beautiful Rutland Water, might they not be tempted by the prospect of occasional publicly-paid-for visits? And certainly, these parish fathers of Whitwell thought they could just about bring themselves to manage reciprocal visits to Paris.

So a letter was written and posted to Paris's mayor, who happened to be Jacques

Chirac, the future president, extolling the copious attractions of Whitwell and suggesting a deal – to which a masterly final sentence was added. We know, it assured the mayor, that you are a busy man, perhaps too busy to deal in good time with all your correspondence. So unless we hear back to the contrary, we'll assume that you have agreed. Sure enough, there was no reply. So signs for the end of the village were ordered and erected, and in time replaced by the official ones that stand proudly at Whitwell's extremities now. Only later did a letter arrive from the Paris municipality regretting that the city was already twinned with somewhere called Rome, and this by a *traité diplomatique* which precluded any further liaison with anywhere else. To which the Noel Arms replied that they were extremely sorry, but Paris had made its decision too late.

Regrettably, no fraternal exchanges between the two communities have yet taken place. But in case one is contemplated by the civic authority in Paris, here is a recommendation. The two greatest attractions at Whitwell are reached by roads from the western end of the village. One of these, to the south, Bull Brigg Lane, runs down to Rutland Water, the great man-made lake, occupying 3,100 acres, created in the mid 1970s under the rather less tourist-inducing name of Empingham Reservoir, to satisfy thirsty East Midlanders. There were yachts with bright red sails on the water when I walked down this lane on a bleak afternoon in January. In the summer, when boaters, anglers, walkers, cyclists, and birdwatchers congregate on these shores there must be a profusion. In the summer too you may take a boat called the *Rutland Belle*, which will ferry you to a spot on the southern shore where you may find a church half submerged in the water. This is Normanton church, originally doomed to disappear when the waters flooded in, but reprieved, with the top of the building used to create a museum of Rutland Water.

Turn north off the main road at Whitwell and a walk or drive of a mile and a half will bring you to the village of Exton. (There are also buses from Oakham, the county town.) If visiting Parisian dignitaries want to discover an unspoiled English treasure, they could hardly do better than Exton. Up a narrow street, past a lane that leads to the church, you come to the green: the kind of green that gets put into paintings and used by the tourist industry to show unmitigated England, with an inn called the Fox and Hounds, an array of harmonious houses, mostly in local stone, and one rather grand one, and in the south-west corner, the old schoolhouse, with a sign above the door that says: R. Kimsey, druggist, though in truth this was never a chemist's shop; the sign was put up by a film company and has never been taken down.

Twelve trees in irregular formation stand on the green. The streets that radiate from the green are for the most part equally pleasing. And, as is often the case in places as satisfying as this, one reason for its close approach to perfection is that for many years everything here was owned by a single family, who quashed all attempts to mess it about. This was the Noel family, who in time became the Viscounts Camden and Earls of Gainsborough, and though they sold a lot of it off during the twentieth century, little was done in the process that eroded its integrity and coherence.

The dominance of the Noels and the families with whom they intermarried over the life of this territory is clearest of all when you reach the church of St Peter and St Paul. The sturdy tower has a spire on top – not the original spire since that was struck by lightning in 1843 and crashed into the building below it, mercifully sparing Exton's matchless collection of monuments. It's these monuments which make the place so remarkable, both for the opulent craftsmanship of their construction – one is by Grinling Gibbons and two by Nollekens – and for the language of their inscriptions.

The Gibbons is, for some people's taste, overblown. Indeed, it has to be said that the sense in this place of ravening self-esteem bred of high birth and abundant money may be too much for some tastes. The best, to my mind, are the simplest: the one, for instance, to Anne, wife of Lord Bruce of Kinloss, whose qualities included perpetual cheerfulness and a more than ordinary conjugal affection; she died in 1627, four years and nine months after their marriage, weakened by childbirth, in her twenty-first year... Sometimes the language verges on the excessive, but there's compensation in the richness of the history it recounts. Here is the third Viscount Campden, who left this life for a better one in the seventieth year of his age in 1683, saluted for his eminent loyalty to two sovereigns, Charles I and II, but also for his conjugal affection for four wives and his paternal indulgence to nineteen children. His hospitality and liberality to all who desired and deserved it (notwithstanding inestimable losses in his estate, frequent imprisonments of his person, spoil and havock of several of his houses, besides the burning of that noble pile of Campden) have justly rendered him, it says, the admiration

of his contemporaries and the imitation of posterity.

John Harington of Exton, knight, is commemorated here with his wife Lucy, who bore him eighteen children. The said John and Lucy lived fifty years in wedlock. She died first, in her seventy-second year. He departed this life when 80 years old in the year of man's redemption 1591, the thirty-fourth of Queen Elizabeth. Their son James erected the monument and caused to be written upon it (in Latin: but the church provides translations) this valediction: 'If any old family and the ancient busts on the walls, if the badge of knighthood, the reward of peculiar virtue; if a numerous offspring and the absence of all complaint through fifty years of married life; if late decay and a rapid death; lastly, if a happy estate, and more happy than any estate, a liberal hand, untainted honour, reverence for Heaven, have made either a happy life or a blessed death, they have made both life and death blessed for us. Now when the fates have bid us to have done with this life, and the stars demand our spirits, the affection of our heir has gathered our ashes and bidden them rest under this mausoleum.'

Most touching of all, perhaps, is the gorgeous monument to Robert Kelwey, also spelled 'Keylwey': a distinguished esquire, it says (as translated), renowned for talent, learning and virtue, who loved retirement, lived as a Christian, and died in the Lord on the 21st of February in the year of our salvation 1580, and the eighty-fourth year of his age. His daughter Anne married Sir John Harrington, and produced two grandchildren: a son, Kelwey, and a daughter, Lucy. Lucy, says the inscription is still surviving and may God grant her a long life. But Kelwey died at twenty-one weeks and lies buried here with his grandfather.

Beyond the graveyard, behind the tower, as an epilogue to this grandeur, there's a dignified fragment of a former glory of Exton, a Jacobean manor house, the rest of which has gone. *The Shell Guide to Rutland*, by the great W. G. Hoskins, says one should save Exton church for the end of the day: 'after this feat of sculpture and language it would be unjust to look at any other church until one has cooled off'. I think that goes for the village too. If I ever drop into the Noel Arms at Whitwell I'm going to suggest that they ask Rutland Council to amend their nameplates. Not, certainly not, to remove the news that they're twinned with Paris, but to make the signs also exhibit a perhaps even nobler claim: Whitwell, gateway to Exton.

WIDMERPOOL

WIDMERPOOL, par. and vil.... 8½m. SE. of Nottingham...
in vicinity is W. Hall, seat.

IF, DESPITE ITS APPARENT obscurity, you have heard the name of this parish and village, it's probably because the novelist Anthony Powell chose it as the surname of the most odious character in his twelve-novel *roman fleuve, A Dance to the Music of Time* (1952–75). Kenneth Widmerpool, later Lord Widmerpool, is a man ominously possessed of the notion that one's life must be shaped by one's will; who, investing in this belief, rises from schoolboy duffer and butt to be a successful businessman, a Labour MP, minister and life peer, before dying an ugly death in the midst of a circle of cultist obsessives, led by a wild, criminal, and probably insane, fanatic called Scorpio Murtlock.

Powell's books are full of characters whose surnames are also place names, though this is often because they are aristocrats, and so have become Viscount Warminster (a town in Wiltshire) or Lord Vowchurch (a village in Herefordshire) or Lord Goring (Oxfordshire has one and Sussex another). But there are others too. Ada Leintwardine (another village in Herefordshire) is no kind of aristocrat. Nor is the scheming don, Sillery: Sillery Sands is a place on the Devon coast. Barnby, Stepney, Isbister, Offord – all are places in Bartholomew as well as people in Powell. Widmerpool too is no aristocrat. The name, I used to assume, was simply plucked out of the air, rather as Gamp and Drudge and Jellyby and Tulkinghorn floated into the head of Dickens. But it may not be as simple as that.

Kenneth Widmerpool makes his memorable first appearance in *A Dance to the Music of Time*, looming up out of the mist and drizzle, at dusk, solemn and clumsy, engaged on a solitary run, at the school that Powell never names, though it's clearly Eton. We know little until the fourth book in the series, *At Lady Molly's*, about his origins. His mother lives in Victoria Street; later she has a cottage at Hinton, festooned with roses. Little is said of his father. But that changes when Nicholas Jenkins, Powell's infuriatingly self-effacing narrator, is asked by some of the future bride's relatives to tell what he knows about Widmerpool, who is shortly to marry the Hon. Mildred Haycock. Her relatives are unhappy about the match. Where do the Widmerpools come from? asks the Hon. Mrs Conyers anxiously. And Jenkins tells her: 'from Nottinghamshire, I believe'; though later he thinks it was possibly Derbyshire. He decides not to add that another figure who moves in these circles, Lord Goring, used once to buy his liquid manure from Widmerpool's father.

There are other fictional Widmerpools too, no more alluring. J. L. Carr of Kettering wrote a novel called *The Harpole Report* (1973) about a headmaster (Harpole) and his tribulations with officialdom, with his staff, with his pupils and with his pupils' parents. The Widmerpools – slobby father, fat and jovial but complaining mother, and the four of their tribe of eleven turbulent offspring with whom Harpole finds himself saddled, are about the worst; especially the fourth of them, Ringo, aged eight (reading age five) who so incenses Harpole that he gives him four hard smacks with a copy of *Janet and John* (Book Three); which, he explains, is a hardback.

People who may be offended when the name of the place they live in is taken in vain – in this case, it seems serially taken in vain – have no redress. There must have been those in Weston-super-Mare who groaned, even raged, when they heard that Jeffrey Archer, on taking his peerage, had tacked the name of their town on to his title. Even after his downfall, it stays there. People in Weeford, Staffordshire, who did not share his robustly Thatcherite views had no right of reply when Woodrow Wyatt chose the title, Lord Wyatt of Weeford. No poll was taken in Widmerpool, Notts, before Powell abstracted its name for his unalluring creation. Did Widmerpool, Notts, I wondered when I spotted its name on the map, resent this blight on its reputation? Or might Widmerpool even deserve it?

You come to it down pleasant lanes from the A46, a neat and blameless place, though drastically changed since Bartholomew's day. Very few who live there now, it is said, are native Widmerpudlians. Little new had been built in a hundred years until the 1960s, but thereafter a rash of well-to-do detached residences began to appear on either side of the stream that runs through it. The effect is disconcerting. Given the kind of statement that people who covet such houses probably want to make (which roughly translated might be: all things considered, I've done pretty well, thank you), they are too close together. Homes with such pretensions need more room to breathe. Here and there you pick up a clue to what's happened: a gardener's cottage, 1832, with a prominent clock, put there no doubt to ensure that the gardener turned up for duty promptly; a coach house, verging on the baronial in its own right… this must have been part of a proud estate.

And there, up the hill, is a tower, suggesting a quite considerable house. Sure enough, just up the main village road you come to Widmerpool Hall, the seat listed by Bartholomew. Once the family seat, not of the Widmerpools, sellers of liquid manure, but of the Robinsons (sometimes Robertsons), Nottingham mill-owners, but with its grounds now sold off to accommodate all these mini-seats down below. Built in 1832, it was never a house in the premier league, and since the Robinsons/Robertsons left it, it has gone through various transitional phases, including a spell as a headquarters for the Automobile Association's patrolmen. When I was there in the spring of 2007, heavy amendments were under way. The house was being divided into nine apartments, plus eleven mews and four detached houses fitted in alongside.

Some parts of the village are much as they must have been when the Robinsons/Robertsons moved there. Often these too look quite affluent. The Old Rectory is imposing even by Old Rectory standards. Houses which bear this name are usually in my experience occupied by rising industrialists or by Tory MPs, the old rectors having moved somewhere much cheaper decades ago. There was certainly a very sought-after breed of motor car parked in the Old Rectory yard. I saw no one while I wandered through Widmerpool, except a delivery driver looking for an address that did not seem to exist. He knocked on a couple of doors seeking guidance, but nobody answered. I had hoped to ask in the pub what people thought about Anthony Powell helping himself to the name of the village – but there isn't a pub. This is not a very villagey village.

The day I went there, as it happened, was misty, and that seemed very appropriate, since it's out of the mist that Kenneth Widmerpool first appears, running; and it's in the mist, running again, this time naked, in accordance with the doctrines of Scorpio Murtlock, that he dies. In line with his almost religious belief in willpower, he has insisted, though now in his seventies, on running faster than his younger companions. 'I'm leading, I'm leading now,' he cries as he fades into the mist.

> 'When they came round a corner, out of the trees, [someone who saw these events tells Nicholas Jenkins], 'he was lying just in the road.'
>
> 'Collapsed?'
>
> 'Dead.'

That comes only three pages from the end of the final chapter of the twelfth and final book in the *Music of Time*. Maybe Nottinghamshire Widmerpudlians sometimes have cause to regret that this tragedy didn't occur at least a thousand pages earlier.

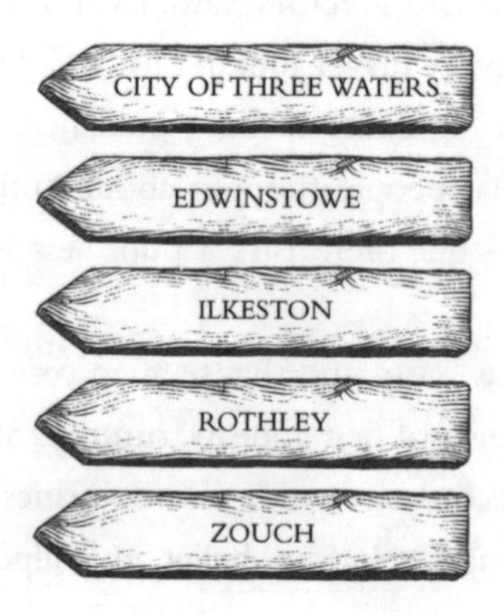

WIGAN

WIGAN, parl. and co. bor., mfr. town and par., with ry. stas. L.M.S. and L.N.E, SW. Lancs, on r. Douglas… Its mfrs. consist chiefly of calicoes, checks, fustians and other cotton fabrics. It has also linen works, iron foundries, iron forges, iron rolling-mills, railway waggon works, chemical works, etc. …

SOME TOWNS ARE ROUTINELY singled out for mockery: Slough, Swindon, Surbiton, Basingstoke, always good for a bit of a laugh; Wigan's another, chiefly, though not exclusively, because of its pier. A pier? In Wigan? In the midst of its mills and its mines, and twenty miles from the sea? How very droll! Also, some assumed the pier was pure invention – but it wasn't. For years it stood, largely unremarked, a practical working pier, on the banks of the town's canal.

Wigan is no longer embarrassed by references to its pier. It's become a tourist attraction, proclaimed as much as the town itself on the road signs in the outskirts, something to boast about, alongside the frequent reminders that Wigan nowadays has teams not only in the rugby league superleague but in the soccer premiership too. One has to admire Wigan's cool in putting these signs up, knowing how close both Wigan Athletic and even for a while their far more famous rugby equivalents came to losing their premiership status at the end of the 2006–2007 season.

The pier is set about now with standard tourist accoutrements: the museum, the café, the visitor centre and the rest. It also has a great big pub called the Orwell, after George Orwell, who in 1937 made it famous by calling a book (which in fact was equally outraged about conditions of working-class life in places like Barnsley and Sheffield) *The Road to Wigan Pier*. Wigan wasn't

so pleased with him then. Why, it was asked, had he deliberately sought out houses of exceptional squalor for a taste of the lives of the working poor? As the *Wigan Observer* put it: 'Mr Orwell has taken great care with his book, and all who wish genuinely to play their part in the modern world may profit in some way by reading it. But Wigan people, one feels, will feel a little hurt and heartsore that the blackest part of a borough that has fought well for centuries should be so held up for exhibition. This is only part of Wigan, as all who know Wigan well would agree.'

This was a fair complaint. When he wrote of his filthy room over a tripe shop: 'It struck me that this place must be fairly normal as lodging houses in the industrial areas go', he had reason to know that this was not true. He had left the first lodgings friends found for him. Why? They were too salubrious for his purposes.

Even setting aside the pier there's much to savour in today's post-Orwellian Wigan. The heart of it is the market square at the top of the hill, from which roads fan out in several directions. Much has changed since the 1930s, when Orwell was there, or the 1940s when as a child I lived there briefly, being woken each morning if I remember (though sometimes early memories become romanticized, and what never happened becomes as real as what actually did) by the sounds of clogs clattering on the pavement as the mill hands made their early morning journeys to work.

The mills have gone, the mines have gone, much of the housing that horrified Orwell has gone. The names on the larger shop fronts are much the same as you'd find in Bristol or Bournemouth; the Grand Hotel ceased long ago to be grand and when I was there in the summer of 2007 it appeared to be abandoned. Other uses have been found for once – thriving theatres. The old, sternly panelled, scholarly library in which Orwell dug out his damning statistics is now called The History Shop, while the new public library eschews such forbidding words as library in favour of the title: 'Explore'. (The street in which the History Shop stands is still known as Library Street, but no doubt they'll find something less stuffy soon.)

Yet the centre has been modernized with a greater respect for the history of the place than one finds in some other towns. It's got the ubiquitous glitzy shopping malls (towns that don't have them see their custom bleeding away to those that do), but Wigan's 1989 Galleries shopping centre has been spatchcocked into the main street without destroying its continuity. There may be a great splash of glass at a moment like this, but the sequence is largely unbroken: these are still recognizably the streets that Victorian Wigan shopped in. Note, too, how much the view down Market Street gains from the continuing presence of the little tower above the ecclesiastical building which now houses the Queen's Hall Methodist Mission. So often in less fortunate towns familiar landmarks like this have been swept away, an unintended but deathly part of the process in which everywhere becomes more and more like everywhere else. The closed market is still a good solid north-country closed market, with butchers' stalls where Wigan still queues for its favourite Lancashire delicacies.

Central Park, on the edge of the town centre, the home of Wigan rugby league football club – for so many years so much the most famous and successful in the land that even Manchester United in the association game is barely a parallel – has been overtaken by progress, though happily the new ground is no great distance from the centre of town. But Mesnes Park remains much as it was when I saw it first in the 1940s, a kind of template for what a good public park ought to be: a place where you'll find a lake with ducks and eager children feeding them; a bandstand to accommodate the brass and silver bands of surrounding villages, playing to people in Sunday afternoon deckchairs; a bowling green – a crown green in the north of England, of course – where men in white caps and women in long practical skirts are in solemn action; a café with passable coffee, strong tea, and if possible, rock cakes; and a statue close to the centre of some stout and puissant late nineteenth-century alderman. Rather than an alderman, Mesnes Park has a former Tory MP, Sir Francis Sharp Powell, Bt, who served the town at Westminster from 1885 until 1910, seated, hand on chin, looking thoughtful while gradually turning green. Its bandstand when I was there showed no sign of recent use and was overdue for repainting, and the twin buildings at the entrance – the lodge and the matching house alongside it – were ready for demolition, but the rest of my Parks Department desiderata were in place, with all seats taken on the terrace in front of the café.

To anyone who has recently been to somewhere like Blackburn or Burnley – in Burnley, particularly, a modern shopping centre has obliterated any sense of what the heart of old Burnley must have been like – what is striking and heartening in Wigan is the sense of continuity balancing change. You would not, I imagine, have cause in Wigan to feel, as so many must do in Blackburn and Burnley, that your town has been taken from you and changed into somewhere else, an experience that inevitably results in a loss of that sense of identity which people need to sustain their lives. A great part of that, it has to be said, reflects the extent to which Blackburn and Burnley have become what we nowadays call multicultural, which means in effect that great swathes have been taken over by households from ethnic minorities, a process made even more fracturing, as official reports have established, by the effective segregation of schools, which tends to march ahead of the segregation of communities as a whole.

Ted Cantle, who wrote the report on the riots in Burnley, Oldham and Bradford in 2001, told the *Observer* newspaper in the summer of 2007 that schools sometimes reached a tipping point 'where one side or the other feels this school is no longer for them'. In Burnley, this has led to a radical redrafting of the pattern of schooling, with eleven schools closing at the end of the summer term in 2007. The 2001 census found that 26 per cent of the population of the Blackburn parliamentary constituency was of Indian or Pakistani origin, ranking it sixteenth of all constituencies in this category, though in Burnley, which had riots, the figure was only 7 per cent.

In Wigan, 98.6 per cent of the population were classified 'white' in the census and 0.44 per cent were of Indian or Pakistani origin. Race is far from the only factor in these equations. The steady decline of the manufacturing industries that had once been the staple of all three towns was also reflected in these figures. The statistics show where each of 659 constituencies ranked on the national scale. The proportion of 'economically active' people in Blackburn (that's to say, people able to work) who had found full-time employment was 58 per cent, placing it 527th, against Burnley's 63 per cent, equal with Wigan's, putting them in 201st and 200th place respectively. In a happy departure from Orwell's day, Wigan's housing stock, as measured by the number of households with central heating and their own bathrooms and lavatories, scored far better than the other two, putting it in 287th place against Blackburn's 578th and Burnley's 607th. And Wigan had a higher proportion of people in managerial jobs, putting it 450th in the national league against Burnley's 531st place and Blackburn's 611th.

Even so, the signs of a changed community that register most immediately, and which tend to cause the most rancour where good housing and jobs are scarce, are colour and accent; together with the proliferation of institutions, especially mosques, which seem strange and alien to some old inhabitants. If Wigan, compared with these two Lancashire counterparts, seems so much more settled, that is one potent part of the mix.

You can judge these things another way too: by looking in the local studies library (or History Shop) at the local papers that reflected the life of the town in the past: its political institutions, its civic occasions, the cases that came before magistrates' courts, its sporting achievements, the lives of its churches and sometimes their interaction, and perhaps above all those particular dates in the year when the whole town turned out to celebrate feast days, to take part in or watch and applaud processions, and in general to honour the life of the town, cementing its sense of identity. These used to be so much stronger in the self-contained, locked-in times when local papers were full of local events, and radio, television and mass advertising had not yet begun to home in on us, so that the wider world in those times seemed less relevant, and certainly less intrusive. The old civic passions are not entirely extinguished, though they tend to surface now mainly in sport: Blackburn v. Burnley is a no less potent concept today than it was in the 1890s, but because there is so much more money in Blackburn Rovers FC than there is in Burnley, their clashes no longer occur so often.

There's another heartening sign that old Wigan still prospers. For years, along with most reporters going to and fro between London and Blackpool during the party conference season, I always used to look out as the train approached Wigan North Western station for a sign on a wall which proclaimed: 'Santus. Uncle Joe's Mint Balls Keep you all aglow'. Today Virgin trains have low windows which seem designed to make you think that you're travelling by aeroplane, which is why nowadays I always miss it. But I've checked, and it is still there. I hope, though I don't really dare to expect, that for the rest of my lifetime Uncle Joe will continue to market his inspiring confectionery, that Wigan will continue to prosper in both premiership competitions, and that crown bowls, ducks on the lake, brass bands in the bandstand, and the reassuring presence of Sir Francis Powell, Bt, MP, will continue to ennoble Mesnes Park.

WOLVERHAMPTON

WOLVERHAMPTON, parl. and co. bor., manufacturing town and par. … Staffs, 12¾m. NW. of Birmingham. Wolverhampton stands on the summit of an eminence, amid a network of railways and canals… has long been noted for its locks and keys.

AN OLD THEATRICAL TALE, in which no doubt the location of the theatre depends on who is telling it – but when I first came across it, Wolverhampton was specifically mentioned – goes as follows. A touring company is playing *Hamlet*. Two subordinate actors are in the pub when the actor-manager, of whom they are somewhat in awe, appears and demands to know what they are talking about. About the play, of course, they assure him. The question they've been debating is whether Hamlet and Ophelia ever consummated their love (though 'consummated their love' was perhaps was not the term the actors actually used). 'I can answer that,' says the actor-manager with his usual roaring confidence. 'Of course they did. On our opening night at the Theatre Royal, Wolverhampton.'

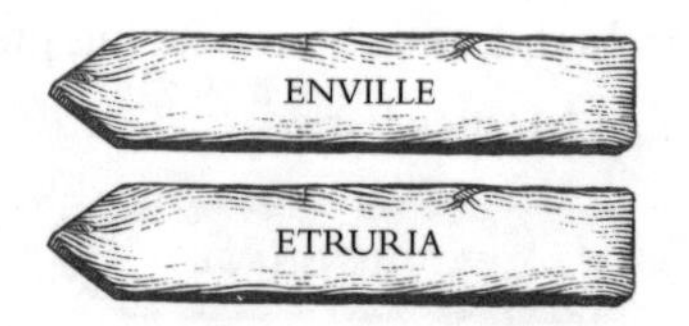

WYTHENSHAWE

WYTHENSHAWE, seat, Cheshire, 3m. ENE. of Altrincham, gifted to Manchester.

IN THE MIDST OF the large and well-tended space dedicated to public enjoyment on the southern edge of Manchester, known as Wythenshawe Park, is a Tudor house, now greatly amended, called Wythenshawe Hall, once home of the rich and influential Tatton family. They lived here from the 1540s until 1926, when the house and its estate were bought by Lord Simon of Wythenshawe, who gave them to the city of Manchester as a playground and breathing space and haven for quiet reflection for the thousands who moved into the vast new Wythenshawe housing estate.

An epic encounter took place at this spot in 1641 when the royalist Sir Robert Tatton mustered his tenants and servants in a doomed attempt, lasting several months, to defend it against the parliamentarians. The house was taken by Oliver Cromwell and used to station his troops, though later the Tattons, on payment of a substantial sum, were allowed to return. But who is this, on a plinth, directly confronting the house, though with his gaze a little averted, as if he had more important things to think about? It is Oliver Cromwell, no less, scourge of the Tattons. It is almost as if Manchester Corporation had placed him here to remind the tourists who visit an establishment which sided with the king against Parliament that Parliament came out on top. Monarchists who visit the Hall must surely find it unsettling. Yet they can take some satisfaction from its history. For Cromwell's presence opposite

Wythenshawe Hall amounts to a relegation – once he commanded a far more eminent site at the very heart of Manchester.

In the mid nineteenth century the city's radical Liberals, and especially a man called Thomas Goadsby (who was mayor in 1861–2), resolved that the city should honour Cromwell. A statue had already been proposed in Leeds, but there opposition was so ferocious that the project was dropped. Manchester radicals, however, were determined to proceed, whatever the objections of the Tories, one of whose newspapers denounced it as 'an odious effigy of a traitor and a regicide', and of the Manchester Irish.

Goadsby did not live to see his cause succeed, but the campaign was taken up by a fellow radical called Abel Heywood, who had married Goadsby's widow, Elizabeth. As it says on a plaque at Wythenshawe, she bestowed the statue – commissioned from Matthew Noble, and very well done – on the citizens in August 1875. There are four steps up to the plinth. Cromwell stands on the top of a rock, looking strong and confident and inevitably after so many years rather green, his hands outstretched in a protective gesture. The site that the Liberals chose for him was the junction of Deansgate and Cateaton Street, close to the Exchange and the cathedral, the spot at which the first blood was spilled in Manchester in the Civil War. Having placed it there, they found themselves forced to defend its continuing presence. When the city built its new town hall in 1877 it naturally thought that given the city's importance the only fit person to open it was the queen. So an invitation was duly issued with high hopes that she would accede. Instead, the message came back that she could not comply with the city's request while a statue of Oliver Cromwell stood in a prominent place in its midst.

The Liberals of Manchester were not to be blackmailed. Though the city recognized the sensitivity of the occasion – the painter Ford Madox Brown, commissioned to decorate the interior with great scenes from the city's history, had to be dissuaded from commemorating the battle of Peterloo – they resolved to hang on to the architect of the Commonwealth even if it meant losing the queen. The honour of declaring the new town hall open was given instead to the mayor.

And there Oliver, on his plinth and in all his imperiousness, remained for a century, until a redevelopment plan threatened his site. Undisturbed by the wrath of a monarch, he now had to yield to an even mightier power: through traffic. The chief campaigner for the statue's removal had been a Conservative alderman, and some on the left objected that the redevelopment was being exploited as an excuse to settle old scores. Cromwell, however, was duly banished, and resettled where he is now.

In 2007, a belated campaign was under way to establish a memorial in the city to the victims of Peterloo, its only recognition until then having been evasive and perfunctory. Were that to succeed, some Manchester radicals hoped, maybe the time would be right for Cromwell to return to the heart of their city.

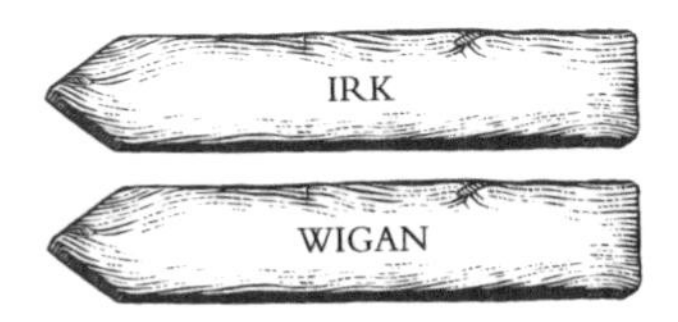

A B C D
E F G H
I J K L
M N O P
Q R S T
U V W XYZ

XI TOWNS

RUYTON OF THE ELEVEN TOWNS, par. and vil., Salop, on r. Perry, 2½m. W. of Baschurch and 8½m. NW. of Shrewsbury…

NOT MUCH OF THE world has this problem. In world gazetteers there's a fine array of places whose names begin with the letter X, not all of them in China. But poor uningenious Britain does not provide even one. There is none in Bartholomew's 748 pages and none in the 791 pages of the 1999 edition of the *Ordnance Survey Gazetteer.* Claims are said to be made for somewhere in Somerset fancifully called 'Xanadu', but the *OS Gazetteer*, now the supreme authority, does not recognize it, so neither shall I. What a missed opportunity, that the people who gave little townships in County Durham names like Quebec and Toronto failed to borrow as fetching a name as Xai-Xai (Mozambique) or Xin Barag Youqi, which is not very far from Xin Barag Zuoqi in China, or Xique-Xique (Brazil).

Yet there's one place in Britain which ought logically to start with an X. Though Bartholomew lists Ruyton of the Eleven Towns, it's more usually spelled Ruyton-XI-Towns. Even that is not logical. It's like calling the England cricket team, when it thrashed the Australians, Flintoff-XI-Players. This odd entity is made up of eleven towns of which Ruyton is only one. So plain 'XI-Towns', or if pedants prefer, 'XI-Towns-including-Ruyton', is the designation the county council should resolve to adopt.

The names of these towns are Coton (or Cotton), Eardiston, Haughton, Rednal, Ruyton, Shelvock, Shotatton, Sutton, Tedsmore, West Felton and Wykey. Though to call them all towns is illogical too. Some are so modest that I passed straight through them without realizing I'd done so. It is only when you encounter a signpost, pointing back to the place you thought you were going to, down the road you just came on, that you realise you've been there already. Even Ruyton, which I suppose is the capital, is a village rather than a town.

An 1868 gazetteer included only six of them: Cotton, Eardiston, Ruyton, Shelvock, Shotatton and Wykey, which seems odd since it omits West Felton, quite a sizeable place today and, because it's on the A5, busier now than Ruyton. It ought also to be said that in my experience if you set out to collect all eleven towns you'll keep coming to somewhere called Grimpo. Grimpo is a bit of a cuckoo. It doesn't belong to this group, but it's grown to a point where it's more substantial than most that do. Developers seem to be irresistibly drawn to Grimpo, and far more families live there now than in Shelvock and its equivalents.

Ruyton itself is a long straggling village, at one end of which is the Talbot Inn, a kind of knockabout black and white building, across the road from a shop which could offer me maps of the Oswestry area but had none that covered Ruyton and its compatriots. The road climbs steadily through the village, detaching itself from the valley. The further you go, the more you notice the stream far below, with the trees reflected in it. On the opposite side there are sandy crags with enviable houses – at least for the views they enjoy – on the top. The war memorial, a shelter cut into the rock, has an unexpectedly large collection of Welsh names, but then we are little more than five miles from the border. Past the church and past the castle, the road descends again past a pub and a site for exclusive development of four- to five-bedroom houses to Telford's bridge at the bottom: a perilous place for pedestrians. 'Like Rome,' says a book called *Life in Ruyton-XI-Towns 50 Years Ago*, 'Ruyton-XI-Towns lies on a river winding its way among the Severn Hills…' A pun on Severn/seven, one has to assume. The river here is not, however, the Tiber, but the rather less internationally famous Perry, which having left the marshy flats of Baggy Moor, plunges its winding way, my book informed me, to join the Severn near Bromley Forge in Mytton.

The walk back to the Talbot Inn (which like so many country pubs these days was shut, although it was lunchtime) was, for some reason, more enjoyable than doing the route the other way around. This time one was more aware of the church, St John the Baptist, twelfth century, built in the characteristic red of the area, with a rather fierce red battlemented tower. Stumps and stubs are all that remain of the castle, which is older than the church and historically more important. Two workmen were cheerfully busy here, one of whom was enthusiastically singing: 'I'm a star in New York, a star in LA', although he broke off to say 'Good Morning'.

Beyond the Talbot Inn there's a road signposted for Wykey and Eardiston. Though it is said to have been an important manor at the time of the Domesday Book, there isn't much left at Wykey – a couple of cottages and a call box – and before long I found myself in Haughton, where there's a C of E church called St Chad's. This meant I had failed to register Eardiston. Beyond, the road, hitherto hedged and treelined, was open and flat. A wholly different landscape presented itself. A large sign saying 'Storm The Embassy' announced the immediate presence of the Rednal Paintball Arena. There were transport depots with large, vaguely menacing lorries and the usual industrial and leisure mixture you find on abandoned air sites: all very unShropshire. Housman – I think, would have fled. On the main road, a notice told me to kill my speed as I passed through the village of Rednal, though it's hardly begun before it is over.

West Felton has a presence about it, but rather a noisy presence because of the A5 traffic. This village can boast not only a church but a shop, a public hall and a pub called the Punch Bowl Inn. No time for that now, though, with a further V towns to find. Sutton I think I found, just to the west of Grimpo. Tedsmore, at which I at last arrived after further flirtations with Grimpo, had two-storey lodges and decorative gates and a drive leading to Tedsmore Hall. The roads down here are narrow, high-hedged, mysterious: this is part of that secret, almost conspiratorial England which lurks down byways, unsuspected by those who journey on serious roads. There were faint signs of Shelvock, which once had a quarry, though nothing much seems to happen there now.

Arthur Conan Doyle lived for a brief time in Ruyton, as a medical assistant to a Ruyton doctor. This was not a success; he did not get on with his senior. And he wasn't impressed with Ruyton. 'It is not big enough to make one town,' he is supposed to have said, 'far less eleven.' It's sometimes claimed that he named his famous detective Sherlock because he'd discovered Shelvock. On the principles enunciated by Holmes, only if every other possible explanation had been eliminated would I believe this.

Coton, described in 1851 as 'a small township in a salubrious situation one and a quarter miles out of Ruyton, population 14', hides its salubrity well, and I failed to find it. That left only Shotatton, which now gives its name to a terrible spot called Shotatton Crossroads, the point at which traffic coming west out of Ruyton and heading west towards the Welsh border is required to fight its way across the ferocious A5. A coach full of children thirteen to fourteen years old was trapped in the fuming queue. By the time they're across, I thought, they'll be too old for university.

YARM

YARM, mkt.-town and par., with ry. sta., L.N.E., N.R. Yorks.
on r. Tees, 4m. SSW. of Stockton…

YARM IS A PLACE that people look down on. You see it from trains engaged on grand journeys from London to Edinburgh as they travel across the viaduct which marches imperiously right through the town. It's not one of the very best thrills on the east coast line, not in the stand-up-and-gape league of Durham Cathedral, the Newcastle bridges, or the first sight of the sea near Alnmouth, but it's a place that some travellers always like to look down on and wonder about – as I did for many years, until at last I got out at Yarm station and went to investigate. (That's the replacement Yarm station, not the original one at the northern end of the viaduct, where in the early days at least one traveller misjudged his descent from his train and fell off the viaduct to his death.)

And the high street, which is what the town is really about, is almost as good as it looks from above. Where it's not, that is because of the traffic, which mooches through the town in numbers you'd hardly expect now the A19 southbound for York, which used to run through it, has been made to take its business elsewhere. But when I was there, a steady crawl of disconsolate traffic ground slowly along the main street, while those who wanted to stop conducted grumbling searches for parking space on the cobbled roadside.

I think you could call it quite posh. There are good Georgian houses at the southern end of the street and towards the northern end, a Bang and Olufsen showroom, which you wouldn't normally find in a place this size. This is where Middlesbrough comes when it makes its money, and that includes Middlesbrough's football stars – initial lack of enthusiasm when expensive imports contemplate moving to Teesside is dissipated, it's said, when they are offered the prospect of living in Yarm.

In the midst of the street is a building which some call elegant but which seemed to me in its present condition to amount to a comic masterpiece. This is the 1710 town hall, once the lord of the manor's court house, now an information centre with downstairs arcades into which they have crammed public lavatories. The town hall's walls commemorate a number of famous occasions in Yarm. There's an unexpected war memorial to those who fought, whether slain or not, in the South African wars. There's a record of the level of various floods over the centuries: 1880, up to my elbow; 1771, a good 10 feet high. Water is very dominant here.

Yarm – in this sense resembling Durham – is set on a peninsula, and close to the confluence of the rivers Leven and Tees, which is one reason for the floods. From the twelfth to the eighteenth century Yarm was the principal port of the Tees, and until 1771 the lowest crossing point on the river. The rise of Stockton put paid to that. The third of the wall's commemorations, one of several in Yarm, celebrates the birth of the Stockton and Darlington Railway, the world's first public railway (or so it says on the plaque: it's a claim that is often disputed). The names of those who sat around the table when the decision was made, with Thomas Meynell as chairman, are recorded, each suffixed by the proud designation, 'of Yarm'. The George and Dragon hotel, where this deed was done in February 1821, celebrates it as well. Yarm had to wait rather longer for a railway of its own. The viaduct, which is 2,280 feet long, was built between 1849 and 1851 for the Leeds Northern Railway company.

In 2007, Yarm high street was voted the best in Britain by viewers of the BBC News 24 breakfast programme, who, before they made their decisions, must, one assumes, have assiduously matched it up against all the rest. Perhaps some of the voters had merely seen it from passing trains. If challenged, though, they could have quoted the teaching of Harriet Martineau, who said that whenever she visited a fresh city, she would go to the highest available point in the place, from where she could see it as a 'living map' before her. 'It is scarcely credible', she wrote in her *Retrospect of Western Travel*, published in 1838, 'how much time is saved and confusion of vision obviated by this means.' So perhaps travellers on the east coast mainline who get the chance to look down on the place and admire it don't really need to get out at Yarm after all.

YARROW

YARROW, par., Selkirkshire, on Yarrow Water; 48,851 ac., pop. 495. YARROW WATER, Selkirkshire, rises on borders of Dumfriesshire, flows through Loch of the Lowes and St Mary's Loch, 14½m. NE. to Ettrick Water, 2m. SW. of Selkirk.

A BEAUTIFUL LONELY ROAD runs from Selkirk to Moffat, following to its source the river called Yarrow Water. A beautiful lonely road in winter, that is: the size of the car parks along the way suggest that its loneliness, its precious sense of remoteness, are lost in summer. But in bleak November, when I was there, one could understand why this border country was so extolled by writers, and particularly by poets, who pined for it when they could not be there.

Its two most celebrated writers, not pilgrims in search of romantic landscape but men born in this region, were an oddly assorted pair. Walter Scott, son of an upper-class family, born in Edinburgh in 1771 though much of his early life was spent in Roxburghshire and Dumfriesshire, lawyer, sheriff at twenty-eight of Selkirkshire, one of the lions of Scottish literature and Scottish society, wrote late in life of this place:

> By Yarrow's stream still let me stray,
> Though none should guide my feeble way;
> Still feel the breeze down Ettrick break,
> Although it chill my wither'd cheek.

And James Hogg, born in 1770 (though he falsely claimed he was born, like his hero Burns, on 25 January and in 1772) and always known, as he wished to be, even in his days of comparative eminence, as the Ettrick shepherd. Hogg was the child of a poor rural farming family, given only rudimentary schooling, became a cowherd at seven, a Shepherd thereafter, so socially maladroit as to cause well-bred households embarrassment, and a self-taught writer who produced one of the most remarkable and mysterious books to appear in his lifetime.

They were brought together, these two, by a common interest in the poetry and legend of the border country: Scott as a collector who intended to weave them into a book, and Hogg as one who knew them by heart, having learned them all from his mother – from whom Scott, on his way to making his reputation with *The Lay of the Last Minstrel*, probably garnered more than he did from her son. An acquaintance that began on this simple basis, supply and demand, grew into something much warmer, which survived through the many excitements and tribulations of both men's lives.

In time Hogg had to leave his shepherding to manage his ageing parents' farm at Ettrick. His passion was always poetry, and with Scott's encouragement and assistance he published a book of poems – signalling his twin commitments, however, by publishing at about the same time a treatise on the treatment of sheep. In the hope of supplementing his meagre income, he went into farming on his own account, which left him bankrupt. But by now he had influential friends and admirers. In 1813, Byron sent a copy of Hogg's *The Queen's Wake* – a series of ballads supposedly recited at a competition of bards to Mary Queen of Scots – to John Murray, telling him he should publish it.

Then came an even more practical kind of assistance. In 1815, the Duke of Buccleuch, whose Duchess had recently died, wrote to Hogg to tell him that in accordance with her wishes he would set him up at a farm at Altrive. For a time all went well, but then Hogg rashly resolved to acquire a neighbouring farm. It failed, and he had to abandon it. His literary reputation, though, was growing; more admirers (he claimed) were turning up at Altrive than he wished for. In 1824, in his middle fifties, he published the book for which he is best remembered: *The Confessions of a Justified Sinner* – or, more properly, *The Private Memoirs and Confessions of a Justified Sinner*, though because of the outrage evoked by the concept of justified sin, it was also known for a time as *The Confessions of a Fanatic*. It's a book full of guilt and fear and obsession in which a young man called George Colwan falls under the spell of a mysterious figure who may or may not be the devil. It's hard to believe as the story develops that he isn't the devil, but one's never entirely sure, and there's a sense now and then that the author himself is not entirely sure either. A series of increasingly terrible murders follow, narrated in the second part of the book by Colwan himself:

> My life has been a life of trouble and turmoil; of change and vicissitude; of anger and exultation; of sorrow and of vengeance. My sorrows have all been for a slighted gospel, and my vengeance has been wreaked on its adversaries. Therefore, in the might of heaven I will sit down and write. I will let the wicked of this world know what I have done in the faith of the promises, and justification by grace, that they may read and tremble, and bless their gods of silver and of gold, that the minister of heaven was removed from their sphere before their blood was mingled with their sacrifices...

The world duly read and trembled, though often with outrage. It is a story – a legend – of extraordinary power, and hugely unsettling.

Throughout these years Scott kept a kindly if sometimes exasperated eye on his strange and difficult friend – 'the honest grunter', as he sometimes called him, or 'the great Caledonian bear'. 'Scott's unwearied interest in James Hogg, despite the waywardness of this imaginative genius,' David Douglas, who edited and published Scott's *Journal* comments, 'is one of the most beautiful traits in his character... from the outset of their acquaintance in 1801 until the end of his life.' 'Poor James Hogg, the Ettrick shepherd, came to advise with me about his affairs,' Scott recorded in 1826, two years after the *Confessions* appeared. 'He is sinking under the times; having no assistance to give him, my advice, I fear, will be of little service. I am sorry for him if that would help him, especially as by his own account, a couple of hundred pounds would carry him on.' Three months later he wrote: 'Hogg was here yesterday, in danger from having obtained an accommodation of £100 from Mr Ballantyne who he is now obliged to repay. I am unable to help the poor fellow, being obliged to borrow myself. But I long ago remonstrated against the transaction at all, and gave him £50 out of my pocket...'

Though by this time he was enshrined as one of the kingdom's greatest writers – one of such influence that he's nowadays credited with re-establishing, some would even say, inventing, the romantic tradition which is one of Scotland's most successful tourist appeals – Scott's life was turbulent too. In 1826, at a time when his wife was gravely, and as it proved, incurably ill, a publishing venture had failed, which was why he felt he could not help Hogg (though he did). Like Hogg, he went bankrupt. His wife of thirty years died a week after that second visit of Hogg's. The last words Scott heard her speak were: 'You all have such melancholy faces.'

Hogg too had been fond of Scott's wife. The first time he came to dinner, 'dressed like any other shepherd, and his hands... stained with sheep-dip', he found Charlotte, whose health was never good, stretched out on a sofa. He immediately lay down on a second sofa, believing, as he later explained, that one could not go wrong by copying the lady of the house. Unused to the kind of formalities which came naturally to Scottish society, he dined heavily, drank well, told stories and started to sing. From 'Mr Scott', he proceeded to 'Scott', then to 'Walter' and finally, 'Wattie'. A shiver seems to have run through the company when he started addressing his hostess as 'Charlotte'.

Scott describes himself in his journal at the time of Charlotte's death as 'lonely, aged [he was fifty-five] and deprived of family'. He never regained financial security. Some of the pain occasioned by this experience lasted the rest of his life, and his circumstances drove him to churn out a series of novels which came nowhere near matching those he had written in easier days. One of these was *Castle Dangerous*, which even his keenest admirers do not recommend.

Driving west out of Selkirk you come to an inn called the Gordon Arms, which proudly proclaims that this was the scene of the final meeting of Scott and Hogg. I was eager to see the room where this last encounter took place, and heartened that even on this empty day in November a sign outside said 'Open'. Unhappily, to my chagrin, and the boiling resentment of a man who had driven some distance in search of his pint, the doors were implacably shut. But in any case, the claim of the Gordon Arms is hardly a match for that which is justly made at a second inn some way along the valley, at the point where St Mary's Loch meets the Loch of the Lowes. This spot, one might say, is sacred to Hogg. Here, amid the high hills with their scattered white cottages, and above the tranquil waters of the great grave lochs – not as wild a scene as it once was, but not yet irrevocably smoothed into a tourist honeypot – you will find a monument to him. Two thousand people came here in 1860 to see it unveiled. Hogg is seated.

'The Ettrick Shepherd,' says the plaque 'born 1770 [he might not have been happy with that], died 1835':

> Instead of arms or golden crest,
> His harp with mimic flowers was drest;
> Around, in graceful streamers, fell
> The briar rose and the heather bell.
> At evening fall, in lonesome dale,
> He kept strange converse with the gale;
> Held worldly pomp in high derision,
> And wandered in a world of vision.

I left my car in the empty car park and made my confident way to the Tibbie Shiels Inn, named after the widow who kept it from 1824 to 1878. She is said to have been devoutly religious; her picture makes her look stern in a recognizably Presbyterian way, but certainly not too austere a soul for innkeeping. Scott and Hogg met frequently here, sometimes joined by such other eminent persons as Thomas Carlyle. But my hopes of inspecting the spot where these great men had sat were again disappointed; as the kindly present-day landlady who saw me prowling about gently explained, she had to take a break sometimes, and in winter she opened the inn only on Thursdays and Fridays and at the weekend. In September 2007, I saw it reported that she planned to dispose of the inn after nineteen years, the first ten with her husband; she was seventy-four, she said, and not in the best of health.

Scott, increasingly debilitated by illness, died in 1832 – the year of the great Reform Act, which he strongly opposed. Hogg, who claimed to be younger than Scott, though in truth he was older, outlived him by three years. Wordsworth was fascinated by Yarrow. Having written a poem in 1803 about falling to see it ('Yarrow Unvisited'), he wrote another, 'Yarrow Visited', in 1814, which begins:

> And is this Yarrow? – this the stream
> Of which my fancy cherish'd

So faithfully a waking dream,
 An image that hath perish'd?
Oh that some minstrel's harp were near
 To utter notes of gladness,
And chase this silence from the air,
 That fills my heart with sadness!

A third – 'Yarrow Revisited' – followed in 1831. When he heard the news of Hogg's death he responded with what he called an 'Extempore Effusion Upon the Death of James Hogg' – the word effusion suggesting then something rather more desirable than it does now.

When first, descending from the moorlands,
I saw the stream of Yarrow glide
Along a bare and open valley,
The Ettrick Shepherd was my guide.

When last along its banks I wandered,
Through groves that had begun to shed
Their golden leaves upon the pathways,
My steps the Border-minstrel led.

The mighty Minstrel breathes no longer,
'Mid mouldering ruins low he lies;
And death upon the braes of Yarrow,
Has closed the Shepherd-poet's eyes…

Wordsworth, born in 1770, was much of an age with the Border-minstrel, Scott, and the Ettrick Shepherd-poet, Hogg. His verse, gliding gently on like the stream of Yarrow, brings him to other lost friends: Coleridge ('the rapt One, of the godlike forehead'); Charles Lamb, George Crabbe and Felicia Hemans, another, much younger poet, dead at forty-one. Proud as he was of his shepherd origins, the Ettrick poet would surely have been honoured to find himself in such company – though not for one moment doubting that his inclusion in this eminent congregation was thoroughly justified.

ZOUCH

ZOUCH MILLS, locality, Notts, in Leake rural dist.

MOST GAZETTEERS OF BRITAIN nowadays end at Zouch, though Bartholomew, for reasons which will soon be made clear, does not. This Zouch is not to be confused with the famous Leicestershire town of Ashby-de-la-Zouch, though that's not an error likely to be made by anyone who has been to them. There isn't a great deal of Zouch: it is merely a few fleeting moments on the A6006 westward from Melton Mowbray before it collides with the mighty A6, by which time you are in Leicestershire. Later generations may even come to believe that the name 'Zouch' is simply a corruption of 'Zilch'. But it does have a river, the Soar, and a canal, and a marina, and a pub called the Rose and Crown from where you may take a boat trip on a craft called *Le Mardi Gras*.

So, in its way, it's a fun place, an impression confirmed when you see in the gents at the Rose and Crown a machine which will supply you with an 'erection booster': a herbal concoction to be taken, it says, '45 minutes before intimacy'. What a splendid old word it is, that 'intimacy'. It's a term that used often to be employed in the *News of the World*: 'intimacy', they used to report in those dear dead decorous days, 'then took place'. And what do you do, I wonder, with the intervening forty-five minutes? Not zilch, presumably.

So, farewell, Zouch. You only got in by accident. I intend to conclude as does my old friend Bartholomew at a place in Cornwall which is blessed with the tantalizing name: Zoze Point. Or is it?

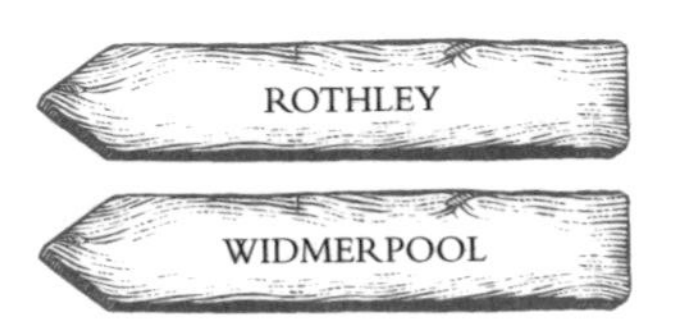

ZOZE POINT

ZOZE POINT, THE, at SW. extremity of Gerrans Bay, Cornwall, 3m. SE. of Falmouth.

SO TO THE VERY last entry in Bartholomew's 748 pages, one of a small but distinguished collection of places beginning with Z, more than half of them in Devon and Cornwall. I came to this part of the coast by a boat from Falmouth on a stormy autumn morning, with the water looking so turbulent that there seemed little chance that the boat across the Carrick Roads to St Mawes would run. But an optimistic crowd was gathered on the quayside, among them a contingent of primary school children from Hackney who seemed to be expecting the time of their lives – and were not disappointed. The boys, and a few of the girls, hung over the edge as the breakers tossed us about so violently that now and then passengers were thrown to the floor. 'Here comes another one!' they gleefully yelled as the rest of us hung pathetically on to whatever support we could grasp at.

The little white town of St Mawes was just waking up for the day, the shops were opening, and soon warm welcoming cafés were busy restoring the equilibrium of those who had made the crossing. From St Mawes, another, smaller boat, for which I was the only customer (and steered by a man who was full of grim predictions for what might become of those who did not get back to St Mawes pretty soon) took me across the bay to a landing stage close to a handsome Victorian building called Place House. A stirring tramp down an old military road on a day of sunshine – but today an almost malevolent wind – brought me to what I expected to be the Zoze Point.

And here at last it was, in all its September splendour, with a huge panorama westward back towards Falmouth and Pendennis Castle, and southwards, limitless views across a dazzling silver sea towards the north coast of Spain. Like stout Cortez on Darien (but Keats got it wrong, of course: he should have said Balboa), I gazed on this place with a sense of achievement. Yet something was wrong. The National Trust signs on the path told me that I had reached, not the Zoze Point, but Zone Point; which was not the same thing at all, since, had Bartholomew called it Zone Point it would have ceded last place in his book to Zouch.

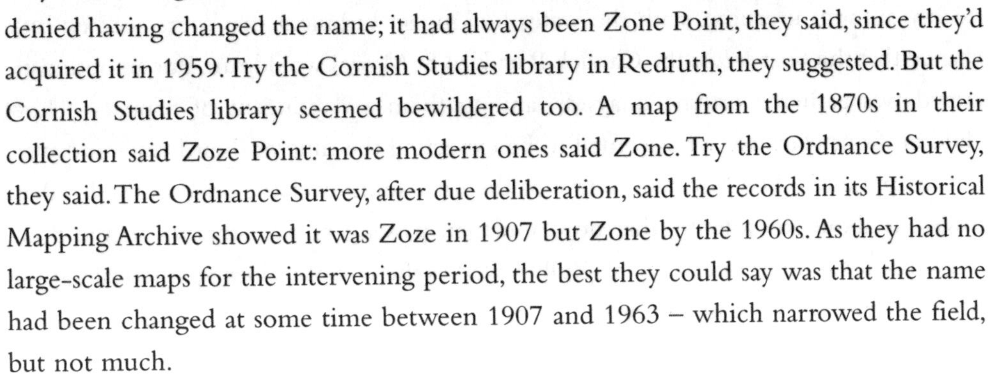

Perplexed, I made my way back to the Trust headquarters at St Anthony Head. No enlightenment there. Later, when, as they advised, I got in touch with their London office, they denied having changed the name; it had always been Zone Point, they said, since they'd acquired it in 1959. Try the Cornish Studies library in Redruth, they suggested. But the Cornish Studies library seemed bewildered too. A map from the 1870s in their collection said Zoze Point: more modern ones said Zone. Try the Ordnance Survey, they said. The Ordnance Survey, after due deliberation, said the records in its Historical Mapping Archive showed it was Zoze in 1907 but Zone by the 1960s. As they had no large-scale maps for the intervening period, the best they could say was that the name had been changed at some time between 1907 and 1963 – which narrowed the field, but not much.

Now, I am happy to say, I am able to unravel the mystery which left these great institutions baffled. The explanation is to be found in *A Popular Dictionary of Cornish Place-Names*, by O. J. Padel. The name Zone Point, he says, derives from the Cornish word Sawn, which means a cleft. The cleft at Zone Point, he adds, is still visible, though most of it has now fallen in. Around 1870, a mapmaker wrote the Anglicized name Zone Point so clumsily that the 'n' was misread as a 'z', and Zoze Point was born. Because it was sanctified by the Ordnance Survey, the wrong version became a popular usage in this region of Cornwall – an interesting case of feedback from a written to a spoken tradition.

Alpha to omega: the river Aan, where I started, was once the river Aan but is now the Water of Aven; Zoze Point, where I end my journey, was never really Zoze Point at all. Still, curious things do occur on this Cornish coast. At about the time I went to the Zoze Point, I saw a report in the national press of a strange event in the Carrick Roads. It said: 'A search-and-rescue operation launched after a lifeguard said he saw a body floating in the sea off St Just, Cornwall, fell flat when a lifeboat found a 2ft 6in (76cm) inflatable copy of Po, the Teletubby. Falmouth coastguards said: "It was an easy mistake to make, except for the antenna coming out of its head."'

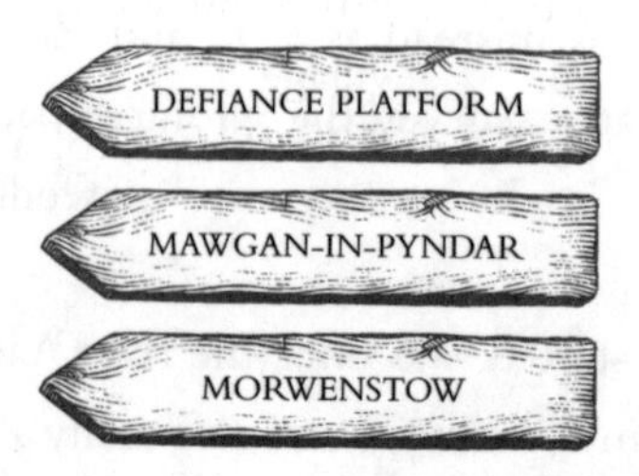

A BARTHOLOMEW GLOSSARY

Abbreviations used in Bartholomew's *Gazetteer of the British Isles*, 9th edition (1943), as reproduced in the introductions to the places listed in this book.

ac.	acres
alt.	altitude
bor.	borough
bur.	burgh (Scottish borough)
cem'y.	cemetery
civ.	civil
co.	county
dist.	district
div.	division
E.R.	East Riding (of Yorkshire)
eccl.	ecclesiastical
ft.	feet
G.C.	Great Central railway
G.W.R.	Great Western Railway
ham.	hamlet
ind.	industry
isl.	island
L.M.S.	London Midland and Scottish railway
L.N.E.	London and North Eastern railway
loc.	locality
m.	mile or miles
met.	metropolitan
mfr.	manufacture, manufacturing
mfrs.	manufactures
mkt.	market
mt.	mountain
mun.	municipal
N.R.	North Riding (of Yorkshire)
par.	parish
parl.	parliamentary
pl.	place
P.O.	Post Office
pop.	population
prom.	promontory
r.	river
roy.	royal
ry.	railway
spt.	seaport
S.R.	Southern Railway
sta.	station
sub.	suburb
urb.	urban
urb. dist.	urban district
vil.	village
W.R.	West Riding (of Yorkshire)

BIBLIOGRAPHY

This book draws throughout on the *Oxford Dictionary of National Biography*; Nikolaus Pevsner's Buildings of England series; the *Shell Guides* to counties in England, Scotland and Wales; *England's Thousand Best Churches* and *England's Thousand Best Houses*, both by Simon Jenkins; the *Ordnance Survey Gazetteer of Great Britain*; and the *New Grove Dictionary of Music and Musicians*. Other sources consulted and cited – some not in the British Library catalogue, but available locally as shown – include the following titles.

Abse, Dannie, *Intermittent Journals*, Bridgend, 1994

Anderson, J. R. L., *The Oldest Road: an exploration of the Ridgeway*, London, 1975

Arnold, Ralph, *The Unhappy Countess and her Grandson John Bowes*, London, 1957

Austin, Alfred, *The Garden that I Love*, London, 1894

Baring-Gould, Sabine, *The Vicar of Morwenstow: being a life of Robert Stephen Hawker*, London, 1949 (first published 1876)

Beazley, Elisabeth, *Madocks & the Wonder of Wales: the life of W. A. Madocks, M.P., 1773–1828: Improver, 'Chaotic', Architectural and Regional Planner, Reformer, Romantic; with some account of his Agent, John Williams*, London, 1967

Benson, E. F., *As We Were: A Victorian Peep-show*, London, 1985 (first published 1930)

Berlioz, Hector, *The Memoirs of Hector Berlioz, Member of the French Institute, including his travels in Italy, Germany, Russia and England 1830–1865*, translated and edited by David Cairns, London, 1990

Betjeman, John, *Collected Poems*, compiled and with an introduction by the Earl of Birkenhead, 4th edn, London, 1988 (first published 1958)

Black, William B., *The Bennie Railplane*, Kirkintilloch, 2004

Boghardt, Thomas, *Spies of the Kaiser*, Basingstoke, 2004

Bragg, Melvyn, *The Adventure of English: 500 AD to 2000: the biography of a language*, London, 2003

Bremner, Geoffrey, *Two centuries of a Cumberland Village, Blennerhasset*, Carlisle, 2006

Brendon, Piers, *Hawker of Morwenstow: portrait of a Victorian eccentric*, London, 1975

Brewer, E. Cobham, *Dictionary of Phrase and Fable, giving the derivation, source, or origin of common phrases, allusions, and words that have a tale to tell*, London, 1870 (and many subsequent editions)

Brewer, E. Cobham, *The Reader's Handbook of Allusions, References, Plots and Stories*, London, 1892

Briggs, Asa, *Victorian Cities*, Harmondsworth, 1968 (first published 1963)

Briggs, Asa, *Victorian People: a Reassessment of Persons and Themes, 1861–1867*, Harmondsworth, 1967 (first published 1954)

Brown, John H., *The Valley of the Shadow: an account of Britain's worst mining disaster, the Senghenydd explosion*, Port Talbot, *c.*1981

Burney, Charles, *Account of an Infant Musician (William Crotch)*, read at the Royal Society, 18 February 1779

Calder, Angus, *The People's War: Britain 1939–45*, London, 1969

Cannadine, David, *The Decline and Fall of the British Aristocracy*, London and Basingstoke, 1996

Carr, J. L., *Carr's Dictionary of English Kings, Consorts, Pretenders, Usurpers, unnatural Claimants & Royal Athelings*

Carr, J. L., *Carr's Dictionary of extra-ordinary English Cricketers*

Carr, J. L., *Gidner's Brief Lives of the Frontier*

Carr, J. L., *Welbourn's Dictionary of Prelates, Parsons, Vergers, Wardens, Sidesmen & Preachers, Sunday-School Teachers, Hermits, Ecclesiastical Flower-arrangers, Fifth Monarchy Men and False Prophets*

(All Carr's titles above republished by the Quince Tree Press, Bury St Edmunds, no dates)

Carr, J. L., *The Harpole Report*, London, 1973

Clare, John, *John Clare: Selected Poetry and Prose*, London, 1986

Clark, Leonard, *Alfred Williams: His Life and Work*, Newton Abbot, 1969 (first published 1945)

Coates, Chris, *Utopia Britannica: British Utopian Experiments: 1325–1945*, London, 2001

Cole, G. D. H., and Raymond Postgate, *The Common People 1746–1946*, London, 1964 (first published 1938)

Constantine, Matthew, *The Remarkable Story of Ernest Terah Hooley*, Ilkeston, Erewash Museum Service

Cossons, Neil and Barrie Trinder, *The Iron Bridge: Symbol of the Industrial Revolution*, Bradford-on-Avon, 1979

Cross, Colin, *The Liberals in Power, 1905–1914*, London, 1963

Cruden, Alexander, *A Complete Concordance to the Old and New Testaments: or a Dictionary and Alphabetical Index to the Bible*, London, 1889 (first published 1737)

Cunliffe, Hugh, *The Story of Sunderland Point from the Early days to Modern Times*, published by the author, 1984 (available at Lancashire County Library and Information Service)

Darley, Gillian, *Villages of Vision*, London, 1975 (reprinted Nottingham, 2007)

Day Lewis, C., *The Buried Day*, London, 1960

Dew, Simon, <http://www.jabadaw.freeserve.co.uk/simon/shires.htm>

Dutt, W. A., *The Norfolk and Suffolk Coast*, London, 1909

Ekwall, Eilert, *The Concise Oxford Dictionary of English Place-names*, Oxford, 1951 (first published 1928)

Ekwall, Eilert, *English River-Names*, Oxford, 1968 (first published 1928)

Evans, Marion, *A Portrait of Rhymney*, Abertillery, 1994

Faber, Geoffrey Cust, *Jowett, a portrait with background*, London, 1957

Fairs, Geoffrey, *A History of the Hay. The story of Hay-on-Wye*, London and Chichester, 1972

Falk, Bernard, *The Way of the Montagues: a gallery of family portraits*, London, 1947

Fraser, George MacDonald, *The Steel Bonnets: the story of the Anglo-Scottish Border Reivers*, London, 1971

Fraser, Gordon, *Wigtown and Whithorn: Historical and Descriptive Sketches, Stories and Anecdotes, Illustrative of the Racy Wit & Pawky Humour of the District*, Wigtown, 1877

Freeman, Kathleen and Barry, *Herefordshire: The Spirit of England's Most Rural County*, Eardisland, 2000

Gerald of Wales, *The Journey through Wales; the Description of Wales*, translated with an introduction by Lewis Thorpe, Harmondsworth, 1978

Gissing, George, *The Odd Women*, Oxford, 2000 (first published in 1908)

Gosse, Edmund, *Father and Son: A Study of Two Temperaments*, Harmondsworth, 1970 (first published 1907)

Glover, Judith, *Sussex Place-Names*, Newbury, 1997

Grahame, Kenneth, *The Wind in the Willows*, London, 1941

Gray, Cecil, *Peter Warlock: a memoir of Philip Heseltine*, London, 1934

Green, Basil, *Portrait of a London Borough*, London, 1953 (City of Westminster Archives)

Griffith, Edward C., *The Bishop's Castle Railway, 1865–1935*, Farnham, 1948 and 1969

Gronow, Rees Howell, *The Reminiscences and Recollections of Captain Gronow, being anecdotes of the Camp, Court, Clubs and Society 1810–1860*, abridged with an introduction by John Raymond, London, 1964

Gronow, Rees Howell, *Regency Recollections. Captain Gronow's Guide to Life in London and Paris*, edited by Christopher Summerville, Welwyn Garden City, 2006 (based on 4 vols first published 1862–6)

Groome, Francis H., *Ordnance Gazetteer of Scotland*, Edinburgh, 1882–5

Grossmith, George, *The Diary of a Nobody*, London, 1940 (first published in 1892)

Haddon, Mark, *A Spot of Bother*, London, 2006

Hadfield, Alice Mary, *The Chartist Land Company*, Newton Abbot, 1970

Halliwell, James Orchard (later Halliwell-Phillipps), *A Dictionary of Archaic and Provincial Words, Obsolete Phrases, Proverbs and Ancient Customs, from the Fourteenth Century*, in Two Volumes, London, 1847

Hammerton, Howard Jagger, *This Turbulent Priest: the story of Charles Jenkinson, Parish Priest and Housing Reformer*, London, 1952

Hardy, Dennis, and Colin Ward, *Arcadia for All: the Legacy of a Makeshift Landscape*, Nottingham, 2004 (first published 1984)

Hardy, Thomas, *Poems of Thomas Hardy. A New Selection*, selected, with an Introduction and Notes by T. R. M. Creighton, London and Basingstoke, 1974

Hayes, T. Wilson, *Winstanley the Digger: a literary analysis of radical ideas in the English Revolution*, Cambridge, Mass., and London, 1979

Hockey, S. F., *Quarr Abbey and its Lands 1132–1631*, Leicester, 1970

Hogg, James, *The Private Memoirs and Confessions of a Justified Sinner*, Oxford, 1981 (first published 1824)

Hood, John and others, *The History of Clydebank*, Carnforth, 1988

Hooley, Ernest Terah, *Hooley's Confessions*, London, 1925

Hutchinson, Roger, *The Soap Man: Lewis, Harris and Lord Leverhulme*, Edinburgh, 2003

Huxley, Aldous, *Texts & Pretexts: An Anthology with Commentaries,* London, 1932

Jacobs, Norman, *Frinton & Walton: A Pictorial History*, Chichester, 1995

Jarvis, Eric, *City to City: a journey through Whitwick from the City of Dan to the City of Three Waters*, Whitwick, 1994

Jenkins, Susan (compiler), *Compton Verney Handbook*, Compton Verney, 2004

Keay, Julia, *Alexander the Corrector: the tormented genius who unwrote the Bible*, London, 2004

Ketton-Cremer, R. W., *Norfolk Assembly*, London, 1957

Kilvert, Francis, *Kilvert's Diary*, chosen, edited and introduced by William Plomer, 3 vols, London, 1938–40

King, Peter, *Hurstpierpoint College 1849–1995: the School by the Downs*, Chichester, 1997

Knott, Simon, <http://www.SimonKnott.co.uk>

Knox, Ronald, *Literary Distractions*, London, 1958

Laing, Samuel, *Atlas Prize Essay. National Distress; its causes and remedies*, London, 1844

Laing, Samuel, *Problems of the Future, and essays*, London, 1889

Laing, Samuel, *Human Origins*, London, 1892

Lawson, William, and C. D. Hunter, *Ten Years of Gentleman Farming at Blennerhasset with Co-operative Objects*, London and Glasgow, 1874

Leyser, Henrietta, inaugural lecture of the Islip Millennium Festival 2005, <http://www.islip.org.uk/oldindex.html>, click on link 'Who was Edward?'

Lovett, William, *The Life and Struggles of William Lovett*, London, 1826

Lyons, Mary, *The Story of the Jaywick Sands Estate*, Stroud, 1996

Macaulay, Thomas Babington, *Prose and Poetry*, selected by G. M. Young, London, 1967

McDonald, Erica, and David J. Smith, *Artizans and Avenues: A History of the Queen's Park Estate*, London 2004

McKie, David, *A Sadly Mismanaged Affair: a Political History of the Third London Airport*, London, 1973

MacGill, Patrick, *Children of the Dead End*, Edinburgh, 2005 (first published 1914)

Maclean, Loraine, *Discovering Inverness-shire*, Edinburgh, c.1988

Matthews, Ronald, *English Messiahs: Studies of Six English Religious Pretenders, 1656–1927*, London, 1936

Mawson, Chris, <http://www.shellguides.freeserve.co.uk>

Mayhew, Henry, 'A visit to the cholera districts of Bermondsey', *Morning Chronicle*, 24 September 1849; <http://www.bl.uk/learning/histcitizen/21cc/publichealth/sources/source1/morningchronicle.html>

Moore, Andrew (ed.), *Houghton Hall: The Prime Minister, the Empress and the Heritage*, London, 1996

Morgan, John Scott, *Bishop's Castle: Portrait of a Country Railway*, Bishop's Castle, 2003

Morris, Chris, *On Tour with Tomas Telford*, Longhope, Glouco., 2004

'*Mountain, Moor and Loch' on the route of the West Highland Railway* (1894: no author given); republished as *Victorian Travel on the West Highland Line*, Colonsay, 2002

Muir, Richard, *The Lost Villages of Britain*, London, 1982

Nairn, Ian, *Nairn's London*, Harmondsworth, 1966

Nairn, Ian, *Outrage*, London, 1955

Nelson, Ian (ed.), *Hurstpierpoint – Kind and Charitable*, researched and written by Hurst History Study Group, Burgess Hill, 2001

Nicolson, Nigel, *Lord of the Isles – Lord Leverhulme in the Hebrides*, London, 1960

Noble, Henry and Marjory Gordon, *The Potato Famine in the Highlands 1846–9*, Ullapool Museum

Orwell, George, *The Road to Wigan Pier*, London, 2001 (first published 1937)

Owen, Hugh, *The Lowther Family: eight hundred years of 'a family of ancient gentry and worship'*, Chichester, 1990

Padel, O. J., *A Popular Dictionary of Cornish Place-Names*, Penzance, 1988

Parr, Martin, *The Last Resort: photographs of New Brighton* by Martin Parr; text by Ian Walker, Wallasey, 1986

Peacock, Thomas Love, *The Works of Thomas Love Peacock*, 3 vols; vols 1 and 2 (*Crotchet Castle, Headlong Hall, Melincourt* and *Nightmare Abbey*), London, 1905–6

Pearce, Edward, *The Great Man: Sir Robert Walpole, scoundrel, genius and Britain's first prime minister*, London, 2007

Perry, Hilda and Edmund, *Tottington: A Lost Village in Norfolk*, Wymondham, 1999

Phillips, J. Basil, *Senghenydd: a brave community*, Abertillery, 2002

Pike, E. Royston, *Human Documents of the Victorian Golden Age*, London, 1967

Poplett, Bob, *Peacehaven: A Pictorial History*, Chichester, 1993

Porter, Roy, *A Social History of Madness: stories of the insane*, London, 1987

Powell, Anthony, *A Dance to the Music of Time*, 4 vols, London, 1997 (novels first published between 1952 and 1975)

Pride, Glen L., *The Kingdom of Fife: an illustrated architectural guide*, Edinburgh, 1999

Rennert, Jonathan, *William Crotch 1775–1847: composer, artist, teacher*, Lavenham, 1975

Roberts, Andrew, *Salisbury: Victorian Titan*, London, 1999

Rogers, Byron, *The Last Englishman: the life of J. L. Carr*, London, 2003

Rogers, P. G., *Battle in Bossenden Wood: the strange story of Sir William Courtenay*, London, 1961

Ross, David, *Scottish Place-names*, Edinburgh, 2001

Russel, Nick, Poets by *Appointment: Britain's laureates*, Poole, 1981

Salmon, Arthur L., *Literary Rambles in the West of England*, London, 1906

Scott, Clement, *Poppy-land papers, descriptive of scenery on the East Coast*, London, 1886

Scott, Sir Walter, *The Lay of the Last Minstrel*, Edinburgh, 1805

Scott, Sir Walter, *Castle Dangerous*, Edinburgh, 2006 (first published 1832)

Scott, Sir Walter, *The Journal of Sir Walter Scott: from the original manuscript at Abbotsford*, Edinburgh, 1890

Sebald, W. G., *The Rings of Saturn*, translated from the German by Michael Hulse, London, 1999

Shaw, Nellie, *Whiteway. A Colony on the Cotswolds*, London, 1935

Shaw, Robert, *The Flag*, London, 1965

Simmons, Jack, and Gordon Biddle (eds), *The Oxford Companion to British Railway History from 1603 to the 1990s*, Oxford, 1997

Simpson, David, <http://www.northeastengland.talktalk.net>

Smith, Brian, 'The mystery of Philip Heseltine's death' in David Cox and John Bishop (eds), *Peter Warlock, a centenary celebration: The man – his music – his world*, London, 1994

Smith, Ian, *Tin Tabernacles: Corrugated Iron Mission Halls, Churches & Chapels of Britain*, Pembroke, 2004

Steel, Duncan, *Marking Time: the Epic Quest to Invent the Perfect Calendar*, New York, Chichester, Weinholm, Brisbane, Singapore, Toronto, 2000

Stisted, Georgiana M., *The True Life of Capt. Sir Richard F. Burton*, London, 1970 (first punlished 1896)

Styan, Del, *Lost Cromer: a guide to Cromer that has gone and where to see what remains*, Cromer, 2003

Subterranea Britannica, <http://www.subbrit.org.uk>

Tavenor-Perry, J. (ed.), *Memorials of Old Middlesex*, London, 1909

Tennyson, Alfred, *In Memoriam, Maud and other poems*, London, 1974

Thomas, Donald, *Swinburne: the poet in his world*, London, 1979

Thwaite, Ann, *Edmund Gosse: A Literary Landscape 1849–1928*, Oxford, New York, 1985

Timbs, John, and Alexander Gunn, *Abbeys, Castles and Ancient Halls of England and Wales: their legendary lore and popular history*, 3 vols, London, 1872

Tomlinson, Charles, *Eden: Graphics and Poems*, Bristol, 1985

Townsend, George, Canon of Durham, *Journal of a Tour in Italy in 1850 with an account of an interview with the Pope at the Vatican*, London, 1850

Trevelyan, George Otto, *The Life and Letters of Lord Macaulay*, Oxford, 1978

Treves, Sir Frederick, *Highways and Byways in Dorset*, London, 1906

Waller, Robert, *The Dukeries Transformed: the Social and Political Development of a Twentieth-Century Coalfield*, Oxford, 1983

Ward, Maisie, *Gilbert Keith Chesterton*, New York, 1943

Watts, Kenneth, *Snap: the history, depopulation and destruction of a Wiltshire village*, Trowbridge, 1989

Watts, Victor E., with contributions by John Insley, *A Dictionary of County Durham Place-Names*, Nottingham, 2002

Wedgwood, C.V., *William the Silent: William of Nassau, Prince of Orange, 1533–1584*, London, 1944

Welton, Ann and John: *The Story of Montgomery*, Woonton*, 2003

Williams, Alfred, *Life in a Railway Factory*, Stroud, 1984 (first published 1915)

Winstanley, Gerrard, *The True Levellers Standard Advanced; or, The State of Community Opened, and Presented to the Sons of Men*, London, 1649

Wordsworth, William, *The Poetical Works of William Wordsworth*, edited by E. de Selincourt, Oxford, 1950/1969

Wright, Thomas, *The Life of Sir Richard Burton*, 2 vols, London, 1906

Yelland, Charles (compiler), *The Gipton Story from 655 AD to 1990*, Leeds, c.1990

*WOONTON, vil. Herefordshire, 4m SE. of Kington.

INDEX

Note: Page numbers in italics refer to illustrations. Personal names beginning 'Mc' are indexed as if spelled 'Mac', and personal and place names beginning 'St' are indexed as if spelled 'Saint'.

Aabe (Shetland) 4
Aan (river; E. Grampians) xvi, 3–4, 643
Aaron Crags (Cumbria) 4
Aaron Hill (Calderdale) 4
Aaron Slack (Cumbria) 4
Aaron's Hill (Surrey *and* Somerset) 4
Aaron's Town (Cumbria) 4
Ab Kettleby (Leics.) 4
abbey ruins:
  Isle of Wight 445–8
  Scotland 241
  Wales 5–6, 302–7, 383
Abbeycwmhir (Radnors.) 5–7
Aberdeen 8–13
Abney, Elizabeth 11–12, 16
Abney Park cemetery (N. London) 14–16, 488
Abramovich, Roman 456
Abse, Dannie 533
Adam, Robert 81, 106, 323
Adrian's Wall 264
Airyhome with Hawthorpe and Baxton Howe 531
Akroyd, Edward 192–5, 437
Akroydon (Yorks.) 193–4
Alkan, Charles-Valentin 91
Allerton Mauleverer with Hopperton 531
Allward, D. R. Stewart 428
anarchy *see* Whiteway
Anderson, J. R. L. 582
Andrewes, J. Floyd 591–2
Andrews, John 468
Appin Murder 388, 429
Arabella (Ross & Cromarty) 32
Arbuthnot, Forster Fitzgerald 373
Archer, Jeffrey 612
Armstrong, William George, Baron 471–4
Arnold, Matthew 480
Arnold, Ralph 519, 520
Arnold, Samuel 91
Arriaga, Juan Crisóstomo de 188
Arthur, Duke of Connaught 356, 500, 507
Artizans', Labourers' and General Dwellings Company 452–6
Ashford (Kent) 17–21
Ashwell (Herts.) 22–4, 35, 216
Asquith, Herbert 289, 344, 467
Assheton-Smith, Sir Charles 73
Aston (Warks.) 25–8
Atherton, James 390
Austin, Alfred 17–20, 134, 589
Austin, William 452
Ayto, John and Crofton, Ian 146

Babington, Thomas 475, 476
Bacon, John Henry Frederick, *The Wedding Morning* 438
Baldwin, Stanley 551
Balfour, Arthur 517
Balham (London) 31
Bannon, Martin 453
Barbaraville (Herts.) 33–5
Barbaraville (Ross & Cromarty) 32–3
Baring-Gould, Sabine 218–19, 375–6, 377
Barnard Castle, Bowes Museum 472, 518
Barnet, battle (1471) 360
Barrington, Shute, Bishop of Durham 133, 135
Barry, Charles 191, 195, 215
Barry, E. M. 195
Bartholomew, John xvi–xvii, 3, 32, 47, 53, 65, 116, 459, 529–30
battles *see* Barnet; Bossenden; Dunkeld; Langport; Sedgemoor; Shrewsbury; Stalc; Turnham Green
Beazley, Elizabeth 571
Beckford, William 127–8, 555
Beddington, Jack 422
Bedford (Beds.) 36–40
Bell, Henry 364–5

Bell, Irvine 497
Bellot, Paul 446–7
Bennie, George 362–4, 365
Benson, E. F. 17–18
Berg, Alban 91–2
Berkeley, Bishop George 196, 197
Berlioz, Hector xvi, 348–51, 511
Betjeman, John 100, 191, 256, 366, 421–3, 508, 541, 595
Bettaney, Michael 434
Bevin, Ernest 508
Bianchi, Francesco 90–1
Biffen, John 311–12, 315
Bingham, G. Clifton 559
Birkett, Sir Norman 229
Bishops Cannings (Wilts.) 122
Bishops' Castle 41–7
Black, Bill 273
Black, William B. 362–4
Blackburn (Lancs.) 357, 617–19
Blackpool (Lancs.) 363, 390–1, 496
Blake, George 434
Blakehopeburnhaugh (Northumbria) 530–1
Blennerhasset (Cumbria) 48–51
Bletchley (Bucks.) 594
Bloemfontein (Co. Durham) 450
Blogg, Henry 504
Bloom, Ursula 168
Bodiam Castle (Sussex) 548–52
Body, Richard 61
Boghardt, Thomas 434
Bolckow, Henry 355–6
Bolingbroke, Henry St John, 1st Viscount 328
Bolingbroke, Henry St John, 5th Viscount 327–9
Bonar Law, Andrew 517
Bonchurch (Isle of Wight) 587–8, 590–2
bookshops
  Devizes 124
  Hay-on-Wye 196, *197*
  St Helens (IOW) 485
  Swaffham 132
  Tewkesbury 556
  Wigton 239
Booth, Bramwell 15
Booth, Charles 454
Booth, William 15
Boothville (Northants.) 52
Bosanquet, B. J. T. 360
Bossenden (Kent) 53–9
Boston (Lincs.) 60–3
Boston Stump 60–1, 63
Boswell, James 323
Bottomley, Horatio 228
Bournville 195, 437
Bowes, Mary Eleanor, Countess of Strathmore 518–22
Bowles, Stan 456
Boyson, Rhodes 461–2
Bragg, Melvyn, *The Adventure of English* 247–8
Bragg, Robert 526
Braid, James 165
Braine, Sir Bernard 161
Brandon, Vivian 431–2
Bremner, Geoffrey 49, 50–1
Brendon, Piers 375–6, 378
Brentford (Middlesex) 359–60
Brewer, E. Cobham 81, 144–6, 147–8, 202, 461
Brian, Havergal 155
Briggs, Asa 355–6, 408
Bright, John 438
Brindley, Joseph 152
British National Party 275
Britten, Benjamin 403, 405
Broadstairs (Kent) 64–6
Brockham Green (Surrey) 39
Brookfield, William Henry 100
Brougham, Henry Peter, Baron 133, 324
Brown, Ford Madox 622
Brown, John H. 501
Brown, T. E. 100
Bruff, Peter 165
Buchan, John, *Thirty-Nine Steps* 65
Buchanan, Colin 159, 160
Bunyan, John 37
Burne-Jones, Sir Edward 168
Burney, Charles 187, 395, 398

Burnley (Lancs.) 617–19
burns, names 237
Burrow (Somerset) 67–9
Burrow Mump 67–8, *68*
Burton, Sir Richard 369–74
Burtt, Joseph 600
Butler, Samuel (architect) 463
Buttocks Booth (Northants.) 52
Byett, Henry 342
Byron, Lord George Gordon 635

Caen Hill locks (Wilts.) 389
Caernarfon 73–6
Caithness, George Sinclair, 4th Earl 200–1
Calder, Angus 103–4
Caledonian Canal 86, 387–9, *388*, 576
Callaghan, James 104
Camilla, Duchess of Cornwall 473
Canada (Co. Durham) 450
Cannadine, David 108
Cantle, Ted 618
Cape Famine *see* Sunderland Point
Cape Wrath (Sutherland) xvii, 77–9
Capel-y-ffin (Monmouths.) 306
Cardiff *see* Temperance Town
Carlisle (Cumbria) 322–3, 324
Carlisle, Rosalind Frances, Countess 48
Carlyle, Thomas 246–7, 251, 480, 638
Carnarvon *see* Caernarfon
Carnegie, Andrew 103, 274
Caroline, Queen 9–10
Carr, J. L. 8, 10, 209, 276–8, 313, 557, 612
Carroll, Lewis 15
Carter, James (Jimmy) 104
Cartland, Barbara 33–5
Cartwright, John 567
Cassel, Sir Ernest 107, 108
Castle Campbell *see* Castle Gloom
Castle Cluggy (Perths.) 80
Castle Dangerous (Lanarks.) 80–2
Castle Drumin (Banffs.) 80
Castle Gloom (Clackmannans.) 83–5, *84*
Castle Rising 207
Castle Spiritual (Inverness) 86–7
Castle Stalker 427–8
castles *see* Bodiam Castle; Caernarfon; Dolbadarn Castle; Grimsthorpe Castle; Lowther Castle; Montgomery; Orford; Streatlam
Cat and Fiddle Inn (Derbys.) 183
cathedrals
  Durham 132
  Peterborough 421, 423
Catherine the Great, Empress of Russia 205, 207
cemeteries *see* Abney Park; Kensal Green
Chamberlain, Austen 517
Charborough Tower (Dorset) 127
Charles, HRH Prince of Wales 473
Charles, John 7
Charlton (Wilts.) 125–6
Chartism 54, 194, 348–9; *see also* O'Brien, Bronterre; O'Connor, Feargus
Chelsea 88–93
Chesterton, G. K. 340
Chiocchetti, Domenico 172
Chirac, Jacques 606–7
Chisholm, Sir John 162
Cholmondeley family 208
churches *see* Ashwell; Boston Stump; Devizes; Exton; Frinton-on-Sea; Frodsham; Hurstpierpoint; Mawgan-in-Pydar; Montgomery; Morwenstow; Orford; Steeple Ashton; Tattenhoe; tin tabernacles; Tottington
Churchman, Sir Arthur 403
Cibber, Colley 17
City of Three Waters (Leics.) 94–7
Clacton (Essex) 165, 262, 263–5
Clare, John 141–2
Clark, Leonard 342, 343, 345
Clarke, Jeremiah 90–1
Claux, Kleber 602
Clavell Tower (Dorset) 127
clearances *see* Highland clearances; slum clearance
Clevedon (Somerset) xvii, 98–101
Clubmen 251–2
Clydebank (Dumbartons.) 102–5

coalmining 84, 94, 147, 317–18, 321–3, 449–51, 498–501
Coalville (Leics.) 94
Cobden, Richard 512
Cole, G. D. H. and Postgate, Raymond 513
Cole, Henry 406
Coleman, Alice 455
Coleridge, Samuel Taylor 100, 639
Coleridge-Taylor, Samuel 92
Collins, John Churton 492
composers, deaths 90–3
Compton, Denis 360
Compton Verney (Warks.) 106–9, 131
Conan Doyle, Arthur 629–30
Connaught, Prince Arthur *see* Arthur, Duke of Connaught
Coolidge, Calvin 555
Cooper, William 171
Copley (Yorks.) 192–3, 195
Corrour 388
Cossons, Neil 255
Coton/Cotton (Shrops.) 627–8, 630
Cottonshopeburnfoot (Northumbria) 530–1
Courtenay, Sir William 53–9, 333
Cowdenbeath (Fife) 316–17, 318–19
Crabbe, George 639
Cragside (Northumbria) 471–4, *471*
Cranbrook (Kent) 548
cricket
  and Carr 277, 278
  Enville 149–51
  Middlesex county team 360
  Risley 229
  Sidmouth 506
Cromer (Norfolk) 502–5
Crompton, John William 467
Cromwell, Oliver 211–12, 251–2, 276, 438, 621–3, *621*
Cromwell, Thomas 445–6
Crosland, Anthony 161
Cross, Colin 517
Crossland, W. H. 193
Crossley family 194
Crotch, William 187, 395–8
Croy Brae 285–6
Cruden, Alexander xix, 8–13, 16, 277
Cryer, Ann 275
Cullen, Gordon 38
Cullingham, Henry 514
Cumming, Mansfield 432
Cunliffe, Hugh 527–8
Cupar (Fife) 316
Currie, Edwina 214
Curzon, George Nathaniel, Marquess of Kedleston 551–2
Cwrt Herbert 383, 385

Dabble Duck (Co. Durham) 450–1
Dalton, John Neille 280, 283
Danby, Thomas Osborne, 1st Earl 212
Darwin, Charles 411, 490–1
Davis, Sir Colin 349
De La Warr, Gilbert George Reginald Sackville, 8th Earl 227
Debatable Land (England/Scotland) 113–15
Defiance Platform (Cornwall) 116–18, *117*
Denbigh, Basil Feilding, 4th Earl 202–3
Destitution Road 575–6, 578
Devil, placenames 119–21
Devil's Quoits (Oxon.) 119–21
Devil's Staircase 120, 280
Devizes (Wilts.) 122–6
Dew, Simon 464
Dickens, Charles 56, 64–5, 259–60, 261, 461, 556, 588
Dicksee, John Robert 473
Disraeli, Benjamin 408, 409
Dolbadarn Castle (Gwynedd) 127, 130–1
Donizetti, Gaetano 201
Douglas, David 636
Douglas Castle *see* Castle Dangerous
Dresden (Staffs.) 154–5
Droop, H. R. 454
Drummond, Sir William 135
Drury, Alison 544
Duck, Stephen 125–6

Dukeries 146–7
Dundas, Henry 145
Dunkeld, battle (1745) 428
Dunning, Sir Leonard 603–4
Durham 132–5
Duruflé, Maurice 92
Dutt, W. A. 503, 505

Eardisland (Herefords.) 139–43
Eardisley (Herefords.) 139–40
Eardiston (Shrops.) 627–8
eccentrics and eccentricity *see* Beckford, William; Carr, J. L.; Courtenay, Sir William; Cruden, Alexander; Hawker, Robert Stephen; Whiteway
Edrich, Bill 360
Edward the Confessor 245, 248–9
Edward I 394
Edward, Prince of Wales (later Edward VII) 208
Edward, Prince of Wales (later Edward VIII) 167
Edwinstowe (Notts.) 144–8
Ekwall, Eilert
  Concise Oxford Dictionary of English Place Names 120–1, 374, 579
  English River-Names 237
Electric Brae 285–6
Eliot, George 28
Elland (Yorks.) 195
Elton, Jane Octavia 100
Elton, Sir Charles 99–100
Emerson, Ralph Waldo 589
Engels, Friedrich 236, 510
English language 247–8
Enville (Staffs.) 149–51
epitaphs 239–40, 377–8, 522
Errwood Hall (Ches.) 184–5
Estcourt, Thomas Sotherton 123
Etruria (Staffs.) 152–5
Eusden, Laurence 17
Evans, Henry 501
Evans, Marion 426
Exton (Rutland) 607–10

Fairbanks, Douglas 167
Fairs, Geoffrey 197–8
Felbrigg Hall (Norfolk) 504
Fernyhough, W. 152
Florence (Staffs.) 155
Fogg, Eric 92–3
Fokker, Anthony 418
Fonthill Tower (Wilts.) 127–8
Foot, Jesse 519, 520, 522
football
  clubs 318–19, 357, *357*, 392, 455–6, 466, 469
  competitions 313–14
  rivalries 232, 233–4
  see also rugby football
Fort Perch Rock (New Brighton) 392–3
Fort Widley (Hants.) 430–5
Fosse Way 202
Foster, Myles Birket 437
Foulness (Essex) 159–63
Fox, Charles James 438, 567
Franck, César 91
Fraser, George Macdonald 113
Freeman, Edward Augustus 247
Freeman, Kathleen 141
Frinton-on-Sea (Essex) 164, 166–8, 507
Frith, W. P., The New Frock 438
Frodsham (Ches.) 169–72, *170*
Fuchs, Klaus 434
Fuller, Thomas 210

Gads Hill (home of Dickens) 64, 121
Gainsborough, Thomas 187
garden cities *see* Gipton; Letchworth; Peacehaven; Port Sunlight
gardens
  Compton Verney 106
  Inverewe 230–1
  Swinford Old Manor 17, 19–20
Gatting, Mike 475
Gatton (Surrey) 39, 175–6
Gauntlett, H. J. 397
Gavin, James 82
Gee, Ethel 434
Gentle, Sir William Benjamin 23–4
George III 11, 396

Gerald of Wales 303–4, 338
Gesualdo, Carlo 91
Giant's Staircase 389
Gibbons, Grinling 608
Gibson, Steve 357
Gill, Eric 306
Gipton (Yorks.) 177–82
Gissing, George 98–9, 100, 345
Gladstone, W. E. 46, 298, 356, 472
  and Lord Leverhulme 436, 438
  and Macaulay 476–9
  and Samuel Laing 406–9
  and Swinburne 18–19, 588–9
Glancey, Jonathan 447
Glasgow *see* Clydebank; Milngavie
Glasson Dock (Lancs.) 528
Glover, Judith 440
Glyndwr, Owain 6, 337–8, 339
Glyndwr's Way National Trail 7
Goadsby, Thomas 622
Gomorrah 426
Gordon, Marjory 578
Gosse, Edmund 15, 488–93, 555, 589
Gosse, Emily 15
Gosse, Philip 411, 488–92
Goudhurst (Kent) 548
Goyt Valley 183–5
Grace, G. F. 150
Grace, W. G. 149–51
Graham of Claverhouse, John 82
Grahame, Kenneth, *Wind in the Willows* 560–1
Granados, Enrique 92
Grant brothers 460–1
Graves, Robert 590
graveyards
  Bonchurch 590–2
  Mortlake 369–70, *370*
  Morwenstow 377–8
  see also Abney Park; Kensal Green
Gray, Cecil 89
Gray, George 519–20
Gray, Thomas 17, 559
Green, Basil 453
Grey, George Harry 149–50
Griffin, Nick 275
Griffith, Edward 47
Grigson, John 6
Grimethorpe (Yorks.) 102, 182
Grimpo (Shrops.) 628, 629
Grimshaw family 184–5
Grimsthorpe Castle (Lincs.) 186–8, 204
Gronow, Rees Howell 383–6
Groome, Francis H., *Ordnance Gazetteer of Scotland* 82, 83, 86, 201, 242, 317
Grossmith, George and Weedon, *The Diary of a Nobody* 65–6
Grove, George 406
Grundy, Isobel 213, 214
Guardian newspaper, printing errors 73–6
Guéranger, Prosper 446
Guillan, Joe 33

Haddon, Celia 119
Haddon, Mark 423
Hadfield, Alice Mary 511
Hague, William 465
Haldane, Richard Burdon, 1st Viscount 433, 604
Halifax (Yorks.) 191–5, 215
Hallam, Arthur 99–100
Hallam, Henry 99
Halliwell, James Orchard, *Dictionary of Archaic and Provincial Words* 67
Hardie, Keir 500
Hardwick, George 357
Hardy, Dennis and Ward, Colin 263–4, 266
Hardy, Thomas 127, 592
Harries, E. Howard 533
Harris, Isle of 295, 298–301
Harris, Robert 508
Harrison, Brian 545
Hartwell, John 25–8
Haughton (Shrops.) 627, 629
Havercroft with Cold Hiendley 531
Havergal, W. H. 155
Hawker, Robert Stephen 375–9
Hay-on-Wye 196–8

Healey, R.M., *Shell Guide to Hertfordshire* 23
Hearne, J. W. 360
Heath, Edward 160
Heathrow 361
Heights of Alma (Co. Durham) 450
Helensburgh (Dumbartons.) 32, 364
Helm, Siegfried 430–5
Helmsdale (Sutherland) 199–201
Hemans, Felicia 639
Hendren, E. H. 360
Henry II 248, 403
Henry III 6, 366, 440
Henry IV 338
Henry VIII, dissolution of the monasteries 6, 304, 445–6
Herbert, George 366
Herbert, Sir John 383
Heseltine, Michael 98
Heseltine, Nigel 89
Heywood, Abel 622
High Cross (Leics.) 202–3
Highland clearances 171, 199–200, 296
Hitchens, Christopher 196, 197
Hogg, James 634–40
Holy Island (Northumbria) 243
Holyoake, George Jacob 49–50
Hood, John 104
Hooley, Ernest Terah 223–9
Horsham St Faith with Newton St Faith 531
Hoskyns, W. G. 609–10
Houghton, Henry 434
Houghton Hall (Norfolk) 204–8
Howard, Ebenezer 195, 437, 546
Howard, John 37
Humber estuary 209–10
Humble, Tom 541, 542–3, 544
Humphreys, J. C. 171–2
Humphreys, Travers 433
Hunt, Henry 'Orator' 123
Hunter, Charles 50
hunting 108–9, 581
Huntingdon (Cambs.) 211–14
Hurstpierpoint (Sussex) 215–19
Huskisson, William 117
Hutchinson, Roger 298, 300
Huxley, Aldous 560
Huxley, Thomas 409
hymnodists *see* Watts, Isaac
Hythe (Kent), tin tabernacle 171

Ilkeston (Derbys.) 223–9
Imber (Wilts.) 562, 565
Ingram, Herbert 61
Ingrow (Keighley) 271
Inkerman (Co. Durham) 450
Innes, John 546
Inveraray Castle 81
Inverewe House (Ross & Cromarty) 230–1
Invergordon mutiny 32
Ipswich (Suffolk) 232–4
Irk river 235–8
Ironbridge (Shrops.) 255–8
ironmonger, Montgomery 367
Isaacs, Rufus 433
Ishiguro, Kazuo 100–1
islands 243-4, *see also* Holy Island; Jacob's Island; Orkney
Isle of Whithorn (Wigtons.) 239–44
Isle of Wight *see* Quarr Abbey; Ventnor
Islip (Oxon.) 245–9
Iwerne Courtney (Shroton; Dorset) xviii, 250–2

Jackfield (Shrops.) 255–8, 366
Jacob's Island (London) 259–61
James of the Glen 429
James II 330, 333
James IV of Scotland 241–2
James, P. D., *The Black Tower* 127
Jarvis, Eric 96–7
Jaywick (Essex) 262–7, 416
Jefferson, Thomas 246
Jemimaville (Ross & Cromarty) 32
Jenkins, Roy 508
Jenkins, Simon 186, 504, 515
Jenkinson, Charles 178–82
John Brown (shipbuilders) 102, 103–4

Johnson, Samuel 197
Jowett, Benjamin 553–4, 556, 593–4
Joynson-Hicks, William 603
Jupp, Henry 150

Keats, John 587, 642
Keay, Julia 11–12
Keighley (Yorks.) 271–5
Kell, Vernon 432–4
Kensal Green cemetery 452, 513
Kent, William 208
Kettering (Northants.) 276–8
Ketton-Cremer, R. W. 206, 208, 504
Killin (Stirlings.), tin tabernacle 171
Kilpeck (Herefords.) 143
Kilvert, Francis 198, 306, 390–1
King, Peter 218
Kingsley, Charles 260, 491
Kinlochleven (Argyll) 279–83
Kitchener, Horatio Herbert, 1st Earl Kitchener of Khartoum 289–94, *291*, 333, 347
Knapman, Roger 526
Knight, Charles 260
Knight, Matthew 553–4, 556
Knockin (Shrops.) 284, 312
Knott, Simon 565
Knoweside (Ayrs.) 285–6
Knox, John 84
Knox, Ronald, *Literary Distractions* 132–3, 134
Kroger, Peter and Helen 434

Lady Lever Art Gallery (Port Sunlight) 437–9
Ladybower reservoir 183
Laing, Malcolm 406
Laing, Samuel (1st) 406
Laing, Samuel (2nd) 406–11
Lamb, Charles 639
Lambert, Constant 89
Lambert, Margaret 106
Lambert, Richard Cornthwaite 582
Lambeth 289–94
Lambholm (Orkney), church 172
Lampeter (Carmarthens.) 308–10
Landor family 306
Landor, Walter Savage 304–6
Langport, battle (1645) 68
Lansbury, George 263, 266, 293
Lawrence, Sir Thomas 123
Lawson, Harry 227
Lawson, Robert 528
Lawson, Sir Wilfrid Wybergh (father) 48
Lawson, Sir Wilfrid Wybergh (son) 320
Lawson, William 48–51
Le Queux, William 430, 434
Leach, Charles 454
Leclair, Jean-Marie 91
Lee, Jennie 317
Leeds *see* Gipton
Lees-Milne, James 421, 422
Letchford, Leonard 217–18
Letchworth (Herts.) 195, 437, 546
Lethaby, W. R. 473
Lever Park (Lancs.) 295, 436
Leverburgh (Harris) 295–301, 436
Leverhulme, William Henry Lever, 1st Viscount 295–301, 436–9, 467–9
Lewes, battle (1264) 440
Lewes, Betsy 324–5
Lewis, Daniel 391
Lewis, Isle of 295, 296–9
Lewis, Sir William Thomas 498–501
Leyser, Henrietta 248–9
libraries
  Queen's Park 454
  Sidmouth 507
  Stromness 523
  Wigan 616, 619
lighthouses
  Cape Wrath xvii, 77–9, *79*
  Cromer 567
  New Brighton 391
  Orford 403
  Port Appin 429
  Shipden 504
Lillywhite, James 150
Linger and Die (Co. Durham) 450

Linley, Thomas 92
Linley, Thomas (Jr) 186–8, 396, 398
Lismore (Argyll) 428
Liverpool, and Rivington 467–8
Livett, R. H. 179
Llandrindod Wells 422
Llanllwchaiarn 394
Llansantffraid yn Mechan (Montgomerys.) 312–14
Llanthony Abbey (Monmouths.) 302–7
Llanthony Secunda (Glos.) 303–4
Llanthony Tertia (Montgomerys.) 306
Llanwrda (Carmarthens.) 308–10
Llanyblodwel (Shrops.) 311–12, 314–15
Llewellyn, Richard, *How Green Was My Valley* 451
Lloyd George, David 73, 107, 290, 517
Llywelyn I the Great 6
Llywelyn ap Gruffydd 6, 130
Loch, James 408
Lochcarron (Janetown/Jeantown) 32
Lochgelly (Fife) 316–19
London
  cemeteries 14–16
  as Sombragloomy 145
  see also Balham; Chelsea; Jacob's Island; Lambeth; Marylebone; Mortlake; Queen's Park
Long, Walter 516–17
Longtown (Cumbria) 113–15
Lonsdale, Gordon (Konon Molody) 434
Loudon, John Claudius 537
Loutherbourg, Philip James de, *Coalbrookdale by Night* 256
Love, Graham 162
Lovett, William 509–10, 514
Lowe, Edward 218
Lowry, L. S. 354
Lowther (Cumbria) 320–6
Lowther Castle 323, 325–6, *326*
Lowther, James (Wicked Jimmy; later 1st Earl of Lonsdale) 320, 321–6
Lowther, Sir John I 321
Lowther, Sir John II 321
Lowther, Sir John IV 321
Lowther New Town 321
Lully, Jean-Baptiste 91
Lumbertubs (Northants.) 52
Lyall, Sutherland 266
Lydiard Park (Wilts.) 327–9
Lyell, Charles 411
Lyme Regis 330–3
Lyne, Joseph Leycester (Fr Ignatius) 306
Lyons, Mary 264
Lytton, Edward Bulwer, *The Last of the Barons* 505

Macaulay, Thomas Babington 204, 331–2, 475–81, 554
Macaulay, Zachary 476
McCarthy, Justin Huntly 370
McCorquodale, Ian 34
McDonald, Erica and Smith, David J. 453–5
MacDonald, Ramsay 32, 345
MacFisheries 297
MacGill, Patrick 280–3
Machynlleth (Montgomerys.) 337–9
Mackay, Mrs I. P. 77–9
Mackenzie, Osgood 230–1
Mackerras, Sir Charles 155
McKie, David (banker and poet) 242
Maclean, Loraine 87
Madocks, William Alexander 566–72
Madog 566
Major, John 214
Mallon, Ray 357
Manchester, town hall 622
Mannion, Wilf 357
Mansfield, P. J. F. 266
Marches, Welsh *see* Abbeycwmhir
market cross, Devizes 123, *123*
Market Harborough (Leics.) 340
Marriott, Sir William 227
Marsh, Rodney 456
Marston, South (Wilts.) 341–6
Martelli, Horace de Courcy 430–1
Martineau, Harriet 632–3
Marvell, Andrew (sr) 209–10, 278
Marwick Head (Orkney) 347
Marx, Enid 106

Marx, Karl 409, 410, 510, 588
Marylebone 348–51
Masefield, John 17
Matthews, Jacob Scott 545–7
Matthews, Ronald 54–5
Mawer, A. and Stenton, F. M. 440
Mawgan-in-Pydar (Cornwall) 352–3
Mawson, Chris 422
Maxwell, Robert, 6th Earl, Warden of Scotland 113
Mayhew, Henry 259–61
Meades, Jonathan 40
Melbourne, William Lamb, 2nd Viscount 479–80
Merthyr, Lord *see* Lewis, Sir William Thomas
Merton Park (Wimbledon) 546
Middlehaven 357
Middlesbrough 354–8, 631
Middlesex 359–61
Mill, J. S. 409, 605
Millais, John Everett, *Bubbles* 438
Milnes, Richard Monckton 589
Milngavie (Dumbartons.) 362–5
Milton Keynes (Bucks.) xvii, 542–3
Mitchell, W. S. 415
Mitchell, William 367
Mittal, Lakshmi 456
Moeran, E. J. 92
Molloy, James L. 559
Monk, Thelonious 559–60
Monmouth, James Scott, Duke, rebellion 330–5, 480
Monopoly (board game) 233–4
Montagu, Edward 212–14
Montagu, Lady Mary Wortley 212–13
Montagu, Ralph, 1st Duke 212
Montgomery 41, 47, 366–8
Montgomery, Robert 476
Moores, Sir Peter 106, 109
Morgan, John Scott 47
Morris, Jan 100
Morris, William 168
Morrison, J. 77–9
Mortlake 369–74
Morwenstow (Cornwall) 375–9
Motley, John Lothrap 554
Mozart, Wolfgang Amadeus 91, 187
Muggeridge, Malcolm 600
Muir, Richard 563
Mumpinday 79
mumpoker 67
museums
  Ashwell 23–4
  Bishop's Castle 47
  Boston 62
  Cromer 502, 504
  Etruria 154
  Halifax 194
  Hurstpierpoint 216
  Kinlochleven 283
  Lyme Regis 330
  Montgomery 367
  Normanton church (Rutland Water) 184, 607
  Richmond 463, 464
  Ullapool 575–6, 578
  Wigan 615

Nairn, Ian 36, 37–40, 175, 176, 191, 217, 415, 447
National Trust
  Bodiam Castle 552
  Burrow Mump 67
  Cragside 472–4
  Felbrigg Hall 504
  Zoze Point 643, *643*
National Trust for Scotland 230
Neath (Glam.) 383–6
Nelson, Horatio, Lord Nelson 364
Neptune's Staircase 87, 387–9, *388*
Neville, Charles William 415–18, 420
Nevin, Charles 419
New Brighton (Merseyside) 390–3
Newport (Cornwall), town hall 176
newspapers
  printing 73–6
  reporters 271–5
Newton, Hannah 520
Newtown 394
Nightingale, Florence and Parthenope 595

No Place (Co. Durham) 450
Noble, Henry 578
Noble, Matthew 622
Noel, Conrad 62–3, 178
Nollekens, Joseph 438, 608
nomenclature, indecision about 250–2
Norman Conquest 245–9
North Leverton with Habblesthorpe (Lincs.) 531
Norwich 395–8
  and Ipswich 232–4
Nowheresville 399

Obbe *see* Leverburgh (Harris)
O'Brien, Bronterre 15, 509
O'Connor, Feargus 15, 295, 348, 509–14
O'Connor, T. P. 469
Official Secrets Acts 433–5
Ordnance Gazetteer of Scotland 82, 83, 86, 201, 242, 317
Orford Ness 404–5
Orford (Suffolk) 403–5
Orkney 406–11; *see also* Lambholm; Marwick Head; Stromness
Orwell, George 283, 493, 615–17
Ouseley, Frederick 397
Owain Goch 130
Owen, Hugh 322, 323, 324
Owen, Robert 394
Owen, Robert Dale 115

Padel, O. J. 643
Page, Walter H. 290
Paine, Tom 49, 246
Paladini, Gianni 456
Palmer, Samuel, *Coming from Evening Church* 5
Palmerston, Henry John Temple, 3rd Viscount 408, 430, 481
paper mills
  Ramsbottom 459–60, *460*
  Somerset 485
Papworth (Cambs.) 225–8
Paradise (sites) 262
Parker, John 314–15
Parr, Martin 393
Partridge, Maureen 97
Paxton, Joseph 194
Peacehaven (Sussex) 415–20
Peache, Barbara 88–9
Peacock, Thomas Love 128–30, 551, 567–8
Pearce, Edward 204
Pease, Joseph 354
Peel, Sir Robert 154, 459, 476, 583
Pell, Robert 589
Pembridge (Herefords.) 140
Perry, Hilda and Edmund 564
Peterborough (Cambs.) 421–4
Petworth (Sussex) 39, 215
Pevsner, Nikolaus, Buildings of England 39–40, 175, 191, 192, 217, 273–4, 415, 515, 563, 581
Philadelphia (Co. Durham) 450
Phillips, J. Basil 501
Piper, John 423, 541
Pitt, William the Younger 323, 325
Pity Me (Co. Durham) 450
Pius IX, Pope 133–4
placenames
  long 529–32
  misuse 611–12
  from personal names 35-8, 130, 338, *see also* Akroydon; Saltaire; Talbot
  and saints 485–6
plotlanders 262–7, 416
poet laureates *see* Austin, Alfred
Ponting, Clive 434
Pontlottyn (Glam.) 252, 425–6, 499
Pooter, Mr and Mrs *see* Grossmith, George and Weedon
Pope, Alexander 18, 119, 128, 212–13
Port Appin (Argyll) 388, 427–9
Port Sunlight (Ches.) 296, 297, 436–9, *437*, 546
Porter, Roy 12
Porthmadog (Gwynedd) 566, 567, 569–70
Portland, Isle of (Dorset) 243
Portmeirion (Gwynedd) 571
Portobello (Co. Durham) 450
Portsdown (Hants.) 430–5

potato famine, Scotland 576–7
Potter, Dennis 492, 493
Pound, Guy Peter 539
Poverty Bottom (Sussex) 440–1
Powell, Anthony, *A Dance to the Music of Time* 611–14
Powell, Enoch 555
Powell, Felix 93, 417, 419
Powell, George Henry 417, 419
Powell, Sir Francis Sharp 617, 619
Powell Cooper, Richard 167
Power, Frank (Arthur Vectis Freeman) 290–4, 347
Presley, Elvis 486–7
Price, Morgan Philips 603
Pride, Glen 318
Prime, Geoffrey 434
printing errors 73–6
progress, opposition to 255–8
prophets, self-styled 25–8
pubs
  Ashwell 23
  Corrour 388
  Devizes 123
  Dunkirk 58–9
  Hurstpierpoint 216
  Jackfield 255–8
  Tewkesbury 556
  Whitwick 94–5
Pugin, A. N. W. 563, 565
Pugin, E. W. 563
Pulteney, Sir William 575
Pusey, Edward Bouverie 464
Pye, Henry 17

QinetiQ 162
Quakers 217–18
Quarr Abbey (Isle of Wight) 445–8, *447*
Quarrell, Johnnie 163
Quarrendon (Bucks.) 542
Quebec (Co. Durham) 449–51
Queen's Park (London) 452–6, *453*

railplane 362–4, *363*
railways
  Bishop's Castle line 41–7
  Defiance Platform 116–17
  East Lancashire 459
  expansion 407–9
  Heart of Wales 308–9
  Kent and East Sussex 549–50
  parliamentary tickets 407
  station names 252, 308, 593–6
  Stockton and Darlington 354, 632
  Swindon works 327–9, 342–4
  and time-keeping 524–5
  Universities line 593–4
  Vale of Towy 308–9
  West Highland line 310, 387–8
Ramsbottom (Lancs.) 459–62
Rannoch Moor 279–83, 388
Ravel, Maurice 92
Raymond, John 385–6
Rednal (Shrops.) 627, 629
Redvers, Baldwin de, Earl of Devon 445, 446
Rees, Richard 309
Rees-Mogg, Lord William 27
reservoirs 183–4, 279, 467; *see also* Rutland Water
Richmond (Yorks.) 463–5
Richmondshire 464–5
Ridley, Nicholas 530
Risley Hall (Notts.) 224–5, 228–9
rivers
  names 236–8
  see also Aan; Goyt Valley; Humber estuary; Irk; Yarrow
Rivington Hall 467–9
Rivington Pike (Lancs.) 436, 466–9
Roberts, Andrew 19
Roberts, Evan 171
Robin Hood story 147–8
Robson, Eric 115
Rochester, John Wilmot, 2nd Earl 359–60
Rodney's Pillar (Montgomerys.) 312
Rogers, Byron 278
Rogers, P. G. 55

Rogers, Samuel 384
Rope, Emmeline 403
Roskill Commission 159–60, 161
Ross, David 33
Rothbury (Northumbria) 470–4
Rothley (Leics.) 475–81
rugby football, clubs 615, 617
Rutland 359
Rutland Water 184, 606–7
Ruyton-XI-Towns (Shrops.) 627–30

Sadler, Sir Samuel Alexander 355
St Elvis (Pembrokes.) 485–7
St John, Sir John, 1st Baronet 328
St Marychurch (Devon) 488–93
St Mawgan *see* Mawgan-in-Pydar
saints, in place-names 485–6
Salinger, J. D. 266
Salisbury, Robert Cecil, 3rd Marquess 19, 589
Salmon, Arthur L. 100
Salmond, Lieut. 430–1
Salt, Sir Titus 152, 192, 195, 437, 454, 545
Saltaire (Yorks.) 152, 192, 193, 545–6
Sandtoft (Lincs.) 494–7
Santa Claus brawl 394
Schafernaker, Tomasz 399
Scots Dike 114–15
Scott, Clement 503
Scott, Sir George Gilbert 194
Scott, Sir Walter 79, 84, 115, 247, 361, 438
  Castle Dangerous 81, 637
  and Hogg 634–7, 638–9
Scoular, William 438
Scrymgeour, Edwin 291
Sebald, W. G. 405, 556
Sedgemoor, battle (1685) 68–9, 333
Seldom Seen (Co. Durham) 450
Selwood, Emily 99
Senghenydd (Glams.) 498–501
Shakespeare, William 201
Shapps, Grant 34–5
Shaw, George Bernard 178
Shaw, Nellie 599–601, 603, 605
Shaw, Richard Norman 471
Shaw, Robert, *The Flag* 62–3
Shell Guides 94, 130, 140, 309, 415, 421–3, 451, 525, 541–3, 609–10
Shelley, Percy Bysshe 570
Shelvock (Shrops.) 627–8, 630
Sheridan, Richard Brinsley 187, 385
shipbuilding 102–5, 387
Shipden (Norfolk) 502–5
shires, sub-county 464–5
Shobdon (Herefords.) 142–3
shops
  Devizes 123, 124–5
  Knockin 284
  Sidmouth 507
Shotatton (Shrops.) 627–8, 630
Shrewsbury 339
Shrewsbury, battle (1403) 338
Shroton (Iwerne Courtnay; Dorset) 250–2
Sidmouth (Devon) 506–8
Siemens, Ernst Werner von 495
silence and taciturnity 553–6
Sims, George 418
Singer Manufacturing Company 102–3, 104, *104*, 105
slavery *see* Sunderland Point; Wilberforce, William
slum clearance 178–80
Smirke, Robert 325
Smith, F. E. 467
Smith, Ian 170–2, 446
Smith, Juliet 421, 422
Smith, Len 435
Smith, Stevie 236
Smith, Sydney 479
Snap (Wilts.) xviii, 581–3
Snig's End (Glos.) 295, 509–14
Snowden, Philip 604
Sodom (Wilts.) 426
soke 421–2
South Marston (Wilts.) 341–6
Speight, Christina 153
Spender, J. A. 553
spies and spying 430–5, 599, 601–3

Spilsbury, Sir Bernard 292
Stacpoole, Horace de Vere 588
Stainer, Sir John 397
Stalc, battle (1468) 427
Stamp, Gavin 40
Stansfeld, James 327, 329
Stanton Harcourt (Oxon.) 119, 128
Stedman, Frank Christopher (Foff) 262–7
steel industry 355–6
Steeple Ashton (Wilts.) 515–17
Stephen, Leslie 555
Stephens, Holman Fred 549
Stephenson, Martin 33
Stert (Wilts.) 126
Stevenson, R. L., *Kidnapped* 429
Stewart, Sir John, Lord of Lorn 427
Steyn, Mark 27
Stisted, Georgiana M. 372–3
Stoat's Nest (railway station) 117–18
Stocks, Mary, Baroness Stocks 161
Stoke-on-Trent (Staffs.) 152–5
Stokes, O. B. 272, 273
Stoney Bowes, Andrew Robinson 518–22
Stornoway (Lewis) 297
Stradella, Alessandro 91
Streatland (Co. Durham) 518–22
Stretford Bridge Halt 43
Stromness (Orkney) 523
Stroud (Glos.) 524–6
Stukeley, William 202
Styan, Del 502–3
Subterranea Britannica (website) 117
Subtopia 38
Sulhampstead Banister Lower End (Berks.) 532
Sulhampstead Banister Upper End (Berks.) 531–2
Summerville, Christopher 385–6
Sunday Referee 290–3
Sunderland Point (Lancs.) 527–8
Sutherland, George Granville Leveson-Gower, 1st Duke 154–5, 199–200, 201
Sutherland, George Granville Sutherland-Leveson-Gower, 5th Duke 298
Sutton (Shrops.) 627, 629
Swansea (Glam.) 533
Swift, Jonathan 212
Swinburne, Algernon Charles 19, 370, 554, 587–92
Swindon (Wilts.) 327–9, 342–4
Swinford Old Manor 17, 19–20
Syre (Sunderland), tin tabernacle 171

Talbot, Marianne and Georgina 537–40
Talbot Village (Dorset) 537–40
Tan Hill Inn (Yorks.) 183
Tardebigge locks (Worcs.) 389
Tattenhoe (Bucks.) xviii, 541–4
Tattershall Castle (Lincs.) 551–2
Tatton, Sir Robert 621
Tavenor-Perry, J. 360
Taylor, A. J. P. 552
Tchaikovsky, Peter Illych 91
Tedsmore (Shrops.) 627, 629
Teise river (Sussex) 237
Telford, Thomas 3, 86, 199, 202, 387, 389, 575, 578, 628
Temperance Town (Glam.) xviii, 545–7
Templars 475–6
Tennyson, Alfred, Lord 18, 99–100, 376, 588
Tenterden (Kent) 548–52
Terrible Down (Sussex) 440–1
Tewkesbury (Glos.) 553–6
Thackeray, William Makepeace 100
Thanet, Isle of (Kent) 243
Thatcher/Thatcherism 177, 181, 311, 410, 465, 530, 612
theatres
  Richmond 463–4
  Sidmouth 507
  Wolverhampton 620
Thetford Forest, abandoned villages 562–5
Thompson (Norfolk) 562–3
Thomson, James and George 102
Thoresby (Notts.) 147
Thorold, Henry 451
Thwaite, Ann 490, 491, 492
Tickell, Kathryn 474
Timbs, John 213–14, 521–2, 551, 587